Feasting on the Gospels
Matthew, Volume 1

Editorial Board

A Feasting on the Word® Commentary

Feasting on the Gospels

Matthew, Volume 1
Chapters 1–13

CYNTHIA A. JARVIS and E. ELIZABETH JOHNSON

General Editors

WESTMINSTER
JOHN KNOX PRESS
LOUISVILLE · KENTUCKY

© 2013 Westminster John Knox Press

First edition
Published by Westminster John Knox Press
Louisville, Kentucky

13 14 15 16 17 18 19 20 21 22—10 9 8 7 6 5 4 3 2 1

Scripture quotations from the New Revised Standard Version of the Bible are copyright © 1989 by the Division of Christian Education of the National Council of the Churches of Christ in the U.S.A. and are used by permission. All rights reserved.

Excerpt from Ken Sehested, *In the Land of the Living* (Raleigh: Publications Untld., 2009) is reprinted by permission of the author.

Book design by Drew Stevens
Cover design by Dilu Nicholas

Library of Congress Cataloging-in-Publication Data

Feasting on the Gospels : a feasting on the WordTM commentary / Cynthia A. Jarvis and E. Elizabeth Johnson, general editors. — First edition.
    volumes cm
  Includes index.
  ISBN 978-0-664-23540-6 (v. 1 : pbk.)
 1. Bible. Matthew—Commentaries.   I. Jarvis, Cynthia A., editor of compilation.
  BS2575.52.F37   2013
  226'.2077—dc23
      2013004484

PRINTED IN THE UNITED STATES OF AMERICA

♾ The paper used in this publication meets the minimum requirements of the American National Standard for Information Sciences—Permanence of Paper for Printed Library Materials, ANSI Z39.48-1992

Contents

Publisher's Note

Feasting on the Gospels is a seven-volume series that follows in the proud tradition of *Feasting on the Word: Preaching the Revised Common Lectionary*. Whereas *Feasting on the Word* provided commentary on only the texts in the lectionary, *Feasting on the Gospels* will cover every passage of the four Gospels. *Feasting on the Gospels* retains the popular approach of *Feasting on the Word* by providing four perspectives on each passage—theological, pastoral, exegetical, and homiletical—to stimulate and inspire preaching, teaching, and discipleship.

Westminster John Knox Press is grateful to the members of the large *Feasting* family who have given so much of themselves to bring this new series to life. General editors Cynthia A. Jarvis and E. Elizabeth Johnson stepped from their service on the editorial board of *Feasting on the Word* to the editorship of *Feasting on the Gospels* without missing a beat. Their commitment, energy, and unflagging enthusiasm made this work possible. The project manager, Joan Murchison, and project compiler, Mary Lynn Darden, continued their remarkable

work, bringing thousands of pieces and hundreds of authors together seamlessly.

The editorial board did enormous work under grueling deadlines and did it with excellence and good humor. The hundreds of writers who participated—scholars, preachers, and teachers—gave much of themselves to help create this bountiful feast. David Bartlett and Barbara Brown Taylor took the time and care to help conceive this new project even as they were finishing their excellent work as general editors of *Feasting on the Word*.

Finally, we are again indebted to Columbia Theological Seminary for their partnership. As they did with *Feasting on the Word*, they provided many resources and personnel to help make this series possible. We are grateful in particular to seminary President Stephen Hayner and Dean of Faculty and Executive Vice President Deborah Mullen.

It is with joy that we welcome you to this feast, in hopes that it will nourish you as you proclaim the Word to all of God's people.

Westminster John Knox Press

Series Introduction

At their best, people who write about Scripture are conversation partners. They enter the dialogue between the biblical text and the preacher or teacher or interested Christian and add perspectives gained from experience and disciplined attention. They contribute literary, historical, linguistic, and theological insights gathered over the millennia to the reader's first impressions of what is going on in a text. This conversation is essential if the reading of Scripture is to be fruitful in the church. It keeps reading the Bible from being an exercise in individual projection or uncritical assumption. That said, people who comment on the Bible should never become authorities. While a writer may indeed know more about the text than the reader does, he or she nevertheless writes from a particular perspective shaped by culture, ethnicity, gender, education, and theological tradition. In this regard, the writer of a commentary is no different from the writers and readers of Scripture.

The model for this series on the Gospels is the lectionary-based resource *Feasting on the Word* (Westminster John Knox Press, 2008–2011), now widely used by ministers as they prepare to preach. As central as the task of preaching is to the health of congregations, Scripture is the Word that calls the whole community of faith into being and sends those addressed out as witnesses to the Word in the world. Whether read devotionally by those gathered to pray or critically by others gathered to study, the Bible functions in a myriad of ways to undergird, support, and nurture the Christian life of individuals and communities. Those are the reasons that Westminster John Knox Press has taken the next step in the *Feasting* project to offer *Feasting on the Gospels*, a series in the style of *Feasting on the Word* with two major differences. First, all four Gospels are considered in their entirety, a *lectio continua* of sorts that leaves nothing out. Second, while *Feasting on the Word* is addressed specifically to preachers, *Feasting on the Gospels* is addressed to all who want to deepen their understanding of the Gospels—Bible study leaders and class members, seasoned preachers and seminarians, believers and skeptics.

The advantage of *Feasting on the Gospels* is that the reader encounters multiple perspectives on each text—not only the theological, exegetical, pastoral,

and homiletical emphases that shape the essays, but also the ecumenical, social, ethnic, and cultural perspectives of the authors. Unlike a single-author commentary, which sustains a particular view of a given interpreter throughout, *Feasting on the Gospels* offers readers a broad conversation that engages the text from many angles. In a church as diverse as the twenty-first-century church is, such deliberate engagement with many voices is imperative and, we hope, provocative.

A few observations about the particular challenges posed by the Gospels are in order here. The Gospels were written in a time when fledgling Christian communities—probably in their second generation—were just beginning to negotiate their relationships with Judaism (within which they were conceived and born), a community that was itself in the process of redefinition after the destruction of the Second Temple in 70 CE. Some of that negotiation was marked by great tension and sometimes outright hostility. The temptation for Christian readers to read anti-Semitism into texts that portray intra-Jewish conflict has beset the church almost from its beginnings. Our editors have been particularly mindful of this when dealing with essays on texts where the temptation to speak contemptuously of Jews and Judaism might threaten faithful interpretation.

A second observation involves the New Testament manuscript tradition. In *Feasting on the Gospels* we identify and comment on significant manuscript variants such as Mark 16:9–20 and John 7:53–8:11, something we did not have to contend with in *Feasting on the Word*. We identify those variant readings the way the NRSV does, except that we talk about "other ancient manuscripts" rather than the "other ancient authorities" of the NRSV notes.

The twelve members of our editorial board come from a broad swath of American Christianity: they are members or ministers of Presbyterian, Baptist, United Church of Christ, Roman Catholic, and Disciples of Christ churches. Some of them are academics who serve on the faculties of theological schools; others are clergy serving congregations. All of them are extraordinarily hardworking, thoughtful, and perceptive readers of Scripture, of the church, and of the world. The writers whose work comprises these volumes represent an even wider cross-section of the church, most of them from North America, but a significant number from around the world, particularly the global South.

We could not have undertaken this work without the imagination, advice, and support of David Dobson, Editorial Director at Westminster John Knox Press, and his colleagues Don McKim, Marianne Blickenstaff, Michele Blum, and Julie Tonini. We are deeply grateful to David L. Bartlett and Barbara Brown Taylor, our mentors in the *Feasting on the Word* project, who continued to offer hands-on assistance with *Feasting on the Gospels*. We thank President Stephen A. Hayner and Dean Deborah

F. Mullen of Columbia Theological Seminary and the congregation of The Presbyterian Church of Chestnut Hill in Philadelphia, Pennsylvania, who made possible our participation in the project. Joan Murchison, who as Project Manager kept all of us and our thousands of essays in order and enforced deadlines with great good humor, is once again the beloved Hammer. Mary Lynn Darden, our compiler, who corralled not only the essays but also information about their authors and editors, brought all the bits and pieces together into the books you see now.

To the preachers, teachers, Bible study leaders, and church members who will read the Gospels with us, we wish you happy feasting.

Cynthia A. Jarvis
E. Elizabeth Johnson

*Feasting on the Gospels
Matthew, Volume 1*

¹An account of the genealogy of Jesus the Messiah, the son of David, the son of Abraham.

²Abraham was the father of Isaac, and Isaac the father of Jacob, and Jacob the father of Judah and his brothers, ³and Judah the father of Perez and Zerah by Tamar, and Perez the father of Hezron, and Hezron the father of Aram, ⁴and Aram the father of Aminadab, and Aminadab the father of Nahshon, and Nahshon the father of Salmon, ⁵and Salmon the father of Boaz by Rahab, and Boaz the father of Obed by Ruth, and Obed the father of Jesse, ⁶and Jesse the father of King David.

And David was the father of Solomon by the wife of Uriah, ⁷and Solomon the father of Rehoboam, and Rehoboam the father of Abijah, and Abijah the father of Asaph, ⁸and Asaph the father of Jehoshaphat, and Jehoshaphat the father of Joram, and Joram the father of Uzziah, ⁹and Uzziah the father of Jotham, and Jotham the father of Ahaz, and Ahaz the father of Hezekiah, ¹⁰and Hezekiah the

Theological Perspective

One of the dominant theological motives in the Bible is a messianic hope. From beginning to end in the Scriptures there is a sense of waiting for God's action and presence with faith and hope. We need a messianic hope so that we do not lose track of God's project of redemption, fulfillment, and destiny for all of creation. We also need a new vision to imagine and dream new realities in the midst of our present crises. Indeed, we need to believe in God's promises and the coming of God's reign.

The Gospel of Matthew makes a theological statement from the very beginning: Jesus is the Messiah, the one announced to and expected by the people of Israel. There is a connection and continuity with the dreams and aspirations of the Jewish people in the coming of a Messiah to establish a reign of peace and justice. The story stresses the relationship of this Messiah with David and Abraham as their descendant. God's action in history is fulfilled now in the life and ministry of Jesus. All the messianic titles are selected to demonstrate this divine presence in Jesus. He is the chosen one, the anointed, in whose life the messianic hope is finally revealed. Peter's confession, "You are the Christ, the son of the living God" (Matt. 16:16), confirms this hermeneutical principle, Jesus is the Messiah. This is the key element of Matthew's theological perspective. Matthew emphasizes both

Pastoral Perspective

Sonia was obsessed by her past. Adopted by an abusive family as an infant, she always felt like a stranger to herself. When she gave birth to a daughter and held the infant in her arms, Sonia simply fell apart. Stunned by the realization that someone had held her thirty years earlier and then rejected her, Sonia was filled with a grief and a self-loathing that shaped her adult life. After an exhaustive search through phone books, hospital records, and birth registries, Sonia discovered a clue that led her to the place where she had been born. Then she began pursuing her birth parents with a passion that infuriated them. They simply did not want to be found.

Slowly, Sonia gave up her search, finding her only solace in the promises of her faith. She found comfort in the knowledge that she—like all of us—is adopted, welcomed, wanted in the family of God, and that Jesus cherishes her as a sister. Her spiritual family helped her mourn the physical family she never knew, but rootlessness wounded her for the rest of her life. As creatures shaped by the womb of history, we all yearn to know where we have come from.

In contemporary family-systems theory, the genogram has become a valuable tool in helping individuals identify values and relationships that have shaped their character and values over the years. By "mapping" three or four generations, we can identify

father of Manasseh, and Manasseh the father of Amos, and Amos the father of Josiah, [11]and Josiah the father of Jechoniah and his brothers, at the time of the deportation to Babylon.

[12]And after the deportation to Babylon: Jechoniah was the father of Salathiel, and Salathiel the father of Zerubbabel, [13]and Zerubbabel the father of Abiud, and Abiud the father of Eliakim, and Eliakim the father of Azor, [14]and Azor the father of Zadok, and Zadok the father of Achim, and Achim the father of Eliud, [15]and Eliud the father of Eleazar, and Eleazar the father of Matthan, and Matthan the father of Jacob, [16]and Jacob the father of Joseph the husband of Mary, of whom Jesus was born, who is called the Messiah.

[17]So all the generations from Abraham to David are fourteen generations; and from David to the deportation to Babylon, fourteen generations; and from the deportation to Babylon to the Messiah, fourteen generations.

Exegetical Perspective

Years ago there was a popular book well suited for settling bar bets: *The Book of Lists*. The book decontextualized whole swaths of human knowledge by placing any conceivable achievement or curiosity into a listed series. Contemporary readers may be forgiven for passing over Matthew's genealogy at the beginning of his eponymous Gospel as poor form—or worse, just another list. If they do, however, they will miss an opportunity to understand something of the Gospel's vision for naming who Jesus is and what he is about. The text is not just another list at all. It merits a careful and close exegetical reading.

We begin with the superscription. Already Matthew is cuing readers about how to take in the two series of genealogical lists given in double-sacred-number size (2x7=14 generations). The superscription calls it the "book of the birth of Jesus Christ, Son of David, Son of Abraham," although the word for "birth" also means "genesis" or "genealogy." Before all that biblical begetting really gets started, Matthew provides readers with a framework for understanding the list that is to follow. Its subject matter is the birth of Jesus Christ, to be sure, but the interpretation of that reality is unique to Matthew's theological and literary vision: this Jesus must be understood as broadly as the Abrahamic promise and as royally as the Davidic promise of kingship

Homiletical Perspective

Do you have a famous relative? Often people name-drop their historical connections to enhance their social, political, or religious prestige. Being a Daughter of the American Revolution or a Kennedy or a Rockefeller engenders associations with American royalty. People take pride in genealogies because these names orient their location in history by establishing continuity between then and now.

Remember the first time you attended your spouse's family reunion. You learned not to confuse venerable Uncle John with gnarly Uncle Joe. Eventually, you learned their names and stories. Even then, some stories were kept silent. No one spoke of Uncle John's experience in Albany. Even an allusion to the memory caused relatives to wince. The memory became elusive more than allusive.

Our cultural fascination with ancestries might be a place to begin as the preacher seeks to engage this text. Likewise Jesus' ancestry has powerful allusive names, but also elusive details. Some names are forgotten and irretrievable. Prestigious connections are made in a list that includes Abraham, Judah, Ruth, David, Solomon, and Josiah. Also, disconnections occur, due to lost registries or differing motives for record keeping. Moreover, names like Manasseh cause readers to recoil. Israel's deportation to a refugee camp stings, as it resembles their Roman occupation. When

Matthew 1:1–17

Theological Perspective

the presence of God's reign in history ("kingdom of heaven") and the church as the affirmation of Jesus as the "Son of the living God."

A genealogy serves the purpose of establishing Jesus' identity and place in salvation history. This genealogy is directly related to the book of Genesis. There are forty-two generations from Abraham to Jesus. Matthew is a storyteller and interpreter of God's saving acts, not a chronicler. His style moves between the facts selected to probe Jesus' origin and a narrative that interprets theologically that Jesus is the Messiah. Matthew introduces Jesus as an authorized teacher and interpreter of the law and the prophets, in whom the new commandment of love with justice is fulfilled. The undergirding hermeneutical principle is the authority of Scriptures. Matthew is constantly making references to the Old Testament in order to show that Jesus fulfills what the Scriptures predicted.

Genograms are assessments that are used to help counselors record family history through the lives of each of its members. Genograms graphically portray family trees that show marriages, divorces, conflicts in dysfunctional families, adoptions, and strained relationships. Matthew's genealogy is a genogram with a theological dimension, an effort to emphasize that Jesus is part of this sacred story, but also very much part of the human stories of common people.

The women in the narrative play an important role. They too are God's instruments, and the majority of them are of Gentile origin. There are four references to women before Mary: Tamar, Rahab, Ruth, and Bathsheba. As Gentile women they are outsiders. Mary, a young Jewish woman, becomes the chosen vessel "of whom Jesus was born" (v. 16b).

Matthew's narrative has caught the attention of filmmakers, novelists, and storytellers. One of these creative spirits is Pier Paolo Pasolini, an Italian filmmaker, actor, and poet. In 1964 Pasolini made an important film on the life of Jesus, based on the Gospel of Matthew. Pasolini was a communist (at times at odds with the Communist Party in Italy!) who considered himself an atheist, but he dedicated most of his filmmaking to religious themes, particularly depictions of Jesus in the four Gospels. For many critics Pasolini was an eccentric filmmaker, sometimes a mystic, most of the time a heretic. He dedicated *The Gospel of Matthew* to Pope John XXIII. The film was very popular all over the world, particularly in colleges and universities.

The film is a retelling of the New Testament story as written by Matthew and interpreted by Pasolini.

Pastoral Perspective

patterns of behavior and uncover emotional legacies. Such an exercise in my early adult years uncovered both the joy and tragedy buried in my familial pedigree. I am descended from a Norwegian queen, a German farmer, a Moravian musician, and a Scottish alcoholic who abused his wife and children. Discovering a pattern of miscarriages and infant deaths has helped me understand deep depression in both of my grandmothers. The role of the church as a haven for immigrants and emotionally abused children keeps reappearing in my genogram. Certainly God has been at work in the generational texture of my life, weaving into my story a pattern of suffering and redemption, industry and artistry, that has framed my call to ministry.

The beginning of Matthew is a genogram of Jesus' life. Tracing forty-two generations all the way back to Abraham, we travel through triumph and tragedy, exaltation and exile, lostness and foundness. What we discover are patterns that define the very providence of God—Gentiles being welcomed, sinners being changed, transgressions nurturing transformation, fear fueling courage. It is out of a ghastly, goodly heritage that Jesus is born. Weaknesses in the family tree form strong branches upon which God brings forth the fruit of the incarnation.

When interpreting and exploring a genogram, the surprises as well as the patterns help shape an individual's self-understanding. We worship a God of surprises who cannot be captured by precedent or prediction. In Joseph's genealogy, the surprises abound. Four women make the list—all of them Gentiles, three of them defined by sexual sins—and yet all of them play redemptive roles in God's unfolding drama of salvation. Are we surprised that God uses what culture abuses to plant life in a broken world? Do we wonder why Jesus is so predisposed to love the marginal and despised among us? Such a surprising compassion is simply part of our Savior's spiritual DNA.

Perhaps the biggest surprise in Matthew's genealogy is the presence of Joseph. Come again? The doctrinal foundation of the Christian faith insists that Jesus was born of a virgin—that Mary had not "known" Joseph in any physical way when she became pregnant with Jesus. Why is Joseph listed as a progenitor? By confusing us, God surprises us and encourages us to dig deeper into the complexity and contradictions of the faith. We are pushed to understand generativity and birth in a spiritual way, not just a physical way. We are assured that our lineage comes from all the people who nurture us and confront us and protect us and change us.

and rule. As if to underline its meaning, the Hebrew consonants of the name David add up to fourteen—a possible signal of Matthew's thinking. (Each Hebrew consonant has a numeric value. D=4 and V or W=6. The name David is 4+4+6=14.) This Jesus of promised Abrahamic lineage is also royal "son of David" from the beginning.

What makes this more than an exercise in following listed names, some of which deviate from other biblical chronologies anyway, is not just who stands in succession, but *how* they do so. Lists of patriarchal begetters should be, well, patriarchal. Yet this one is different. Just when you think that the indispensable chain of male succession is going to guarantee the promised pedigree of Jesus, something interrupts the flow. Sometimes someone other than the firstborn male carries the line forward. Sometimes a known king or three are left out of the succession to ensure numerical symmetry (cf. 1:8 and 1 Chr. 3:11–12).

Even this otherwise predictable succession of male pronouns, names, and articles is broken up with the occasional feminine in Matthew's list. Matthew's genealogical picture is not just another photograph of the biblical Old Boys Club, because there they stand: abused Tamar (v. 3), resourceful Rahab (v. 5a), and that foreigner Ruth (v. 5b) are themselves key to the unfolding promised succession. Lest we think that Matthew's vision is just about females of a scandalous sort, the list also includes King David's manifold misdoings, thanks to the less directly named Mr. and Mrs. Uriah the Hittite. She (Bathsheba) is not named in verse 6, but the scandal (here interpreted as King David's own) only helps to underline the dogged way in which the promises of God deal particularly with male messiness in the line.

All this prepares the way quite nicely for the end of the genealogy, which words the outcome of the twofold promise of Abraham and David in a strangely phrased sequence (v. 16): "and Jacob begat Joseph, the husband of Mary, from whom Jesus was born, the one called Christ" (KJV). Clearly this unusual genealogical list has prepared us for a bumpy, sometimes even scandalous ride to the promise. Human begetting can do only so much. The rest is up to God and God's strange, marginal way of making promises come to fulfillment. (It also sets up the necessity of the Holy Spirit "how?" to follow in 1:18–25!)

In the end, Matthew is careful to give us the genealogical review so we do not misunderstand his list. Verse 17 clearly reminds us of the fulfilling symmetry of the divine promise. Fourteen generations from Abraham to David, fourteen more from David to the

the wife of Uriah is mentioned, the memory mortifies the soul. Genealogies highlight Israel's greatest moments and expose her darkest days. Now as then, some stories do both. Hezekiah's faith and arrogance are side by side in their retelling. Matthew's genealogy delineates accolades and baggage.

Numerous commentaries highlight the four women who appear unexpectedly in an otherwise patrilineal list. Other OT genealogies catalog women, but typically list Sarah, Rebecca, and Rachel, not Tamar, Rahab, Ruth, or Uriah's wife. These women draw our attention to the fifth woman: Mary, the mother of Jesus. What these women share with Mary eludes interpreters. Sermons often retell their narratives as sinners or foreigners, or by the irregularities of their unions, or through their bold initiatives to partner with God's purposes. When the homiletical tradition offers multiple conflicting options, the preacher often arbitrarily picks one. However, as Raymond Brown indicates in *The Birth of the Messiah*,[1] all the interpretive options pertaining to the women have limitations.

Considering the theological themes explicit in the whole genealogy presents a compelling option for the preacher. Brown recognizes how readers today overlook the function of genealogies, reading them as though they are lists of grandparents in the "frontispiece of the Family Bible."[2] While he cites various reasons for the existence of ancient genealogies, the preacher could explore why our fascination with ancient genealogies persists. People scour census reports, immigration data, and military records for clues about their family histories. Social media tap people's impulses to unlock the secrets of their past with sites like ancestry.com. The British television series asks the intriguing question, "Who do you think you are?" How much more intriguing is the question about Jesus' roots! This is the family tree of our Lord. In all their mess and glory, these names are his kin.

The *inclusio* of the pericope also invites the preacher to pursue a global reading. "The account of the genesis of Jesus the Messiah" (v. 1, my trans., and truncated in v. 18) recalls God's activity in the redemption of humanity from the beginning (Gen. 2:4; 5:1). Generations come and go. The endless ages roll by without consideration, but now Jesus is the fulfillment of Israel's hopes. The stylized account of three sets of fourteen generations signifies that God works to fulfill God's intentions (v. 17). In God's

---

1. See Raymond E. Brown, *The Birth of the Messiah: A Commentary on the Infancy Narratives in the Gospels of Matthew and Luke*, rev. ed. (New York: Doubleday, 1993), 71–74, 590–96.
2. Ibid., 65.

Matthew 1:1–17

Theological Perspective

The words, deeds, and scenes of the script are very close to Matthew's text, but Pasolini's eclectic style is also predominant. He combines the music of Johann Sebastian Bach (Mass in B Minor and *Saint Matthew Passion*) and Wolfgang Amadeus Mozart. Pasolini also selected the *Missa Luba*, a Congolese mass sung to African instruments and rhythms. Behind scenes of Mary and the baby, the Negro spiritual "Sometimes I Feel Like a Motherless Child" was also sung. Finally, Pasolini included *Alexander Nevsky Cantata* of Sergei Prokofiev behind Herod's slaughter of the infants and the scene of Jesus' removal to Golgotha.

From the very first scene, in which Mary is shown as a pregnant woman in front of Joseph in disbelief, the film makes a compelling argument: these are very human, everyday persons with their anxieties, doubts, and hopes. The film moves in this dynamic, making visible the hidden stories of peasants and common people. Jesus is portrayed as a young man searching for his destiny, struggling to become the messianic figure in the midst of a very conflicted reality.

A final theological element to consider in any reading of Matthew's Gospel is the role of the Holy Spirit. The Holy Spirit is an active agent, with a diversity of actions in different contexts. The overall theological principle is that God is present as Father, Son, and Holy Spirit in these different contexts. The Holy Spirit is not acting alone but as part of an intercommunion of the Trinity. In Jesus' baptism this perspective, implicit in the birth of Jesus, is confirmed (3:13–17). For Matthew, the Holy Spirit confirms Jesus' authority in word and deed.

Matthew has developed a theology of history in his Gospel. Jesus, the Christ, is the awaited Messiah, announced by the Scriptures. Jesus is incarnated in human reality with a redemptive message of salvation and hope, calling people to follow him, discerning their own vocation and destiny in life. Jesus is the fulfillment of the messianic hope of the people of Israel. Starting with a genealogy that establishes God's purpose for humanity in the first chapter and ending with a mission to the world, Matthew points to the divine realm that now permeates all reality as a transforming power. The church is a witness to the world of God's redemptive love manifested in Jesus Christ.

CARMELO E. ÁLVAREZ

Pastoral Perspective

Congregations, as well as individuals, have genograms—patterns of behavior, surprises of history, stories of generations that indelibly shape who they are. In the 1980s a religious sociologist named James Hopewell suggested that narrative history can help a congregation define their unique call and propel them into a fresh history. By creating a timeline of stories, drawn deeply out of the soul of those who have come before, a central, defining metaphor or image can emerge. Using this metaphor to imagine the future allows a congregation to draw on its legacy in order to continue to change the world. In the congregation I served for seventeen years, such a storytelling journey helped us identify the central pattern of our history. Born as a Sunday school in a renovated stable—and resurrected as a suburban congregation during a meeting in a cemetery—the congregation discovered during its fiftieth anniversary year that it really was the resurrected body of Christ called to transform the world. For both congregations and individuals, patterns lead to surprises and surprises call us to new life.

Harold Kushner recalls the Hasidic tale of a man who received a telegram from a rabbi informing him that a relative had died and left him some valuable property. Eager to claim his inheritance, the man rushed to the rabbi's office, only to learn that the relative was Moses and the valuable property was the Jewish tradition. For Jesus and for the rest of us, God shapes us most distinctively by the promises and peculiarities of our spiritual legacy.

By prefacing the story of Jesus with such a rich and ridiculous genealogy, Matthew sets the stage for the rich and ridiculous power of the gospel. The good news is that God creates us out of our history in order to re-create us for our future. Our past births us—but it does not control us. We are adopted into God's future—new creatures in Christ, where the past is finished and gone, and the new has come. Thanks be to God!

SUSAN R. ANDREWS

Exegetical Perspective

Babylonian exile, and fourteen more from the exile to Christ. The promise is good, yes; but it is being read stylistically through an important counterimperial lens. The promise to Abraham and the promise to David, which are constitutive for the claims of who Jesus Christ is, need to be read through the realities of exile.

In the midst of the lines that run from promise to fulfillment, there is a sense that they pass through scandal, yes, but public catastrophe, too. The mention of Babylon is not just for historical reasons. It is a reminder of the strange shadow under which even this story of a child unfolds: the pain of being under the thumb of the Roman Empire. NT scholar Warren Carter goes so far as to say that what we have here is an anti-imperial statement.[1] Just as Babylon has come and gone, so also are the new empire's days numbered, as assuredly as 2x7=14.

The upshot, of course, is that this not just your average, run-of-the-mill genealogical list. Like *The Book of Lists* it seems to be something less than pure, holy history. There is a whiff of scandal in the air, just as a book suitable for settling bar bets probably reeks a bit of old beer and cigarettes. Unlike *The Book of Lists*, however, there lurks here the dogged nature of the promise to work newness, even through stale patriarchies and tired old successions. God is up to something new in the empire's shadow. The question is no longer *if*, but *how* this will happen. So perhaps the list in 1:1–17 was really about setting the stage for the action to follow.

It has been claimed that there are four indispensable elements to a good narrative: religion, money, sex, and mystery. The proof of this assertion can be given in a single narrative sentence: "Oh, my God," said the banker's daughter, "I'm pregnant . . . and I don't know who the father is!" Well, for Matthew, three out of four may suffice. Matthew has one plot element sufficient to hold together his story from musty list to birth narrative: a promise that will not be waylaid—whether by patriarchs, scandal, or even empire.

DAVID SCHNASA JACOBSEN

1. Warren Carter, *Matthew: Storyteller, Interpreter, Evangelist*, rev. ed. (Peabody, MA: Hendrickson, 2004), 108.

Homiletical Perspective

providence, marriages are arranged, offspring are produced, and people are rescued from peril. Matthew's genealogy documents Jesus' lineage as an Israelite and provides a unifying link between the necessary figures that authenticates him as God's chosen.

While Abraham and David function as anchors for fourteen generations, the exile is brought to prominence as a third anchor. The anomaly in the register shouts for due time. The directory of names is interrupted by an event. The exile (vv. 11, 12, 17) carries the same rhetorical weight as "son of David," and "son of Abraham." Both Abraham and David represented covenants (Gen. 12:2–3 and 2 Sam. 7:16) that became foundational for Israelite identity. The reality of 586 BCE changed everything. What had become of God's promises of nation and king? Israel's relationship to God's faithfulness became tenuous. Matthew's readers resonated with the plotline of exile and liberation. Abraham, yes: Jesus is an Israelite. David, yes: Jesus is a son who is a king. Deportation, yes: Jesus is a Messiah who will deliver God's people from exile and occupation.

The genealogy orients us with bookends that reveal the denouement of God's promise-keeping activities. Matthew begins with a proclamation of Jesus as the Messiah, the son of David, the son of Abraham (v. 1). As son of Abraham, Jesus is the culmination of Israel's faith. As son of David, Jesus is the fulfillment of Israel's hope for a future king. As Messiah, Jesus is the salvation of God's people from the dominion of others. When people turn to God's Messiah, God will deliver them from sin's consequences. The *inclusio* emphasizes God's role in the unfolding of the generations from Abraham to David to Babylon to Messiah (v. 17). In case you missed it, the *inclusio* double-stamps the proclamation of Jesus as the Messiah (vv. 16, 17). The climactic conclusion of the genealogy arrives at the last name on the list, one who will redeem. This one will not be an allusion but will have a concretization in the stories that follow.

The Eyes Glaze Over (the TEGO Effect) when reading biblical genealogies. A more global reading brightens people's eyes on three primary levels. First, an introduction on our cultural fascination with ancestries and the importance of family instills a sense of identity and belonging. Second, a sweeping retelling of the stories in Jesus' family tree unfolds the grand epic of Israel's narrative with all its drama. Finally, the climactic birth of the Messiah opens the possibility for all who are listening to be part of this same redemptive lineage.

TIMOTHY R. SENSING

Matthew 1:18–25

¹⁸Now the birth of Jesus the Messiah took place in this way. When his mother Mary had been engaged to Joseph, but before they lived together, she was found to be with child from the Holy Spirit. ¹⁹Her husband Joseph, being a righteous man and unwilling to expose her to public disgrace, planned to dismiss her quietly. ²⁰But just when he had resolved to do this, an angel of the Lord appeared to him in a dream and said, "Joseph, son of David, do not be afraid to take Mary as your wife, for the child conceived in her is from the Holy Spirit. ²¹She will bear a son, and you are to name him Jesus, for he will save his people from their sins." ²²All this took place to fulfill what had been spoken by the Lord through the prophet:

²³ "Look, the virgin shall conceive and bear a son,
    and they shall name him Emmanuel,"

which means, "God is with us." ²⁴When Joseph awoke from sleep, he did as the angel of the Lord commanded him; he took her as his wife, ²⁵but had no marital relations with her until she had borne a son; and he named him Jesus.

Theological Perspective

We are waiting for the Messiah. That is the spirit of the season. The celebration is fast approaching. Our expectations are high because we need to celebrate and rejoice. We are surrounded by too much trouble and pain. We need a fresh breeze.

This text is exactly that: it is a fresh look at the many ways God is revealed to us, often in unexpected places and persons. Mary, Joseph, and Jesus are introduced as nothing more than common people. They look a lot like other folks of their time, and a lot like us. In this text we see that God uses what looks insignificant to reveal what is significant and transcendent. Ordinary humans are transformed into divine vessels. Humans are shown to be part of salvation history. The objective is to demonstrate that Jesus is the incarnate one from God, and his birth is a historical event. Jesus' birth is the concrete demonstration of God's incarnation among the poor and marginalized of the world, then and now.

The story itself is dynamic. God is active in history. Mary is an instrument of God's grace. Joseph is portrayed as a man who trusts in God, and Jesus is Immanuel, God with us. At the center of the story is an overwhelming experience of believing. This is what Christmas is all about!

The text in Matthew 1:18–25 poses two key questions: How does God intervene in history? What

Pastoral Perspective

In this text from Matthew we are invited inside the Joseph version of the annunciation story—not a virgin story, but a vision story. We meet Joseph the dreamer—a righteous man who trusts relationships rather than rules—an obedient man who responds to dreams rather than to demands. In this ancient story, we twenty-first-century disciples discover fresh insight about living and believing in highly anxious times.

It is appropriate in these postmodern days to consider dreams as the place where we find hope. The great promises of the Enlightenment, which offered reason and human potential and scientific truth as the answers to all our problems, have turned out to be bogus promises that have crumbled all around us. Science has given us nuclear destruction and technological mania and a thousand ways to pollute the earth. Reason has led us to exhausting debates about who is right and who is wrong. Human potential has created war and worry and a busyness that bores us. None of it has done much to feed our soul. Somewhere along the way, the church has gotten gobbled up in all this modernity—forsaking the gospel of Jesus for a gospel of junk.

As the faithful remnant amid the institutional ashes of mainline Protestantism, many of us identify with Joseph. Caught in a culture and a religious institution that is deteriorating, we yearn for a new

Exegetical Perspective

Matthew's birth/genesis of Jesus continues the genealogy's vision by turning to how this Jesus gets included in Joseph's "son of David" line so carefully listed in 1:1–17. As we turn to this perhaps overly familiar text, so beloved at Advent and Christmas, we need to screen a few things out of our mind.

First, we may be predisposed to read this text in light of the many Christmas pageants we have endured, where Luke's shepherds and Matthew's wise men are harmonized into a high-traffic manger scene that would have even put Tatian's *Diatessaron* to shame. Matthew's Joseph is the focus here; Mary gets no speaking role, no Magnificat recitative to sing. Matthew's singular focus is *how* this Jesus Christ gets into Joseph's line. In his unique narrative nativity, it hinges on the gracious initiative of Holy Spirit and, in turn, Joseph's inspired obedience.

Second, the text is based on the genealogy's carefully laid groundwork. If the genealogy begins with a pun on birth/genealogy (*geneseōs*), Joseph's dream likewise begins with the nominative case of the same double-sided Greek word (*genesis*) in 1:18. For all the familiarity of the Joseph story of Jesus' birth, the genealogical interest in Abrahamic and Davidic sonship and its connection to the birth is still front and center.

Third, we are also mistaken if we try to read later christological developments into Matthew's

Homiletical Perspective

Christmas is a time to retell familiar stories. When the preacher uses Matthew's version, the retelling will necessarily be more sober. The scandal at Joseph's house, the gossip around town, and the rumors that followed even in Matthew's day are not the stories for little children. Joseph is a righteous man who is faithful to the demands of the law, yet he desires mercy more than sacrifice. Background understandings about Jewish marriage laws and customs, divine communications through angels, dreams, and OT texts give the story greater texture, the grit of reality. However, be warned. Do not turn story into commentary. The clarity of the story's denouement and Matthew's economy of words provide a model for the preacher.

When retelling Matthew's version, the preacher will want to plot the sermon in a way that emphasizes Matthew's climax. The literary structure suggests one way to determine the focus of the sermon: (a) Mary's unusual pregnancy (v. 18); (b) Joseph's dilemma and initial decision (v. 19); (c) the message of the angel (vv. 20–21); (c′) the message from Scripture (vv. 22–23); (b′) Joseph's new resolution (v. 24); (a′) Mary's unusual pregnancy and birth (v. 25). A chiastic reading of the text focuses the sermon on the messages from characters outside the immediate scene. The angel's message emphasizes both the identity of

Matthew 1:18–25

Theological Perspective

is the role of belief in God's supernatural action in human history? These questions can help us in discerning God's will.

In the first place, Matthew stresses three fundamental theological affirmations: God is incarnate in Jesus Christ, God is an active agent in the incarnation through the Holy Spirit, and God participates actively in the human condition. The incarnation of Jesus Christ became a fundamental principle in christological discussions, particularly the person and work of Jesus Christ. The direct action of the Holy Spirit is a witness of divine power and Trinitarian intercommunion. A divine energy and presence in the midst of human life is further evidence of a God who cares and is involved in creative and redemptive action.

Given these three theological affirmations, it may be helpful to make two distinctions: what is defined as mystery and how we understand the miracle. God is the mystery of our lives. We are reminded of Rudolf Otto's definition of mystery as "fearful and fascinating mystery" (*mysterium tremendum et fascinans*).[1] The idea of the holy, according to Otto, is the "numinous" in the mystical experience of the sacred that inspires awe and wonder. In theological terms it means that God is hidden (the realm of the unknown) and revealed (the realities of human history); God is transcendent and immanent.

A miracle is a "remarkable act of God, especially suspension of normal working of the laws of nature by supernatural intervention."[2] Matthew describes the roles of divine and human agents in the miracle: an angel, Joseph, Mary, and a baby, Jesus, in a providential and eschatological manifestation of God's purpose. God's mystery and presence permeate these eight verses.

In the second place, in the naming of Jesus, God confirms our human identity in relation to God. Matthew invites us to see this act through the lens of prophetic fulfillment in Matthew 1:23 (1662 Book of Common Prayer): "Behold, a Virgin shall conceive and bear a Son, and shall call his name Immanuel, which being interpreted is God with us." In naming, God names God's self, names Jesus (Joshua), Lord, the Messiah, the Anointed. God also names us. We are God's own people, remembered by God.

In Handel's oratorio *Messiah* this verse is used in an alto recitative, immediately after the famous chorus

Pastoral Perspective

way of seeing, a new way of trusting, a new way of coping with problems that seem insurmountable. Our pews are empty, our buildings are crumbling, and our young people have wandered away toward the cathedrals of pop culture. As biblical history reminds us, this is exactly the kind of scenario that God most desires. It is when we are vulnerable and lost and anxious—and out of control—that God can finally discover a way into our hearts.

Walter Brueggemann has written about the power of dreams in the Bible.[1] From Jacob terrified and exhausted by his guilty fleeing to OT Joseph shackled in a prison cell in Egypt, from Daniel doing a death dance in the lions' den of King Darius to the magi pondering how to escape the clutches of Herod, dreams are the way God frees us and rebirths us and pushes us into new life. So it is with Joseph, confused and scared and wanting to do what is right. So it is with us, wondering what God can possibly be up to. God turns us all into dreamers—we who know that the past is gone and that the new has come, but have no idea how to survive in our deserts of unfulfilled dreams.

Brueggemann reminds us that all the dreams in Scripture have something in common. They represent the intrusion of God into a settled world—an unbidden communication in the dark of the night that opens sleepers to a world different from the one they inhabit during the day—an intrusion that generates a restless uneasiness with the way things are until the vision and the dream come to fruition. Jacob woke from his dream as a restless wrestler but was blessed in the end. OT Joseph woke from his dream and saved his people. The magi woke from their dream and went home another way. In this text, NT Joseph wakes from his dream and embraces the Savior of the world. Having been changed by their dreams, all these pilgrims discover purpose. They discover a promise. They discover a passion to live life for someone and something beyond themselves. So the story of God's goodness and grace is written on one more human heart.

Joseph is described by Matthew as a righteous man—a description that has led to all the rigid, silent Josephs hiding in the shadows of our Christmas pageants. Joseph's righteousness, however, is based on love, not on law. It has to do with trusting intuition and imagination—being in right relationship with the dreams of God. By so doing, Joseph becomes

---

1. "Mysteries, Mysterium Tremendum et Fascinans," in George Thomas Kurian, ed., *Nelson's New Christian Dictionary* (Nashville: Nelson Publishers, 2001), 534.
2. "Miracle," *Nelson's New Christian Dictionary*, 512.

1. Walter Brueggemann, "The Power of Dreams in the Bible," *Christian Century*, June 28, 2005, 28–31.

story. Issues of virgin birth need to be considered in light of at least two exegetical problems. On the one hand, there is the way we read a virgin birth in terms of divine *being*. Matthew's way of viewing the story is much more functional—the birth is more about divine purposes than divine pedigree. On the other hand, the whole virgin-birth issue hinges on a messy translation of a Hebrew prophecy in Isaiah 7:14 about a birth-giving young woman (*almah*); the unfortunate Greek translation of this word in the Septuagint as virgin (*parthenos*) can, but does not actually have to, mean "virgin." This has bequeathed to us a lot of confusion in the history of interpretation. In light of these two potential misunderstandings, it is best to focus on what Matthew is really saying about this birth: that it is Holy Spirit work in the midst of a messy, but promising genealogical lineage in the shadow of empire.

How do we know? Matthew's own rhetoric makes the point. In both verses 18 and 20b, Matthew places the name of the agent of the child's origin at the very *end* of a long, periodic sentence: Holy Spirit. There is a mystery to this birth, a strange, convoluted path of unwinding promise that ends, tellingly, with the only One who could possibly beget such newness: the Holy Spirit. For that matter, all the talk about ancient marriage practices, the sequencing of promised betrothals, and Deuteronomistic divorce laws is there in the narrative in order to remove possibilities of human paternity. This child is Holy Spirit work and, as such, eschatological earnest and messianic material.

Joseph underlines this reality through his narrative role. Although we readers are privileged to learn the Holy Spirit's agency in the pregnancy in verse 18, Joseph can see the dawning truth only in his dreams. He has made righteous plans to dismiss Mary quietly and avoid a stoning for his apparently scandal-prone wife, only to be briefed by an angel, a divine messenger, who brings him on board with the rest of us readers. In fact, the only way this child gets grafted into Joseph's Davidic line is because of Holy Spirit labors. Joseph's chief role is to respond to such dawning grace with a relational obedience ("taking [Mary] as his wife" in v. 24b, "had no marital relations with her until she had borne a son" in v. 25a, and "[naming] him Jesus" in v. 25b) that corresponds to the angel's dreamy commands (vv. 20a, 20b [Roman Catholic tradition], and 21 respectively).

In the middle of this circle of the Holy Spirit's initiative and Joseph's obedience is the first of Matthew's twelve Scripture-citation fulfillment formulae (they tend to come fast and furious in this opening

the child being "from" the Holy Spirit (v. 18) and the meaning of the name Jesus, "for he will save his people from their sins" (v. 21). The message from Isaiah 7:14 highlights the miraculous nature of the child's conception and identity. This time, his name will be Immanuel, meaning "God is with us." Both messages reassure Joseph that Mary's pregnancy is not a result of promiscuity but the action of God through the Holy Spirit in order to save God's people. While some preachers bog down in the "how" of the conception or the associated apologetics, Matthew does not. The preacher should proclaim in the present tense the timeless significance of Jesus as the fulfillment of God's messianic purposes.

Another way to plot the retelling is to use the Jewish technique of "lesser to greater." The angel's announcement and the OT texts underscore the child's holiness and uniqueness because no conception before or after has been by the agency of the Holy Spirit (vv. 18, 20). Jesus' origin is from God. While Jewish and Greco-Roman literature both contain many stories of extraordinary births, none parallels Matthew's. Jesus' birth is not analogous to but different from and greater than the rest. The lesser to greater comparison also holds with our own birth announcements in relation to this birth announcement. Couples often find imaginative ways to reveal their news to their parents and friends. While we rejoice with the parents-to-be, how much more joyous is the birth of the redeemer of the world!

The preacher also may retell the story with an eye to the way Matthew clears up some legal matters by setting the record straight. Matthew 1:1–18 states that Jesus is the son of Abraham and the son of David. How Jesus is David's son needs further explication. A messenger signifies Matthew's intent by stating, "Joseph, son of David" (v. 20, the only time that someone other than Jesus is given this title). Joseph legally adopts Jesus so that the title son of David is legitimately conferred upon him. For the law to take effect, Joseph is instructed in the text to do something. Joseph's actions affirm his desire to take the role as father. Joseph keeps his marriage covenant by taking Mary into his house. Next, Joseph assumes responsibility for mother and child. Finally, Joseph exercises his right to name his son Jesus. Joseph's actions point to his position as a legal father, but not the boy's natural father. So Matthew addresses the gossip with the legal facts and in yet another way makes it clear that Jesus' conception was divine.

Retelling the story could also call attention to Matthew's intentional plotline. For example, if the

Matthew 1:18–25

Theological Perspective

"And he shall purify." The sequence of a bass recitative, bass aria, and the chorus points to the coming of the Lord, the Messiah and High Priest. The alto recitative moves into a sober, joyful, and expectant moment. The alto whispers the promise of the prophet with a sense of awe in the presence of a mystery: God's mystery now made manifest. The announcement is that the virgin is conceiving this baby, Immanuel, God with us; in a soft and tender voice the alto conveys the message: God is here, God is with us.

Matthew has made two very relevant theological statements in this text. First, God's mystery and presence permeate the eight verses (vv. 18–25). Second, in naming, God confirms who we are and whose we are. Joseph, the one passive actor in the saga, names Jesus.

Going forward in the Matthean narrative, how will "God is with us" save us from our sins? Jesus will call his followers to the path of radical obedience, an experience of humility in fidelity, a true vocation (4:12–25). This is a free decision, accepting an obligation in action (5:13–16). Christian mission is really a call to obedience rather than a quest for victory; it is a call to be faithful, not successful. Discipleship, as the grace of God, is a privilege of living this obedience in every situation (chap. 25).

Discipleship occurs in concrete and transparent self-giving, like the self-giving of Jesus (5:38–48). In his actions and his words, his miracles and his parables, Jesus models a life that rejects selfishness (21:33–46). He asks believers to follow his example and accept the risk of being a witness to the faith so that others might live (11:25–30). So there opens before our eyes the path of truth and life. To spend our life in the fulfillment of this commitment is the privilege of every Christian (20:20–28).

Matthew, the storyteller and narrative theologian, has inspired filmmakers, novelists, poets, and musicians. Cesáreo Gabaráin, the late Spanish Catholic composer, wrote a song based on Matthew 4:18–25 that became a favorite of Pope John Paul II. It speaks of the Lord who came to the lakeshore:

Looking neither for wealthy nor wise ones;
You only asked me to follow humbly.[3]

This is a very accurate summary of Matthew's theology!

CARMELO E. ÁLVAREZ

Pastoral Perspective

faithful not to the conventions of the world, but to the heart of the Holy One.

Our young adults are caught in a media world embraced by paradox. Reality TV competes with fantasy films. YouTube immediacy wrestles with dancing pigs and romantic vampires. It is as if the rawness of reality needs to be balanced by the freedom of dreams. The fear and ugliness of the way things are needs to be softened by the promise and power of the way things might be. Practicality duels with possibility. Yes, we live in a searching time, a chaotic time, a biblical time—a time when a dreamer like Joseph can set us free from the complexities that confine us.

Advent is the most countercultural time of the liturgical year. With our purple shadows and doleful music and eschatological terror, the church clashes with the culture. Refusing to escape into a womb of sentimentality and materialism, we dare to look at the darkness of our days, so that we might imagine the brightness of a new way. Joseph is our guide. He invites us to a seasonal slumber party—daring us to share our dreams about new life, our dreams about what we need, our dreams about everything we have been too afraid to dream about. He shows us how to welcome incarnation—the radical intrusion of a flesh-and-blood God into the dreariness of our human condition—the full embodiment of God's dream of shalom and compassion and justice and grace and wholeness and abundance. He shows us how to name our dream—to name our dream "Jesus, God with us"—a dream even more vivid in the sunshine than it is in the dark.

SUSAN R. ANDREWS

---

3. Cesáreo Gabaráin, "You Have Come to the Lakeshore (*Tú has venido a la orilla*)," trans. Gertrude Suppe, George Lockwood, and Raquel Achón, in *Glory to God* (Louisville, KY: Westminster John Knox Press, 2013), 721.

part of Matthew; see 2:15, 17, and 23). All this happened to fulfill the Scriptures (v. 22). In this case, Isaiah 7:14 is cited and the point is made. It is not so much about the divine being of virgin-born demigods, as the Greeks might claim. It is really about a divine purpose that reaches back to the promises of God and forward to an eschatological fulfillment that will not be waylaid. It is in this sense a hope that is thoroughly Jewish and ancient. This one named Jesus, whose Hebrew rendering as Yeshua *means* "God saves," is not some modern-day Plan B. Jesus is a promise as old as the patriarchs and as recent as a new *genesis* in our present. What is different is whom this Jesus will save and what he saves them from. This Jesus saves "the people" from "their sins." The vision is not confined to our individual souls, but is related to the people (note the singular collective *ho laos* in the Greek), living in an age where sin is not just a painful heritage, but a shared living burden in a world gone awry.

Matthew does not pass up the opportunity to score his point in the midst of the circle of Holy Spirit's grace and Joseph's obedience. The throne name of this miraculous child is *Immanuel*, "With-us God." This particular fulfillment formula is first and programmatic. The "with us" (*meth' hēmōn*) of this text in verse 23 stands in a bookend relationship with the promise of the risen Christ in the last verse of Matthew 28: "Remember, I am *with you* (*meth' hymōn*) always, to the end of the age" (emphasis and parentheses mine). The birth of Jesus is a birth of a new world, even as the old one is tottering around us. Matthew's text is not just about Jesus' first birthday, but a new birthday for the world, which in the midst of its own birth pangs, receives a startling promise of divine solidarity to see it through to the crowning of a new *genesis*, a new creation.

DAVID SCHNASA JACOBSEN

episodes of the story are retold as three acts in a play, then a common refrain of naming closes each scene. Act 1 (vv. 18–21) opens with an impending scandal and Joseph's quandary. Then the Lord appears to Joseph in a dream to help Joseph mediate his dilemma. The scene closes with the first refrain: "you are to name him Jesus, for he will save his people from their sins." The name of Jesus vividly portrays the character of Jesus that Matthew displays throughout his Gospel.

Act 2 (vv. 22–23) is a word from the narrator to the audience about Jesus' relationship to Scripture. This OT prophecy is the first of five fulfillment passages in the next four pericopes (2:1–12; 2:13–15; 2:16–18; 2:19–23). Matthew claims that the audience will understand Jesus only by understanding that he is God's chosen one. The scene closes with another naming refrain: "'and they shall name him Emmanuel,' which means, 'God is with us.'" The name Immanuel also provides an *inclusio* with Matthew's Gospel, reminding the audience of God's abiding presence with God's people (Matt. 28:20).

The Fourth Sunday of Advent, Year A, follows Matthew's lead and pairs the text with Isaiah 7:10–16. The prophecy refers to a child born in the immediate context during the troubling days of Ahaz. Craig Blomberg calls this text a bifocal vision that

> prepares the reader for 9:1–7. In this context appear the words musically immortalized by Handel, "for us a child is born, to us a son is given" (9:6a). Against the current critical consensus, it is difficult to identify this son, who is an heir to David's throne, "Mighty God," "Everlasting Father," "Prince of Peace," and governing eternally (9:6b–7), with anyone other than Isaiah's royal Messiah.[1]

The promised child is a child in Isaiah's day (Isa. 8:18), but the promise is also of the Immanuel to come.

Act 3 (vv. 24–25) completes the drama with Joseph's obedience. The scene and the entire play closes with the final naming refrain: "and he named him Jesus." The climax of the drama reaches its apex with the naming of Jesus. Act 1 and Act 3 echo Jesus' name as the name that towers over all other names anyone can speak.

TIMOTHY R. SENSING

1. Craig Blomberg, "Interpreting OT Prophetic Literature in Matthew: Double Fulfillment," *Trinity Journal* 23 (2002): 17–33.

Matthew 2:1–12

¹In the time of King Herod, after Jesus was born in Bethlehem of Judea, wise men from the East came to Jerusalem, ²asking, "Where is the child who has been born king of the Jews? For we observed his star at its rising, and have come to pay him homage." ³When King Herod heard this, he was frightened, and all Jerusalem with him; ⁴and calling together all the chief priests and scribes of the people, he inquired of them where the Messiah was to be born. ⁵They told him, "In Bethlehem of Judea; for so it has been written by the prophet:

⁶ 'And you, Bethlehem, in the land of Judah,
　　are by no means least among the rulers of Judah;
　for from you shall come a ruler
　　who is to shepherd my people Israel.'"

Theological Perspective

The Epiphany is one of the most cherished and ecumenical feasts in Christendom. It is deeply rooted in celebration of the visit of the magi to Bethlehem, as recorded in the Gospel of Matthew. An epiphany is a divine manifestation in the midst of human history. This text points to the birth of Jesus as an incarnational event that involves the daily experience of simple and humble people who are transformed into chosen vessels of God's purpose and blessing. In Matthew's narrative the epiphany is closely related to symbols like the magi and a star. They represent and point to something beyond what is normal and natural. They are signs communicating a meaningful, transcendental revelation.

Matthew insists on making the case for a "theology from the underside of history," a phrase made popular by liberation theologian Gustavo Gutiérrez, from Peru.[1] The God of the king-persecuted child is the God hidden in poverty yet sought out by "kings from the East" and so revealed in honor and dignity. God comes into human situations and achieves the miracle of power and wisdom. Blessed are those who realize they are privileged in the divine plan (Matt. 5). God raises the poor and marginalized from the dust, bringing justice and equality to them.

1. Gustavo Gutiérrez, *Teología desde el reverso de la historia* (Lima: CEP, 1977).

Pastoral Perspective

When I was in college I fulfilled my science requirement by taking astronomy. Our main assignment for the semester was to study the stars, to carefully draw the changing heavens over a four-month period. So every night, with a flashlight, mittens, and my dog-eared notebook, I would climb to the roof of my dorm and gaze starward. Soon the close and holy darkness began to pulse with wonder. It became clear to me how reasonable the skies are, how predictable the patterns, and how logical the language of those glowing gases inching themselves across the sky night after night after night. It also became very obvious when something did not fit the pattern—a falling star or an airplane light or a meteor streaking across the sky.

Those wise men from Arabia would have easily spotted that strange star so long ago, and having exhausted the reason of nature, they would quickly have turned to a second kind of reason: the reason of knowledge. What would other wise seers in other parts of the world know about the stars, and what was written down about the truth of the heavens? This is how they ended up in Jerusalem, picking the brains of Herod's scholars.

Is it not odd that it took pagans from the East to invite the Jews to remember their own tradition? Is it not odd that Gentiles were the ones to remind the

Feasting on the Gospels

⁷Then Herod secretly called for the wise men and learned from them the exact time when the star had appeared. ⁸Then he sent them to Bethlehem, saying, "Go and search diligently for the child; and when you have found him, bring me word so that I may also go and pay him homage." ⁹When they had heard the king, they set out; and there, ahead of them, went the star that they had seen at its rising, until it stopped over the place where the child was. ¹⁰When they saw that the star had stopped, they were overwhelmed with joy. ¹¹On entering the house, they saw the child with Mary his mother; and they knelt down and paid him homage. Then, opening their treasure chests, they offered him gifts of gold, frankincense, and myrrh. ¹²And having been warned in a dream not to return to Herod, they left for their own country by another road.

Exegetical Perspective

With this text we are again in overly familiar territory. We need to read with discernment to understand it beyond the gauzy vision of Christmas manger-scene coziness. As the wise men opened their treasures when they saw the child, we certainly can do no less than pause and open our minds.

We might begin with the new characters. With a bow to Herod, Matthew narrates the magi (*magoi*) entering from the East. We may struggle to name just who these people are. They are not kings. They are better understood as wise men or astrologers, representing something of Eastern wisdom here. Their significance is twofold. First, they are Gentiles. Because they bring gifts, they embody the prophecy that "the nations" will bring their wealth when God's kingdom is established. Second, when magi arrive, they come to worship. Their astrological wisdom tells them that something in the cosmos is changing. This causes them to come and bow down. Their actions contrast in important ways with those of other characters in the pericope.

Our familiarity with this text may cause us also to miss its political edge. Matthew sets the story in Bethlehem of Judea, which prophecy itself anticipates as the messianic birthplace (vv. 5b–6, actually a conflation of Mic. 5:2 and 2 Sam. 5:2). Matthew also plots this episode in the days of Herod the king.

Homiletical Perspective

If you consider most Christmas nativity scenes, you will find a conflation of Matthew's and Luke's narratives. Fortunately, the calendar separates Matthew's version from Luke's and associates this text with Epiphany, thus providing a distinctive liturgical context for the preacher to interpret. The restoration of Epiphany to the church's memory is still under construction. The theophany of the holy nativity of Jesus calls the preacher to construct the liturgy around this story. Here, as is the case with other manifestations of God, the congregation is standing on holy ground; no one leaves unchanged.

Initially, the preacher will need to retell Matthew's version with its grit of promise and threat intact. If adapted into a play, Matthew's story shifts dramatically between scenes set in a house of promise and a palace of threat. Since the story has two noticeably different points of view, the preacher's entry into the play is crucial. Let us suppose the preacher focuses the congregation's attention on the two scenes from a balcony perspective. Such an angle allows the congregation to shift between scenes without experiencing whiplash. Maybe they could see the action from an insider's point of view. The preacher would transition from scene to scene by maintaining the gaze of one of the characters. Points of view and points of entry are key elements

Matthew 2:1–12

Theological Perspective

The magi are "the priestly sages from Persia." These astrologers come with sincerity to the Christ child, guided by God. They come with joy to adore! Interestingly enough, the magi were transformed in the popular religion of the Middle Ages into kings. In countries like Spain, with a profound Catholic faith and culture, a whole tradition of royalty and luxury evolved.

The star is a symbol of direction and knowledge for the magi. It is a manifestation of God's guidance, the light for the way. It is a sign of hope and vision for humanity. The small village of Bethlehem of Judea becomes the center of human aspirations and dreams, the city of God in which Jesus, the Messiah, is king. The tradition added the names of Melchior, Gaspar, and Balthazar and spiritualized the gifts the three kings from the East brought: gold, a symbol of royalty; frankincense, a symbol of divinity; and myrrh, a symbol of death.

An important and relevant element in this narrative is the story that follows this text. Jesus, Joseph, and Mary migrate to Egypt; they are now in exile as expatriates in a strange land. This reminds us of the people of Israel in exile and captivity in Egypt. Jesus, the Messiah, is now the liberator of the new Israel of God, becoming the stranger and persecuted, reversing the history of oppression to turn humankind toward a new horizon of freedom (Matt. 2:13–23).

In reading, studying, theologizing, teaching, and preaching on this powerful story of migration, marginalization, and displacement, let us remember the tragic situation of so many children. The reading can provide an opportunity to raise consciousness in our seminaries and churches on issues that affect the majority of children in the world today. The little babe shines with hope for all these children in need of hope, care, love, compassion, and solidarity.

The Jesus born in Bethlehem was a stranger, a marginalized person, an innocent victim who transformed suffering into joy. Let us rejoice in his coming, and pray and act for the justice and equality of God's reign.

A key issue in the text is tradition. The Jewish people knew all too well the richness and value of history and God's intervention in it. Tradition is transmitted from generation to generation. There is a sense of continuity, meaning, and purpose in human pilgrimage (*diaspora*) and a close relationship with God.

The late Jaroslav Pelikan, Orthodox historian of dogma and historical theology, coined a sentence that summarizes the importance of a living tradition,

Pastoral Perspective

religious authorities in Jerusalem of the great promises of the Hebrew prophet: that a light will arise and shine and usher in the promised kingdom of God? Is it not odd that wise scientists—who made their living on the merits of reason and research—were wise enough to go beyond reason and follow the intuitive tug of their wondering hearts? Is it not odd that this ancient story should surface in our modern times—just when we are hearing voices from within the scientific community beginning to whisper the name of God? As physicists break through the world of quarks and neutrons, some are beginning to wonder if there could be a clear pattern of creation—even amid the mystery of chaos.

In order truly to follow the star, the wise men had to move beyond reason to intuition. They had to move beyond science to faith—trusting the journey even though they did not know where they were going, trusting a wisdom beyond their own to take them where they needed to go. Yes, the wisdom of the wise men was a wondering, wandering kind of wisdom that ended up in worship, in their offering homage to the wider and more wonderful Wisdom of God.

In these postmodern times, many within the younger generations are moving away from the rationalism of their parents and grandparents. Through incense and meditation and experience and beauty, they are seeking mystery and embracing wonder. Rather than doctrine, they seek delight. Rather than ideas, they explore imagination. Rather than rationality, they yearn for relationship. Like the magi, they are willing to take risks and explore the unknown in order to find the Holy. Ask and keep on asking. Seek and keep on seeking. Find and keep on finding. Their faith is a Jesus faith—a journey faith—and like the wise men, their intellectual curiosity and spiritual hunger give them courage to leave behind all that is familiar.

Biblical scholar Ken Bailey has opened our hearts to a fresh understanding of the Christmas story, based on his own experiences living and studying in the Middle East. Jesus was not born in the cold stink of a barn, rudely marginalized by an insulting innkeeper. Instead, consistent with the ethic of hospitality ingrained in the cultural DNA of Arab and Semitic peoples, Mary and Joseph were warmly welcomed by their relatives in the countryside of Judea. They were invited to sleep in the warmth of a big family room—a gracious, but well-used space commonly shared with the animals of the family. Yes, Jesus was born in a living room—and continues to dwell in the living room of our lives.

Exegetical Perspective

When the magi ask, "Where is the one 'born king of the Jews'?" it is more than just an innocent question. Herod's own claim to the throne was less than sure, since he was born Idumean. More than that, Herod's title was "king of the Jews." The simple statement by the magi seems to bring another will into play: this child is "born" to be king of the Jews, and that means Herod was not.

This political edge becomes most clearly manifest in the reaction to the wise men's question. Herod is "frightened," and so is "all Jerusalem." The power center is shaken. The reappearance of the word for people (*laos*) in verse 4 reminds us of those whom this child is destined to save from their sins (Matt. 1:21b). Promise and threat usually go together; and the people of the city and their religious and political leaders are plenty threatened by the astral birth announcement. By verse 8 Herod too is asking where the child is, though by now his stated desire to "pay him homage" seems less than genuine.

Of course, if anything is familiar about this text, it is the star. The history of interpretation has also been troubled here—in this case desiring to explain how this peripatetic star could possibly be. A connection to Halley's comet has been ventured, and star patterns in this period have been dutifully charted too. As readers today, however, we are probably best advised to stick close to Matthew's theological agenda, rather than assuming he wants to compete with contemporary astrophysicists. The star illumines the wonder of the magi. Since 1:1, Matthew's Greek has been aligning the book of Genesis, Jesus' genesis as birth, and the genesis of "genealogy," in order to describe the particular Jewish claim and the cosmic, Gentile news that this son of David/son of Abraham represents. It is not so much science as a social and theological "world" that Matthew's narrative is describing. "We observed his star at its rising," the wise men said (v. 2), and we contemporary readers, looking over their shoulders, get to witness a sparkling new age dawning with a child's birth star ascending.

Of course, we readers have to admit that nobody else looks all that good in the narrative either. Religious leaders are happy to parlay their Scripture knowledge about Messiah's birth to help out the illegitimate king. Even the magi look a little disingenuous for saying yes to the king while circumventing his command to send news of where the child was born. Keep in mind that this is also part of the world of empire. The power differentials in a Roman client state are such that ruler and ruled do not always say what they really mean. Postcolonial interpreters

Homiletical Perspective

that must remain coherent throughout any narrative reconstruction.

Everyone finds a seat, cell phones are silenced, and the orchestra begins. Enter stage right, "Where is the one who has been born king of the Jews? We observed his star in the East and have come to pay him homage" (v. 2). Inquisitive magi from a distant land come to the seat of power seeking one who is truly worthy of their life's devotion, although without the human knowledge to find him. The signs in the heavens only partially lead these magi to their destination. They arrive in Jerusalem seeking further directions. Herod then turns to those who have the wisdom to know. He calls together the chief priests and scribes to inquire of them the Messiah's birthplace. These leaders know their Bible. Herod knows the right question to ask, and these scribes know the answer, although knowing the answer does not lead them to the way of wisdom. The irony of the scribes' proof-texting Micah is that Israel missed it. Betwixt threat and promise, Israel did not see their salvation. Herod's men at court also miss it.

However, this is no children's play. Sitting on his throne is King Herod, one who is already designated "the king of the Jews." If the wise ones had known Herod, they would not have come. A despot capable of genocide, Herod rules unpredictably. When they later realize his wickedness, they return on another road. How they survive their first encounter is a mystery. The key is found deep in Herod's treachery, for he too asks, "Where indeed is he?" (v. 4). Herod and all of Jerusalem are disturbed. The talk of Messiah, a sign from God in the heavens, is both a promise and a threat to them. In his fear, Herod says, "I too want to go and pay him homage" (v. 8). Let the word "homage" linger in the ears of the audience. The weight of Matthew's theological focus settles on this word. Only the magi continue the journey to find the one for whom all eternity longs. The lights fade as the scene closes and the curtain falls.

During intermission, the preacher can talk to the patrons about how we always live in the tension between threat and promise. Whether the examples are economic, political, social, or psychological, the crux of the matter is spiritual. The promise of Messiah fills the room with the hope of God's dawning restoration, even as we look at our neighborhoods, cities, and nations and see that it is not yet so. In their angst, people fill the vacuum with false hopes, empty promises, and void dreams. They long for and pay homage to lesser virtues and deceitful vices. Phillips Brooks's words in his 1868 "O Little Town

Matthew 2:1–12

Theological Perspective

the one that Matthew is narrating in this text. For Pelikan, "tradition is the living faith of the dead; traditionalism is the dead faith of the living."[2] "Jesus is the Son of the *living* God," Matthew insists in his Gospel.

The tradition of the three kings, the magi who came to Bethlehem, runs deep in the Catholic cultures of Latin America and the Caribbean. For people in Mexico, Cuba, Dominican Republic, and Puerto Rico, the tradition is very strong. On the eve of Three Kings Day, January 5, children get a shoebox and put fresh grass in it. The shoebox is left under the Christmas tree or under the bed (as we do in Puerto Rico!). Very early on the morning of January 6 children look under the Christmas tree or under the bed to unwrap the gifts left by the three kings. The grass is eaten by the camels or horses (a Puerto Rican tradition). Joy and celebration follow during the whole day on January 6, with the reenactment of the coming of the magi to the place where the Christ child was born and the sharing of good food!

A few years back I was lecturing at Uppsala University in Sweden and stayed at the Good Samaritan Guest House of the Lutheran Church. On the eve of January 5, I was told, they had a surprise for me. I waited in my room with anxiety and expectation. Around 7:00 p.m. a group of children in their traditional dress for the occasion came to my room, inviting me to the chapel to honor, celebrate, and rejoice, because the magi, the three kings, were coming to the Good Samaritan Guest House! We sang and enjoyed the reenactment of the story of the magi! "Jesus, the Son of the living God," the living tradition of the Christian faith, was present!

CARMELO E. ÁLVAREZ

Pastoral Perspective

What this means, of course, is that the wise men followed their intuition and their hearts to this same living room—discovering the meaning of the star not in the corrupt halls of Herod's power, but in the swaddled heart of everyday life. So, in the fullness of time, wholeness was born. Mind and heart, Jew and Gentile, rich and poor, powerful and simple: they all meet in the living room of God's imagination—God fully alive in the fragile familiarity of flesh. Incarnation can be understood only through intuition and imagination, through the real stuff of real living.

Contemporary Christian educator Jerome Berryman has discovered a fresh way for small children to learn about the immediacy of a living God. Through "Godly Play," he encourages children to crawl inside imagination and intuition. In a quiet, simple space children are invited to sit on the floor and gather around a storyteller. With concrete objects—velvet sand, wooden figures, glittery props—the storyteller slowly spins out a story from the Bible. The star, the camels, some kings, a scary Herod, a simple home, a mother and a father and a baby. No theology. No interpretation. No doctrine. Just the story. Then the storyteller invites the children—age three or four or five—to wonder. I wonder . . . what did Mary do when the kings showed up? I wonder . . . how did the wise men change? I wonder . . . how did God feel when Jesus was born? I wonder . . .

Albert Einstein captures the necessity of wonder: "The most beautiful emotion we can experience is the mystical. It is the source of all true art and science. The one to whom this emotion is a stranger, who can no longer wonder and stand rapt in awe, is as good as dead."[1]

Thanks be to God!

SUSAN R. ANDREWS

---

2. "Tradition" in Jaroslav Pelikan, *The Melody of Theology* (Cambridge, MA: Harvard University Press, 1988), 252.

1. Barbara Brown Taylor, *The Luminous Web* (Cambridge: Cowley Publications, 2000), 100.

Exegetical Perspective

will sometimes speak of the mockery of a colonial subject. However, Matthew sees God at work even in that. It is, at the end of our pericope, a divinely ordained dream that drives their subterfuge. Recall the positive association with Joseph's dreaming obedience in 1:20 and note the divine passive in the verb of warning ("having been warned") in 2:12. Apparently God has purposes that go far beyond ours, our desire to please our potentates, and our potentates' imperial pretensions to power.

Where the text ends, however, is with a generous scene of worship—and one thoroughly rooted in Matthew's literary and theological vision. The visitors intend to worship (v. 2), Herod pretends to worship (v. 8), but now the wise men *extend* worship—and with doxological gusto. Case in point: when the magi saw the star, as the Greek puts it, "they rejoiced a great joy very much" (v. 10, awkward trans. mine). The logic of worship is superabundant, rejoicing joy—even in the midst of long journeys and tedious visits with imperial hacks like Herod. To top it off, seeing the child causes the wise men to fall down in worship and "open their treasure chests" (v. 11) to him. What are the three presents? Two gifts fit for a king, one less so. There are royal gold and priestly frankincense to be shared. In addition and in a nod to a Matthean literary vision that culminates in crucifixion, there is also among the three treasure gifts an odd gift of myrrh, a burial spice that prepares the child for *cruciform* kingship.

With this, Matthew sets the stage. Biblical scholar Krister Stendahl famously titled Matthew's opening narrative "*Quis et unde?*" that is, "Who is he and where is he from?"[1] It is that, no doubt, but also more. Matthew prepares us for a narrative to come that helps us see this Jesus in all his paradox. He is the child of promise, yet bears this promise in the midst of threat. That is not just who he is or where he is from, but where he is going.

DAVID SCHNASA JACOBSEN

Homiletical Perspective

of Bethlehem" capture the sentiment of Matthew's day: "Yet in thy dark streets shineth the everlasting Light; the hopes and fears of all the years are met in thee tonight." Will anyone follow the magi on their journey? Will shrines along the way lure captives to idolatry, or will the fainthearted cower in hiding?

Enter stage left. As the curtain rises, the tenor of the scene changes. The magi come to Bethlehem overjoyed. Their first response when they see Jesus is to kneel down and pay him homage (v. 11). They bow down before him with gifts and adoration. To adore and offer is a definition of worship in any language. However you say it, "to praise and sacrifice, magnify and forfeit, glorify and relinquish, revere and give, exalt and dedicate, honor and consecrate, love and devote," the couplet defines a disciple's only response. Consequently these foreigners become prototypical disciples and anticipate the gospel going out to the ends of the world (Matt. 28:17–20). The houselights come on, and the only response for the congregation is to join with the magi in paying homage to the king.

Like many good stories, this one is followed by an epilogue. Figuratively, outside in the parking lot, the preacher gathers the congregation to proclaim the meaning of these scenes. The little baby in Joseph's house grew up and got killed—not by Herod and the religious establishment of his day (although not for a lack of trying), but by Pilate and the religious establishment of his day. Jesus came and was a threat. From the beginning, he was a threat. Because of that threat, they destroyed him. From his birth, they sought to kill him, and, in a different time and place, they thought they succeeded.

Whether it was in Bethlehem or on a hill, Jesus was also a promise. In the midst of our fears, with threats to our faith, homage is often a lost practice. While folk often leave the playhouse entertained, the congregation must leave Matthew's play moved to adore and to offer.

TIMOTHY R. SENSING

---

1. Krister Stendahl, "Quis et unde? An Analysis of Matthew 1–2," *The Interpretation of Matthew*, ed. Graham N. Stanton (Edinburgh: T. & T. Clark, 1995), 69–80.

Matthew 2:13–15

¹³Now after they had left, an angel of the Lord appeared to Joseph in a dream and said, "Get up, take the child and his mother, and flee to Egypt, and remain there until I tell you; for Herod is about to search for the child, to destroy him." ¹⁴Then Joseph got up, took the child and his mother by night, and went to Egypt, ¹⁵and remained there until the death of Herod. This was to fulfill what had been spoken by the Lord through the prophet, "Out of Egypt I have called my son."

Theological Perspective

Matthew's story of Joseph, Mary, and the child occurs in a world that looks very much like our own. There are paranoid and corrupt politicians, dangers, and crises, but there are also people who are faithfully trying to respond to God's will. These few short verses of Matthew seek to describe this stark contrast in terms of a collision between two dominions. This confrontation is nothing new; in fact, Matthew describes it in terms that reenact stories from the OT. The narrative of the magi in Matthew 2:1–12 points to this conflict by describing foreign, Gentile kings who seek to honor a child king, Jesus, while the king who should be faithful to God, Herod, is characterized by fear of the potential this new baby holds. The outcome of this clash of dominions is described by Matthew 2:13–15, contrasting God's intervention in the Holy Family's life through dreams and prophecy fulfillment with the ever-present reality of danger, death, and fear.

The central focus of these verses is the statement the angel of the Lord makes to Joseph in a dream: Joseph is to "get up, take the child and his mother, and flee to Egypt, and remain there until I tell you, for Herod is about to search for the child, to destroy him" (v. 13). Of course, a striking point of this passage is the means by which Joseph hears this message: by an angel in a dream. This method involves a

Pastoral Perspective

God leads with cords of human kindness and bands of merciful love. God speaks through angels and dreams, people and circumstance. God sends stars with light into a dark, birthing sky and sends wise people home by a way they might never have imagined.

Maybe a visit to your widowed mother in her independent living facility brings a change you least expect. After a long day at work, you travel to this place explicitly to get the ball rolling on moving her from independent to assisted living. You rehearse the words you will say. You know you cannot say them too directly. However, you cannot come every time she has an incident, loses her purse, or complains that the neighbor has taken her favorite library book.

When you arrive, something shifts in you. Your small group at church has been discussing Exodus and Moses' journey. The group has discussed the power of observation and how small decisions can lead to big changes. Moses' mother, his sister, and the Egyptian princess all played a role by paying attention to that baby boy.

From afar you watch how your mother knows her neighbors and how they move together. You observe how they stand at the plateglass window and name the birds gathering at the feeder right outside, laugh with joy when they cannot remember the genus

Exegetical Perspective

Celebration and recognition dominated the previous scene with the magi (wise men), chief priests, and scribes all unfolding the identity of Jesus. Nevertheless, a hint of the sinister hung over the scene, beginning in verse 3. The narrator's comment that Herod felt "frightened," along with the whole city of Jerusalem, interjects a curious note into an otherwise joyous scene. The reader does not know the extent of the fear, or its cause, or the true purpose of Herod in calling for the magi.

What the story has only suggested becomes clear in these verses. The scene stands in contrast to the reverent gift giving in the previous scene. The last sentence of that scene (v. 12) reminds the reader of the possible treachery of Herod and the threat that has hovered over the story. The angel knows what the reader has only suspected. Herod feels threatened by the baby and has no intention of honoring him. The three verses in this passage intensify the conflict and the danger to Jesus. Joseph and his family must flee.

Matthew makes intentional connections between Jesus and Moses, introducing the idea of Jesus as the new lawgiver/interpreter/fulfiller (Deut. 18:15). In this episode the experience of the baby Jesus echoes the experience of baby Moses. Just as the supposedly mighty Pharaoh felt threatened by Hebrew baby

Homiletical Perspective

Some texts are not first about the well-educated, well-positioned persons in many of the pews certain preachers might address on Sunday morning. Sometimes it is important to talk about where such texts touch down—even when they touch down on the other side of town or the other side of the world. This is a story about refugees under the threat of death, who are forced into hiding.

Given such a short and telegraphic text, it may be important to draw connections to other parts of Matthew to reinforce its message. In this case those connections are many, and two of those related texts are well known.

This text follows immediately after the story of the magi, and it can be helpful to draw out the parallels. Like the magi, the Holy Family is in dire straits. The magi come to Herod from the East; they are courtiers from Rome's primary enemy in the East, Persia. They approach Rome's puppet king asking, "Where is the one to usurp your title?"—king of the Jews, a title specifically given to Herod by Mark Anthony. Mary and Joseph are harboring this usurper and so fall under the same danger.

The magi address Herod with unhypocritical transparency; they seem to be more forward than Joseph, but in the end they "withdraw" to their own country by another road and avoid conflict. The

Theological Perspective

means of revelation that has precedent in Scripture (notably Gen. 37–50 and Dan. 2). Matthew has narrated other dreams. Joseph was told in a dream to stay with Mary, given that her pregnancy was brought about through the Holy Spirit (1:18, 20), and the magi dreamed that they should not return to Herod, thereby preventing him from knowing more about Jesus (2:12). God continues to use dreams to intervene in Joseph's life to protect the child; here, Joseph is told specifically to protect Mary and the child by taking them to Egypt.

Most modern readers of these texts will find God's revelation through dreams strikingly strange. While some of us have had experiences where a dream may clarify a situation in life, we live in a post-Freud era where dreams can be psychologically revealing and even dangerous. Whether clarifying or dangerous, dreams are not generally thought to be the means of God's communication with us. The ancient world knew that dreams were not easily understood. In fact most of the prominent narratives about dreams in the OT involve not the dreams themselves, but the interpretations of them. Daniel was a prophet known for interpreting Nebuchadnezzar's dreams (Dan. 2:1–45). Daniel's own dream interpretation was based on Joseph, the dream interpreter par excellence in the narratives of Genesis 37–50. It is easy to see how the story in Genesis of an earlier Joseph is reenacted in Matthew 2. Joseph's brothers intend to kill him (Gen. 37). Instead they sell him into slavery, and he goes to Egypt, where he eventually finds safety and prosperity, in part by interpreting Pharaoh's dreams (Gen. 41). In both Genesis and Matthew, a Joseph is the recipient of God's revelation for the good of God's people.

This link with the Joseph of old is cemented by the prophetic word that concludes this passage: Joseph and his family will go to Egypt and thereby fulfill Hosea's words: "Out of Egypt I have called my son" (v. 15; cf. Hos. 11:1). In this way, Jesus becomes a new proxy for God's original son, Israel (see Exod. 4:22). Just as the OT Joseph and his father, Israel (Jacob), went to Egypt for safety from a famine in their land, so now Joseph takes God's Son, Jesus, and once again travels to Egypt to escape danger at home. Matthew further solidifies this link between previous interactions with God's child, Israel (God's Son, Hos. 11:1; Matt. 2:15), and the Jesus of the present by describing Joseph and Mary's offspring simply as "the child" (v. 14), rather than naming him as Jesus. God's actions in a new situation look very much like God's actions in a previous situation,

Pastoral Perspective

name for the red bird—the *Cardinalis, cardinalis*—then realize that it is painted on the decorative plate hanging on the wall next to the window.

Maybe you *had* gone to visit with the strict intention to facilitate a move into assisted living, convinced she would be safer, less likely to fall and not be found, *but* you come away having seen something, almost like a dream. This window-watching, neighbor-loving, name-forgetting woman raised you, then freed you to do what is right. That dreamlike intuition leads you to be free. When it is just the two of you, questioning and confessing, you say, "Mom, I'm afraid for you as you get older. What do you need, how do I protect your dignity and balance being your caregiver? How will we know together when it is time to move from independent into assisted living?" God's cords of human kindness and bands of merciful love hold you together for an intimate and difficult life-passage conversation. You leave that night by a way you could not have imagined. What had been a private burden, shifted to the shared joy of light shining against the darkness that still lies ahead.

Following a star and Herod's secret instruction, the magi have been led to Bethlehem, the house of bread, to see Mary and the infant Jesus. When they stand face to face with the living Lord, they experience the infectious and overwhelming joy that leads to the beginning of change.

Having met the infant Christ, one dream leads the magi to turn toward change and a new pathway for life. They do not go home by the same way. Avoiding Herod and his death-dealing ways, they choose a different path. Meeting Christ leads to transformation, the freedom to be changed.

For some who meet Christ, life can shift with a subtle awakening that feels like a nudge of "something needs to be different because of this joy." There is a willing spirit to be changed, to be different, to be transformed. For others who meet Christ, life decisions can be given a certain clarity that feels like the surge of contrast dye in your veins before an MRI. There is an impulse that leads to change, to do and say what is just and right, to be transformed.

The dream energy that directed the magi to change continues to flow as it settles upon Joseph, and continues to lead to movement and freedom for change. This is not Joseph's first dream. Initially he had hoped to quietly dismiss pregnant Mary, not wanting to expose her to any disgrace. A dream changes that preconceived plan. To fulfill what has been spoken by the prophet, he takes on a pregnant wife and names the child "God with us."

boys, so Herod the Great feels threatened by one baby boy. The mother of Moses protected him within Egypt, and the father of Jesus protects him by taking him to Egypt.

The passage provides an interesting insight into Matthew's understanding of revelation from God. Three sources of revelation, of gaining information into God's ways, appear in these three verses. The wise men appear only as a vestige, but their departure reminds the reader of how they came to find Jesus. Matthew introduces a curiosity into his story: astrology, a Babylonian religion, leads the magi to Jesus. Even the practice of a foreign religion, from former oppressors, draws Gentiles to Jesus! As Christians celebrate in Epiphany, the presence of the magi in the story expands the understanding of the salvation offered by God to all people. Their use of astrology suggests that God speaks, even through discredited means of gathering information, to draw outsiders into Jesus' presence.

Joseph learns of Herod's treachery through a dream, a frequent vehicle of revelation in these early chapters of Matthew. Dreams play a prominent role in Daniel, Zechariah, the Joseph narrative, and other parts of the Old Testament. A consistent theme in dream interpretation is that dreams reveal what a person's senses cannot detect. Among people, only Herod knows his true intentions, but God knows and sends the dream.

In addition to astrology and dreams, the final verse of this section announces that the flight into Egypt "fulfills" Hosea 11:1 about God calling the son out of Egypt. Astrology, dreams, and prophecy all reveal God's ways. This section depicts a God intent on communicating, even by unexpected means. Later in Matthew, the teachings of Jesus will provide the definitive way of knowing God's will. A variety of sources of revelation points to Jesus, who becomes the authoritative source of revelation about God.

Matthew consistently portrays Jesus' life and ministry as a "fulfillment" of prophecy, even when he does not carefully document the source (e.g., 2:23). Though Matthew's use of this fulfillment motif contains much substance, he does not carefully explain his understanding of "fulfill." The contemporary reader should avoid the understanding that the prophets "predicted" the events of Jesus' life. Matthew understands fulfillment in a much deeper way. The verse from Hosea originally referred to divine tender care for Israel, and the process of forming the people into a community of faith and witness. The people rejected the God who called and formed them

word translated "they left" is a word for a military retreat—an expression of meekness. The same word is repeated when the text says the Holy Family "went" to Egypt. Both the magi and Joseph retreat. Both are directed by dreams. Both demonstrate integrity.

All these virtues—integrity, prudence, meekness—are lifted up in the Sermon on the Mount. Blessed are the meek. Blessed are the peacemakers. Be perfect (*teleios*) as God is perfect (*teleios*; Matt. 5:5; 5:9; 5:48). *Teleios* is the usual translation of the Hebrew *tamim*, which means to be consistent or to have integrity—to do what you say. The opposite is to be hypocritical—like Herod: "Oh, tell me when you find the child, and I will come and worship him." Joseph, like the magi, demonstrates these virtues lifted up in Matthew 5–7. This is a paradigm for Matthew that this tiny passage reinforces, and here the emphasis is on meekness and humility.

We know that Jesus will not always "withdraw" from Roman authority but will ultimately stand before a Roman judge; he will not avoid conflict throughout Matthew but will ultimately confront the powers. The "now" of *this* text is not that time. God will wait for now, until the immediate threat is gone—until the right time, when the powers can be exposed in their violence and hypocrisy.

Nevertheless this waiting until the right time is a difficulty. Why not face down that evil now, even meekly? In a course on Christian ethics Father Daniel Berrigan once said, "Don't be a small tinder in a big flame." His point was that timing matters. Getting arrested when no one is paying attention is not necessarily a helpful witness. Foolish bravado is sometimes just foolish. We do not think of Jesus' meekness as avoiding conflict, but the timing of the confrontation is surely a part of how Matthew's first chapters report his story. The closing line of the passage underscores this divine intent in directing the Holy Family to avoid conflict until the *kairos*.

So, here is a refugee family: meek, hidden, and buffeted about by the powers. Tragically, we do not have to go far to find the story of refugees under death threats. In an unpublished paper delivered at a gathering of clergy in Atlanta, Leanne Pearce Reed offered a clear picture of that reality from Gregory Boyle's *Tattoos on the Heart*.

> In 1987 Dolores Mission Church declared itself a sanctuary church for the undocumented, after passage of the Immigration Reform and Control Act of 1986. Soon, recently arrived undocumented men from Mexico and Central America would

Matthew 2:13–15

Theological Perspective

as Matthew continually demonstrates, emphasizing God's constancy and faithfulness in the process of redemption.

Readers of Genesis and Exodus have seen the conflict of dominions before: the dominion of Pharaoh collided with the dominion of God, yielding costly plagues and a dramatic exodus from Egypt that exhibited God's consistent love for Israel. God's desire and ability to rescue Israel does not mean God keeps Israel completely out of danger and away from the risk of death: Israel was constantly jeopardized by Pharaoh's destructive and oppressive policies. In many ways, the human situation has not changed from Pharaoh to Herod to us. From Matthew's perspective, we are called to discern God's will in the midst of current conflicting dominions, whatever the cost, just as foreign, Gentile magi followed a star to Bethlehem to worship the true king (2:2).

The challenge for Pharaoh, for Herod, and often for us, is that revelation comes—if not in a dream, perhaps through the confirmation of another person or circumstances—and we are blind to its meaning and impact on our lives. Part of the power of these few verses in their narration of Jesus' birth is that they testify to the multiple ways in which God reveals a purpose for Jesus' life, even though the participants may be unaware of the significance of their actions. First, Joseph receives the direct revelation in a dream. Second, Joseph reenacts events of Genesis and Exodus as he and his family go to Egypt to flee from danger in Israel, only to return from Egypt again. Third and finally, God's purpose for the life of this new child is illuminated through the fulfillment of Scripture (v. 15). The combined testimony of revelation in dreams, reenacting OT events, and fulfilling Scripture points to God's continued intervention, an intervention that does not erase the danger, risks, and death inherent in life as we know it, but reveals God's presence and activity in the darkness. By tracing the parallels between God's actions in Israel's exodus and God's actions with Jesus, Matthew shows that God's dominion will clash with and triumph over Herod's, whose days are numbered.

LAURA C. SWEAT

Pastoral Perspective

In Joseph's second dream he hears another strong imperative from an angel of the Lord. It is an imperative that seeks to protect his newly formed family unit and their life together, but also speaks against a system of authority out to destroy and cause death to the least of these.

Joseph's dream leads him to take his family back to a land of bondage, embittered slavery, and harsh oppression. Joseph has to take a risk to go back to a place that had been hard, trusting the irony that this would protect—literally save—his family.

The journey of Joseph, Jesus, and Mary into Egypt broadens the road for our life together as the church, particularly as we minister with those who live on the edges—those who are older and widowed; shut in by loss of independence and alone in age's rapid advance. An infant's rescue models a way to be present with the other side of the age spectrum.

We—like Joseph, gathered and called out by God—are free to be led by God's cords of human kindness and merciful love, a freedom like no other. We are free from bondage to the things of the world. We are free, along with members in the covenant community, to join, take, and be in different places along the Christian journey.

Maybe like that exchange in the nursing home, there are conversations you have learned how to have at church in a small group. You learn how to listen and speak honestly, not always asserting your opinion. You learn how to be held accountable in Christ's authority and how to test authority through Scripture: Is God's love known here? Is this a life-giving situation? Which way must we travel if we are to have life as the body of Christ in the world?

How has God come before you in cords of kindness or dreams? How has God led you to move in ways that you never could have expected? How has God carried you and the community in which you worship into places of light and life, and away from darkness and death?

ANNE H. K. APPLE

Exegetical Perspective

by their infidelity. Jesus lives out the history of Israel and fulfills its mission, participating in the events of Israel's life, such as time in Egypt and temptation. In Hosea, God refuses to give up on the people, despite their failure. The birth and protection of Jesus represents God's continuing faithfulness to Israel and, through the magi, Gentiles as well. The arrival and security of Jesus teaches that God acts decisively now as in the exodus event and the return from exile.

Quite a dramatic vignette emerges here. For the second time Joseph has had to trust a dream that contradicted what his waking senses told him or could not tell him. This part of the narrative presents a striking contrast to the previous episode. At the arrival of the magi, the family experiences honor and deference. Immediately after, the family must furtively flee from danger, trusting the message of an angel in a dream for simple survival. The family that had just received the royal treatment becomes a band of refugees, living in an unfamiliar place, waiting for further instructions before returning. The certainty of the message of the magi becomes wondering what will happen next.

A preacher working through Matthew in *lectio continua* might simply tack this story on to the heartwarming narrative of the magi, or the more dramatic narrative of the killing of the babies. These few verses make their own contribution to the faith of the contemporary church. Life can turn on events. A family receiving accolades one minute can find itself in crisis the next. A person, family, or church may have to change plans and venture out in faith with something that seems no more substantive than the voice of an angel in a dream for guidance.

The various sources of revelation in the passage raise the question for the contemporary reader of how we discern God's will and direction. The passage gives the preacher the opportunity to wrestle mightily with an issue of God's goodness. God acts behind the scenes to warn Joseph to protect Jesus. Why do the other families looking on their sons with adoration not receive dreams? The answer that God absorbs their grief into the larger plan of salvation might make intellectual sense, but the preacher must sensitively ask how to proclaim that message in a way that brings healing, not resentment. A passage that calls the preacher/teacher to address this agonizing issue demands attention not neglect.

CHARLES L. AARON

Homiletical Perspective

sleep each night in the church . . . and women and children in the convent. . . .

Attention followed and lots of it. The media swarmed the place in these earliest days. As almost always happens, attention begets opposition. I used to dread clearing the parish's answering machine during this period. It always had a handful of hate messages and vague (and not so vague) death threats.

Once, while I turn the corner in front of the church, heading to a CEB meeting in the projects, I am startled by letters spray-painted crudely across the front steps.

WETBACK CHURCH

The chill of it momentarily stops me. In an instant, you begin to doubt and question the price of things. I acknowledge how much better everything is when there is no cost and how I prefer being hoisted on the shoulders in acclaim to the disdain of anonymous spray cans.

I arrive at the meeting and tell the gathered women about our hostile visitor during the night.

"I guess I'll get one of the homies to clean it up later." . . .

Now, I was new at the parish and my Spanish was spotty. I understood the words she spoke but had difficulty circling in on the sense of it.

"You will not clean this up. If there are people in our community who are disparaged and hated and left out because they are *mojados* (wetbacks) . . ." Then she poised herself on the edge of the couch, practically leaping to her feet. "Then we shall be proud to call ourselves a wetback church."[1]

Sometimes people live with humility, meekness, and integrity—proudly, even while living under the threat of great powers beyond our control. Sometimes even the enemy's blows, on either cheek, expose the perpetrator and ourselves for who they and we are, as well as God's beatitude and timing.

CHANDLER BROWN STOKES

---

1. Gregory Boyle, *Tattoos on the Heart: The Power of Boundless Compassion* (New York: Free Press, 2010), 72–73.

Matthew 2:16–23

¹⁶When Herod saw that he had been tricked by the wise men, he was infuriated, and he sent and killed all the children in and around Bethlehem who were two years old or under, according to the time that he had learned from the wise men. ¹⁷Then was fulfilled what had been spoken through the prophet Jeremiah:
¹⁸ "A voice was heard in Ramah,
    wailing and loud lamentation,
  Rachel weeping for her children;
    she refused to be consoled, because they are no more."
¹⁹When Herod died, an angel of the Lord suddenly appeared in a dream to Joseph in Egypt and said, ²⁰"Get up, take the child and his mother, and go to the land of Israel, for those who were seeking the child's life are dead." ²¹Then Joseph got up, took the child and his mother, and went to the land of Israel. ²²But when he heard that Archelaus was ruling over Judea in place of his father Herod, he was afraid to go there. And after being warned in a dream, he went away to the district of Galilee. ²³There he made his home in a town called Nazareth, so that what had been spoken through the prophets might be fulfilled, "He will be called a Nazorean."

Theological Perspective

Matthew's account of the Christmas story does not involve twinkling lights or feel-good Christmas music, nor does it reflect the warm glow of a Thomas Kinkade Christmas painting. Instead, in Matthew 2:16–23 tragedy intersects with the Christmas story. Matthew portrays the unfolding drama of God's continuing story with Israel in light of Jesus' birth. In this passage, Matthew describes the liberation of God's people once again. Matthew does not shy away from the fact that redemption always comes at a cost, which Israel's earlier history also demonstrates. It is sobering that the cost is once again the lives of innocent children.

While Luke emphasizes the reality of this world with the smells and the sounds of the stable outside Bethlehem, and augments his story of humility by inviting shepherds to the party (Luke 2:1–20), Matthew highlights the dangers and the costs inherent in challenging the world's dominions and structures. This is a text that we often avoid at Christmas, even though modern readers recognize the tragedy revealed in this passage. We know too many instances of genocide, both ancient and modern. Matthew reminds us that Jesus came into the world we know, with all of its problems, with all of its sin, and with all of its challenges.

Pastoral Perspective

Down the street from St. Jude Hospital in Memphis, Tennessee, a church by the name of Friendship Nazarene sits up on a hill at the corner of Manassas and North Parkway. In a windstorm years ago, the large wooden cross that guarded the north side of the property tumbled. The cross splintered apart and crushed the concrete retaining wall, falling across the sidewalk. As drivers passed by, it might have gone unnoticed. However, if you walked along the sidewalk, you had to take a detour around the wood remnants from the disintegrating cross.

Herod is incensed. How dare the magi change their course and go home by another way? How dare the magi not reveal the identity or location of the "king of the Jews"? Herod manipulated the circumstances so that the babe-born-a-king might be destroyed without much effort. Herod would control the fissure that fractures God's entry into the world. When the magi do not report Christ's location and when Joseph, Mary, and Jesus flee to Egypt, events turn against Herod and his anger rages. He orders the massacre of innocent children—*all* children under the age of two—taking life from the most vulnerable. Herod's anger is rooted in the fear of losing his authority and power. His wicked response is to cut at the quick, to fell the life force of a new

Exegetical Perspective

Great horror erupts in the heart of this section of Matthew. The narrator describes the actual scene in a restrained and understated way. He leaves unspoken the pools of blood, the mangled little bodies, the self-loathing of the soldiers required to carry out the order. Although no one can confirm the historicity of this particular event, the historical Herod earned a reputation as a brutal, heartless, narcissistic ruler. The storyline leading to this section has demonstrated great narrative skill. The magi have played a complex role, starting as witnesses to Jesus' royal identity but ending as a kind of catalyst in Herod's murderous spasm. The story reveals a great irony, as a remarkable act of devotion becomes a prelude to terror. The killing of the children carries layers of meaning, but the psychological, political, and theological dimensions deserve comment.

Matthew does not provide a deep psychological understanding of Herod, as is typical of biblical writers. The biblical writers often show the reader the actions and words of a character, but do not always reveal the thoughts or mental states of those characters. Matthew does give the readers some psychological insights, however, and places those insights into a theological context. In 2:3, the reader learns that the arrival of the magi (wise men) has "frightened"

Homiletical Perspective

If a preacher brings this text to worship, proclamation will require negotiating the Scylla and Charybdis of its great difficulties. On the one hand, one rightly treads gently where the death of children is so prominent. On the other hand, one rightly does not avoid the obvious horror in the text.

This is a chilling text: "he sent and killed all the children in and around Bethlehem who were two years old or under." Herod uses the information given by the wise men to calculate his slaughter: cold calculation. The brute exercise of power and its icy reality are front and center. Painting the text in winter seems fitting.

There are many elements of the text that can be illumined to good advantage, but its central horror does not need focus. The slaughter of the innocents is an all too real part of our world: Rwanda, Kosovo—it is too easy to make the connection. I heard a student sermon on this text once that included the phrase "dead babies" a dozen times—eleven more than necessary. As much as one cannot ignore the horror, there are always those in worship for whom the death of a child is close at hand. A gentle touch is required.

Herod's rage can be illumined. Herod is exposed, though he knows not how; his is the reaction of

Matthew 2:16–23

Theological Perspective

The theological problem of this text is best posed as a question: Why is God willing to alert Joseph to the ensuing danger before Herod has even formulated a plan to kill infants and toddlers, and yet does not seem to be concerned to extend the same kind of foresight to the families of other children? Does this mean that God is unjust or that the end justifies the means?

These are difficult questions with no clear answers. At the same time, Matthew provides material for a few initial reflections. It is Matthew's determined emphasis on God's revelatory intervention in the previous passage (2:13–15) that leads us to wonder where God is in this passage. Because God intercedes in various ways to protect Jesus, who is the new representative for Israel, we wonder why God does not keep the other children safe too. The only way to avoid this theological problem is to posit a God who does not intervene in history, which disregards the testimony of Matthew's Gospel: this child who is fleeing to Egypt is Immanuel, God with us (1:23–24). In other words, God does intervene, but as a helpless, vulnerable child.

As we are faced with this conundrum, it is helpful to remember the context in which Matthew is telling his story of Jesus' birth. Just as Joseph's dreams remind Matthew's readers of a previous dreamer named Joseph who ends up in Egypt (see Gen. 37–50), so too God's desire to bring Jesus' family back out of Egypt mirrors God's initial liberating intervention in the exodus: through Moses, God frees Israel from Egyptian slavery; through Matthew's Joseph, God saves the child from Herod. God still redeems the oppressed from the oppressor, whether that oppressor is Egyptian (Pharaoh) or Judean (Herod).

Both God's redemption in Exodus and God's redemption in Matthew come at a cost, however. In Exodus, the firstborn sons of Egypt tragically bear the cost of Egypt's sins (Exod. 4:22–23; 12:29–32). Here in Matthew, the roles of oppressor and oppressed have switched. The oppressor is not a Gentile who worships other gods; Herod identifies with the Jewish people and claims the title "king of the Jews" (Matt. 2:3). Joseph and his family do not flee persecution in Egypt for safety in the promised land; rather, they leave apparent safety in Egypt only to find the land of Israel still in danger from Herod's descendant, Archelaus (2:22). Herod's actions in murdering children recapitulate Pharaoh's actions of old, but unlike the story of the exodus, in Matthew there is no sense of divine justice

Pastoral Perspective

generation. That such unmitigated anger could lead to such unspeakable violence is unfathomable.

It would be easier to say that this story is just a myth from time past, dismissing violence born out of anger with the sweep of time's advance; but the truth is that anger is misemployed daily, even by good churchgoing folk. Sometimes right behind the mask of anger is raw fear. There is a spectrum to anger and its expression.

Reflect on the places where anger has played a role in your own life. Did your heart rate increase? Did your blood boil and your teeth clench? Did you draw a line in the sand? Anger can begin like a small spark and accelerate into a raging fire.

Maybe, when considering the addition of an alternative worship service to your church program, the worship committee meeting becomes intense, and behind the intensity is a sense of real fear. A stalwart of the congregation barks, "You will *absolutely never* lead worship in *this* church, in *that* way, *ever*. Even when I am gone, I will be watching over you from the columbarium." Behind the bark might be not only the fear of one's faith system falling apart as different forms of worship open others to the gospel, but also a real fear of the end of life.

In the church how do we take the time to dissect anger's roots when it surfaces? In Ephesians 4:26–28, we hear a word offered to a particular community about anger with three negations as a caveat. "Be angry but do not sin; do not let the sun go down on your anger, and do not make room for the devil." Scripture validates anger as normal but calls the angry person to account for the anger.

Accountability for Herod's anger is absent. How might the church both anticipate anger and account for it? When training persons to be church officers or before they begin serving on the church governing board, we might ask, "What role will fear play for us as the leaders in this body of Christ?" "What sorts of things might bring us to anger?" "How will we discern when conflict among us leads to anger?" "How will we work together and not be splintered apart?"

Intentional discernment is a tool for finding a sure balance between a certain righteous anger that can lead to mighty acts of justice and an anger that is rooted in fear. Herod's order to silence a generation actually gives voice to the righteous anger of an often silent minority, the voice of women. Herod's misappropriated anger leads Matthew to hear the sobs of many mothers.

During the civil war in El Salvador, a community called Mozote was wiped out, nearly 1,000 killed.

Herod. This term carries the connotation of "stirred up" or "agitated." Herod's words in 2:8 do not conform to his true motives, indicating deception. In 2:16 the narrator tells the reader that the passive resistance of the magi leaves Herod "infuriated." The root of this term can suggest treacherous anger, as in Sirach 45:18, or a character trait that undermines true discipleship in a believer, as in Colossians 3:8. These three insights combined portray a leader whose passions control him.

The wisdom teachers of Israel warn of the dangers posed by persons who cannot control their anger (Prov. 29:22) or who act deceptively (Prov. 11:3). Matthew teaches that good trees produce good fruit (7:17). Herod's evil psychological traits produce evil fruit. Herod's actions arise from disharmony in his soul, character flaws that lead to disruption in the community, especially the families of Bethlehem. This repulsive story teaches that much damage can arise simply from a lack of control by one powerful person.

Matthew's political insights instruct about the role of leaders, again in a theological context. Although the text refers to him as "King Herod" (2:1), Herod did not have absolute power. Judah lived under Roman control. Nevertheless, Herod exercised power and authority to some degree among the Judeans. He had the ability to order the deaths of the infants, and (within the narrative world of Matthew) Roman authorities did not intervene or investigate. The Bible contains many narratives that speak to the role and responsibility of leaders. Part of the significance of the David and Goliath story is that young David assumed the role rightly belonging to Saul: protecting the people against the Philistine threat. Daniel 4 describes the expectation of even a foreign ruler to provide security, safety, and communal fulfillment for his subjects. Nebuchadnezzar relates his dream of a tree under which the birds, animals, and other living things flourished (4:10–12). When the king receives divine punishment for his sins and iniquities, all of the living creatures who had previously flourished under the tree flee away from their security (4:14). Herod fails to understand his task to protect his people. He seeks power for its own sake, doing the unspeakable because of a threat years away. All of the evidence (magi, prophets, and scribes) points Herod to Jesus as the Messiah, so Herod's actions become an attempt to thwart God's prerogative to assign leaders (Dan. 4:17).

The theological dimension of the passage portrays the resistance to God's gift of the Messiah. The other Gospel writers also describe resistance to the coming

those found out. The uncovering of hypocrisy brings embarrassment that, among the powerful, finds easy expression in violence. That the dream-warned magi ignored his disingenuous desire to worship the new king and returned home by another way, enrages Herod, and the result is murderous rampage.

Rachel's inconsolable weeping can be illumined. The Greek says that Rachel *does not want* to be consoled. When we lose someone, our mourning honors them. To cease mourning feels like we have ceased honoring them. Her children are no more; she has nothing left but her tears over them. If she gives up the tears, all seems lost.

The prophetic witness can be illumined. There is a kind of background assurance in the quotation of Scripture in Matthew 2. The impact of these witnesses is clear: this time of mourning is also a time of God's presence. God has been present and still is present, in Rachel's mourning and in ours. Even this is not unknown to God, but, as Scripture witnesses again and again, it is part of the ongoing journey of God with God's people, from Jeremiah to Jesus to us.

That is still perhaps cold comfort, and the sermon's hope must be commensurate with the horror of the text. More than Herod's rage, Rachel's weeping, and the prophetic witness, what most needs illumination is the hope that is obscured by this horrific passage. The Holy Family waits for Herod to die and end his vicious killing; even so, it is still a time of God's promise. When Archelaus shows up with an all too familiar edge, how hard it is to hold to that promise in such darkness and cold. Still, it is a time of promise.

Our hope is rooted in that promise. As Vaclav Havel once said, "Hope always comes, as it were, from elsewhere."[1]

Tom Long's treatment of *No Country for Old Men* in his *Preaching from Memory to Hope* is perhaps one resource that can measure up to the demand for preaching hope in the face of this text. Long makes it clear that Sheriff Ed Tom Bell, the main character in *No Country for Old Men*, knows the darkness of Rachel. Bell sees evil with an honesty born of his hard failures to bring justice, and he wavers in the sight of all that is frozen and impossibly broken, what he has experienced is so much bigger than himself.

As the novel drives to its end, after dark and chilling and unredeemed violence, Bell reflects

---

1. Vaclav Havel, *Disturbing the Peace: A Conversation with Karel Huizdala* (New York: Alfred A. Knopf, 1990), 181.

Matthew 2:16–23

Theological Perspective

being accomplished. Jesus escapes, the children are murdered, and Herod seems to go free without judgment.

The only response to this tragedy comes once again through the voice of Scripture. Matthew quotes a text from Jeremiah 31:15, collapsing different time periods and scriptural traditions. Matthew employs Jeremiah's imagery of Rachel, the beloved wife of Jacob/Israel, weeping loudly for the children of Israel, because they are no more. The original setting of this prophecy refers to the conquering and dispersion of the nation of Israel in the eighth century BCE. Jeremiah places Rachel's mourning in a context of consolation, emphasizing hope to come. Matthew does not appeal to the hope found in the surrounding verses in Jeremiah 31, yet we know that a thread of hope remains in the form of the child who has fled to Egypt. In Bethlehem, however, Matthew highlights the fact that tragedy and genocide have now come upon Israel from within. Rachel's loud cries and mourning give voice to the cries of those who long for redemption and liberation throughout all time: God, be merciful; come and save us from ourselves.

The gospel, in its promised victory over sin and death, does not erase or absolve the deaths of these children, any more than the gospel excuses the tragic acts we commit against one another today.[1] The coming of the child, Immanuel, does not instantaneously create a world in which sin and tragedy are joyfully absent. Nevertheless, the broader testimony of the gospel is that with the coming of Immanuel there is someone to weep with Rachel over the personal and corporate tragedies of this world and to promise that there will come a time when God's dominion will conquer the Herods of this world.

LAURA C. SWEAT

Pastoral Perspective

Villagers gathered in the town square to receive promised food. What unfolded was not justice and distribution of food to the least of these, but violent death. Herded like animals, an entire community was massacred. A mother's voice is heard. Rufina Amaya reports, "We could hear the women and girls being raped on the hills . . . and the soldiers talking and joking, saying how much they liked 12 year olds."[1]

On a youth mission trip, youth studied the theological concepts of hope and despair working alongside local children building a school. The youth asked, "Where do you find hope?" One woman responded, "I have hope when you hear my story and work with these children. Your listening to the pain in my story helps me to heal." One woman's answer harks back to the fulfillment of the prophet, "Rachel weeping for her children."

Maybe this story, like Herod's massacre of the innocents, is one in which we can distance ourselves from the depth of the pain and the sound of a mother weeping. However, within our congregations, and in the cities where our congregations are located, there are mothers who weep for children: infertile, desperate to feel life in the womb; worried, watching children suffer the consequences of a failed marriage; weary, longing for the wholeness of a teenager lost to addiction. Do we hear their voices?

Christ's birth led to Herod's unchecked anger and senseless violence against the least of these. As Christ's disciples, whether along dusty footpaths in foreign countries or on sidewalks in our own cities, we must seek to hear the voices of mothers weeping; seek to right the wrongs of misused anger. Like splinters of a cross strewn on a city sidewalk, amid the splinters of suffering pain, Christ's love and merciful healing break in through the simple task of listening. May we be the body of Christ, persons who not only rightly recognize and discern anger, but who have the collective ears to hear the voices of women weeping for their children.

ANNE H. K. APPLE

---

1. For more information on the continued, pervasive problem of genocide, see Ben Kiernan, *Blood and Soil: A World History of Genocide and Extermination from Sparta to Darfur* (New Haven, CT: Yale University Press, 2007), and for further information that calls the United States to account for its position in terms of global genocide, see Samantha Power, *A Problem from Hell: America and the Age of Genocide* (New York: Harper Perennial, 2002).

1. Mark Danner, "A Reporter at Large, The Truth of El Mozote," *The New Yorker*, December 6, 1993, 82.

of Jesus into the world. Mark presents a scene of an unclean spirit challenging Jesus early in his ministry (Mark 1:21–28). John gives a cosmic overview, in which light and darkness battle within creation itself (John 1:5). The threat and resistance in Matthew takes the form of Herod's violent jealousy. Theologically, these examples of resistance confirm that even though Jesus embodies good news, the evil in creation continues to exercise power. The reader notes the irony that Jesus comes to save the people from their sins (Matt. 1:21), but cannot save the children of Bethlehem from Herod's sin. Just as the genealogies speak to God's long-range plans that take centuries to unfold, so the killing of the children in Bethlehem indicates that, even though God has acted in Jesus, the true redemption of creation has not yet occurred. Evil may seem to have the upper hand, but God's plans continue to develop.

Matthew writes cryptically and enigmatically in the last vignette in this section. God continues to act behind the scenes by sending dreams. The immediate threat to Jesus has changed, but apparently not completely ended. Joseph and the family can leave Egypt, but must relocate to Galilee. Matthew and Luke agree that Jesus was born in Bethlehem and raised in Nazareth, but they present entirely different scenarios for how that happened. Luke portrays Jesus' family as poor and powerless, but Matthew presents a threat to Jesus' very life. In Galilee, Jesus grows up outside the seat of power in Jerusalem.

The passage contains powerful material for proclamation. The connections between Exodus/Moses and Matthew/Jesus convey both the consistency of God's actions and God's freedom to act in unexpected ways. No one expected such a vulnerable Messiah, but God had acted before in the protection of a boy child. The story of the killing of the infants in Bethlehem shatters any sentimentality to which the church feels tempted, especially at Christmas time. Despite the appeal of children's pageants at this time of year, the birth of Jesus concerns serious matters of violence and suffering. That the Holy Family has to retreat and then lie low, even after the death of Herod the Great, suggests that even though passivity is never in order, the church must choose the right time for certain confrontations.

CHARLES L. AARON

on [why he first went into law enforcement and says, "It was because] . . . I always thought I could at least someway put things right and I guess I just don't feel that way no more. I'm being asked to stand for somethin that I don't have the same belief in it I once did." Sheriff Bell reflects to himself about the only hope he can imagine, a hungering for redemption that transcends the powers of humanity. "I wake up sometimes way in the night and I know as certain as death that there ain't nothing short of the second comin of Christ that can slow this train."

Then Bell remembers a dream he had about his father. . . . "I was on horseback goin through the mountains of a night. Goin through this pass in the mountains. It was cold and there was snow on the ground and he rode past me and kept on goin. Never said nothin. He just rode on past and he had this blanket wrapped around him and he had his head down and when he rode past I seen he was carryin fire in a horn the way people used to do and I could see the horn from the light inside of it. About the color of the moon. And in the dream I knew that he was goin on ahead and he was fixin to make a fire somewhere out there in all that dark and all that cold and I knew that whenever I got there he would be there. And then I woke up."[2]

Dreams delivered the Holy Family, and a dream delivered Sheriff Bell into hope. It is the preacher's task with such a text to share these dreams of God's redemption and repeat the promise, to carry the fire or light the fire or at least report the dream of lighting the fire for the people lamenting in Ramah, for "hope lies in the God who goes ahead of us, 'to make a fire out there' in all the dark and cold."[3]

CHANDLER BROWN STOKES

2. Thomas G. Long, *Preaching from Memory to Hope* (Louisville, KY: Westminster John Knox Press, 2009), 121–22.
3. Ibid., 122.

Matthew 3:1–6

¹In those days John the Baptist appeared in the wilderness of Judea, proclaiming, ²"Repent, for the kingdom of heaven has come near." ³This is the one of whom the prophet Isaiah spoke when he said,
"The voice of one crying out in the wilderness:
'Prepare the way of the Lord,
    make his paths straight.'"
⁴Now John wore clothing of camel's hair with a leather belt around his waist, and his food was locusts and wild honey. ⁵Then the people of Jerusalem and all Judea were going out to him, and all the region along the Jordan, ⁶and they were baptized by him in the river Jordan, confessing their sins.

Theological Perspective

After leaving Jesus and his family in Nazareth (2:22–23), Matthew transitions to another figure, with no introduction or preamble except for the vague phrase "in those days" (3:1). This transition marks a tremendous spatial and temporal shift for the Gospel. Thus far, the narrative has described events that occur in towns or cities (Bethlehem, 2:1, 5–6; Nazareth, 2:23). Most of the stories we have heard describe interactions with rulers and politicians, like Herod (2:1–22). Now Matthew takes us out to the wilderness to hear a rough prophet's preaching. The passages that immediately precede this one reenact God's liberation of Israel in terms that mirror Israel's exodus, through the child Jesus.

This passage pushes the current people of Israel to be accountable for their new liberation. As the redeemed Israel wandering in the wilderness became the people of God by submitting to God's laws and dominion, the same is true here. John the Baptist proclaims: "Repent! For the kingdom of heaven has come near" (v. 2). Reenacting the role of the prophets of old, John prepares the way of the Lord, who is coming and who will offer the same message of repentance and promise to the people (4:17), the way of redemption.

The role of John the Baptist is striking in each of the Gospels, inaugurating Jesus' ministry and taking

Pastoral Perspective

When John appears in the wilderness, he starts with a shout: "Repent!" As if his locust-eating, sartorially inelegant self would not grab enough attention, John shouts, "*Turn around, people!*" After he clears his throat, he says, with what must be a bit of a closed-lipped smile, a harsh whisper, and the lifting of an eyebrow, "The kingdom of heaven is drawing near."

When the kingdom of heaven has come near, how will we know? Is it something that a "we" may know as the gathered body of Christ? Is the kingdom of heaven something only an "I," a single disciple, may know? Is it either-or, or is it both-and?

Try sitting with a nine-year-old whose mother has died of complications from chemotherapy and insidious cancer and ask, "Is there anything you would like to talk about or ask me?" The child's memory is overwhelmed in the flood of emotion, having last seen her body and then watched his feet walk on the straight red-carpeted aisle as he followed her casket out of the sanctuary when he was six. Three years later, he asks with precision, "What will happen when I die? Will I join my mother in heaven? Is heaven above the trees, inside the clouds, or in the ground beneath the dirt?"

Behind the child's questions is a quiet desperation for the assurance of things hoped for and the conviction of things unseen (Heb. 11:1). Behind the child's

Exegetical Perspective

Matthew's transition from chapter 2 to chapter 3 might cause a reader to scratch her head. The narrative about Jesus growing up in Nazareth simply fades out, with no follow-up, while John suddenly emerges in the wilderness with no back story. The narrator does not clarify "those days." Nevertheless, Matthew's juxtaposition carries much power. John's mighty proclamation about the nearness of the kingdom of heaven follows immediately after a sickening story of cruelty and suffering. The narrative of the killing of the children creates a yearning for the kingdom of God, surely an elusive term, but in broad strokes a time and place marked by justice and peace, where children and families fear no such intrusion (see Isa. 65:20).

Even given the paucity of information about him in the Gospels, John appears as one of the most colorful and compelling characters in the New Testament. The brief portrait of John captures our attention. The Gospel writers perhaps intentionally withhold information about him because many in the crowds took him for the Messiah. The scholarship about the "historical John the Baptist" will continue, seeking answers about his likely relationship to the Essenes and his connection to Jesus. Even if these verses deny us insight into such matters, they provide much material for reflection by the contemporary church.

Homiletical Perspective

There are a number of stumbling blocks to preaching this text. One of them is that the fulcrum and strength of the reading, the quotation from Isaiah, rather than reinforcing Matthew's Gospel word, can distract the contemporary hearer. When Matthew says, "In those days," part of what he intends to convey is that the events of "those days" are to be understood as a fulfillment of Scripture. The scriptural context of John's appearance "in those days" is critical to Matthew's telling of the gospel, but we do not read Scripture the way first-century scribes did. Matthew's approach seems like proof-texting. How does the preacher appropriate a feature of the text that is awkward, yet essential?

Without going into a long dissertation on the character of first-century exegesis and modern hermeneutics, it is possible to claim a legitimate function for the series of quotations from Scripture that are so important to Matthew. Rather than ignoring the citations, the preacher should emphasize them. From Matthew 2:1 through our text, Matthew explicitly quotes Micah, Hosea, Jeremiah, and now Isaiah. He also makes countless other allusions to Scripture, including the characterization of Joseph as a dreamer from Genesis and of John as wearing Elijah's leather belt from 2 Kings.

This wash of quotations from Scripture forms a landscape for the telling of the story. Each quotation

Matthew 3:1–6

Theological Perspective

part in its proclamation of repentance. John is similar to the prophet Elijah, who also appears in the scriptural narrative with little introduction (1 Kgs. 17), lives mostly in the wilderness, and prophesies the need for repentance (e.g., 1 Kgs. 18:21; 19:19–21). The fact that John resumes Elijah's ministry serves not only as a call to realize the timing of these "days" (v. 1)—they must be the last days, for that is when Elijah would appear again (Mal. 4:5–6)—but it also provokes the audience to remember that people did not listen to the first Elijah when he called for repentance, and Israel was judged accordingly. If John's audience, then and now, misses the point of his message or thinks it is meant for others, what prevents us from falling victim to his judgment too?

The message of John the Baptist, as summarized above, sounds simple: repent. In most church contexts, repentance is associated with guilt. People repent because they want to absolve themselves of the guilt incurred by sins they know they have committed. John's repentance has little to do with the guilt that causes us to wallow in despair. Repentance for John is an action. John Howard Yoder understands clearly what this repentance looks like: "To repent is not to feel bad, but to think differently," and therefore, to act differently.[1] Luke's summary of John the Baptist's preaching highlights quite clearly the change in action called for: "Whoever has two coats must share with anyone who has none; and whoever has food must do likewise" (Luke 3:11), with variations for different people in the crowd (Luke 3:10, 12–14). In Matthew, we see the difference that repentance should make by understanding the kingdom of heaven better.

The dominion of heaven has been contrasted with the reigns of worldly leaders from the beginning of the Gospel of Matthew. Based on this contrast, Matthew shows us the ways of this new kind of rule, God's rule, and its transforming presence. First, the clash between God's reign and Herod's makes it clear that God's rule challenges the current political and religious authorities. Being an insider of the status quo in Matthew is not a comfortable, safe position, and insiders seem to know this. Herod acts against the child Jesus in fear and paranoia, rather than in humility, admiration, or worship. Likewise, if we are insiders in our political and religious cultures now, our own status is put in jeopardy by John's words. More than others, insiders need to hear John's clear

1. John Howard Yoder, *The Original Revolution* (Scottsdale, PA: Herald Press, 1971), 31.

Pastoral Perspective

questions is a deep trust and love for God. All his life this child has heard, "God loves you." Most of his life he has known that love in the care of a congregation that took their baptismal questions seriously. Now, as this boy's birthdays come and go, and he opens gifts prepared by a dying mother, with handwritten notes attached in lasting love that he traces with a finger, he wonders aloud with aching questions about life, death, and love. Listening, what you know is that behind the child's questions is John the Baptist crying out to you, "The kingdom of heaven has come near."

Jesus implores us to listen to children, to welcome their questions and presence among us. Children teach us how to listen from the margins and to be open to God's kingdom as it draws near.

Like storm chasers who follow potentially dangerous winds, the people of Jerusalem had come down off the hill. The folks of Judea had wandered into the wilderness. All these people were making their way to this prophet ministering in the wilderness, John the Baptist. Maybe as a group they made their way to get a glimpse, to say one day, "I remember when we sat in on the wilderness . . ." Like the crowds we may make our way to be part of a dangerous history, of following Christ, of being a disciple.

When Hillary Clinton ran for the Democratic nomination for president in 2008, she had a slogan that said, "Make history." Once while she was wearing the slogan on a shirt in an airport, an older man, somewhat prophetically, walked past her, quickly saying over his shoulder, "Listen, lady, every day we get the chance to make history—just not everybody gets to read about it in textbooks."

Maybe those Judeans and folks from Jerusalem were surprised at the way they had come through the baptismal waters. Dripping with river water, they found themselves in a place of confession, of turning back to God, of sputtering and spilling out the truth of what was separating them from God. They found themselves in a place of knowing, "The kingdom of heaven has drawn near." They found themselves participating in history.

Maybe what we know in the church and as individuals is that there is a wilderness in each one of us—a gnawing feeling that lurks right beneath the surface and taunts, "You are not enough." Something is not quite right, and you feel edgy. Maybe some imperfection rides along the surface of your life like a small splinter, an ebbing and flowing of pain: an intermittent insecurity feeding your tendency to isolate and put on masks, a divorce and your broken heart for what could have been, an illness and your

A careful reading of Matthew's use of Isaiah in this section demonstrates the significance of interpretation. Matthew's use of Isaiah's call to prepare in the wilderness makes the wilderness the location of the voice. As with Matthew's other uses of the fulfillment motif, we read his message as the assertion that God acts in a time when the community needs God's intervention, whether the wilderness is exile or Roman oppression.

In the early part of this chapter, John appears as a unifying figure, a somewhat curious role for a prophet. People who would not have much in common all respond to his ministry: urbanites from Jerusalem, more rural folk from Judea, Pharisees and Sadducees (v. 7). Does John preach in such a compelling way that his message breaks through barriers? Does his proclamation of the kingdom of heaven tap into such a deep longing that his listeners forget their differences? John's early ministry—keeping in mind his prison experience later—helps the community of faith hear and holds out some hope that people will respond together to God's impending action.

John's preaching seems to presuppose that his listeners had some basic understanding of the kingdom of heaven (Matthew's phrase for the "kingdom of God" used by the other Gospel writers). John does not describe the kingdom of heaven; he announces its nearness. At its most basic, the kingdom of heaven connotes the time when and place where God will intervene to transform creation, restoring creation to its intended state of harmony. God gave Abraham the mission of blessing all the families of the earth, and the prophets and visionaries wrote of a situation in which God would act, bringing justice and stability (see Isa. 11:2–9, Dan. 2:44). John's declaration that this situation has "come near" intrigues, encourages, and mystifies. That God stands ready to work decisively in a world marked by corruption and grief catches the attention of even the most jaded listener.

What exactly does John (or Matthew) mean by the assertion that the kingdom of heaven has come near? The arrival of Jesus marks a momentous event of God's grace and power, but the disharmony in creation continues. As the next section of Matthew indicates, even John himself may have misunderstood the significance of the coming near of the kingdom. He may have expected a full-blown purging of evil that no one could miss. In chapter 11 he seems disappointed that such a cleansing did not take place. The church continually works out the exposition of the reality that Christ has made a decisive difference in creation, yet everything seems the same as before.

suggests continuity with God's previous activity with Israel, but all of them collectively make the point powerfully. As one reads through these opening chapters of Matthew, the impression is unmistakable: "God has been here before. God's people have been here before. This territory is not alien. This landscape is known to God and to God's people."

At a minimum, these quotations say that what we witness in Jesus Christ is in keeping with the God of Israel. "In those days" says that as God *was*, so God *is:* faithful and active. Whether or not we understand the promise of Scripture to be fulfilled in precisely the same way as Matthew did, the experience of the first-century church resonated with their understanding of how God was, and always had been, with the people of God.

"In those days" also means, literarily, like the days that precede this story in chapters 1 and 2: the days of the slaughter of the innocents, the days of God's watching over the life of God's Son, the days of his protection, the days of his waiting for the right moment to reveal the truth about the vicious rulers of this world. "In those days . . . John appeared," and the reader knows that John's story will also end in slaughter. Those days, these days, are bloody days.

Nevertheless "in those days"—John appeared, proclaiming, "Repent"—is a hopeful word in any day. The root of the word "repent" communicates change, a turn in life. To proclaim repentance is to say that change is possible. A life headed off the road need not end at the bottom of the cliff. A life at the bottom of the cliff need not remain there. Because John preaches repentance, "in those days" is a time of beginning—right in the middle of life. Here at the muddy Jordan, in the wilderness of Judea, a real place with a name and a history and its own particular mess, there is still a place where the hopeful word of repentance is spoken and new beginnings are live options.

We claim baptism as a new beginning and as a new creation. A friend suggests that, as we are met by John "in these days," the question for us becomes,

> Where did you begin? Where did the story of you begin? Is it a birth story? Did you begin at your birth? Did you begin farther back in history? Are you part of a long line? Did your life begin in the new world? Are you part of one of the great migrations? Were you forcibly brought here in slavery? Did you come seeking liberation?
>
> Some of us are not even as old as our bodies. Maybe you began the day of the great awakening of your mind, or the day you met your soul mate

Matthew 3:1–6

Theological Perspective

call to repentance, but the insiders are the ones who are most likely to ignore it (3:7–10; cf. 2:16).

To this end, the second point Matthew makes about the advent of God's dominion is that it questions the presumed identities of insiders and outsiders. While there are faithful people in Israel, like Joseph and Mary, the best examples of characters that understand what God is doing in Jesus are the magi, who are foreign Gentiles, the consummate outsiders (2:1–12). Even though John looks like Elijah and Jesus has taken on the role of Israel, God is doing something new, and people are responding to it in new and surprising ways.

Finally, in this dominion of God, the impossible is made possible. Mary is made pregnant by the Holy Spirit, with no commentary about how this could happen (1:18, 20). Joseph, fully within his right to divorce Mary, believes the dreams and stays with her, thereby protecting both Mary and the child (1:24). The child is spared the disastrous tragedy of slaughter in Bethlehem and grows up in Nazareth, fulfilling a prophetic word that remains unknown to us (2:23). The fact that the kingdom of God comes in surprising ways, making the impossible possible, fuels human hope for the one John promises is to come. Even so, prophets seldom live to see the fulfillment of their efforts, and John is no different from those who have come before him (cf. v. 5 and vv. 7–10). He has been sent only to announce the nearness of the kingdom, and to make the paths straight for the one who is to come (v. 3), who will not only proclaim the need for repentance and the advent of God's dominion, but who also embodies the reign of God himself.

Now the church sits in the position of the Pharisees and Sadducees, needing to hear John's cry for repentance (vv. 7–10). At the same time, the church, like John, on account of God's grace, is to prepare the way for Christ's final victory and the consummation of God's reign. With this dual vision, Jesus' followers now make his paths straight as they turn and think and act differently, announcing and making visible the difference between God's dominion and the dominions of this world.

LAURA C. SWEAT

Pastoral Perspective

recognition of life's frailty. The kingdom of heaven seems distant when we live seeking something, grasping at wholeness but achingly aware that we are not finding it—in our own lives or in the life of the church.

Try sitting in a hospice room with a veteran of a world war. Holding on to each breath, not able to let go or to die, his lingering question pierces the silence, "Do you think it matters?" The response "Do I think what matters?" opens him to sobs. Between the gasps flood the memories of his life as a military tank commander. The war was officially over, but he had issued an order that resulted in the death of his entire convoy. His decision brought him face to face with the sensory onslaught of the death of every man with whom he had shared pictures of home and laughed in the cold of battle's fear. His was a kingdom question, "Will God forgive me?"

For some, thinking about the kingdom of heaven drawing near leads to thoughts of what happens after death: For a veteran, what does judgment look like? For a motherless child, with whom will I be? For others, it is as if they are hearing John's very shout, "Turn around!" daily.

John's cry harks back to Isaiah's plea out of the wilderness. Isaiah summoned a people to make a straight path, to walk level with the Lord. When we walk on a level path, we live with a certain awareness of how Christ indwells our lives, despite our imperfect faith, and meets us with an upholding love. These moments are known both in community and individually. Thanks be to God.

ANNE H. K. APPLE

Exegetical Perspective

John calls his audience to repentance, a thorough change of heart, mind, and actions. Repentance literally means "turning around," moving in an opposite direction. The harsh, no-nonsense John, whose overall message certainly contains judgment (v. 10), actually teaches the contemporary church a needed message about repentance. Repentance arises not so much out of fear of punishment as it does out of the sense of passion about the nearness of the kingdom of heaven. Sinners repent in order to participate in what God does in bringing near the kingdom.

The action that gives John his moniker carries inestimable value for the church. John's baptism, an action accompanying the repentance of the community in anticipation of the nearness of the kingdom, became a sacrament for the church. How could an act that apparently brought a measure of unity to the fractured Jewish community of the first century CE have so deeply divided the Christian community? Even if the church cannot agree on the time and method of baptism, perhaps it can learn from John that baptism cleanses from sin and incorporates the one baptized into God's action to bring near the kingdom.

John appears as a preacher/prophet nearly antithetical to the contemporary institutional church. One can hardly imagine a situation in which he would fit. His attire would draw stares in "cowboy" churches or in mainline congregations, even given the current trend of dressing casually. His contribution to a potluck supper would sit untouched. How would his uncompromising message affect church-growth strategies? He points the institutional church back to its pre-Christian roots, where the church has much to learn.

Our deepest longing for God's intervention bringing peace, stability, and justice unites us, even where we have created lasting divisions. The recognition of our shared sinfulness and need for repentance crosses human-made boundaries. We reclaim our mission to foster a sense of anticipation for God's action on behalf of creation, as we work out what it means that somehow in Jesus that action has come near.

CHARLES L. AARON

Homiletical Perspective

and began living for one another. Some of you began the day you went sober for good.

"In those days"—those bloody, broken days—the hopeful word of repentance and the promise of a new beginning in baptism were heard in the wilderness. When we are desperate for a new beginning, we have this story in these days. We have a creating and re-creating God, who shapes chaos into order, and even beauty.

There is not one beginning in the Bible; creation stories abound. Psalms, Genesis 1, Genesis 2, the resurrection stories, and the stories of baptism in each Gospel: all witness to the fact that there is no disorder that the love of God cannot remake, no chaos that God's love cannot turn into a thing of beauty.[1]

As Scripture testifies, beginnings happen every day, and, now as then, those beginnings happen in a world that is broken. John did not show up at a perfect time. As Madeleine L'Engle has written: "God did not wait till the world was ready, /. . . God did not wait for the perfect time. / God came when the need was deep and great."[2]

You can begin again—"in these days." The "Spirit of God hovers over the chaos of your life, calls you by name, and longs to deliver you into a good, a blessed place. This is how God is, was and ever shall be."[3] "In those days, in these days"—the bloody days and broken days—are days full of the promises of our faithful God, days in the wilderness where God has always accompanied God's Son, Israel, and us.

CHANDLER BROWN STOKES

1. David Lewicki, paraphrased from an unpublished paper for the Moveable Feast—January 2012 in Atlanta.
2. Madeleine L'Engle, "First Coming," in *The Ordering of Love: The New and Collected Poems of Madeleine L'Engle*, Random House, Inc. Kindle Edition.
3. Lewicki, op. cit.

Matthew 3:7–12

⁷But when he saw many Pharisees and Sadducees coming for baptism, he said to them, "You brood of vipers! Who warned you to flee from the wrath to come? ⁸Bear fruit worthy of repentance. ⁹Do not presume to say to yourselves, 'We have Abraham as our ancestor'; for I tell you, God is able from these stones to raise up children to Abraham. ¹⁰Even now the ax is lying at the root of the trees; every tree therefore that does not bear good fruit is cut down and thrown into the fire.

¹¹"I baptize you with water for repentance, but one who is more powerful than I is coming after me; I am not worthy to carry his sandals. He will baptize you with the Holy Spirit and fire. ¹²His winnowing fork is in his hand, and he will clear his threshing floor and will gather his wheat into the granary; but the chaff he will burn with unquenchable fire."

Theological Perspective

With all of Matthew's readers through the generations, John beckons us to cross the threshold of a new age through the passageway of baptism. John the Baptist, as we all know, prepares the way for the Messiah. In Matthew's Gospel, he introduces the refrain that Jesus will take up in just a few verses, "Repent, for the kingdom of heaven is at hand" (3:2; 4:17). Up to this point in the narrative, Matthew reveals Jesus' identity and purpose by recapitulating the history of Israel. In the genealogy, Jesus is connected with all the great events and people in the scriptural narrative. In his sojourn to Egypt, Jesus and his family relive the exodus experience. Now an eschatological prophet, in the image of Elijah, announces the arrival of "the Messiah, the son of David, the son of Abraham" (1:1).

The dramatic confrontation with the Pharisees and Sadducees in the current passage makes clear the threat presented by the advent of the kingdom of heaven. Suddenly King Herod's violent response to the Messiah's birth makes sense. The new age takes no prisoners and offers no quarter. John the Baptist is a frightening messenger of doom, with fire flying from his eyes and thunder rumbling deep in his throat. The foundations are shaking and about to collapse! "Even now the ax is lying at the root of the trees" (v. 10). There is no escape from the crisis at

Pastoral Perspective

We are uncomfortable with this text. We *say* that we are uncomfortable with this text because we do not like the harsh judgments of John the Baptist. However, if we probe a little deeper within ourselves, we may find that our discomfort actually stems from our own desire to be that judging voice. As children, we love to tell on other children. Teenagers evaluate the clothing and appearance of other teens. As adults, we judge others for their sexual behavior, their views on abortion, their treatment of the environment, the way they raise their children. As pastors, we judge our congregants for their attendance, their involvement in the church, their financial giving. I suspect we would relish the opportunity to call our enemies a "brood of vipers" or to impress upon them God's coming wrath (v. 7). Our problem with this text may be that we really would like to be John the Baptist.

However, the writer of the Gospel of Matthew does not intend John the Baptist to be an example to follow. He is intended instead to be a forerunner to Jesus. John the Baptist takes great pains to describe Jesus as a figure of greater importance, authority, and power than himself. John the Baptist declares to the crowd, "I baptize you with water for repentance, but one who is more powerful than I is coming after me; I am not worthy to carry his sandals" (v. 11). He also

Feasting on the Gospels

Exegetical Perspective

After introducing the messianic identity of Jesus as the son of Abraham, son of David, and the new Moses (chaps. 1–2), Matthew introduces John the Baptist in 3:1–6. The real purpose of introducing John the Baptist is to introduce through his prophetic words the messianic identity of Jesus as the eschatological judge. Matthew 3:1–6 ends with a brief summary of John's successful mission of baptism (3:5–6), and functions as a preface to the next two passages (3:7–12, 13–17).

Matthew 3:7–12 comprises John's prophetic preaching. The major themes of John's preaching include the urgency of the final judgment, the coming of the messianic figure, the comparison of role and status between John the Baptist and the messianic figure, and the image of bearing "good fruit," a metaphor for a life spent doing good works, the essential criterion for salvation.

The parallel passage in Luke is nearly a verbatim copy of Matthew, with one key difference. In Luke, the entire preaching is addressed to all those coming for baptism, whereas in Matthew, the first half of the preaching is addressed to the Pharisees and Sadducees. The preaching to the Pharisees and Sadducees is a harsh condemnation against them, with a warning about the imminence of divine judgment (vv. 7–10); the preaching to everyone is a proclamation

Homiletical Perspective

In many ways it is hard to discern why John was such a threat to political rulers like Herod or religious leaders like the Pharisees and Sadducees. Verses 2–4 certainly depict someone outside of the mainstream. Perhaps preachers could find significant validation here for being countercultural. Certainly John was that! Matthew's depiction of John and his message includes at least two charges: repentance and judgment. Both charges press upon the hearers immediate and future exigencies: to "prepare the way of the Lord" (v. 3), through the baptisms with water and then again with fire. Each involves rejection of the prevailing customs of political and religious life.

Matthew's account moves beyond the other Synoptic Gospels to include the baptism with fire from the Q source (v. 11). Preachers should be careful to weigh critically the correlation made here between the Holy Spirit and fire, because it is unclear in Matthew. The juxtapositions in the Gospel are many: between John and Jesus, between baptisms of water and fire, between the current age and an age to come. These juxtapositions offer resources for understanding John's sermonic message in the balance between repentance and judgment, or more effectively between grace and judgment.[1] The

1. Charles J. Daryl, "The 'Coming One'/'Stronger One' and His Baptism: Matt. 3:11–12, Mark 1:8, Luke 3:16–17," *Pneuma* 11, no. 1 (Spring 1989): 37–49.

Matthew 3:7–12

Theological Perspective

hand, no matter who you are. This is no mere reformation; it is a revolution! Everything will be turned on its head, and nothing will be left as it was.

This passage is the first of five times the author of Matthew mentions the Pharisees and the Sadducees together (the others: 16:1, 6, 11, 12). This unusual pairing is found nowhere else in the Gospels. The Pharisees and Sadducees are not obvious partners in anything. On most significant issues, both religious and political, they took different positions and ended up on opposite sides. Their disagreements and conflicts are not surprising. The Pharisees and Sadducees represent different classes, institutional loyalties, intellectual traditions, and theological heritages, but in Matthew they are united by their shared resistance to the coming kingdom of heaven. Beside the Jordan River, John the Baptist initiates a conflict that builds throughout the Gospel and leads straight to the cross. It is a conflict not with one party or another but with everyone and everything that resist God's heavenly kingdom for the sake of their crumbling fiefdoms.

None will be protected from the "wrath to come" by belonging to any particular group or heritage. Not even being a descendant of Abraham himself guarantees safety. It is neither a Gentile kingdom nor a Jewish kingdom that is at hand. It is God's kingdom! Therefore, all those for whom the identities and distinctions of the world are the source and goal of their striving will find themselves and all they value destroyed in "unquenchable fire." God's kingdom does not exist for the sake of anything or anyone. Rather, everything exists by, through, and for God's kingdom.

Struggling with similar issues in the early church, Paul makes an analogous point to the Christians in Galatia: "There is no longer Jew or Greek, there is no longer slave or free, there is no longer male and female; for all of you are one in Christ Jesus. And if you belong to Christ, then you are Abraham's offspring, heirs according to the promise" (Gal. 3:28–29). In the eschatological crisis, things will be united either in their celebration of God's reign over everything or by their resistance to God for the sake of their own partial and passing kingdoms. The Pharisees and Sadducees will find themselves arm in arm one way or another, either as wheat or chaff.

This is a lesson worth remembering in a church and world divided into different parties. We are so busy vilifying our enemies that we seldom see the ways in which we have become comrades in hostility to God's kingdom. We imagine that our enemies

Pastoral Perspective

describes Jesus' unique authority to judge the world with his "winnowing fork" (v. 12). We can assume that the writer of the Gospel of Matthew intends for us to follow the teaching of Jesus, rather than the example of John the Baptist.

Given the greater prominence of Jesus in this passage, it is useful to note that just a few chapters later within this Gospel, Jesus teaches the crowds, "Do not judge, so that you may not be judged" (7:1). This is not meant to convey that we are to be unrepentant or that we should not differentiate between right and wrong in our thoughts and actions. Indeed, Jesus certainly makes these judgments and encourages his disciples to do so as well. We are instructed to judge the integrity of a spiritual message as Jesus warns us, "Beware of false prophets" (7:15). He instructs his disciples to "shake the dust off your feet" as a judgment against those who would not welcome them or listen to their message (10:14). It is clear that we are to discriminate in the messages we hear and the treatment we receive from others. There is a place for judgment in our lives.

We are not, however, to judge hypocritically. Jesus follows his well-known statement "Judge not" by saying, "Why do you see the speck in your neighbor's eye, but do not notice the log in your own eye?" (7:4). Jesus endorses the kind of judgment that discerns the right path to follow in one's life, but he teaches against the kind of judgment that casts a critical eye on faults that one also shares. This kind of judgment is disingenuous. Jesus calls us to repent of our own sin before we attempt to call another to account.

Jesus calls us to suspend judgment of another, and to forgive others for the faults we have judged them to have. Jesus teaches us in the Lord's Prayer to pray, "And forgive us our debts, as we also have forgiven our debtors" (6:12). He urges us to forgive one who has wronged us "not seven times, but, I tell you, seventy-seven times" (18:22). Our orientation is to be one of personal repentance and forgiveness toward others, before judging others' sins.

Consistent with the larger message of Jesus' teaching, we must read John's baptism, not as a call to engage in self-righteous judgment of others, but as a call to personal repentance. Immediately preceding our pericope, we read, "and they were baptized by him in the river Jordan, confessing their sins" (3:6). John's baptism was inextricably connected to this confession, and it is on this point that John critiques the Pharisees and Sadducees. John the Baptist demands of them, "Bear fruit worthy of repentance"

of the messianic figure's imminent coming as the eschatological judge (vv. 11–12).

Warning to the Pharisees and Sadducees. Why does Matthew single out the Pharisees and Sadducees? Some exegetes have interpreted John's condemnation of the Pharisees and Sadducees, alongside Jesus' severe condemnation of the Pharisees and other Jewish leaders found in Matthew, as a Christian condemnation of Judaism. Does this anti-Jewish interpretation have any merit?

Under the Roman imperial subjugation, several reformist movements competed in Judaism. Pharisees, Sadducees, Essenes, and the Jesus movement were some of those. In Matthew, the Pharisees are Jesus' main antagonists, more so than in Mark or Luke. They challenge Jesus and his disciples for not keeping Jewish law and tradition (e.g., 9:11; 12:2); they also try to discredit him and even plot to assassinate Jesus (e.g., 9:34; 12:14). Jesus harshly condemns them as hypocrites and blind leaders who do not do God's will (e.g., chap. 23). However, the portrayal of the Pharisaic group as Jesus' main antagonists is historically implausible, as the Pharisaic group gained dominance only after the destruction of the Jerusalem temple in 70 CE. Until then, the Sadducean aristocrats held religious and political power over the Jewish people and persecuted Jesus some four decades earlier. It was the Matthean Jewish community—not Jesus—that experienced marginalization at the hands of the Pharisaic leadership and thus from the wider Jewish society.

In presenting the story of Jesus from the sociohistorical context of his community, Matthew blends his historical sources (the Sadducean aristocrats' marginalization of Jesus) and his community's experiences of marginalization at the hands of the Pharisaic group into a single narrative. Both sources reflect internal conflicts within Judaism. As a skilled storyteller, Matthew also dramatizes the tensions among the characters and groups. It is important to understand John's harsh preaching to the Pharisees and Sadducees in verse 7 as an example of this literary move.[1] With this understanding, the reader will find that anti-Semitic interpretation of the Gospel of Matthew is unjustifiable.

It is not surprising, then, that John's two seemingly separated preachings actually contain one core message: the urgent need to live a life that produces good fruit. Neither baptism with mere water nor the privilege of being a descendant of Abraham warrants

balance here is struck in the confrontations. The language Matthew attributes to John is harsh, but it mirrors the language of Jesus in the Gospel. For instance, John harshly challenges the integrity of the Pharisees' and Sadducees' approach to his call for repentance and baptism. Do they stand under the divine election of their sacred inheritance? Does anyone hold claim to divine inheritance in the face of judgment? The grace offered instead is the call to repentance. Baptism is our sign in this age and our promise in the coming age. That Jesus will baptize with the Spirit (or wind) and a purging fire in an eschatological age holds God's grace in tension with God's judgment.

So why the threat? Why is John's message threatening politically or religiously? Why is John's message conditioned in a threat? Preachers may be tempted to relegate this passage to our sacramental rites of baptism, claiming to escape divine wrath without critical attention to the challenges baptism signifies in our various circles of life. Scholars suggest that the passage reflects Wisdom literature and the rhetorical patterns of prophetic judgment. Preachers should resist earmarking an alleged rejection of Israel under the impending wrath of judgment. While the rejection of the gospel message might be a question in the Q source, even there the intent of Wisdom literature marks judgment with the message of love in the Gospel. Similarly, some scholars point to a critical relationship undergirding the hortatory nature of John's message, which places the wisdom appeal in dialectic tension with Q's prophetic appeal to a fire of judgment in an eschatological future. John's message may be one of reproach, seeking to arrest the attention of those scorning the divine call to repentance, and thereby rooting believers in the desired way of life in God. The prophetic appeal to judgment is the work of admonition and God's insistence upon transformed life that is the Gospel's understanding of Jesus.[2]

The message is not some distorted rejection of Israel, in the form of the Pharisees and Sadducees, as the divine judgment of the gospel. We are included among any who hold the divine call for repentance and new life in disdain or contempt. Preachers may appeal to John here in pronouncing God's utter judgment of those who reject repentance and the gospel message of love as revealed in Christ. God's own response to judgment is the grace of the appeal in preaching as evidenced in Christ. John's message is

---

1. We see a similar event again in Matt. 16:1–20.

2. Alan Kirk, "Upbraiding Wisdom: John's Speech and the Beginning of Q (Q 3:7–9, 16–17)," *Novum Testamentum* 40, no. 1 (January 1998): 1–16.

Matthew 3:7–12

Theological Perspective

are also God's, never recognizing that both we and those we oppose may be equally distant from God's kingdom (and equally close). Religious conservatives blame the sorry state of the church on religious liberals, and vice versa. Perhaps the church is in such a state because each is committed to its own party's victory rather than the reign of God. The same may be said of our national politics and international relationships. We each claim God for our purposes, rather than offering up ourselves and everything else to God's sovereign cause.

In the waning days of the Civil War, one of America's greatest prophets described God's work in the midst of that terrible conflagration. In his Second Inaugural Address, Abraham Lincoln did not proclaim God's vindication of the Union cause, though its victory was all but assured. Rather, he presented both North and South in a larger, more ultimate context:

> Each looked for an easier triumph, and a result less fundamental and astounding. Both read the same Bible, and pray to the same God; and each invokes his aid against the other. . . . The prayers of both could not be answered; that of neither has been answered fully. *The Almighty has his own purposes.*[1]

God's wrath was not carried out by one against the other, but was borne by both for their shared opposition to God's reign. The only appropriate response to such an apocalypse was repentance. So, like John the Baptist, Lincoln begged Americans to bear fruits worthy of repentance:

> With malice toward none; with charity for all; with firmness in the right as God gives us to see the right, let us strive to finish the work we are in; to bind the nation's wounds; to care for him who shall have borne the battle, and for his widow and orphan—to do all which may achieve and cherish a just, and a lasting peace, among ourselves, and with all nations.[2]

In the name of the one who baptizes with fire and the Holy Spirit, here on the threshold of the kingdom of heaven, may we bear the fruits of such repentance.

TIMOTHY A. BEACH-VERHEY

Pastoral Perspective

(v. 8). In John's view, the Pharisees and Sadducees are unrepentant. John regards them as hypocritical leaders who are overconfident of their own religious status, and he shows this by saying, "Do not presume to say to yourselves, 'We have Abraham as our ancestor'; for I tell you, God is able from these stones to raise up children to Abraham" (v. 9). John is calling the Pharisees and the Sadducees away from their smug assuredness of their status before God and to an orientation of personal accountability.

While we are not called to judge others, John foretells Jesus' authority to judge all of us. Uncomfortably for us, John describes Jesus holding a "winnowing fork" (v. 12) and separating the wheat from the chaff. This description is difficult because it is not our preferred depiction of Jesus, and it certainly is not the image we aspire to teach our children. John's description of Jesus must again be tempered by the example of Jesus, who consistently forgave his followers and who, in the Lord's Prayer, urged us to confess to a forgiving God. We must remember that the focus of John's message is on personal repentance.

It is easy to see the negative effects of judgment within the church today. Preachers scold not only their congregations, but also society at large, for everything from their political views and their spending habits to their sexual lives. If we are attentive to the stories we hear, we may notice that these critical voices do not lead to repentance and the furthering of the gospel. They lead rather to self-righteous pride in our perceptions of our own spiritual purity. We are to preach the message of repentance and forgiveness and to leave the "brood of vipers" language to John the Baptist.

PATRICIA J. CALAHAN

---

1. http://usgovinfo.about.com/library/blabe2.htm, accessed November 21, 2012.
2. Ibid.

salvation. Only those who "bear fruit worthy of repentance" (v. 8; see also 7:16–20; 12:33; 13:23; 21:34–43) will be saved, but those who do not will be thrown into unquenchable fire (vv. 10, 12; see also 5:22; 7:19; 13:40, 42, 50; 18:8–9; 25:41). John does not explain what the fruit means; Jesus will, through his teaching, ministry, and entire life. One of the most vivid examples of the essence of Jesus' elaboration of the "fruit" is found in 25:31–46, where the "fruit" explicitly signifies working for justice by caring and providing for the essential needs of the underprivileged.

The Coming of the Messianic Figure, the Eschatological Judge. In early Judaism, a servant would carry his master's sandals when they traveled. John says that he is even lower than a servant in relation to the messianic figure, whose coming as the eschatological judge is imminent. John, the Elijah figure and precursor to the Messiah, baptizes with water to prepare people for the Messiah's coming (11:7–15; cf. Mal. 4:5–6). The eschatological judge, however, will baptize with the Holy Spirit and fire.

One may interpret this dualistically, holding that the Holy Spirit is for salvation and the fire for condemnation, because fire is often related to condemnation in Matthew. However, an alternative and more compelling interpretation understands the Holy Spirit and fire to be complementary rather than oppositional aspects of baptism. This was a popular interpretation until the Middle Ages. Moreover, Acts describes the Pentecostal gift of the Holy Spirit with the metaphor of fire (Acts 2:3). In fact, in the Old Testament and related literature, the Holy Spirit often appears as destroyer (e.g., Isa. 4:4), and fire often appears as sanctifier and purifier (e.g., Ps. 66:12).

We may, then, interpret the image of the Holy Spirit and fire as evoking Jesus' seemingly incompatible dual identity: the human (Son of Man) Messiah who has already come to sanctify, purify, and save people through his own example, and the divine (Immanuel) eschatological judge who will come ultimately to choose people for salvation or condemnation. In this sense, the baptism with the Holy Spirit and fire indicates both the ethical responsibility to do God's will, as Jesus exemplified, and the limitless grace of promised sanctification. Today many Christians understand baptism as a one-time rite that grants them salvation. The Matthean community certainly understood their practice of Christian baptism to include ethics and eschatology (see 28:19–20).

SEUNG AI YANG

not the eschatological threat per se; nor should ours be. Any eschatological move in our preaching needs to underscore God's unrelenting and uncompromising appeal to repentance and new life. John points to the advent of Jesus as the call and means to that repentance and new life.

The threat then in our preaching, like John's, is the extent to which social, cultural, political, or religious life is called to repentance and transformation. The public outrage over such a call, especially when couched in God's disfavor or judgment, is no less real today. Consider the American outrage during a presidential primary race over the Rev. Jeremiah Wright's warning of God's looming disfavor with and judgment of American culture, global political power, and economic privilege. The risk in preaching repentance is the threat it poses to theological and political worldviews of divine election or divine sanction.

The gospel call to new life reorients the way we relate to God and to each other. It also continually reorients the way God relates to us or how God is present with us to transform life. The challenges John places before preachers are these: How shall we strike the critical admonition to repentance in the grace of Christ? How dare we preach divine disfavor or divine judgment without the grace of God in Christ as the appeal? In our sermons is Christ the grace and means to new life or the threat?

In Matthew, both John and Jesus rely on this call to repentance, even though the words are open to the charge of stark judgment (cf. 3:7 and 23:33). "Brood of vipers" is not inviting! The threat of eschatological judgment admonishes us, even threatens us (cf. 3:12 and 23:33). This is a threat to our political ways of life with one another, as well as our spiritual ways of living. Perhaps God's judgment is intentional and should be present in our preaching. The challenge for preachers is to proclaim the grace of God that works unrelentingly to overcome God's own judgment or disfavor.

DALE P. ANDREWS

Matthew 3:13–17

¹³Then Jesus came from Galilee to John at the Jordan, to be baptized by him. ¹⁴John would have prevented him, saying, "I need to be baptized by you, and do you come to me?" ¹⁵But Jesus answered him, "Let it be so now; for it is proper for us in this way to fulfill all righteousness." Then he consented. ¹⁶And when Jesus had been baptized, just as he came up from the water, suddenly the heavens were opened to him and he saw the Spirit of God descending like a dove and alighting on him. ¹⁷And a voice from heaven said, "This is my Son, the Beloved, with whom I am well pleased."

Theological Perspective

In the Gospel of Matthew, Jesus Christ is presented as the Messiah, the anointed one. He is the true king of Israel. His royal pedigree establishes his claim to the messianic title. The special character of his birth and the pattern of his early life further reinforce this identity: he is conceived by the Holy Spirit and recapitulates Israel's history by sojourning in Egypt. However, it is his baptism that finally realizes the identity and purpose that had been previously intimated. It is the coronation of the true king, the Messiah, the Son of God.

Through this baptismal rite, Jesus Christ was formally invested into the high office to which he had been called and for which he had been prepared by God. Kings were merely anointed with oil, but God's Holy Spirit descended upon Jesus, in the form of a dove, and touched him. Then the voice of God spoke the words of investiture: "This is my Son, the Beloved, with whom I am well pleased" (v. 17). These words reflect God's promise to David in 2 Samuel 7:12–14, "When your days are fulfilled and you lie down with your ancestors, I will raise up your offspring after you, who shall come forth from your body, and I will establish his kingdom. He shall build a house for my name, and I will establish the throne of his kingdom forever. I will be a father to him, and he shall be a son to me."

Pastoral Perspective

Mario was a formerly homeless man who lived in a church shelter. He had lived on the streets of New York City for half of his life. He spent his sixtieth birthday with friends at a church dinner at the shelter. Several people at the dinner claimed that Mario did not appear to be sixty years old. Responding to this comment, Mario reached into his coat pocket to produce his birth certificate, which showed that he was indeed sixty years old. Mario said, "Want to see my baptismal certificate?" His baptismal certificate showed that he was baptized as a baby at an Episcopal church on the Lower East Side of Manhattan. What a remarkable thing! Why would Mario have carried his baptismal certificate with him for all those years as he wandered the streets of Manhattan?

Jesus comes to the Jordan River to be baptized by John the Baptist. John protests, saying, "I need to be baptized by you, and do you come to me?" (v. 14). Our text is clear that John says this because he does not want to assume a superior position to Jesus. Then Jesus responds, "Let it be so now; for it is proper for us in this way to fulfill all righteousness" (v. 15). We may wonder why Jesus is so insistent that he be baptized.

One answer to this question lies in the next portion of our text. The writer tells us that after Jesus was baptized, "suddenly the heavens were opened to

Exegetical Perspective

Our passage marks both the ending of the story of John the Baptist and the return to the story of Jesus the Messiah. Here comes Jesus, as John the Baptist prophesied the coming of the more powerful one (3:11–12). Jesus must go through two rites of passage, baptism (3:13–17) and testing (4:1–11), before he begins his mission. Our passage is about the baptism.

The fact that Jesus received John's baptism of repentance has been a puzzle or even an embarrassment to Christians throughout the history of Christianity. How can Jesus receive baptism from his inferior, who is even lower than a servant in relation to him (Matt. 3:11)? Moreover, if Jesus is not only human but also divine, why does he need a baptism for repentance? For Matthew, however, Jesus' baptism is not only far from an embarrassment; it is a key to understanding Jesus' true sonship with God, as well as true discipleship.

Both Mark and Luke also include the story of Jesus' baptism. When comparing the parallel versions, we find two significant differences between Matthew and the other Synoptic Gospels. First, in Matthew, John is startled by Jesus' coming and respectfully expresses his hesitance to baptize Jesus. Jesus persuasively explains the necessity of his baptism; in response, John baptizes Jesus. In Mark and Luke, there is no dialogue between John and Jesus.

Homiletical Perspective

Perhaps the most immediate distinction Matthew makes in his account of Jesus' baptism is to excise the explicit reference to forgiveness of sin as the work of baptism. Mark includes this orientation. However, Matthew resolves that the work of Jesus' baptism is caught up in his obedience to fulfill righteousness (v. 15). Why is obedience a fulcrum here? Preachers may find some answers in the historical, cultural usage of the term "to fulfill righteousness." In the ancient cultural, religious usage, righteousness typically means to seek or to follow God's will.[1] John preaches that all should "repent" and employs the act of baptism as a sign to new life; yet John approaches Jesus differently. Are we to teach that Jesus needed to repent and only Jesus knew it?

Theological traditions struggle with any notion of the incarnate Christ needing to repent from sins. This question may be an important focus of the sermon if you determine that the nature of Jesus' personhood is at stake in the baptismal understanding of your hearers. However, preachers may find it more useful to question further the actual encounter that takes place in this passage. The Baptist recognizes the irony of the encounter. When John objects, does he couch his question in worthiness or relatedness? In either case

1. Andrew Foster Connors, "Matthew 3:13–17," *Interpretation* 64, no. 4 (October 2010): 402–4.

Matthew 3:13–17

Theological Perspective

This is the true king of Zion, to whom God says, "You are my son; today I have begotten you," and who God promised would rule not only over Israel but over the whole earth and all nations (Ps. 2:7–8). After generations of false kings, the line of David seemed completely defunct. Now the messianic promise was realized: "Here is my servant, whom I uphold, my chosen, in whom my soul delights; I will put my spirit upon him; he will bring forth justice to the nations" (Isa. 42:1).

Jesus' baptism marks him as the true king, the Messiah, the Son of God, but this is a strange and humiliating sort of coronation for a strange and humble sort of king. John the Baptist voices his discomfort with what is being requested of him. "I need to be baptized by you," says John, "and do you come to me?" (v. 14). John baptizes people as a sign of repentance in preparation for the coming of the kingdom of heaven, but Jesus has no need of repentance; he is himself the embodiment of the kingdom. Things seem just backwards in Jesus' coming to John for baptism. It would be as though the king were putting himself in the place of his subjects. Jesus' enigmatic response to John the Baptist has puzzled biblical scholars and theologians ever since: "Let it be so now; for it is proper for us in this way to fulfill all righteousness" (v. 15). Righteousness denotes a right relationship with God; but Jesus already possessed this righteousness. He was himself the fulfillment of it. So why should he be baptized?

The answer lies in the character of kings in general and of this king in particular. Kings have always claimed to have a special relationship to God. Part of their legitimacy comes from being God's representative among the people. From the ancient pharaohs who claimed to be the embodiment of the sun god, Ra, to European monarchs who presented their power as bestowed by God, kings have always relied on the Divine as the source of their authority. On the other hand, monarchs have always seen themselves as the representation, in one person, of the whole people. They have been the embodiment of the unity and character of the people. This has been the other source of their legitimacy. Monarchs exist as mediators between God and the people, presenting God to the people and the people to God.

Tragically, throughout human history, monarchs have embraced this rhetoric of legitimacy but have failed to embody it. They have claimed divine sanction but have not represented the ways of God. They have presented themselves as the embodiment of the whole people, but they have ruled in accord

Pastoral Perspective

him and he saw the Spirit of God descending like a dove and alighting on him. And a voice from heaven said, 'This is my Son, the Beloved, with whom I am well pleased'" (vv. 16–17). The baptism of Jesus reveals his identity to Jesus and to us as well. Jesus is the beloved Son of God. This identity must give him confidence as he carries out his ministry, defending himself to those who question his message. This voice must bolster him as he is later declared a criminal and crucified. Others declare him to be a liar and a criminal. God declares him to be God's beloved Son.

As Christian people, we take our understanding of baptism from this text. We understand that, through God's grace, we stand alongside Jesus as God declares, "This is my Son, the Beloved, with whom I am well pleased" (v. 17). This is our Christian identity, the loved of God. Through this identity of grace we experience our own value and are motivated to see and proclaim all people to be children whom God loves.

Of course, the difficulty is that, as we grow, we sometimes forget the heavenly voice, and we begin to listen to other voices that confuse us. Perhaps we hear voices when we are children through report cards that tell us that we are not smart enough. As teenagers, we hear voices through the cruelty of other teens who tell us that we are not cool enough. As adults, we hear voices that tell us that we are not successful enough or that we do not have enough money. We often hear voices through media and unkind people that our bodies are not attractive enough. Somehow, as God's voice gets drowned out, we listen to these other voices, and we are tempted to forget who we are. We are tempted to forget that God and a congregation of Christians have claimed us as beloved children of God.

We are tempted to forget that God has claimed all people as beloved children. There are times when we forget this identity in others, as we meet homeless individuals, perceive others as unattractive, or interact with those we feel are lazy, dishonest, or even cruel. Sometimes there are people who just get under our skin for some indefinable reason, and we see them as annoying or difficult. If we are not attentive, we find that God's voice gets drowned out by our own judgments, and because of our words and actions, God's love shines a little less brightly for our world.

We can imagine Mario living on the streets for those thirty years. Passersby must have called him many things: a bum, homeless, panhandler. People avoided him and tried not to look at him. We have

Exegetical Perspective

The narrator simply says that Jesus came, and John baptized him. Second, whereas in Mark and Luke the heavenly voice says, "*You* are my beloved Son," in Matthew it says, "*This* is my beloved Son."[1] These differences are the primary lens we will use in our interpretation.

Dialogue between Jesus and John. John's attitude and speech well match what the crowd has just heard from him about the coming of the more powerful one (3:11). It effectively reminds the reader that John is even lower than a servant in relation to Jesus. In this context, Jesus' response is astonishing when he says that his baptism is necessary to fulfill all righteousness. What does he mean? The key word in his speech is "righteousness," which is a central term in Matthew. Matthew uses this term (*dikaiosynē*) seven times (3:15; 5:6, 10, 20; 6:1, 33; 21:32, all uniquely in Matthew). In the OT and early Jewish literature, when used for human character and behavior, "righteousness" and related words refer to one's ethical response to God: obeying and doing God's righteous will. Matthew uses these words in the same way. Jesus' response to John, "Let it be so now; for it is proper for us in this way to fulfill all righteousness," signifies that it is God's will that Jesus be baptized by John, despite Jesus' superiority to him; therefore they must obey it.

This is more than an eloquent speech from one who has knowledge of God's will. As the very first words Jesus ever says in the Gospel, it exposes the most characteristic feature of who Jesus is: Jesus the Messiah is the Son of God, who humbly obeys the will of God. Immediately after Jesus' baptism, this is what the heavenly voice authenticates by saying, "This is my beloved Son."

"This Is My Beloved Son." The scene about the heavenly voice follows after Jesus' baptism. Matthew presents this scene as a public revelation to the crowd, in contrast to the other Synoptic Gospels, which describe the scene as a private vision to Jesus. The difference in the wording of the heavenly voice confirms this. Whereas "*You* are my beloved Son" (Mark 1:11; Luke 3:22) is addressed to Jesus, "*This* is my beloved son" (Matt. 3:17) is addressed to the crowd present for the baptism (see 3:5). They have already witnessed the dialogue between Jesus and John, Jesus' baptism by John, and the opening of the heavens. The heavenly voice proclaims to them that the Jesus they have just witnessed is God's beloved

1. Or as in NRSV, "This is my Son, the Beloved."

Homiletical Perspective

the need of sinfulness for absolution is not hidden behind his objection. Rather, "who Jesus is" becomes central to John's encounter. Does Jesus need to confess sins? Why would he approach John for baptism? Even John has to ask! Jesus' response, however, is a critical one; diligence or obedience to serve God's will now permeate the sign of baptism itself.

Repentance remains central to *preaching* the baptism of Jesus, in that repentance marks the turn to new life. The preaching ministries of John and Jesus mark that turn in their call to new life and in the eschatological anticipation of the reign of God. Matthew 3:6 clearly underscores the confession of sins as an act in the sacred ritual. No less significant to our understanding of repentance as vital to new life is Jesus' call for repentance as he preaches the inbreaking reign of God (4:17). Since Jesus' own preaching ministry will also begin with this call to repent, surely John cannot be completely off the mark. John recognizes the inbreaking of God's reign with Jesus' approach to baptism, even if he does not fully understand his own role in the encounter.

How powerful is this encounter for our preaching! John preaches repentance, calls for the submission and integrity of a new life in God through confession, and still cannot fathom his own call in service—or perhaps he can! The encounter reveals his unworthiness to the call of herald or messenger. How do we reconcile our message and who we are, in the midst of that encounter? This passage teaches us that we cannot!

Our message may be defined by this encounter between John and Jesus as much as it is by the sacramental ritual of baptism signifying repentance and new life. John discovers anew that he cannot possibly be worthy of any anointing office—even as unglamorous as his is. Our sermons can therefore wrestle with who we are in relation to the very nature of our call and our service to that call. Does baptism change us? We see ourselves in John's encounter with Jesus as we question who we are in calling people to repentance, who we are in daring to stand in the waters of baptism as one who anoints.

Matthew 3:7–12 exposes the questionable integrity of our approach to the baptismal event. Here in verses 13–17 we encounter the character of any baptizer, the character of the seeker, and the nature and mission of the One whom baptism signifies. Perhaps our hearers will get the point before we do. Notwithstanding, preachers may find it necessary to explore this encounter to get at the relationship between John and Jesus. Why Jesus would seek out

Matthew 3:13–17

Theological Perspective

with much more limited interests and aims. In his baptism, Jesus shows himself to be the one true king, who represents God to humanity and humanity to God. He is invested with divine authority and power through the descent of the Holy Spirit and God's proclamation to the whole world, "This is my Son, the Beloved, with whom I am well pleased" (v. 17). He also embodies and represents lost humanity, by appropriating the human responsibility to repent and turn toward God in the face of the impending kingdom of heaven. In his baptism by John, Jesus identifies himself with the human condition and represents them in his right relationship with God. This baptism, therefore, not only bestows upon him the mantle of divinity; it also marks his *kenōsis* (self-emptying) on behalf of humanity. He is the king, the true and only mediator between God and humanity.

For Karl Barth, the atonement is embodied in Jesus' mediatorial identity: "In [Jesus Christ] that turning of God to man [*sic*] and conversion of man [*sic*] to God is actuality in the appointed order of the mutual interrelationship, and therefore in such a way that the former aims at the latter and the latter is grounded in the former. In Him both are in this order the one whole of the event of reconciliation."[1] This is the image of Jesus Christ we receive in Jesus' baptism. In Jesus Christ, God condescends to humanity, and humanity responds in faith and repentance to God. This is what makes Jesus the Messiah. This is what drives the true king relentlessly toward the cross and the atonement it accomplishes.

TIMOTHY A. BEACH-VERHEY

Pastoral Perspective

all watched as people like Mario are declared to be undeserving by our government and our society. We have all watched as our system refuses to provide the health care or financial assistance that would permit someone like Mario to live more successfully on the streets. We have all watched as our government underfunds programs intended to provide food and shelter for a child of God such as Mario.

Even as others, through their actions and words, declared Mario to be worthless, he carried his baptismal certificate and his birth certificate in his pocket. His birth certificate recalled his parents, who named him out of love. His baptismal certificate recalled the God and the congregation who loved him and claimed him. Here he was, sixty years later, sitting in a church and having dinner with his friends. A congregation had once again acknowledged Mario's true identity, claimed him as one of their own, and extended love and care. Mario is a beloved child of God.

As we walk through our days and hear others judge us, we need to remember God's voice at Jesus' baptism. As we hear ourselves disparage another, we need to listen for that heavenly voice. As Jesus walked forward into the Jordan River, we walk to the baptismal font. As all those who listened carefully then heard a voice from heaven, so all who listen carefully now may hear God say, "You are my son, my daughter, my beloved, with whom I am well pleased."

PATRICIA J. CALAHAN

---

1. Karl Barth, *Church Dogmatics*, IV/1, *The Doctrine of Reconciliation*, ed. G. W. Bromiley and T. F. Torrance (Edinburgh: T. & T. Clark, 1956), 122.

Exegetical Perspective

Son. Why does Matthew present the heavenly proclamation as public revelation? It is because in the Gospel of Matthew humble obedience is the essence not only of Christology but also of discipleship.

In chapters 1 and 2 Matthew repeatedly alludes to, but does not explicitly mention, Jesus' identity as God's Son. The reader finds the first explicit statement of his identity only after Jesus actually demonstrates his humble obedience to God. Throughout the remaining chapters, Matthew portrays Jesus as the humbly obedient Son of God who fulfills God's will (5:17). The apogee of his humble obedience is the passion and crucifixion, in which Jesus' submission to God's will is absolute. This structure of the Matthean story lucidly reveals that Jesus' true sonship has to do with his humble obedience to God's will.

In our passage, the evangelist artistically connects Christology and discipleship by presenting the scene of the heavenly voice as the public revelation of Jesus' sonship. The people who are there to be baptized now learn from this revelation that their relationship with God should be marked by humble obedience to God's will, as Jesus has just exemplified. In the remaining chapters, the disciples (and all others) will learn this over and over through Jesus' teaching and exemplary life. Even though they may worship Jesus and do many miracles in the name of Jesus, they will not enter the place promised to God's people unless they humbly do the will of God (7:21–23). As discipleship demands higher righteousness than that of scribes and Pharisees (5:20), those who work for peace and justice and love others, including their enemies, in accordance with the will of God will be called sons and daughters of God (5:9, 44–45).[2] As Jesus and John the Baptist must fulfill all righteousness, discipleship too demands a life of doing God's will thoroughly (see 5:20, 48).

SEUNG AI YANG

Homiletical Perspective

baptism remains the wonder of this passage. Jesus submits to this relationship with John as much as John seeks to submit to Jesus. Jesus acts in obedience to some understanding of righteousness. His submission, however, is to his relation to God and to humanity together, and our need for new life—our need marked by this baptism.

The significance of Jesus' baptism does not end with his obedience. His obedience serves as a sign itself. The referential language of the text helps the preacher to explore the implications. Most prominent are the consecrating servant language of relationship and the anointing language from the Spirit or voice of God (vv. 16–17). Many scholars correlate Psalm 2:7 with this spoken relationship between Jesus and God. For many also, the servant character of his manner of life and mission reflects Isaiah 42:1.

The servanthood of Jesus here may actually stand in contrast to the rather common interpretations of inherited royal lineage in much of our preaching of Jesus' baptism, which points to the theological claims of the Davidic strain implicit in the suggested correlation to the Psalter. This association with the royal line of anointing is probably more adequately reflected in the two earlier chapters of Matthew. Alternatively in chapter 3, Jesus stands in the shadows of Israel's relationship to God as beloved child and the sacred servanthood that comes with that relationship. Like Israel, Jesus' sacred relationship to God carries a mission that defines his identity and the nature of his obedience. The ritual of baptism is a sign of new life, a new life in service to its relationship with God, or servanthood.[2] Can our preaching speak into this encounter?

DALE P. ANDREWS

---

2. In contrast to Matthew, the Gospel of John seems to suggest that people may become children of God by receiving and believing in Jesus (John 1:12; cf. Rom. 8:14–17; Gal. 4:5–7).

2. Jeffery A. Gibbs, "Israel Standing with Israel: The Baptism of Jesus in Matthew's Gospel (Matt. 3:13–17)," *Catholic Biblical Quarterly* 64, no. 3 (July 2002): 511–26.

Matthew 4:1–11

¹Then Jesus was led up by the Spirit into the wilderness to be tempted by the devil. ²He fasted forty days and forty nights, and afterwards he was famished. ³The tempter came and said to him, "If you are the Son of God, command these stones to become loaves of bread." ⁴But he answered, "It is written,

'One does not live by bread alone,
    but by every word that comes from the mouth of God.'"

⁵Then the devil took him to the holy city and placed him on the pinnacle of the temple, ⁶saying to him, "If you are the Son of God, throw yourself down; for it is written,

'He will command his angels concerning you,'
    and 'On their hands they will bear you up,
so that you will not dash your foot against a stone.'"

Theological Perspective

The Spirit descended upon Jesus during his baptism, investing him with the messianic office to which he had been called and for which he had been prepared. It was the coronation of a new king, who mediated God to the people and the people to God. The question at hand, for the reader of the Gospel, is whether his promise and potential would be realized. Is this the true Messiah or just another pretender to the throne? So the Spirit led him out into the wilderness, where he was tested. Forty days in the wilderness would assure Matthew's audience that this really is the "Son of God."

This time of testing is a clear reflection of Israel's forty years in the wilderness. In fact, biblical scholars note that Israel had faced each of Jesus' trials during its wilderness wanderings (Exod. 16, 17, and 32). Not only the temptations, but also Jesus' responses come from Israel's time in the desert (Deut. 8:3; 6:16; 6:13). Jesus' early life had recapitulated Israel's sojourn in Egypt (Matt. 2:13–15, 19–21). Now he relived their time in the desert, with one fundamental difference, according to Matthew: while Israel had failed the tests, Jesus passed them. Like Israel, Jesus was called "God's Son" (Deut. 8:5; Hos. 11:1). However, where Israel had turned to other gods, Jesus held fast to God alone.

This time of trial would show Jesus to be the true Messiah, the true king, who embodied true

Pastoral Perspective

Who are we? What is our identity? These are questions we ask when faced with difficult choices. As Christian people, this question is even more significant. Our identity is more than a collection of individual characteristics and personality traits. We may also ask, "What does it mean that I am a Christian?"

Jesus also faced questions of identity. At Jesus' baptism, a "voice from heaven" reveals his special identity: "This is my Son, the Beloved, with whom I am well pleased" (Matt. 3:17). As Jesus is tempted, he must decide what this identity means. What will be the character of the Son of God? Similarly, we are also given an identity at our baptism, as a child of God. We must decide how we will live into this identity. Who are we, really?

Our identity is challenged most significantly when life is hard. Our text states that Jesus is "famished" (v. 2) when he is tempted by the devil. We may find ourselves faced with temptation when we are stressed, overtired, anxious, or sick. It was in the wilderness that the Israelites struggled to identify themselves as people of God, creating a golden calf to worship in the place of God (Exod. 32). Churches are tested when they face financial problems, internal disagreements, or external threats. During these times it is the hardest for us to be the people God has called us to be.

⁷Jesus said to him, "Again it is written, 'Do not put the Lord your God to the test.'"

⁸Again, the devil took him to a very high mountain and showed him all the kingdoms of the world and their splendor; ⁹and he said to him, "All these I will give you, if you will fall down and worship me." ¹⁰Jesus said to him, "Away with you, Satan! for it is written,

'Worship the Lord your God,
  and serve only him.'"

¹¹Then the devil left him, and suddenly angels came and waited on him.

Exegetical Perspective

Matthew 4:1–11, a masterpiece of the evangelist's artistic skill, serves two purposes in the narrative design. First, it is a story of Jesus' second rite of passage, following his first rite of baptism, before he begins his messianic mission. The parallel phrases in the introduction of each story—"to be baptized by him" (3:13) and "to be tempted by the devil" (4:1)—underscore the pairing of the two rites. At the baptism, the heavenly voice proclaimed Jesus' identity as God's beloved Son. Now the Spirit of God, who came to him at that baptismal proclamation, brings him to the devil, who will test Jesus' true sonship. After Jesus withstands all the temptations, the narrative moves to begin the story of Jesus' ministry (4:12–17).[1] Second, the story serves as a condensed, symbolic preview of the life of Jesus the Son of God, which the evangelist will unfold in the remaining chapters. This second aspect will be the focus of our interpretation.

Matthew 4:1–11 is simply but meticulously organized. It contains three temptation episodes (vv. 3–4, 5–7, 8–10) bracketed by the narrator's introduction (vv. 1–2) and conclusion (v. 11). The introduction describes the setting of the temptation: the Spirit's initiative and Jesus' fasting and hunger. The three

1. The temptation as a rite of passage for a religious founder or hero is a widespread motif in ancient culture (e.g., Buddha, Zarathustra, Heracles).

Homiletical Perspective

How do we interpret for our hearers' lives Matthew's careful account of the testing of Jesus in the wilderness? Was Matthew characterizing the temptations that were before the church? If we build upon the work of chapter 3 in Jesus' baptism and anointing, we find extended threads from that story woven into the Gospel's wilderness narrative that begins Jesus' mission. The baptism reveals the manner of Jesus' righteousness in seeking to fulfill God's desires. The anointing by the Spirit announces his identity and signifies his relationship to God as the beloved child and servant of God. Both depictions are at work in this story and reflect the relationship to God and the servant mission of Israel.

Matthew continues to look at Jesus through the mirror of Israel in chapter 4. Here, however, the reflections are not always dependent on Israel's gifts, as they weigh in more heavily on Israel's struggles. As soon as Jesus receives his anointing, the Spirit leads him into the wilderness (v. 1). So far, the positive correlations seem intact. Israel wanders in the wilderness and learns to trust in God through many pivotal experiences between struggle and dependence on God. The Spirit drives Jesus to test his faithfulness. In the wilderness, Israel's faithfulness wavers. From here on, Matthew draws out the variances between the identity and mission of Israel and

Theological Perspective

"righteousness" (Matt. 3:15)—a right relationship between God and the people. At the conclusion of these trials, all questions about whether this was the Messiah were set to rest. In the remainder of the Gospel, the drama would not be generated by whether Jesus would be faithful to the kingdom of heaven but by how the disciples and the crowds would respond to his faithfulness.

These temptations, therefore, not only provide a sign of the true Messiah, but also foreshadow the temptations facing those who encounter him and those who would follow him. In each of the trials, Jesus embodies a genuinely theocentric piety and rejects an anthropocentric orientation. When we are confronted by God's kingdom, the temptation is always to see it through the narrow lens of our own interests and aims. Each of the tests revolves around whether the kingdom of heaven is welcomed for God's sake or the sake of something else. Do people love the kingdom of heaven itself or the prosperity (vv. 2–4), protection (vv. 6–7), and power (vv. 9–10) it provides for them? Through Jesus' miracles the hungry are fed, the sick are healed, the dead are raised, and demons are cast out. These are signs that he is the Messiah and the kingdom of heaven is at hand. If these are the reason people love him and desire the kingdom, then they are far from it indeed. The kingdom of God is realized in those who, like Jesus, orient their lives toward God and not around the things that God provides.

There is a subtle difference between celebrating the good gifts of God and turning them into idols. God is the source of our sustenance, but Jesus resists the temptation to allow physical well-being to become the point. So he replies to the tempter, "One does not live by bread alone, but by every word that comes from the mouth of God" (v. 4). God intends the well-being of God's people, but Jesus refuses to make it the measure of God's glory. So he says to the devil, "Do not put the Lord your God to the test" (v. 7). Power allows God's people to serve God's purposes, but Jesus will not allow power to become an end in itself. So he dismisses Satan's offer with the words, "Worship the Lord your God, and serve only him" (v. 10). Like us, Jesus is tempted to place God at his own disposal, but he proves himself to be the true Messiah by remaining, always, at God's disposal. The question for all who encounter the new life that Jesus offers is whether we fall prey to the temptation to ask first what is in it for us.

The temptation of Israel was to love the gifts of God more than the giver. Similarly, in the church

Pastoral Perspective

The first two of Jesus' temptations address the issue of his identity directly. "*If* you are the Son of God," the devil challenges (vv. 3, 6). The implication is that, if Jesus is to prove his identity as the Son of God, he will succumb to the devil's wishes. Through these struggles, Jesus claims a different character for the Son of God.

The devil first tempts him to alleviate his hunger with divine power: "If you are the Son of God," he says to a hungry man, "command these stones to become bread" (v. 3). How human will the Son of God be? Jesus later miraculously feeds others, but here he does not choose to feed himself in the same way. Jesus decides not to escape human pain and suffering, but to be more fully one of us.

The devil next challenges Jesus to test God's faithfulness by throwing himself down from the "pinnacle of the temple" (v. 5). "If you are the Son of God," the devil says to him (v. 6). Here Jesus must decide what the nature of his faith will be. Will he choose to test God's faithfulness by asking for grand demonstrations? Will his faith rely on knowing the character of God?

In the final test, the devil offers Jesus authority over "the kingdoms of the world," if "you will fall down and worship me" (vv. 8, 9). Jesus must decide whom he will serve. Will he serve God, or will he serve evil? He must decide how he will use his authority. Will he choose a life of power, or will he choose the life of a servant? Just who is this Son of God going to be?

We also must choose what it means to be a child of God. Who are we going to be? Will we respond with anger toward others when we are irritable or tired? Will we take the time to listen to someone who is hurting when we are in a hurry? When we are financially struggling, will we continue to give charitably? Will we be the giving, honest, and loving people we are called to be?

Who are we going to be as a church? How will we spend our money when our resources are scarce? Will we continue to support mission? Will we be fair to our staff? How will we handle disagreements? Will we be an example to the world by responding with love? How will we treat those from the outside who threaten our church? Will we respond as any other institution would, by protecting ourselves and our corporate interests? Will we respond with sacrificial love?

In addition to resisting the temptation to do harm, we can also live into our Christian identity through positive actions. We can choose to sacrifice.

episodes develop with multiple climaxes: in locality, from wilderness to high mountain; in the devil's tempting suggestions, from a private miracle to the rulership of the entire world; in Jesus' response, from God's Word in general to the core of God's Word. The conclusion announces the departure of the devil and the approach of the angels to Jesus.

The first sentence of the introduction implies that God has purposely brought Jesus to the wilderness to let the devil tempt him (v. 1). This is in line with Israel's understanding of God as the tester of people, sometimes of the righteous in particular. God is said to test all humans (e.g., Ps. 7:9), Israel (e.g., Exod. 15:25), and the righteous Abraham (Gen. 22:1–19). God may use a proxy tester, as in Job's case, in which God lets the Accuser (literally, "the Satan"), one of God's ministers (literally, "sons of God"), test Job (Job 1–2). Although tempting is not what God intends when testing (see Jas. 1:13), the tested person may confront temptations to defy God's will, due to the hardships that the testing involves. Echoing Job, Jesus is tempted by the devil, while the ultimate origin of the testing is God. The complex relationship between God's testing and the devil's temptation[2] reflects a Jewish (and Christian) monotheistic interpretation of God as the ultimate authority of all.

In the first two episodes, the devil makes clear that the testing is about Jesus' divine sonship: "If you are the Son of God . . ." Avoiding the devil's first temptation to perform a miracle that would end his starvation, Jesus quotes God's Word and thereby shows that he is truly God's Son, who lives "by every word that comes from the mouth of God" (Deut. 8:3). In the second episode, the devil tempts Jesus, by quoting Psalm 91:11–12, to throw himself from the top of the temple (God's earthly place!) to show off his divine sonship, which God should be obliged to protect (v. 6). Jesus responds by citing Deuteronomy 6:16: "Do not put the LORD your God to the test" (v. 7).

In the remaining chapters of Matthew, the reader will easily find many stories that echo these temptations. Jesus constantly confronts such temptations from his contemporaries. They test his divine sonship by demanding a sign from heaven (16:1–4), and by asking a question concerning the greatest commandment in Jewish law (22:34–40). They test him by means of a difficult legal question to which the Mosaic law gives no definite answer, such as on divorce (19:3–9) or imperial tax (22:15–22). They do so to trap, accuse, or slander him, and thereby tempt

2. "Testing" and "tempting" are one and the same word in both Hebrew and Greek.

Jesus. The parallels are built on their differences in faithfulness. Preachers need to exercise extreme caution to avoid making claims that Jesus' faithfulness and anointing indicate some rejection of Israel now. Such claims are terrible distortions of this text.

At least with Israel the wilderness narrative demonstrates God's faithfulness in working with this beloved child and servant, even in the face of the stark realities of human depravity or at least human frailty. Scholars of the Matthean narrative point out that in Deuteronomy 1, according to Moses, it is God who drives Israel into the wilderness to test the character of their hearts. In Matthew, preachers may struggle with such a notion of testing Jesus. Why would the Spirit need to test him? Is Jesus just a pawn in this wilderness narrative to demonstrate God's sovereignty or demand for blind submission? Does the mark of one's relationship with God or servanthood really rest in being a willing pawn to the arbitrary sovereignty of God? Is this brokerage the character of God that we inherit as preachers? Matthew gives us a Jesus fully submissive to the testing. Jesus does not appear to mind being a pawn. Matthew even sees it as intrinsic to his identity and mission. Jesus begins with the assurance of his relationship to God and anointed service as he emerges from baptism (3:17).

Our sermons could wrestle with that liminal space between anointing and the realities of the wilderness. Matthew does not indicate that Jesus understood why he was being driven into the wilderness. Obviously the Gospel does not intend to claim the divine omniscience of Jesus as much as it is concerned with making his identity and mission clear. This narrative intends to demonstrate that Jesus is faithful in his human struggles in the wilderness, where Israel was not so successful. Would followers of Jesus be any more successful than Israel?

The correlation of Jesus with Israel becomes somewhat more stark in the actual temptations Jesus faces (vv. 3, 5–6, and 8–9). Jesus' responses to each temptation not only cite lessons from Israel's wilderness experiences in Deuteronomy (8:3; 6:16; and 6:13); the lessons or temptations mirror those particular struggles when Israel failed to sustain their trust in God. For Matthew, the parallels uphold Jesus' anointing and inheritance as God's beloved child from Israel and their shared servanthood, which defines life in relationship with God. Jesus' anointing establishes his inheritance and his obedient triumphs over temptation. It also establishes his faithfulness, whereas Israel had failed in the

Matthew 4:1–11

Theological Perspective

today, we are tempted to measure God's value by the realization of our own desires, rather than to conform ourselves, our desires, and our values to God's will. In an age when American Christians and the mainline churches feel threatened, this temptation is particularly acute. We long for a prosperity, security, and power that we no longer possess. We grasp for ways to return to a former glory, imagining that the kingdom of heaven consists in these things. Israel expected this same sort of renewal from the Messiah in the first century, an age when these things were as absent as they had been during their wilderness wanderings. The true Messiah died on a cross and demanded that those who would be his disciples "deny themselves and take up their crosses and follow me" (Matt. 16:24). This is the meaning of the exhortation of John the Baptist and Jesus, "Repent, for the kingdom of heaven has come near" (3:2; 4:17). Turn from these temptations—prosperity, security, and power—and return to God.

It is not as though any of these things is bad or evil. They are temptations for us because they are genuine goods that come from God. It is only when we prefer them to God that they betray our true purpose and joy. In his *Confessions* (1.1), Augustine famously says, "You have made us for yourself and our hearts find no peace until they rest in You."[1] Jesus says something similar in the Sermon on the Mount: "Therefore, do not worry. . . . Your heavenly Father knows that you need all these things. But strive first for the kingdom of God and his righteousness, and all these things will be given to you as well" (6:31–33).

TIMOTHY A. BEACH-VERHEY

Pastoral Perspective

For example, I know of a contractor who, even during lean financial times, offers a $50 discount off the price of his services if his customers will donate to a charity listed on his Web site. The charities include groups that help the hungry, build shelter for the impoverished, and contribute to a healthier environment. The contractor is voluntarily reducing his income in order to serve those in need.

I know of a church that was picketed by abortion protestors because of the church's views. These protestors harassed worshipers as they came to Sunday services, and particularly directed their messages and graphic pictures toward the children of the church. The church was in turmoil, and many members responded angrily to the picketers. Retrospectively, one member says, "I wish we had offered the protestors donuts and coffee as they picketed our church. This would have been a loving response to those who threatened us." This is a Christian identity.

Through his temptations, Jesus shows us that it is when our lives are difficult that we choose who we will be. Like Jesus, we will be hungry. We will have times when we are tempted to doubt God's faithfulness. We will be tempted to reach for power, rather than to live the life of a servant. To live as a child of God we must serve God even when our circumstances are hard. This is when we choose just what it means to be a child of God.

"*If* you are the Son of God." *If* we are children of God, who will we be?

PATRICIA J. CALAHAN

---

1. Augustine, *Confessions*, trans. R. S. Pine-Coffin (London: Penguin, 1961), 21.

Exegetical Perspective

him to show off the power of his divine sonship. The temptations reach a climax during his passion on the cross, where we see a near-verbatim repetition of the devil's words. Those who pass by deride Jesus: "If you are the Son of God, come down from the cross" (27:40). The chief priests and other elites similarly say: "Let him come down from the cross now. . . . Let God deliver him . . . God's Son." By mocking and tempting Jesus, they put God to the test, as the devil did. Jesus renounces all these temptations because he "fulfills the scriptures," as God's true Son, by humbly obeying God's will (26:54).

In the third episode, the devil plays God's role and offers to give Jesus the whole world, if Jesus will worship him. "Away with you, Satan!" shouts Jesus; then he solemnly recites a core tenet of Judaic teaching, that one should worship and serve God alone (Deut. 6:13). Later in the Gospel, the reader will find a story that is strongly reminiscent of this episode. When Peter argues that Jesus, as the Son of God, should not suffer through the passion and death, Jesus rebukes him: "Get behind me, Satan!" (16:23).[3] By insisting on his own definition of divine sonship for Jesus, Peter is no different from the devil, who tempted Jesus by playing the role of God.

It was on a high mountain that Jesus renounced the devil, who falsely offered him authority over the world. The story concludes that after the devil left, angels came and served him (v. 11). The reader will find a parallel finale at the end of the Matthean Gospel. After renouncing all temptations and thoroughly obeying God's will, the resurrected Son of God meets his disciples on a high mountain and says that all authority in heaven and on earth has been given to him (28:18).

SEUNG AI YANG

Homiletical Perspective

wilderness.[1] Preaching these parallels from Matthew should not become some triumphal supersessionism, judging the covenant or the covenant people. Jesus' relationship to God, to Israel, and to us defines his own discipleship and his identity. Matthew roots his Christology in the nature of Jesus' anointing and connects the character of his faithful obedience as servant to his relationship with God and humanity.

Preachers may find that the paradigm of wilderness experiences help us understand Matthew's efforts to clarify the messianic identity of Jesus or the character of discipleship. Much as this passage reflects a rabbinic tradition that uses stories to debate or interpret Scripture, preachers can learn from Matthew how to use narrative. Matthew's wilderness encounters illustrate how we may understand the exigencies in our own lives when learning about the intimate and yet difficult relationships between God, Jesus, and Israel in our faith identity and the character of discipleship. For instance, the very nature of the temptations may illustrate the struggles of discipleship itself.

Sermons might construct contextual stories to reflect or to dialogue with the wilderness struggles of Jesus, and thereby also with the Israelite wilderness journey—the temptations of plenitude in relation to the resources we need or desire in life (vv. 3–4), the temptations of privilege that claim divine favor (vv. 5–7), and the temptations of power that assert divine inheritance or sanction (vv. 8–10).

Does the Spirit lead us or drive us (v. 1) into the wilderness of discipleship? How do our hearers perceive their faith identity or anointing as they discover their own faithlessness or failures in the wilderness? How do different people or cultures of difference experience these struggles in particular narrative constructions of plenitude, privilege, or power? Answering these questions within our contexts will be critical to the character of anointing and the character of faithfulness we mirror in our sermons on this biblical narrative, answers that ultimately reflect upon the messianic identity and servanthood of Jesus. How we construct our claims of divine call, election, or inheritance from Matthew's wilderness will reveal our understanding of the discipleship or the character of servanthood in the relationship of God and humanity together.

DALE P. ANDREWS

---

3. In Greek, Jesus' word to Peter is exactly the same as his word to the devil, except that some manuscripts include "behind me" in 16:23.

1. William Richard Stegner, "The Temptation Narrative: A Study in the Use of Scripture by Early Jewish Christians," *Biblical Research* 35 (January 1990): 5–17.

Matthew 4:12–17

¹²Now when Jesus heard that John had been arrested, he withdrew to Galilee. ¹³He left Nazareth and made his home in Capernaum by the sea, in the territory of Zebulun and Naphtali, ¹⁴so that what had been spoken through the prophet Isaiah might be fulfilled:

¹⁵ "Land of Zebulun, land of Naphtali,
     on the road by the sea, across the Jordan, Galilee of the Gentiles—
¹⁶ the people who sat in darkness
     have seen a great light,
 and for those who sat in the region and shadow of death
     light has dawned."

¹⁷From that time Jesus began to proclaim, "Repent, for the kingdom of heaven has come near."

Theological Perspective

Herod Antipas, one of the sons of Herod the Great, and a Roman client king governing Galilee and Perea from 4 BCE to 39 CE, has John the Baptist imprisoned. After John's arrest, Jesus withdraws to Galilee to begin his ministry in a formal way, preaching repentance and the imminence of God's reign. Matthew's summary of Jesus' message is identical with what he depicts as the proclamation of John (cf. 3:2 and 4:17). For Matthew and the rest of the Gospel writers, John is a significant figure. Indeed, as Matthew frames the story, in looking at John's life, Jesus and later the disciples can anticipate some of what will characterize their own trajectory: reliance on God for sustenance and guidance, resistance to imperial common sense, and a deadly backlash from the reigning powers. John functions both as a forerunner to Jesus and as a model for Christian discipleship: he is a person of integrity who recognizes the presence of God in Jesus (3:13–15), who wrestles openly with doubt (11:2–6), and who is recognized by Jesus for his fidelity to God's reign (11:7–15).[1]

The public ministry of Jesus is bracketed by the actions of the local representatives of empire: it begins with John's imprisonment, and it seems to end with crucifixion at the hands of the Romans.

1. Cf. Lisa Bowens, "The Role of John the Baptist in Matthew's Gospel," *Word and World* 30, no. 3 (2010): 311–18.

Pastoral Perspective

Famine that causes the deaths of thousands of children in Africa. A broken immigration system that brings about increasing death, division, and fear on America's southern border and growing family separation and apprehension in the interior of the country. The urban crisis, the financial crisis, the crisis of trust in our political leaders.

The untimely death of a beloved spouse. The addictions to drugs and alcohol that wreak havoc on the lives of individuals and their loved ones. The dread of facing the reality of a family member with Alzheimer's or some other debilitating disease.

"Bad news" is something that surrounds our congregations and is a reality in all of our lives. In response we often seek to hide the suffering and the pain of our lives and to ignore or inoculate ourselves from the bad news of the wider world. When we do choose to acknowledge the bad news, we are often too overwhelmed and paralyzed to do much more than be depressed.

After the devil has left Jesus and the angels are attending him (4:11), Jesus is confronted with some really bad news. Jesus hears that John the Baptist— the voice of one calling in the desert, calling for repentance and proclaiming that the kingdom of heaven was at hand—has been put in prison.

Exegetical Perspective

The Gospel of Matthew begins with a portrayal of Jesus as one who is rooted in Judaism. He is the Messiah whose lineage emanates from the Jewish patriarch, Abraham. Matthew's Jesus is the fulfillment of Jewish heritage and expectation. His actions situate him as the link between the Judaism of the past and the Judaism of the first century CE. The author's use of geography connects Jesus not only to past and present people, but to past and present places within Jewish life. Early references to "Bethlehem" (2:1, 5, 6, 8), "the land of Judah" (2:6), and the "holy city" (4:5) all serve as cultural and historical reminders to Matthew's Jewish readers.

However, the writer of Matthew also uses geography to give cues to non-Jewish members of Matthew's audience. Whereas Jesus is born in Bethlehem, he makes his home in Nazareth (2:23). Although he endures a temptation in Jerusalem (4:5), he travels from Galilee before returning to Judah. John the Baptist preaches, "Repent, for the kingdom of heaven has come near," in the wilderness of Judea (3:2). Matthew portrays Jesus as declaring the same in Galilee (4:17). Thus the Gospel employs geographical shifting to identify the social location and cultural composition of Matthew's audience. The author also uses such moves to show the fluid nature of the ministry of Jesus. As Jesus goes, so go the

Homiletical Perspective

Preachers who pay careful attention to the lives of those around them struggle with the temptation of pessimism. The world is at war without an exit strategy. Ministers see so much pain that they easily become numb to suffering. Darkness is overwhelming.

We want to believe that life—especially for good people—should be easier, but the painfully obvious truth is that life is hard. Most of us have more medical tests in our future than in our past, more tears to come than we have already shed. The carefree days never last long.

Do you remember the story of Sisyphus, condemned to push a huge rock up a hill over and over again, only to have it immediately roll back down? We know his frustration. Some of us worry about being alone. Others worry about family. Will our marriage get better? We fear for our children. Will they turn out as we hope? We fear the complications of our parents growing old. How will we care for them? We worry about our health. We are growing old. Life is hard.

We are "the people who sit in darkness." We sit in the darkness of fear, conflict, and confusion. The daily news is filled with stories of darkness. The finest films embody the darkness we feel. The best literature explores the darkness that surrounds us.

Matthew 4:12–17

Theological Perspective

The nearing of God's commonweal or reign, a theme woven throughout this time of ministry, is rightly understood as a challenge to the imperial governmental structure. The proclamation and actions of Jesus reflect his conviction that God desires to establish a reign of justice in the world, in a way that contradicts the logic of empire. God's reign therefore has not only an individual dimension but also a wider structural one. The implications of the gospel should not, in other words, be privatized.

Therefore an important theological question to ask, if we are to remain faithful to the gospel as portrayed by Matthew, is always: Is the gospel as it is preached and embodied in a given time and place really "good news"? Why or why not? Even more pointedly: For whom is the gospel good news? If it is not good and transformative news for those most marginalized by the empires and powers of the prevalent economic and political systems, then it has little to do with the reign or commonweal of God that Jesus begins to announce in Galilee.

Consequently one of the responsibilities of Christian theology is to be vigilant about the church's tendency to lose the gospel's anti-imperial edge. We should lovingly warn the church when it loses sight of the materially transformative nature of the gospel; when it falls into an easy spiritualization of the message of Jesus that offends no one in power; when it offers no sustaining hope for the weakest and most vulnerable in the world.

Theologically speaking, place matters: where and how Jesus embodies the reign of God is part of the gospel message. We should therefore pay attention to geographical clues that can shed light on Matthew's narrative. Significantly, Galilee is the place where Matthew has the work of Jesus begin and, after the resurrection, culminate with the Great Commission (28:16–20). It is a fertile and beautiful region, but in the time of Jesus it bears a heavy burden of taxation and oppression. Within Galilee, a rather marginal area in a geopolitical sense, the village of Capernaum, the place to which Jesus withdraws to begin his ministry, is a further symbol of marginality. As a small agricultural and fishing village, it is very different even from the larger cities in the area, such as Sepphoris or Tiberias. It is in Capernaum that Jesus will seek his first disciples: not among the wealthy and powerful, but among those bearing the brunt of imperial greed on their very bodies, as they try to make ends meet.[2]

2. Cf. Paul Hertig, "The Galilee Theme in Matthew: Transforming Mission through Marginality," *Missiology: An International Review* 24, no. 2 (1997): 154–63.

Pastoral Perspective

John has caused the ire of the authorities with his call to revival and repentance and talk of the kingdom of heaven. He is facing the death penalty under Herod's rule and is later beheaded (14:1–12). There are many reasons Jesus could take this news as a sign that the time is not right to take his place as the leader of God's revival and plan of redemption for Israel and for the whole world.

On a personal level, John, Jesus' cousin according to Luke's Gospel and the one who has baptized him, is in grave trouble. In addition to the grief, sadness, and anger that the news could provoke, Jesus' family and friends could argue that if Jesus continues on the path that John has prepared for him, he too could find himself in grave trouble, perhaps even facing the death penalty himself.

On a strategic level, perhaps it is not the right time to start preaching about the kingdom of heaven, when that message has obviously not found a good hearing among the leaders. Perhaps continuing to preach and embody the kingdom of heaven in public will once again draw the fury of the leaders, and God's intentions for repentance, revival, and redemption could be squelched before they gain sufficient traction. It would be better to wait and let things cool down.

However, it is precisely in the face of the bad news of John's arrest that Jesus leaves the wilderness, returns to Galilee, and begins to call for repentance. It is precisely in the face of the bad news—of Herod and his government attempting to silence the voice crying in the wilderness—that Jesus proclaims, "The kingdom of heaven is near" (4:17). Throughout the Gospel, Jesus not only proclaims with his words but also embodies with his life and ministry the reality of the kingdom of heaven breaking forth in the midst of the bad news of the kingdoms of this world.

Jesus' hearing of the bad news and his subsequent response to it bracket another prophetic text from Isaiah 9:1–2. The text focuses on both the reversals, from darkness to light and death to life, and the location of Jesus' proclamation.

First, it is in the darkness of life that Jesus comes and shines. For those of us living in the shadow of death, Jesus brings forth life. It is precisely in the midst of that bad news, both personal and corporate, that God has called us to repent and follow Jesus in proclaiming and living the reality that the kingdom of heaven is at hand. It is precisely as the darkness seems to overwhelm us that we are called to seek the great light.

We are not called to ignore or dismiss the reality of the bad news that exists, but rather to "repent"

Feasting on the Gospels

racial, cultural, and ethnic width and depth of those who would heed his message.

This geographical code switching becomes more evident in what appears after Matthew's account of the temptations of Jesus. The author does not offer any explanation or details of the arrest of John the Baptist. It is almost unexpected. There is nothing to indicate that John is in trouble with Roman officials or that there is resistance to his proclamation. However, it is John's imprisonment that spurs Jesus to go back home. Upon hearing that John is in jail, Jesus withdraws to Galilee (4:12). After his encounter with the devil, Jesus leaves one area of turmoil and disease and goes to his place of security and familiarity. Jesus goes home.

Jesus does not make his home in Nazareth (2:23), but establishes a new place of comfort in Capernaum (4:13). It is here that the territories of Zebulun and Naphtali are located. Perchance Matthew's geographical move of establishing Jesus in this area undergirds the literary inclusion of the Isaiah reference (Isa. 9:1) to the lands of Zebulun and Naphtali (4:13).

These eponymous areas refer to two sons of Jacob. Zebulun's mother was Leah, and Naphtali was the son of Rachel's maid, Bilhah. Genesis records Jacob on his deathbed blessing Zebulun and declaring that he "shall settle at the shore of the sea" and "be a haven for ships" (Gen. 49:13). After the conquest of the promised land, descendants from Zebulun and Naphtali receive land in what would later become Galilee (Josh. 19). Isaiah later includes a reference to the tribes to set the stage for a deliverer who would bring a "great light" to "those who lived in a land of deep darkness" (Isa. 9:2). For a group of people once cast out and "out of place," the time would come for heirs of Zebulun and Naphtali to return to their rightful standing. Isaiah connects geography with sociology and theology.

Matthew's use of fulfillment language redirects the Isaiah passage to highlight Jesus as the Messiah who some seven centuries after Isaiah's words has come to give light to the Gentile darkness. Therefore, the Gospel of Matthew, by altering the location of Jesus, also shows a connection to a broader racial group who would hear the message of Jesus. No longer situated in Judea, but now back in Galilee, Matthew's Jesus fulfills anew the prophecy of the light coming to the darkness. Jesus is a Jewish Messiah whose message is not limited to Jews. Instead, by expanding the metes and bounds of where Jesus goes, Matthew broadens the parameters of those who would hear his word and receive his redemption.

When life is darkest, even the faintest flicker makes us breathe a little faster and open our eyes a little wider. We long for light, because we understand that the world is dark. Light is the promise that something important is on its way. When the night seems long, honest preachers may find it hard to speak of dawn.

The darkness is about to descend on a preacher in Nazareth. Jesus wipes the sawdust from his hands when a customer says: "Did you hear what happened to John the Baptist? He was so busy getting everyone else in the water that he did not see the hot water he was heading for. You would think he would know better than to cross King Herod."

Jesus stops sanding a table long enough to hear the whole story. After their neighbor leaves, Jesus tells Mary that it is time for him to go. He packs what he can carry in a bag and heads out the door. As he walks to Capernaum, he thinks about the preacher who baptized him. Jesus has picked a bad time to begin a ministry. If John could be arrested for what he said about the king's marriage, what will happen to Jesus when he proclaims a whole new kingdom?

Matthew describes the compulsion Jesus feels as prophetic fulfillment. When Isaiah wanted to speak to our deepest longings, the prophet chose light as the symbol because he knew how dark the world could be. Zebulun and Naphtali were the two northernmost tribes of Israel. Whenever anyone invaded, they were the first and last to bear the brunt of it. When the Assyrians overran Israel, they annexed these two tribes. Naphtali and Zebulun were cut off from the rest of Israel, separated from their country and family. What can Isaiah say that will bring them hope?

Isaiah preaches, "You live in darkness, but take hope, for a light is shining. I know things are dismal, but your despair will become joy. The enemy has killed people you loved and taken your land, but your oppressors will be driven away. A child will be born that will make things right. This one who comes will be a wonderful Counselor, acting as a true friend; a mighty God, ruling in power; an everlasting Father, caring for you; the Prince of Peace, bringing harmony to a war-torn world. His kingdom will last forever. Light will come in the child that will be born."

The magnificent vision seems more like a fantasy than a promise. The hurting people in Zebulun and Naphtali must have said, "The world still looks dark to us. We have seen no great light." Isaiah's response is, "You will one day." Matthew says that he has seen Isaiah's vision in the person of Jesus.

Matthew 4:12–17

Theological Perspective

By placing Capernaum in "the territory of Zebulun and Naphtali," Matthew taps into a rich reservoir of meaning. The area has a long history of experience with empire and oppression, but also a deep narrative of hope for transformation by the grace of God. Zebulun and Naphtali were two of the ancient Hebrew tribes that had colonized northern Palestine. These territories fell to the Assyrian empire in 722 BCE, and by the time of Jesus had come in turn under Roman domination.

In order to frame the initial announcement of God's good news in the ministry of Jesus, Matthew puts together a medley of quotations and references that allude loosely to Isaiah 9:1–2. When he mentions "Galilee of the Gentiles," quoting Isaiah 9:1, it becomes a many-layered reference to the fact that Galilee is an occupied territory. "Across the Jordan" evokes the rich history of God's acts of liberation in the exodus. Whereas the Hebrew text and the Septuagint have the people "walking" and "dwelling" in darkness, Matthew depicts them as "sitting" in darkness, perhaps a nod to Psalm 107:10, which continues, "prisoners in misery and in irons." It is as if they had been pushed down even further into despair by a succession of empires. In the context of Isaiah, the people have already suffered unspeakably from the wars with Assyria. In Matthew, they are suffering anew, now under the Roman yoke.

As both Isaiah and Matthew show us, what the empires of the world actually offer, despite their glitter, is nothing but darkness. Reweaving the theme of hope he has found in the Hebrew Bible, Matthew proclaims, for those living in the shadow of empire, that the light of God has already dawned and is now manifest in the proclamation of Jesus. The opportunity to receive that hope is to be marked by repentance: not by any sort of solemn self-flagellation, but by turning away from the false hopes offered by reigning imperial common sense and turning toward the way of Jesus Christ.

NANCY ELIZABETH BEDFORD

Pastoral Perspective

from (turn our backs on) the power of bad news to control our lives, and instead to trust in the power of God in Jesus Christ to bring healing and wholeness, redemption and salvation, to our broken lives and our broken world.

We as Christians are called to proclaim and live out the good news amid the bad news. Precisely in the face of the growing fear, division, and death, we are called to put flesh on God's good news of hope, peace, and life. We are called to repent from the simple path of only denouncing or describing the bad news, and to be proactive, trusting and living out the good news of God that the kingdom of heaven has come near.

How are we responding to the bad news within our church, our community, and our world? Do we allow the complexity of the situations to paralyze us? Do we allow our own fears and prejudices to guide our response? Do we rely on our faith in the One who brings forth light to those living in the shadow of death to guide us?

Second, Matthew addresses location. Most religious folks were anticipating that the Messiah would be revealed in Jerusalem—the religious, political, cultural, and economic center of power for the Jewish people—but Jesus' ministry is begun and largely is based in "Galilee of the Gentiles" (4:15). God's revelation in Jesus Christ takes place in an unexpected place. Even within Galilee, Capernaum was not the center of power.

While this foreshadows the expansion of God's mission to include not only Jewish people but Gentiles as well, it is also an important reminder for the church, that God speaks in places that surprise us. Perhaps God will speak more clearly to us outside the comfort of our sanctuaries.

Where are the places in your community that are outside the centers of power? How can your church be present in them and be open to experiencing and embodying the reality that the kingdom of heaven is at hand?

MARK S. ADAMS

Exegetical Perspective

So, even as Jesus returns to a place of familiarity, Galilee, he branches out into a different territory, Capernaum. It is in this new place that he proclaims a repeated message, "Repent, for the kingdom of heaven has come near" (4:17). Although the place has changed, the message is the same. These are the very first words John the Baptist speaks in the wilderness (3:2). Matthew has Jesus reiterate these words after his temptation experiences in the wilderness and after Jesus transitions to a new place. What was first John's disheveled land of the Jews is now Jesus' unkempt land of the Gentiles. However, for Matthew, both areas are populated with people who need deliverance and salvation.

This deliverance is rooted in the idea of the kingdom of heaven coming near, coming now. The use of *basileia* (kingdom) follows Matthew's narratives involving King Herod and Archelaus as key figures in the Roman Empire (chap. 2). The author does not discount the kingdom of the *Pax Romana* (Peace of Rome). However, the writer from the onset wants the readers to know that there is another kingdom present—a kingdom that is not of this world. It is a kingdom from heaven that will triumph over the political prowess of the earth. Just as Roman rulers could not stop the birth of Jesus the Messiah, these same authorities are no match for the ministry or message of the Messiah. Matthew's Jesus as an infant had to move from place to place in order to elude Roman figureheads. As an adult, this same Jesus declares that God's presence is here and now, front and center.

Matthew employs changes in geography to show the expansive nature of the message of Jesus. By portraying Jesus as relocating and moving from place to place, Matthew demonstrates through a theology of geography how the message of Jesus is not confined to one place or one people.

STEPHANIE BUCKHANON CROWDER

Homiletical Perspective

Christ proclaims that peace will overcome hostility. Love will defeat hatred. Fears will become laughter. One day we will not learn war any more. One day those committed to the way of repentance will be proven right. One day the light will overcome the darkness.

We let our pessimism keep us from dreams as big as Isaiah's and hopes as dazzling as God's light. We ignore the deepest longing of our hearts. We need to help one another see Christ's light. God will teach us to recognize it when we catch a glimpse: when a young father takes his newborn daughter into his arms for the first time; when a troubled couple falls in love again; when a family makes a pilgrimage to the bedside of a dying loved one and feels an unexplainable peace; when a single woman comes home to her solitary dwelling not as a place of emptiness but as a nest sheltered under the wing of God; when the light of Christ shines into the darkest places in our lives.

The Talmud tells of a rabbi who was asked what questions a Jew would have to answer at the Last Judgment. What would God ask? First, the rabbi thought of the obvious things: Were you honest in business? Did you seek wisdom? Did you keep the commandments? Then a question about the Messiah came into his mind that surprised the rabbi himself. God will ask, "Did you hope for my Messiah?"

Is that not the question Christians will be asked? Did you hope for Jesus? Did you long for the kingdom of heaven Christ proclaimed? Did you put your faith in Christ, even when you thought about giving up? Did you live in Christ's light? Since Jesus left home to begin his ministry, countless people have been caught up in Christ's life. God's preachers invite God's people to believe in God's power to bring light into the darkness.

BRETT YOUNGER

Matthew 4:18–22

¹⁸As he walked by the Sea of Galilee, he saw two brothers, Simon, who is called Peter, and Andrew his brother, casting a net into the sea—for they were fishermen. ¹⁹And he said to them, "Follow me, and I will make you fish for people." ²⁰Immediately they left their nets and followed him. ²¹As he went from there, he saw two other brothers, James son of Zebedee and his brother John, in the boat with their father Zebedee, mending their nets, and he called them. ²²Immediately they left the boat and their father, and followed him.

Theological Perspective

Jesus takes the initiative. He proceeds in a way that would probably have been unusual for a rabbi: teachers normally accepted disciples who requested the honor of sitting at their feet, but they did not necessarily go out on the road to seek out their apprentices. The way Matthew structures the scene implies that Jesus' word is endowed with a certain divine fiat: he speaks, and it is so. He is presented as having an authority that is difficult to withstand. At the same time, and somewhat paradoxically, there is no sense that the fishermen are forced to follow him; they are depicted as making a free decision to do so, leaving behind their trade and their means of livelihood, symbolized by the nets, the boat, and the family business.

It is possible that these men already knew Jesus and even that they had been sympathizers or followers of John the Baptist (cf. John 1:35–42). That does not dampen the force of the command "Follow me," nor does it lessen the deep personal consequences of the decision to follow him for the two sets of brothers. In following Jesus, they will find both continuity and discontinuity with their former activity; they will still require patience, endurance, strength, and skill, but their efforts will now be concentrated on the human dimension of God's reign of justice in the world.

Fishing in the Sea of Galilee was grueling, backbreaking work, involving nights spent out on boats

Pastoral Perspective

After Jesus began his public ministry by preaching, "Repent, for the kingdom of heaven has come near," he immediately began to gather around him a group of disciples, companions on the journey of faith who will later form the church. Jesus will not be alone in proclaiming and embodying the reality that the kingdom of heaven is near. Walking by the Sea of Galilee, Jesus told Simon called Peter and his brother Andrew and James and his brother John: "Come, follow me."

The amazing thing is that they immediately left their nets, their boat, their father, and followed Jesus. The Scriptures do not give us any indication about their thought process or their emotional state at hearing the call of the Lord. The Scriptures just say they obeyed Jesus' call. Discipleship is just that: hearing God's call and obeying it—even if it means radical changes of direction in life.

A danger in the church today is the tendency for us to define our mission and then invite Jesus to tag along with us. Christian discipleship does not begin with our seeking out Jesus and calling him to participate in what we are doing. Discipleship has to do with Jesus' call on our life and our response. As Dietrich Bonhoeffer said in *The Cost of Discipleship*, "Discipleship is not an offer [humans] make

Exegetical Perspective

In leaving Judea, Jesus moves away from the center of political and religious power. According to Matthew, after he settles in Capernaum by the sea, Jesus acquaints himself with people who earn a living from the sea. The geographical move Jesus undertakes serves as a relocation of power. Here at the Sea of Galilee Jesus does not befriend political potentates. Instead, he calls to himself persons who have no power at all. He beckons fishermen to follow him. Through his physical act of moving from Judea to Galilee, Jesus employs a social reversal. It is a reorientation that includes common members of the society.

First-century fishermen were not at the top of the economic pyramid in the Greco-Roman world; neither were they at the very bottom like shepherds. They belonged to a "middle poor"; the fishing industry was as ubiquitous as the sea itself. Fishermen in Capernaum could not determine how much they earned, as there was a political and economic system that regulated taxation. Any subsequent remaining profit went to the elite and those who controlled the fishing process from the top. Thus the system was not one that allowed for entrepreneurship or capitalism as in our modern-day thinking. It was a matter of fishing to eat and survive.

In addition, persons in the fishing industry depended on people in various professions to help

Homiletical Perspective

Much of a preacher's life is routine. We return phone calls, respond to e-mails, attend meetings, write sermons, and plan worship services. We typically have a dozen administrative details to finish. The urgency in what preachers do is usually the urgency of keeping up.

Routine rarely feels holy. Preachers do not generally distribute medicine, deliver meals to the hungry, or fight for laws to protect the uneducated. Preachers try to help people who are already interested to love the church more. We preach sermons to the converted. We try to be kind, to listen, and to tell people what we hope is true about God. The preachers' work is enjoyable, but it does not feel as adventurous as the story of the disciples leaving their nets and following Jesus into the unknown.

Shortly after moving to Capernaum, Jesus is walking beside the lake one afternoon when he sees two men in a rowboat waiting for unsuspecting fish. What happens next is hard to believe. Jesus offers them a job with no pay and they accept: "Come with me and I will make you fish for people." Why should they follow someone who uses such tortured metaphors? Nevertheless they leave their boat and follow.

Had the sales pitch been, "Come and make more money selling iPads than you could ever make fishing," then it might make sense, but this invitation

Matthew 4:18–22

Theological Perspective

on the temperamental lake, the hauling of great nets, the constant labor of repair, and the prospect of an insecure livelihood made even leaner by the quotas, taxes, and tolls required by the regime of Herod Antipas. The demand for Galilean fish products across the Roman Empire provided a pretext for tightening the screws ever more tightly. In this context, Jesus offers the possibility to fish not for the good of Herod Antipas or of his imperial masters, but to fish in a new way, in anticipation of God's reign of justice and peace on earth.

The calling has a dynamic quality that pops up in the repetition of the adverb "immediately" in verses 20 and 22. Jesus does not call the four fishermen to sit at his feet, but rather to follow in his footsteps. As opposed to those in Galilee who had been sitting in the darkness of imperial injustice (v. 16), the disciples are called out to walk in the light of God's coming reign. Their discipleship or "following" constitutes an incipient confession of faith: they are putting aside their old way of life in the confidence that, in the way of Jesus, God's justice and grace will be found.

Beyond reflecting particular traditions about the actual disciples, the stories of the calling of the first disciples are paradigmatic. They reflect the early faith community's experience of discipleship, specifically the insight that discipleship is not believing certain "facts" about Jesus, but following him in specific contexts and in concrete, material ways that are traversed with hope.[1] While all followers of Jesus are called out from a given time and place, their backgrounds and identities are not denied. On the contrary, they are challenged to put the skills and knowledge that they already have to work for the good of the many. This intersection, of the particularity of each disciple's story with the universality of God's reign of justice, keeps theology in balance. As in the story of the incarnation itself, in which the God of the universe becomes identified with one particular, fragile baby, God's dealings with creation are never about negating the beauty and worth of each individual life. Still, structural dimensions are also always at stake, and the arc of justice is wider than any one person's vision.

Later in the Gospel (16:13–20) Peter will articulate a verbal confession that Jesus is indeed the Messiah, the Son of the living God. Now that confession begins to emerge already in a practical way with the decision by the fishermen to leave their nets behind.

Pastoral Perspective

to Christ. It is only [God's] call which creates the situation."[1]

One of my favorite songs, which I learned serving as a mission coworker, is "Tomados de la Mano con Jesus." The song speaks about how we will walk "hand in hand with Jesus." The image is that, when he says we should leave everything behind, we put our hand in his and go where he goes. I am not sure why this is one of my favorite songs, because if we live by it, we will end up in places we never imagined being, doing things we never imagined ourselves doing, and sharing life, fellowship, service, and worship with people we would have never imagined ourselves interacting with.

Simon Peter, Andrew, James, and John all "put their hand in Jesus' hand" and followed—and they had no idea where Jesus was going to lead them. Despite not having a road map for the journey that lay ahead of them, they obeyed the call of Jesus and followed. A crucial part of discipleship is trusting in the One who has called us to faithfully lead us from what is known and comfortable into what is unknown and perhaps uncomfortable. Through following Jesus, we come to know the fullness of God's mission and purpose for our lives.

In our ministries of "discipleship making" (new member/evangelism), we often follow a model of "know, grow, go"—teaching the doctrines of the church, trusting in Christian growth through knowing, and then embracing folks into the fellowship and ministry of the church. In Jesus' plan, our plan is reversed: go (or follow), grow, know.

The fact that these first four disciples left behind nets, boats, and fathers is a sign that discipleship is not cheap. God's call in our lives is not convenient. For disciples, Jesus' claim upon our life is more important than our careers, our material possessions, and even our family. If anything gets in the way of our call to follow Jesus, we are to leave it behind. Our careers—read vocations, material possessions, and families—are to function in the service of God's mission. If they are in any way embodying the powers of the kingdoms of this world that promote oppression, greed, or brokenness, we are called to repent and reorient them so that they reflect and embody salvation, justice, and wholeness—the realities of the kingdom of heaven that are breaking forth in our lives and in our world.

The calling of the disciples is the beginning of the formation of the church—the community of

---

1. See Warren Carter, "Matthew 4:18–22 and Matthean Discipleship: An Audience-Oriented Perspective," *Catholic Biblical Quarterly* 59 (1997): 58–75.

1. Dietrich Bonhoeffer, *The Cost of Discipleship* (New York: Macmillan, 1959), 68.

supply nets, boats, and other needed materials. Processors, distributors, buyers, and sellers partnered with those whose primary responsibility it was to catch fish. Thus fishing was not an individual commercial endeavor. It was one grounded in relationships akin to present-day unions.

Another note about fishing during Matthew's time concerns the familial nature of the profession. Jesus calls two sets of brothers who are fishermen (vv. 18, 21). The author narrates that James and John leave their father Zebedee. Jesus' calling these fishing siblings is the first of many references in the Gospel of Matthew to life lived of and by the sea (7:9–11; 8:23–27; 12:38–40; 17:24–27).

Jesus does not ask any of the men in the text to follow him. Instead, he issues an imperative, a command. The irony is that perhaps many Roman officials had commanded Peter, Andrew, James, and John to go and/or to do something. They were residing in Capernaum of Galilee, an area under the political auspices of King Herod's son, Herod Antipas. Soldiers and military personnel populated the area in order to ensure civil obedience and to dissuade any who might consider uprisings. Thus the people residing in the territory were accustomed to commands delivered with physical and even verbal insults.

However, just as Matthew has Jesus relocating from religious and cultural centers and associating with those of limited authority, the readers "hear" Jesus' command as still reversing the sting of imperialism. The directive Jesus gives is not to incite fear or terror. His command emanates from love. Jesus issues an order of social transformation. When he says, "Follow," it is not grounded in social hierarchy, but in an ethic intent on leveling the playing field.

Nevertheless there is a cost to "fishing for people" (v. 19). Simon Peter and Andrew have to leave what is their only source of income. They are men who have to reconfigure their family obligations in order to go with Jesus. In patriarchal, patrilineal, patrinominal society, adhering to the command of Jesus puts any women and children in the families of Simon Peter and Andrew in jeopardy. The price of discipleship is paid by those who are left behind, even as it is a price John and James, sons of Zebedee, have to pay. Matthew maintains that they disregard the holes in their fishing nets and immediately leave their father (vv. 21–22). Once again, the author gives a cultural cue to the familial ties of fishing.

There is no indication that any of the men who follow Jesus resist. Matthew says they all "immediately" cease what they are doing to go with Jesus

and this response seem unlikely. Four fishermen drop what they are doing and head off to maybe-God-knows-where. They do not know what is coming next, but they do know what happened to John the Baptist.

People typically try to explain away big fish stories, and this one is no exception. Some commentators suggest that the response of the disciples was not uncommon, that young men often left their occupations to become a rabbi's students. We read the story and assume that this is not the disciples' first encounter with Jesus, that they must have known Jesus before this. Matthew, however, does not feel any need to explain why they would follow Jesus.

The disciples' instant acceptance of Jesus' peculiar invitation is as dramatic as any moment we will encounter. We occasionally stand at a fork in the road, facing big decisions about jobs, retirement, or where to live. We have moments when we act in a particular way for reasons that we cannot completely explain. Some have an extraordinary moment when they decide to be a teacher who makes a difference for children, a businessperson who makes the world better, or the kind of Christian who tries to become more like Jesus. Some women and men live astonishing, heroic lives because of their faith.

Most of the time our work is not that dramatic. We do not often drop everything to start a new life. Maybe someday we will do something spectacular. For now, most of us feel called to less dramatic discipleship. The calling of the disciples is more spectacular than what happens to us on most Tuesdays.

Maybe Jesus' disciples had days when it did not seem sensational, as they walked up and down Galilee from village to village, through Samaria to Jerusalem and back again. Maybe they had days when they thought things were slow, when Jesus did not heal anyone. Matthew chose not to write much about the days when nothing happened. On those days, maybe the disciples followed as we follow: with modest faithfulness.

We tend to focus on dramatic conversions, overwhelming encounters with God, and powerful moments of prayer. We search for peak experiences and assume that some disciples are born with spiritual gifts that we do not have. We forget that God calls us every hour of every day. God is in the details, inviting us to be friends with one another, practice kindness, and pray for our daily bread. We live out our faithfulness in worship, work, and study.

The routine, everyday ways in which we follow Jesus—the way we read Scripture, welcome strangers,

Matthew 4:18–22

Theological Perspective

Following Jesus means entering into a way of knowing God and God's reign that requires embodiment, never simply a verbal assent to a concept. Jesus will embody what it means to seek out God's ways of justice and peace in the world, and the disciples who follow him will learn to do the same. For some, that will mean suffering imprisonment and violent death at the hands of the local agents of imperial power (see Acts 12:1–4), like John the Baptist and Jesus.

It is perhaps significant, in the apparently male-centered framework of the narrative, that James and John, the sons of Zebedee, leave their father behind in order to follow Jesus. Although the church has rarely taken Christian discipleship as an opportunity to go beyond the logic of patriarchal common sense, the call of Jesus to follow in the ways of God's reign and God's justice does open up that opportunity. The story of the call of the disciples appears between the temptation narrative and the depiction of Jesus' ministry of healing. What follows immediately after is the Sermon on the Mount, which proposes a way of life in the world contrary to all prevailing systems that abuse power.

Matthew thus places the paradigmatic call to follow Jesus as a hinge between the temptation to misuse power and the possibility to use it for justice and peacemaking. James and John are called to leave behind both their investment in the prevailing economic order (the boat) and their attachment to patriarchal structures (their father), in order to practice a more excellent way of relating to other human beings and to God. That kind of apprenticeship has never been easy for the Christian church to pursue. It is only by the creative power of the Holy Spirit that such a relationship can be experienced at all, yet it is always a subversive possibility for those attentive to the call of Jesus.

NANCY ELIZABETH BEDFORD

Pastoral Perspective

men, women, and children "called out" to be agents of God's mission in the world. The church is not an end in itself, but rather a means through which God works to fulfill divine purposes. The church is not the destination of discipleship, but rather the vehicle through which a community of disciples is joined together to fulfill God's purposes in the world.

When I was ministering with the children in a summer camp, I led a study on the church. To begin the lesson, I asked the children to draw a picture of the church. My assumption was that the children would draw a picture of the church building. One eight-year-old girl did not "go along with the program" and stole my lesson.

She had five pictures drawn on her paper. In the upper left corner, she drew a picture of a woman in bed with people surrounding her. She explained that that was her grandmother in a hospital bed and the people around her were the pastor and members from the church praying for her healing. In the upper right corner, she drew a picture of a can. She said that there were hungry people in the world and God does not want people to be hungry so the church shares its food. In the bottom right corner, she drew a picture of a group of children playing. In the bottom left corner, she drew music notes with people of different sizes and of different colors. She said that God loves all people, and the church gathers to sing thank-you to God. In the middle of the paper, big enough to invade the space of each picture's space and to unite them, she drew a big heart—God is love, and we are called to love God and to love our neighbors as ourselves.

What does your picture of the church look like?

MARK S. ADAMS

Exegetical Perspective

(vv. 20, 22). It is possible that, being accustomed to following imperial orders, the fishermen do as they are told. The Gospel writer does not extrapolate the political and economic variables from what could easily become a theological lesson. Fishermen had some value in Matthew's day, as so many depended on their livelihood, but even with this little "power," they were still not in control. Therefore in addition to the compelling command of Jesus, the urgency with which this initial group of disciples leaves and goes is an indication of their place in the power pyramid of the day.

Jesus comes to show fishermen the proper use of power that, at the same time, reveals the kingdom of heaven come near. Their task will be to "fish for people" (v. 19). They will no longer fish and be subject to exploitation. They will no longer have to worry about how much of the catch will be compromised. Instead of viewing the creatures of the sea as a means to eat and stay above ground, Jesus offers a different perspective on God's creation on land and on sea. As fishers of people, Simon Peter, Andrew, James, and John will use what is familiar to them to embark on a new and different work. They will join a new profession.

The author of the Gospel of Matthew highlights Jesus' use of culturally loaded language to inaugurate a new social order. The fishermen are to continue fishing. They are to continue to cast their nets. This has been their life's work. Jesus speaks to the newly minted disciples on their own terms, in order to compel and conscript them to a new work. Jesus does not discount their profession or place in society. On the contrary, he calls them and commands them to rethink their position, in order that they might help others to do the same.

STEPHANIE BUCKHANON CROWDER

Homiletical Perspective

and love the lonely—are crucially important. God works in quiet ways. God is present whenever we live with hope and forgiveness. Our calling is faithfully to live God's grace on routine days in ordinary ways. Love spreads word by word. The bucket fills drop by drop. Wrongs are righted one by one.

We can hear Jesus' call even in the cluttered busyness of our days. We cannot be sure that any decision is unimportant, because the sacred is present in the ordinary. Every moment matters, because life is holy. God speaks to us in the ordinary and the routine. If we pay attention, we will see that even as unsurprising a life as most of us think we live is extraordinary: waking up after a good night's sleep; frying an egg; hugging someone we love; taking a child to school; eating lunch with a friend; trying to do a decent day's work; reading a good book; reading the Good Book; preaching, praying, and thinking about the wonderful, normal possibilities.

No event is so commonplace that God is not present. Every moment and every word have possibilities. We grow in faith not only in memorable, never-to-be-forgotten moments, but also in forgettable moments: when we decide to pray instead of turning on the computer, to say something kind instead of something clever, to offer help when we do not have to.

Grace comes in unspectacular deeds. The novelist John Updike said, "I will try to work steadily in the spirit of those medieval carvers who so fondly sculpted the undersides of choir seats."[1] We learn to follow in simple acts. Slowly but surely our priorities change. On the day they first followed Jesus, the disciples were brash, impulsive, and stubborn. They smelled of fish and were not always kind. Day by day they had to learn to be the church. Every worship service is an opportunity for preachers to offer the hope of following Jesus again.

BRETT YOUNGER

---

1. Frederic Brussat, *100 Ways to Keep Your Soul Alive: Living Deeply and Fully Every Day* (New York: HarperOne, 1994), 4.

Matthew 4:23–25

²³Jesus went throughout Galilee, teaching in their synagogues and proclaiming the good news of the kingdom and curing every disease and every sickness among the people. ²⁴So his fame spread throughout all Syria, and they brought to him all the sick, those who were afflicted with various diseases and pains, demoniacs, epileptics, and paralytics, and he cured them. ²⁵And great crowds followed him from Galilee, the Decapolis, Jerusalem, Judea, and from beyond the Jordan.

Theological Perspective

After they lay their former identities on the Galilean shore and leave behind their kin to "fish for people" (whatever could Jesus have meant by *that*?), the first disciples disappear. In this miniature travel narrative they go unmentioned. Are they watching as Jesus teaches and heals? Presumably. In any case, they disappear as they follow him, like initiates in a rite of passage. The disciples are in what Victor Turner calls "liminal" space; they are marginal, "betwixt and between" who they were and who they will be. True, they vanish for only three verses; but in a story covering much geography, this is a long time to be without role or status. The attention is now on the countless multitudes approaching Jesus.

Here the differences between the disciples as "insiders" and others as outsiders are not emphasized. Nor, apparently, are boundaries between Jews and Gentiles. In one breathless sentence, Jesus teaches in synagogues *and* proclaims the kingdom *and* heals "the people" (*tō laō*, v. 23). While there is suffering—the physically, mentally, and spiritually afflicted come to him—it is as if Jesus were moving in a space without lines of demarcation. Borders and differences between Galilee and Judea, between Jerusalem and Syria and places beyond the Jordan, disappear for a while in the seemingly global activity of following him.

Pastoral Perspective

Now Jesus' public ministry begins in earnest. With this preliminary work—baptism by John, trial in the wilderness, calling the first disciples—behind him, in these three verses Jesus "goes public," as we say. Days, weeks, perhaps even months pass in the space of a few dozen words in this text. The Sermon on the Mount is fast approaching, of course, arguably the most famous, beloved sermon in the Christian tradition, and many readers may well be eager to lean forward into those familiar terms of blessing. Do not rush things. Dwell in the preamble. For here, in these modest, often overlooked lines, the stage is set—and the crucial pastoral key is provided—for that blessing, that sermon, and that public ministry.

Pastoral care is often cast as a sedentary, even domestic activity, something done in the house of the Lord (say, in the pastor's study), in the house of a layperson (say, in the living room), or at the quasi-domestic hospital bedside. These scenes of pastoral work are common enough, of course, but passages like this one can be occasions to remember that the word "pastor" means shepherd, and shepherding is nothing if not an outdoor, itinerant form of life, immersed in the wilderness of the world.

The shepherd's primary task is to safeguard the sheep, and he or she does so in at least three ways: by protecting them against nearby threats, by

Exegetical Perspective

This summary of Jesus' ministry describes the inbreaking of the kingdom of heaven through his teaching, preaching, and healing. Because this is a transitional summary, it is helpful to understand its literary context. Jesus begins his Galilean ministry by calling his first four disciples (4:18–22; cf. 4:17 and 16:21, which signal important geographical and chronological shifts in the development of the narrative). Our passage outlines Jesus' ministry, as also in 9:35, and describes the effects of this ministry. Some scholars see 4:23 and 9:35 as shaping an *inclusio* summarizing Jesus' words and deeds at the beginning and end of the section. This larger section consists of two parts: his words in the Sermon on the Mount (chaps. 5–7) and his deeds (chaps. 8–9). In both his words and his deeds, Jesus is presented as having authority or power (*exousia*, 7:29; 9:6, 8). He will confer this authority upon his disciples (10:1).

Jesus' ministry of teaching, proclaiming, and healing covers the "whole" area of Galilee. Matthew presents Jesus as teaching first in the synagogue. Discourses composed of Jesus' teaching take up a big portion of Matthew's Gospel: (1) the Sermon on the Mount (5:1–7:29); (2) the mission discourse (9:35–10:42); (3) the parables (13:1–53); (4) the ecclesiastical discourse (18:1–35); and (5) the eschatological discourse (24:1–25:46). Each discourse ends with the

Homiletical Perspective

As soon as John the Baptist was arrested, Jesus got to work. At first his followers numbered only two pairs of brothers: the fishermen Simon Peter and Andrew; and James and John, the sons of Zebedee. Then, as Jesus proclaimed the good news of God's kingdom and taught in the synagogues, others followed. As he cured people with diseases and sickness—healing those afflicted with demons and pains, saving those struck by epilepsy and paralysis—his fame spread rapidly. Soon crowds flocked to him, from rural areas of Galilee and the urban center of Jerusalem, from the Jewish homeland of Judea and the Greco-Roman Decapolis, from the Diaspora throughout Syria and across the Jordan.

Why did the crowds follow Jesus? We would be naive to think that they had no other options. The crowds could have followed the leaders of other kingdoms: there were countless military officers and political figures with whom they could try to curry favor. The crowds could have followed other teachers: there were myriad Jewish rabbis and Greek philosophers under whom they could study. The crowds could have followed other healers: there were numerous faith healers and mystery cults from whom they could seek comfort and cure.

Two thousand years later, crowds are still following Jesus. Why?

Matthew 4:23–25

Theological Perspective

This space-time of following, of being taught and healed, is perhaps a prolepsis or foretaste of the reign of God, a present trace of eschatological fulfillment. The word for healing here relates to "therapy"; it is not *sōzō*, which can be translated "save" as well as "heal." The range of maladies Jesus heals in verses 23–24 is suggestive of salvation, and there may even be a glimpse of another possibility of salvation. The healing of the afflicted suggests what redemption could be like without crucifixion, atonement without the Messiah's sacrifice, apocalyptic revelation without destruction. Jesus has confronted the tempter (4:1–11) and is defeating the demons, so the eschatological challenge to evil and suffering is certainly in play. Do these verses not envision the *freedom* of God's possibilities for salvation? Do they not show God's will to save realized in another way, one of numberless ways we can but dimly imagine?

Consider that those brought to Jesus are afflicted physically, psychologically, and spiritually. The category "demoniac" overlaps all three. Interestingly, sinners and the social ramifications of sin are not specified in verses 23–24 (though they certainly will be elsewhere in Matthew). Many cultures have correlated illness with sin, but that is not the point here. These afflicted persons do not suffer the consequences of sin so much as they reflect tragic suffering due to contingency and finitude. Forms of epilepsy (the word here, *selēniazomai*, "to be an epileptic person," suggests the moon causes it) were invasive of spirit and body, disturbing connections between the individual and society, even the mundane and the sacred. The seizures mark the vulnerability of being an *embodied spirit*.

There was also demon possession, which most would now consider a form of mental illness. While in late antiquity the harmful demon would be thought of as an invisible creature of evil—and demons might be considered punishments for prior sins—demonic possession also denoted a person's vulnerability to unseen though finite forces, a "super-nature." Demons, then, were among the dangers of the finite and fateful world, much as material causes of illness are recognized today.[1]

So Jesus is addressing persons in all their fragileness and contingency and is touching the permeable boundaries of mind, body, and spirit. The healing miracles become an image of the transforming kingdom, where creaturely vulnerability—while not finally set aside by God—is nonetheless being

Pastoral Perspective

guiding the flock to good pasture, and by navigating any rough terrain along the way. Indeed, the iconic shepherd's crook is designed to help on all three of these fronts: it is a weapon to ward off wolves, a tool for catching and guiding sheep, and an aid for the shepherd's own sure footing. Accordingly, the shepherd—that is, the pastor—is characteristically on the move, following the example Jesus sets in passages like this one.

How does the Good Shepherd carry out this crucial work at the outset of his public ministry? On one hand, he preaches, "proclaiming the good news of the kingdom"; on the other hand, he heals, "curing every disease and every sickness among the people" (v. 23). Preaching and healing, encouraging and restoring—these are the signature moves of Jesus' public ministry from the very beginning, and in that sense they establish the terms through which that entire ministry is properly understood. Both moves are paradigmatically pastoral in character, of course, and each belongs with the other. Every great sermon or Christian education class, for example, is properly delivered for the sake of the community's health and restoration, just as every act of restoration is properly carried out for the sake of the gospel. Jesus breaks onto the public scene precisely as a preaching healer, a healing preacher. Like an overture the orchestra plays before the curtain rises in a Broadway musical, these three verses introduce the key themes that will unfold over the course of Matthew's testimony as a whole.

As word gets out about Jesus, his fame spreads "throughout all Syria" (v. 24). This verse's clear implication is that while his ministry ambidextrously includes both preaching and healing, the crowds are initially drawn to the curative dimension of his work. In fact, Matthew goes out of his way to emphasize that Jesus' growing renown has to do with his reputation as a healer: "they brought to him all the sick, those who were afflicted with various diseases and pains, demoniacs, epileptics, and paralytics" (v. 24).

Matthew's emphasis here is analogous to the episode in the Gospel of Luke in which Jesus, preaching in his hometown synagogue, announces that God has sent him "to bring good news to the poor . . . to proclaim release to the captives" (Luke 4:18; cf. Isa. 61:1). It is as if Matthew's Jesus declares, in effect, that God has sent him "to declare good news to the sick, to proclaim restoration to the afflicted." In Matthew and Luke alike, then, Jesus frames his public ministry at the outset as an exercise in encouragement and repair, a mission meant primarily for those

---

1. Peter Brown, *The World of Late Antiquity* (New York: Harcourt, Brace, Jovanovich, 1971), 53.

formulation, "When Jesus finished (all) these sayings/parables/instructing . . ." The beginning and end of the Sermon on the Mount, for instance, identify the Sermon as a teaching. After this teaching is delivered, the crowds acknowledge Jesus' authority, which is superior to that of "their scribes" (7:29). This may explain why the summary statement in 4:23 describes Jesus as teaching like a scribe "in their synagogues."

Synagogues, which developed after the exile to Babylon, functioned as the center of Jewish communal and religious activity such as prayer and the studying of Scripture, particularly the Torah. Generally, the scribes and the Pharisees are assumed to succeed to the authority of Moses (23:2). While Jesus' teaching on the mountain recalls Moses on Mount Sinai, Jesus is one who teaches, not merely the one who delivers the law. Jesus is portrayed as the authoritative interpreter of the Torah (chaps. 5–7). Matthew often adds the word "their" to synagogue, which indicates Jesus' distance from the religious leaders (9:35; 10:17; 12:9; 13:54). Some scholars view this distance as reflecting tension between Matthew's community and rabbinic Judaism in the making.

Jesus' ministry and teachings fulfill the law and the prophets rather than supersede them. In Matthew, teaching is presented as a unique ministry of Jesus, because the disciples are appointed to preach and heal (chap. 10), and only after Jesus' resurrection are they commissioned to teach (28:20).

Jesus' proclamation is focused on the good news of the kingdom. Matthew 4:17 puts the content of his preaching in a direct statement: "Repent, for the kingdom of heaven has come near." This proclamation is exactly the same as that of John the Baptist (cf. 3:2; 10:7). Matthew uses the term "kingdom" (*basileia*) 55 times out of its 162 occurrences in the NT. In most cases, "of the heaven(s)," instead of "of God," modifies "kingdom" (cf. 12:28; 19:24; 21:31). The coming of the kingdom of heaven denotes movement in both temporal and spatial senses. Thus the kingdom is already experienced by or belongs to some people (5:3, 10; 19:14; 21:31), or they will enter or participate in the kingdom in the future (5:19–20; 7:21; 8:11; 18:3; 19:23; 21:43). The kingdom is not something that can be achieved by human effort, although one can still seek it, for it is described as an agent (6:10, 33).

Jesus is the one in whom God's end-time rule comes near to humanity. The kingdom is a present reality, a reality to be fully realized only in the future. Jesus speaks about the kingdom of heaven in parables to illuminate the characteristics of the kingdom

For centuries in the West, being a Christian was a cultural assumption. Now it is different, much more like how it was before the fourth century CE, when the whole empire became Christian through the force of imperial edict. Now following Jesus is increasingly a choice we must make, whether we live in the global South or the industrial North, the Anglo West or the Asian East. Like the crowds who first followed Jesus, we follow, not because it is the only option, but because something compels us to make that choice. What prompts us to *choose* to follow Jesus?

Our answers will vary. Some of us grew up following Jesus, even if we barely knew what it meant. We spent the Sunday mornings of our childhood going to church school, learning Bible stories, and singing hymns, after which we were rewarded with Kool-Aid and cookies. Later, there came a time when we had to ask ourselves: Will I make the choice to follow Jesus?

Some of us rejected following Jesus for a period of time. Perhaps as young adults, or later in our lives, we quietly questioned everything about him: Did he really heal people? Was he really the Son of God? Did he really rise from the dead? Even if all of that were true, why should we follow him?

Some of us went through the motions of believing. We went to church, supported our congregation with money and volunteer time, sent our children to Sunday school and confirmation. Then, once the children grew up and left home, we began to consider what it meant for us to follow Jesus now.

Following Jesus is no longer an obvious choice; it is certainly not the default option for postmodern people. Our time, energy, passion, and resources can be spent in countless other ways. If we are just looking for a diversion, we can follow every move a celebrity makes; TV and Twitter make it easy. If we are looking for a "team" to belong to, we can follow any sport's games and ranking; cable and the Web make it effortless. If we are interested in trendsetters, we can follow fashion and jewelry, home decor and gardening; magazines and commercials make them hard to miss. If we are interested in creative genius, we can follow comedy or cooking, dancing or music on any number of competitive "reality" shows. If we want more serious reality, we can follow political and economic news 24/7; news shows and pundits guarantee it. If we are looking for inspiration, we can follow numerous self-help gurus; media doctors and advice columnists proliferate.

In our advertising-drenched, celebrity-filled, information-saturated age, we have endless options

Matthew 4:23–25

Theological Perspective

held in God's life of love. If we also say that human vulnerability is being transformed, the Sermon on the Mount will point to its being transformed into new possibilities for love and justice.[2] *All this—during these travels of Jesus—the disciples would be observing.*

Then there is a subtle, tonal shift in verse 25. News of the healings is spreading fast, and big crowds are pressing after Jesus. No longer are we glimpsing an alternative configuring of divine salvation; rather, we see an ordinary instance of crowds seeking what they need and desire. Notice that it is the healings that attract them, not Jesus' prophetic lessons in the synagogues (as in Luke 4:16–21). The transcending of boundaries is affirmed; but the popular, poignant, human rush for healing (like the "See me . . . heal me" lyric from Pete Townshend's rock opera *Tommy*) is implicitly disturbing. *This too the disciples would have observed.*

So the Sermon on the Mount, soon to begin, will be a response to what the disciples have seen and heard while following Jesus. Jesus will lead them to a "mountain," to a place at some distance from the people. (This movement is often compared to Moses ascending Mount Sinai to receive the commandments.) While the Sermon will not create simple oppositions between human needs and what God desires for humans, Jesus will show how the latter transforms the former. If it is the disciples that Jesus will teach, it becomes apparent by 7:28 that the crowds hear him too, just as the disciples now witness him teaching and healing the crowds. The people and the disciples share the space of transformation.

Turner reports that in the liminal phase of a rite of passage, special knowledge is imparted to the initiates. Jesus is creating receptivity to the kingdom. He invites all who would hear him into the transforming event, into the eternal happening of new creation. In the dangerous liminality of this event, those who are risking the transformation of their lives must not be left without knowledge. It is time for the Beatitudes and the extraordinary lessons of covenantal love of God and neighbor. It is time for the disciples to return to the scene.

LARRY D. BOUCHARD

Pastoral Perspective

who need these things the most: the suffering, the downtrodden, the downhearted.

In this way, these verses provide the interpretive key for understanding the upcoming Sermon on the Mount. This is no conventional congregation. The crowds are not made up of a random cross-section of curious locals, or even of the especially devout in any typically religious sense. Rather, the gathering is constituted by "all the sick, those who were afflicted with various diseases and pains, demoniacs, epileptics, and paralytics," as well as those caregivers who bring them to Jesus. Perhaps the closest parallel today would be an outdoor "healing service," a tent revival meeting on the outskirts of town. The afflicted, the suffering: *they* are the addressees of Jesus' pastoral work of encouragement and restoration. *They*, along with the disciples, are the congregation he summons in order to deliver the Christian tradition's most famous sermon (cf. 7:28). They come from far and wide—"from Galilee, the Decapolis, Jerusalem, Judea, and from beyond the Jordan" (v. 25)—having heard the Good Shepherd's voice, so that he might protect them, guide them to pasture, and lead them, sure-footed, through the wilderness along the way.

Does this mean that Jesus' ministry is meant exclusively for the afflicted and their caregivers? In one sense, yes; it is primarily meant for them. So if we do not count ourselves among those ranks on any given day, we are actually bystanders to the gospel. Our mission may then be faithfully to preserve and pass on that good news to its intended recipients. In another sense, on any given day, each one of us has our own struggles, our own ways in which we urgently require an encouraging word or a healing touch. Properly understood, then, the Christian church is never a circle of prestige or self-sufficiency. On the contrary, it is always a pastoral circle of vulnerability, a flock of "those afflicted with various diseases and pains." On this basis, and on this basis alone, we may then sit at God's feet and hear the breathtaking news of blessing to come.

MATTHEW MYER BOULTON

---

2. Kristine A. Culp, *Vulnerability and Glory: A Theological Account* (Louisville, KY: Westminster John Knox Press, 2010), 95, 99–101.

Exegetical Perspective

(chap. 13; 18:23–35; 20:1–16; 21:33–43; 22:1–10; 25:1–13; 25:31–46). Whereas in Mark's Gospel the secret of the kingdom itself is given to the disciples, Matthew clearly states that what is given to them is "to *know* the secrets of the kingdom of heaven" (13:11; cf. Mark 4:11).

Alongside the significance of Jesus' teaching and preaching about the kingdom of heaven, our passage highlights his healing. Jesus' healing is comprehensive to such an extent that he is presented as curing every disease and every illness among the people (4:23). As a result of his ministry of teaching, preaching, and healing in Galilee, his fame spreads throughout the "whole" region of Syria, an imperial province. Again, Matthew stresses and repeats that he cures "all" those who are sick with various diseases and pains, those who are demon possessed or epileptic, and paralytics from the extended area (v. 24; cf. 8:16; 9:35; 10:1).

Some Greek words, such as those for sickness (v. 23) and epileptic (v. 24), are used only in Matthew among the NT writers. Here Jesus' exorcism is also regarded as healing. Even his calling of sinners is related to his role as a physician in 9:12. Although this saying of Jesus appears in other Synoptic Gospels (Mark 2:17; Luke 5:31–32), in Matthew such holistic healing that includes sinners is based on God's mercy (Matt. 9:13; 12:7; cf. Hos. 6:6). Further, Matthew understands Jesus' healing as the fulfillment of Isaiah 53:4, "He took away our infirmities and bore our diseases" (Matt. 8:17).

This summary of Jesus' ministry of teaching, preaching, and healing is followed by verse 25, which illustrates the far-reaching consequences of such ministry. Great crowds "follow" (*akolouthein*, v. 25) Jesus from Galilee, Decapolis (literally, the "ten cities," a group of Hellenistic cities southeast of Galilee, administered from Syria by the Roman Empire), Jerusalem and Judea, and the other (east) side of the Jordan River. These places cover not only Jewish but also Gentile territories.

This transitional summary functions as the narrative setting for the Sermon on the Mount and also demonstrates that the wholeness of Jesus' kingdom ministry of teaching, preaching, and healing responds with power and impact to both spiritual and physical needs of all people across territorial boundaries. This is the ministry that disciples of Jesus are called to continue.

JIN YOUNG CHOI

Homiletical Perspective

for following entertainment, self-improvement, partisan opinion, personal fulfillment. So why should we follow Jesus?

Our decision to follow him may have started out of curiosity or habit, a friend's invitation, or a compelling altar call. Chances are good that we were hungry for some good news for a change, some hopeful word in contrast to the distressing problems of the day.

If we continue to follow Jesus, I suspect we will follow him for the some of the same reasons the crowds first followed him. We continue to follow because we are seeking a kingdom that has eternal values, like justice and generosity, freedom and fairness; and that is what Jesus is proclaiming. We continue to follow because we are yearning for teaching that guides the heart as well as the head, that leads to wisdom as well as knowledge, that values righteousness even more than being right; and that is what Jesus is teaching. We continue to follow because we are longing for healing of body and soul, for ourselves and those we love; we are longing for wholeness for a broken world; and that is the healing Jesus promises. We continue to follow because we are longing to find God's nearness; and that is what Jesus is sharing, as we discover in him that God has come to seek us.

That is why some of us have become devoted to Jesus, having chosen to follow him with all our heart and mind and strength.

Why did the crowds follow him? The crowds probably followed Jesus because they were filled with the same human longings we share. They had fewer options that promised to fulfill those yearnings, and maybe that was a blessing. In that ancient day, there were far fewer purveyors of false hopes, entertainers promising distraction, gurus peddling self-improvement.

Still, they were not without choices, false prophets and messiahs. They saw in Jesus someone who invited them into God's kingdom, run by the power of love instead of the power of soldiers; who taught them God's righteousness, shaped by wisdom instead of esoteric knowledge; who reached out to them with God's healing, promising not just a cure but the fullness of life.

CHRISTINE CHAKOIAN

Matthew 5:1–12

¹When Jesus saw the crowds, he went up the mountain; and after he sat down, his disciples came to him. ²Then he began to speak, and taught them, saying:

³"Blessed are the poor in spirit, for theirs is the kingdom of heaven.

⁴"Blessed are those who mourn, for they will be comforted.

⁵"Blessed are the meek, for they will inherit the earth.

⁶"Blessed are those who hunger and thirst for righteousness, for they will be filled.

⁷"Blessed are the merciful, for they will receive mercy.

⁸"Blessed are the pure in heart, for they will see God.

⁹"Blessed are the peacemakers, for they will be called children of God.

¹⁰"Blessed are those who are persecuted for righteousness' sake, for theirs is the kingdom of heaven.

¹¹"Blessed are you when people revile you and persecute you and utter all kinds of evil against you falsely on my account. ¹²Rejoice and be glad, for your reward is great in heaven, for in the same way they persecuted the prophets who were before you."

Theological Perspective

"How happy are the depressed!"

Well, no. This is *not* really a plausible reading of "poor in spirit," but it hints at how startling are the first words Jesus teaches the disciples—as provocative as Luke's "blessed are the poor" (Luke 6:20). Matthew does not "spirit away" material poverty; rather, he deepens its significance. How? Let us take bearings. The Sermon on the Mount is a religious-ethical discourse, one of five in the Gospel of Matthew that interpret the Torah and the message and mission of Jesus. It may have been a unitary composition of its own; it may predate Matthew.[1] It likely contains historical teachings of Jesus on the kingdom of God and repentance, some from the hypothetical Q source. If we can discern these strands as all being reflective of the witness to Christ, it remains hard to say any one is theologically decisive (e.g., passion over teachings, resurrection over miracles, Matthew over Luke). Nor do they make one pristine whole. We can only follow the texts wherever they push.

The first beatitude locates the world, with its tragedy and sorrow, in the milieu of spirit and in the arrival of God's transforming love and righteousness.

1. W. D. Davies, *The Setting of the Sermon on the Mount* (Cambridge: Cambridge University Press, 1966), 13; Hans Dieter Betz, *Essays on the Sermon on the Mount*, trans. L. L. Wellborn (Philadelphia: Fortress Press, 1985), 17–18.

Pastoral Perspective

The Sermon's setting is more complex than might appear at first glance. Jesus sees the crowds of the sick and afflicted, goes up the mountain, and sits down—thereby taking up both the traditional position of revelatory authority (a mountain) and the paradigmatic posture of a teaching rabbi (sitting down). However, Jesus does not thereby *retreat* from the crowds. On the contrary, his new post likely makes him more visible and audible to them; in any case, Matthew reports, they hang on every word (7:28). Jesus' most immediate addressees are his disciples, who come near and form an inner circle of instruction. There is thus a kind of double audience in this tableau, and we should therefore do our best to hear the Sermon in stereo. On one hand, Jesus speaks to his closest followers; on the other, he simultaneously speaks to the crowds. He is teaching and preaching, advising and consoling—all at once.

He begins with blessing. Who are the blessed, the truly favored of God, the ones with the most justifiable right to be happy, hopeful, content? Not who you might think. In fact, if you and I were to draw up a list of relative blessedness, we would likely put the rich and healthy and carefree at the top of the list, and the poor and afflicted and mourning down at the bottom. That sequence would be perfectly reasonable, of course, but it would also be utterly upside

Feasting on the Gospels

Exegetical Perspective

Three paired elements constitute the framework of Matthew's first discourse in chapters 5–7: Jesus' ascending to and descending from the mountain; his sayings as "teaching"; and the crowds' following of Jesus (4:25–5:2 and 7:28–8:1). The setting on a mountain in Galilee evokes primarily the imagery of Mount Sinai, where God's will for Israel was revealed through Moses. "Sitting down" (v. 1) and "opening of his mouth" (a literal rendering of v. 2) seem to be incidental features, but actually suggest Jesus' divine authority (cf. 4:4; 13:35). Jesus addresses his teaching primarily to his disciples (v. 1), but its power is demonstrated in its impact on the crowds, who are astounded at his teaching and follow him (7:28).

The first part of the Sermon, 5:3–12, is known as the Beatitudes because of the repeated word "blessed" (Latin, *beati*; Greek, *makarioi*), which indicates God's favor toward certain types of people. There are eight beatitudes; the last two (vv. 10 and 11), which concern persecution, are counted as one. Each characteristic or action of those blessed is followed by a promise that carries an eschatological ring. The first and eighth beatitudes anticipate the same reward, the "kingdom of heaven," while "righteousness" is mentioned in the fourth and eighth beatitudes.

The first beatitude blesses "the poor in spirit, for theirs is the kingdom of heaven" (v. 3; cf. Luke

Homiletical Perspective

What does it mean to be blessed, or, to use different translations of the Greek word *makarios,* what does it mean for us to be fortunate, or happy?

Every culture has its own definition of success. In Jesus' time, it would probably feature freedom from domineering rulers, oppressive tax collectors, and capricious soldiers. It might well include the respect that comes from savvy negotiating skills in the marketplace. In the Near East—ancient and modern—the list would certainly include the ability to provide for one's household, and having one's family enjoy health and prosperity.

Every culture promotes some vision of what happiness looks like. In postmodern America, the list would also include health, prosperity, and the ability to provide for one's family. In addition, our society has long promoted the goals of accumulating wealth and amassing power. Individual freedom is high on the list, as is the respect of one's neighbors and colleagues. Popularity, recognition, and prestige are also lifted up as worthy of pursuit. Political debates assume that disparagement and condescension are appropriate tools to use in pursuit of happiness. So-called reality television runs on the premise that everyone wants to have his or her day in the sun. Men's magazines promote virility and ambition; women's magazines promote perfect beauty and ideal

Matthew 5:1–12

Theological Perspective

God's reign interrupts the usual expectations of life, and its language can sound odd. The Beatitudes are so familiar that "accurate" translations risk losing this oddness. Verses 3–12 proclaim a prophetic, eschatological logic: the future of God challenges and transforms the present of those who hear. If we imagine these words spoken by the historical Jesus, they reflect eschatology in the process of realization or in its advent; the kingdom *to come* already *is* appearing. They may also reflect early Christian anticipations of Christ's return (*parousia*).[2]

In any case, each beatitude expresses existential and communal tensions between *will be* and *is*. As each penetrates those who hear, there breaks into personal and social imagination the criterion of God's steadfast love. Ordinary expectations—for example, that ultimate value lies in political, economic, or personal power to "make things happen"—are reversed. The extraordinary expectation is that the poor—those who are unable to make things happen and those who lay aside that value—are God's priority. This can seem impossible to grasp. To begin grasping it, Jesus insists, is itself a blessing.

The Beatitudes, however, do not each express their unexpected logic in the same way. "Blessed are the merciful" (v. 7) comes closer to common wisdom than "blessed are the meek" (v. 5). The former seems intuitive ("If I forgive him, he might forgive me"), the latter counterintuitive. That some beatitudes sound reasonable is not surprising if God's righteousness leaves traces in creation and history. Even so, their strangeness and their reasonableness must always be reimagined. Again, "Blessed are the poor" (v. 3) should sound odd. Can we listen for both oddness and wisdom in the remaining blessings?

Mourning takes many forms. Even when coming with relief, after a loved one's long dying, the ache of memory floods over us, wave after wave. Grief's pain can also be speechless: after sudden illness, a child's accident, murder, the loss of communities to natural catastrophes or historical hatreds. Then what is "inconsolable" exceeds expression and comprehension; to hear how, in God, grief will be consoled takes us beyond the edge of language.

Perhaps only the powerful wonder that the meek shall inherit the earth. Given the ubiquity of the powerless, they obviously have already inherited it! However, Jesus may refer to those who set aside anxiety for control. They are those who move, amid the

2. Norman Perrin and Dennis C. Duling, *The New Testament: An Introduction*, 2nd ed. (New York: Harcourt, Brace, Jovanovich, 1982), 276, 414.

Pastoral Perspective

down. Insofar as Jesus directly addresses his disciples with these words, the force of his message amounts to this: *You are the so-called inner circle of my followers, but the true "insiders" are in fact down around the foot of this mountain, the empty handed and empty hearted. The least of these—they are the truly blessed, the ones whom God favors.*

Like a thunderclap, these opening words are meant to directly contradict conventional wisdom. The world seems to favor those who look out for themselves, the miserly and the prideful, those who rely on strength and swords and cunning. In truth, Jesus contends, divine blessing attends the gentle and the merciful, those who do the right thing, even and especially when the odds seem stacked against them: peacemakers in a world infatuated with war, for example, or visionaries in a world that routinely persecutes prophets. To help us catch Jesus' meaning here, a preacher might begin a sermon by composing a kind of photonegative version of these declarations, a "business-as-usual beatitudes" that lay bare the wisdom by which most human communities still operate today:

> Blessed are the rich, in things and in self-assurance.
> Blessed are those untouched by loss.
> Blessed are the powerful.
> Blessed are those who are "realistic" about righteousness, compromising at every turn.
> Blessed are those who demand and exact an eye for an eye.
> Blessed are the crafty and opportunistic.
> Blessed are those bold enough to make war.
> Blessed are those who, doing good things, receive many accolades.
> Blessed are those who, following Jesus, are widely praised and adored.

Again, from a different angle of contrast, substituting "woe" for "blessing": "Woe to the poor in spirit, for they will be trampled and left behind in a dog-eat-dog world. . . . Woe to the peacemakers, for the human appetite for retribution is surely insatiable. . ." And so on.

The trick here is to uncover what we routinely take for granted, the deep logic by which we often assume the world actually works. Jesus is saying, in effect:

> No. That is not how the world actually works, no matter how things may seem. On the contrary, as God has ordained the deep, emerging order of creation, the truly blessed are ultimately and actually the gentle, the merciful, the peacemakers, the

Feasting on the Gospels

Exegetical Perspective

6:20). The "kingdom of heaven" refers to God's reign, rather than a place. Who are "the poor"? When Jesus speaks about the good news brought to the poor and orders the young man to give his possessions for the poor, Jesus means those who are literally poor (11:5; 19:21). Material impoverishment on earth—whether imposed or chosen—is germane to participation in the realm of heaven (cf. 4:17, 23). The poor, who suffer from economic distress but completely count on God, recognize and receive God's rule as a gift.

The second beatitude, "Blessed are those who mourn, for they will be comforted" (v. 4), alludes to Isaiah 61:2–3, where the prophet's mission involves comforting those who mourn over the destruction of the temple in Jerusalem. In Matthew, the mothers, represented as Rachel, weep at the loss of their children and refuse to be comforted (2:18; Jer. 31:15). Only when Jesus is taken away from the disciples will they mourn (Matt. 9:15). For those who mourn due to oppression or deprivation, God will be manifest as one who comforts.

The third beatitude refers to "the meek," who "will inherit the earth" (v. 5; cf. Ps. 37:11). Jesus himself best exemplifies the character of the meek: he accepts those who carry heavy burdens (11:29; 21:5). Similarly, those who treat well any of the destitute, who are identified as sisters and brothers of the Son of Man, will inherit the kingdom (25:31–40; cf. 18:3–5; 19:29).

"Blessed are those who hunger and thirst for righteousness, for they will be filled" (or satisfied; v. 6) draws from Psalm 107:5, 9. As in Matthew 25:31–46, righteousness involves human relationships and actions (6:1). While "your righteousness" should be better than that of the scribes and Pharisees (5:20), "doing your righteousness" should ultimately imitate God's righteousness (5:43–48). Righteousness can also be translated as justice, suggesting the vindication of the righteous at the Last Judgment. Hence, the disciples seek God's justice in the eschatological hope of satisfaction from God and as a witness to the realization of this promise in Jesus' ministry (3:15; 6:33; cf. the feeding of the multitudes: 14:20; 15:33, 37).

The fifth beatitude, "Blessed are the merciful, for they will receive mercy" (v. 7), lifts up one of Matthew's signature themes. Matthew later stresses God's desire for mercy by quoting Hosea 6:6 (9:13; 12:7). Jesus' healings demonstrate his mercy as the sign of the kingdom of heaven at work (9:27, 36; 15:22; 17:15; 20:30, 31). Jesus teaches that those who receive mercy from God should have mercy on their fellows (18:33). Finally, those who practice mercy will receive mercy at the Last Judgment.

Homiletical Perspective

relationships; trade magazines promote financial success; sports magazines promote strategies to win.

This is why Jesus' list is so jarring. Contrast his words with the goals our culture says we ought to pursue:

Our culture says, Happy are those with great prospects for marriage and work, because they will be successful.

Jesus says, Happy are the destitute, because the kingdom of heaven is theirs.

Our culture says, Happy are those whose loved ones enjoy health, because they will not worry.

Jesus says, Happy are people who grieve, because they will be made glad.

Our culture says, Happy are those who enjoy power, because they will be in charge.

Jesus says, Happy are people who are humble, because they will inherit the earth.

Our culture says, Happy are people who can buy any pleasure, because they can do whatever makes them feel good.

Jesus says, Happy are people who are hungry and thirsty for righteousness, because they will be fed until they are full.

Our culture says, Happy are people who have power to sit in judgment over others, because they can boss people around.

Jesus says, Happy are people who show mercy, because they will receive mercy.

Our culture says, Happy are people who can run down their opponent by whatever means possible, because they will see victory.

Jesus says, Happy are people who have pure hearts, because they will see God.

Our culture says, Happy are people who can beat their opponents, because they are winners.

Jesus says, Happy are people who make peace, because they will be called God's children.

Our culture says, Happy are people whose lives are lived in total freedom to do whatever they want, because they do not have constraints.

Jesus says, Happy are people whose lives are harassed because they are righteous, because the kingdom of heaven is theirs.

Our culture says, Happy are people who are popular, because you will be rewarded with a great reputation.

Jesus says, Happy are you when people insult you and harass you and speak all kinds of bad and false things about you, all because of me. Be full of joy and be glad, because you have a great reward in heaven. In the same way, people harassed the prophets who came before you.

In the Sermon on the Mount, Jesus proposes a definition of happiness wildly different from

Matthew 5:1–12

Theological Perspective

troubles of today, in sight of the divine horizon. They live, as Stanley Hauerwas says, "out of control."[3]

We rationalize our desires. We think we are right; we wish to be thought "in the right," whereas Jesus blesses the desire for righteousness that transforms even our desires for a just and caring society. However, when we do hunger and thirst for God's righteousness, which will only rarely jibe with our desires, the kingdom draws near. Joy of desire, for God's love and justice, is a gift that grows toward fulfillment.

Mercy, as forgiveness, is said to be the grease of interpersonal life; it smoothes countless faults and frictions. It may carry expectations of return, like gift exchange; sometimes to withhold forgiveness appears wrong. Forgiveness can also seem impossible, even beyond morality. With Jesus, all these "mercies" are being transformed. The imperative to forgive even the unforgivable turns us in repentance toward the cross, and then beyond.

"They will see God" (v. 8). Here the future tense avoids simple equations of goodness and godliness. The pure in heart set aside (they are purified, freed from) anxious obstacles to hope. Their blessing, now, is the freedom to expect the kingdom.

"Peacemakers" (*eirēnopoioi*, v. 9) distantly echoes a poetic sort of making. In poetry, metaphors *atone*. They bring distant things together, in harmony and dissonance; some chaos remains in metaphor, inviting still more creation. Peacemaking too requires creation and improvisation. The peacemakers have a gift for imitating God on the run—as if children.

To think we are persecuted for our goodness is usually delusional. Most persecution stems from others' anxiety, prejudice, and hatred for our status, race, or identities. Even when we are persecuted for doing justice and love, the last beatitudes remain difficult. At peace with God, but laboring under oppression, we find it hard to be told, "Rejoice, you are prophets!" (like v. 12). These last beatitudes anticipate the cross. Not with solemnity, however, but with the joy of a shepherdess, surprised to find that safety had unexpectedly "arrived" while she was taken up with guarding the sheep. Is there a test for whether these beatitudes apply to our persecution complexes? Yes. If we think they do, we are probably not tending to the kingdom.

LARRY D. BOUCHARD

Pastoral Perspective

poor. It appears to be otherwise, I understand—and that is precisely why I am beginning this way, the better to dispel the commonplace illusions, to clarify reality, to declare the dawning reign of God, and so to help us find our bearings as we live into God's future.

In this sense, the Beatitudes are an early, implicit example of the formula Jesus later makes explicit: "You have heard it said . . . but I say unto you" (e.g., Matt. 5:21–22).

The Beatitudes are not an ethical code—at least not in the familiar sense of instructions for righteous living, or a list of tasks that, once discharged, may win God's favor. Whenever we read these lines this way, we demonstrate yet again our tendencies toward acquisitive forms of reading Scripture, that is, attempts to *acquire* from a text some recipe for spiritual triumph. On closer inspection, the Sermon itself rebuffs these attempts, since the idea cannot be for us to seek out additional mourning in our lives, for example, to say nothing of persecution or slander!

Indeed, rather than an ethics, the Beatitudes are more like a twofold pastoral gift. First, they mark out a map of divine blessing—a map strikingly different from the conventional one, which tends to identify "blessings" as positive goods, gifts, talents, and so on. By contrast, in the Beatitudes Jesus highlights not goods already granted but rather empty spaces, longings, hungers, and so on. In this way, his map is fundamentally eschatological—and therein lies the gift's second and decisive aspect.

This map is also an encouraging promise, an atlas of "not yets," homiletically refigured into sites of hope, foretastes of heaven. Most of the verbs here are in the future tense: "they will be comforted," "they will see God." Here is good news spoken in full view of the world's longings—and yet so vividly promising blessings as to make them available by anticipation here and now, even as Jesus, God incarnate, declares them in our midst. If those disciples have ears to hear, this testimony may just be enough to reorient them so that they might turn and behold—in the crowd's countless, astounded faces—a teeming sea of blessedness all around.

MATTHEW MYER BOULTON

---

3. Stanley Hauerwas, *A Community of Character: Toward a Constructive Christian Social Ethic* (Notre Dame, IN: University of Notre Dame Press, 1981), 11.

"Blessed are the pure in heart, for they will see God" (v. 8; cf. Ps. 24:3–4) seems a conundrum. Humans cannot see the face of God (Exod. 3:6; 19:21; 33:20, 23). In Matthew, only the heavenly angels of the "little ones," the humble, continually "see" the face of God in heaven (18:4, 10). The purity of one's innermost being, in contrast to an outward or legalistic purity, leads to the eschatological blessing of seeing God. The righteous encounter God's presence among the least ones—the sick, the hungry and thirsty, the naked, and prisoners (25:31–40).

"The peacemakers" will be called "children of God" (v. 9). This beatitude speaks of active engagement in peacemaking. In the setting in which Rome's peace (*Pax Romana*) is propagated, practicing peace (*eirēnopoioi*) means to embody *shalom* as a wholeness that God's reign brings, while resisting the false peace imposed under military rule by human empires (cf. 10:13). As Jesus is called Son/Child by God (3:17; 17:5), those who practice God's impartial love and thus imitate the perfection of God will be called children of God in the kingdom that breaks through into the present whenever disciples pray to their heavenly Father (5:43–45; 6:9).

The final two-part beatitude focuses on "those who are persecuted for righteousness' sake" (vv. 10–12). Jesus reaffirms the same promise as in the first beatitude, "theirs is the kingdom of heaven." Verses 11–12 amplify the descriptions of persecution and make them more personal, shifting to the second person plural in direct address ("blessed are you"). Here persecution for righteousness' sake is treated as persecution for Jesus' sake. The disciples' suffering is compared to what the prophets went through. These descriptions may reflect conflicts between Christians and other Jews, when Christians adopted new ways of living the Jewish traditions, or the oppression they endured while living in the Roman Empire. In the midst of present suffering, they rejoice and even "shout for joy" because of their future bliss.

Despite strong ethical implications, the Beatitudes are not to be understood as prescriptions for entrance into the kingdom of heaven but as descriptions of the characteristics and actions appropriate for life in God's kingdom. The Beatitudes evince beliefs and practices of Christlike people living under God's rule, which may cause derision and hostility. The promises proclaiming God's future actions provide urgent encouragement to these who live distinctively as disciples.

JIN YOUNG CHOI

anything we are accustomed to hearing. How do we square these two vastly diverging road maps?

The problem may well be that we are trying to overlay Jesus' road map on top of our culture's. Instead of trying to synchronize them, the better option may well be seeing where the paths end up.

In Robert Frost's famous poem "The Road Not Taken," he writes of the choice that lay before him, and indeed before us all:

> Two roads diverged in a yellow wood,
> And sorry I could not travel both
> And be one traveler, long I stood
> And looked down one as far as I could
> To where it bent in the undergrowth . . .

For many of us who follow the road our culture sets out for us, the initial way may look very appealing. Who would not want to have a healthy family or provide for their household? Although we recognize the "undergrowth," that is, the tangled roots that might trip us up, the trouble appears to be worth it.

Then somewhere down the way, the culture's promises turn out to be erratic, and there are traps and dead ends that we did not expect. We hurl ourselves at work, yet we find ourselves spending more and more time there at the expense of our relationships, with no guarantee of success. We pursue every medical test available, yet sooner or later our bodies fail us. We chase after power, but then find out that we always have to defend it. We aspire to popularity, but then can never say anything controversial, lest someone dislike us.

The path that Jesus offers may not initially look as appealing, but the farther down the road of faith one travels, the more truth one finds. We discover that humility, unlike power, needs no defense. We realize righteousness—doing the right thing—is its own reward. We find that a pure heart is much easier to live with than one filled with jealousy, resentment, or cynicism. Step by step, we learn that following Jesus—even if we are persecuted for it—leads to a joy that nothing can take away.

As Robert Frost's poem concludes:

> I shall be telling this with a sigh
> Somewhere ages and ages hence:
> Two roads diverged in a wood, and I—
> I took the one less traveled by,
> And that has made all the difference.[1]

CHRISTINE CHAKOIAN

1. Robert Frost, "The Road Not Taken," in *Mountain Interval* (New York: Henry Holt and Company, 1920), 9.

Matthew 5:13–16

¹³"You are the salt of the earth; but if salt has lost its taste, how can its saltiness be restored? It is no longer good for anything, but is thrown out and trampled under foot.

¹⁴"You are the light of the world. A city built on a hill cannot be hid. ¹⁵No one after lighting a lamp puts it under the bushel basket, but on the lampstand, and it gives light to all in the house. ¹⁶In the same way, let your light shine before others, so that they may see your good works and give glory to your Father in heaven."

Theological Perspective

If Matthew's Beatitudes are the inaugural moment in the disciples' training, then Jesus' metaphors of identification—*you are salt, you are light*—set the terms of their calling. If Jesus is *heard* by the disciples and *overheard* by the crowds, then who are we: hearers or overhearers? The Sermon on the Mount's drama of speaking, hearing, and overhearing creates the promise of such a question.

Speaking. Another inaugural moment, Luke 4:16–21, occurs when Jesus reads aloud from Isaiah, "The Spirit of the Lord is upon me." He concludes, "Today this scripture has been fulfilled in your hearing." Language philosophers might say that Jesus' Sermon is "performative speech," speech whose meaning is a relationship created in being said or performed.[1] A common example is "I promise." A new social reality—the promise—appears *in the act of speaking*. Probably all discourse is performative to a degree, but especially speech that alters relations between speaker and audience. Much of the Sermon is performative; certainly the Beatitudes and the metaphors of salt and light are. The kingdom of heaven is being realized or "fulfilled" in the speaking and hearing.

1. J. L. Austin, *How to Do Things with Words* (New York: Oxford University Press, 1962).

Pastoral Perspective

Jesus begins the Sermon on the Mount with a kind of map of divine blessing, a portrait contrasting sharply with conventional wisdom about who is truly fortunate and who is not. Now Jesus pivots to the question of the true identity of his listeners, in effect locating them on the map of blessing, and at the same time charging them with a particular mission for the sake of creation as a whole. In short: "You are salt and light." Let us take these terms one at a time.

"You." Who are Jesus' addressees here? Matthew has composed a complex communicative scene: an inner circle of disciples who join Jesus on the mountainside (5:1); an outer circle of sick and afflicted people who both prompt the Sermon in the first place ("When Jesus saw the crowds . . . ," 5:1) and avidly attend to the Sermon as it unfolds ("the crowds were astounded at his teaching," 7:28); and finally, a third circle comprised of all those listening in via Matthew's proclamation through the ages—including you and me. Up to this point in the discourse, Jesus has been speaking in the third person about blessing and God's promises. He has only just shifted into the second person ("Blessed are you when people revile you . . . on my account," 5:11), underscoring the threat of persecution in Christian life.

Exegetical Perspective

The switch from the third-person plural address in the Beatitudes to the second-person plural ("blessed are you") in 5:11–12 prepares for the following passage in which Jesus declares, "You are the salt of the earth," and "You are the light of the world" (vv. 13–16). While similar sayings appear in Mark and Luke, Matthew's use of these two metaphors is distinctive. In Mark, Jesus relates the use of salt as seasoning food to one's character and peaceful relationships with others (Mark 9:49–50). In Luke, tasteless salt is mentioned in terms of discipleship (Luke 14:34–35). In Mark and Luke, Jesus' saying on light is given after his explanation of the parable of the Sower and the Seeds (Mark 4:21–22; Luke 8:16–17). In these literary contexts Jesus' saying on light is related to hiddenness and manifestation, that is, to understanding Jesus' parables. Here at the close of the Beatitudes in Matthew, Matthew's Jesus identifies the disciples with "the salt of the earth" and "the light of the world." Thus, in Matthew it is not Jesus' teaching or certain practices that are "salt" and "light," but the witness of the disciples themselves.

First, Jesus' followers are defined as salt. Salt was widely used for various purposes in the ancient world, such as preserving, seasoning for food (Job 6:6), fertilizing soil (Luke 14:34–35), sacrificing (Lev. 2:13; Ezra 6:9; Ezek. 43:24), covenanting (Num. 18:19; 2

Homiletical Perspective

Year after year, for close to half a century, the church in America and Europe has been in decline. Not that long ago, the church was at the center of society. Its leaders enjoyed public admiration. Its opinions were valued at the civic table. Its ethics were lifted up as a guide to appropriate behavior. Its services were sought after for the edification of young people.

All that has changed. Now the church is rarely mentioned in the news, except when it is shamed by its leaders' malfeasance. Its voice is silenced, except when extremists are lifted up as examples and caricatures. Its values and services are considered ancillary, rather than essential to the formation of young adults.

One would hardly describe the church as indispensable—especially as indispensable as salt or light.

If that is true for our age, how much more was it true for Jesus' earliest disciples! From what we can surmise through the Gospels and Paul's letters, they were an odd lot of fishermen, homemakers, tax collectors, and, eventually, former Pharisees and assorted Greco-Romans. They were small in number; they had no organized church; there were no goals or vision statements. According to every standard by which we currently measure the health of congregations, the early church would be deemed anemic at best.

Matthew 5:13–16

Theological Perspective

The Beatitudes announced renewed realities—the "happiness" of the poor, the "blessing" of the persecuted—that, though proclaimed by the prophets, are exceedingly hard to grasp or accept; and to accept them is to be transformed. Now, through the metaphors of salt and light, Jesus attaches these realities to the disciples' lives. The associations of salt and light seem limitless. The disciples are to be hidden, like salt, suggesting goodness—yet visible, as light, manifesting truth. The point is not that they are remarkably good or wise. Nor is it to predict what they will become (recall the failings of Peter).

The point is that if the kingdom is the extraordinary realization of God's love and righteousness, then the disciples are part of the kingdom's embodiment. They join in the event of incarnation realized in the entrance of Christ into the world, Israel's call to embody the Law, and the covenants with Noah and Abraham. With "You are the salt . . . you are the light" (vv. 13, 14), Jesus means the kind of community for which the world hungers—one where God's love and life illuminate and liberate—is finding a new occasion in the disciples.

Hearing. If the disciples understood the Beatitudes even a little, they likely resisted being named *salt* and *light*. Sensing what was at stake, they probably thought about declining the nomination.

Consider that for Paul Ricoeur, the figurative "is" of a metaphor is in tension with a literal "is not," and a metaphor's meanings spring from the tension.[2] A disciple figuratively "is" *and* literally "is not" salt. I think the disciples would have resonated more with the "is not," as would I. Partly I would resist performative speech. It would hedge my options and impose on my life. Partly I would resist out of realism. I am unworthy to be salt or light, certainly not a light to the nations. What have I gotten into? Evidences for this hesitation can be found in the counterfactuals Jesus appends to each metaphor. "If salt has lost its taste . . . it is no longer good for anything, but is thrown out and trampled under foot" (v. 13). "A city built on a hill cannot be hid. No one after lighting a lamp puts it under the bushel basket" (vv. 14–15). Jesus is not telling the disciples they are exceptionally strong or good, nor does he mean, "Don't be so modest." He basically says, (1) this is real: the kingdom is joined with you; and (2) this is not really "about you." It is not even about the

Pastoral Perspective

Here, in verse 13, Jesus not only addresses his listeners directly; he also sums up their mission and character. He describes them. He tells them who they are. Who is the "you" in this passage? Jesus' disciples, the crowds, and the broad congregation of listeners over the centuries—we dare not exclude any of these pastoral circles of addressees. Listening to Jesus' Sermon afresh from each of these angles may give rise to a rich array of interpretive options.

"Salt." In the ancient world, salt was a prized preservative—a function all but forgotten today in most of the industrialized world, where refrigeration is now the rule. Likewise, salt was also part of the paraphernalia of ancient sacrifice, another sign of its extraordinary status (e.g., Lev. 2:13). Most immediately, however, Jesus has in view here the mineral's savory function, the role it plays in enhancing the taste of food. For all three of these reasons—preservative, liturgical, and culinary—salt was a precious commodity in Jesus' day.

This basic sense of prestige is perhaps the first thing a preacher or teacher needs to establish in order to properly evoke the force of the phrase "the salt of the earth." After all, in a world full of saltshakers on virtually every dining-room table, salt is easy to overlook or regard as humdrum. In fact, human history has long been shaped in deep and crucial ways by salt, from trade routes to government monopolies to popular protests as recent as Mahatma Gandhi's "Salt March." Even our everyday vocabulary includes traces of salt's longstanding influence on human affairs: the word "salary," for example, derives from a Latin term for "a soldier's allowance for the purchase of salt."

Whether we focus on salt's preservative, liturgical, or culinary functions, it is difficult to miss the point that salt is a small thing of great value. Just a pinch of it can make a tremendous difference. It also has another important property. It not only adds flavor; it spices things up. As both cooks and chemists will attest, salt brightens and sharpens other flavors already present. Pepper can only add more or less of a peppery taste. Salt, if added in the right amount at the right time in the right way, enlivens and enhances a meal's other flavors. It brings them out. It makes them themselves, only more so—and the Christian community can and must do the same. We should bring our own flavor to the mix, of course, spicing things up here and there. Then, just as much, we should work to enhance other flavors, enliven other tastes, making the world more savory,

2. Paul Ricoeur, *Interpretation Theory: Discourse and the Surplus of Meaning* (Fort Worth: Texas Christian University Press, 1976), 50.

Feasting on the Gospels

Exegetical Perspective

Chr. 13:5), purifying (Exod. 30:35; 2 Kgs. 2:19–21), cleansing (Ezek. 16:4), and signifying loyalty (Ezra 4:14). Unlike Mark's and Luke's parallels (seasoning and fertilizing, respectively), Matthew 5:13 does not indicate a specific function of salt. Thus one can assume that the general benefit of salt applies to the disciples' positive influence on the earth.

In Matthew, the earth is characterized in several ways. The earth is the place where human kings rule (17:25). However, God is the Lord of heaven and earth, and believers call God "Father in heaven" (6:9; 11:25; 23:9). At the end of Matthew, God will give Jesus all authority in heaven and on earth (28:18). Through Jesus' kingdom ministry, the disciples are given the keys of the kingdom of heaven, and so their ministry on earth operates in heaven (16:19). Especially when two of them on earth agree about anything they ask for, the Father in heaven will make it happen (18:18–19). Thus what disciples should do is pray that God's will be done on earth as it is in heaven (6:10). While Jesus' followers are poor and meek on earth, they do not store up for themselves treasures on earth, but in heaven when they inherit the earth (5:3, 5; 6:19–20). In the parables (chap. 13) the earth is the field of the disciples' actions as well as the object of their mission; the parable of the Seeds represents different types of earth as people who receive the word of the kingdom (13:3–9).

As such, disciples should actively engage in making God's will and rule realized on the earth. Just as the salt that has lost its saltiness (*mōranthē*, literally, "become foolish") is good for nothing and thrown out and trampled under foot, when disciples lose their competency and are unfit for their mission, they are treated with disdain by people (v. 13).

In the second metaphor, the disciples are as "light." While Rome and the emperor were proclaimed as a "light to the entire world," Matthew depicts the launching of Jesus' ministry in "Galilee of the Gentiles [*ethnōn*]" as fulfilling the prophecies of the Old Testament for light that shines upon those in darkness and in the shadow of death (Matt. 4:16; Isa. 9:1–2). As Israel's vocation in the Old Testament is "a light to the nations [*ethnōn*]" the disciples, who succeed to Jesus' ministry, function as light to the world (Isa. 42:6; 49:6; 51:4–5). The disciples' identity as light is further illustrated by two images: "a city built on a hill" and "a lamp under the bushel basket."

The image of a city laid on a mountain recalls Jewish images of Jerusalem, from which it was believed that God's presence beams over the world. Whether Jesus alludes to Jerusalem or not, it is the

Homiletical Perspective

None of these things that seem to us to be measures of strength appear to be conditions Christ sets for usefulness in the kingdom. Note that Jesus does not say, "You *should* be the salt of the earth," as if we are responsible for making ourselves into something useful or writing our goals and objectives to encourage measurable outcomes. Nor does Jesus say, "You *will* be the light of the world," as if to suggest that God will make this happen in the completion of time.

Instead, Jesus says, "You *are* the salt of the earth," and "You *are* the light of the world." Already. Right now.

So what might it mean for our churches not to try to retrieve our former "glory," but instead to explore what it looks like to be salt and light for the world today?

We might begin by exploring the nature of salt and light. Both are God-given; they are elements in nature, rather than things that human beings can produce. So it is with the faithful who follow Jesus. As followers of Christ, we are not self-made; rather, we are created by pure grace, out of the will of God.

Neither salt nor light is rare; they are the most ordinary of elements. So it is with the faithful. We are valuable not because the world deems us a tradable commodity, or because we are rare and precious and costly. Rather, we are common, humble elements whose existence could well be overlooked.

Still, both salt and light are essential to life: salt, for taste; light, for finding one's way. They are good for the world, and their value is found in their usefulness. So it is with followers of Jesus. Our goal is not to be valuable according to the world's standards; our worth is not measured by whether we have the largest budget or staff, measured like a corporation. Our goal is not to have the most popular youth program or most professional choir, as if we were a franchise or a touring company. Like ordinary salt, or ordinary light, our goal is to be beneficial, useful, *life-giving* elements in the world. To the extent we are able to stay true to this calling, we will give glory to God.

While it is always dangerous to measure another's faithfulness, one might point to examples of "success" according to the qualities of salt and light:

We tend to measure a church's success by the prominence of the congregation, and while it is altogether likely that faithful disciples are to be found in tall-steeple churches in the center of town, they are just as likely to be found in tiny emerging communities in the city, gathering young adults in coffeehouses for safe and honest conversation.

Theological Perspective

good *you* will do or truth *you* will bring. "Let your light shine before others, so that they may see your good works *and give glory to your Father in heaven*" (v. 16)—as if to say, "The credit is not even supposed to be yours, if that is what is bothering you."

Overhearing. We know implicitly how the disciples heard: they kept following Jesus. Later we learn explicitly (7:28) how the crowds responded: what they overheard astonished them. Did they follow? Some did, some did not. *What is revealed in Jesus' strategy of being overheard?*

Overhearing first suggests how the Sermon's performative range extended far beyond those it addressed. That can be said of other remarkable discourses. What brings us closer to the distinctive content of Jesus' teaching is its resistance to paraphrase. As he elaborates on the kingdom of heaven—in metaphors, parables, and other figures—its meanings come alive yet remain elusive, as in "How happy are the poor. . . . How blessed are the persecuted." If the kingdom resists direct communication, perhaps allowing itself to be overheard is part of how it reveals and transforms lives.[3] Some may have overheard Jesus and said, "I cannot say for sure what he meant, but . . . well, somehow it has authority, somehow it applies to me." Overhearing is a strategy of transmission common to other authoritative teachings. Martin Luther King's "I Have a Dream" wanted to be overheard and is overheard anew today.

King's speech itself overhears the kingdom. Its freedom has roots in "You are salt. . . . You are light." Freedom from bondage is the clue. Remember, the disciples—already called, already in training—had chosen to follow. Jesus was not coercing them but intensifying their choice. *Those who overhear receive a larger space for response.* They are made free to discover salt and light, to discover that they too are salt and light. They will choose or not, then or later. They may have to choose again. The kingdom is not coercive. Its freedom is a gift. It allows borders to be crossed, spaces to merge, just as salt and light mix and move across boundaries. Overhearing may be how a peaceable kingdom wills to be heard.

LARRY D. BOUCHARD

Pastoral Perspective

more delicious, more beautiful. If we do not, what good are we?

"Light." Again, the accent of the image is on both audacity and service: a relatively small thing that, handled well, can make a big difference. A hillside city may guide a traveler along the way or usher someone into safe harbor. A lamp may illuminate a house, thereby making a host of other activities possible long after the sun has set. Moreover, it is worth noting that the act of putting a basket over a burning lamp is not only absurd; it is also dangerous. It involves a fundamental, even reckless misunderstanding of what a lamp is, how it works, and what it is for. "You are not made to be hidden," Jesus insists. "You are made for shining, for illuminating, for giving light to all in the house"—a mission that, if taken seriously, would fundamentally shift how we plan our days, in terms of both what we do and how we do it.

Any teacher will encourage students to "do good works," for example, but here Jesus articulates a particular underlying basis for that work, a motive and framework within which it properly takes place. Do not do good works in order to enhance your standing or status, he seems to say; do them because that is exactly what you are made to do. Do them because "doing good works" is one and the same as "being who you really are." Do them not to gain stature, but rather as an outworking of the stature you already enjoy. For you are the light of the world, the salt of the earth, the small and unimpressive band of brothers and sisters—reviled and persecuted—that can and must, God willing, make a broad and inspiring difference.

MATTHEW MYER BOULTON

---

3. Søren Kierkegaard, *Concluding Unscientific Postscript*, trans. Howard V. Hong and Edna H. Hong (Princeton, NJ: Princeton University Press, 1992), 242–43.

disciples who are visible to the world and reflect the light of Jesus Christ upon the world, like a city on a mountain. On the other hand, an oil lamp functions to light up a household. Just as a city on a hill cannot be hidden, so it would be absurd if one were to place an oil lamp under a basket, rendering it invisible.

This light corresponds to the good deeds of disciples (v. 16). Disciples should shine their light before people so that the people encounter God's presence through their good deeds and praise God. This consciousness of the importance of witnessing or practicing one's faith "before people" is prominent throughout Matthew (5:16; 6:1; 10:32–33; 23:13). The purpose of such practice is not to show off, but to bring glory to the "heavenly Father," an important image for God in Matthew (9:8; 15:31; cf. 23:5). The significance of practice is explicated in 5:21–48, but prevails in the entire Sermon on the Mount and throughout the Gospel, being expressed in the verb form "to do" (*poiein*, 3:8, 10; 5:19, 46–47; 6:1–3; 7:12, 17–26; 12:12) and by the metaphor of "fruit" (*karpos*, 3:8, 10; 7:16–20; cf. 12:33; 13:8, 26; 21:19, 33–43). What is stressed here is not human-initiated effort but human response to "the will of the Father in heaven," which will lead one to enter the kingdom (7:21). This understanding of "light" corresponds to an understanding of the Beatitudes as characteristics that describe disciples who are attuned to God's actions as the promise of hope, not as imperatives demanding what human beings ought to do.

As the Beatitudes also attest, the two images of salt and light thus highlight the distinctive character and actions of disciples. Salt and light are the disciples' identity and way of life. Their identity is formed and stands out in order to influence and provide orientation for people in the midst of the world.

JIN YOUNG CHOI

We tend to measure a church's value by numbers at worship, and while it is quite likely that faithful disciples are attending a megachurch in the suburbs, it is just as likely that they are attending a tiny rural congregation that makes sure its elderly neighbors are regularly visited or that new immigrants have food to eat.

We tend to measure a church's worth by the power its members have accrued; while it is likely that faithful disciples are to be found among titans of commerce or politics, they are just as likely to be found among the unemployed who volunteer to help homeless people or battered women or underprivileged children, serving those who are in at least as much difficulty as they are.

Our effectiveness as disciples does not depend on our success according to the world's standards. Moreover, if we are working only to have the most prominent, well-attended, powerful congregation, then we are working toward the wrong goal. The point is not to give glory to ourselves, but to give glory to God. Doing that requires nothing more than the humility of being who we really are: salt and light.

If we fail to be true to God's purpose for us, then what good are we to the world? If we bear the name of Christ but have lost our true essence as salt, then people stop seeing us as useful for anything, and Christ's good name is squandered. If we say we are followers of Jesus but have hidden Christ's light under buildings, bureaucracy, and budgets, then we have robbed the world of God's good gift.

Salt and light may not be the most glamorous elements in the universe, but they are worth more than silver or gold. They are life giving and useful, for the well-being of the world. That would be a worthy goal indeed.

CHRISTINE CHAKOIAN

Matthew 5:17–20

[17]"Do not think that I have come to abolish the law or the prophets; I have come not to abolish but to fulfill. [18]For truly I tell you, until heaven and earth pass away, not one letter, not one stroke of a letter, will pass from the law until all is accomplished. [19]Therefore, whoever breaks one of the least of these commandments, and teaches others to do the same, will be called least in the kingdom of heaven; but whoever does them and teaches them will be called great in the kingdom of heaven. [20]For I tell you, unless your righteousness exceeds that of the scribes and Pharisees, you will never enter the kingdom of heaven."

Theological Perspective

Why is it important that Jesus fulfills, even to the last stroke of a letter, the law and the prophets? Why must the righteousness of Jesus' disciples exceed that of the scribes and Pharisees? These questions are rooted in the foundational concerns of Jesus' Sermon on the Mount, concerns that also run through the long history of God's people, especially the central elements of Israel's Scriptures, the law and the prophets: does God need a special people, and what makes them special?[1]

The "law and prophets" refers not only to the most venerated portions of the Hebrew canon, but more broadly to the story of Israel's often troubled, but always mercied relationship with God. The Scriptures record, again and again, God's yes to the question about a special people, even in the face of Israel's persistent resistance to God's call and will. God needed a people to come out of slavery and empire; to endure judgment, wandering, and exile; and to repent and be redeemed. God did not need an imperial juggernaut, an unconquerable military power, or a people who outdid the surrounding nations in building cities and temples, although Israel tried at times to be and to do just that.

1. These questions are the focus of Gerhard Lohfink's book *Does God Need the Church? Toward a Theology of the People of God* (Collegeville, MN: Michael Glazier/The Liturgical Press, 1999).

Pastoral Perspective

Oh, how difficult for those dedicated to a life of faithfulness: to go from the soaringly beautiful bravo blessings of the Beatitudes to the difficult teachings of Christ that follow almost immediately. In this pericope we hear Jesus' teachings regarding the eternal law that he comes into our lives to fulfill (Greek, *plērōsai*), to make complete or to fill full of meaning "the law" and not to abolish it. We who rely on the unconditional grace of God have been tempted to think that "our" salvation by grace is somehow superior to salvation by the law. However, as this passage shows, this arrogantly and willfully misunderstands the message Jesus proclaims.

Let us remind one another of what we know of Jesus' own (Jewish) tradition when speaking of "the law." When speaking of the law, Jesus and his rabbinic colleagues meant a variety of things, depending upon context. The law could refer to the Ten Commandments, the core of ethical teaching in Jesus' faith. The law could refer to the Pentateuch, the first five rolls or books of Hebrew Scripture. "The law and the prophets" was and is used to refer to the whole of Hebrew Scripture and the essential themes to be found there. Finally, "the law" could refer to the whole complex of oral and written tradition about the essential teachings. This final usage is similar to what we mean when we speak of precedent in civil

Exegetical Perspective

In these transitional verses within the Sermon on the Mount, Jesus moves from delivering blessings and encouragement for the crowds to addressing issues surrounding the "law." Here we find clear support for the Gospel writer's argument that Jesus was an observant Jew and a "new" Moses. Jesus did not do away with the requirement of following the commandments, nor did he replace them. Rather, Jesus strongly emphasized the necessity of following even the "least of these commandments" (v. 19). While continual interpretation of the "law" was necessary to meet changing circumstances, the content of the Torah was eternal (v. 18a). No one had the authority to make any changes to God's law (v. 18b), not even Jesus.

Many issues in this passage need close attention, not the least of which is the word "law." The phrase "the law [and] the prophets" in Jesus' opening line may confuse the modern reader. The word "law" is the translation of *nomos,* the word that the Greek translation of the Hebrew Bible, the Septuagint (LXX), used most often to render the Hebrew word *torah. Nomos* has the primary meaning of "legislation or a legal system"; it is not an adequate equivalent for *torah,* which has a root meaning of "teaching," not "law" or "legislation." The reliance on the LXX by early Christian communities has resulted in a common misunderstanding of Torah, with it

Homiletical Perspective

It was the night before "graduation" from first- and second-grade Sunday school into the prestigious third-grade class. On this occasion each year my home church would give young Bible scholars their first Bible. My devout grandmother prepared me for the big day by emphasizing that I was about to receive a book that had changed her life and, by implication, would change mine.

On that special Sunday morning, each student was called forward and given a King James Version, red-letter edition of the New Testament with the Psalms. The red letters were the publisher's attempt to focus our eyes on the words of Jesus, long before the Jesus Seminar's color scheme claiming to zoom in on the "authentic" sayings of Jesus. The Psalms were included in this otherwise New Testament version of the Bible, no doubt as a nod to our Old Testament heritage and most likely because Jesus was a direct descendant of the believed author of the psalms, King David.

Implicit in my childhood red-letter edition of the New Testament was a Jesus who had come to set us free from the strictures of a legalistic Judaism and to release us from the harsh chains of Old Testament law. This kind of reductionist theology was also echoed in the same Sunday school classes of my childhood, when teachers were often proud to boast,

Matthew 5:17–20

Theological Perspective

God needed instead a people through whom mercy, love, forgiveness, and faithfulness—in short, God's own righteousness—would be evident. From beginning to end, the Sermon on the Mount addresses these same questions. This passage in particular affirms the integral continuity between Israel's story and Jesus, and thus between Israel's vocation and that of Jesus' followers. The scribes and Pharisees, mentioned at the end of this passage, represent not Israel as a whole, but a particular way of forgetting Israel's distinctive vocation to strive for justice, wholeness, and reconciliation—a forgetfulness to which Christians have been no less susceptible.

A deep Protestant suspicion of "law-keeping" has led interpreters to narrow our focus in these verses to how Jesus and his followers "fulfill" Israel's law. We look for ways to wriggle out from under Jesus' apparent blanket affirmation of the law—"until all is accomplished." Some interpreters attribute this sweeping claim to Matthew, locating the evangelist at the far end of the theological spectrum from Paul's supposedly "law-free" gospel. Some hold that the law was only an interim measure until Jesus came, and was then rendered obsolete by grace. Others argue that Jesus affirms only the written law, not the oral traditions—the special interest of scribes and Pharisees—that had grown up around it over the centuries. Still others claim that Jesus upholds the "moral law," but dispenses with the ceremonial and purity laws. Even then, we have read the "moral law" selectively, highlighting, for example, teachings on sexuality while ignoring more frequent injunctions against usury. All of these approaches attempt to narrow the reach of Jesus' claims in these verses, which are nothing less than a sweeping, comprehensive affirmation that he fulfills the whole law, which continues to be valid in all its details, without restriction. Why?

The whole law, all 613 commandments, was meant to reveal to Israel—and to enable Israel to reveal to the nations—what it means to be God's people. To us it seems that keeping the law is a personal, individual matter, but for Israel, and especially for Jesus, it was the redemptive and revelatory expression of God's presence in the life of the whole people. God's aim in giving the law and prophets to Israel was not to produce a collection of heroically righteous individuals but to shape a just and faithful society that would be a light to the nations. The law was meant to create a particular kind of community, a model for how to live peaceably, justly, and faithfully with others in God's good creation—precisely what Jesus seeks to accomplish in the Sermon on

Pastoral Perspective

jurisprudence or of "tradition" in a local congregation.[1] It may be this last understanding to which Jesus is referring here.

We have all read and heard the rather dishonest and anti-Jewish explanation that "the Pharisees" had layered the essential law with trite and oppressive extraneous laws that contradicted the essence of "the law." This is dishonest, because these tendencies are not limited to "the Pharisees." Every congregation, every organized gathering of faith begins to develop traditions that can harden quickly into rules. We seem prone to develop behavioral expectations that have far more to do with our own anxieties and fears about whether we "belong." The tandem temptation is to define who does *not* belong in order to prove that we do. While I feel sure there were those in Jesus' faith community who held tight to just such extraneous traditions and saw them as "laws," I would say the same of every group to which I have ever belonged. (Just try changing one of the regular practices of the youth group in your congregation to discover how universal this temptation is. Youth can be the most conservative of groups, in my experience, precisely because of the strong emotional need of adolescents to belong.) It is our clinging to fear-filled and anxiety-motivated cultural traditions and "rules of behavior" that Jesus objects to in other powerful passages about the abuse of "law."

In every faithful gathering (including those of the Jewish faith, from which Jesus never transferred his membership) there are people filled with an authentic and passionate desire to understand how to apply faithfully the teachings of that group's ethics to real-life situations. How does a people of faith, for example, live out the gospel commitment to the poor, the hurting, the homeless, the imprisoned? Too often the desire to fit in with those around us can suppress these faithful concerns and questions. There is within our corporate responses a very real temptation to stay away from anything that might be controversial and uncomfortable. When we fall prey to the temptation to steer clear of controversy, even within our own faith communities, our faith remains blissfully irrelevant to the real world.

In many faith communities there is an equally damaging temptation to cling with arrogance to a far less liberating set of rules, expected behaviors, and beliefs that identify us as committed insiders, but that in the end only replace faith in God with

---

1. Jesus' tradition included a much stronger oral tradition than we know in contemporary Western culture, making this understanding of "the law" more like our understanding of a local tradition.

often being equated with "legalism" and contrasted with "grace."

The Torah ("Teaching of Moses") was given to Israel by God as a way of living in covenant relationship with God and with neighbor; it was how Israel (and the later Jewish community) were to distinguish themselves from Gentiles (i.e., those who did not worship the God of Israel). These commandments were seen not as a burden but, rather, as a way of reflecting, in their behavior, the kind of God that Israel served. There was never a sense that one must follow these rules in order to earn God's salvation; Israel's foundational stories (e.g., the ancestors, the exodus, etc.) show that God's steadfast love was offered freely and without consideration of merit. The Jewish community's obedience to Torah was a response to God's saving acts.

In Matthew 5:17, the pairing of *nomos* with "the prophets" is probably a reference to the first two sections of the Hebrew Bible: the Torah (first five books of the Hebrew Bible, Gen.–Deut.) and the *Nevi'im* (the second section of the Hebrew Bible, Josh.–2 Kgs.). During Jesus' lifetime, this would have constituted the whole of the Hebrew Bible. The third section, the *Ketuvim* (Writings), was not accepted as authoritative until late in the first or early second century CE.

The more difficult question is to determine the meaning of "to fulfill" (v. 17). Matthew shows that Jesus is not doing away with the Torah or the prophets, but how does he "fulfill" them? Within this Gospel, there are numerous places where the writer references prophetic texts from the Hebrew Bible as a way of showing Jesus' true identity and Jesus' continuity with Jewish tradition. Some have misunderstood these references as the Gospel writer's attempt to show that the prophets "predicted" Jesus and only Jesus.

The more appropriate understanding is that the writer's use of these citations stands within the Jewish interpretive practice of showing how an ancient text can speak to a new audience. In the eighth century BCE, Hosea was not predicting that Herod would try to kill Jesus, forcing his family to flee to Egypt, but the words of the prophet (Hos. 11:1, "Out of Egypt I have called my son") receive new meaning in the life of Jesus. When Jesus states he has come to "fulfill" the Torah and the prophets, the implication is that he will perform the commandments and further expand on their meaning, as he does for the words of the prophets.

In emphasizing the importance of the commandments, Jesus declares that anyone who attempts to "annul" one of them, and teaches others to do the

"I have never even read Leviticus or Numbers or Deuteronomy. Why should I?"

These childhood memories collide with an adult reading of this text from Matthew. In his Sermon on the Mount, Jesus does not give the audience a red-lettered pronouncement that leaves behind the witness of Hebrew Scripture. Whatever the antitheses (that follow this text in 5:21–48) mean in Matthew's Gospel, they are not intended as "replacement commandments" for the old, arcane, and outcast Mosaic law. Lest the crowd be tempted to see the antitheses as "new and better commandments," Jesus takes that option off the table in these short and intense verses. Far more than that, Jesus stresses that his teaching and life are not about diminishing the law and the prophets or abolishing them or replacing them with a new and better version, but about fulfilling them.

Matthew's Jesus leaves preachers with a direct challenge to wrestle blessing from the Hebrew law and prophets, to preach from the full canon of Scripture, and to resist the temptation to make the New Testament witness the real canon, with the Psalms a lovely traveling companion. In fact, in this text, Jesus calls those who would follow him to attend to the law and the prophets in an even more intentional and faithful way than the scribes and Pharisees do. Preachers and teachers would be well served to remember that over his thirty-two years of teaching Martin Luther devoted seven-eighths of his time to Hebrew Scripture, one-eighth to the New Testament. For preachers today, then, this text is an invitation to help Christian congregations not only feast on the Gospels and the rest of the New Testament canon, but feast on the *entire* canon of Scripture.

Again, these childhood memories collide with an adult reading of this text from Matthew. On the heels of pronouncing the Beatitudes, Matthew moves quickly to have Jesus refute any kind of Christian antinomianism. Not only does this text assert that the law and the prophets are intact for those who would follow Jesus. For Matthew's Jesus, they hold the key to entering the kingdom of heaven. As Jesus contends tenaciously here, those who follow him are set free to follow the law and the prophets in ways yet to be imagined by the religious leaders of the day, ways that lead into the reality of God's reign. Jesus himself is the "imagination" needed to interpret and to embrace fully the law and the prophets. This is a message for congregations ready to move beyond rote religiosity to engage the divine imagination, to move from a child's to an adult's reading of Scripture.

Matthew 5:17–20

Theological Perspective

the Mount, in his ministry, and especially through his death and resurrection. Jesus supplants neither the law nor Israel itself, but redeems and fulfills the intention of both.

In our rush to figure out what Jesus is saying about the law, we usually neglect the parallel claim that Jesus fulfills the prophets, which does not mean only that he fulfills particular Old Testament prophecies. More importantly, Jesus fulfills the prophetic vocation, most clearly in his willingness to suffer for the sake of God's reign. The prophetic vocation is, in fact, the focus of the material that immediately precedes this portion of the Sermon. Jesus has just warned his disciples that they too will suffer in the same way as the prophets before them (5:11–12). He then says that in fulfilling their prophetic vocation, the disciples are salt and light for the world (5:13–16). This prophetic witness is integrally related to the surpassing righteousness to which Jesus calls his disciples (5:20).

What then does it mean to practice a "righteousness" that surpasses that of the scribes and Pharisees? We often think that righteousness is a matter of being a better, nicer, more ethical person: the righteous attend church regularly, give when the offering plate is passed, avoid common vices, and treat others kindly—essentially a pale version of what the scribes and Pharisees were devoted to. For Jesus, however, righteousness is concerned with mercy, forgiveness, and, most of all, justice—the practices that have been the focus of the Beatitudes (5:3–11) and that will be illustrated in a variety of ways in the "antitheses" (5:21–48) that immediately follow this section. This righteousness is the sum of our relationships, restored to their God-intended blessedness, completed by mercy and grace. This righteousness surpasses because it seeks above all else the restoration of whole and just relationships.

Does God need individuals who outdo the scribes and Pharisees in moral purity and rectitude? Does God need people who pursue the kind of morality that divides the world into the righteous and the unrighteous? Does God need people whose sense of righteousness denies the reality of grace? Does not God, rather, need a people whose righteousness consists of mercy, love of neighbors and enemies, and relationships made whole?

STANLEY P. SAUNDERS

Pastoral Perspective

something idolatrous. We think it necessary to affirm this political cause, that mission emphasis, or this cultural practice or perspective, in order to conform to patterns of our social group and to be seen as faithful to the teachings of Jesus. That one must dress up for worship in order to show proper respect and reverence for God is far more cultural than biblical. The kind of music one uses in order to praise God says far more about one's cultural background than one's faithfulness or lack thereof. What reality one names as God is usually shaped in light of our prejudices and preconceptions, whereas God is, in reality, bigger than any one community's way of conceiving and naming God. When we regard our political and social opinions as if they were essential laws of God, we unwittingly dedicate ourselves to the things "of this world," as Paul put it, which by definition fail to transcend messy human reality and always fall short of God's saving grace.

We are saved by grace alone. Only when our salvation is assured by God's unconditional love can we truly respond with an authentic love of our own. Otherwise we remain trapped in our fears and the desire to placate the gods of our multitudinous anxieties. Having been saved by grace, however, we cannot separate our faithful response to the divine love from a desire to share the gospel in word and deed. The English word we translate as "gospel" is, in the Greek, *euangelion*, which means "good news" or "glad tidings" of the great joy that is God's love of all and expectation of justice for all. As Jesus so rightly points out in this powerful passage, only when the law of divine love is fulfilled and its command that we treat both stranger and friend with justice and love obeyed, will God bring about the liberation for all that God has promised (and we have glimpsed) through the life and witness of Christ.

BARBARA BLAISDELL

same, "will be called least in the kingdom of heaven" (v. 19a). The opposite will be true for those who observe and teach the commandments. It is interesting that even those who break the commandments are part of the "kingdom of heaven." Jesus, however, also states that "unless your righteousness exceeds that of the scribes and Pharisees, you will never enter the kingdom of heaven" (v. 20). These seem like contradictory claims.

What is the "kingdom of heaven," and who gets to be a part of it? In Matthew, the "kingdom of heaven" is synonymous with the "kingdom of God." This "kingdom" is not a geographical region or heavenly abode, but a reality brought into being by Jesus and still evolving. It includes those who acknowledge God as sovereign and follow the Torah, as exemplified in the life of Jesus. Although the Gospel writer seems to be arguing against those who claim that Jesus "abolished" the Torah, she/he ultimately does not condemn these opponents as being outside of the "kingdom of heaven." When Jesus addresses the crowd (including those in Matthew's audience), however, he declares that they are held to a higher standard than even those who know the Torah intimately and claim to be strict adherents to it (i.e., the "scribes and Pharisees").

In the sections that follow, Jesus will expand on the meaning of this "higher standard" to which his followers are held. Employing Jewish methods of interpretation common in first-century Judaism, Jesus will acknowledge some of the important commandments (re: murder, adultery, divorce, etc.) and provide an intensified expectation for their fulfillment. In Matthew, Jesus addresses not only the prohibited behaviors but also their root causes (e.g., anger, lust). The dominant tradition in the Christian interpretation of Matthew 5:21–48 has labeled these six sections as "antitheses," claiming that Jesus was contradicting or superseding the Torah. Jesus' expansions of the commandments, however, fall within the broader conversations and teachings taking place in the Jewish communities at that time.

LISA WILSON DAVISON

In the worship services of some of the Reformation churches, the Ten Commandments were a regular part of the spoken or sung liturgy. John Calvin and other Protestant Reformers did not contrast the teaching of Jesus with the Ten Commandments, but saw in Jesus the fulfillment of the Commandments, the lens through which they were to be understood and embraced. Jesus thus invites preachers to reclaim and proclaim the witness of the Ten Commandments, as well as the whole of Hebrew Scripture.

To embrace the challenging words of Jesus in Matthew 5:17–20 means resisting two extremes often heard in Christian pulpits. We must resist, first, preaching a red-letter Christianity that understands itself to be the new and improved, replacement people of God. Then we must avoid contenting ourselves with wooden and literal readings that fail to engage Hebrew Scripture from the perspective of the life and witness of Jesus.

Matthew's Gospel will continue to challenge readers, not only to embrace Hebrew Scripture, but to push deeper to discern the true intent of the law. A quick, careless reading of this passage could lead some preachers to pit the Old Testament righteousness of the Pharisees and scribes against the New Testament righteousness of Jesus and his followers. A more careful, nuanced, and constructive reading affirms that "Jesus is not calling his hearers to determine how righteous the scribes and Pharisees are and then to do them one better. . . . No, the followers of Jesus are called to a different *kind* of righteousness, a righteousness that seeks to be ever expressive of the merciful, forgiving, reconciling will of God that lies at the center of the law."[1]

Preachers, take this text into your study, chew on these words until any anti-Judaism taste has disappeared from your mouth. Now taste the exquisite gospel promise awaiting those who wrestle with these words from Jesus. Then go preach!

GARY W. CHARLES

1. Thomas G. Long, *Matthew*, Westminster Bible Companion (Louisville, KY: Westminster John Knox Press, 1997), 54.

Matthew 5:21–26

²¹"You have heard that it was said to those of ancient times, 'You shall not murder'; and 'whoever murders shall be liable to judgment.' ²²But I say to you that if you are angry with a brother or sister, you will be liable to judgment; and if you insult a brother or sister, you will be liable to the council; and if you say, 'You fool,' you will be liable to the hell of fire. ²³So when you are offering your gift at the altar, if you remember that your brother or sister has something against you, ²⁴leave your gift there before the altar and go; first be reconciled to your brother or sister, and then come and offer your gift. ²⁵Come to terms quickly with your accuser while you are on the way to court with him, or your accuser may hand you over to the judge, and the judge to the guard, and you will be thrown into prison. ²⁶Truly I tell you, you will never get out until you have paid the last penny."

Theological Perspective

Jesus now offers the first of six antitheses in which he takes up and interprets anew an old accepted teaching based on the Law of Moses. He is not replacing the older teaching with something new. Jesus has asserted moments before (5:17) that his teaching is neither a replacement nor an abolishment of Moses' law, but rather a new interpretation—a reclaiming or realization, if you will—that focuses on the original intent of Moses' law.

Jesus frames these teachings as a polemic, "You have heard that it was said . . . but I say to you . . ." This polemic is the basis for understanding the distinction between the righteousness of the scribes and Pharisees and the surpassing righteousness to which Jesus calls us to aspire in verse 20. Followers of Jesus accomplish this surpassing righteousness when they strive for restored, reconciled relationships, rooted in justice and immersed in God's grace.

This kind of righteousness is impossible for those who are focused merely on their own standing before God or their personal sense of merit in comparison to other people. There is no way to achieve this righteousness as an individual in isolation from others, for the very attempt to establish one's own (self-)righteousness leads inevitably to the alienation, divisiveness, and even violence that Jesus ascribes to those who oppose his way. This is as hard a lesson

Pastoral Perspective

Jesus was a rabbi, steeped in the rabbinic tradition that seeks wisdom through the very public forum of debate, conversation that speaks and listens to contrasting views. Jesus and his collegial rabbis would have debated the fuller meaning of such passages from the Hebrew Scriptures as "Death and life are in the power of the tongue" (Prov. 18:21a) and "Which of you desires life, and covets many days to enjoy good? Keep your tongue from evil, and your lips from speaking deceit" (Ps. 34:12–13). The teachings of Christ in Matthew 5 were not offered so that we could claim that Christianity is superior to Judaism (or the Christian superior to the scribe or the Pharisee or any other human being). Indeed, to do that is to violate the heart of Christ's teaching here. When we judge others more harshly than we want to be judged, or see in others worse motives than we are able to see in ourselves, we damage our souls and put ourselves in peril of being unable to grow and mature either in our moral character or in our practice of faith.

When God placed the Decalogue before that straggling, struggling band of recently released slaves, God was offering a hedge against the worst of human behavior. When we reflect on the Ten Commandments at any depth, however, those with eyes to see discover that God is also offering in those

Exegetical Perspective

This is the first of six sections within the Sermon on the Mount where the writer of Matthew portrays Jesus expanding some commandments of the Torah. For a primarily Jewish audience, the Gospel of Matthew demonstrates how Jesus was of the Davidic lineage, a faithful follower of Torah, and that his teachings were consistent with the traditions of the Jewish community. More specifically, this portion of the Sermon on the Mount (5:21–48) paints Jesus as a "new" Moses, delivering his teaching (*torah*) from a mountaintop. The preceding section (5:17–20) provides the setup for Jesus' expositions on the commandments. The Gospel writer argues against the competing claim that Jesus did away with the Torah and thus his followers were no longer expected to follow the commandments. In contrast, Jesus not only declares the validity of the Torah; he intensifies the requirements of some commandments. This move by Jesus is consistent with the broader interpretive practices at work in the Jewish community during the first century CE.

While scholars debate which teachings in these six sections actually are the words of Jesus, most agree that the writer of Matthew has provided the literary framework for each expansion on the Torah. All but one (vv. 31–32) begin with the introductory phrase, "You have heard that it was said [to those of

Homiletical Perspective

Preachers are stewards of words. Good preachers never forget the nature of this stewardship. They are entrusted with words intended to give life, shape identity, inspire justice, and resound with praise to God. This brief but pointed passage from Jesus' Sermon on the Mount challenges preachers not simply to be good stewards of words, but, of equal importance, to be careful interpreters of Scripture.

In this text, Matthew's Jesus gives the first example of his claim that he has come to fulfill the law (5:17). He focuses on the commandments about killing/murder as set forth in Exodus 20:13 and Deuteronomy 5:17. Preachers and congregations must occasionally deal with murder and its devastating consequences to a Christian community. Far more frequently, however, they must face the devastating consequences of murderous behavior and attitudes that result from shallow worship and alienated relationships within the community.

No doubt worship would come to a screeching halt if Matthew 5:21–26 were the call to worship that opened each service. The world may know "we are Christians by our love," but even a brief tour of church history reveals that anger, rage, and embittered judgments are also well earned and are far less flattering identity marks for the church. Given how hard it is to live lovingly in any Christian community

Theological Perspective

for modern Christians to learn as it was for the scribes and Pharisees in Jesus' audience.

Everyone understood that one should not murder. The taking of a human life was wrong (sin), and the penalty for that was strict (Lev. 24:17). Jesus says in verse 22, however, that even anger and insults directed toward a brother or sister render one liable to judgment, even to the judgment of "the hell of fire." Jesus is posing a powerful ethical question: how can you make sacrifice upon the altar of God while harboring anger, malice, and even insulting words in your heart? Jesus then goes on to radicalize even this challenging teaching. Even if you do not harbor something in your own heart against a brother or sister, if you remember that someone has something against you, you are to reconcile with that person before coming to the altar.

The priority here is clear: right relationship with God is predicated upon having a right relationship with your neighbor(s). Jesus' teaching challenges not only the scribes and Pharisees of his day, but religious people, even Christians today, who focus exclusively on their personal relationship with God to the neglect of others, as if we could have a relationship with God apart from our relationship with our neighbors. Here Jesus teaches us that the relationship with one (God) is predicated upon the relationship with the other (neighbor).

How striking it must have been for those first witnesses to have heard Jesus say, "Leave your gift there before the altar and go; first be reconciled to your brother or sister" (v. 24). What a radical concept that must have been to those first witnesses! Jesus is clearly making a very important point: anger and malice in one's heart are cancers that over time will metastasize and grow, and can be deadly both to those holding the anger and to those against whom the anger is directed. It is deadly to the individual holding the anger because, in the words of Martin Luther King, it distorts the personality.[1] It can destroy the very center of your creative response to both life and the universe. It is deadly toward the persons to whom the anger is directed because anger festered and metastasized turns to vengeance and seeks ways of expression that are destructive. These destructive things may be hidden within the heart of the individual and masked by the outward appearance of piety when one makes sacrifice. Jesus calls us to be sure our outward piety matches our inward

Pastoral Perspective

commandments a vision of what the best of humanity can attain. In today's passage, Christ quotes the sixth commandment (Exod. 20:13) and then shows us the depth of that commandment and the height and breadth of God's hope for us, saying, "You have heard that it was said to those of ancient times, 'You shall not murder'; and 'whoever murders shall be liable to judgment.' But I say to you that if you are angry with a brother or sister, you will be liable to judgment" (vv. 21–22a). This is not a replacement of the commandment against murder. It is a searing insight into all that God desires for and from us: that we refrain not only from killing but from nursing the anger that also kills. As it is written in 1 John 3:14–15: "We know that we have passed from death to life because we love one another. Whoever does not love abides in death. All who hate a brother or sister are murderers; and you know that murderers do not have eternal life abiding in them."

To nurse anger is to kill divine love. To kill love is to kill our human capacity to love. When our hearts are clenched in anger, they are shut tight against love. We have only one heart, so a clenched heart is also clenched against God and the healing God provides. Jesus shows a deep and abiding respect for what the human spirit can attain, both in goodness and in evil, when he goes on to give an example of anger that kills: "If you insult a brother or sister, you will be liable to the council; and if you say, 'You fool,' you will be liable to the hell of fire" (v. 22b). When we insult another and call another names, we not only nurse our own anger; we help birth a soul-killing anger in the person we verbally abuse. This teaching is consistent with Genesis 1 and John 1 in claiming that words have power, the power to create and the power to destroy. Indeed, Christ as much as says, "*Words kill!*"[1]

What is the prophylactic to fight the murderous power of angry words? Before we approach God in worship, before we offer praise or prayer or song or sacrifice, we are to go to anyone who might have something against us and seek reconciliation. Is anything harder than deliberately seeking out someone with whom we have had a conflict? Why does Christ ask so much from us? It is because we each have only this one heart.

If our whole heart has not been offered to God, if we keep some part of it back, so that we can hold onto our anger, then God does not want our

1. See Martin Luther King's sermon, "Loving Your Enemies," November 17, 1957: http://mlk-kpp01.stanford.edu/index.php/encyclopedia/documentsentry/doc_loving_your_enemies/.

1. See R & B artist Dave Barnes's powerful lyric at http://www.stlyrics.com/songs/d/davebarnes18573/sticksandstones846049.html; accessed October 23, 2012.

ancient times] . . . but I say to you . . ." (vv. 21, 27, 33, 38, 43). This was a common pattern in rabbinic teaching; a biblical text would be cited, along with its traditional interpretation, and then a new meaning given for that text. In the same way, Jesus introduces a commandment and then gives an explanation of what more is required.

These six verses actually address three different situations. First, Jesus quotes the commandment, "You shall not murder" (Exod. 20:13), adding the consequence for this act, "whoever murders shall be liable to judgment" (possible paraphrase of Exod. 21:12 or Lev. 24:17, etc.). Then Jesus expands this prohibition to include anger and verbal violence, both insults (the meaning of the Greek word *raca* is unclear) and name-calling (v. 22). Each of these additions carries a more intense punishment; one who insults another person will face the "council," and one who calls another person "fool" is "liable to the hell of fire." What the NRSV has translated as "council" is most likely a reference to the Sanhedrin, the Jewish high council in Jerusalem, and "hell of fire" is the rendering of "fires of Gehenna," a reference to the Hebrew word *ge-hinnom*, a valley south of Jerusalem that was linked with the practice of child sacrifice by the followers of Molech (see 2 Kgs. 23:10 and Jer. 7:31). After the Hebrew Bible was written, Gehenna became associated with a place where dead people go to suffer for their sins.

Jesus addresses the motivation for murder (anger) and the possible escalation of behaviors (e.g., verbal abuse) that could lead to murder. One should not read this passage as a condemnation of anger by Jesus, who also is portrayed as getting angry. The emotion is not, in and of itself, a sin; it is what one does with anger that matters. Unexpressed anger can do harm either to the person harboring the emotion or to the object of that person's anger. Matthew's Jewish audience might recall the story of Cain and Abel (Gen. 4), in which God asked Cain what he was going to do with his anger and warned that, if Cain did not get control of his emotions, "sin" (perhaps violence) "is lurking at the door" (Gen. 4:7). While verbal abuse is certainly less violent than murder, Jesus teaches that such language dehumanizes other persons, making it easier to mistreat them.

In the second part of this section, Jesus moves from the abstract to a specific situation. "When you are offering your gift at the altar, if you remember that your brother or sister has something against you," go and reconcile with her or him before making the offering (vv. 23–24). While one might think

and how easy it is for misunderstanding within community to lead to anger and estrangement, should Jesus not have been satisfied that people were coming to the altar at all? Is Jesus not pushing the worship of God beyond any reasonable limit when he insists that the angry worshiper do an about-face and make amends with her or his estranged sister or brother before giving a gift to God?

Jesus must have preached many sermons and taught his disciples even more than we hear in the Sermon on the Mount. So why did Matthew include these particular verses? After all, what church in any era could survive if it required its members to be reconciled with estranged neighbors, spouses, business partners, and declared enemies before worship could begin? Why is Jesus not satisfied when worshipers obey the commandment not to murder? Later in Matthew's Gospel, Jesus himself will have religious leaders breathing down his neck, resisting his teaching, challenging his authority, and insulting his integrity. By the close of this Gospel, if anyone has cause to nurture righteous anger, it is Jesus. If anyone has good cause not to suffer fools gladly, it is Jesus. So why does Jesus insist—foolishly it seems— that worshipers deal with anger or rage before coming to worship and bringing their gifts to God?

Archbishop Desmond Tutu has spent a lifetime, not only listening to Jesus, but arguing that this part of Jesus' Sermon on the Mount is anything but nonsensible and nonachievable piety; it is, in fact, the unfailing path to redemption and new life. Tutu argues:

> True reconciliation is based on forgiveness, and forgiveness is based on true confession, and confession is based on penitence, on contrition, on sorrow for what you have done. . . . Only together, hand in hand, as God's family and not as one another's enemy, can we ever hope to end the vicious cycle of revenge and retribution.[1]

Throughout his service on the Truth and Reconciliation Commission in South Africa, Tutu drew on the wisdom of Jesus in today's text to differentiate vengeance from justice. Tutu recognizes that the judgment to which Jesus refers in this text is not a call for vengeance, not a call for preachers to wave Bibles and wag fingers and threaten congregations with the fiery flames of hell. It is a call for preachers to look again at the remarkable and inexplicable

---

1. Desmond Tutu, *God Has a Dream* (New York: Doubleday, 2004), 53, 58.

Matthew 5:21–26

Theological Perspective

piety. The place where God dwells with us must be pure; so Jesus tells us to leave our sacrifice and go, be reconciled with our neighbor(s).

It is in actions directed toward reconciliation with neighbors and even enemies (5:38–48) that our righteousness rises above the usually self-interested practice of religion—religion that people believe in, instead of loving God and neighbor. The act of reconciliation is an extension of the grace that God has extended to us. God has reached out to us with grace in order to bring reconciliation in our broken relationship. From the grace, through which we are reconciled with God, flow the grace we extend to others and the grace in which we are reconciled one to another. We are called to offer forgiveness to those who have angered and wronged us and to seek forgiveness from those we have wronged. The importance of this is very clear: God's grace and forgiveness come first, but our ongoing experience of that grace is dependent in turn on our sharing it with others (cf. 6:14–15). Grace that is interrupted, no longer passed along, is no longer grace.

Jesus' orientation to the law is both ethical and social; it calls us into a right relationship with our neighbors as an essential element of being in right relationship with God. So it is not enough to say that we have never murdered anyone; rather, we must be wary of whatever we hold in our hearts that displaces and denies the grace of God at work in the lives of others as it is in our own. When we do discover the wrong, whether in what has been done to us or what we have done to others, we must leave our sacrifices—our acts of worship and celebration—at our altars and seek to be reconciled with our neighbors. We do so, not only because Jesus commands us to do so, but because the denial of God's grace at work in "the other" ultimately chokes and denies the power of God's grace in our own lives. Forgiveness, reconciliation, and grace are not merely experiences of the individual's heart, but the experiences and practices by which we bear witness to God's transformation of the world.

REGINALD BROADNAX

Pastoral Perspective

sacrificial service or our songs. Nor does God desire our prayers and praise if we will not give our whole heart to the divine Love first. There is no placating the God who is and was and shall forever be Love; no bargaining by saying, "God, I'll increase my pledge this year, or I'll offer to teach Sunday school or promise to preach better sermons, but let me hold on to my anger, my bitterness, and my unwillingness to forgive."

Jesus teaches something approximating this: if you hold onto your bitterness and anger, then the bitter, ungenerous judgment you have meted out will be the same bitterness and ungenerous judgment that comes back to you. In contrast, however, if you work at giving your whole heart to God, there will be room only for generosity, for thinking the best of people until proven otherwise, for offering forgiveness when someone has acted less than the best. When our whole hearts are given to God, we are honest enough to know that—if not at this very moment, then soon—we will be the ones in need of forgiveness.

The gospel is that God has given us, in Christ, God's whole heart first. In him we behold that God's heart is not clenched against us. The forgiveness God asks of us has already been given to us in the one who is speaking. Now think about that brother or sister in Christ with whom you may be at odds, at odds for reasons trivial or profound. Do you realize what Jesus is saying to us? He is asking that we comprehend the true force of the commandment and apply it with its full force to that person from whom we are alienated. Christ also promises that in so doing, our hearts will grow more flexible and strong for this rigorous exercise of forgiveness and an all-inclusive love.

BARBARA BLAISDELL

Feasting on the Gospels

Exegetical Perspective

that Jesus is speaking specifically about temple worship, this is not necessarily the case. Jesus is addressing a Galilean audience. Their access to the temple in Jerusalem would have been severely limited, due to both geography (ability to make the trip to Jerusalem) and religious restrictions (only the priests received offerings and made sacrifices at the temple altar). In addition, the date of composition for Matthew (post-70 CE, after the destruction of the Second Temple by the Romans) would mean that the Gospel writer's intended audience would not be worshiping at the temple. It seems more likely that Jesus is referring to altars in local shrines, which were more accessible to the laity.

The importance of reconciling with another human, before one could be reconciled with God, was already present among Jewish teachings, especially in relation to the Day of Atonement. Jesus, in line with many of Israel's prophets (Amos, Micah, etc.), is acknowledging that it is impossible to worship God with integrity if we are not in right relationship with our neighbors.

In verse 25, a legal scenario is introduced in which one person owes another a debt. Jesus advises his followers that it is better to settle "out of court" than to face the legal system and its possible repercussions. A dispute between two people about a debt can be addressed through dialogue, and arrangements for repayment can be negotiated. Once the judge gets involved, however, the required punishments for breach of an agreement go into effect. If the plaintiff wins her or his case, then the law requires that the accused be put in jail until the debt can be paid (v. 26). Of course, being imprisoned makes it nearly impossible for the person to repay the amount owed, unless a relative or friend provides the necessary money. Jesus has made the case for why his followers should make every effort to reconcile (whatever the problem may be) with their sister or brother before things go too far, resulting in violence and/or punishment.

LISA WILSON DAVISON

Homiletical Perspective

ways in which God administers judgment and to proclaim the merciful judgment of God far and wide.

Tom Long, another preacher who cares deeply about the intersection of justice and worship, judgment and compassion, offers a related angle of vision into this passage. Long writes:

> Judgment is God's repairing of the broken creation. Judgment is God's scalpel carefully removing the malignant tissue that threatens life. Judgment is God's burning away of all that is cruel and spirit killing in order that we may breathe the air of compassion. Judgment is good news; it is God setting things right.[2]

This text gives preachers a chance to refresh the congregation's theological imagination around God's good and merciful judgment. It gives preachers compelling gospel words about a God who does more—and expects more—than that we merely patch or repair relationships that have been damaged or broken. This God makes all things new, no matter how damaged or broken the relationship.

In addition, this text invites and urges preachers to remind congregations that worship is tied integrally to ethics. Reconciliation is not an impossible ideal toward which Jesus encourages us to strive, doing the best that we can. It is the foundation upon which genuine worship and authentic relationships are founded. Praise of God will always ring hollow when colored by rage against our neighbor. Writing to a Christian community some years later than Matthew, the author of the Johannine epistles makes a similar, if not even more pointed, appeal: "Those who say, 'I love God,' and hate their brothers or sisters, are liars; for those who do not love a brother or sister whom they have seen, cannot love God whom they have not seen" (1 John 4:20).

In a world that continues to build walls of division and to sow seeds of divisive rhetoric, this passage calls forth preachers who are careful interpreters of Scripture and true stewards of the gospel words that renew worship, seek reconciliation, and restore sanity within and beyond the church.

GARY W. CHARLES

2. Thomas G. Long, *Matthew,* Westminster Bible Companion (Louisville, KY: Westminster John Knox Press, 1997), 56.

Matthew 5:27–32

27"You have heard that it was said, 'You shall not commit adultery.' 28But I say to you that everyone who looks at a woman with lust has already committed adultery with her in his heart. 29If your right eye causes you to sin, tear it out and throw it away; it is better for you to lose one of your members than for your whole body to be thrown into hell. 30And if your right hand causes you to sin, cut it off and throw it away; it is better for you to lose one of your members than for your whole body to go into hell.

31"It was also said, 'Whoever divorces his wife, let him give her a certificate of divorce.' 32But I say to you that anyone who divorces his wife, except on the ground of unchastity, causes her to commit adultery; and whoever marries a divorced woman commits adultery."

Theological Perspective

Perhaps more than any other people before us, our imaginations are saturated with desire. Desire drives our economy. Advertising, books and magazines, movies, television, all create a climate of desire for both things and persons, often mingling the two. Images of glamorous, sexy people are used to sell products, everything from cars to plumbing fixtures, especially things that we do not really need. If we buy this product, we are told, we will surely be like the glossy, happy people portrayed next to the product. In this climate of desire, we measure our status and self-worth by our ability to possess these idealized objects, whether products or people, rather than by the character and quality of our relationships.

How radically different are the words of Jesus. In this passage, Jesus deals with two related commandments, one focused on adultery and one on divorce. Both refer to transgressions of our most important social relationships. Both topics were also used metaphorically in the prophetic tradition to describe Israel's idolatrous transgressions of the covenant with God. The seventh of the Ten Commandments is clear: "You shall not commit adultery" (Exod. 20:14). This commandment goes beyond just marital and sexual purity; it aims also to protect the lineage and inheritance rights of fathers to sons. Numbers 5 gives an elaborate and disturbing ritual for determining

Pastoral Perspective

In twenty-first-century American culture, where so many marriages end in divorce, is there anything more difficult to hear than Christ's teaching on adultery and divorce? However, Jesus' teaching is not offered in order to shame us. It is given from the mouth of the One who would not let anything kill his love for us—not human anger, not human folly, not human hatred against the world and other humans, not our very real willingness to kill one another, even those whose only offense is that they refuse to share in our moral folly, frailty, and fratricide. No, this teaching is offered not to shame but to lure and lead us, to help us imagine that we, who are so morally fragile, might find a more loving way to live.

Jesus' teaching is likewise not intended to "better" the teachings of Judaism. Indeed, what Jesus calls for in these verses falls well within the highest standards of rabbinic moral thought. The Talmud teachings on marriage state, "One who gazes lustfully upon the small finger of a married woman, it is as if he has committed adultery with her."[1]

What then shall we say to this troubling teaching: looking with lust equals adultery, and divorce is hated by God?[2] Can we begin honestly to confess

1. *Kallah* 1, in H. L. Strack and P. Billerbeck, *Kommentar zum Neuen Testament aus Talmud und Midrasch* (Munich: Beck, 1926), 1:299.
2. Malachi 2:16a: "I hate divorce, says the LORD, the God of Israel."

Exegetical Perspective

This section of Matthew's Sermon on the Mount (vv. 27–32) contains two of Jesus' six expansions on the Torah, covering adultery (vv. 27–30) and divorce (vv. 31–32). Like the preceding expansion (5:21–26), the discussion of adultery opens with a frame provided by the writer of Matthew ("You have heard that it was said . . . ," v. 27), but the text dealing with divorce has an abbreviated form: "It was also said . . ." (v. 31). This gives the impression that perhaps these last two verses have been tacked on to the primary expansion on the commandment against adultery. Both sections are linked by the topic of adultery and what constitutes this prohibited behavior.

It is important first to understand the socio-historical context of the commandment that Jesus quotes: "You shall not commit adultery" (Exod. 20:14). In ancient Israel, women were considered the property of men: of their father prior to betrothal/marriage and then of their betrothed/husband. Adultery was understood as a betrothed or married woman having sexual intercourse with a man other than her betrothed/husband. One intent of the law prohibiting adultery was to protect the paternity of any children the woman might produce, but a deeper concern was that the "other" man had trespassed on the property of the betrothed/husband. Jesus affirms the commandment and then expands it to prohibit

Homiletical Perspective

Adultery. Lust. Plucking out an eye to avoid boarding the express train to hell. Divorce certificates from husbands to wives. Wives who are deemed adulteresses by holding a divorce certificate. Men who commit adultery by marrying a divorced woman. Preachers, welcome to Matthew 5:27–32!

Many passages within the Sermon on the Mount are delights awaiting a deft homiletical hand. This is not one of them. These words from Jesus are charged with theological and pastoral land mines. It is no surprise then that there are few sermons preached on Matthew 5:27–32, and even then this passage is often "preached against."

Former President Jimmy Carter was widely ridiculed when, citing this text, he said that he had lusted in his heart. If adultery is considered only a matter of physical actions, then many can claim to be fully obedient to the Mosaic law. When adultery is understood to be also a matter of the heart, as President Carter well understood, following this commandment is far more complex and challenging.

This passage sounds a deafening alarm across the centuries to a modern society that markets sensuality and specializes in titillating sexual exploits. How many women are abused annually because this warning from Jesus is dismissed as puritanical nonsense? How many marriages are destroyed annually

Matthew 5:27–32

Theological Perspective

whether a woman has committed adultery. Thus narrowly defined, adultery concerns the sexual act itself. As long as one has not committed the actual sexual act, one neither has broken the commandment nor is in danger of judgment.

This, however, is not sufficient for Jesus and his followers. Jesus tells his disciples that even lust or desire for a woman is tantamount to committing the act of adultery itself. It is not sufficient to say that one has never committed adultery; for if one has lusted or had a desire for another, then he or she also has committed adultery. Lust and desire linger in the heart. Jesus' teachings invite us to consider what is really within our hearts, for if our hearts are not clean, our actions will not be either. He also effectively levels the playing field of judgment. Often our judgment of others gives rise to a sense of our own superiority. According to Jesus, even those who have only lusted or harbored desire are just as guilty as those who have committed the act itself. It is not only the act of adultery itself, but the lust and desire that precede it, that are idolatrous, that turn others into objects to be possessed and consumed, and thus rupture our relationships with both God and those around us. To follow Jesus, we must live counter to the desires our culture dictates to us. To follow Jesus, we can never "conform to this world."

In the Sermon on the Mount, Jesus is calling his disciples to a surpassing righteousness rooted in just relationships. Jesus employs two hyperbolic images concerning the eye and the hand to underscore the threat that idolatrous desire poses to the pursuit of righteousness. The eye—the right one is usually understood as the dominant one—symbolizes perception and thus the source of desire. The right hand symbolizes the strength by which we take what we desire. Better to lose these than lose one's whole body. Jesus is not advocating literal dismemberment. The theological question is this: What brings wholeness and just relationships? Are wholeness and righteousness accomplished by taking possession of the things, including people, that our culture tells us we need in order to be whole? Is there another way?

Jesus' discussion of divorce (vv. 31–32) continues to focus on the ideal of whole and just relationships. The law of Moses gives a man the right to divorce his wife (Deut. 24:1–4). He did not need to give any substantial reason for the divorce, but only to write her a letter of divorcement. This gave undue power to the husband and often left the woman destitute, without means of support if she could not return to the home of either her father or her eldest brother.

Pastoral Perspective

that no one, least of all ourselves, has managed a life free from failure in this regard? Even those who are happily married stretch all credibility if they claim they have never looked with sexual longing, even briefly, at someone other than their spouse. Many good people who join with God in hating divorce find themselves nevertheless deciding to divorce—not as a good thing, but perhaps as the least bad of the alternatives available. Given this honesty, we would do well to remember that we have been saved by grace, because none of us has managed to live up to the unconditional love of God and neighbor.

So we come before the throne of God on our knees, confessing our sin, our foibles and failures. Relying on the love and grace of God to receive and forgive us, we are set free from who we have been so that we might live into our future as forgiven Christians, that is, as people who just may be more forgiving than we have been able to be in our past. This is true for all Christian teaching, by the way. Whenever we would claim to have the moral high ground, we deceive ourselves and deny that we live by grace. We live better than we might otherwise live due only to the liberating forgiveness of God. Reinhold Niebuhr has famously and richly argued in *The Irony of American History*:

> Nothing that is worth doing can be achieved in our lifetime; therefore, we must be saved by hope. Nothing which is true, or beautiful, or good, makes complete sense in any immediate context of history; therefore, we must be saved by faith. Nothing we do, however virtuous, could be accomplished alone; therefore, we must be saved by love. No virtuous act is quite as virtuous from the standpoint of our friend or foe as it is from our own standpoint; therefore, we must be saved by the final form of love, which is forgiveness.[3]

I would argue that amid culture wars and religious wars and the valuing of self-esteem over self-awareness, self-entitlement over honesty and authenticity, we should bind Niebuhr's words on our foreheads, tie them to our hands, and place them on the doorposts of our houses. If we passed these words every day, if we looked at the world through them, as if in a phylactery, they were tied to the hands we write with, I for one would be required to be a bit more humble, a little less certain, a bit more willing to listen to God and to those who share this beautiful blue planet floating in space.

3. Reinhold Niebuhr, *The Irony of American History* (New York: Charles Scribner's Sons, 1953, Kindle Edition), 63.

looking at a woman "with lust" (v. 28). As in the previous example, here the Gospel writer portrays Jesus as moving beyond an act (committing adultery) to a motivation (lust).

Jesus' prohibition of "lust" was not a new idea in Jewish thought; lust was a concern in the Hebrew Bible. The Greek word translated as "lust" can also mean "covet," and it is the same word used in the Septuagint (the Greek translation of the Hebrew Bible) for the tenth commandment: "You shall not covet your neighbor's house; you shall not covet your neighbor's wife . . ." (Exod. 20:17). This last commandment also addresses motivation; if you covet what someone else has, object or human, it could lead to one of the behaviors proscribed in the preceding commandments (e.g., murder, stealing, adultery). The Greek phrasing for Jesus' expansion has the sense of looking "with the purpose of lust." The idea is not that one may not look at a woman and admire her beauty, or that a husband may not look at his wife with desire. What is prohibited is looking at another man's betrothed/wife with the purpose of lust, which could lead to the "taking" of the woman to satisfy one's own desires.

The punishment for adultery was death for both the woman and the man (see Lev. 20:10). What is the punishment for lust? Jesus commands that the organ responsible for looking "with the purpose of lust" (the eye) should be removed from the body, along with the part that would be used in taking the object of lust (the hand). The commands to gouge out the eye or cut off a limb are also found in Matthew 18:8–9, where the Gospel writer includes cutting off the foot as well as the hand, anything that "causes you to stumble." Matthew's source is the parallel text in Mark 9:43–47, but only in Matthew 5:29–30 are these commands to remove offending body parts connected to lust. Although there was precedent for this kind of punishment by amputation, Jesus is probably using hyperbole to drive home the seriousness of adultery and lust.

The final two verses of this section, along with the text in Matthew 19:3–9, have produced heated debates over the centuries about whether Jesus prohibited divorce and remarriage. We will only deal with verses 31–32, but this passage must be understood in the context of the whole book. Jesus here takes up a topic not covered in the Ten Commandments. The Gospel writer portrays Jesus as quoting some known text: "Whoever divorces his wife, let him give her a certificate of divorce." While no explicit command like this is found in the Torah,

because partners underestimate the devastating power of lust? What if preachers were to engage this text and then speak honestly and forcefully against many of the self-indulgent and destructive sexual and marital practices so prevalent in society? How many preachers must remain silent, lest it be found out that Jesus' words expose their own broken lives?

The jarring and violent image of tearing out an offending eye is a hyperbole, not intended to be taken literally, but intended to be taken nonetheless with utter seriousness. It would be easy to chastise Jesus, or Matthew, for using such violent hyperbole. Better, though, that we should thank Jesus and Matthew for reminding us of how devastating uncontrolled sexual desire and behavior can be. Whether adultery is understood as sexual impulse or as a matter of property theft as in antiquity, existing relationships are cast aside and people around us are cast aside, reduced to objects or possessions to be used or collected. That deprives everyone, perpetrator and victims alike, of their humanity. Therefore, this hyperbole is not a nice morality lesson on "safe sex," but a call to understand the power and responsibility of being sexual beings in faithful relationship with another and the violence and horrors that inevitably ensue when covenant relationships are violated.

The final verses in this passage only get more difficult. How do preachers who themselves lust and who are themselves divorced preach this text to congregations filled with those who lust and are divorced? Jesus' teaching here is based on Deuteronomy 24:1: "Suppose a man enters into marriage with a woman, but she does not please him because he finds something objectionable about her, and so he writes her a certificate of divorce, puts it in her hand, and sends her out of his house." Deuteronomy clearly assumes the privileged position of the male in the relationship, viewing the woman as a male's property. By requiring a "writ of divorce," Deuteronomy seeks to mitigate some of the abuses women experienced in the patriarchal structures of ancient Hebrew society, but it does nothing to challenge or overturn the patriarchal structures themselves.

How does Jesus engage this ancient ethic? His response does implicitly challenge patriarchal assumptions by implying that God's will is not for divorce, even under carefully structured legal guidelines, but for the preservation of faithful relationships (see this argued more explicitly in 19:3–9). The priority of maintaining faithful relationships, an image central to the relationship between God and Israel, fundamentally undermines both divorce and

Matthew 5:27–32

Theological Perspective

For her economic survival, remarriage was vital. The husband who divorced his wife thus forced her into a crisis: in order to survive, she had to remarry, but when she married again, both she and whoever she married became adulterers. Jesus' teaching, in contrast, both upholds the original sanctity of marriage and protects women from economic abuse by their husbands. This is a radical interpretation, in that it shifts the onus of responsibility from the woman to the man. If *he* divorces *his* wife, *he* causes her to commit adultery.

It has been all too easy for Christians to read this teaching as a new law, especially as a word of judgment against those who experience broken relationships. Jesus does not condemn those who experience divorce. Instead, he names the consequences of a system that granted most of the power to men and had become more concerned with legal technicalities (e.g., just cause and the bill of divorce) than with the fate of the people—especially the women—involved.

To be sure, Jesus provides us with strong warnings in this passage about the importance of preserving relationships, but with condemnation only for those who break their relationships while insisting that they have met the requirements of the law. That would seem to be a firm warning to us too, not to think ourselves to be righteous when we avoid breaking the technicalities of the law, even while we treat others as objects to be possessed and later disposed of, or leave them in situations of brokenness that render them vulnerable to sin. In a world that constantly invites us to turn people into objects to be consumed and exploited, Jesus calls his followers to discover wholeness and righteousness in relationships of equity, mutuality, compassion, mercy, and solidarity—in a word, relationships that manifest the same justice and love that God constantly shows toward each of us.

REGINALD BROADNAX

Pastoral Perspective

A word needs to be said about the text's use of bodily mutilation as an example of "a better way." There is very similar language in Jesus' teaching regarding those leaders of faith who would cause a little one to stumble. That passage says, "And if your eye causes you to stumble, tear it out and throw it away; it is better for you to enter life with one eye than to have two eyes and to be thrown into the hell of fire. Take care that you do not despise one of these little ones; for, I tell you, in heaven their angels continually see the face of my Father in heaven" (Matt. 18:9–10). In both cases, it must be argued that Jesus could not have intended to invite self-mutilation. Rather, this language speaks metaphorically of the severe spiritual mutilation that comes when we disregard the humanity of those with whom we are most intimate (or with whom we have the desire to be intimate). Turning another into a mere body for one's use and abuse cannot help but mutilate the soul.

Finally, each of us stands before Jesus Christ as a sinner redeemed, not by our own goodness but by God's. Daily I fall short of the glory God has envisioned for me, and sometimes I surprise myself because by God's grace I rise to the occasion and manage to love, to forgive, to live a better life than I ever imagined I could. Then I stumble and fall again and must rely, once again, on God's forgiveness. I stand before these teachings that follow the Beatitudes in just the same way: a sinner redeemed by God's goodness and love, one who falls short, so very short of the grace given to me through Christ, but also one who has been freed from that sin enough to get up and try again and again to live up to the vision God has for me and for us all.

BARBARA BLAISDELL

a close reference is found in Deuteronomy 24:1–4, where Moses instructs the Israelites about the proper procedures for a man to divorce his wife, if she "does not please" him.

At first it appears that Jesus is prohibiting divorce, by declaring that a man who divorces his wife causes her to "commit adultery," along with any man whom she might remarry. A closer examination, however, reveals that Jesus simply describes the outcome of the divorce process set forth in Deuteronomy 24, when viewed from the perspective that marriage is a permanent relationship that cannot be ended by a legal process. Many Christian interpreters of this passage have claimed that Jesus was trying to protect women by not allowing divorce, that he was concerned about what would happen to a woman without a husband to support her.

This approach, though, seems to overlook two key elements of the text. First, Jesus' discussion presumes the traditional Israelite practice that allowed only men to initiate divorce, but by the first century CE, some Jewish communities permitted a woman to divorce her husband. Second, there is one caveat to Jesus' supposed prohibition of divorce: a man can divorce a wife for "unchastity" (Greek, *porneia*). The exact definition of this word has been heavily debated across the centuries, with answers ranging from her not being a virgin on the wedding night to adultery to some other sexual sin. Perhaps the exact exception that Jesus allows is not as important as is the fact that he allows one in the first place.

Read with a critical eye (both ancient and contemporary), Jesus' declaration about divorce and remarriage actually further disadvantages a woman. Either she is stuck with a man who does not want her, or she can never remarry. Unlike the preceding Torah commentaries Jesus gives in Matthew 5, which are simply expanding the commandments in ways that were in line with broader Jewish conversations in the first century BCE, here the Gospel writer shows Jesus contradicting one of Moses' teachings and, in so doing, reneging on one of the rights women had gained. Clearly, the ideal is that marriage vows will be kept and relationships will be egalitarian. When that is not possible, there must be consideration for the well-being of all those involved.

LISA WILSON DAVISON

the assumptions of a patriarchal social order, including the male's prerogative in divorcing a wife. Jesus here is not issuing a "new" law; he is saying that giving a bill of divorce is not a real solution. He does not issue a new edict: "Thou Shalt Not Divorce." He just exposes the negative consequences, even when we follow the letter of the law.

A careful reading of this passage will caution preachers against using this text to rail against divorce and to pontificate definitively on the sacred marital relationship between a man and a woman. Jesus here describes an outcome of Israel's practice of divorce, and thus implies an alternative ideal that neither Israel nor we often realize. He also keeps reminding us that God is a God of mercy, forgiveness, healing, and inclusion, known especially well by those who know themselves to be sinners. On an issue like divorce, it is a fatal homiletical, ethical, and theological mistake to leave aside either the ideal or the promise of forgiveness.

Jesus may not as explicitly challenge the male-oriented prerogatives of his society as much as one would wish, but he does tell us that the system is broken; even the legal directives meant to inhibit abuse of women nonetheless lead to more damage and alienation and brokenness. This will not come as news to any pastor. Pastors minister within human brokenness every day—brokenness of their parishioners and their own brokenness. Pastors see too many marriages that have been entered into unwisely, even frivolously, and with far too little commitment. They also see too many divorces that are tragic but necessary. "Most divorced people, however, have left their marriages because, to the best of their ability to see, they had to. What do the words of Jesus mean for these people?"[1]

It is a long leap from the social context of Jesus to the social context of Western society today. Marriage as a relationship exclusively between a man and a woman is contested by many today. Most Western societies no longer regard divorce as the exclusive right of the male. In a society saturated with divorce and uncertain about how to best understand marriage, I can only imagine what healing and hopeful word could be spoken to a congregation today by a preacher willing not to "preach against" this text, but to wrestle with it until dawn.

GARY W. CHARLES

---

1. Thomas G. Long, *Matthew,* Westminster Bible Companion (Louisville, KY: Westminster John Knox Press, 1997), 60.

Matthew 5:33–37

³³"Again, you have heard that it was said to those of ancient times, 'You shall not swear falsely, but carry out the vows you have made to the Lord.' ³⁴But I say to you, do not swear at all, either by heaven, for it is the throne of God, ³⁵or by the earth, for it is his footstool, or by Jerusalem, for it is the city of the great King. ³⁶And do not swear by your head, for you cannot make one hair white or black. ³⁷Let your word be 'Yes, Yes' or 'No, No'; anything more than this comes from the evil one."

Theological Perspective

No way. No "bleeping" way. How can Jesus expect us not to swear? That preacher in Seattle is famous for swearing in his sermons! What would happen to hip-hop and rap? Jesus never drove on a twelve-lane inner loop during rush hour. If we did not swear and, uh, wave at each other, we might start shooting. This is clearly one of those historically conditioned Jesus sayings. I have been swearing since for-bleepin-ever. Oh. That is not what Jesus is talking about? What is he talking about then?

Jesus is talking about the truth. Nothing but the truth, minus the "So help me God." Not truthiness, an approximation of the truth, plausible deniability, need to know, or any of the other ancient and modern convolutions created to circumvent honesty. Yes means yes, not "It depends." No means no, not "We will see." Sorry, parents, but the saying does not seem to include an exception clause for dealing with one's children.

Jesus' admonition to simple, straightforward honesty is an ancient commonplace, the phrasing of the admonition also used by both Paul (2 Cor. 1:17–20) and James (Jas. 5:12). Matthew has cast the admonition in the larger form of the fourth antithesis. The antitheses follow a common pattern: a command from Torah, a reinterpretation of the command that extends the scope and force of the obligations it

Pastoral Perspective

Is it a matter of integrity, or is it simply about trust? There was a time when a handshake was as good as an oath taken on a stack of Bibles, when members of the community trusted each other sufficiently to open their lives to one another, figuratively and literally, by leaving doors unlocked when one was away from home, day or night. In fact it was considered an insult to ask a neighbor to sign a promissory note or take an oath—formal or informal—in order to participate in any type of transaction, since it indicated a lack of trust. Those days are long gone. The reality of life in twenty-first-century Western culture is defined in part by its litigious nature. We expect compensation for broken promises, whether implied or explicit. Perhaps the source of that distrust is the lack of truthfulness in our interactions with others.

The court system of the United States makes it clear that one is expected to tell the truth when one takes an oath. Truthfulness provides the foundation for trust. There is an expectation of truth telling and the promise of fulfillment when one makes an oath, despite the fact that culture and society may give evidence of the inaccuracy of that claim. The prevalence of divorce calls into question the understanding of the marriage oath. Certainly it seems that persons who make marriage vows today do so tongue in cheek because of the ease with which couples appear

Exegetical Perspective

Jesus' instructions concerning oaths appear as the fourth in a series of six antitheses in the Sermon on the Mount. In these teachings Jesus contrasts the higher righteousness of the age to come with the righteousness of this present age. The structure of these antitheses is entirely consistent with the pattern of rabbinic debates of that era. Those entering a debate on a given topic would summarize the traditional teaching, "You have heard it said . . . ," and then proceed to offer their own interpretation of the tradition.

The topics included in these six antitheses—anger, adultery, divorce, oaths, revenge, and love of neighbor—were all subjects of intense debate in the Judaism of the first century BCE through the second century CE. In transmitting Jesus' teachings on these issues, Matthew is not setting Jesus over against the Jewish legal tradition, but portraying Jesus as an authoritative participant in the law's ongoing interpretation.

The Mishnah has an entire tractate on oaths and another complete tractate on vows. Oaths involve an agreement between two parties in which the name of God is invoked as a guarantor. The assumption—sometime explicit, sometimes implied—is that God will punish the party who has invoked God's name, if the oath is not fulfilled. However, the commandment against taking God's name in vain created within

Homiletical Perspective

The story is told of Mark Twain, who loved to brag about his hunting and fishing expeditions.

> He once spent three weeks fishing in the Maine woods, regardless of the fact that it was the state's closed season for fishing. Relaxing in the lounge car of the train on his return journey to New York, his catch iced down in the baggage car, he looked for someone to whom he could relate the story of his successful holiday. The stranger to whom he began to boast of his sizeable catch appeared at first unresponsive, then positively grim. "By the way, who are you, sir?" inquired Twain. "I'm the state game warden," was the unwelcome response. "Who are you?" Twain nearly swallowed his cigar. "Well, to be perfectly truthful, warden," he said hastily, "I'm the biggest liar in the whole United States."[1]

Truth telling is at the core of every major issue in politics, business, medicine, religion, family life, the economy, international relations, health care, and the judicial system. How do you know what is the truth?

The preacher needs to lay out the historical context of this passage for the listener. It is imperative that they understand the elaborate system of oaths and vows, and their use and misuse, in the Judaism of Jesus' day.

1. "Mark Twain," No. 19, in Clifton Fadiman, ed., *The Little Brown Book of Anecdotes* (Boston/Toronto: Little, Brown & Co., 1985), 556.

Matthew 5:33–37

Theological Perspective

requires, and an argument justifying the reinterpretation. The nature of these arguments varies—logical, legal/practical, and eschatological—and in the case of the fourth antithesis, it is distinctively theological. An oath of any sort is precluded by nothing less than the very nature of God.

"The earth is the Lord's," sings the psalmist (Ps. 24:1), "the world, and those who live in it." You cannot take that which is entirely beyond your purview and influence and make it surety for your oath. If we strive to impress by the grandeur of our claim, "By heaven!" we are reminded that we are making claims on the divine throne room (Ps. 103:19). Something more tangible and visible, perhaps the earth? God's footstool (Isa. 66:1)? Something more personal, say the hair on our head? We have no more sway here than we have over the courses of the stars. Wherever we look, wherever we turn, we are surrounded by the Divine, and must admit there is no basis for the intensification of sincerity we presume in our oath.

As is almost always the case in the teaching of Jesus, the profoundly theological is also the deeply personal. Why is a simple yes or no not enough? When we are honest with ourselves, we find that the problem may be that we are not honest with ourselves. We are not too sure about the other person either. The oath is a substitute, a stand-in, for honesty—I know you probably do not believe me, so I am going to call on heaven and earth to witness on my behalf. Jesus points out that we are not fooling anyone.

Parish clergy and others who have a door that people knock on are familiar with the phenomenon. A person in need tells an amazing story of tragic confluence, been down so long it looks like up from here. They need . . . money. To "prove" to you that they are "telling the truth and not just trying to rip off the church," they reach into a pocket and produce . . . something. A picture, a phone number, a ticket stub, a receipt—some evidence of veracity. Sadly familiar, maybe a little pathetic—except we all do it. What in heaven's name (Oops!) do you think a PowerPoint presentation is? Do you not believe my words? Look at this graph! Our congressional representatives clumsily muster charts, propped up by embarrassed interns, to "prove" the outlandish nature of the other party's position. In the academy we are taught to support every claim with a multitude of quotations and footnotes. I used to be impressed and played the game well, until a mentor pointed out that the people I was trying to impress were not going to read my books, and the people

Pastoral Perspective

to move in and out of marriage contracts. Headlines report regularly the fallout from broken contracts of all kinds, such as betrayal of their office by elected officials and business and world leaders. The myriad crimes of home invasion, theft, mugging, murder, and even the recent epidemic of bullying of children and young people of all ages, all represent a betrayal of the implied promise of care that has been the bedrock of life in community.

As we consider the many issues—political, cultural, and even ecclesiological—that impact and influence our society, Jesus' words in Matthew remind us—or perhaps simply make us aware—of the requirements and the challenge of making and keeping oaths. An oath is a promise or covenant between two parties, and the covenant between God and humanity is the foundation of our lives as the people of God. There is a divine/human covenant that runs through all of Scripture; but unlike God, who keeps covenant with humanity, human beings break their covenant with God again and again. That is the source of most of the problems of our lives as Christians. There are also covenants between individuals, families, and communities that influence greatly both the substance and the quality of life.

Except in the bonds of marriage, it is unlikely that most people consider their relationships as being lived in compliance with or contrary to either a stated promise or a covenant. Generally, the language of covenant is relegated to biblical societies. Most people instead take for granted the relationships they develop, yet both individuals and society as a whole are the victims of broken promises.

In the shaping of the community formed by the people of the exodus, the issue of covenant took center stage. Laws were given to the people to guide most, if not all, aspects of their life in community. The people were expected to commit to the laws given by YHWH. Among these laws was the requirement to keep sacred the name of God. To misuse God's name through the making of false oaths was to violate the integrity of one's place in the divine/human covenant as well as in the human community. It was simply an issue of trust—in God and in one's community. The members of the community were expected to care for each other as God cared for them. Oaths were not necessary nor were they prohibited, but using the name of God to seal an oath or as a guarantee of one's commitment was considered vain use of the name of God, and thus forbidden. The exodus community understood this

Exegetical Perspective

the Jewish legal tradition a robust wariness about invoking the name of God for an oath, because this might cause someone to use God's name in a false or superfluous way. Various rabbis proposed elliptical solutions in which one might swear an oath by something other than God. The list that appears in Matthew—heaven, earth, Jerusalem, and one's own head—covers some of the most popular of these proposed substitutes.[1]

However, these substitutes were themselves problematic. Some authorities contested that swearing by heaven or earth made an idol of creation. Others argued that in swearing by one's head, one made a god of oneself. So the debates about the use and misuse of oaths persisted. Some authorities recommended limiting the circumstances under which an oath should be deemed necessary, thus reducing the frequency with which anyone would have to involve himself or herself in the morally and legally tricky business of oath taking. Sirach 23:9 states, "Do not accustom your mouth to oaths." Sirach 23:11 continues, "The one who swears many oaths is full of iniquity, and the scourge will not leave his house." Philo of Alexandria consistently condemned those who involved the name of God in pointless oaths. He asserted, "The simple word of a brave man shall be an oath." There was also a stream within Greek philosophy that discouraged oath taking.[2] Humanistic thinkers asserted that human integrity should be sufficient in legal agreements and that invoking the gods in such dealings was unworthy of free people.

In his contribution to this ongoing rabbinic debate, Jesus pushes this wariness of oaths even further and argues for a total ban: "But I say to you, do not swear at all" (v. 34). Other authorities seemed to consider swearing oaths, like divorce, a necessary evil. Human beings are prone to speak and promise falsely. Human experience of this reality makes mistrust a given in community relationships. Therefore oaths are necessary as a hedge against deception and a means of repairing trust. Jesus' ban on oaths points toward the higher righteousness of the age to come. In the realm of God, the community of God's people will be freed from legal provisions that accommodate the human propensity toward false speech. In the new age that is dawning with the gospel, all speech will be grounded in God's love and truth and will, therefore, be entirely trustworthy. Jesus urges his followers to begin to live this way now, using speech

Homiletical Perspective

Clarence Jordan writes, "They admitted that an oath should be binding, but then they said that it should be no more binding than the thing sworn by."[2] In other words, your word needed collateral, and the collateral was not to be more than was needed to cover the oath. Interesting.

Jesus basically cuts through all of that manipulation of truth and integrity. His yes or no is a reflection of God's kingdom, which exceeds rules and regulations written for evil people in order to make them do the right thing. Jesus is calling for a change of heart that needs no wiggle room or maneuvers. What is inside a person determines what is outside.

At the heart of the oath issue are commitment, integrity, truthfulness, and trust. Consider the multiple ways in which the erosion of these qualities has had an impact on our society. At any given moment in our society, the preacher has a storehouse of examples that will illustrate how dishonesty and manipulation of the truth have caused great pain and suffering. The list is always too long. However, let us be careful not to project all of our sins onto others. Scapegoating is an old trick that does not really work. We all have manipulated the truth.

Think of this. A faithful person would not need to swear by an oath at all. Oaths are only necessary because there is evil in the world. In the ideal world, we would not need oaths or vows. We would say what we mean and mean what we say. However, we live in a world of polygraphs and lie detectors. Getting at the truth can be difficult.

How many decades ago was President John F. Kennedy assassinated, and we still do not know the truth about that event? When you listen to political candidates debate, how do you know what the truth is? What is the truth about our nation's financial situation?

The people in the pew struggle with the truth in their own lives too. Truth telling and integrity, in business, in marriage, with family and friends, even from the church and the pulpit (!), have many dimensions. Jesus is obviously raising the bar and challenging the system. Simply tell the truth. Replace legalism with faithfulness. Replace manipulation with commitment. Be congruent. This is true community and a reflection of Christ himself.

Why is this so difficult for us to do? Like Adam and Eve, we hide. Our motives are tainted by our sinful nature. We lie. We manipulate the truth. We are

1. Ulrich Luz, *Matthew 1–7: A Commentary* (Minneapolis: Fortress Press, 2007), 263.
2. Douglas R. A. Hare, *Matthew* (Louisville, KY: John Knox Press, 1993), 55.

2. Clarence Jordan, *Sermon on the Mount*, rev. ed. (Valley Forge, PA: Judson Press, 1970), 82.

Matthew 5:33–37

Theological Perspective

whom I was writing for would buy the book because they wanted to read what I had to say, not for the footnotes.

Yes and no is not just about oaths. It is about a deeper truth, the deeper truth of our lives and manner of being, and, in the saying's context in the Sermon on the Mount, the place of unvarnished honesty in the life of discipleship. Like most of the Sermon, what we often take to be about someone else is really about us. Because the person we are most likely trying to impress with our sincerity and honesty is not the other, but the self. I am so sure this is what I think, believe, saw, remember, that "I swear" it is so.

Whom do we think we are fooling? Not Jesus. Nevertheless, if we succeed in fooling ourselves a little bit, then we can make it through another day. Is that the truth of what is happening here? Depicting the high cost of maintaining such self-delusion is central to much modern and postmodern fiction, theater, and cinema—appearances trumping reality until death do them part. Frequently some disarming character, Alyosha or E.T. or Benjamin Button, captures our attention precisely because he or she does not project a facade, swear an oath, or beg a question.

"But that is not the real world, you say." Sorry, no buts, just yes and no. Either Dostoevsky and Spielberg are telling the truth, or they are not. Preachers, rightly wary of giving offense and alienating listeners, may need to take Jesus' words to heart. If it is the truth, perhaps especially if it is a truth that hurts, do not qualify, hedge, and on-the-other-hand the truth into oblivion. Yes or no, remember?

WILLIAM F. BROSEND II

Pastoral Perspective

prohibition, and it became an important part of their tradition.

Both Jesus and the community of Matthew's church were inheritors of this tradition. As Judaism developed, it carried forward the abhorrence of misusing the name of YHWH. The antithesis named by Matthew forbids persons the use of God's name as the guarantee of truthfulness in speech or in relationships with others. Jesus' teaching directs his followers to live a life that does not require anything other than their word as a guarantee of their truthfulness. That life involves more than simple trust; it is more than a matter of integrity; it is evidence of Christian faith that demonstrates the disciple's commitment to Christ's teachings. Living such a life means that the relationship among members of the community will be based on truth in their dealings with one another and identifies them as the beloved community where Christ is head.

Through Christ, not only has a new community been called into being; a new covenant has been established between Christ and his church. Like Israel of old, the church has fallen victim to the influence of the society in which it resides, and the issue of trust has become a major challenge for the Christian community. In many cases, promises are not expected to be made or kept. The words "I swear" are met with skepticism and given little or no credence. This teaching of Jesus calls us to live a life of truth where one's word can be trusted. As members of the beloved community, there should be no distrust of one another and therefore no need for oaths to guarantee the truth. So perhaps integrity is a starting point for developing fully as Christians, but truth is even more basic to the Christian life. Living a life of truth signifies faithfulness to the baptismal oath: to live according to the example of Christ. Such a life should require no further oath on the part of the Christian believer.

GENNIFER BENJAMIN BROOKS

that is simple and truthful and honors God's purposes for humanity.

Later in Matthew's Gospel, at his trial before the high priest in 26:63–64, Jesus demonstrates this principle in practice: "Then the high priest said to him, 'I put you under oath before the living God, tell us if you are the Messiah, the Son of God.' Jesus said to him, 'You have said so. But I tell you, From now on you will see the Son of Man seated at the right hand of Power and coming on the clouds of heaven.'"

Also, in James 5:12 it is clear that Jesus' teaching continues to be the rule for that emerging Christian community: "Above all, my beloved, do not swear, either by heaven or by earth or by any other oath, but let your 'Yes' be yes and your 'No' be no, so that you may not fall under condemnation."

Jesus' teaching on oaths expresses his desire for a community that points toward the coming realm of God. In this present age, communities are organized around suspicions of deceit and the assumption that much of what people say and promise will not be truthful. The community of Christ's disciples, however, will be a sign of the age to come, not only in their obedience to the commandment to honor God's name, but also in their simple speech that assumes honest, fair relationships among those equal before God. This passage speaks an important word to Christians living in a culture in which much of public speech is assumed to be false.

The proper formula for oaths is no longer a matter of great concern. People of faith, however, are struggling to discern in what manner it is desirable for them to employ marketing techniques to put forward their message or to participate in the burgeoning realm of social media. How do Jesus' followers today respond to his teaching to let our yes be yes and our no be no?

KAREN C. SAPIO

deceptive. "If we say that we have no sin, we deceive ourselves, and the truth is not in us" (1 John 1:8).

Jesus said, "The truth will set you free" (John 8:32), but it does not always feel as if it will set us free. The truth can put you in jail. The truth can cost you your marriage. It can cost you your job or a relationship with a friend or family member. Saying "Yes" or "No" is not so easy, Jesus.

In the 1992 film *A Few Good Men,* Lieutenant Danny Kaffee, an inexperienced U.S. Navy lawyer, leads the defense of two Marines accused of murdering a fellow Marine in their unit at Guantanamo Bay Naval Base in Cuba. Jack Nicholson plays the part of Col. Nathan Jessup. When pushed for the truth while on the witness stand, Jessup replies with an angry voice, "You can't handle the truth." The truth was, *he* could not handle the truth. Who among us can?

In the 1997 movie *Liar, Liar*, Jim Carrey portrays a fast-track lawyer who cannot lie for twenty-four hours, due to his son's birthday wish after his dad had broken yet another promise. Imagine not being able to lie or to conceal the truth. It is comical in the movie, but in real life it could be extremely painful.

Jesus is not directing us to be brutal with the truth. To let your answer be "Yes" or "No" does not imply we forgo discretion or speaking the truth in love (Eph. 4:15). The raw truth can be a deadly weapon.

This text may feel far away from our reality, but how far is it? Manipulating the truth, using God's name like a rabbit's foot, issues of integrity, truthfulness, and trust—how far away is all of that from our world today?

Make the commitment. Do what you say you will do. Take the vow. Honor it. Be transparent. Tell the truth, the whole truth, and nothing but the truth; and leave off the "so help me God." Your word should be enough, without using God's name to close the deal.

STEVEN P. EASON

Matthew 5:38–48

³⁸"You have heard that it was said, 'An eye for an eye and a tooth for a tooth.' ³⁹But I say to you, Do not resist an evildoer. But if anyone strikes you on the right cheek, turn the other also; ⁴⁰and if anyone wants to sue you and take your coat, give your cloak as well; ⁴¹and if anyone forces you to go one mile, go also the second mile. ⁴²Give to everyone who begs from you, and do not refuse anyone who wants to borrow from you.

⁴³"You have heard that it was said, 'You shall love your neighbor and hate your enemy.' ⁴⁴But I say to you, love your enemies and pray for those who persecute you, ⁴⁵so that you may be children of your Father in heaven; for he makes his sun rise on the evil and on the good, and sends rain on the righteous and on the unrighteous. ⁴⁶For if you love those who love you, what reward do you have? Do not even the tax collectors do the same? ⁴⁷And if you greet only your brothers and sisters, what more are you doing than others? Do not even the Gentiles do the same? ⁴⁸Be perfect, therefore, as your heavenly Father is perfect."

Theological Perspective

Be perfect. Not be pretty good, be prepared, be all that you can be. Be perfect. Not practically perfect, almost perfect, or really something. Be perfect. Somewhere, probably lots of somewheres, a preacher with a little bit of Greek will argue that *teleios* does not so much mean perfect as "complete" or "finished" and is more about our goal or orientation than our destination. Alas, that Greek word for "goal" is *telos*. This one, *teleios*, means what it says, "perfect"; and if the Greek does not convince you, the rhetoric should. At the end of a series of six commands extending the ethical demands of the law, Jesus does not wind things up with, "Be mature/complete/headed in the right direction, as your Father in heaven is mature/complete/headed in the right direction." Rather, he says, "Be perfect, . . . as your heavenly Father is perfect." Now what?

Perhaps we should not be so surprised by this summarizing demand at the end of the chapter. Recall how the chapter begins and how it unfolds—Jesus pronounces a series of patently ridiculous blessings, then seems to moderate with sayings about salt and light that end up making equally ridiculous claims. This is followed by an assertion that he himself has come to fulfill the law, not curtail it in any fashion, and then he tosses in a warning to any who presume to lessen the demands of the law, bringing

Pastoral Perspective

At first glance this law seems to represent justice. "An eye for an eye and a tooth for a tooth" signifies a response proportionate to the evil perpetrated against one's person. In fact the original intent of the law given to the Hebrew people was just that. It was an equalizer that allowed the sufferer appropriate and equal recompense. Jesus knows the law, but he also understands the challenges faced by his community, which is living in a culture of violence under Roman occupation. He understands both their desire to retaliate against the violence done to their persons and their life, and the consequences of that retaliation, which will provoke even greater violence from the occupiers.

In a different yet similar way, the culture of many communities in the United States, especially in large cities, is one of violence. Violent crimes plague neighborhoods, especially poor urban communities, as gangs claim territories and put their markers on streets, thereby defying invasion by rivals. The urban jungle is not the only location for gang activities. Rural and suburban areas, where residents once lived peaceful lives together, have now become private, gated enclaves that are ruled by fear of those who have laid siege to or overtaken surrounding communities. Jesus' teaching just does not work in those scenarios—or does it?

Exegetical Perspective

This section includes the final two of the six antitheses that make up this portion of the Sermon on the Mount. As in the first four, Jesus' teaching here contrasts the righteousness of the age to come with the righteousness of this present age, rather than contrasting Jesus' teachings with established Jewish teaching and practice.

Verse 38 summarizes the *jus talionis* found in Exodus 21:23–25, Leviticus 24:19–20, and Deuteronomy 19:21. The law of "an eye for an eye, a tooth for a tooth" was intended to establish proportionate justice rather than private revenge as the standard for community life. By Jesus' time, many rabbis had recommended that such injuries should be compensated financially rather than physically. This would have been the prevailing practice in first-century Palestine.

The term "evildoer" (*ho ponēros*) in verse 39 is ambiguous. This word can refer to an individual evildoer, to an abstract evil, or to Satan, the evil one. The word for resist (*anthistēmi*) is usually used in military contexts referring to armed resistance. Here, however, it appears to refer to relinquishing one's right to sue for compensation. The appropriateness of violent resistance to the Roman occupation was a matter of intense debate in the Jewish community of Jesus' day. This debate, which continued among the early

Homiletical Perspective

The preacher had better hope that Jesus is not serious here. Surely we are not to take him literally. If so, then there will be a lot of red-faced, coatless, and worn-out people in the world who live like doormats, letting anybody and everybody take advantage of them. You are kidding. Right, Jesus? Maybe we can move this into the parable category.

We could duck this text because it was addressed only to his audience. However, consider who they were. Jesus is talking to people who were religious. So is the preacher. He is addressing folk who have tried to be good. So is the preacher. He is challenging their self-righteousness. So is the preacher. He is raising the bar, ushering in the kingdom of God. You guessed it: so is the preacher.

This is crazy talk. We want to be Christians at covered-dish dinners. We love being Christians at infant baptisms and weddings. We really enjoy being Christians at Christmas. We even like being Christians at a funeral. However, what in the world is Jesus talking about here? This is not Christianity, is it? It is way too extreme. Did we sign up for this at our baptisms? Maybe it signed up for us.

We do not want to be Christians (the word means "like Christ") when it is time to turn a cheek, give away the cloak, go the second mile, give to a worthless beggar, or loan everything we have to anybody

Theological Perspective

the section to a rousing coda with an insistence that his hearers' righteousness exceed the most notable standards of the day. Then come the six "antitheses," concluding with the sayings in Matthew 5:38–47 not to resist evil and to love one's enemies. After all that, are we really going to be surprised that Jesus wraps things up by telling us to be perfect? The entire chapter is crazy. Exactly—and it does not get any better in the chapters to follow.

The ethic explicit in Matthew 5 is impossible to follow in whole and part. No one you or I know or have heard of this side of Jesus has ever lived up to the expectations of the chapter for a day, probably not for an hour. God knows. After all, the law of "an eye for an eye" (5:38, from Exod. 21:24 and Lev. 24:20) was a check on the escalating vengeance of "ten of yours for every one of ours," a standard of vengeance as contemporary as it is timeless. The rest of this antithesis provided practical wisdom for those living in a country under occupation. We should not overestimate the number of times one might have been "pressed into service," because there were not all that many Roman soldiers in Judah and Galilee. Probably about as often as one was slapped on the cheek or sued for their cloak. The last antithesis, however, "love your enemies," was an altogether impossible demand. Nobody loves their enemies. That is what makes them enemies: we hate them! What is the difference between friend and enemy if you love them both? Oh.

The ethically impossible is apparently metaphor for the theologically outrageous. "Be perfect, therefore, as your heavenly Father is perfect." Jesus is taking the *imago Dei* not just seriously, but literally, a truly incarnational theology. What he seems really to be after is not an improvement in our morality, but a recasting of our theology. The challenge, one that Jesus will take up time and time again in the Gospel of Matthew, is to help us see what it means to understand God as "our Father in heaven." Not the problems, although very real, of patriarchy, abuse, neglect, exploitation, and oppression that can tragically attend to the word "father," but the problem of accepting that this theology means we are God's children. We are, Jesus implicitly argues, God's heirs, and also God's flesh and blood, God's family, God's descendants and legacy. We have more to live up to than we ever imagined. Wow.

A good theologian would surely now ask about the nature of the divine perfection we are expected to match. Since the answer will finally be "perfect in every respect," that may not prove to be of as

Pastoral Perspective

Jesus' directive on turning the other cheek is both an act of defiance and a means of bringing shame to the perpetrator of the original act of violence. Likewise, his advice to subject oneself to the injustice of giving up not only the outer garment but the inner clothing as well, and to become a beast of burden by carrying the load twice as far, were all expressions of active, nonviolent response. His distinct purpose is to guide his followers away from retaliatory acts of violence and into ways of peace. The model of nonviolent protest followed by Dr. Martin Luther King Jr. has sometimes been attributed to Mahatma Gandhi; but Gandhi as well as King could trace this model back still further to Jesus himself.

Violence begets greater violence, but history and present society have shown that even a nonviolent response does not prevent further violence. Does that then absolve the Christian from finding other ways of responding to the violence in our societies? I think not. These teachings of Jesus are meant to be taken seriously, and they challenge the church to a new understanding of the reign of God on earth. They commission individuals and the church community to bear witness to their Christian identity by finding just and nonviolent avenues to peace in the midst of violence. Likewise, in the midst of the violence and impoverishment of spirit that have overtaken families and communities because of economic challenges, the church is called to respond to those in need of both peace and justice.

At times it is difficult to give to those who accost us on the street, because of the obvious evidence of their alcoholism, drug addiction, or mental or social illness. We would rather not see such people at all, perhaps because their situations prick us in sensitive places as we are confronted unwillingly by the prosperity that we take for granted. Jesus' call to give to those who beg and to lend to those who want to borrow goes against the world's value system, which admires those who consider themselves self-made successes and admonishes those who are down to pull themselves up by their own bootstraps. Jesus' teaching calls us to do justice as persons of love, and moves progressively from nonviolent resistance to active love.

The teaching of the law calls for love of neighbor. Jesus considered it on par with the first great commandment that required love of God. Here Jesus goes a step further—a giant step. Given the Jews' hatred of their enemies, the Roman occupiers, a call to love even those "neighbors" requires radical change in the thinking of Jesus' followers. That

Exegetical Perspective

Christian communities as well, is an important context to keep in mind when reading Matthew's account of Jesus' teaching on nonviolent resistance of evil.[1]

The first three examples of nonresistance portray situations in which the evil is perpetrated by one with greater power over one with lesser power. A slap on the right cheek indicates a backhand slap delivered with an assailant's left hand. Such a slap would be intended as a rebuke or insult rather than a violent attack. To turn the other cheek in such a situation would be to respond with neither violence nor subjection.

The *chitōn* translated here as "coat" was one of two garments usually owned by people of this era. The coat was the inner garment worn next to the skin, while the *himation* was the cloak, or outer garment. There were legal situations where a person's coat might be taken, as in repayment of a debt; however, there were prohibitions against taking both garments (Exod. 22:25–26, Deut. 24:12–13). To give one's cloak as well as one's coat was to cede one's legal right to enforce this limit.

The third example illustrates the practice of conscripting civilians to transport military gear. The word *angareuō* ("force" or "compel") has Persian origins and originally referred to compulsory service in the postal system. Legally, one mile was the limit that Roman military personnel could require a civilian conscripted into such service to go, but this limit was frequently ignored. To go a second mile willingly would be to submit voluntarily to a Roman's failure to comply with this limit. Perhaps significant is Matthew's use of the Latin word *milion* for the distance described rather than the more commonly used Greek word *stadion*. This suggests that Matthew may intend a clear allusion here to Roman occupation.[2]

The final instructions regarding almsgiving and lending at first seem incongruous. Beggars and those requesting loans are not depicted as evildoers in Jewish law or literature. Rabbinic literature does, however, include debates that attempt to balance commandments to give freely (Deut. 15: 7–11) with other laws that protect personal property and possessions. Seen in this context, this last example continues Jesus' exhortation to a higher righteousness, in which one cedes the legal rights one might invoke in self-protection when faced with matters of giving or lending.

This section ends with a culminating contrast of the righteousness of this age with the righteousness

1. Douglas R. A. Hare, *Matthew*, Interpretation series (Louisville, KY: John Knox Press, 1993), 55.
2. Ibid., 56.

Homiletical Perspective

who wants it. What kind of "like-Christ" person is that? It sounds more like foolishness.

The preacher has a golden opportunity to argue with Jesus a little here. Get over there in the pew with your folks. They will love you for it, because this kind of talk makes no sense to them whatsoever. Therapists call this "building rapport" with the client. Join them. Get on their side—at least for the moment. Help them feel the tension of how difficult it is to live this way.

The phone rang just days before Christmas. It was a young man in my church whom I barely knew. He was obviously upset. He told me his story. "I discovered that my wife has been cheating with my best friend. We have four small children. And right here at Christmas. What in the world am I going to do? We have parties to go to, shopping, Santa—how will I get through it?" I could have said, "Well, Jesus says to love your enemies, turn the other cheek, go the second mile. You just need to do what Jesus says to do. Let me know how that works for you." Seriously?

So then, what are you going to do with this as the preacher? How do you hold the line of pastoral care and offer these ethics of Jesus? Who can actually pull off loving their enemies? Who really prays for those who persecute them? Let us just say it: who can "be perfect"? No one. Total depravity shows up in the newspapers every day. It is in the church. It is even in the pulpit. We cannot do this on our own. So, pick another text. Preach a psalm!

You can help your congregation to feel the overwhelming, futile feelings of this text. Do not skirt the difficulty. Own it. Stand out there in the cold with them, staring at a locked door. Just do not leave them there. What are the preacher's options?

We all know that we cannot offer this as a works-righteousness program. The Sermon on the Mount is not a do-it-yourself kit for getting into heaven. Nor can we simply dismiss this teaching. Maybe you offer that this is the life of Christ lived in and through us. Not easy but possible. Maybe this is what Paul meant when he wrote; "It is no longer I who live, but it is Christ who lives in me" (Gal. 2:20a). Maybe this is Paul's "Do you not know that you are God's temple and that God's Spirit dwells in you?" (1 Cor. 3:16).

Is that not our only hope? No one can produce a Christlike life by sheer will or discipline. How else could the folks in the pew—the banker, the teacher, the lawyer, the business person, the contractor, the teenager, the alcoholic, the hairdresser, or anybody else—do this? There is no way. Christ has to do it in us.

Matthew 5:38–48

Theological Perspective

much help as we might wish, only underscoring the impossibility of the task—if it is a task. What if it is, as already hinted, a metaphor? Perfection is not an accumulation of good deeds, restrained actions, and pure desires. Perfection is a state of being, and if Jesus is to be believed, it is our birthright. The "command" to be perfect is not a call to devout and holy action; it is an invitation to self-recognition, to a level of theological awareness that requires an embrace of the gift given at creation. To be perfect as our heavenly Father is perfect means neither more nor less than to be who we already are, in God's image.

If God is our Father, then we are God's children, not "very God from very God," but not so far removed as to be unrecognizable. There is a family resemblance. Later in Matthew, the reader finds specific language about children, roles, expectations, and welcomes. "He called a child, whom he put among them, and said, 'Truly I tell you, unless you change and become like children, you will never enter the kingdom of heaven. Whoever becomes humble like this child is the greatest in the kingdom of heaven'" (18:2–4).

We spend most of our time wondering what it is about children that makes it possible for them to "enter the kingdom" and how we might somehow emulate that. Except we cannot, any more than, morally, we can match the perfection of God. Children do not know this. They just walk right in, as if they owned the place. Mi casa es su casa, right? We are perfect. We just do not act like it.

WILLIAM F. BROSEND II

Pastoral Perspective

same change is required of Christians today, as we are confronted daily by violence in all spheres of life. Such violence makes life untenable; it systematically destroys not only the peace but the substance of life itself. The perpetrators of such violence cannot possibly be persons to whom we need, or are willing, to show love.

Perhaps this is the key to Jesus' message. Those who perpetrate violence are the very ones we need to love—for our own sake as Christians. While they may need to receive the love that Christ has placed in our hearts, it is perhaps more important that we as followers of Christ offer God's love. We are called to active involvement in spreading the love of God to the lost and the least. Those who are lost in spirals of violence and poverty of body, mind, or spirit require continuous exposure to the love of God that offers renewal and change. God's love extends to all people. The love that Christ places in our hearts must be shared with all persons, regardless of their situation or even the threat they may pose to us. Love has the ability to bring about change. The love of Christ in our hearts changes us. That love not only transcends the need to retaliate when wrong has been done to us; it also compels us to love those who have wronged us.

Christ's teaching is as appropriate for our violence-ridden society today as it was for his community and for Matthew's community. It is the consistent message that Jesus taught and lived throughout his ministry—a message of God's empowering love that enables us to love God and through that love to love our neighbor as we love ourselves. Love opens our eyes and our hearts to seek justice for all people and to work for change in the world. As followers of Christ we are empowered by his love to transform the world and by living a life of love to make real the reign of Christ on earth.

GENNIFER BENJAMIN BROOKS

Exegetical Perspective

of the age to come. "You have heard that it was said, 'You shall love your neighbor and hate your enemy'" (v. 43). Love of neighbor is commanded in Leviticus 19:18, but there is no positive command in Jewish law to hate one's enemies. One might find such a stance implied in the imprecatory psalms or in the harsh condemnation of Israel's enemies in certain prophetic texts. Proverbs, however, also instructs the people not to mistreat their enemies:[3] "Do not rejoice when your enemies fall, and do not let your heart be glad when they stumble, or else the LORD will see it and be displeased, and turn away his anger from them" (Prov. 24:17–18). "If your enemies are hungry, give them bread to eat; and if they are thirsty, give them water to drink; for you will heap coals of fire on their heads, and the LORD will reward you" (Prov. 25: 21–22).

Jesus' commandment to "love your enemies and pray for those who persecute you" (v. 44) should not be interpreted as a negation of Jewish law or practice, but as Jesus' call to his disciples to transcend this righteousness with an even higher righteousness. To support this exhortation, Jesus points out that even those considered outside the circle of the righteous—tax collectors and Gentiles—are able to attain the minimum standard of righteousness set up by a narrow definition of what love of neighbor would require.

Jesus' teaching that his disciples should "be perfect, . . . as your heavenly Father is perfect" (v. 48), echoes the call of God to Israel. The Law in Leviticus is often punctuated with the phrase "I am the LORD your God," or "You shall be holy, for the LORD your God is holy" (Lev. 11:44–45; 20:7; 20:26; and 21:8). To become the son or daughter of a person is to exhibit the qualities of that person. Thus the character of the covenant people should reflect the character of God. In loving our enemies, we reflect the nature of God, whose love extends to all. This is the higher righteousness that will characterize the age to come. This is the righteousness toward which Jesus calls his followers to strive even now.

KAREN C. SAPIO

Homiletical Perspective

Key to the passage may be Jesus' relentless unwillingness for evil to win, though it may appear at times to have the lead. Evil is overcome with good, not with a stronger version of evil. Break the cycle, is Jesus' idea. Break the cycle with your estranged brother or sister. Break the cycle with your spouse or child. Break the cycle with the person at work or a neighbor next door. With God's help, you can do it and be the different one. Christians are called to be Christlike, to counter evil with good, to allow Christ to live through us.

Is Jesus being serious with this? The truth is, Jesus is being really serious. Extreme evil demands extreme good. It requires a good that is tenacious. It requires more than your nominal effort. You have to go deeper.

Can we challenge the church to turn its cheek, give its cloak, go the second mile? Can we challenge the church to give to the beggars and lend to those in need? Can we challenge the church to love its own enemies, within and without, and to pray for those who persecute the church? Can we challenge the church to go deeper and to be that kind of extreme church in the world?

Go past sending get-well cards, visiting a few homebound members, potlucks, Sunday school, Scouts, and preschool. Be such an extreme church that somebody would want to be a part of it. Live in such a way that somebody would beg you to take their money, their time, and their talents to promote such a church in the world today. We had better pray that Jesus was serious and that he still is.

STEVEN P. EASON

3.Amy-Jill Levine and Marc Zvi Brettler, eds., *The Jewish Annotated New Testament* (New York: Oxford University Press, 2011), 12.

Matthew 6:1–6

¹"Beware of practicing your piety before others in order to be seen by them; for then you have no reward from your Father in heaven.

²"So whenever you give alms, do not sound a trumpet before you, as the hypocrites do in the synagogues and in the streets, so that they may be praised by others. Truly I tell you, they have received their reward. ³But when you give alms, do not let your left hand know what your right hand is doing, ⁴so that your alms may be done in secret; and your Father who sees in secret will reward you.

⁵"And whenever you pray, do not be like the hypocrites; for they love to stand and pray in the synagogues and at the street corners, so that they may be seen by others. Truly I tell you, they have received their reward. ⁶But whenever you pray, go into your room and shut the door and pray to your Father who is in secret; and your Father who sees in secret will reward you."

Theological Perspective

Do not be like the hypocrites. How exactly is that supposed to happen? Anonymous gifts and short, private prayers? Invisible Christians? This does not sound promising, but given the source, we should not dismiss the idea out of hand.

Some years ago Archbishop Desmond Tutu gave the sermon at my seminary's graduation. It was a packed church, standing room only, the presiding bishop on hand to celebrate Holy Eucharist. More or less the opposite of what Jesus was talking about, come to think of it. The archbishop, not a large man, was swamped by the massive pulpit, and spent most of the sermon in a losing battle with the sound system. He was clearly tired—Sewanee, Tennessee, is a long way from South Africa—but he had something he wanted to tell us. Except he stopped, or he stopped trying. At first we thought the sound system had finally won, but when we listened more closely we heard his whispering, lilting voice. He waited for us to quiet ourselves enough that he could be heard, and then he spoke. His was the voice of quiet stillness after the earthquake and wind and fire, and his words echoed in our hearts in a way they could not in any hall.

I do not remember what he said. It does not matter. It was the speaker, not the message that mattered. Everything Desmond Tutu had ever done,

Pastoral Perspective

Jesus addresses the religious practices of his day for the distinct purpose of calling his followers to more faithful observance of the traditions that demonstrate their commitment to the worship of God. Contrary to the interpretation given to this text in some circles, Jesus is not pointing fingers at the practices of the keepers of the law in his community. Rather, he is directing the attention of his followers to their own observances as the starting point for their acts of worship and prayer. Jesus does not so much cast doubt on the authenticity of the prayers of either his fellow Jews or the Gentiles in their midst, since their ways of worship fit the accepted customs of the time. Instead, he is setting a higher standard for his disciples, one that reorients the approval of one's worship practices away from the community and toward God, since it is only what God alone sees that matters.

The disciple of Christ is led by love of God, and every action of the Christian is done in praise to God. This is the teaching that Jesus tries to make clear. Disciples' actions give witness to the God they worship, and their practices define their Christian identity. As their new identity becomes obvious to others, it must call attention not to the disciples themselves, but to the God they serve. It is public piety that is practiced, not for the praise it brings to

Exegetical Perspective

These verses introduce a new section of the Sermon on the Mount, in which Jesus offers instruction and interpretation of the three foundational aspects of Jewish piety: almsgiving, prayer, and fasting. Jesus' instructions assume that his hearers are already doing these things and that these practices will continue to form the foundation for piety in the community of Jesus' disciples. Among the community of disciples, however, almsgiving, prayer, and fasting will take on the eschatological function of pointing toward the realm of God that Jesus is now announcing. The word "righteousness" (Greek *dikaiosynē*) links this section with the section before it. The manner in which one undertakes almsgiving, prayer, and fasting is part of the greater righteousness also highlighted by the antitheses concerning murder/anger, adultery, divorce, oaths, and retaliatory violence.

Each practice of piety is examined in three parallel segments, introduced by the phrase "When you . . . (give alms, pray, fast)," followed by a negative example. Then follows a positive command to Jesus' disciples concerning the manner in which they are to undertake that particular practice. A contrast between the practice of the hypocrites and the practice Jesus desires from his disciples introduces all three examples. The former is distinguished by

Homiletical Perspective

Here is an opportunity to awaken the good Christians who dared to get up, get dressed, and come to worship. Who would think that good things like giving and praying could be dangerous? However, there is a dark side to everything. Giving money and praying can be dangerous! (Good sermon title!) It is the motive, not the amount. It is the content, not the delivery. We are prone to get it wrong, even when we are trying to do it right.

A particular church terminated a contract with one of its employees, which upset a small but vocal minority. A meeting was called and the discussion became heated. One of the members stood to say, "There is a lot of money represented in this room, and money talks!" The pastor quietly looked about the room and did the math. There was not $25,000 worth of pledges totaled among them all. The larger contributors to the church were not in the room, and if this vocal minority knew who those folks were, they would be extremely surprised.

Almsgiving can be demonic. Alms can be given out of pride or guilt. They can be given to manipulate or control. They can be given to cover up, silence, buy out, or pay back. Watch your motive when you give your alms. Your left hand always knows what your right hand is doing—and may want everyone else to know too!

Matthew 6:1–6   117

Matthew 6:1–6

Theological Perspective

everything he stood for, every evil he had fought against, spoke for him. He, not his words, was the witness. His presence and not his eloquence was his prayer. Do not be like the hypocrites.

Is there a theology of hypocrisy? Most people know hypocrisy when they see it, but almost without fail they see it in others and not in themselves. Usually when we see it, we attach a label to it, the label making it all the easier to dismiss it. Jews this, Muslims that, Catholics the other, and Mormons . . . you get the idea. Do not be like the hypocrites, Who gets to decide?

Is there anyone more hypocritical than a theologian? What could possibly be more audacious than spelling out precisely what one believes in and why? As soon as you tell me what you believe, then I can point out where your life fails to live up to your creed, and just as quickly dismiss you and your beliefs. Case closed. Here is a theology of hypocrisy for you: all theology is hypocritical!

Yes, it is, as is all belief, and hope, and prayer. We stick our theological necks out knowing they will be lopped off every time. Something about the cross would probably fit in here but that would be both hypocritical and presumptuous.

Take giving; that is where Jesus starts. Every building at my university has a name over the door and a million plaques in the hallway. So do the church where I worship, the hospital where I healed, even the fire engine ready to respond to my emergency. We do not sound the trumpet, but we make sure our name is on the alumni donor list. We even know who "Anonymous" is that gave a zillion dollars. Is that bad? Warren Buffett and Bill Gates have been out and about encouraging their fellow billionaires to give and go public in order to inspire others to do the same. It is a defensible strategy; it just is not the strategy of Jesus. Jesus argues that we have a choice of payback: immediate and public, or private and eternal.

Prayer? The more the better: retreats, workshops, groups, partners, spiritual direction, Ignatian exercises, centering, Taizé, you name it and we have it. Many years ago a pastor attempted to form a prayer group in the congregation, and a parishioner responded that she agreed with Jesus that she should go into her closet and pray privately before the Lord. The pastor asked how often she did so. She responded, "That is not the point! The point is that if I did pray, I should do it all by myself."

Hypocrisy is possibly more difficult to avoid than Jesus allows. The only sure way to avoid hypocrisy

Pastoral Perspective

the individual, but for the testimony it offers to the presence and grace of God operating in the life of the individual. This critical message relating to the public piety of Christians is relevant for any age, and certainly for our own, especially given the almost insatiable need for public recognition that prevails in society. Jesus names two specific issues that were relevant to his time, the giving of alms and public prayer; but the greater issue of the need for recognition makes them just as appropriate for our time.

The people of God are called to do the work of justice and mercy in the name of God. Many churches are to be commended for offering food programs that provide much-needed help to the poor and needy. However, when the persons who run the programs do so with a sense of superiority to those whom they serve, they are just as misguided as the hypocrites of whom Jesus speaks, who seek to earn the praise of the community. As Christians we are given gifts by God for the good of the community. At times there is much fanfare at the start of a program, and the church is commended for its faithfulness, but the program dies once the cameras are turned off. Matthew's community was heir to the same traditions of prayer, fasting, and almsgiving of which Jesus spoke. Matthew's intention was to help his community center their prayer, their worship, and their acts of mercy on God. They were to make God their motive for the things that they did, so that they would know the blessing of God, not merely the approbation of their community.

The ways in which we serve God should give glory to God, not merely result in human commendation for the work we do. To be certain, there is nothing wrong in receiving a commendation. The problem comes when one is motivated by the desire for recognition. In our churches there are many persons who are engaged in different aspects of ministry simply for the praise and recognition they hope to receive. When that recognition is not immediately forthcoming, such persons may either end their service or become a stumbling block to the advancement of the work that the church needs to do.

Jesus' message may help us take the emphasis off of the magnitude and worth of our efforts, which lure us to think in the world's terms and seek what we consider our just deserts with regards to recognition. When we consider that what we have is a gift of God and give from a heart of love, there is no count taken. Giving is done in praise to God at any and every level possible, regardless of how big or how small. Then the blessing from God comes into the

the performance of piety to gain human approval, the latter by a deeper piety that seeks to honor and glorify God.

"Hypocrite" was the Greek word for a stage actor. In ancient times actors often wore masks that hid their true identity. Because of this, the word later acquired the connotation of those who "act" one way in public and another in private, and thus conceal their true nature. Matthew often applies this term to the Pharisees or to others whose observance of the law or other acts of righteousness is undertaken with the desire to gain worldly approval. The term should not, however, be understood as applying to Jewish practices in general.

The hypocrites in the first example make a noisy public display of their acts of charity. There is no evidence that "sounding a trumpet" to announce almsgiving was common practice in the Jewish community. Rabbinic literature of this era, such as the Talmud tractates *Berakot* and *Megillah*, included cautions against seeking praise for acts of mercy.[1] This reference to "trumpeting" might refer to the receptacles set up for almsgiving in the temple courts. One might deposit coins into the receptacles in a way calculated for maximum noise, thus calling attention to one's donation from those nearby.[2] In giving alms so that "your right hand does not know what your left hand is doing" (v. 3), however, one performs this act of righteousness as an act of devotion and service to God. By giving in this way, one also cedes the social prominence and power that go along with being known for great philanthropy. The higher righteousness that points to the realm of God seeks neither human praise nor the trappings of worldly influence.

Verse 5 introduces the contrast between the prayer practices of the hypocrites and the prayers of Jesus' disciples. This condemnation of these hypocrites does not indicate a blanket condemnation of public prayer, but of private prayers conducted in public view for the purpose of seeking human approval. One example might be the custom for pious Jews of breaking their routine each day around three o'clock to offer prayer in conjunction with the evening sacrifice in the temple. This practice was a personal act of devotion, yet some may have performed it in a very public way, deliberately stepping into the street or entering the synagogue so that their

We are all capable of turning a good thing sour. We can exploit a birthday cake! We "sound the trumpet" so others will praise us for our good deeds. "Do it another way," says Jesus. Get under the radar. Give the alms quietly. Turn off the noise. Lay your gift on the table while no one is looking, and seek no praise for it.

When I was a young associate pastor, with small children, I had very little money and lots of debt. One day the senior pastor came to me and said, "Someone has set it up for you to go to a certain men's store and pick out a suit." Of course I wanted to know who had done such a gracious thing. "I promised not to tell you," he replied. Every year this happened. Every year I went and picked out a new suit. Every year I was told, "I promised not to tell you." Every year I still wanted to know.

I do not recall exactly how I figured it out, but I did. It was the senior pastor. He would never tell me and I would never ask, but I think we both knew. He gave his gift quietly, but after all these years it still speaks loudly to me. Almsgiving can be dangerously good too.

Then Jesus moves to the matter of prayer. How dangerous can a little prayer be? Leave it to us to make it extremely dangerous. Jesus warns us to beware of praying for show. Watch your motive. Go to your room, close the door, and talk to God.

In my former church in Mount Pleasant, South Carolina, we were embarking upon a capital campaign. Following the session meeting in which we approved the ambitious goal, I asked the oldest elder to close us in prayer. I had given her no notice. She politely declined, saying that she never prays in public without prior preparation. My bad.

So I spontaneously turned to our young organist, who was Korean. She had broken English and had just recently come to this country. For some reason, I felt compelled to ask her to pray. She replied, "In English?" To which I responded, "No, in Korean." Being a devout person, she proceeded to pray in her native tongue for what seemed like five minutes. No one understood a word. For a moment it was uncomfortable, even comical. Then we all knew that she was talking to God and not to us. It was one of the most powerful prayers I have ever heard and I did not understand the first word . . . or the last.

To whom are we talking when we pray? Prayers can run into the danger zone when they seem more directed to the listeners than to God. Therapists often use a "Gestalt technique" in which the client addresses an empty chair as if someone were present.

1. Amy-Jill Levine and Marc Zvi Brettler, eds., *The Jewish Annotated New Testament* (New York: Oxford University Press, 2011), 12
2. Daniel J. Harrington, SJ, *Luke*, Sacra pagina (Collegeville, MN: The Liturgical Press, 1991), 94.

Matthew 6:1–6

Theological Perspective

is to not believe in anything. Avoiding hypocrisy in giving and praying is another matter altogether. It is entirely possible if you pray before you give and give before you pray. Add in the fasting in the verses to follow, and you have a wonderful plan for spiritual practice. The problems arise when we separate giving and praying, doing one in place of the other, when both are required.

Pastoral leaders are infamous for being lousy givers and pathetic prayers, and there are abundant ecclesiastical scandals to prove it. "Why, I have given my life to the gospel, is that not tithe enough?" No, it is not. "Pray? Why, I prayed four times at the hospital today, and I am on my way to the nursing home where I will lead a prayer service. How dare you ask me about my prayer life!" Someone has to. My own beloved spiritual director at the Mercy Prayer Center in Rochester, New York, Sister Jody Kearney, taught me that the most wonderful and terrifying question in the world is, "How is your prayer life?" Wonderful, because she listened to my answer. Terrifying, because she listened to my answer.

I do not know how Desmond Tutu got to be Desmond Tutu. My guess is that it involved a lifetime of giving and prayer. I do know that one thousand people will never stop breathing, in order to hear what *I* have to say. How one gets to be more like him and less like me is a matter of prayer. Our closets are waiting, and so is our God.

WILLIAM F. BROSEND II

Pastoral Perspective

heart of the giver as God receives the prayerful gift of every faithful heart and recognizes, cherishes, and rewards every gift of every faithful giver, regardless of the content. Each gift represents the love of God in the heart and itself becomes a prayer from the heart of the giver.

The issue of public prayer that Jesus names is less of a problem for the church today. Prayer is conversation that opens the dialogue between God and the person who offers a prayer. Public prayer is not often practiced today in the manner that it was in Jesus' and Matthew's day. It was and, I believe, still is an honor to be able to lead the congregation in public prayer. The problem arises when those so engaged are more concerned with how the prayer sounds than what the prayer means. Many Christian communities cherish the memories of some saints of old who, when called on to pray, could practically "bring down God from heaven" (as some would say). Those saints prayed with sincerity and with faith, and the community was blessed by their prayers.

Then there were those whose prayers were merely self-serving. Such prayers often become rote, lacking the faith that could give life to the words and enable the hearers to experience the presence of God. Jesus' message calls us individually and the church as a community to deep and fervent prayer that is focused on God, thereby enriching the life of the community and bearing witness to the glory of God for the life and work of the whole people of God. Those who pray in the way Jesus taught will do so in the assurance that the prayers of the faithful are heard, accepted, and blessed by God.

GENNIFER BENJAMIN BROOKS

Exegetical Perspective

observance of this personal act of piety would be visible to as many people as possible.[3]

Jesus uses hyperbolic language to urge his hearers to go to great lengths to ensure that their private acts of devotion are directed toward God alone. They are to go into their *tameion* and shut the door. This word is translated in various places as an inner room, pantry, or closet, that is, a room without windows or doors that would open to the street. Prayer in such a room would shield the one praying from even accidental observation by the general public.

Running through each of these parallel segments is the notion of reward. Verse 1 warns that those who perform acts of piety to gain worldly praise will receive no reward from their Father in heaven. Jesus then assures his hearers that both the hypocrites who give alms to win social approval and influence and those who pray in a manner that attracts public attention "have received their reward" (v. 2). This reward, however, is not from God. God's rewards go to those whose practice of almsgiving and prayer is done "in secret" and directed toward God alone.

The Roman system of patronage revolved around very public acts of service and honor to one's patron that were then rewarded by that patron's public approval, protection, and support. It is intriguing to consider that Jesus' condemnation of the practices of the hypocrites may have been a barely veiled critique of this Roman client/patron system and its influence on community life.

Given the current cultural climate of strident individualism, interpreters will want to guard against citing this text as privileging private spirituality over corporate worship and practice. Jesus' desire is for a community that is animated by acts of righteousness that are directed toward God, not calculated toward achieving worldly prestige or influence. His warnings are a hedge against the hypocrisy that would cripple the community's witness to the coming of the realm of God into the world.

KAREN C. SAPIO

Homiletical Perspective

This imaginary person could be a spouse, parent, child, or employer, living or deceased. If successful, the client experiences a cathartic moment by engaging this person in conversation.

Using the Gestalt technique, suppose that Jesus is sitting in a folded chair right in front of the lectern. How would we then pray? My prayers would be much shorter and more humble. That is Jesus' point.

We need to monitor ourselves, lest we drift into an unhealthy piety with lots of pomp and circumstance but very little substance. Could this be one of the many reasons that the church in America is declining? Do visitors come looking for a connection but leave empty? Lots of pomp with little substance quenches the Spirit. Dead. I once heard Fred Craddock say that, in light of the resurrection, the one sin the church cannot commit is that of being dead. Prayer for show is dead.

Jesus is firing a warning shot over our bow. For all the good there is in giving and praying, there is also the possibility of evil. Maybe he was just speaking to a group in front of him, or maybe he knew what was coming. Maybe he could see ahead to the modern church. Maybe he knew that we are all prone to take a good thing and mess it up. Maybe he loves us enough to warn us of things that rob us of our joy and health.

STEVEN P. EASON

3. Douglas R. A. Hare, *Matthew* (Louisville, KY: John Knox Press, 1993), 63.

Matthew 6:7–15

7"When you are praying, do not heap up empty phrases as the Gentiles do; for they think that they will be heard because of their many words. 8Do not be like them, for your Father knows what you need before you ask him.

9 "Pray then in this way:
Our Father in heaven,
    hallowed be your name.
10   Your kingdom come.
    Your will be done,
        on earth as it is in heaven.
11   Give us this day our daily bread.
12   And forgive us our debts,
        as we also have forgiven our debtors.
13   And do not bring us to the time of trial,
        but rescue us from the evil one.

14For if you forgive others their trespasses, your heavenly Father will also forgive you; 15but if you do not forgive others, neither will your Father forgive your trespasses."

Theological Perspective

The teaching of Jesus is a crucial element in the Gospel of Matthew, and his instruction concerning prayer is pivotal, standing at the center of his words to the crowd on the mountain in chapters 5–7. Matthew's account contains no request for instruction on prayer, as in Luke 11:1. Nevertheless, the prayer presented in Matthew occurs in an evident context of instruction concerning the ways of the kingdom of God.

For modern ears, the portion of this passage with the highest potential for impact is very likely the first two verses, verses 7 and 8 (perhaps including the difficult verses on public piety and its rewards in 6:1–6 as well), rather than the last seven verses, verses 9–15. It is certainly not that the words of the prayer itself are unimportant, and most believers know them by heart, at least some version of them. Despite oft-repeated recitations of some version of the prayer, it is very likely that those who utter it seldom note, much less heed, the theological claims central to Jesus' introductory words to the prayer. This is particularly the case in Jesus' assertion concerning the nature of the God whom we worship and to whom we pray: *God knows before we ask*: this is an extraordinary claim on God's behalf! The creator of the whole world and its people is predisposed with intimate interest in individuals' lives and actions.

Pastoral Perspective

Anyone listening to Jesus' teaching on prayer who expects him to offer only a mild alternative to "heaping up empty phrases" like the Gentiles will be alarmed at the audacity of the model prayer he sets forth. This audacity may not be evident, however, on a superficial reading, even to those who pray this prayer frequently. The prelude (vv. 5–8) teases the reader to attention by exposing the hypocrisy of street preachers who seek nothing more than attention. Such an archetype is illustrative no matter which millennium you belong to. Do we not all appreciate a moment of good finger-pointing, especially when the target is in plain sight, loud, and obnoxious? Jesus' prayer, however, will not let us off the hook so easily.

Those of us who worship with congregations in liturgical traditions and pray this prayer weekly (and often meekly) may be surprised to learn that Jesus encourages us to pray in private with simple sentences. Ironically, the frequency with which many of us pray this prayer publicly may have the adverse effect of obscuring the fact that Jesus urges us to pray in silence and alone for the kingdom to come, for God's will to be done on earth, just as it is in heaven.

Jesus' prayer possesses none of the regrettable subtlety common to the prayers of the contemporary church. Instead, the prayer compels us immediately

Exegetical Perspective

The Lord's Prayer is beyond familiar; it is ingrained. The upside to this is that we can turn to it instinctively in time of need, the downside that we may find it tired and stale. Can the old and familiar become unfamiliarly new? It can. That at least is the promise of close reading. The prayer's wording and structure, its origin and expansion over time, have surprisingly broad implications for the Christian life.

Wording and Structure. There are two New Testament versions of the Lord's Prayer: Matthew 6:9–15 and Luke 11:2–4. Some of the wording is identical: "Father, Hallowed be thy name, Thy kingdom come, Lead us not into temptation." Other phrases, though not identical, are close to each other: "Give us today/ each day." Still other words appear only in Matthew: Our; who art in heaven; Thy will be done on earth as it is in heaven; Deliver us from evil. In Luke there are five petitions, in Matthew seven. Luke's version then is shorter; mainly because of this, many scholars think Luke's is the earlier of the two, and that Matthew's version represents a later expansion.

Even though the wording differs a bit and the length varies, the structure of the prayer is consistent. The prayer opens with (a) an *address* to the Father. Then it proceeds to (b) *Thou-petitions* that focus mainly on God. Next it includes (c)

Homiletical Perspective

The Great Sermon within which these verses fall represents a powerful affirmation of both the transcendence of God that is beyond doubt and the coming "reign of God" as present reality and eschatological hope, demanding of those who would share in this reign a life of radical obedience and righteousness. Here is affirmed the power of the rule of heaven intersecting the life of the faithful both in the present and in the ultimate manifestation of the reign of God.

The introduction to this saying on prayer may be a pejorative reflection on pagan religious expression, which is characterized as mere babbling. It is reminiscent of Elijah on Mount Carmel, when the babbling pagans pray and cut themselves (1 Kgs. 18:26–29). A similar idea, not unknown to the Jewish community of the day, is found in the apocryphal book of Ecclesiasticus or Sirach 7:14:

> Do not babble in the assembly of the elders,
>   and do not repeat yourself when you pray.

Jesus' concern here is, first, to take the focus from the act of prayer itself and to turn our attention instead to the one who is supreme and to whom our prayers are directed. This may offer an opportunity for addressing those persons who are afraid to pray in a public context under the pretext that they do not

Theological Perspective

It is also essential to attend to Jesus' remark about Gentiles and what they may think their long-winded prayers accomplish (v. 7), as modern people surely find themselves within earshot of hollow prayers, words piled up more for their own or others' hearing than for God's information. We ought certainly to pause and marvel at verse 8, comprising as it does one of Jesus' most profound claims about the nature of God, a claim that lies at the very heart of Jesus' introduction to the prayer: "Your Father knows what you need before you ask him" (v. 8).

Indeed! Here Jesus lays claim, on God's behalf, to a kind of comprehensive divine knowledge and interest that may well have been alien to common thinking in his own time, and surely remains entirely foreign to the thinking of many people in the modern world.

People of our times are no strangers to excessive verbiage, in every conceivable context, from slick advertising to common, everyday speech, words employed to stall while seeking the right word. Jesus criticizes a piety meant to draw attention to the one who is pious. The multitudinous words of the Gentile babblers are not superfluous "um's" and "er's"—for them at least—but edifying, even eloquent symphonies of holy speech. The problem is that this kind of speech is not really directed to God. Heaps of empty phrases are to be avoided, for *God's* sake.

We can almost hear the trumpet blast (v. 2) intended to garner attention from the maximum number of witnesses and to focus on good works or a gift of alms or an eloquently pious prayer. The meat of Jesus' introduction and prayer provides the opposite to empty or self-serving rhetoric; Jesus models a prayer of depth that is elegantly simple and straightforward.

The people who first received Matthew's Gospel may have been familiar with a ritual repetition of doctrinal formulae in the religious cults around them, and the sheer volume of words may have suggested a need to capture the attention of inattentive gods. People of any era can be encouraged by Jesus' introduction to this prayer to recognize the endless recitation of empty phrases for what it can be: pompous, self-serving, and, most importantly, a denial of the God who is predisposed to hear, to attend, to care in an intimate way. Offerings of extended wordiness may simply go unheeded, as they are not addressed to God, but spoken for the benefit of others who may hear or overhear them. They may be antithetical both to the common good and to the intentions of those who pray.

Pastoral Perspective

to look inward, for it is at once a prayer of adoration and a prayer of confession. How can we ask for our daily bread without assessing (silently) how much bread we throw away? How does one beg for forgiveness without being reminded of a neighbor, friend, or family member who remains unforgiven? Can we ask for protection at the time of trial while remaining blind to the temptation that we willfully invite?

Jesus' prayer thumps along to the beating of our heart. While the beginning lines of the prayer elevate our attention toward the heavens, by the conclusion we are stuck in the belly of our soul, because we are unwilling to forgive others and thereby unable to receive the forgiveness promised us by God. There is no easier character to play than the victim, especially when the claim of victimization conveniently enables us to forget our supporting roles in broken relationships. Imagine what it would be like if forgiveness retained a place in all human relationships. Imagine that instead of pointing fingers at each other we presented gifts wrapped in the fabric of forgiveness. What if, rather than laughing at the predictable fall of hypocrites, we raced to catch them and soften their landing.

If one brings this prayer to life, once one leaves the privacy of the prayer room and returns to the chaos of real life, strange things will happen. The kingdom may actually come. In truth, the kingdom will already be coming if and when we claim Jesus' model prayer as a mandate for daily living.

Still, there is some part of me that cannot help but wonder why a prayer that is frequently recited and widely known seems so often to come back empty. We witness glimpses of the kingdom coming each day, but mere glimpses are not what Jesus encouraged us to pray for. Is God ignoring our consistent pleadings for the kingdom to come? Are we, perhaps, to believe that God's will is being done, just not in the manner we anticipated?

For Jesus' audience, the coming kingdom of heaven represented the sharply contrasting alternative to the Roman Empire. The rule of the Romans was total and absolute. To consider out loud the possibility of another kingdom coming was treasonous and might result in death. In our contemporary context, empires retain the power to punish rabble-rousers. If we dare to be faithful in public to the prayer we utter in private, the absolute rule of the "evil one" manifested in oppressive political, economic, and social systems will be threatened. Praying this prayer, however, does not call forth the violent revolution Jesus' enemies feared. Rather,

We-petitions that focus on our life now: our need for bread, for forgiveness, and for help in trying circumstances. Neither version concludes with a doxology: "For thine is the kingdom . . ." Christians in the second century began using a short doxology; a longer doxology, customarily used in Protestant churches, was appended even later.

Origin and Expansion. The Lord's Prayer has come to us, as its literary features suggest, by a process of development. Jesus probably taught his disciples a model prayer. Luke, decades later, recorded it in a version that may well be close to the original, although we do not know for sure. Matthew rendered it in a slightly fuller form, almost certainly the form that was being used in worship in his community near the end of the first century. Still later, other Christians tacked on endings that reflected their experience of the majesty of God. The prayer then is something of an accordion. As it expanded, it projected a fuller and richer sound—the sound we "sing" today.

Some people find it upsetting that the form of the Lord's Prayer they recite does not come from the lips of Jesus. The fact that the prayer developed has profound, positive implications. It indicates that members of the faith community gradually mingled their voices with the voice of the One they worshiped, his words becoming their words and their words becoming his. With the growth of the tradition, we witness something striking: people living into Christ, bonding with him, identifying with his deeds and words so completely that who he is and who they are begin to merge. They speak with him and through him. Precisely because it has a history, a history of expansion, the Lord's Prayer is an example of participation in Christ. It reflects the participation of earlier generations and enriches our own participation as we voice the prayer together. The prayer is a gift from Christ *to* his church, and a gift from Christ *and* his church.

Substance. The meaning of the Lord's Prayer comes into sharper focus when we clarify a few details. The first petition, "Hallowed be thy name," is an urgent appeal for God to act. In English it may sound like praise, but it is an imperative. The "name" is simply a traditional way of speaking of God. May you—your name—be sanctified, that is, vindicated, recognized as holy, and therefore extolled. God is being called upon to reveal God's glory in a world all too full of ugliness and evil—and to do so soon. The second petition, "Thy kingdom come," is of a piece with the

know how to pray. The right attitude in prayer is that of focusing not on oneself and how one is doing or on the observers and their approval or evaluation, but on God, who is awesome, yet compassionate.

Jesus' teaching also raises serious questions concerning why we pray. It provides a sharp challenge to those who understand prayer as like being in a relationship with Santa Claus, in which the purpose of prayer is to convey to God one's list of wants. Jesus makes it clear, not only that YHWH is real, but that YHWH knows our needs before we articulate them. Jesus here anticipates what he will teach later in the Sermon on the Mount concerning the Father's care for the birds and flowers (6:26–31) and the Father who knows to give good gifts to his children (7:7–11).

Jesus' prayer also serves as a model for his disciples. In Luke 11:1–4, a disciple asks Jesus how to pray, and Jesus then presents them with a model. Here in Matthew, it is Jesus who takes the initiative in offering the model prayer, which challenges conventional understandings of God's relationship to God's people from the very first phrase. "Our Father" introduces a radically new dimension of intimacy between God and the people. It also invites the Christian community to explore how we understand God and God's relationship to us. Jesus renders the relationship between God and humanity in more personal terms and affirms an understanding of human beings as connected by kinship to God as their Father, thus making this the prayer of the Christian family throughout the world. The plural pronouns emphasize the sense of community and family that also find expression in Paul's images of the church as a unified body, a corrective to the individualism that has come to characterize much of life in the Western world.

In the opening address, God who indwells heaven is represented not as some remote figment of the imagination, but as the One who is supreme over human society and in whose sovereignty human history is ultimately fulfilled. For the preacher, this also challenges the perspective of modernity, with its elevation of human beings to a position of supremacy in the universe. The prayer places human beings in a position of dependence in relation to God and stewardship in relation to the created order, both rooted in a perspective of humility from which the name of God is truly hallowed.

From address, the prayer turns to petition. The petition concerning the kingdom asserts the supremacy of God and constitutes a subversive affirmation that all earthly powers are transitory and have no

Matthew 6:7–15

Theological Perspective

Jesus objected to vacant vocalization, not only because it distracts disciples from their true mission and fills the church assembly with babble that is beside the point, but also because it fundamentally denies who God is. The essence of true prayer lies in self-revealing honesty before God, the supreme confessor for those desiring to unburden themselves in order to be reinvigorated for labor on behalf of the gospel. The premise upon which Jesus based this assurance is that petitioners' needs are known before God is even asked. One unnamed early church authority declared, "As soon as sincere prayer issues from the mouth, the angels take it up in their hands and bring it before God."[1]

To avoid empty phrases and reflect in prayer more fully on who God really is, believers may benefit from Jesus' admonition on the strength of simple, single-word prayers that can carry more weight than paragraphs devoid of straightforward, honest communication: "Help!" "Strength!" "Heal!" "Peace!" "Thank you!" Impressive wordiness is rendered unnecessary because Jesus declares that it is in the very nature of God to attend to honest, sincere prayers emerging from genuine faith. God's responsiveness is already poised, out ahead of the one in prayer, prepared to supply what is needed before the petitioner is even finished, before needs are formed into words. This lesson may have been lost on generations of believers following the apostolic era, which provided the ending of the prayer that we know so well in the church today: "Yours is the kingdom, and the power, and the glory."

In the prayer of Matthew's Gospel, God has sized things up already, and awaits believers who turn toward God and boldly pour—*pray*—their hearts out. Apparently it is in the nature of God to pay careful and faithful attention to honest prayer.

ROBERT J. ELDER

Pastoral Perspective

the harder and perhaps more dangerous work is in revolting against our own worst tendencies to covet more than our daily bread and to deny forgiveness to others. The Lord's Prayer calls forth the kind of systemic change capable of ushering in a new kingdom. Such change, though, will be hard to see at first. Initially it will appear as if it is happening in private or is silent.

If the burden of following Jesus' lead in prayer is cumbersome, remember the promise of verse 8: God knows what we need before we ask. The model prayer is then also a road map for our return to God. It is an encouragement for God to come down to be with us and an invocation for our journey toward God. Such a journey is not easy, so it is right that our steps are guided by familiar words. The road toward God is narrow, but it is not hidden.

Even as the prayer is animated by silence, it is also likely that the prayer served the early church as liturgy. Recited in public worship, the collected voices of the church men and women were joined to the voice of Jesus. It is a personal prayer that is nurtured and, finally, lived in public and in the congregation. There is power in praying like this. In fact, it is not possible for us to realize the promises of this prayer absent the encouragement of others. The model prayer asks too much for one person to bear alone. The journey is inward, but inwardness is not the final destination. Contrary to popular opinion, prayer of this sort is not self-serving or valued only for its meditative attributes. Neither is it solely therapeutic. Rather, this discomforting prayer unsettles our assumption that what we see now will forever be true. In short, it is an alternative not only to the street prayers Jesus refers to in his prelude, but also to the paltry and small prayers that we settle for when we do not have a model.

AMOS JERMAN DISASA

---

1. Anonymous, in Manlio Simonetti, ed., *Ancient Christian Commentary on Scripture, New Testament Ia: Matthew 1–13* (Downers Grove, IL: InterVarsity Press, 2001), 126.

first, as is the additional phrase in Matthew, "Thy will be done." These Thou-petitions look to the future, to the end of history, to the culmination of God's saving work. They beg God for a whole new world. They are, by implication, brutally realistic. They know that however much we may succeed in ameliorating the world's major ills—something we should certainly strive to do—there will be no end to any of them until God intervenes and radically reconstitutes everything "on earth as it is in heaven."

In the meantime, there is the matter of getting on day by day. So we have the We-petitions: the request for God to sustain our life, to forgive our sins, to prevent our being tempted to the point where we turn away from him. All three petitions express a humble confidence in God's providential care and a conviction that they will be heard. "Ask, and it will be given you; search, and you will find; knock, and the door will be opened for you" (Matt. 7:7; Luke 11:9).

Implications. We learn from our passage that Christian prayer is fundamentally about asking—five petitions in Luke, seven in Matthew, the totality of the Lord's Prayer. There are, to be sure, other types of prayer, all of them vitally important, but none more basic than petition. At its core, prayer is simply asking, *asking God for appropriate things.*

Of course, that begs the question, what is appropriate? Some people feel guilty asking God for anything concrete, especially for themselves. It seems selfish and pointless. Does not Jesus say the Father knows our needs before we ask him (Matt. 6:8)? Yes, when we ask, we are not informing God of something God does not already know. God knows and wants to provide and, we believe, will do so regardless. Nevertheless, there are some things God wants us to have *precisely as prayed for.* Why? To foster in us a deep sense of gratitude and humility and stewardship. Prayer then is for our benefit. It is, as George Herbert put it, "the heart in pilgrimage."[1]

DAVID R. ADAMS

ultimacy, even as it calls those who pray to participate with God in the realization of the kingdom of heaven within human history.

The petition concerning the will of God speaks in its original context to the openness of the faithful to the will of God for humanity. It places an obligation on the faithful, not only to align themselves with the will of God for humanity, but to seek to discern and live according to that will for the sake of the world.

The fourth petition undermines notions of the Christian faith as something concerned only with ethereal and eternal realities. It expresses God's concern for the things that make for the daily sustenance of human beings. At the same time, it constitutes an imperative for the faithful, as people of the kingdom, to take note of those for whom daily bread is absent and to see to their needs.

The fifth petition acknowledges human estrangement from God and seeks reconciliation with God through his forgiveness. This has been achieved in the saving work of Jesus Christ, but it must now be received by each person. The petition makes clear that reconciliation with God through the exercise of God's forgiveness must be complemented by a similar forgiveness of the neighbor as an expression of the radical values that prevail with the kingdom of God.

The sixth petition may seem at a superficial glance to be suggesting that God is a source of temptation. James 1:12–15 makes it clear that God is not the source of such temptation. Rather, the petition is a plea to God, before whom all powers of evil stand impotent, to save us from ourselves, even when we think that we are in a right relationship with God. This petition needs to be linked with the following one regarding rescue from evil. Together, these two petitions challenge in the faithful any sense of self-assurance and invulnerability.

Seen from an eschatological perspective, the Lord's Prayer is an appeal for the final inbreaking and consummation of the kingdom of God, a kingdom above all earthly authorities, a realm in which God will be acknowledged and God's will will be accomplished, not only for the sake of the elect, but for the whole creation.

HOWARD GREGORY

1. *George Herbert's Work in Prose and Verse* (London: William Pickering, 1848), ii, 48.

Matthew 6:16–18

[16]"And whenever you fast, do not look dismal, like the hypocrites, for they disfigure their faces so as to show others that they are fasting. Truly I tell you, they have received their reward. [17]But when you fast, put oil on your head and wash your face, [18]so that your fasting may be seen not by others but by your Father who is in secret; and your Father who sees in secret will reward you."

Theological Perspective

The contemplation of an unseen yet all-seeing God of secret rewards can intimidate. These three verses provide concise instruction on both superficial and profound motivations for a practice all but lost in modern Western Christianity: fasting as devotion. Anyone taking up a fast as an act of faith would do well to immerse himself or herself in the perspective of the admonitions of these verses.

In earlier years of the church's development, when fasting appears to have been a common accompaniment to religious faith, Chrysostom declared that some believers behaved like actors (Greek: *hypokritēs*), taking up a fast with great outward demonstration of their efforts, striving to outdo others with the spectacle of their fast, resorting to pretence, "even while neglecting to fast, yet still wearing the garments of those who fast."[1] A believer's action can travel in a more faith-filled direction. Still, Augustine wrote that, in what has been termed "the theatre of the locked room," "vainglory can find a place not only in the splendor of pomp and worldly wealth but even in the garment of sackcloth as well. It is then all the more dangerous because it is a deception under

1. Chrysostom, "The Gospel of Matthew, Homily 20.1," in Manlio Simonetti, ed., *Ancient Christian Commentary on Scripture, New Testament Ia: Matthew 1–13* (Downers Grove, IL: InterVarsity Press, 2001), 140.

Pastoral Perspective

Centuries before the proliferation of social media tools that enable us to control our public personas with the click of a mouse, Jesus of Nazareth cautions us to be careful about what we share. There is an unspoken assumption—especially prevalent within generations unable to recall a world without easy, free access to the World Wide Web—that the events that make up our lives, including the banal as well as the more significant moments, are only as real as they are "shared." One might argue that the ability to share the moments of our lives as they happen is a good thing; celebrating a wedding engagement with others, for example, in real time, with complementary video footage, cannot hurt, right? No, but what happens when we share more than the things worthy of community-wide celebration? Should such a reflexive impulse to "share" extend to our suffering, pain, and spiritual disciplines? There is a benefit to journeying together as we follow Jesus. Might it also be beneficial for us occasionally to journey alone?

Jesus reminds us in these verses that we ought to keep the suffering compelled by our spiritual disciplines quiet. He does not trust our motives for sharing. Can you blame him? The self-satisfaction we experience in knowing that others see the suffering we endure in the name of Jesus is a cheap imitation

Exegetical Perspective

Literary Features. The teaching of Jesus on fasting—deliberate, total abstention from food for religious reasons—is the third of three successive warnings in the Sermon on the Mount against practicing one's piety in public so as to call attention to oneself. Whether it be almsgiving (6:1–4), prayer (6:5–8), or fasting (6:16–18), it is to be done either in private or so unobtrusively that no one else is aware.

Jesus' teaching in all three passages has a sharp polemical thrust directed at "the hypocrites" who display their pious deeds ostentatiously in the synagogues and streets of Palestine. Here, as in Matthew 7:5, their identity is not specified any further, but throughout the Gospel Matthew applies the label, usually to the Pharisees and sometimes, especially in the withering denunciations of chapter 23, to the scribes as well. The disciples of Jesus are to differentiate themselves from such people in the way that they fulfill their religious duties.

In what does the hypocrisy of those censured by Jesus consist? There is nothing in chapter 6 to suggest that it is a matter of pretense. At least so far as almsgiving, prayer, and fasting are concerned, Jesus does not fault "the hypocrites" for professing a belief they do not hold, or hiding a vice under the cover of virtue, or living a lie with the aim to deceive. Rather,

Homiletical Perspective

The verse with which this chapter begins introduces a somber, if not awesome warning concerning the practice of religious ritual and deeds of righteousness: "Beware of practicing your piety before others in order to be seen by them; for then you have no reward from your Father in heaven" (6:1).

The sacramental principle is one of the key theological affirmations of the Christian church in its approach to the reality of life and the physical environment. In its simplest form it is an affirmation: the things that constitute physical matter can be the vehicles for the revelation of God and spiritual reality. In some parts of the Christian church, water, bread, and wine—common things in the daily lives of human beings—are seen as the means by which the believer encounters the divine presence, grace, and the deepening of the alliance between God and humankind. We use these physical things, as well as ritual acts from daily life, to give voice and shape to how we experience God and how we encounter God in worship. Fasting constitutes a ritual or spiritual discipline by which the faithful, through a break in the daily round of life and a refusal of physical sustenance, seek to be open to and responsive to God.

In a world in which some have too much to eat and are afflicted with obesity and the consequent

Matthew 6:16–18

Theological Perspective

the pretense of service to God."[2] One fast, the fast on public display, makes the act its own reward. The other fast, a closeted fast, takes place in the solitude of the shuttered room, where it may acquire a solitary satisfaction.

Martin Luther declared, "Fasting and bodily preparation are certainly fine outward training, but a person who has faith in these words, 'given for you' and 'shed for you for the forgiveness of sin' is really worthy and well prepared" (*Luther's Small Catechism*: "The Sacrament of the Altar"). For his part, Calvin declared, "A holy and lawful fast has three ends in view. We use it either to mortify and subdue the flesh, that it may not wanton; or to prepare the better for prayer and holy meditation; or to give evidence of humbling ourselves before God, when we would confess our guilt before him" (*Institutes of the Christian Religion*, 4.12.15).

Jesus characterized the desire to display one's fast to others as a shallow, even hypocritical motivation. Deeper, more authentic incentive leads to fasting that is "not seen by others but by your Father." Looking toward self-denial's chief end, the "reward" for fasting comes from the integrity of a fast that is invisible to all but God, "who sees in secret" and rewards by means invisible to the eyes of others.

Fasting, as a religious practice providing its own reward, makes little palpable sense to many people in the modern world. Moderns prefer fasting as a practical effort: a programmatic thirty-hour famine, the goal of which is some measurable result: raising money to relieve hunger, or losing excess weight. If we desire to comprehend the word about God that drives this text, to know what motivated Jesus to offer it, that desire becomes a serious call to puzzle out what Jesus intends for us to know concerning fasting. Understanding the purpose of a practice involving self-denial is particularly difficult in a twenty-first-century, Facebook world, given as it is to excessive self-concern about even the most inane aspects of life. It is hard to imagine maintaining a more difficult religious practice than fasting in any but a few congregations in our time. Why would God desire it? On the other hand, why do many Christians in the modern West turn a soundproof ear to an unmistakable call for the centrality of fasting in the practice of faith?

Who is this God who sees "in secret"? In considering God's identity and will, prose may fail us. In

2. Augustine, "Sermon on the Mount 2.12.41," in Manlio Simonetti, ed., *Ancient Christian Commentary on Scripture, New Testament Ia: Matthew 1–13* (Downers Grove, IL: InterVarsity Press, 2001), 141.

Pastoral Perspective

of the "reward" promised by Jesus in verse 18. Jesus does not supply a clear definition of the "reward," but it is apparently something deeper, more lasting, and more profound than the "Atta-boy" and "You go, girl" that we expect to hear when our neighbors notice how hard we are working on our faith.

Still, the encouragement to suffer through the fast in secret demands another step. Not only are we to remain silent regarding the reason for our dismal appearance, but it is also necessary actively to disguise our depleted state. In this manner we might follow the example of the desert fathers and mothers, a loose collection of men and women who purposely moved out to the deserts of Egypt in the third century. They left everything behind to seek solitude and grow closer to God. Many of them drove themselves out to the wilderness as a response to the popularization of Christianity after it was established as the Roman state religion. In an unexpected move they withdrew from the world just as Jesus was being accepted by it. They lived an unordinary life—forsaking convention and conveniences and embracing the scarcity of the desert wilderness in an effort to find God.

The results of their quest for a quiet place to practice their faith cannot be overstated. Without the distraction of practicing their faith publicly or, better yet, demonstrating their faith publicly, their attention remained on the reward promised by God. Those of us unable to witness a life of solitude firsthand can still learn from the desert people of the third century through their simple but not quaint reflections on following Jesus. Preachers and teachers looking for practical examples of piety that is not public will find the witness of the desert fathers and mothers more than adequate.

We learn from them that the journey to the cross demands an examination of our willingness to deny certain seemingly innocent things that can get in the way of the "reward." Approval by our peers is one notable example. How so? Fasting is intended to elicit an acute awareness of our ultimate dependence on God. When we are unshackled from the incessant voices reminding us to eat, we can hear other voices that are no less important but normally go unnoticed. First, our own inner voice, powered by the Holy Spirit, tells us the truth when it is not manipulated by alien desires, including the desire for the approval of our peers. Second, the voice of God speaks to us through mundane, ordinary interactions and landscapes, and when the rabid insistence to eat, meet, greet, be busy, create, decide, fix, do, and be loved is set aside. To fast but then allow

he faults them for making an outward show, for performing good deeds in order to be held in high public esteem. That is a far cry from letting your "light shine before others, *so that they may* see your good works and *give glory to your Father in heaven*" (Matt. 5:16, emphasis added). The intention is all-important. At bottom, the sin of "the hypocrites" is the desire for acclaim, which, in its displacement of God by the celebration of self, borders on idolatry.

Small wonder, then, that the accolades they angle for are the only rewards they are to get (Matt. 6:2, 5, 16), meager in comparison to the rewards "your Father who sees in secret" has in store for those who carry out their religious tasks discreetly (Matt. 6:4, 6, 18). It is the very "secrecy" of such piety that stamps it as authentic, utterly devoid of any self-seeking. In this one respect, the threefold mention of future reward anticipates Matthew 25:31–46, the dramatic scene where the coming Son of Man separates the sheep from the goats at the Last Judgment. The sheep, the righteous, are surprised at their fate (as are the unrighteous). The judge explains they have done good works innocently, without calculation, motivated simply by the needs they see in others around them.

Historical Considerations. The assumption in the Sermon on the Mount is that disciples of Jesus do engage in fasting, an assumption made clear in the first phrase of our pericope, "Whenever you fast." Did they? That issue arises from the question posed pointedly in Matthew 9:14 by the disciples of John the Baptist: "Why do we and the Pharisees fast [often], but your disciples do not fast?" (cf. Mark 2:18; Luke 5:33). Jesus parries the implied criticism with a counterquestion of his own: "The wedding guests cannot mourn as long as the bridegroom is with them, can they? The days will come when the bridegroom is taken away from them, and then they will fast" (Matt. 9:15). Matthew's is a slightly abbreviated version of the reply in Mark 2:19–20 and Luke 5:34–35, and it substitutes "mourn" for "fast," but the point in all three versions is the same: the lack of fasting by the disciples of Jesus is/was temporary. That situation would/did change with his crucifixion. Note especially the image of the bridegroom who is to be "taken away."

The exchange with the disciples of John the Baptist in Matthew 9:14–15, where Jesus tacitly grants that his disciples do not fast, is narrated from a post-Easter perspective, and that accounts for the apparent contradiction with the Sermon on the Mount,

physiological challenges, the practice of fasting may not have much appeal (except as a pious cover for dieting). In Scripture the idea of fasting is grounded not in dietary and health concerns, but in the expression of penitence and repentance. In biblical times the observance of certain religious festivals included a period of fasting, which was followed by a communal ritual meal. The reading for Ash Wednesday, the first day of Lent, the season of penitence, usually is that of Joel 1:13–14, the call to repentance and prayer in which the priests are to "put on sackcloth and lament" and to "sanctify a fast" and "call a solemn assembly." The preacher may choose to explore the extent to which the call to national fasting and repentance may be appropriate for the people of God as a corporate body or as an expression of individual contrition. Our complicity with evil and inhumanity calls forth the communal need to repent nationally and globally.

In the New Testament, Jesus and his disciples seem to have turned away from fasting as an appropriate discipline and deed of righteousness. In Matthew 9:14–17 and Mark 2:18–20, people criticize Jesus and his disciples for not fasting like the Pharisees. Jesus' response contrasts the present time of Jesus' ministry with the time when he is "taken away" and crucified. For this moment in Jesus' ministry, fasting is not appropriate, but there will come a time when the bridegroom will be taken away; then fasting will be appropriate. In this story, Jesus seems to associate fasting with repentance and lament, as in the OT. The preacher may choose to explore how these seasons of eating and fasting are enacted within the Lenten discipline, a discipline practiced in certain religious traditions as a way of using ritual to reinforce faith.

Fasting as a spiritual discipline is also a way to deny oneself something that is essential to one's daily sustenance, thereby creating a greater sensitivity and openness to God. The preacher may challenge persons toward the practice of this discipline at times of special challenge and transition, as a way of listening to God. Fasting also may be used corporately by a congregation going through a particularly difficult or significant moment in its common life. The calling of a new minister, a major decision concerning an outreach project, or the planning of a new strategic orientation for the congregation can be moments for individual and corporate fasting.

Given the history of fasting as part of Jewish religious life, it appears that what Jesus was underscoring in his teaching was not the abandonment

Matthew 6:16–18   **131**

Matthew 6:16–18

Theological Perspective

the poetic imagination of Taoist master Chuang Tzu (250 BCE), famously cited by Thomas Merton, we may encounter a fuller expression of this God, who prefers a faithful, private fast to public display:

> Who can free himself from achievement
> And from fame, descend and be lost
> Amid the masses of men?
> He will flow like Tao, unseen,
> He will go about like Life itself
> With no name and no home.
> Simple he is, without distinction.
> To all appearances he is a fool
> His steps leave no trace. He has no power.
> He achieves nothing, has no reputation.
> Since he judges no one
> No one judges him.
> Such is the perfect man:
> his boat is empty[3]

The poet's "boat" to freedom is the very body of the person making fast. It is the incarnation of a self-denial, which, at last, may expand mundane perception into a fuller awareness of God as Other. The gospel sometimes borders on oxymoron: finding comes through losing, fulfillment comes through emptying, satisfaction comes through self-denial, God sees what is hidden, in secret. These are difficult assertions made about the true nature of God's desires for God's people, assertions we may not dismiss lightly while hoping to remain faithful to the call we receive to be participants in the kingdom.

In our era, relatively few modern church bodies in the West ask adherents to take up a fast in any but unobtrusive, symbolic ways. Modern people may wonder about motivation for self-denial of any sort. What kind of religious expression requires abstinence from food, or anything else, and for what reason? What is the benefit?

The secret of a fast may be kept between God and disciple. If those who fast decide it is more important to pursue fasting for the benefit of others, then that demonstration may well become its own reward. If a fast is undertaken in solitude, out of the view of others, a believer may discover what it is to receive a different reward, the gift of an experience shared only with God.

ROBERT J. ELDER

Pastoral Perspective

the life-giving voice of God to be truncated by the approving voices of others—who, by the way, are also seeking the reciprocity of your approval—is to settle for a cheap imitation rather than the eternal reward.

In this way Jesus' instructions on fasting are less about correcting something we might do wrong, and more an encouragement not to exchange the truth that is rooted in God's faithfulness for the temporary satisfaction of human approval. If a tree falls in the forest and no one is present to hear the sound, Jesus might argue, the sound does not go unnoticed. God hears it and responds.

According to the prevailing sentiment within worshiping communities, our faith is best practiced simultaneously and together. Contrast this with the inward journey. Anonymity is not always a bad thing. Not to be noticed, at least when you are fasting or engaged in other spiritual disciplines, may be not only desirable but necessary.

How might a recovery of the inner journey look in a local church or community of faith?

1. Standard retreat formats are altered to invite and encourage an abundance of time for individuals to be quiet and explore the bounty of solitude.

2. Newcomers are allowed to be present in worship for as long as they need before being pushed into small-group settings, service opportunities, and committees.

3. Up-front leaders, especially pastors, are expected to disappear regularly over extended periods (several weeks in a row at a minimum) to practice their faith away from the crowds.

4. Rich, new liturgy is written, and timeless, ancient liturgy is reclaimed with a particular emphasis on personal worship at home.

I suspect that the allure of social media is proportional to the number of relationships it encourages, rather than the quality of the human connections it actually supports. It is impossible, however, to be social through digital media, or just plain social, without first nurturing our relationship with God, a connection that cannot be experienced virtually. To be alone with God, one must reject the cheap thrill of accumulating flimsy relationships to embrace first the one relationship capable of preserving our life.

AMOS JERMAN DISASA

---

3. Thomas Merton, *The Intimate Merton: His Life from His Journals*, ed. Patrick Hart and Jonathan Montaldo (New York: HarperOne, 1999), 211.

Feasting on the Gospels

Exegetical Perspective

where it is assumed that his disciples do fast indeed. In both instances the Matthean Jesus is speaking to and for the post-Easter church. In all likelihood, the very first disciples did not fast, but post-Easter Christians took up the custom of fasting as an expression of penitence or grief. Matthew 9:14–15 explains *why* it was done; Matthew 6:17–19 explains *how* it should be done.

Implications. Most Christians today, if they fast at all, do so as a Lenten discipline, in imitation of the forty-day fast of Jesus in the wilderness depicted in Matthew and Luke, but even then not as a discipline that involves total abstention from food. Is the practice of fasting, however severe or minimal, to be commended? If so, under what conditions?

The early history of Christian fasting demonstrates that this issue, like so many others, cannot be settled by simply asking, "What would Jesus do?" There is nothing in Matthew or Luke to suggest that Jesus expected anyone to imitate his forty-day fast—something specific to his messianic vocation—and there is much in the Gospels, as we have seen, to indicate that his own disciples never fasted while he was alive.

Still there is value to fasting for a season, as a way of sanctifying time. The persistence of Christian fasting from the first century to the present attests to that. Fasting—especially in conjunction with prayer, self-examination, and repentance—can serve as a reminder that in every moment we stand "before God," and it can serve as a vehicle for deepening that relationship. It is a physical discipline that concentrates the mind. As the Sermon on the Mount insists, it is never a matter of self-generated merit. Fasting is solely for the glory of God.

DAVID R. ADAMS

Homiletical Perspective

of fasting as a ritual expression of piety, but those expressions of piety that are directed to an audience other than God—a stage performance that has the wrong motivation. Fasting directed toward human audiences receives the appropriate and intended reward—the praise of men and women—but no acknowledgment from God. Jesus makes it quite clear that the label of "hypocrites" has never been far from the religious community. Indeed, he points to the ease with which we can be overtaken by self-deception and our practice of the faith become like an empty shell.

To be sure, religion is practiced with a mixture of pure and impure motives. Faithful piety and its various expressions begin and end with one's relationship with God, a single-hearted devotion, and lead to change—transformation—in the life of the person. Fasting as a ritual or spiritual discipline must spring from a heart of honorable motivation and be accompanied by a change of heart. The preacher may want to engage the faithful concerning the ways the practice of the faith meets this criterion of authenticity. Does what is being expressed on the outside have any relation to what is going on in the inner dimensions of our life?

Indeed, where it is authentic, the life of faith will be like the very life of Jesus, which was characterized by powerful rituals, from his baptism in the Jordan and his fasting and praying in the wilderness at the beginning of his ministry, to the entry into Jerusalem on a donkey, the washing of the feet of the disciples, and his sharing with them in a ritual meal the night before the crucifixion. How many of the rituals of the church have come directly from the ritual-filled life of Jesus?

A misreading of this passage in Matthew could give one the idea that Jesus is encouraging a nonritualistic, cognitive, internal religion, at best a head trip with no ritual. Religious faith without ritual would be a very sterile affair, just as ritual that is oriented toward human audiences is idolatrous. The practice of true religion is focused on God, who in turn transforms us.

HOWARD GREGORY

Matthew 6:19–21

¹⁹"Do not store up for yourselves treasures on earth, where moth and rust consume and where thieves break in and steal; ²⁰but store up for yourselves treasures in heaven, where neither moth nor rust consumes and where thieves do not break in and steal. ²¹For where your treasure is, there your heart will be also."

Theological Perspective

The main theme in this passage for reflection is treasure and its storage and security. The *Oxford English Dictionary* defines the noun "treasure" as "wealth or riches stored or accumulated, especially in the form of precious metal; gold or silver coin" or "anything valued and preserved as precious." As a verb, *OED* defines "to treasure" as "to put away or lay aside (anything of value) for preservation, security, or future use." Two key words that stand out in relation to treasure are *value* and *storage* or setting apart.

The Bible uses treasure (*genez* in Hebrew; *thēsauros* in Greek) in different ways. In ancient and traditional societies, treasures constituted accumulated wealth stored primarily in palaces and temples. Palace and temple treasuries became principal targets for looting during wars. Nebuchadnezzar looted the Jerusalem temple treasury (2 Kgs. 25:13–17) and palace (2 Kgs. 24:13; 2 Chr. 36:18) and deposited the loot in his god's temple treasury in Babylon (Dan. 1:2). Cyrus later returned the treasure to the Jewish leaders for the rebuilding of the temple (Ezra 1:8–11). Treasure is also used metaphorically in the Bible for wisdom and knowledge (Prov. 2:4; Col. 2:3); Israel is God's "treasured possession" (Exod. 19:5). In the New Testament the kingdom of heaven is likened to a "treasure hidden" (Matt. 13:44), the

Pastoral Perspective

Preaching about wealth and possessions is no easy task. Many of our parishioners will have worked hard Monday through Friday to earn as much as possible, and then will have gone shopping on Saturday to stock up on earthly treasures of one kind or another, only to come to church on Sunday and be told that it was all apparently in vain.

"Do not store up for yourselves treasures on earth," Jesus says, "but store up for yourselves treasures in heaven." There are perfectly justifiable reasons why we feel the need to store up treasures on earth—reasons that have nothing to do with greed or crass materialism. We want to plan for the future. We need to save for retirement. We have to put the kids through college. We are told to stash something away in case of some unforeseen crisis down the road.

So we build up a nest egg—and manage to accumulate a fair number of things along the way—as a means of ensuring our own security—but how much is enough?

Wall Street Journal columnist Robert Frank wrote the book *Richistan*, a travel guide through the parallel universe that the ultrarich in America have built for themselves, complete with Gulfstream jets, 30,000-square-foot homes, and alligator-skin toilet

Exegetical Perspective

Across cultures and history, humans have sought to define and represent themselves by what they possess. In most societies, the accumulation of "treasure," however it may be defined, is also closely associated with power, status, and security. The amassing and hoarding of wealth thus also has a lot to do with the cause and supposed treatment of the underlying human conditions of alienation and insecurity. It is little wonder, then, that the accumulation of possessions may become a consuming passion, a hunger never satisfied, eventually consuming us.

In this brief section of the Sermon on the Mount, Jesus names these dynamics and calls disciples to become discerning consumers of treasure. In a society awash with a seemingly infinite array of products that we evaluate largely in terms of what they say about us, we develop highly refined skills of discernment and discrimination. This discernment and discrimination are usually blinkered and distorted by popular regimes of meaning and worth. As a consequence, many of us, even Christians, spend our lives chasing some version of "the American Dream" or of the life to come, rather than the dream of God's reign on and for the earth.

The "treasure" Jesus calls us to seek concerns primarily the "righteousness" (relationships made right)

Homiletical Perspective

What is the good news here? This is the question always before the gospel preacher. If a sermon is to move beyond teaching (which it certainly also may contain) to proclaim the gospel, then the work of the preacher must begin and end with the question: What is the good news here?

The question may seem a puzzling one when applied to Matthew 6:19–21, for a number of reasons. First, the three verses seem to merely offer another bullet point in a list of prohibitions for the Christian life. "Do not do this. Do not do that." Second, the particular warning not to store up for oneself treasures on earth, but to store up treasures in heaven, seems like a move to detach from the world and any accumulation of wealth, especially when followed by the declaration, "You cannot serve God and wealth" (6:24). In other words, one can read this passage as participation in a dualism that renders the world bad and the heavens good. Worldly wealth is bad; spiritual, heavenly wealth is good. Third, this bit of instruction might then leave one with the impression that any tangible blessing or reward is a delayed one to be cashed in upon achieving a heavenly existence beyond this world. If there is good news at all, it is to be found in delayed gratification.

Matthew 6:19–21

Theological Perspective

gospel message described as a "treasure in clay jars" (2 Cor. 4:7), while believers are referred to as "God's special possession" (1 Pet. 2:9 NIV).

In the Bible treasure, therefore, has a much deeper meaning than riches or material wealth. While the Bible, on the whole, is critical of the craving pursuit of material wealth or riches, treasure is cast in favorable light. Jesus warns in Matthew 6:24 that "you cannot serve God and wealth [or mammon]" and in Matthew 19:24 that "it is easier for a camel to go through the eye of a needle than for someone who is rich to enter the kingdom of God." Paul warns that "the love of money is a root of all kinds of evil" (1 Tim. 6:10). It is important to differentiate greed and craving for material things, which is condemned here, from riches and wealth in themselves.

A treasure is something that we value highly. These are normally things that mean a lot to us because we have invested so much in them or because someone dear bequeathed them to us. It is the value invested in things that makes them treasure, not necessarily the things in themselves. Treasures can include family mementos or words of important figures. A treasure therefore has more than monetary value. Treasures have emotional value. People take pleasure and seek happiness in the things they treasure. Due to the value we put in treasures, we set them aside or seek safe and secure storage for them.

Treasures are meant for use only in very special circumstances, in critical situations, as a last resort. Treasures are a kind of insurance, both materially and emotionally. For such reasons treasures are kept in the most secure and safe places possible, called safes. A treasure, in turn, acts as a safe for our hearts, "for where your treasure is, there your heart will be also" (v. 21). When treasures are stolen or damaged, it is not just a material loss but, even more, an emotional loss, a heartbreak.

The New Testament's warning against storing up treasures on earth, where "moth and rust consume and where thieves break in and steal" (v. 19), seeks to make two important points. First, that there is no foolproof storage place here on earth; therefore it is unwise and risky to store up our treasures here on earth. The earth is riddled with perils: natural, human, and spiritual. To store up treasures on earth is to risk heartbreaks. Second, and more important, the earth is not our "home" and therefore should not be the storage place for our treasures. In the parable of the Rich Fool (Luke 12:13–21) the point is made

Pastoral Perspective

seats. These are people who know a thing or two about storing up for themselves treasures on earth!

Frank interviewed a number of them, and was quite surprised to learn that the inhabitants of Richistan were plagued by anxiety—so much so, in fact, that some had even formed self-help support groups. What could possibly keep these multimillionaires and billionaires up at night? It turned out they were worried about running out of money.[1]

Now that seems crazy—unless that is just the way humans are wired. We never think we have enough.

Frank cites one particular survey of the rich. They were asked, "How much money would you need to feel financially secure?" The results were quite revealing. Those worth $1 million said they needed twice that amount in order to feel secure. Those worth $10 million said they needed twice *that* amount. Those worth $100 million said they needed twice *that* amount. Whatever their level of wealth, no one felt that they had accumulated enough to feel secure.[2]

All of this seems to prove Jesus' point that wealth guarantees no ultimate fulfillment or security. In a world of moths and rust and thieves—not to mention a roller-coaster stock market, volatile housing prices, and corporate downsizing and outsourcing—there is always a certain amount of anxiety. No one is ever satisfied with what they currently have. Everyone wants just a little bit more.

If Richistan is one parallel universe, Jesus came proclaiming another: the kingdom of heaven, he called it. Those who wanted to be a part of it, he called to a different kind of lifestyle. He asked them to leave their occupations behind. He sent them out into the world, telling them to carry no gold or silver or copper, and to wear just the clothes on their back. He urged them not to store up treasures on earth, but instead to invest in the things of heaven.

Frankly, it is hard to imagine what this might look like today. Jesus does not tell us precisely how to store up treasure in heaven. However, he did give us his own life, and he has given us other lives as examples.

Oseola McCarty was an African American woman from Hattiesburg, Mississippi. She left school after the sixth grade to take care of a relative who was sick, and after that she went to work as a washerwoman. For seventy-five years, McCarty washed and ironed and folded the laundry of the wealthy bankers, lawyers, and doctors in town. She earned

1. Robert Frank, *Richistan: A Journey through the American Wealth Boom and the Lives of the New Rich* (New York: Crown Publishers, 2007), 203–18.
2. Ibid., 50.

that is the focus of so much of Jesus' sermon. Righteousness (or justice) is not a matter of spiritual or religious practice alone, but something that permeates the whole of life every day, including our relationships with other people, with the things of this world, and with God. The Lord's Prayer (6:9–13), which precedes this section by a few verses, already articulates the hope of those who follow Jesus into the heavenly kingdom, not in terms of some future, otherworldly realm, but for this very world reclaimed in all its dimensions from those who deny or are blind to God's will. In the heavenly kingdom God's presence, trustworthiness, and power to supply what we need each day are abundantly on display (bread, 6:11), and the debts that keep so many in bondage to human powers are removed (debts, 6:12). Each of the teachings in 6:19–34 in some way comments upon or develops what the Lord's Prayer calls forth in the disciples' relationships with God, with other people, and with material goods. Matthew 6:19–34 may be broken into four subunits, focusing on storing up "treasure" (vv. 19–21); the eye as the lamp of the body (vv. 22–23); serving God or mammon (v. 24); and worrying about life or trusting God (vv. 25–34). In these portions of the Sermon, Jesus is answering the question of how God's rule and will are realized "on earth as . . . in heaven" (6:10).

Matthew's Jesus develops the sweeping contrast set forth in 6:19–20 around the same "on earth" and "in heaven" terminology first articulated in the Lord's Prayer. In Matthew, earth and heaven are not discrete physical spaces but intersecting realms, distinguished ultimately by whether God's presence and redeeming power are named and hallowed, and thus by conflicting visions, values, forms of power, and especially relationships. In these verses, the contrast Jesus draws does not concern present vs. future or material vs. spiritual realms. Nor is the contrast between seeking and not seeking treasure. The focus, rather, concerns whether our discernment of God's presence shapes our vision and values, the kind of power we exercise and its consequences, and the character and well-being of our relationships. As the Lord's Prayer has already made clear, disciples do not hope to abandon earth for heaven, but to perceive and name God's presence and restore the earth and earthly things to their place within the rule of the heavenly Father. The contrast in verses 19–20, as in the other portions of verses 19–34, thus concerns the things and relationships toward which we direct our vision (see vv. 22–23, 24, 33), which in turn reveals where our heart is to be found (v. 21).

Discovering the Architecture of Matthew's Good News. Pressing more deeply into the architecture of the Gospel of Matthew and the particular palette offered us by the Sermon on the Mount, the preacher might discover a word of good news in Matthew 6:19–21. The unique architecture of Matthew's Gospel, as compared to that of the other Gospel accounts, is apparent in Matthew's careful and intentional effort to connect the story of Jesus to the story of Israel. This connection orients a community of Christians that may find itself increasingly alienated from its heritage. In this way, Matthew is providing for Christians continuity with the past that opens onto God's future.

One of the dominant features of Matthew's orienting literary architecture is the structure given the story by five teaching sections. The first of these teaching sections is the Sermon on the Mount, which begins with a pronouncement of blessing (Matt. 5–7). The last of these teaching sections begins with a pronouncement of woes (Matt. 23–25). As architect, Matthew is careful to create an inhabitable space for the reader by using this kind of parallelism. As the preacher takes the time to appreciate Matthew's work in this sort of detail, she or he might discover good news for the sermon.

The Sermon on the Mount begins with the pronouncement of blessing often referred to as the Beatitudes. Matthew is inviting the reader to reimagine the values that emerge from the kingdom of God. The Beatitudes read as a collection of wisdom sayings about the kingdom. There are nine of these sayings. Without pressing Matthew's parallelism too far, it is worth noting that the fifth of these nine sayings, the one that stands at the center of them, declares, "Blessed are the merciful, for they will receive mercy" (5:7). In a similar way, the parallel pronouncement of woes in Matthew 23 contains seven sayings. The one that stands at the center of these declares, "Woe to you, scribes and Pharisees, hypocrites! For you tithe mint, dill, and cummin, but have neglected the weightier matters of the law: justice and mercy and faith" (23:23). Matthew's attention to mercy is a feature that is reinforced by Jesus' instructions, "Go and learn what this means, 'I desire mercy, not sacrifice'" (9:13). Matthew is constructing a house in which God's people live deeply in the mercy of God.

The way of mercy frees one to live more fully and openly in relation to the other. From mercy flows abundance. In the way of the sacrifices, there is always deficit and never enough. One is always

Matthew 6:19–21

Theological Perspective

that not only are things we treasure corruptible and vulnerable, but that also our time here on earth is temporary.

Why heaven? As stated above, in ancient and traditional societies, treasures were stored in palaces, temples, and shrines, because these were the abodes of the rulers and the gods. These places were therefore believed to be the most secure of places. To get to the treasures, one had to go past the rulers and the gods. The Bible teaches that heaven is the dwelling place of God, the King of kings and the Lord of lords. Heaven is therefore the most secure place to store our treasure, "where neither moth nor rust consumes and where thieves do not break in and steal" (v. 20) and where we will spend eternity.

Since believers, like the nation of Israel in the Old Testament, are God's treasured possession, set apart from the rest of the world, it follows that our treasures have to be different from worldly treasures. Jesus identifies giving alms to the poor as one practical way of storing up treasures in heaven (Matt. 19:21; Mark 10:21; Luke 12:33–34; 18:22). Prayer and fasting, when done in the right spirit, are classified alongside alms to the poor as "acts of righteousness" (Matt. 6:1–18) that will be rewarded by God. The New Testament places emphasis on Christian charity, for as James puts it, "faith by itself, if it has no works, is dead" (Jas. 2:17).

The parable of the Sheep and the Goats in Matthew 25:31–46 dramatizes this point vividly. The righteous inheritors of the kingdom of heaven will be those who, as an outworking of their faith in Christ, feed the hungry, give drink to the thirsty, welcome the stranger, clothe the naked, care for the sick, and visit those in prison, not because these acts in themselves can earn us salvation—"all our righteous deeds are like a filthy cloth" (Isa. 64:6)—but because we bear those fruits as branches grafted onto the vine, apart from whom we can do nothing (John 15:5).

JOHN A. AZUMAH

Pastoral Perspective

just pennies, but tried to put away whatever she could, eventually starting up a little savings account at the First Mississippi National Bank. McCarty lived a simple life. Her treasures on earth were few. She lived in a modest frame house, just blocks from the campus of the University of Southern Mississippi. She did not get an air conditioner until she was well up in her eighties, and turned it on only when she had company. She never owned a car. She walked a mile each way to and from the grocery store. She went on Sundays to the Friendship Baptist Church, carrying a Bible held together with Scotch tape.

When she got to be eighty-seven—her hands gnarled with arthritis—McCarty had to retire. She began to put her affairs in order and decide what she wanted to do with the little she had been able to accumulate.

In 1995, the development office of the University of Southern Mississippi received a phone call from the bank. The bank had a check for them from an Oseola McCarty—a check for $150,000.

No one at the college had even heard of Oseola McCarty. She had never set foot on the campus. This washerwoman who had never been to high school—let alone college—gave away virtually every dollar she had ever made for a scholarship fund for minority students.

The gift made front-page headlines. McCarty was invited to the White House and was even awarded an honorary degree from Harvard. In an interview shortly before she died, she was asked why she did not spend the money she had earned on herself. She smiled. "I am spending it on myself," she said.[3]

I do not know exactly what Jesus had in mind when he said that we should store up for ourselves treasures in heaven; but I suspect that Oseola McCarty knew.

WALLACE W. BUBAR

---

3. Rick Bragg, "All She Has, $150,000, Is Going to a University," *New York Times*, August 13, 1995.

What then are these treasures? How do we know what are heavenly as opposed to earthly treasures? Treasure is defined by being a focus of attention, energy, imagination, and resourcefulness. While we often think of the treasures that Jesus warns against as material goods, "treasures upon the earth" is probably a wider category, encompassing not only physical possessions but such values as success, security, happiness, or even life itself. According to Jesus, the problem with earthly treasures is that they are subject to being consumed, whether by moths or rust, and stolen. Earthly treasures, in other words, are vulnerable and ephemeral.

Earthly treasures, even the ones that cannot literally be consumed or stolen, do not satisfy the basic needs for security, meaning, and self-esteem that we rely on them to fulfill. In our culture of superheated consumption, an endless array of new models, new toys, and new programs shout out the promise of satisfaction—but they never deliver.

"Heavenly treasures" (literally "treasures treasured in heaven") are, by contrast, subject to neither decay nor theft. The contrast, again, is not necessarily between material and spiritual entities, but between what lasts and what does not, between what satisfies the deep human longing for whole relationships and genuine security and what fails. The folly of treasuring things that do not last is clear enough. Still, what, more concretely, does Jesus mean by treasures that cannot be consumed or stolen?

"Treasures in heaven" refers not so much to "salvation" (which we often treat as a commodity) or to future, otherworldly rewards, but to the transformed relationships that attend God's presence, whether on earth or in heaven. Throughout Matthew's Gospel, Jesus gives us glimpses of these relationships and values, which include restoration and reconciliation, forgiveness, mercy, grace, and justice. These treasures satisfy our foundational human needs. The goods we treasure, whether material possessions, financial security, worldly power—or mercy and relationships made right—reveal where our "heart" is (6:21), the core of our identity. The heart set on heavenly treasure seeks first God's own presence and power, and in the process discovers all else that is needed (6:33). This is no mere religious ideal, but the only true alternative to the religions of consumerism, whether ancient or modern, that now threaten to consume God's creation and life itself.

STANLEY P. SAUNDERS

compelled to live out of scarcity to secure life and a future. In the way of mercy, there is always enough, and one can live freely and generously with hope.

Proclaiming Treasure in Heaven as Good News.
If the architecture of Matthew's Gospel points to mercy, then the deep structure of mercy becomes the lens for reading the particular teaching of the Sermon on the Mount. Jesus' teaching is to reappropriate the basic structure of life and of keeping the law toward a merciful end. His purpose is to exhort the listener to live more fully into the way of mercy. The preacher finds a deep and rich reservoir for proclaiming good news from this text by holding the instruction of Jesus about "treasures" within Matthew's merciful paradigm for the kingdom.

Treasure stored up "in heaven" need not be interpreted as delayed gratification or Christian living as making deposits in an eternal investment account, the dividends of which will be paid out sometime in the future. These words of Jesus are good news precisely because they free us to live in the abundance of God's gracious and merciful provision right now. They liberate us from the bondage of scarcity and the worry of "not enough." This is good news!

The gospel preacher who takes up Matthew 6:19–21 for preaching will allow the architecture of Matthew's Gospel to meet Jesus' teaching at just this point. The sermon will construct the space to declare the good news of God's merciful abundance. In order to participate with this text in proclaiming good news, the preacher will do well first to describe the way of scarcity, the "never enough." In fact, in order effectively to declare the good news of God, the sermon must first make clear how the way of scarcity is life stealing, closing us off from God and from one another. Having done this, the sermon can then pronounce, with Jesus, another way: the merciful way of abundance, a treasure in heaven, good news indeed!

STEPHEN C. JOHNSON

Matthew 6:22–23

²²"The eye is the lamp of the body. So, if your eye is healthy, your whole body will be full of light; ²³but if your eye is unhealthy, your whole body will be full of darkness. If then the light in you is darkness, how great is the darkness!"

Theological Perspective

Upon first reading, this passage of the eye being the lamp of the body appears to sit oddly between the passages on storing up treasures in heaven and the impossibility of simultaneously serving God and mammon. Upon closer examination, however, the connection will become apparent. The Bible uses the eye in a number of metaphorical senses. In several places the Old Testament talks about "the eyes" of God's favor and displeasure (Gen. 6:8; Amos 9:8). The apostle Paul talks about the enlightenment of "the eyes of your heart" (Eph. 1:18), and in the passage under consideration, Matthew talks about the eye as "the lamp of the body."

The biological function of the eye is obviously for sight or vision, which means that, literally, the passage is teaching that the eye is to the body what the sun is to the universe in the daytime, or a lamp or candle to a house at night. The metaphorical sense in which the eye is used in this passage, however, goes beyond the biological function of the eye. The meaning of the passage includes perception and vision, with implication for the choices we make. Jesus taught in parables because "seeing they do not perceive, and hearing they do not listen, nor do they understand" (Matt. 13:13).

Good vision and perception are crucial in terms of the choices we make. For instance, Eve ate the

Pastoral Perspective

"God be in my head," reads the old prayer from the *Sarum Primer*, "and in my understanding." The second line has always intrigued me: "God be in mine eyes, and in my looking." What might it mean to have God "in mine eyes, and in my looking"? This is something Jesus sheds some light on—as it were—in this passage.

It is a strange passage, at first glance. Biblical scholars tell us that, in order to make sense of it, we must first know something of the way that the ancients understood eyesight. Whereas we see the eye as a window that lets the outer light in, the ancients saw the eye as a lamp that projected the inner light outward, illuminating the world.[1]

"The eye is the lamp of the body," says Jesus. Its health and soundness determine the well-being of one's whole existence. This understanding perhaps explains why Jesus made restoring people's vision so central to his ministry. Jesus wants all of us to be able to see things aright.

Of course, no one should treat the New Testament as a textbook on ophthalmology, about which we know a great deal more in the twenty-first century than in the first. We have a much better grasp of

1. M. Eugene Boring, *The New Interpreter's Bible* (Nashville: Abingdon Press, 1995), 8:210.

Exegetical Perspective

With its focus on inner illumination, we might expect this passage to be a spiritual classic, but Jesus' discussion here of sight and light has generated among modern readers a stronger sense of obscurity than enlightenment. Countless discussions of this passage open with something like "These verses are difficult." The first level of difficulty arises from the differing ways ancient and modern people think about the function of the eye. Whereas we imagine the eye as a window that receives and filters light from outside sources, translating the light into signals that eventually reach our brains, in Jesus' day it was much more common to think of the eye as a "lamp," the source of illumination. When we speak of someone having "fire in their eyes," or of the light of life leaving one's eyes at death, we may be closer to the ancient conception that Jesus here presumes.

A second source of obscurity concerns what the eye/lamp illuminates. Does the eye shine light onto the world around, thus projecting what is within the body, or does the eye project its illumination into the body itself? The first view seems to be favored in the variant of these verses found in *Gospel of Thomas* 24: "There is light within a man of light, and he [or: it] lights up the whole world. If he [or: it] does not shine, he [or: it] is darkness." In this reading, it is the inner light of the person that illumines the world.

Homiletical Perspective

It is noticeable that these two verses tucked away in the Sermon on the Mount do not appear in any of the common lectionaries. They disappear into the ethereal air of the preaching schedule. On the surface, I can understand why. These two verses contain only several short sentences that appear to be disconnected from those that precede (vv. 19–21) and follow (v. 24) them. Verses 19–21 speak of storing up treasure in heaven as opposed to earth. Verses 22–23 speak about the eye as the lamp of the body, while verse 24 returns us to the question of serving God or money. What is the eye doing there, amid all this talk about treasure and money? Verses 22–23 seem to interrupt the natural flow of the passage. It is no wonder they disappear from the lectionary.

A closer look reveals that verses 22–23 speak about the good eye and the bad or evil eye. The good eye fills one with light. The bad eye fills one with darkness. The problem here is the evil eye. One scholar suggests that speaking idiomatically the Master generously suggests that "the evil eye, which can take over a person and cause him to say more, act less constructively than he intends, is to blame."[1] The

1. Robert T. Fortna notes a connection between the occurrence of "evil eye" in this passage and in Matthew 20 (Fortna, "Exegesis and Proclamation: 'You have made them equal to us' [Mt. 20:1–16]," *Journal of Theology for Southern Africa* 72 (1990): 66–72.

Matthew 6:22–23

Theological Perspective

forbidden fruit partly because "it was a delight to the eyes" (Gen. 3:6). In other words, good sight alone is not enough when it comes to making the right choices. As a lamp that lights the entire body, the eye serves as the entrance to our hearts and minds, thereby providing a doorway to our whole being. Healthy eyes are those that not only see well, but also perceive well. It is not only what we see, but how we perceive what we see, that makes the difference between godliness and ungodliness, between light and darkness. Bad eyes lead to bad perception, but if our eyes are good, our whole person will be illuminated.

In ancient Greece and in Hindu, Jewish, and Islamic societies, there are strong beliefs in the "evil eye" or "bad eye." An evil eye was a phrase in use among the ancient Jews to denote an envious, covetous person or disposition; a person who repined at his neighbor's prosperity, coveted their own money, and would do nothing in the way of charity. A person with an evil eye represents a great danger to our moral purity and fabric of society. A "good eye," on the other hand, represents an attitude of good will, generosity, and kindness toward other people. In Islamic traditions, "evil eye," *Isabat al-'ayn,* is a common belief that individuals have the power to look at people, animals, or objects to cause them harm.

Instead of a healthy and unhealthy eye, the King James Version of our passage has "single" and "evil" eye respectively. This makes sense against the background of the teaching on the evil eye in the Jewish context and in the wider context of Jesus' teaching against greed and materialism in the Sermon on the Mount. To fully appreciate this teaching in the wider context of the New Testament, consider Matthew 20:15, where the landowner rhetorically asks the grumbling workers: "Am I not allowed to do what I choose with what belongs to me? Or are you envious because I am generous?" The King James Version renders this passage as follows: "Is it not lawful for me to do what I will with mine own? Is thine eye evil, because I am good?" In this passage, the generous spirit of the landowner is contrasted with the mean-spiritedness of the earlier-hired workers.

In societies with strong belief in the evil eye, where people lived in constant fear, religious leaders found a number of ways to ward off the evil. In Islamic societies, invoking the blessings of God upon the victim or reciting particular verses or chapters of the Qur'an are believed to serve as protection against the evil eye. Some religious Jews avoid talking about valuable items they own, good luck that has come

Pastoral Perspective

the anatomy of the eye and its functioning and of the way that the eye and the brain work together in the process of visual perception.

However, perhaps there is a sense in which the ancients were onto something. Namely, we do not all "see" the world in the same unfiltered way. We do project something of our inner selves onto the world around us, dramatically shaping the way we see and experience things. So, if we were to see with the eyes Jesus wants us to have—if we were to have God in our eyes and in our looking—we would see the world in a very different light.

As a pastor, I am very interested in how people perceive the world around them, and I never fail to marvel at how that perception differs from one person to another. A situation one person sees as a burden, someone else sees as a gift. An individual whom one person dismisses as worthless, another sees as a treasured child of God. A job one person may consider a menial task, someone else sees as a way of fulfilling God's calling. An event one person may chalk up to random chance or coincidence, another sees as within the scope of God's providence and grace.

What accounts for that difference? Might faith play a role in it somehow? I have to believe that it does. Faith seems to offer a unique way of seeing the world. It enables us to see things differently and—we trust—more clearly. Because the light of Christ is in us—the light that first shattered the darkness and makes all the stars to shine—we are able to see things as they truly are.

In the first church I served as pastor, there was a much beloved older couple—members for sixty years—named Orville and Woodye Kessler. They were salt-of-the-earth folks—simple, kind, and faithful. The light of Christ shone brightly in them. One thing the Kesslers were known for in both the church and the community was their jail ministry. It was something the two of them had started and led together. They went every Thursday morning to the Johnson County jail to lead a Bible study and to pray with the inmates. They befriended them. They had birthday parties for them. They wrote letters—thousands and thousands of letters over the years—to people in prison and just out of prison. They invited ex-convicts into their home for supper and for the holidays. Orville and Woodye did this faithfully for nearly thirty years, and countless people would testify that their lives had been transformed as a result.

What was it like to see the world through the Kesslers' eyes? The average person looks at people

Exegetical Perspective

The absence of this light, perhaps a metaphor for moral character, yields a dark world.

On the other hand, many readers believe that Matthew's construction of these sayings points toward the light of the eyes illuminating the body. This would suggest that what we look at, our focus of attention or "treasure" (6:19–21), shapes our inner person or character. Both perspectives are well represented in ancient discussions of the eye. The irreducible ambiguity of Jesus' sayings, however, invites us to entertain and embrace both ways of imagining the flow of light through the eyes. When Jesus says that "the eye is the lamp of the body," he identifies the eye as the conduit of relationship, the portal between the world within us and the world around us, between ourselves and others, and between us and God (who sees what is really in our hearts). Whether the light shines from or upon the inner person, the eye is "the lamp of the body."

A third layer of difficulty revolves around the adjectives Jesus uses here in conjunction with the eye. The Greek word *haplous* in verse 22 can by extension mean "good" or "sound," but more precisely carries valences such as "direct," "sincere," and "uncomplicated." The contrasting term in verse 23 is *ponēros*, which is often translated simply "evil" but also conveys a sense of jealousy or stinginess. Among Greek-speaking Jews the contrast here would have focused on generosity and a lack of envy, as opposed to selfishness, a niggardly spirit, and meanness. The contrasts are thus thoroughly relational in nature and embrace both perception (what one seeks and receives from others, including God) and projection (what one conveys toward others). The envious eye fills the whole body with darkness, shrouds whatever light is within (v. 23), and destroys relationships with those upon whom it is cast. The eye that is generous both fills the body with light and transmits light to others. When Jesus says, "If the light in you is darkness, how great is the darkness!" he describes the black hole of the envious, destructive spirit. The simple and generous eye discerns and broadcasts the light of grace.

If an evil eye represents greed, envy, conniving, or hexing, and a sound eye means honesty, integrity, and generosity, the relationship of these sayings to their immediate context, which has focused on "treasure" and will next turn to "mammon," becomes clearer. Here, as in the context, it is not possible to draw a sharp distinction between what we do and who we are, between what we set our hearts on and how we treat other people. While Jesus continues to

Homiletical Perspective

evil eye is that which allows so much darkness to encroach that one is unable to see the generosity of the master. The evil eye in Matthew 6 is that which has been so clouded by the hegemony of scarcity that it can no longer see the abundance of God's provision. The evil eye is a way of seeing oneself, the world, and others in which there is never enough. That way of seeing is an enfolding darkness that is indeed great. In contrast, the good eye sees the abundance of God's provision, provision that is brimming from the storehouses of heaven. The good eye allows one to see the world and others as the occasion to live freely into the abundance of God's provision. The good eye floods one's life with light.

Preaching from Matthew 6:22–23 will require the preacher to draw forth both the bad news and the good news implied in this text.

I am reminded of the story recounted by a colleague who was teaching in Accra, Ghana, a course from the Hebrew Bible. He asked the students, "Is God just for allowing some people to have so much and other people to have so little?" One of the Ghanaian students replied, "I have always wondered that myself, because I think about how much I have in my country of Ghana and how little my friends just to the north in Burkina Faso have." My colleague described how completely reorienting it was in that moment as the student became the teacher.

One might say that the Ghanaian student possessed "good eyes" filled with light and allowing him to recognize the generosity of God.

This is the good news in the text that can be proclaimed in the sermon. There is a way of seeing, a gift of grace, that floods one's life with light. This way of seeing refuses to live in scarcity, but lives in the abundance of God's provision. Stories such as the one recounted above or drawn from the preacher's own experience or context will allow the concept of the bad versus the good eye to become more than ideas or concepts.

Beyond the immediate context in which these verses exist, verses 22–23 appear in form like a wisdom saying. Wisdom sayings are about not only what one knows but who one is. What is the character of the person, and how does one live? On the whole, the Sermon on the Mount casts a vision for how one thinks and lives or, put another way, how one sees the world and therefore lives in it. As a wisdom saying, verses 22–23 make the point that how we see the world, others, and ourselves shapes our lives and floods our lives with either darkness or light.

Matthew 6:22–23

Theological Perspective

to them, and, in particular, their children. If any of these are mentioned, the speaker and/or listener will say, *b'li ayin hara*, meaning "without an evil eye," or *kein eina hara* (often shortened to *kennahara*), "no evil eye."

The passage under consideration can be seen as representing Jesus' remedy for the evil eye. Here Jesus extends and sublimes the understanding of the evil eye, as he does on other subjects in the Sermon on the Mount, and uses the healthy or good eye as a metaphor to point out the simplicity of intention and purity of affection with which his followers should pursue the supreme good for themselves and for all. Instead of focusing on the evil eye, which is destructive to the individual and society, Jesus points to the good eye, which builds both the individual and society as whole.

Additionally, the eye as the lamp of the body not only illuminates the path for the body, but also acts as an instrument that projects the inner light onto objects so they may be seen. In other words, the world around us will identify us through and with the choices we make in life. By locating the passage in this context, Matthew is relating the saying to the issue of the disciples' attitude toward material wealth, declaring that if the eye is not clear on this matter, the whole of one's life is perverted. It is in this light that Paul's counsel in Philippians 4:8 becomes imperative: "Finally, beloved, whatever is true, whatever is honorable, whatever is just, whatever is pure, whatever is pleasing, whatever is commendable, if there is any excellence and if there is anything worthy of praise, think about these things"—for ourselves, but above all, for others!

JOHN A. AZUMAH

Pastoral Perspective

in jail and sees only criminals. Thugs. Delinquents. Predators. Dangers to society. Woodye and Orville Kessler looked at those very same people and saw something quite different. Human beings made in God's image. Beloved children of God. Men and women whom Christ died to save.

Faith makes a difference in how you see things. It makes all the difference in the world.

Perhaps as pastors, one of the most important things we can do for our parishioners is to attend to their vision, to enable them and invite them to see the world and their own lives with eyes illumined by the light of Christ. Perhaps—as in the case of the Kesslers—sometimes our parishioners will help us to do this.

Incidentally, one of the treasures I have kept from Woodye and Orville is a picture they gave me many years ago. It is a simple black-and-white pixilated sketch of Jesus' face. The instructions below tell you to gaze intently at the image, to focus intently on it for thirty seconds, then look away at a blank wall. When you look away, the image of Jesus' face is supposed to reappear suddenly on the wall. I do not pretend to understand the physiology of it—it has something to do with retinas and rods and cones—but sure enough, that is exactly what happens. Jesus' face shows up everywhere you look.

It is just a little optical illusion, of course. Stare at a pixilated sketch of a duck, and you would be seeing ducks.

Orville and Woodye Kessler would tell you that, for them, that image of Jesus never did go away. Spend enough time looking at Jesus, allow him to open your eyes and give you his vision, and sooner or later you will start seeing Jesus everywhere. You will never look at things the same way again. Your whole body—the Gospel tells us—will be full of light.

WALLACE W. BUBAR

Exegetical Perspective

focus at least superficially on possessions, especially the ways our pursuit and use of material goods may either destroy or nurture our relationships with God and others, these verses do not permit us to limit their scope to economic relations, as important as these may be. It is possible, after all, to use what appears to be generosity to control and manipulate others. Our charity often serves to preserve rather than tear down walls. An eye that is truly open and generous, in contrast, seeks nothing but the well-being of the other—not least economically, but ultimately for the transformation of broken, alienated relationships into whole, restored relationships.

At one level, these sayings about light and the eye can be easily turned into a simple moralism: make a choice for the good, be generous rather than greedy. Jesus does not say anything here about our choices. He is simply describing the inevitable alignment of our inner being with what we seek and bring about in our relationships with others and with God. Remember, Jesus is still commenting here on the Lord's Prayer, with its primary plea for God's name to be hallowed and God's will to be done.

Ultimately the possibility of having a simple, generous eye and a body that is full of light springs not from our own volition but from the recognition of God's glory and light. The light within comes from and reflects God presence. In Jewish tradition, when Adam and Eve turned away from God, the light of God's glory that had shown in their eyes and illumined their whole being was diminished and darkened. Those who have turned from God will stumble in darkness, alone and hostile. Sin is not the cause of moral blindness, but its inevitable consequence. Where a sense of alienation from God and from the world dominates our perception and practice, the darkened eye and body is the necessary, inevitable consequence. The only real alternative, the only choice we have, is to turn once again toward God, the source of all light.

STANLEY P. SAUNDERS

Homiletical Perspective

It is one thing for the sermon to declare these things as true. It is another thing for the sermon to so narrate the "good eye" so that the listening community is formed to live in this way.

After lunch at the restaurant, she asked me if it would be okay if we took the leftovers and gave them to the homeless people at the bridge. "I have plenty, and they could probably use a little." I would say she had the good eye. I pulled the car to the side of the road, and we approached a man sitting on the ground. As we handed the man the food, he looked inside the take-out container and back at us. He said, "I'm going to share this with my friends." She beamed at the man and then smiled at me. We turned to leave and he called out, "Thanks for sharing!" I would say he had the good eye.

In this way, the preacher might speak to a way of seeing and being in the world that liberates one to choose the way of life over the way of death in all its forms. The evil eye is turned in upon itself and the preservation of oneself. The evil eye robs life from the other, in order to build up its own life. Darkness closes in. That is not the eye we have received. The good eye is turned toward the other, lives with open hands and open hearts. The good eye extends the gift of life to others. There is light. If we have been given healthy eyes, we not only see one another differently with them, but the light that fills us transforms our speech and shapes our passions.

STEPHEN C. JOHNSON

Matthew 6:24–34

24"No one can serve two masters; for a slave will either hate the one and love the other, or be devoted to the one and despise the other. You cannot serve God and wealth.

25"Therefore I tell you, do not worry about your life, what you will eat or what you will drink, or about your body, what you will wear. Is not life more than food and the body more than clothing? 26Look at the birds of the air; they neither sow nor reap nor gather into barns, and yet your heavenly Father feeds them. Are you not of more value than they? 27And can any of you by worrying add a single hour to your span of life? 28And why do you worry about clothing? Consider the lilies of the field, how they grow; they neither toil nor spin, 29yet I tell you, even Solomon in all his glory was not clothed like one of these. 30But if God so clothes the grass of the field, which is alive today and tomorrow is thrown into the oven, will he not much more clothe you—you of little faith? 31Therefore do not worry, saying, 'What will we eat?' or 'What will we drink?' or 'What will we wear?' 32For it is the Gentiles who strive for all these things; and indeed your heavenly Father knows that you need all these things. 33But strive first for the kingdom of God and his righteousness, and all these things will be given to you as well.

34"So do not worry about tomorrow, for tomorrow will bring worries of its own. Today's trouble is enough for today."

Theological Perspective

Whom or what do you love? Whom or what do you fear? These are two questions that underlie these teachings of Jesus in this portion of the Sermon on the Mount. Answering the first question implied by verse 24 helps listeners determine how they will answer the second question implicit within verses 25–34. For if they love God rather than wealth, it follows that there will be no reason to fear not having enough food, clothing, and other material needs. Loving and serving God means being able to trust that one's basic needs will be provided. By the same token, if they love and serve Mammon (the god of Prosperity), which is nothing more than a projection of their own hands and imaginations, they will find that there is never enough, and they will suffer from constant misplaced worry.

Of the many false gods Jesus could have named, the fact that he chooses Mammon as his foil alerts us to the theological frame he is setting up for what follows. Variously depicted in art history as a ravenous wolf or a seething demon, its association with avarice gives us the background to understand that behind our supposed needs is often the god of greed. As Jesus will demonstrate, this is a god that can never be satisfied.

Jesus' words are reminiscent of Joshua's to the Israelites to choose which god they will serve as they

Pastoral Perspective

This passage is a continuation of the admonition that begins about five verses earlier with "Do not store up for yourself treasures on earth" (Matt. 6:19), chiding the listener not to be too attached to possessions or overly concerned with money. In the opening lines of this particular pericope, which perhaps are more aptly connected to what has come before, the clarity about right priorities stands out starkly beside what many know their priorities actually are. The language of slave and master may be distant, but the meaning of the metaphor is as true as ever. Many a sermon has been preached on the clichéd, yet resonant, idea that a person can tell you what her priorities are by showing you her credit-card statement and checkbook register.

Still, when we hear Jesus speaking in such a declarative manner, "You cannot serve God and wealth" (v. 24), some will want to attempt a challenge, to cite examples of the good that money can do. Even if those in the pews do not debate this critique of wealth and treasure, just about every facet of American society sets itself up against this message from Jesus. At any time and season, you can identify numerous examples of the destructive influence of money; yet beware setting up a straw man. Money itself is neutral. It is how we feel about money that distorts our priorities and judgment. Jesus' words remind us that the

Exegetical Perspective

This hauntingly beautiful but seemingly poetic impracticality is far from impractical if one reads it as a missional text, that is, a text about the sending out of the disciples. While it is positioned strategically in the Sermon on the Mount, it appears also in Luke 12:22. Its original context most likely was not as a part of the great Sermon of Jesus at the outset of the Galilean mission. These stirring words were presumably directed to the disciples, as Luke explicitly states (12:22). The classic text reflects a thought-out attitude toward the mission Jesus had discerned personally, probably hammered out in part from his own temptation experience. The text certainly represents a classic case against worry (note the reiteration at vv. 25, 31, 34) and in favor of a profound trust in God, but its immediate significance may have been poignantly more specific and strategic. While there are substantial parallels with essays on anxiety in both Greco-Roman and Jewish sources, these admonitions of Jesus contain a unique kingdom vantage.

The structure of this address to those of little faith represents a case against worry (vv. 25–30), answering anxieties about survival needs and the offer of a kingdom alternative (vv. 31–34). The major premise, that life is more than food, the body more than clothing (v. 25), is supported by illustrations of a provisioning

Homiletical Perspective

The pericope opens with an assertion, "No one can serve two masters" (v. 24a). It is an assertion calling for, even demanding, single-mindedness, commitment, devotion. A slave belonging to more than one master is completely committed to neither. The illustration itself is troublesome. Though Jesus draws from his experience of first-century Palestine, where enslavement was so common that it was observable virtually everywhere, the idea of such servitude is bothersome to the postmodern mind. There are so many forms of slavery, so many ways that human beings are being robbed of their freedoms, that one scarcely wants to suggest yet another form of enslavement, even if the idea originates with Jesus.

Jesus, though, is not thinking of unjust social, political, and economic covenants and arrangements. He is not validating the misuse of power and the crass, vicious, and violent grasping for domination and control over others, as far too many women and men have done through the ages. Rather, Jesus is asserting, first negatively, that it is impossible to have two masters; then positively, that whether one has a master or not is her or his decision. The master to whom Jesus refers is not born of flesh and blood, but is pure and everlasting, an ever-living, life-giving, and life-sustaining Spirit.

Matthew 6:24–34

Theological Perspective

stand ready to enter the promised land of Canaan (Josh. 24:15). At this in-between place they are reminded of the gods their ancestor Abram served before he was called by God, and the Egyptian gods they were *forced* to serve. No longer naive or subjected to circumstances beyond their control, they are going into a land where they will be tempted with idolatry and can plead neither ignorance nor innocence. Now they know better. Now they must make a choice.

Jesus too is with the Hebrew people at an in-between place on the mount. They may choose to lavish their offerings on any number of gods from among the vast cast of mythological figures in the Greco-Roman pantheon. They are forced daily to choose whether to worship the human god of Caesar, who holds them in the servitude of empire. Either choice will lead to frantic worrying about whether enough has been offered to a self-serving god to secure the needs and wants of the misguided idolater.

Jesus then makes a brilliant rhetorical move. He states that for the birds and flowers, the idea of having to make such a choice about whether or not to trust God is not only unnecessary; it is downright silly. Jesus encourages his listeners to learn from their kin within God's creation to gain insight into what it means to trust the Creator. There is a twinkle of humor in his word pictures of birds pushing plows and piling seeds into silos, lilies spinning yarn and knitting sweaters. Then the visual image of Solomon—the wealthiest, most richly clothed king in Israel's history—contrasted with the vibrant colors of the flowers of the field serves to further illustrate his point about God's ability to care and provide for all of creatures.

From an ecological-theological perspective, this passage poses some interesting questions. Could Jesus' illustration of birds and lilies be seen as an example of inviting creation to be his "teaching partner" in his didacticism about how to live into a life that reflects trust in God? Does, rather, the fact that Jesus places humans in a position of having higher value than the birds and the lilies contribute to an anthropocentrism that reinforces the potentially damaging notion of humans over and above the rest of creation? Paul Santmire, for example, cautions against using this passage to paint a romanticized picture of Jesus and nature.[1]

Perhaps more troublesome is the question this passage raises regarding a prosperity theology that "promotes a God that meets congregants in this

1. H. Paul Santmire, *The Travail of Nature: The Ambiguous Ecological Promise of Christian Theology* (Philadelphia: Fortress Press, 1985), 200.

Pastoral Perspective

real warning is not strictly about money, but about our service to money, and ultimately our love and devotion to anything that is not God.

In some communities, the preacher or teacher will need to consider the scope and reach of the so-called prosperity gospel. Whether formally preached or casually accepted, the message that God rewards the faithful monetarily and materially will be part of the worldview of some listeners to this gospel. Countering this message should be done carefully and forcefully.

Beginning with the word "therefore," the pericope becomes a poetic discourse on the uselessness of worry. Jesus' focus on our worry about material matters continues the strain begun in prior verses. When the admonition against worry at large is yoked with the idea that money is not the highest goal, we find ourselves on the receiving end of one of the most countercultural sermons that Jesus preaches. His words certainly have the potential for daily and even hourly relevance. Worry has no boundaries: where the next meal will come from, if a cure can be found, where a child will go to school. Worry lives in the homes of the poor and the wealthy, the young and the old. Worry is a part of the lives of people of every race, in every region. Men and women worry; married folk and singles worry. Worry is a part of distracted days and sleepless nights. Worry takes on the past and the future. It is to everyone then that Jesus preaches with image-rich assurance, "Do not worry about your life, what you will eat or what you will drink, or about your body, what you will wear" (v. 25). While these verses are clearly directive, they are intended to offer freedom and release. A question for the preacher, the teacher, and the congregation is whether this passage feels like an invitation to live in a new way or criticism about the way we live—because, of course, it is both.

Though "Do not worry" is repeated three times, it seldom is experienced as a pastoral response. When someone seeks counsel—from a minister, a friend, or, for that matter, a stranger on the street—in the vulnerable moment of sharing a deep concern, what that person does not want to hear is, "Don't worry, everything will be fine." This response negates the reality, or at least the perceived reality, of the person in need. This response tells the person that his or her feelings are wrong, a word that goes against a century of therapeutic theory. This response feels like criticism. How then does the preacher/minister/priest balance the need to comfort her congregants, who come with their own concerns and even a

God feeding the birds (vv. 26–27) and clothing the lilies (vv. 28–30). Jesus drew sensitively from both the masculine (v. 26) and feminine (v. 28) worlds. Jesus apparently gave the category of life/self/soul considerable philosophical reflection (see Luke 12:15). The rhetorical language of persuasion abounds with words of argumentation ("more," v. 25ab; "but," vv. 27a, 30a, 33a; "therefore," vv. 31a, 34a; "for," 32ab, 34b; "if," 30a; English wording may differ slightly), alerting the reader to the intention of Jesus to bolster faith. Jesus utilized the rabbinic argument of "light to heavy" (*qal wahomer*). He unmasked the powerlessness of anxiety to add even a single hour of longevity (v. 27). To avoid misconstrual, take due note that Jesus did *not* advise the farmer to stop sowing and reaping.

A major step forward in understanding may very well derive not only from the recognition and implications of the text addressed to the disciples, but more to those erstwhile disciples whom Jesus dubbed "you of little faith" (v. 30). This text was not addressed universally, but to disciples of little faith. Our text is not addressed to those without faith but with too little. The Greek word *oligopistos* means literally "little faith," and Jesus applied that designation to his disciples. Of the five usages of this term in the New Testament, four are in Matthew and the fifth, in Luke 12:28, parallels Matthew 6:30, reflecting Q and further suggesting its primitive character in Palestinian Jewish Christianity.

Jesus characterized his frightened disciples in a nocturnal storm as lacking in faith (Matt. 8:26). Again frightened while in a boat on the Sea of Galilee in the midst of menacing winds and waves, Peter attempted to walk on the water but was overtaken by fear and doubt (Matt. 14:28–30). Jesus addressed him, "You of little faith, why did you doubt?" (14:31c). Fear and doubt appear comingled. Finally, at 16:8 the disciples felt inadequate because they had no bread, so Jesus reminded them of the feeding of the five thousand, characterizing them one final time as of little faith.

Hence, all of the applications of the term "you of little faith" are addressed to the disciples and upbraid them for lack of sufficient faith, particularly in the presence of Jesus. Smallness of faith then relates to disciples who stumble as believers when facing trials such as danger (8:26; 14:31), lack of food (6:30; 16:8), and inability to heal someone (17:17). The usage may very well go back to Jesus, but Matthew apparently has found in this characterization a favorite category.

We can and must go further then, building upon this particular insight about those addressed as

The preacher might even press the point that in this broader discussion about the kingdom of God (4:12–17)—which I prefer to call "the Reigndom of God," just to assure that no one is left out or left behind because of gender—the other "master" in Matthew's mind may be the Roman Empire, along with the apparatus and functionaries that sustain it, including the Jewish temple. It is within this broader religious-social-political, economic, and military context that the assertion "No one can serve two masters" is made. Now the rope gets tighter, the proverbial plank thinner. In a system where wealth "makes a way out of no way," where "mammon" equates with status and power, a choice is required. "You (second person plural/all of you) cannot serve God and wealth" (v. 24).

It may be that Jesus had the first Jesus (Joshua) in mind when he made this assertion. One fateful day, after conquering the enemies of Israel, Joshua summoned all of the elders to Shechem and required of them an answer, after rehearsing for and with them the mighty acts of YHWH (Josh. 24:15). Just as those in the Matthean community, and the reader along with them, are being required to decide whether God or empire and the thing empire values most (mammon) will be master; so too in Joshua the twelve-tribe coalition that was becoming a nation had to choose.

In verses 25–33 Jesus offers the comforting assurance of God's provision of life's essentials—food, drink, and clothing. No preacher should ignore the rich imagery embedded in these verses. The thing that beats back the worry lines that wrinkle an anxious brow; the cure for a stomach churning in fear of failing to access daily bread and clean, drinkable water or tatterless clothing; the prescription for deep down uneasiness born of agonizing over the day's provision is choosing the right master: God. God provides!

A word of caution is appropriate here.

It is easy for Christians to speak glibly about God's provision if they enjoy the privileges of well-ordered and wealthy societies, societies that are also relatively free of unexpected natural disasters—especially if they are middle income or above. Jesus spoke not to the privileged, but to ordinary people, many of whom were poor, suffering brutal oppression and therefore legitimately concerned about daily bread, water, and clothing. Emotional signs like worry and anxiety and fear were ever present for those to whom Jesus spoke, simply because life was so uncertain. Indeed, the majority of people in the

Matthew 6:24–34

Theological Perspective

world and provides them with the knowledge to obtain wealth and to be healthy."[2] Jesus' words may be interpreted to mean that as long as believers "strive for the kingdom of God," God will see that they get the best food and most expensive drink, the most extravagant clothes and the finest luxury cars. This theological perspective ignores verse 25, in which Jesus clearly states that life is more than the pursuit and attainment of the choicest gourmet diet and raiment.

Indeed, in North America, the idolatrous worship of this god of prosperity (Mammon!) has increased the number of people across the globe who worry with good reason about what they will eat and whether they will have clean water to drink. This is not the kind of frivolous worry Jesus is speaking about here. This is the anguished cry of "the least of these" in chapter 25 later in the Gospel, who languish, waiting for the unresponsive goats to share their food, drink, clothes, and ministry of presence—not to mention that the worship of this Mammon-god has driven countless species of birds and plants to extinction. How would Jesus preach this sermon today, looking for birds and finding the skies empty due to lost habitats and poisoned ground and water? To what stunning flowers of the Amazon would Jesus point, given the relentless human invasion and destruction of "the lilies of the field"?

Unlike Mammon, which is concerned only with sating its voracious appetite through the consumption of its worshipers, who sacrifice themselves for its own unchecked, cancerous growth, God desires only life in abundance equitably shared by all—human and other-than-human. Loving, worshiping, and serving Jesus' Abba leads even those of us with "little faith" to begin to see that there is great peace and contentment to be had in learning to live with "just enough."

LEAH D. SCHADE

Pastoral Perspective

willingness to spend some moments considering the prayer concerns of others, with the need to bear witness to the countercultural message of Christ?

Some attention might be given to the difference between prayer and fretfulness. Seize the moment to teach about fruitful prayer as a more faithful response to our very real worries than futile anxiety. Drawing a distinction between "striving first for the kingdom" and secondarily "all these things" (v. 33) gives the preacher/minister/priest an opportunity to speak in the language of invitation rather than harsh criticism. Our concerns and our basic needs are not unimportant, but in light of the hope of God's reign, they are somewhat diminished and put in their rightful place.

In a world where the operative fable is of the ant and the grasshopper, many listeners will find these words of Christ to be naive if not irresponsible. Some may walk away from the invitation to "consider the lilies of the field, how they grow; they neither toil nor spin." Some will rightfully want to address the needs of those who really do not know what they will eat and what their children will wear. Here we rest in the knowledge that Jesus spoke clearly at other times about the importance of clothing the naked and tending the sick. Still, for some, turning our attention to this passage and likewise turning our attention to the birds of the air and the lilies of the field may be as difficult as, if not more difficult than, remembering the poor. Knowing the temperament of those in the congregation will allow the preacher/minister/priest to send them out to serve in the homeless shelter or into the world in search of God's creative beauty. For the uninitiated, Mary Oliver, Annie Dillard, and Wendell Berry may be helpful guides about the intersection of the gospel and the natural world.

KATHERINE M. BUSH

---

2. Paula L. McGee, "New Black Church Preachers and a New Definition for Prosperity Theology," presented at the Academy of Homiletics, Austin, TX, December 2, 2011.

disciples of limited faith. Within the text itself the anxious concerns about what can be eaten or drunk or worn exemplify the nature of the little faith. We may hazard the reconstruction that these anxious feelings were quite real and were actual words or feelings of the disciples, jitters at the thought of going on the kind of mission Jesus envisioned. Indeed he would send them out without money with which they could buy food (Matt. 10:9; cf. Peter at Acts 3:6), nor would they receive payment for healing (10:8). Those on mission would, in fact, be quite vulnerable, explicitly disallowed to take a staff to defend themselves or a bag or extra clothing (10:10). They would go without provisions and without shelter. This represented quite a daunting mission. The disciples' anxious queries about survival needs are understandable.

If our reconstruction is well founded, we can go further to speak of the intention of the text. Jesus addressed premission jitters with a conception of God; his understanding of the character of God profoundly influenced his teaching. The mission is God ordained. Jesus not only promised the general provision of God (vv. 26–30) but, in the mission instructions themselves, revealed a divine plan based upon the hospitality of worthy houses (10:11–12). This implied dependence on God for daily bread sheds light on the petition in the Lord's Prayer (6:11). John the Baptizer depended upon the general provision of God with his diet of locusts and wild honey (3:4b). Hungry disciples of Jesus gleaned on the Sabbath (12:1). Jesus himself experienced hospitality (Luke 19:1–10; 10:38–42; 11:37; Matt. 8:15). Jesus offered a dramatic counterpart to anxiety in his strong admonition to seek the kingdom of God as the life-controlling priority (v. 33). The final Matthean verse urges a focus on the present as an alternative to being paralyzed by fear of the future (v. 34).

This "Franciscan" text, greatly admired by the Christian philosopher Kierkegaard, still speaks, but from a rarefied eschatological realm. Jesus named and calmed the fears of disciples; that liberated them to venture. Anxieties can dissuade from mission, but a Jesus conception of a provisioning Deity, one modeled by Jesus himself, can empower. The effectiveness of the text may be confirmed by the disciples' mission and its outcome (Luke 10:17–18).

PETER RHEA JONES

world today know about the tenuousness of life in the twenty-first century.

It helps a little to note that Jesus is contrasting the *psychē* soul with the *sōma* body. Life/*psychē*/soul is more than food and clothing (v. 25b). The human soul is of more value to "your heavenly Parent" than the birds of the air for whom God provides, though they neither sow, nor reap, nor gather into barns (v. 26). God places great value on who and what human beings are in essence. Choosing God, who provides even for the birds, over empire, whose only interest is self-preservation, reconstructs human identity, self-understanding, and socioeconomic arrangements. God provides.

Implied in the words of Jesus is the vision of a compassionate and considerate God with power to undergird and sustain the creation of which human beings are a significant part. In view of such a reality, worry and anxiety are unnecessary emotional weights. "Strive first for the Reigndom of God and God's righteousness, and all these things will be given to you as well" (v. 33). Striving for God's Reigndom and righteousness are the essential priorities for people of faith. God's Reigndom is the realm of God's governance. God's righteousness is the justice characteristic of a compassionate and considerate God. The sort of poverty typified by hunger, thirst, and nakedness simply does not exist in God's Reigndom. Since the Reigndom is proleptically present, do not worry about tomorrow (v. 34). The Reigndom of God is present today, and it is unfolding in the morrow, even though the morrow has its own particular issues and evils.

Making the choice for the God who is compassionately mindful of all creation transforms human self-understanding, human identity, and socioeconomic arrangements. Making the choice for God is simultaneously choosing to value life in all of its manifestations, including the environment, ocean depths, and outer space. Making the choice for God and God's Reigndom is tantamount to asserting the propriety of relationships rooted in justice and tempered by compassion of the sort that Jesus reputedly possessed for the lepers and the blind and tax collectors. Choosing God has revolutionary implications when contrasted with the policies and practices of contemporary economic and political leadership.

MARK A. LOMAX

Matthew 7:1–6

¹"Do not judge, so that you may not be judged. ²For with the judgment you make you will be judged, and the measure you give will be the measure you get. ³Why do you see the speck in your neighbor's eye, but do not notice the log in your own eye? ⁴Or how can you say to your neighbor, 'Let me take the speck out of your eye.' while the log is in your own eye? ⁵You hypocrite, first take the log out of your own eye, and then you will see clearly to take the speck out of your neighbor's eye.

⁶"Do not give what is holy to dogs; and do not throw your pearls before swine, or they will trample them under foot and turn and maul you."

Theological Perspective

Rhetoric sometimes communicates theology. In other words, how we say things may convey something of our beliefs about God and God's relationship to us. In this section of the Sermon on the Mount, Jesus uses certain rhetorical and literary devices that express three unique aspects of who God is, how God gets through to us, and what God is calling us to in our human community.

The first device is literary. Had this section been heard immediately following the previous chapter, the first thing Jesus' listeners would have noticed is that there is a shift in tone and style. Verses 1–6 sound as if they could have been lifted straight from the book of Proverbs. This carries interesting implications from a perspective of feminist Sophia theology. Could the use of wisdom sayings in itself imply something to Jesus' listeners? Is Jesus perhaps stepping into the role of Lady Wisdom? In any case, he is certainly taking on the role of the sage, indicating that part of who God is for us is our teacher, parent figure, mentor, and trusted advisor, handing down these precious nuggets of wisdom that have been distilled from a vast store of experience. Another way to think of these proverbs is as little pearls that have been brought up from the depths after long exposure to constant motion and pressure, shaping them into tiny round glistening treasures.

Pastoral Perspective

Jesus' preaching in Matthew's Gospel is full of practical counsel. Some people expect advice for daily living from the Bible; others believe it to be more esoteric. Whatever it is that readers expect from an encounter with Scripture will color how they hear Jesus speaking. Here we have Jesus seeking to guide in the most earthly of ways the behavior of those who will listen. How to get along in community, you ask? Start by not judging. Do not judge. The simplicity and clarity of these three words belie their import and the difficulty that many will have living into them.

A crucial first step for readers of any text is to consider the personal implications. Without examining the ramifications of the message on the messenger, the interpreter is likely to reach shallow insights. When someone is preaching on a text that touches on the issues of judgment and hypocrisy, it seems even more important that he or she engages the words honestly. This is not to hold the preacher to an impossible standard of perfection when it comes to specks and logs, nor should the congregation expect a confession of every misstep from the pulpit. Rather, the preacher should be expected to take seriously the role of interpreting a text about judgment without being judgmental.

Is Jesus telling his listeners not to judge? Is he, rather, telling these listeners how to judge, or only

Exegetical Perspective

This promising text "On Judging Others" is addressed directly to the new community ("you," vv. 1–4), who are accosted as hypocrites (v. 5). This text stands in considerable parallel to a similar text in the Sermon on the Plain (Luke 6:37–38, 41–42), suggesting its critical role in the inaugural sermon for building the community of the kingdom. Here Jesus reflects a particular sensitivity to the possibility of a contagious censorious spirit spoiling a new movement and embodying an attitude not belonging to the character of God. Jesus envisioned a nonjudgmental community.

This historically important passage rather naturally divides into 7:1–2, 3–5, and 6. Key argument signals appear (in Greek, though not always apparent in English translations), such as "in order that" (v. 1b), an inferential "for" (v. 2a), rhetorical questions (vv. 3–4), "but" (v. 3ab), "or" (v. 4a), and "then" (v. 5b), which allow one to follow more closely the unfolding of the unit.

Jesus, who sought to persuade, not only declares the categorical prohibition of judging others (v. 1a), but also offers a motivation/revelatory disclosure (v. 1b) expressed with a purposive clause, "in order that" you may not be judged. He immediately makes a correlation between the actions of his community and the divine decisions. Already in the Lord's Prayer (6:12), a correlation is drawn as to forgiveness

Homiletical Perspective

Throughout the entire Sermon on the Mount, Jesus constructs a different, if not new, ethic. The overall point being made in the Sermon on the Mount is that the ethical and moral principles that undergird the Reigndom of God are different from those of the Roman Empire and even the Jewish temple. The compassionate consideration seen in God's character is to typify human relationships in God's reign. Therefore one person is not to judge another.

Jesus does not identify specific ways that his followers are to refrain from judging one another or even strangers. He simply says, "Do not judge" (v. 1a). This terse imperative has the potential of completely transforming social interactions. Judgments are rendered when judges have enough evidence or information to determine a particular course of action in consonance with predetermined legal standards. Jesus' command against rendering judgment may issue from the recognition that human beings rarely possess sufficient evidence and/or information to draw accurate conclusions about one another, especially as it pertains to character. Behavior toward other people that is rooted in half-truths and partial understandings often results in hurt feelings and even broken relationships.

Surely, as colonized peoples, Jesus and those to whom he speaks would have experienced the sharp

Matthew 7:1–6

Theological Perspective

What is so stunning about pearls is that they are eye catching, making us gasp at their iridescence. Therein lies a second aspect of God revealed to us through Jesus' proverbs: God finds beautiful and creative ways to get our attention. The implication for theological teachers (including preachers, Sunday school teachers, and adult Bible study leaders) is that our attempts to communicate to others what we have discerned about God can employ artistic beauty and metaphor, creative language and meaningful symbols. Certainly Jesus' listeners would never have accused their rabbi of being "boring." The Sermon on the Mount is an example of how he varied his tone and style, employing "teaching methods" that engaged his pupils by drawing on narrative, parables, physical props, and, in this case, humor!

Humor? Jesus used humor to teach theology? Absolutely! We hear these sayings so often that we miss the ironic and comic effect they have. These six verses appear as a string of pithy one-liners, each one like a pearl to be examined. As Jesus would have dropped each pearl, laughter would have effervesced from the crowd. Walter Wink, in his book *Engaging the Powers*, describes how Jesus used burlesque, exaggeration, irony, hyperbole, and humor to engage his listeners and communicate a deeper truth they needed to hear.[1]

There is a deeper truth cleverly conveyed under the guise of joking by Jesus the Jester that leads us to the third theological aspect: how God wants us to relate to each other in community. Verses 1 and 2 provide the frame for this passage, the lens of justice and judgment. One definition of justice is "the quality of all created things living together in right relationship."[2] Thus judgment must be tempered with justice if relationships are to be sustained. Standing aloof and aloft in a position of self-righteous arrogance while criticizing others reveals us to be ridiculously clueless about our own foibles. In contrast, Jesus is like a stand-up comedian who is skilled at truth telling through humorous hyperbole. This in turn models how we can relate to each other. When conflicts and tensions rise, good-natured humor can go a long way to defusing tempers. To paraphrase another sage, "A gentle [and humorous] word turns away wrath" (Prov. 15:1a).

The question is, What will we do with these pearls of wisdom that have been dropped into our

Pastoral Perspective

to judge with care? The assumption that Jesus seems to make is that people will judge. This is likewise a fair assumption to make of contemporary listeners. Judgment is a fact of life, and the preacher or teacher would helpfully invite the congregation to consider the difference between making personal choices and making comments about the choices of others. Without encouraging relativism, there is a way to move forward following Jesus' counsel. Responding to the metaphor of specks and logs may offer an approach that allows one to acknowledge the realities of sin, brokenness, and wrongness as we are encouraged to judge with mercy.

An awareness of the congregation's penchant for gossip and cliquishness, each of which is a close cousin of judgment, will provide grounds for pragmatic education and encouragement. These common social realities may be addressed with strength and with tenderness, remembering that judgment itself is often a mask for insecurities. The strength of Jesus' you-language, "You, hypocrite," should stay in Jesus' mouth; the wise preacher or teacher will remember to be a recipient of Jesus' message along with the congregation. To remind the congregation that judging others is condemned here, and likewise that their judgment of themselves is also condemned, may provide an opportunity to speak with tenderness and mercy. For those who worship in higher liturgical forms, it is important to help the congregation to see that confession and absolution are yoked events, and that God alone is holy. This will bring comfort to those inclined to turn on themselves and check those inclined to turn on others.

To address the role of society in judgment provides fertile ground for conversation. Care must be taken to avoid the creation of straw men out of everything from tabloids to the criminal justice system, and so to engage thoughtfully with those timely situations in the local or larger community. It is possible to use any number of cultural examples without making an easy target of the person or situation. A keen awareness of the political and social climate of the congregation and of the community in which the congregation lives is important. Knowing how these may or may not be in tension with each other and with the message that Jesus brings will help preachers/teachers speak directly to the lived experiences of their congregants.

In the last verse of this pericope, Jesus changes direction, to address a different community issue. Intriguingly, he seems to be asking his listeners to make a significant judgment: discerning first what

---

1. Walter Wink, *Engaging the Powers: Discernment and Resistance in a World of Domination* (Minneapolis: Fortress Press, 1992), 175–93.
2. Clark M. Williamson and Ronald J. Allen, *A Credible and Timely Word: Process Theology and Preaching* (St. Louis: Chalice Press, 1991), 103.

(6:14–15). Jesus forged a crucial connection between horizontal relationships with others and vertical relationship with God (cf. 25:31–46). The opening "do not judge" (v. 1a) not only introduces the topic of judging. The emphatic position of the "not" probably implies discontinuing a judging spirit already in progress. If so, this represents a bold intervention, based upon an understanding of God and of end times. The "judgment of God" as a persistent theme is particularly pronounced in Matthew 7.

At verse 2 the support for the admonition at verse 1 comes in terms of an analogy to "measures," entering a familiar marketing world of capacities. Here the parallel in Luke offers illumination. First, one parallel clarifies judging others in terms of condemnation by adding: "Do not condemn, and you will not be condemned" (Luke 6:37; cf. Matt. 12:37). Hence the text has in mind especially *condemnatory judgmentalism*. Furthermore, at least in the Lukan expression, it is not just a symmetric tit for tat. Rather, the Lukan text envisions a measure extraordinarily generous to overflowing, though here in terms of giving (Luke 6:38). The lavish generosity of God exceeds the commensurate acts of disciples. Significantly for our text, the evangelist Matthew has picked up the thread from 5:48 ("Be perfect, . . . as your heavenly Father is perfect") at 7:2. The parallel in Luke bases an injunction to being merciful on the mercy of God (Luke 6:36; cf. Matt. 5:7). The mercy of God and this text on judging are in particularly close proximity.

Commandeering the exegetical method of "interpreting Jesus by Jesus," we can bring a poignant parable alongside 7:1–2. The parable of the Unmerciful Servant (Matt. 18:21–35) narrates mercifulness in relationships. The parable portrays in its first segment the divine propensity to forgive extravagantly on the one hand (Matt. 18:23–27). However, when the forgiven servant acts in a flagrantly unmerciful fashion toward a fellow servant, the potentate takes definitive judgment out on the unmerciful.

The ensuing text in our pericope (vv. 3–5) engages the readers/hearers with its "why" (v. 3) and "how" questions (v. 4) as it develops the imagery of the eye. Worthy of note is the surprising frequency of eye imagery in the Sermon on the Mount (5:29, 38; 6:22, 23). The Greek word for "eye" appears no less than six times in three verses. The image is literal and more. The eye represents more than optical reality. It refers to perception and observation. Contrast, so common in the parables of Jesus, works memorably here in the juxtaposition of splinter/speck in the eye of the object of condemnation and the beam/log in the eye

edge of unfair judgment. Colonizers historically draw spurious conclusions about their colonized victims. Further, the economic location of the people gathered at the foot of the mount, due to no fault of their own, could have placed them in a position to be unfairly judged by others, in a society where worthiness was measured by wealth. The sad and awful truth is that the poor are often blamed for their impoverishment, even though there are always public policies and social covenants in place to hold them down.

Jesus says, "Do not judge." Though he is not specific, there is sufficient evidence that he understands that human beings need to consider carefully with whom they are in relationship. In 7:15–20, for example, followers of Jesus and people who evidently have heard the commandment against judging are encouraged to be fruit inspectors. "You will know them [false prophets] by their fruits" (v. 16a).

Jesus indicates that judgment begets judgment: "Do not judge, so that you may not be judged" (v. 1). He warns that those who judge will not only be judged; they will be judged in the very same way they rendered judgment. It is impossible to be light-hearted in view of such a hard saying, but it is vitally important to proclaim the truths that reside in these words.

There can be no right judgment without a considerable amount of introspection. Whereas the judge in the hall of justice is to consider the evidence and gather the information about the subject awaiting judgment, in the Reigndom of God the would-be judge must look within herself or himself. There is something about introspection, about being honest and truthful about oneself with oneself, that makes the human heart more pliable and sympathetic in regard to the plight of other people. Those living in God's reign, in particular, are to be extremely careful about casting aspersions on Reigndom kin. The failure to look within and to consider one's own heart and history prior to rendering judgment—regardless of how repugnant the attitude or behavior of the other is—may well render one a hypocrite.

Hypocrisy is as inappropriate for the disciple of Christ as any other sinful transgression. The hypocrite is an actor. Consequently she or he acts and speaks not in truth but deceptively. The deceptive nature of a hypocrite may indeed be the reason an inaccurate judgment of a kin rebounds to the hypocrite. It is the law of reciprocity: one reaps what he or she sows (cf. Gal. 6:7).

The last saying of this pericope is rather harsh. The words "dogs" and "swine" (v. 6) are ostensibly intended as designations for a certain class or kind of

Matthew 7:1–6

Theological Perspective

hands? Will we receive them as precious treasures that remind us of the sagacity of not hypocritically judging others? Will we be able to smooth our rough nuggets of conflict with patience and humor, so that pearls of wisdom emerge from the depths of community? Will we perhaps be nothing more than unappreciative dogs, incapable of discerning aesthetic value, much less holiness?

Worse, will we be like wild boars, not only trampling the pearls underfoot, but turning on and attacking the giver of such treasure? If we were to imagine the gathering of people from all walks of life surrounding Jesus on the Mount, we might see him turning his eyes toward the hostile bystanders in their midst. The crowd, following his gaze, would see the ominous image of these boars lowering their heads, charging, slashing upward with their tusks, biting and cutting their Teacher to pieces.

Thus the greatest pearl Jesus is giving them is the gift of learning how to respond to oppression and conflict in creative ways. These innovative approaches "break the cycle of humiliation with humor and even ridicule, exposing the injustice of the System. They recover for the poor a modicum of initiative that can force the oppressor to see them in a new light."[3] This is, perhaps, one of those "pearls of great price" Jesus speaks about later in the Gospel (Matt. 13:45–46). Because, long after the boars charge the Sage and think his treasures are scattered and trampled, the shining orbs of wisdom reemerge within the community. Not just what Jesus taught, but how he taught, is seen recapitulated in the creative nonviolent movements of humanity in the centuries since, from Gandhi to Martin Luther King Jr. to Wangari Maathai, for example. How might your congregation or faith community begin to think in imaginative and humorous ways about how to live and work together to exchange judgment for justice?

LEAH D. SCHADE

Pastoral Perspective

is holy and then who deserves to receive that which is deemed holy. The preacher or teacher will need to consider how these designations can and do have meaning for the congregation, how to test what is "holy," and to consider corollaries to "dogs" and "swine." Since Jesus is likely speaking about sacrificial meat, reflection about what is set apart in the contemporary setting might be helpful. Then listeners could be challenged to consider what it means today that some are deemed eligible (holy) and others are not. There may be implications for the community in worship and for the community in mission. To push toward honest reflection about who is in and who is out should be done with great care and with a willingness to stay with the conversation, perhaps long after the sermon or the class has ended.

That conversation may expand to include other references to dogs, pigs, and other derogatory language in the Gospels. Particularly remembering the Syrophoenician woman, it may be fruitful or provoke dialogue to suggest that there are times when the best choice is to argue with Jesus. The preacher/teacher will want to maintain sensitivity to contemporary examples of disparaging names. How are these labels a part of the community being addressed? Are those in the pews likely to be labeled or to label others? It seems probable that any one person may be both the giver and receiver of deprecating names, a habit from the schoolyard that we often do not grow out of.

Throughout the Sermon on the Mount, Jesus offers pithy teachings that in many cases have daily relevance. By not making bumper stickers or giving overly simplistic interpretations, the preacher/teacher will help the congregation see that the application of these principles may bring challenge, but also great goodness, to a life in community. In moving away from judgment, individuals may have the opportunity to experience peacefulness within themselves, in their relationships with others, and in their relationship with God. This stability and composure can be part of a path toward wholeness with their fellow travelers and union with God.

KATHERINE M. BUSH

3. Ibid., 185.

of the critic. Some have found the humor of Jesus in the hyperbole of a plank in the eye of the critic. Clarence Jordan in his Cotton Patch style referred[1] to "old Plank-Eye himself." The Greek verb *katanoeō* (v. 3b) as it relates to one's own eye means "to notice, be aware of, direct one's attention to." Jesus named the human tendency to establish one's own superiority by calling attention to the flaws and faults of the other.

Jesus' prescription for how to see clearly reflects a kind of down-home ophthalmology of removing the obstruction out of one's own eye. Such removal may amount to major and not "drive-by" surgery. Hans Dieter Betz raised the possibility of the practice of "fraternal correction" preceded by self-criticism and self-correction.[2] Jesus seeks to protect those who are oppressed by aggressive people who put down others arrogantly but also destructively. He positions himself against the verbally oppressive. Jesus implies that honest confrontation with one's own flaws and frailties can make one more compassionate in assessing another. Lacking such self-awareness leads to unrealistic and cruel criticism.

Again, with verses 3–5 we do well to illustrate Jesus' sayings by his parabolic narratives. Consider the Lukan parable of a Pharisee and a Toll Collector (Luke 18:9–14). The accusation of a hypocritical inconsistency (Matt. 7:5) appears also in the parable, as this religious man excoriates the toll collector for his moral failures, revealing a caustic spirit devoid of grace and reflecting a profound blindness to the log in his own eye. Thankful that he is not like other people, he makes an invidious comparison of himself with this sinner, to feed his voracious appetite for self-congratulation. Praise of God deteriorates into praise of himself. The prideful log in his eye forecloses self-awareness and invites harsh assessment of the other. The wrathful elder brother at Luke 15:25–32 rehearses also his own record of filial service (v. 29b) and castigates the perceived inconsistency of his father (vv. 29–30).[3] He does not fathom the meaning of grace in the actions of his father, nor its abysmal absence in his own judgmental attitude, the log obscuring his vision.

Verse 6, seemingly independent, prohibits possible future action of casting the sacred to ritually unclean swine, possibly a metaphor for cynical mockers or the temptation to apostasy.

PETER RHEA JONES

people. The swine is considered an "unclean" animal in Jewish religious tradition. The word "dog" is used in reference to the Canaanite woman in Matthew 15:26 and may therefore be a slander of non-Jewish people of the first century CE. The "holy" thing is more difficult to determine. "What is holy" may be the teaching Jesus shared with those gathered on the mount or the quality of relationship Jesus has just commanded to be practiced among citizens in the Reigndom of God. Considered positively, Jesus is insisting that Reigndom relationships are of such high moral and ethical quality that they are indeed holy, that they glorify and honor God. The danger in giving the same kind of compassionate consideration to those who do not share Reigndom moral and ethical values is that they will use it against the person offering it, to "trample" and "maul" them—not literally but metaphorically.

This later teaching makes problematic the way evangelization and missions are currently perceived, taught, and sometimes practiced in the Christian West. Those preaching this text may want to consider whether the whole pericope potentially calls into question the assumptions we Christians make about those whom we seek to reach for Christ's sake. We often prejudge those who are not Christians, assuming that their failure to confess faith the way we do means that they lack faith in God altogether. Sometimes it is the mere fact that other peoples do not speak English and therefore use names for God in their own tongue or dialect that render them suspicious in our eyes. In either case we have rendered judgment on the one hand and failed to give witness on the other. If we are not to cast treasure or pearls to "dogs" and "swine," then we have made yet another judgment.

Living lives without rendering judgment may mean that our sole focus in life is bearing witness. We are to attend to the quality of our walk with God and humanity. If we find it impossible to walk blamelessly, can we at least walk honestly? Prayerful, generous, compassionate, and faithful lives lived honestly before God and in the public square will yield a compelling witness to God's Reigndom reality.

MARK A. LOMAX

---

1. Clarence Jordan, *Sermon on the Mount*, rev. ed. (Valley Forge, PA: Judson Press, 1952), 104.
2. Hans Dieter Betz, *The Sermon on the Mount*, ed. Adela Yarbro (Minneapolis: Fortress Press, 1995), 487.
3. See Peter Rhea Jones, *Studying the Parables of Jesus* (Macon, GA: Smyth & Helwys, 1999), 219–21.

7"Ask, and it will be given you; search, and you will find; knock, and the door will be opened for you. 8For everyone who asks receives, and everyone who searches finds, and for everyone who knocks, the door will be opened. 9Is there anyone among you who, if your child asks for bread, will give a stone? 10Or if the child asks for a fish, will give a snake? 11If you then, who are evil, know how to give good gifts to your children, how much more will your Father in heaven give good things to those who ask him!"

Theological Perspective

What are we to be seeking? For what are we to ask? What is it we hope to find on the other side of the door? This passage begins with bold imperatives to ask, seek, and knock, followed by confident assertions that whatever is being sought is there for the finding. However, it is not immediately clear what we are to be seeking. This enigma is intentional on Jesus' part. He is creating a clever setup to invite the inevitable question that will lead to deeper understanding about what we are to seek and receive from God.

If Jesus would have paused for a moment after presenting the imperatives and assertions in verses 7 and 8, his listeners would have undoubtedly rushed to fill that space with their own ideas. I witnessed this with confirmation students when studying with them about prayer. I simply read these two verses aloud to them to see how they would respond. "If this is true," they said, "then I am asking for (fill in the latest techno-device, brand-name clothing, trip to exotic destination, etc.)." Go ahead, I told them, and ask for those things right now. They happily called out to God their ever-growing list of desires. After the boisterous voices quieted, they went on to bemoan the fact that such magical asking and receiving, Aladdin style, produced no results.

"But Jesus does not say that is what we should ask for," one astute eighth-grade girl responded. Aha! So

Pastoral Perspective

The familiarity of the first verses of this passage can provide comfort to a community feeling adrift. Even singing the Scripture in the canon setting represents a true kind of harmony. The words are a promise offering hope and assurance to those in need of surety. However, for many, this promise may seem to be a broken promise. For many, if not all, believers, there are those prayers that seem to have gone unanswered. A country-music lyric aside, the pain of unanswered prayers is real and deep. Addressing the need of those who hear this as a false promise takes care and thoughtfulness, not trite or overly simplistic answers. The prayer concerns of the congregation will be global, local, and personal. Whether these concerns are shared publicly in the liturgy or held quietly for private devotions, some may want to shake their fists at God with the frustration of prayer. Perhaps this is a better response than simply walking away. There is an opportunity to teach about the struggle to take prayer seriously, to teach about intercessory prayer, and to teach about prayer as listening rather than listing.

Inviting listeners to celebrate that which is given, found, and opened is an important lesson in responding to the gracious actions of God. This is the needed prayer of "thank-you" that rightly follows the prayer of "please." Compassionately inviting

Exegetical Perspective

This self-contained unit or topos encourages prayer. It has been dubbed "The Value of Prayer" (M'Neile), "The Answering Father" (Hagner), "On Answered Prayer" (Guelich), and "Encouragement to Pray" (RSV). It might also be called "Summons to Confident Prayer," "The Imperative of Asking," or "The Promise of Prayer." It reads as extraordinarily winsome, yet troublingly naive. In those two regards it is reminiscent of 6:25–34, with which it might be connected. This passage may also be related to the Lord's Prayer, given its central role in the Sermon on the Mount (Bornkamm).[1]

Matthew 7:7–11 stands between the prohibition of verse 6 and the Golden Rule at verse 12. It is also the last unit before the eschatological epilogue (vv. 13–27). Its structure is readily apparent as it opens with a positive admonition (v. 7), continues with a supporting rationale (v. 8) buttressed by two illustrations (vv. 9, 10) and followed by a conclusion (v. 11) that forms an *inclusio* with verse 7. The illustrations amount to vital questions of engagement with the listener. The steps in persuasion (as the inferential "for," [v. 8a]; "or," [vv. 9a, 10a]; the "if" [vv. 9b, 10, 11] introducing a matter of reality conditional sentence;

1.Bornkamm suggests Matthew 6:19–7:12 is an elaboration on the Lord's Prayer. See Gunther Bornkamm, "Der Aüfbau de Bergpredigt," *NTS* 24 (1977–78): 419–32.

Homiletical Perspective

In these verses Jesus issues three short, sharp commands intended to induce intimacy between God and Reigndom (kingdom of God) citizens. Each command posits a different posture and procedure, though they all desire the same aim and outcome. In asking, the inquisitor is using her or his voice. Searching typically requires the use of the whole body. Knocking compels the use of the arm and hand. All three postures demand mental and moral commitment. All three gestures—asking, searching, and knocking—are grasping for a positive response from God.

Neither asking nor searching nor knocking results in an immediate response from God. None of them is to be preferred above the others. God answers. God satisfies the seeker. God opens the door for those knocking. God is dependable. What cannot always be determined, though, is how God answers; one does not necessarily know what constitutes an answer from God.

It may very well be the case that the ambiguity regarding God's response to the petitioner's plea is intentional. The writer of Matthew's Gospel would know better than to try to prescribe divine activity. So also would a good Christian leader who has lived long enough to observe that life lived in intentional and conscious relationship with God is neither clear

Matthew 7:7–11

Theological Perspective

what *does* Jesus say? He goes on to give an illustration that any child and parent can understand: asking for something to eat. Again, using humor (see theological reflection on vv. 1–6), Jesus asks a rhetorical question that provokes laughter if we imagine a child asking for toast and getting a slab of slate on a plate, or receiving a hissing snake instead of wholesome fish. Of course our parents would not do that, responded the students when I asked if this would happen in their households.

Then they were ready to hear the truth about what they *are* to ask for, seek, and find: to agathon—"The Good." They are to ask for good things. What are "good things"? The students reverted to their wish lists from earlier in our conversation. Are these extravagances *good*, I pressed them? "They are to me!" one boy responded, to the amusement of his peers. I pointed out that perhaps we are confusing "goods" with "the good." Reinhold Niebuhr in *Moral Man and Immoral Society* elucidates the dilemma when the distinction between the two is missed:

> Man [*sic*], unlike other creatures, is gifted and cursed with an imagination which extends his appetites beyond the requirements of subsistence. Human society will never escape the problem of the equitable distribution of the physical and cultural goods which provide for the preservation and fulfillment of human life.[1]

In other words, "the good" of the preservation and fulfillment of human life is threatened by the uneven distribution of "goods" within human society. The students and I discussed the fact that our consumerist society has led to increased poverty, environmental depletion, and wars over the distribution of goods.

At this point I introduced a bit of process theology to the students, explaining that God is not a Santa Claus or genie in the sky, but the One whose *initial aim* of goodness continually invites us or *lures* us to respond in kind. The students began to see that at the heart of their selfish desires listed earlier is a kernel of egotistical evil that seeks only its own pleasure, at the expense of others. Jesus' exhortation to ask, seek, and knock for *the good* enabled them to imagine other good things to ask for—not just for themselves, but for others. Peace, healing, aid for recent natural disaster victims, and less pollution were among the items on their new list.

1. Reinhold Niebuhr, *Moral Man and Immoral Society* (New York: Charles Scribner's Sons, 1946), 1.

Pastoral Perspective

someone who has come to seek your counsel to reimagine and reinterpret both their prayers and the response, even the seeming lack of response, is difficult and necessary work. Remembering those individuals who are known to be struggling will keep the preacher or teacher mindful and tender to their needs and also sensitive to the unknown needs of other congregants.

It is this same active imagination that Jesus demands as he continues teaching, about the gifts parents give to their children and the parallel of God's gifts given to God's children. Jesus invites his listeners to assume the good intent of a parent for the child and in so doing to magnify the good intent of God. For many, this bridge is an easy bridge to cross; for others, the parent-child relationship is marked by failure, brokenness, and in some cases cruelty. For some individuals and for some congregations, the preacher or teacher may need to be sensitive to histories where need has not been met, or where a need has been mocked.

The intentional substitution of stone or snake seems appalling, but is a reality. For Jesus' listeners, the connection between bread and stones and between fish and snakes is a visual one. A small loaf of bread could resemble a stone. The imagination of those who have been hurt in the past may see the stone, even when bread is offered. How can we address the pessimistic and the damaged vision of those who have been wounded, not only by parents, but also by other loved ones and even by the church? Demonstrating that bread and fish are in the outstretched hand can be a wondrous moment. Showing the beauty of God's gifts can be a joyful task. Helping others to learn to see this beauty again or for the first time is one of the higher callings for a preacher/minister/priest.

Similarly, taking the occasion to create some distance between parental models and models of God may be life giving and freeing. Ask the same question that Jesus asks, "How much more . . . ?" in order to demonstrate the difference between humanity and divinity. This difference can be lost in a world where hierarchies are flattened (a good thing among equal citizens) but is an important distinction for us mortals to hold onto when we encounter God. The preacher/pastor can invite listeners to move beyond models of God that limit or hamper true relationship and devotion, and encourage them to see that the relationship and devotion can flourish in new and creative ways.

If one of the questions for this text is how to unlock its meaning with those who know suffering,

the "therefore," [v. 11a]) signal a conclusion based upon prior argument. If these steps are underlined by the interpreter, the movements of the argument are easy to follow. Note also the typical question from Jesus, "Who among you?" (v. 9a) and the rabbinic "How much more . . ." (v. 11b).

This Matthean text finds parallel in an extended Lukan form (Luke 11:1–13). The wording of Matthew 7:7–11 and Luke 11:11–13 is quite similar. Luke points toward a historical context when Jesus had finished praying. His disciples requested that he teach them to pray as had John (Luke 11:1). The ensuing paragraphs include first the Lord's Prayer (Luke 11:2–4), a parable concerning the friend at midnight requesting bread (Luke 11:5–8), and then the summons to pray and its corresponding promise (Luke 11:9–13), forming a kind of prayer *didache* (teaching). Some or all could go back not only to Jesus but to a particular time. The parable itself includes request and gift. For Luke, the parable is connected to the saying on prayer by the words "And I say to you" (Luke 11:9a).

The Matthean passage begins with the necessity of persistent asking (v. 7a) and may well be rendered "keep on asking." As a present imperative, it suggests a "continuous process of asking." If so, an element of persistence in prayer is implied. Verse 7 contains a threesome of synonymous parallels ("symmetric tautologies") saying essentially the same thing, with the second and third (v. 7bc) portraying the first figuratively. The Greek for "asking" regularly refers to prayer in Matthew (Matt. 6:8; 18:19) and elsewhere in the Gospels (Mark 11:24; Luke 11:10, 13; cf. Eph. 3:20). Seeking God's face in the Hebrew Scriptures means to pray (2 Sam. 21:1; Ps. 23:6; Prov. 8:17). The imagery of knocking metaphorically pictures petitionary prayer as standing in front of a closed door, expecting it to be opened. A promise, as well as a summons to pray, is reiterated three times. "The promise here," as Howard Marshall put it, "is that God is waiting to be found by those who will seek after him (cf. Deut. 4:29; Isa. 55:6; 65:1; Jer. 29:18; cf. Prov. 8:17)."[2] The object of the prayer is not iterated here but implied later in terms of "good gifts" (v. 11).

Verse 8 represents more than a repetition or support for an audacious claim. It asserts and reveals a truth about God and prayer. It is reassurance but more. This surety grows out of the experience not only of Israel but of Jesus himself. Quite noticeably Jesus not only practiced withdrawal and prayer, but

2. Howard Marshall, *Commentary on Luke* (Grand Rapids: Eerdmans, 1978), 467.

cut nor determinable. Ask, seek, and knock, knowing that God hears and sees and will answer in God's own way and time.

This pericope is ultimately about faith—persistent, unrelenting faith. It is about faith that simply will not give up on the God whose very nature requires those who possess faith also to be possessed by faith. The experience of being possessed by faith is an experience of living in relationship to the God who has given faith as a gift. Paradoxically, in making an appeal to God, we are possessed by faith and relinquish all need—and maybe even all desire—to control the relationship.

Asking, seeking, and knocking become ways of being in relationship with God. Each implies dependence. Each is indicative of the fact that one is relying completely upon God for whatever is being sought. The inquirer does not possess the answer. The seeker does not possess the treasure. The knocker does not also open the door. Appeals are made to God, and God responds in God's time.

Asking, seeking, and knocking are ways of acknowledging that God is the ultimate and trustworthy authority in the Reigndom of God. As the sovereign One, God alone possesses the power to determine when the appropriate response is given. God even has the right to decide what the right response is.

A child sits at the feet of her mother, unable to speak in language the mother understands cognitively, but the mother knows what her child is asking of her. The mother knows this because she knows her child. She also knows whether her child truly needs what she is requesting at the moment, or some later time. The mother, in her love for her child and because of her wisdom as the mother, will give her child what she needs, when she needs it. She will also, for the same reasons, deny her child what is being sought, should it not be in the child's best interest.

Whether or not the thing requested is given, the mother answers. Mother and child are bound together by their mutual love. The child trusts her mother, loves her mother, and seeks her mother's acceptance and approval, whether or not she receives what she has requested. So also does the mother love, care for, and earnestly seek the best provision for her child. She is present and available and open to every appeal.

Jesus assures his followers that God is far more deserving of fealty and more worthy of trust than human parents. God is our "Parent [*sic*] in heaven" who knows how to give "good things" (v. 11). What

Matthew 7:7–11

Theological Perspective

"Maybe we should also pray for kids who actually do not get enough to eat and kids whose parents really are abusive to them, like giving them stones and snakes when they should be giving them bread and fish," said the boy who had earlier insisted on wanting "the goods." The class nodded thoughtfully.

Well, go ahead, I told them once again, and ask for those things right now. This time there was no rambunctious calling out. Their voices were more subdued. There were spaces of quietness between their petitions. When it felt as if they were done, I repeated once again verse 8: "Everyone who asks receives, and everyone who searches finds, and for everyone who knocks, the door will be opened." However, that was not the end.

"How can we be sure that this is true?" a girl asked. "How will we know that we've gotten what we asked for? Because there are still a lot of abused kids and pollution and war and stuff," she pointed out. Yes, how will we know? Jesus was being naive, unrealistic, or, worse, lying to us.

The astute eighth-grader chimed in once again. "It doesn't say *when* all these things will happen." Stretching them even further, I explained how the Greek verb tenses in verse 7 are indicative future, meaning that they have not happened yet, and there is no specific indication of the time when they will come to pass. The paradoxical phrase "already and not yet" is apt to describe the fulfillment of God's work in the world.

"So you have recognized the 'not yet' aspect of all this," I said. "Where is the 'already'?" We began making a third list—evidence that prayers were being answered, doors were being opened, and people were finding the *agatha* for which they were looking. Our church's food boxes for the hungry, the ecology ministry's work on protecting God's creation, the abused foster child being adopted by a loving family, the soldiers coming home. The young theologians decided to continue in the weeks thereafter asking for the good, and then listing the signs that the future indicative of Jesus' promised future was already making itself known.

LEAH D. SCHADE

Pastoral Perspective

without trivializing or offering cheap answers, then the combination of the two sets of verses into one pericope is helpful. The same conversation that offers the faithful answers and opened doors can also speak of God as a giver of good gifts that are by definition beyond our imagining.

Preachers, teachers, and listeners alike are aware of the sufferings and tragedies that mark life in the world. Given the darkness of these times, there is a need to speak about the futility sometimes felt in prayer and the frustration when miracles are not forthcoming. Sometimes a belief that we operate and understand on the same plane as God inhibits our ability to imagine; this may keep us from even seeing bread or the opened door. Without criticizing the needful mourning of those who suffer loss and without offering trite answers, the voice of the church can remind the faithful of the difference between wishing and praying. Both are legitimate responses, yet prayer allows for answers and even miracles that do not look like what we think they will look like. Prayer allows us to see bread instead of a stone. Prayer does not teach what to ask for, but how to ask; prayer reminds us of our place and of our limits; prayer recognizes the difference between human comprehension and God's vision.

There will be times and situations when a person or a congregation cannot hear this. Sometimes the best pastoral response is not to leap to insist that we trust in God, but rather to allow the asking and the searching and even the wishing to play through. Holding fast to the belief in God's provision for someone else can be the private role of the counselor and the public role of the preacher. The preacher is asked to keep faithful to a vision of God who faithfully keeps promises and to articulate that faith for those who lack it, without suggesting a critique of their faith or doubt.

KATHERINE M. BUSH

his healing and exorcism were predicated upon the answer to prayer (Mark 9:29: John 11:41). This text reflects a conception of God willing to respond with an accent upon the promises.

Verses 9 and 10 shift from confirmatory assertion to questions of engagement. Jesus frequently appealed to the common experience, inviting a nod of agreement. First, he envisions a son *asking* for bread. Interlocking with the hearers, he interrogates whether such a father would give an inedible stone instead of nutritious bread. Were this ordinary father to be asked for fish, would he proffer a dangerous snake? Of course not! Bread and fish were staples for daily food around the lake of Galilee. This may well provide us a clue to the object of the prayer at verses 7 and 8. We see here connection with the Lord's Prayer and its petition for daily bread (Matt. 6:11). This may also suggest a context of mission, as in Matthew 6:25–33. Prayer in the context of the Sermon on the Mount may well encompass requests for forgiveness and deliverance from evil (Matt. 6:12–13). Indeed, it was likely a kingdom-oriented prayer passionately urging the outbreak of the will of God on earth. Transcendent blessings may be implied.

Building upon the two examples at verses 9 and 10, Jesus concludes then that if sinful human fathers know how to give good gifts to their children, then surely the heavenly Father does, arguing in rabbinic fashion from the lesser to the greater (v. 11). The Greek word translated "evil" or "sinful" as a characterization of a human father seems to assume the sinfulness of humanity (cf. Mark 7:21–23). This characterization does not eliminate the possibility of relatively good human acts, but it does intensify contrast with the implied character of God.

Because this text standing alone is expressed in such unconditional and universal terms, one does well to reckon with and interact with qualifications concerning prayer found elsewhere. Believing that you will receive (Matt. 21:22; Mark 11:24) is inherent to adequate prayer. In John, prayer must be in the name of Jesus (John 14:13–14; 15:16; 16:24, 26). Most critically, prayer must align with the will of God (Matt. 26:39).

This text on prayer implies a conception of God as giving generously, as listening and responding to his children praying. The text encourages prayer because the efficacy of the Christian mission depends on it.

PETER RHEA JONES

a bold statement, considering the audience of Jesus! What an audacious statement, considering the vicissitudes of our own life experiences! We know and love and serve a sovereign God who possesses all power and knowledge and whose presence is ubiquitous. This same Deity knows, has the experience, and, yes, even the reputation of giving "good things." Still, every day thousands if not millions of poor, suffering peoples in every nook and cranny of the globe make sorrowful, desperate appeals to this God, this Creator, this Deity whom we claim and love and worship.

There is a silence in response to the asking, the seeking, and the knocking. The suffering is ubiquitous. The pains and traumas of life seem as omnipotent as the Creator, and a yawning silence continually, perpetually, permanently fills the space between loving Creator and suffering people—except the privileged perhaps. At least among us there is no physical hunger, no perpetual fear of annihilation by armed men and women with minds poisoned by ideological or racial or gender-based hatred. The women and men of Jesus' day, particularly those who may have heard words like those in this pericope, were overcome by the viciousness of their Roman colonizer and the sympathizers who worked alongside of him. Given life's vagaries, how dare one claim that God answers? Such a claim can only be made by faith—sincere, earnest, belligerent faith in a God who has always been and will forever be bigger and more powerful than relatively petty human interests. What are the "good things" God reputedly gives anyway?

According to the pericope the examples of "good things" provided by God are "bread" (v. 9) and "fish" (v. 10). Interestingly the "good things" are not luxury vehicles, vacation homes, and closets full of clothes and shoes. "Good things" are not perpetual safety and rest and peace. The "good things" are not the love, joy, and happiness of the sort that we Westerners are accustomed to demanding and expecting. The "good things" spoken of in the text are staple foods, life's bare essentials.

The particular postures of prayer are unimportant. What is important is faith in the God who hears and who sometimes answers with provision and at other times answers with silence.

MARK A. LOMAX

Matthew 7:12

> [12]"In everything do to others as you would have them do to you; for this is the law and the prophets."

Theological Perspective

There is a danger lurking when Matthew 7:12 is given a special place all to itself. This danger, in fact, is fatal to the gospel if we succumb to it, because it turns the gospel into an idea, a philosophy, an ethical principle or norm of behavior. In which case, the sum of "the law and the prophets" becomes detached from the person of Jesus. It becomes an abstract entity called the Golden Rule. This means not just the detachment of the teaching from the teacher, as if we just fail to note the author of the teaching. The danger at hand is the detachment of the disciple from Jesus Christ, in which we fail to recognize that the teaching is given on the ground of the presupposition of an exclusive attachment to Christ, as a result of our response to his call, "Follow me." This verse is not to be interpreted as a universal truth, even as a universal truth taught by Jesus. Detached from the disciple being in relationship with Jesus, even accepting it as taught by him, the text becomes that most unchristian entity, a *logos asarkos*, a word without flesh. It becomes a Golden Rule, another expression of a general law that is unbearably hard to obey.

Our text must be read in theological context, as Matthew's Sermon on the Mount drives to its conclusion. That is to say, the text must be read in terms of Jesus' claim upon his disciples to leave everything and follow him. It must be interpreted

Pastoral Perspective

Far more people know the so-called Golden Rule as expressed in Matthew 7:12 than realize that it may be found in the New Testament. This can be accounted for, in part, by the fact that whether the rule is stated in the positive form found in Matthew ("Do to others . . .") or the negative form ("Do not do to others . . ."), some version of the principle can be found in many different religious and ethical systems. This failure to connect the Golden Rule to the New Testament is also surely a function of the fact that it has become for many people nothing more than a statement of the need for basic politeness. It ranks right there with your grandparents' advice: "If you cannot say something nice about someone, then do not say anything at all."

Two researchers studying the religious/moral attitudes of contemporary American youth documented both the pervasiveness and the limitations of this understanding. They found that one core belief of young people was that "God wants people to be good, nice, and fair to each other, as taught in the Bible and by most world religions." Coupled with that was the conviction that "the central goal of life is to be happy and to feel good about oneself."[1] If one overlays those

1. Christian Smith and Melinda Lundquist Denton, *Soul Searching: The Religious and Spiritual Lives of American Teenagers* (New York: Oxford University Press, 2005), 162–63.

Exegetical Perspective

Our focus is the so-called Golden Rule, a widely known ethical maxim in the ancient world: "In everything, do to others as you would have them do to you; for this is the law and the prophets." (The last clause is unique to the biblical tradition.) How might we read this maxim located near the end of Matthew's Sermon on the Mount (chaps. 5–7)?

Interpreting this verse is affected by how we read Matthew's Sermon on the Mount. One reading strategy understands Matthew's Sermon to set out an impossible ideal that causes the reader to repent and seek God's mercy. This approach sees 7:12 as setting the bar of interpersonal relationships so high that we repent of our failures. Another reading strategy understands the Sermon as providing a perfectionist ethic (5:48), an ideal way of being for which disciples are to aim. In this reading, 7:12 establishes an ideal standard of interacting with other human beings. A third option sees the Sermon, contextualized by Matthew 1–4, as providing a vision of discipleship shaped by God's gracious initiative in commissioning Jesus to manifest God's saving presence. This reading of 7:12 offers an example or summary of this way of life, in which love for neighbor and enemy is central. I will pursue this third option here.

Matthew's Sermon on the Mount (chaps. 5–7) appears after the Gospel's opening four chapters

Homiletical Perspective

A beautiful thing about the Golden Rule is that you do not need to be a devout Christian to understand it. In fact you do not need to be religious at all. It is one of those rare axioms whose simple truth stands on its own merit. However, like Einstein's brilliant formula $E=mc^2$, contemplation of it encourages one's imagination to dig deeper into the wisdom tucked in its lining.

This simplicity also presents a predicament for preachers, especially those who have encountered this text many times over the years. In an effort to have something coherent and concrete to preach, the busy homilist may overlook that deeper wisdom and leap too quickly to simple, timeworn phrases. While this passage provides temptation enough to do so, a more contextual approach will unearth greater riches.

One context to be considered is the longtime, universal nature of this ideal. Before it appeared in Matthew, the prudence of ego-based altruism was woven into the community fabric of many cultures throughout the world. Wise people, contemplating the dynamic of human relationships, seemed to know instinctively the worth of this nugget. Far removed from us in time and culture, the philosophy of Confucius proclaimed this connection, as did the Code of Hammurabi and ancient Greek

Theological Perspective

in terms of faith in Jesus as the Christ to whom the disciples know they belong, because he has called them to belong to him and so names them accordingly "blessed." The text cannot be interpreted as if it stands alone, apart from Jesus' call to exclusive attachment to himself.

The modern classic on the theological interpretation of the Sermon is Dietrich Bonhoeffer's *The Cost of Discipleship*, published in 1937. Bonhoeffer's main point is that Christian discipleship arises from a singular attachment to the call of Jesus to follow him. In his now-famous distinction between cheap grace and costly grace, with which he opens his discussion, Bonhoeffer warns against what we might be in danger of doing if we preach Matthew 7:12 as a stand-alone verse. Cheap grace means grace as a doctrine, a principle, a system, a general truth, an intellectual idea. It is grace construed without Jesus Christ, apart from what it means that the disciples are called to follow him. Grace is only grace, costly grace, when it calls first the disciples and then us to follow Jesus. The Sermon is to be understood theologically in terms of the mutual relation between grace and discipleship, that is, in terms of an exclusive allegiance to Jesus. Bonhoeffer argues that the Sermon can only be understood on these terms, summing up his position in an often-quoted sentence: "When Christ calls a man [*sic*] he bids him come and die."[1]

Turning specifically to Matthew 7:12, the radical framework within which we interpret Jesus' teaching is that we who follow Jesus already know how Jesus has treated us. Between us and God's law stands Jesus as the one who has fully fulfilled the law on our behalf and called us to share in that righteousness. Bonhoeffer states bluntly that Jesus "is the righteousness of the disciples. By calling them he has admitted them to partnership with himself, and made them partakers of his righteousness in its fullness."[2] In academic terms, here we are confronted with the two doctrines without which there is no understanding of Christian life: (1) the vicarious humanity of Christ, in which he stands in for us before God, and God's law, doing for us what we can never do for ourselves, and (2) union with Christ, by which in the Holy Spirit Christ binds us to himself, thereby to share in that which is his. With regard to Matthew 7:12, this means that there is no possibility whatever of allowing our interpretation to go forward on the basis of a general moral teaching as a kind of Golden

Pastoral Perspective

ideas on the "Golden Rule," then what God expects persons to be is "good, nice, and fair to each other," with those standards defined in terms of those things that allow one "to be happy and to feel good about oneself." As another commentator observes in reflecting on this research, "when contentment becomes an end unto itself, the way that human contents express themselves can look an awful lot like vanity and decadence." In the end the "vanity and decadence" of the individual trumps concern for others: "Learning to love ourselves and love the universe isn't necessarily the best way to learn to love our neighbor as ourselves, it turns out, and an overemphasis on the essential unity of all things—the Creator and creation, God and humanity—may be a good way to dissolve more intermediate loyalties completely."[2]

A difficulty with the Golden Rule can arise, then, when it is viewed through the lens of either cultural or individual narcissism. In such cases, what *I* consider good *for me* becomes the measure of what is good for all. However, reading Matthew 7:12 through narcissistic lenses is not the only thing that contributes to this difficulty. There is also the failure to read Jesus' full statement. He not only said, "In everything do to others as you would have them do to you"—which would leave ourselves as the only standard of judgment. He went on to add, "for this is the law and the prophets." One way to summarize what "the law and the prophets" teach us is that we recognize what is holy by its value not primarily to *us*, but to *God*. If what I desire for myself is founded upon the sacredness and value God places in people and on treating the blessings of life, so they are not abused in destructive ways, then I will have removed my personal desires from being the sole or even the determining standard for my actions.

For the Golden Rule to function in a distinctively Christian way, rather than as one among many aphorisms that might be espoused by Miss Manners, it must be located within its broader scriptural context. The answer to the prior question, "Just what would I have others do for me?" is to be found not in the "vanity and decadence" of self-indulgence, but rather in "the law and the prophets." When we understand God's justice as the standard that defines what is best for us, we will understand that justice is not only good for us as individuals, but can truly exist only in communities where that same justice is extended to all by all.

1. Dietrich Bonhoeffer, *The Cost of Discipleship*, trans. R. H. Fuller, with revisions by Irmgard Booth (London: SCM Press, 1959), 79.
2. Ibid., 113.

2. Ross Douthat, *Bad Religion: How We Became a Nation of Heretics* (New York: Free Press, 2012), 234 and 241.

have accomplished two crucial tasks. The first task is to establish the identity of Jesus as God's agent. God begins the action in the conception and commissioning of Jesus to manifest God's saving presence (1:21–23). Thereafter, protected by God from imperial mayhem (chap. 2), witnessed to by John (3:1–12), sanctioned by God in baptism (3:13–17), tested unsuccessfully in his loyalty by the devil (4:1–11), and confirmed by the Scriptures (4:12–16), Jesus begins his ministry (4:17). He carries out his task of manifesting God's saving presence in proclamation (4:17, 23) and in compassionately healing those damaged by the imperial world in which they live (4:23–25).

The second key thing accomplished in chapters 1–4 is that Jesus calls disciples to encounter God's reign and saving presence (4:18–22). Immediately thereafter, in the Sermon on the Mount, Matthew's Jesus begins the process of shaping their identity and way of life (along with that of the Gospel's readers) based on their encounter with God's reign and saving presence. The Sermon provides "for examples," of what such a way of life and identity might look like. The Gospel's post–70 CE readers lived in a world in which Roman imperial power had been asserted in the destruction of Jerusalem and its temple. The Sermon reimagines a world of quite different priorities, societal structures, and social interactions.

Among that reimagining are human interactions where, instead of domination and exploitation, integrity and concern for the other—love—are primary. The Sermon ends chapter 5 with a "for example" concerning love not only for neighbors but even for enemies (5:38–48). Such love that seeks the good of the other—whether friend or enemy—reflects God's way of working in the world. It mirrors God's generosity and life-giving graciousness in indiscriminately shining the sun on the evil and the good and sending rain on the just and the unjust (5:43–48). In the context of chapters 1–4, it reflects God's gracious and loving initiative to disclose God's saving presence among humans in Jesus. Later in the Gospel, Jesus tells the young man trying to find life that loving his neighbor as himself is part of the finding (19:19). In 22:34–40, Jesus sums up the tradition of "the law and the prophets" in terms of love for God and neighbor.

Not surprisingly, then, Matthew's Jesus concludes the middle section of the Sermon with this instruction in 7:12 about loving and just social interactions. The reference to the "law and the prophets" links back to 5:17, where Jesus declares that he does not abolish them but fulfills or enacts them. He does

philosophers like Pittacus, who said: "Do not do to others what would anger you if done to you by others."[1] Also, more modern sages, such as the philosopher Immanuel Kant and the venerable former New York Yankee catcher Yogi Berra, have added their insights on the subject. Kant spoke of his categorical imperative in lofty terms: "Act only according to that maxim whereby you can, at the same time, will that it should become a universal law."[2] Yogi was reported to have said it more humbly: "Don't do nothin' you wouldn't want done to ya." So basic is this ideal and so widespread its use that it must be considered a moral law underlying all human interaction.

When we turn our attention to the context of Christian ideals, this imperative emerges from the very teaching and preaching of the early church. It became the way to inform and instruct the people of the day about the practical life their faith yields. Now that teaching challenges the homilist of today to help the seeker with the faith, mind-set, and ethics of a people trying to be loyal to and living out the meaning of Jesus' life, death, and resurrection.

Matthew must have understood how perfectly this teaching related to the faith and practice of the early Christian community. By invoking the law and the prophets, he draws this ethical ideal into the full tradition of the faith. He is announcing that this is not some disembodied, ethereal thought floating from culture to culture, but the very essence of a people whose community has a reason and a purpose. By remembering the law and the prophets, the church community clothes itself in the rich beauty of the family garments. Its life together gives credibility and authority to the point being made and the teaching being provided.

As a boy, I had a rather unlikable aunt whom our extended family enjoyed ridiculing. I noticed, however, that they never did so in our home. My mother gave the reason. She said my father would not allow it. It was his expectation that in our home, every guest would be treated with respect, because that is the way he was brought up. Calling up the law and the prophets produces more than a history lesson for the first-century community and for us: it is a reminder of who and whose we are.

So, perhaps a focus of this sermon could be, What tells us who we are as a people? What is it about Jesus that convicts and challenges our hearts? What makes sense to us above all the competing ideas and

1. H. G. Wells, *The Outline of History* (New York: Macmillan Co., 1924), 272.
2. William S. Sahakian, *Ideas of the Great Philosophers* (New York: Fall River Press, 2005), 44.

Matthew 7:12

Theological Perspective

Rule, apart from Christ's righteousness for us and our participation in his life.

Thus, following Bonhoeffer's teaching, we are not to judge, for we have no objective righteousness in ourselves by which we could judge another. We own no new standard, but we are disciples because of Jesus Christ. Always, Christ stands between believer and unbeliever, neither free as such, but free only insofar as either may be in communion with Christ. The disciple of Jesus has neither special privileges nor power to call his or her own. Everything arises from the call of Jesus, the fellowship with him that the call entails, and one's obedience to that call and fellowship.

In union with Christ, participating in his righteousness and in obedience to his claim upon us, Christians accept what Bonhoeffer calls "a simple rule of thumb"[3] (how less grand that "rule" is than The Golden Rule!): "to say 'I' instead of 'Thou', and put himself [sic] in the other man's [sic] place." That is, the disciple lays aside any advantage over others he or she might feel, and will no longer excuse those things in him or herself that he or she condemns in others. The wickedness in others is no more or less than the wickedness within the disciple. Believing in Jesus Christ, we will look upon other people as forgiven sinners who owe their lives to the love and mercy of God. In so doing, we will fulfill the great commandment to love God above all things and our neighbors as ourselves.

ANDREW PURVES

Pastoral Perspective

Within the context of Matthew's Gospel, "the law and the prophets" are associated not only with God's justice but also with the fundamental commands to love God and to "love your neighbor as yourself" (Matt. 22:34–40, esp. v. 39). Some commentators suggest that this connection with the "Rule of Love" is important in understanding the positive formulation of the Golden Rule within the gospel. Because it is thus grounded in love, the Golden Rule is an affirmative demand placed upon us. It is not sufficient for us simply to avoid doing things that we would find objectionable if directed at us. We have an obligation to act with love toward others "in everything." Even should others fail to reciprocate those actions by doing the same things for us, the Rule of Love must determine our actions, not simply an avoidance of things that are hateful or harmful. Seen within this context, the Golden Rule "is not primarily a basic ethical principle; it is an aid in helping love become concrete and find the right track."[3]

Certainly we live in a time when the coarsening of the culture generally points up the need for reminders that people owe each other at least the common civilities they themselves expect to receive. All people really should be "good, nice, and fair to each other." However, within the context of the teachings of Jesus, the Golden Rule requires more than simple politeness. It is an expression of the deeper obligation that we are to "love [our] neighbors as [ourselves]." The standard from our own lives that we are to apply in determining our actions toward others is the love we have experienced from God. Loving God and loving others in response to God's love for us is not just a Golden Rule; it is a demonstration of "the law and the prophets."

TIMOTHY B. CARGAL

---

3. Ibid., 167.

3. Ulrich Luz, *Matthew 1–7*, Hermeneia (Minneapolis: Fortress Press, 2007), 267.

Exegetical Perspective

so, as 22:34–40 indicates, in expressions of love. Another feature reinforces this linking of the Golden Rule in 7:12 to 5:17. The regular translations of 7:12 ("In everything, do to others . . .") miss a key little word in the Greek that a more literal and somewhat clumsy translation highlights: "All things *therefore* whatever you wish that people do to you, thus also you do to them." The "therefore" and its reference to the law and the prophets link 7:12 to 5:17, bookending the Sermon's middle section. The Golden Rule of verse 12 does not exist in isolation from this context, but sums up the middle section of the Sermon (5:17–7:12).

What constitutes the "all things . . . whatever you wish"? Is this a blank check that we can fill in for whatever we like? In the context of the Sermon and evoking the law and the prophets, such an open reading is not likely. Rather, both Jesus' teaching and the law and the prophets focus on doing God's will. So in the Lord's Prayer Jesus teaches disciples to pray for God's will to be "done, on earth as it is in heaven" (6:10). The Sermon ends with contrasting the wise who hear and do Jesus' teaching with the foolish who hear but do not do (7:24–27). As with the rest of the Sermon, disciples are to imagine what God's will, God's reign, might look like as the basis for their social interactions. Disciples are to imagine and understand how God acts—indiscriminately generous in seeking the good of all people, exhibited in the sun and rain of 5:45—and act accordingly to others. By so imagining and acting, love is made explicit and concrete in specific interactions.

Such actions, then, are not about manipulating the other for our own advantage. They are about the other's well-being. There is a risk, of course, in urging disciples to initiate actions that reflect God's generous and gracious actions. While many respond positively to being treated with generosity and love, others respond with manipulation or rejection or misunderstanding or suspicion or abuse or . . . Nevertheless, even in this way, disciples imitate God, who also takes such a risk in chapters 1–4, in commissioning Jesus and in shining the sun on the good and the bad.

WARREN CARTER

Homiletical Perspective

ideals in life? Why do we choose to be in worship rather than the myriad of places the culture offers at the same hour (some of which admittedly outdazzle our rubrics by quite a bit)?

Still, the lining of this garment is not yet finished revealing truths. Like the Ten Commandments that define the relationships within Israel's covenanted community, "Do unto others . . ." takes the primary commitment to human interaction built on justice and righteousness, expands it, and applies it to the community of relationships everywhere. The transforming life and death of Jesus not only renew the heart of the believer, but transform the context of ethics from provincial to universal.

This universal context means the church has a new task if it is to fulfill its enduring purpose. That task is to live out this ethic in a new day. The new day of our era opens us to interaction with all the world's peoples. Community no longer concludes at the end of the street or the city limits, but includes all the families of the earth. Applying the universal aspect of this ethic fits perfectly for today's complex relations, whether they are personal or international.

Each generation creates new human struggles that must be addressed. Before they are addressed, we must be clear on one thing: it is not enough to remember or even encouragingly preach this commandment. As it walks its way, the church must be weaving this ethic into the fabric of its own life—not because we must, as the saying goes, but because we may. Not because we are commanded, but because we are persuaded.

Then, once persuaded, we can address many of those struggles by becoming this ideal's great advocate. Whether speaking truth to power or whispering guidance to children, we can proclaim the gospel in a few easily remembered words. The ethical banner we unfurl now becomes worthy of display, because it has been woven with the threads of our commitments and the integrity of our actions. Then, when the world's eyes fall upon it, all can see the vision we hold for the basis of relationships everywhere.

RICHARD WILLIAM HARBART

Matthew 7:13–20

¹³"Enter through the narrow gate; for the gate is wide and the road is easy that leads to destruction, and there are many who take it. ¹⁴For the gate is narrow and the road is hard that leads to life, and there are few who find it.

¹⁵"Beware of false prophets, who come to you in sheep's clothing but inwardly are ravenous wolves. ¹⁶You will know them by their fruits. Are grapes gathered from thorns, or figs from thistles? ¹⁷In the same way, every good tree bears good fruit, but the bad tree bears bad fruit. ¹⁸A good tree cannot bear bad fruit, nor can a bad tree bear good fruit. ¹⁹Every tree that does not bear good fruit is cut down and thrown into the fire. ²⁰Thus you will know them by their fruits."

Theological Perspective

Everything we have read from the Sermon on the Mount leads us to expect the conclusion that following Jesus is going to be demanding. We cannot say that *much* is demanded from us; rather, we must say that *everything* is demanded of us. Now the distinction and separation between discipleship and worldliness is progressively pushed to mark the division that obedience to the call of Jesus entails, even to the point of forcing that division into the church itself. The severity of Jesus' teaching is surely indicative of both our capacity, even as Christians, for self-deceit and of the power of evil, even within the church.

The first teaching is the requirement to enter into discipleship through the narrow gate and thereafter to walk the road that is hard. Already having read through the Sermon on the Mount, we have found solid content to give to this narrow gate and hard road. From Matthew 5 we know that the disciple is called to a way of life characterized at verse 47 as *perisson*—a way of life that is extraordinary, "much more than," not the usual matter-of-course but the unusual.[1] This is the life of the Beatitudes; it is the city set on a hill; it is the life of going the second mile, turning the other cheek, love, purity,

1. Dietrich Bonhoeffer, *The Cost of Discipleship*, trans. R. H. Fuller, with revisions by Irmgard Booth (London: SCM Press, 1959), 136.

Pastoral Perspective

Overfamiliarity can be the death of a good metaphor. Metaphors are intended to open up the possibility for discovering new meanings and connections. Through the juxtaposition of dissimilar things, the speaker or author nevertheless suggests that there are important similarities. When everyone already knows the answer, then the possibilities for discovery are prematurely foreclosed. The two primary metaphor sets within this passage—the "gate" and "way" that are to illuminate "destruction" and "life" (7:13–14), and the "fruit" that should identify "false prophets" (7:15–20)—are ready examples of metaphors that suffer from the problem of overfamiliarity.

What everyone knows about these particular metaphors is that they reveal something of the sectarian outlook of the Matthean community. Jesus (generally for those who agree with the view of the world expressed by this understanding of the metaphors)—or at least the evangelist (generally for those who are less certain or are at least troubled by this understanding)—insists that there "are few who find" the "way" to live in the manner that God intends and so fail to "enter through the narrow gate . . . that leads to life" and salvation. Instead, they are carried along with the masses through the wide gate and easy road/manner of life "that leads to destruction."

Exegetical Perspective

After summing up the Sermon's demand for love in 7:12; the Sermon's remaining verses (7:13–27) comprise three warnings and exhortations. One section concerns two different ways of living and their respective goals (7:13–14); one section concerns false prophets (7:15–20, 21–23); and the last one employs house building as a metaphor for living (7:24–27).

The language of 7:13–20 highlights the section's emphasis on living faithfully now, in order to participate in the yet-future (eschatological) completion of God's purposes. This emphasis is carried in the verses' common language of "entering" (2x in 7:13), "knowing" (2x; 7:16, 20), and "doing" (7:17–19). In order to enter into God's purposes, doing God's will and knowing or discerning (and rejecting) false options are necessary. The language in this section is frequently dualistic. Opposites such as wide and narrow, easy and hard, many and few, destruction and life, good and bad, set out the alternative ways of living. One way of living—the wide and easy—leads to destruction in the judgment. The other—the narrow and hard—leads to life. The four other major collections of Jesus' teaching in the Gospel (chaps. 10, 13, 18, and 24–25) similarly end with warnings about eschatological destruction if disciples do not "do" Jesus' teaching.

Verses 13–14 contrast two ways of living and their respective destinations. The initial imperative

Homiletical Perspective

As we come near the close of the Sermon on the Mount, there seems to be a shift in mood. The final admonitions are lacing up this three-chapter package of teachings with a high sense of urgency and drama. This is not your mother casually reminding you to pick up your socks or brush your teeth. This is an urgent alert to look both ways before crossing the street and a stern warning to pick your friends carefully. It is Matthew's reminder to the newly forming community that what it believes and how it proceeds will have concrete and direct consequences, not just about their style of life but about whether they will have life at all.

The stakes are high, and the historical circumstances show there will be no ease to the journey ahead. They must know the places of danger and the people of treachery, so that they do not fall prey to external wiles. At the same time they must be faithful to Jesus' teachings, so that they do not crumble from within. In Matthew's mind a letdown of diligence to either part would tarnish the relationship between Christ and the fledgling church that the teachings are attempting to describe. That is why the language is large and the images are pressing and rigorous.

The images of the gate and road turn on the thought that it is especially important to stay

Matthew 7:13–20

Theological Perspective

truthfulness, and meekness. It is a way of life known by its fruits.

From Matthew 6 we know that the disciple is called to "single" (*haplous*) sightedness (v. 22), looking only to Jesus, the pioneer and perfecter of our faith (Heb. 12:2). We cannot serve two masters. Thus, entering through the narrow gate and walking the hard road are what it means to have an exclusive attachment to Jesus, for only he is the way (John 14:6), and apart from that attachment we will not know the Father. Because it is an exclusive attachment to Jesus, this narrow gate is the gate of grace, and this hard road is the road of grace—and thus good news for the disciple. The yoke of Christ, the burden of discipleship, is grace; therefore the yoke is easy and the burden is light (Matt. 11:29–30), because it is Christ who calls us.

The second teaching concerns fruitfulness as the criterion of truthful discipleship. The teaching is cast in an ominous tone. The call is for the church to be vigilant: beware! The division between true and false discipleship now enters into the precinct of the church, and the consequences will surely be anxiety, untruth, and confusion. The trumpet of the gospel will give an uncertain note, an indistinct sound (1 Cor. 14:8). Some people will claim to have a word from the Lord; they will be wrapped in the mantle of piety and gentleness, but they will be hell-bent on destruction. Evil is at work under the cover of discipleship. Such a disciple appears to be faithful to the call of Christ, appears to have entered through the narrow gate and to walk upon the hard road, but is in fact under the call and tutelage of evil.

Can we trust our Christian neighbor? Can Christian appearance conceal a lie? Is it necessary for us, however discomfiting, to speak of evil people in the church—among leaders and clergy, among theologians, as well as within the broad populace of the body itself? The thought is shocking, but experience most likely confirms the truth of our text. Forbidden to judge, Christ's disciples nevertheless need a criterion of discernment. It is too dangerous to the health of the body to let evil go unchallenged. The heartening word, as Bonhoeffer notes, is that "All this distrust would ruin the Church but for the word of Jesus which assures us that the bad tree will bring forth bad fruit. It is bound to give itself away sooner or later."[2]

Three brief points may be emphasized. First, evil disguised as discipleship is to be anticipated in the

2. Ibid., 171.

Pastoral Perspective

However, it is not just the press of the unwitting masses that prevents them from finding "life." There are also "false prophets" who disguise their true loyalties and intentions ("in sheep's clothing but inwardly are ravenous wolves") and so contribute to their destruction. The only way to recognize them is "by their fruit." These "false prophets," who are intent on the destruction of others, will in the end, like "every tree that does not bear good fruit," be destroyed themselves ("cut down and thrown into the fire"). Those who seek "life," then, must not only be willing to travel the "hard" road created by obstacles others throw in the path of those who commit themselves to living as God intends, but also pay close attention to the effects of others' lives ("their fruits"), so as not to be deceived by "false prophets."

Promoting a sectarian view of the Christian life is probably not a tactic that pastors should be utilizing within their work. Even if you are convinced that some are heading down the road to destruction, should not your goal be to reduce their numbers to the "few," so that it is instead "many" who find life? Rather than using these metaphors as lenses through which to view others ("*They* are the ones, deceived by false prophets, who have entered the wide gate and travel the easy road"), perhaps it would be better to use the metaphors as means for examining our own individual lives.

What if the admonition to "enter through the narrow gate" were not seen as a one-time decision? What if, instead of a once-in-a-lifetime conversion experience, the decision to "enter the narrow gate" was the kind of moment-by-moment experience such as is described in 12-step programs where each day and in particular situations within each day one must make the decision to remain sober? Seen from that angle, the very idea that one could make a single decision to enter "the gate [that] is narrow" and travel "the road [that] is hard" might itself be recognized as the "wide" and "easy" choice that actually "leads to destruction." The "hard" part of the "road" is that it in fact confronts us with many, many gates, and at each one we must again choose to "enter through the narrow gate." Those who find "life" are those who come to recognize that it is not some grand prize hidden behind Door Number 2. They are the ones who learn that life is making the hard choices, again and again, to conduct oneself as God intends; they are the ones who despite the necessity of repeated choices find joy in the journey.

What if the "false prophets" are not others who disguise themselves in order to deceive us, but are

of verse 13 directs attention to entering "through the narrow gate." The Sermon has used the verb "enter" in 5:20 to speak of participating in the full and final establishment of God's rule or empire (so also 7:21). The notion of "entering the gate," then, along with the subsequent image of "the road," presents discipleship as a journey that begins with Jesus' calling disciples and their initial, partial experience of God's rule (4:18–22). The journey ends with the eschatological destiny of either "destruction" or "life." The subsequent descriptions of the gate and the road as either wide and easy (7:13b) or narrow and hard (7:14a) denote the ways of living that lead to these destinations. The easy road and wide gate have "many travelers" (7:13c). The narrow gate and hard road, the way of discipleship, have "few" (7:14c).

This image of two ways of living, with life-and-death consequences, is found in a number of places in ancient literature (e.g., Deut. 30:1–5, 15–20). Why is the way of discipleship hard, the gate narrow, and the travelers few?

The Sermon has made clear that the way of life that enacts God's reign or empire is counter to normal societal expectations. So God's blessing is found, surprisingly, not with the rich and powerful, but with the apparently cursed, "the poor in spirit" (5:3), those who are so desperately poor materially that it corrodes their very being, their spirit. God's blessing is with those who "hunger and thirst for righteousness" (5:6), a way of life that embodies God's justice in social interactions and societal structures. This life of justice (5:20) challenges the interests of those with status, power, and wealth; predictably, they retaliate to defend their interest (5:10–12, 38–42). This just way of life enacts God's reign or empire, which has come among people in part, but not yet in full, with a different set of priorities and focus (6:32–33). This minority, difficult, and countercultural way of life is missional (chap. 10), communal (chap. 18), and preparatory for the future establishment of God's reign.

Part of the journey's difficulty is its vulnerability. Disciples on the journey can be vulnerable to opposition (5:10–12), to losing their distinctive identity and calling (5:13), to anger (5:21–26), to lust (5:27–30), to unjust male power (5:31–32), to speech that lacks integrity (5:33–37), to retaliation (5:38–42), to restricted love (5:43–48), to social conformity (6:1–18), and to wealth and anxiety (6:19–34). In 7:15–20, disciples are alerted to another danger, that of false prophets.

There has been extensive discussion about the possible identity of these false prophets. Some

intentional and directed. Not all roads "lead to Rome." Different decisions lead to different destinations. Different intentions lead to different outcomes. Matthew's Jesus calls the reader to reflect on the choice at hand. The wide gate calls for no particular thought or serious purpose, but the narrow one calls for both. The wide gate allows everyone and everything to pass through without much consideration. So, "What shall it be? The gate of ease or the gate of principle?" Matthew asks those who have "ears to hear." The physical image invokes the spiritual here. Not everything one believes or every ethic one embraces can be carried into the kingdom of God. The straight gate calls for discernment and intention. To be a follower of Jesus, a choice must be made regarding what you will take with you in your heart, remembering that not everything fits through the narrow gate, because not everything is fit for the kingdom of God.

It is difficult to appreciate this struggle, due to the ease of being Christian in our culture. One need not work especially hard to be faithful in the social sense of religion today, and the cunning words of false prophets, now or yet to come, are thoughtlessly embraced and readily accepted as holy mantras. Civil religion fuses God and country so completely that to question the superiority of either may well be considered blasphemous and traitorous. The acceptability of wealth and status is so ingrained in our faith systems that even to hint that God favors the poor becomes irritating and openly laughable to more than a few. Is this indictment too severe? To our ears, perhaps. The text, however, may not think so. The radical message of the kingdom of God must in the end be embodied by the radical commitment of its followers.

The admonition to pick your friends carefully is as important as picking your way carefully. The warning against false prophets is another dimension of the same issue. In a time of many dangers and wiles, being innocent as doves must be contoured by snakelike wisdom, or the outcome is certain ruin. Many first-century prophets were mercenaries of thought and part of an industry that was hired to give advice to kings and commoners alike. Speaking messages pleasing to the ear, they offered solutions that did not fit the character or purpose of the kingdom of God. They could not be trusted, because they came to transmit their own agenda. They created a facade that looked to satisfy another's needs only so that they in the end would find their needs satisfied.

Therefore pick those friends inspired by God's Spirit. Good friends look out for your best interests

Matthew 7:13–20

Theological Perspective

church. That need not lead to a Manichean dualism between good and evil or impress the need to map out a metaphysic of evil. Jesus' teaching does not lead there. The emphasis is on alertness and expectation rather than explanation: there will be evil in the church.

Second, like fruit from a bad tree, the results will become clear in due course. The emerging reality will name the lie of the appearance.

Third, when the bad fruit appears, the body must be ready to act decisively to cut down the bad tree and throw it into the fire. This is undoubtedly a most awkward and difficult duty, but the health (single-sightedness) and truthfulness of the body depend upon it. In different language, this is the time for church discipline, a topic largely left alone today, apart from quasi-judicial processes mostly having to do with clergy misbehavior. The guiding metaphor of false prophets suggests teaching that is untrue (heresy), that leads the flock of Christ astray, or that in the extreme case attempts to destroy it. Timidity in the face of false prophets compounds the evil already spread among the body.

To this point, study of an important but neglected text from the Reformation period is strongly recommended: Martin Bucer, *Concerning the True Care of Souls.*[3] Bucer's discussion is a major treatment of pastoral discipline. While there may be good reasons to think that we approach the problem of false prophets in the church in a manner different from Bucer, his book is a forceful reminder of a ministry within the church that needs to be attended to in every age.

ANDREW PURVES

Pastoral Perspective

instead the many ways we disguise our truly selfish motives as noble purposes and so deceive ourselves? What if we do not take a long and careful look at the "fruits" of *others'* actions, but instead seek the truth about who *we* are from the effects of our own actions? It may now be as overly familiar as the other-focused, sectarian understanding of the metaphor, but a different analogy might shift the focus onto ourselves. Instead of Jesus' statement to his primarily agrarian culture, "Thus you will know them by their fruits," maybe we would say to our consumerist society, "You will know yourself by your checkbook."

Even in choosing to view these metaphors as primarily about ourselves rather than others, it is still possible to expand their scope beyond the individual. Within our communal associations—our families, our faith communities, our neighborhoods, and so forth—we can collectively ask ourselves these same questions. What decisions have we made that we continue to fall back upon as the easy path of least resistance, rather than to face the hard choices that now confront us in the changing circumstances of life? What inconsistencies are laid bare by comparing things we believe true about ourselves with facts about how we live? Are our mission statements, whether in the church or on the job, in reality nothing more than "sheep's clothing" thrown on the backs of "ravenous wolves" who are concerned about themselves far more than about others?

Perhaps even the different ways of understanding these metaphors are themselves gates—not only into the text but also out into the world—between which we must choose. If so, which approach to this passage—a sectarian view of others, or an inward look at ourselves and our communities—would you identify as the wide gate and the easy road that leads to destruction? Which would be the narrow gate and the hard road that leads to life?

TIMOTHY B. CARGAL

---

3. Martin Bucer, *Concerning the True Care of Souls*, trans. Peter Beale (Edinburgh: Banner of Truth Trust, 2009). See also Andrew Purves, *Pastoral Theology in the Classical Tradition* (Louisville, KY: Westminster John Knox Press, 2001), for a chapter on Bucer's pastoral theology.

have suggested specific groups of opponents such as Pharisees. Others have suggested that they are Jesus-followers that have been in conflict with the Gospel's author and of whom the author does not approve. Another option is to consider the warning hypothetical and stereotypical. That is, it does not refer to an identifiable group but to false prophets who will arise as the end approaches. Deciding among these options is difficult, but there does not seem to be any doubt that various groups in the early Christian movement had trouble discerning true and false prophets (Mark 13:22; Acts 20:29–31; Rev. 2:20; 1 John 4:1–6). With few processes in place for sanctioning legitimate leaders, the issue was a very practical one.

Matthew's Gospel has mentioned prophets positively previously in relation to the central teaching of love (5:17; 7:12). It has also honored prophets in the tradition who are understood to have correctly anticipated Jesus' ministry (1:22; 2:5, 15, 17, 23). It also recognizes that true prophets are active in the community's ministry (10:41).

Verses 15–20 warn of the danger of false prophets and propose a way of identifying them. The danger is conveyed in the initial image of wolves and sheep, in which the former endanger the latter (so the peaceful vision of Isa. 11:6; 65:25). The image of wolves frequently denotes people who bring danger and destruction (Gen. 49:27; Jer. 5:6; Ezek. 22:27–28). The image of sheep commonly denotes God's people (Num. 27:17; Ps. 100; Ezek. 34). Here, danger threatens God's people.

The danger comes by the way of disguise and deception. The wolves appear to be sheep, but they are disguised by sheep's clothing (7:15). The challenge is to identify the wolves on the basis of their actions or "fruits" (7:16a, 20). The logic is that since thorn bushes do not produce grapes and thistles do not produce figs (7:16), false prophets will not produce good fruit or actions shaped by Jesus' teaching, thereby disclosing themselves (7:17–18). This identification is difficult, however, given the role of disguise (7:15) and of the limited vision of disciples, who do not always see clearly (6:22–23; 7:1–5). So the passage leaves the final condemnation of false prophets to God (7:19). Disciples are to "beware," but they are not judge and jury.

WARREN CARTER

even when it is difficult. They share the same goal and understand the same purposes in Christ. They see your failures as impermanent and believe with all their heart you will improve next time. False prophets, however, care little for your well-being or the well-being of that which you cherish. They are certain to undermine valued purposes and introduce toxic messages, thereby poisoning persons and the community whose task it is to live out and speak out the kingdom's message of loving-kindness.

"What is your business," Matthew asks of all the people and dynamics swirling around the fledgling community (and ours), "the kingdom of God, or feathering your nest or worse?"

The challenge is timeless. Each age must engage the struggle. False prophets and foxes are foiled in the end not with force but with wisdom and discernment. Once these are employed, contrary spirits are discovered for their malevolent intent, and they lose their power to inflict harm on those who embrace the teachings and lifestyle of Jesus. The false prophets, whatever bruised or rotted fruit they market, become as no fruit at all. What they say is fit only to be gathered off the ground and thrown out with the trash.

In the end we must remember we are not talking about gates or wolves or fruit-bearing trees, but the rich integrity of a community that has been transformed by Jesus' dynamic spirit of life. This is a community that embraces without exclusion and without prejudice and without parsimony. Our faith is not an armchair religion, nor was it ever meant to be. Created in a living crucible, the way forward is never going to be easy, the vision will be difficult to maintain, and the pursuit will always be treacherous. To the faithful, however, it is the path to triumph over the forces that militate against God's loving-kindness for the whole human family. Like good fruit, these stories stand ripe for the homilist's voice. They are filled with as much challenge to the present day as they were to the first-century fledgling church.

RICHARD WILLIAM HARBART

Matthew 7:21–29

21"Not everyone who says to me, 'Lord, Lord,' will enter the kingdom of heaven, but only the one who does the will of my Father in heaven. 22On that day many will say to me, 'Lord, Lord, did we not prophesy in your name, and cast out demons in your name, and do many deeds of power in your name?' 23Then I will declare to them, 'I never knew you; go away from me, you evildoers.'

24"Everyone then who hears these words of mine and acts on them will be like a wise man who built his house on rock. 25The rain fell, the floods came, and the winds blew and beat on that house, but it did not fall, because it had been founded on rock. 26And everyone who hears these words of mine and does not act on them will be like a foolish man who built his house on sand. 27The rain fell, and the floods came, and the winds blew and beat against that house, and it fell—and great was its fall!"

28Now when Jesus had finished saying these things, the crowds were astounded at his teaching, 29for he taught them as one having authority, and not as their scribes.

Theological Perspective

The Sermon on the Mount ends with a terrifying question, the answer to which is the sole ground for justification: Are we known by Jesus? That is to say, the church's confession and ministry have their ground in him, precisely at the point where we have no confession or ministry of our own but have them derivatively, by sharing in Christ's confession of us to the Father (Rev. 3:5) and in Christ's ministry through us from the Father (John 17:18).

To begin with, not everyone who says, "Lord, Lord," will enter the kingdom of heaven. The late T. F. Torrance of Edinburgh, the leading British theologian of the twentieth century, once wrote that "the very beliefs which we profess and formulate as obediently and carefully as we can in fidelity to God's self-revelation in Jesus Christ are themselves called into question by that revelation, for they have their truth not in themselves but in him to whom they refer."[1] Jesus Christ, Lord, is our truth, not our words about him. Only derivatively, and in reference to and controlled by Jesus, is doctrine true. Because he is Lord, we do not own him, no matter how seemingly true our words about him intend to be. He is not putty in our religiously or theologically creative hands. He is Truth as such, in his own freedom and

Pastoral Perspective

At a time when many question what it will mean to be the church in a post-Christendom world, it is important to stop and think for a moment about what Jesus had in mind when he said that "only the one who does the will of my Father in heaven" fully participates in the realm of God (v. 21b). What does it mean to do the will of the Father?

First, notice that Jesus rules out what are now some standard answers to that question. Simply declaring, "Jesus is Lord," is not enough, even if asserted emphatically ("Lord, Lord," v. 21a). Neither is engaging in specifically religious activities like prophesying, performing exorcisms, and "doing deeds of power"—even when all the while giving credit and glory to Jesus for what has been accomplished ("in your name," v. 22). To be sure, Jesus does not criticize these activities. He does not even tell those doing them to stop. What he does say is that they are to "go away" from him, rather than "enter the kingdom of heaven," because he "never knew" them (v. 23). There was no genuine relationship between themselves and Jesus. At least there had been no fully transformative relationship, since they remained "evildoers," even as they also engaged in religious acts.

Some might conclude, then, that "the will of [the] Father in heaven" involves nothing more than

1. Thomas F. Torrance, *Reality and Evangelical Theology* (Philadelphia: Westminster Press, 1982), 18–19.

Feasting on the Gospels

Exegetical Perspective

Dividing the passage between verses 20 and 21 is awkward and not very convincing. There are good reasons for taking verses 21–23 with verses 15–20, rather than as a separate subsection. For example, verse 22 identifies those who are condemned as being prophets who spoke falsely, thereby continuing the focus on false prophets. The wolves who appear as sheep but are not sheep (vv. 15–20) are those who appear as Jesus' disciples but are not disciples (vv. 21–23). The wolves that cannot do good actions (vv. 15–20) are those who claim good actions but are sent away in the judgment (vv. 21–23). Moreover, there are some significant parallels between the false prophets who are described in chapter 24 and the characters of 7:21–23. The false prophets of 24:24 who come in Jesus' name (24:5) do great signs and wonders (24:24), just as the characters of 7:21–23 claim to prophesy in Jesus' name and do many deeds of power (7:22).

Verses 21–23 continue the focus on false prophets rather than introduce a new section. They elaborate the judgment on the false prophets mentioned in verse 19 with its reference to being cut down and thrown into the fire. Matthew has John the Baptist use this image for judgment in 3:7–10.

Verses 21–23 offer a glimpse of a judgment scene with Jesus as the judge of the world. What exactly do

Homiletical Perspective

This pericope is the final wrap to the Sermon on the Mount, which Matthew has used to feature the earliest church's remembrances of Jesus' teachings. When approaching this material for homiletical purposes, there are some biblical dimensions that need to be taken into account. These last words of the Sermon on the Mount draw together three individual yet connected stories. Seemingly disparate, they are linked together to create some lively options for the homilist.

If the sermon highlights the first story (vv. 21–23), it will necessarily embrace the issue of the motivation and sincerity of today's church. Among human beings—including the early church and us—talk is cheap, and so are deeds done ostensibly for the kingdom, but used primarily to advance one's position. It is likely that "many" were using Jesus' name and charging fees for prophecy and healings, a common practice in that day. This demonstrated that the underlying motivation was not first to advance the cause of the kingdom or to show the power of God to overcome the powers of evil, but to serve their own interests.

While the historical circumstances are different, human nature today seems much the same. The purpose of the kingdom of God is to serve before being served, as in the marvelous prayer of Francis

Theological Perspective

reality. We did not invent him or coin him out of our fervid theological imaginations and religious neediness.

Even the most faithful confession of faith—"Lord, Lord"—does not have its truth in itself. Truth lies in the one to whom reference is made. We are not justified through our confession of the lordship of Jesus; we are justified by Jesus' call and claim upon us. "You did not choose me but I chose you" (John 15:16).

So: be more than people who say the seemingly right words, who get their theology right; be doers of the will of God. However, danger lies even in apparent obedience to the will of God in the work of ministry. The illusion of discipleship is now stripped down further. Cannot the church's ministry speak for itself? If by our fruit we will be known for whose we are—the conclusion of the preceding paragraph—do we not now have the building of faith finally on solid rock (v. 24)? What Jesus teaches here is the development of what he has taught already: truth, whether in word or act, does not lie in what we do, but in him. "I am the truth" (John 14:6). No matter how seemingly good and evangelical our acts, insofar as they are *our* acts, they are not true. As Calvin used to say, we must repent even for our virtues.

The issue here is not lack of good intention or even a lack of love. The issue—indeed, the danger Christ warns against—is the displacement of Christ's ministry with the ministry of the church. Bonhoeffer hits the point exactly: "In all this activity the activity of discipleship is absent, namely that activity the doer of which is in the last resort none other than Jesus Christ himself."[2] It is within this perspective, then, that the final words of Jesus (v. 23) make sense. We may paraphrase them this way: "Go away from me, evildoers, for you said what you said and did what you did, even using my name, but they were not my words and they were not my ministry." This conclusion is also the meaning of the words of Jesus at John 15:5: "Apart from me you can do nothing."

Thus the disciple has now nothing of his or her own to offer, neither confession nor works. As Bonhoeffer says, "There is only [Jesus'] word: 'I have known thee', which is his eternal word and call. . . . [I]t is always *his* word and *his* call, his alone. If we follow Christ, cling to his word, and let everything else go, it will see us through the Day of Judgment. His word is his grace."[3]

2. Dietrich Bonhoeffer, *The Cost of Discipleship*, trans. R. H. Fuller, with revisions by Irmgard Booth (London: SCM Press, 1959), 174.
3. Ibid., 174.

Pastoral Perspective

being engaged in a relationship with Jesus so as to be known and recognized by him when calling upon him as "Lord." Anyone who might draw that conclusion after reading through the full Sermon on the Mount has not been paying attention. If the point is a relational one, then the transformational nature of that relationship must be emphasized. Jesus, after all, is the one who challenges: "Be perfect, therefore, as your heavenly Father is perfect" (5:48). Just being in relationship (saying, "Lord, Lord," v. 22a) is not enough. Just knowing God's purpose (prophesying) and acting upon it (casting out demons and doing "deeds of power") are not enough. Entering "the kingdom of heaven" is clearly a both-and proposition. It is doing God's will, not simply because you know Jesus' name ("Lord"), but because knowing and being known by him have transformed your own will by bringing it into accord with God's will.

Just how thoroughly the relationship and the actions of those who "enter the kingdom of heaven" are enmeshed is demonstrated in an interesting way by how the parable of the Two Houses (vv. 24–27) resists being allegorized. It would be tempting to identify the respective foundations of the houses ("rock" and "sand") with those who know and are known by Jesus and those who are not in relationship with him, respectively. "Hear[ing]" Jesus' words would correspond to the relationship/foundations, and "act[ing] on them" would be the building of the houses. That, however, is not the comparison actually established by the parable. The "rock" is both hearing *and* acting on Jesus words; the "sand" is hearing *but not* acting on them. In either instance the construction of the house takes place, just as those who called Jesus "Lord, Lord" had prophesied, performed exorcisms, and done "deeds of power," even though they had no true relationship with him. It is the joining of the relationship and the actions that results in being "founded on the rock." The same actions, if they do not arise from that relationship, rest on "sand" and will ultimately fall—"and great was its fall" (v. 27).

What is true of individuals is also true of churches. A church that has become only a venue for adoration of the Divine (proclaiming, "Lord, Lord") has not fully become a part of the realm of God. A church that has become only a social service agency, even if openly stating that its own motivation comes from Christ, is also not really inside "the kingdom of heaven." A church that is, at least provisionally, demonstrating the reality of the reign of God in the world will be a gathering of people who seek to deepen their relationship with Christ and who,

these false prophets do wrong? Why is it that they do not "enter the kingdom of heaven" even when they address Jesus as "Lord"?

They are certainly not condemned for claiming in the judgment that they have performed actions. Jesus requires actions of disciples, as 7:12 makes clear: "do to others as you would have them do to you." They are certainly not condemned for doing miraculous actions such as prophesying and exorcizing. Jesus casts out demons (9:33–34; 12:24–27), as disciples are to do (10:8), and Jesus also performs deeds of power (11:20–23; 13:54, 58).

The key aspect of the scene seems to be found in verse 21b. Only those who "do the will of my Father in heaven" enter into God's purposes. These "many" who claim miraculous actions but nothing else are on the wrong road. They are on the easy road leading to destruction (7:13). They lack, so Jesus discerns, doing God's will as an expression of an inner commitment to that will. They are not what they appear to be. They are wolves dressed up as sheep. They lack integrity or wholeness (5:48). They do not seek God's reign and justice (6:33–34). As "workers of lawlessness" (7:23, a better translation than "evildoers"), they have not heeded the "law and the prophets," which require love.

The Sermon's third concluding scene underlines the goal of the journey of discipleship (destruction or life, 7:13–14). Two brief scenes contrast two responses to Jesus' teaching and two eschatological destinies (7:24–27).

The opening "then" links the first scene to all that has come before it in the Sermon. The scene exemplifies everyone who hears and does Jesus' teaching. The one who exercises judgment (7:21–23)—Jesus—reveals in his teaching the instruction and criteria needed to be vindicated in the judgment. In the Sermon he has interpreted the tradition (5:21–48). He has countered the false practices of the hypocrites (6:1–18), Gentiles (6:7, 32), the anxious person (6:25), the hypocritical judge (7:1–6), and the false prophets (7:15–23). He has announced what God desires (5:3–12; 7:12). Repeatedly he has underlined the obligation of disciples to do or to perform "these words of mine" (7:24).

When they do this, disciples are like the wise person. The wise person is a regular character in Wisdom literature, fearing the Lord, turning from evil, accepting correction, and gaining understanding. The house in Wisdom literature represents human life as part of a larger world, ordered either according to or in opposition to God's will (Prov. 9:1–6).

of Assisi: "Lord, make me an instrument of thy peace . . ." Those using the kingdom of God to "feather their nests" will not be claimed, because there is nothing about them to claim for God's kingdom. Their purposes are the opposite of God's. The homiletical connection between this first-century admonition and the twenty-first-century church is clear. In ways large and small we find ourselves eroding the purposeful activity of our calling with words of worship and prayer that are left inert on the sanctuary floor. We neutralize our full participation in the kingdom when we assume that speaking or singing "Lord, Lord" finishes the task and fulfills our responsibility. It slips our attention that we run the risk of being "unknown" when we are known only for thin and frail participation in the kingdom's purposes.

If the second story becomes the highlight of the message (vv. 24–27), the sermon's purpose is to subvert the temptation of the congregation to embrace shallow, one-dimensional thinking. Wisely placed in the final folio of the Sermon on the Mount, this story hearkens to Socrates' challenge: "The unexamined life is not worth living." The text challenges us to examine the dimensions and depths of inviting the kingdom into our lives through listening and doing the whole of Jesus' teaching. It does not wrap up the didactic collective with a wagging finger or say, "You must," or "Thou shalt not." It is appropriate that the final admonition appeals to our thoughtful and judicious side. It is a call to embrace wisdom—wisdom for the day, wisdom for the journey, wisdom for life.

Wisdom in every age is the basis of discernment, which is the forerunner of good decision making. Matthew calls us to be wise—perhaps above all. This is a special wisdom that is more than philosophical gymnastics. It is wisdom that calls a follower to be more than an unthinking slug who slavishly follows plodding instructions for rote behavior in the kingdom of God. It is wisdom that employs our active participation in the daily process of living, wisdom that inspires both character and actions. It calls us to live with full focus on the world around us. It wants the best of who we are, energetic and prepared to meet the faith challenges of every day. It wants to see a more mature part of our human nature step forward and take charge of the future. In plain terms, we are to discern that the fruits of the kingdom (kindness, gentleness, humility, patience, etc.), connected to the missional qualities of the faith (justice and righteousness), are the very ingredients that make up the rock-solid future upon which healthy generations of Christians are to be built.

Matthew 7:21–29

Theological Perspective

The only word of hope, then, is Christ's declaration, "I have known you." This is the rock. It would now be a mistake of alarming proportion to put a subjective interpretation on to this final metaphor, as if *our* faith and *our* obedience, the confession and ministry of the church, were the rock on which to build. Building on our own piety, faith, and ministries, the storms will rage and we will be destroyed. Thus Jesus, as it were, bumps aside our assertions and deeds, even said and done in his name, and, in what amounts to a soteriological displacement, stands in for us at every turn. That is why it is grace. Only when this happens, come the rain and the winds, the house still remains, because it has been built on the rock of Christ, rather than the sand of our faith and works.

Once more allowing Bonhoeffer to be our teacher, we may conclude in this way: What is there now for us to say and do, when the one word that had to be spoken has been spoken and the one work of obedience that had to be offered to the Father has been offered? Our call is to hear the words of Jesus and act on them, not picking among them or selectively obeying them. Christ gives us his word on condition that we understand it as the demand for an exclusive attachment to him. Of course this is costly for us, but it is grace because it calls us to follow *Jesus Christ*.

The crowd was astonished at this teaching: indeed!

ANDREW PURVES

Pastoral Perspective

transformed by that relationship, engage others both within the church and beyond it in the world in ways that make real God's just will for all.

The evangelist provides an interesting commentary at the conclusion of the Sermon on the Mount that might also be a telling critique upon much of the Christendom that is passing away. What "astounded" (v. 28) the crowds about the Sermon, the evangelist insists, was not the content of what Jesus said. Rather, it was that "he taught them as one having authority," which was in contrast to their usual experience of religious teachers (v. 29). At one level, this response focused on "authority" rather than content testifies to the truth of Jesus' statement earlier in the Sermon that he had "come not to abolish [the law or the prophets] but to fulfill" what God had revealed through them (5:17). On another level, perhaps the "authority" they experienced in him came from a sense that indeed the fullness of God's reign was present among them in Jesus (cf. 1:22–23).

One thing that the church has lost with the passing of Christendom—certainly in the eyes of the broader culture, but also to a degree among Christians—is a sense of the church's "authority." That loss of authority could be attributed to many causes. People see the hypocrisy in those who proclaim Jesus as Lord and yet do not live in ways fundamentally different from others in society. Christians may actively engage the world in the name of Christ, yet seem apathetic about their own spiritual relationship with him. Christians may help others in Jesus' name, yet seem unconcerned whether those served seek a relationship either with Jesus or with the "Father in heaven." Perhaps one way for the church to reclaim some of its lost authority is by a renewed emphasis, both individually and institutionally, on what should be the essential identity between a relationship with God in Christ and how one lives in and on behalf of the world.

TIMOTHY B. CARGAL

Exegetical Perspective

This house's foundation on a rock (cf. 16:18–19) means the house withstands the storm. Storm imagery regularly depicts the lives of the righteous assailed by the wicked and misfortunes (Ps. 69:1–4; Prov. 28:3). Through the storms, the wise and righteous person (6:33–34) remains faithful to God. Here the storms particularly depict the eschatological woes and judgment that drive out the false prophets (7:23) but pose no threat to the person who hears and does Jesus' teaching. Obedience secures their destiny in the judgment.

However, this is not so for the contrasting scene (7:26–27). Those who hear Jesus' teaching but do not do it are foolish. In contrast to the wise person, the foolish person is not concerned with God's purposes or will; in fact the foolish person declares there is no God, does corrupt and abominable acts, and does not do anything good (Ps. 14:1). "The foolish woman" builds a house of death (Prov. 9:13–18) and evil (Prov. 5:1–14). While the wise person's house stands in the midst of the storm, the foolish person's house falls (Matt. 7:27). The storm reveals the lack of foundation, the failure to do Jesus' words. The journey of the many to destruction is completed (7:13).

For disciples the two scenes offer both warning and encouragement. They are warned to do Jesus' teaching in lives of obedience. They are encouraged that, if they so live, they will be vindicated in the judgment.

Such eschatological thinking is basic to Matthew's Gospel. The Gospel is very dualistic, moving continuously between vindication and condemnation, between encouraging disciples and bullying them into compliance with threats of frightening eschatological destiny. There are also glimpses in the Sermon that God operates in a quite different way. Instead of vindication and judgment on the basis of how people live in response to Jesus' teaching, the Sermon envisages life-giving mercy and divine favor on all. As 5:45 points out, God "makes the sun rise on the evil and on the good, and sends rain on the righteous and on the unrighteous." However, this profound vision of God's indiscriminate and life-giving goodness to all people does not seem to carry the day in Matthew's Gospel.

WARREN CARTER

Homiletical Perspective

Highlighting in the homily the third piece of the trilogy (vv. 28–29) puts the exclamation point on both the pericope before us and the whole of the Sermon on the Mount. The final sentence testifies to the power and gravity of this truth. It legitimizes all the teachings of the last three chapters. The depth of it was so profound and the adherence to it so transforming that the crowd knew instinctively that Jesus was set apart from and above anyone and anything they had heard before: *he taught with authority.* The scribes and Pharisees were given authority by temple decree, but Jesus had authority because he was congruent inside and out with the Spirit of God. His words were not the memorized and oft-repeated phrases of those acting as temple utensils. He was energized by a creative, life-giving spirit that offered in love and service the very same life-giving spirit to people of his and every age.

It behooves us to remember the implications for our own faith lives. The congruency of strong belief and worthy action becomes the basis for a testimonial life. If we truly believe the teachings, we will become the teachings in our daily lives. Then, when the world sees us, it will see also the very presence of the kingdom of God here on earth. A tall task? Why would we assume something so profound could be anything less?

Still, the homilist has yet another option when these stories are taken together as a whole. The preached word could show how our embracing of these beliefs becomes the profound change mechanism that allows the person and community an opportunity to step into the new mind-set and lifestyle the kingdom offers. As they are embraced, these beliefs become the great "game changer," as the empty tomb was to Mary and the disciples when they thought everything was lost and gone. They become the spiritual mind expander and "eye-opener" whereby the human focus on selfish needs is put aside. Once done, the altruistic principles of the kingdom of God and Jesus' teachings become the new center of thought and action, not only for the Christian community, but for the whole human family.

RICHARD WILLIAM HARBART

Matthew 8:1–4

¹When Jesus had come down from the mountain, great crowds followed him; ²and there was a leper who came to him and knelt before him, saying, "Lord, if you choose, you can make me clean." ³He stretched out his hand and touched him, saying, "I do choose. Be made clean!" Immediately his leprosy was cleansed. ⁴Then Jesus said to him, "See that you say nothing to anyone; but go, show yourself to the priest, and offer the gift that Moses commanded, as a testimony to them."

Theological Perspective

Yes, Jesus knew how to make boundaries. We never hear Jesus saying, "I am burnt out," or complaining about his "private space." Jesus knew how to find times and places to build his strength, confirm his own sense of mission, and renew his love for God and people. There is no dichotomy between Jesus' time at the mountain and his time with the crowds. Mountain time meets sick, troubled, exhausted people, and it is at this thin/thick moment that Jesus lives in its fullness. It is neither alone on the mountain nor only with people that he lives his life fully; rather, empowered by God, Jesus fulfils his mission and shines God's glory fully to the world in living with the excluded ones.

So a leper comes to him. Perhaps bruised and disfigured, he appears before Jesus and kneels. I can only imagine how painful this gesture might have been for this man. I imagine his body utterly aching; still, he kneels down. His desperation is as acute as his pain and his brave faith. He knows he is unclean, not supposed to get closer to anybody; yet he drops himself in front of this rabbi. The movements of the body are enormous theological statements. A body bent, curved, thrown, now on the floor. What does it say about this man—belief, trust, hope, desire? What is it that this desperate body claims beyond words?

Pastoral Perspective

No matter how moving and inspirational mountaintop experiences are, eventually we have to return to the world of suffering and discord. Here is Jesus, like Moses coming down from Sinai, seeing the pain of those around him. In a divine reversal of "show and tell," we get instead "tell and show," the mountain Sermon being the "tell" and the miracles in Matthew being the "show."

Jesus immediately sees something revolting, something that would make most of us avert our eyes and turn away. What he notices is the leper everyone has seen every day on the street. The leper is so ugly and disgusting, however, that no one can look at him anymore. He is like the homeless in our cities, who disappear, practically blending into the urban landscape.

I remember serving a church with a large ministry to street people and being initially turned off by their outward appearance. Then, after working with them over a long period of time, I began to realize these are real people with real stories and real lives. I began to "see" them in a different way. Once, as I swished in my robe, moving quickly toward the chapel on my way to officiate at a wedding, a tattered-looking young woman, face smudged with dirt, stopped me in my tracks and said, "I need some milk for my baby, and I need it now!" She opened her coat

Exegetical Perspective

The Sermon on the Mount (Matt. 5–7) has concluded with the crowd's being astonished at Jesus' teachings because he taught as one having authority. Now the evangelist continues to build on the theme of Jesus' authority with a collection of miracles that demonstrate his power and serve to fulfill Scripture. Reference to Jesus' descent from the mountain links Jesus to Moses. Reference to the mountain and to the great crowds following him in Matthew 8:1 links the great authority demonstrated in his teaching in chapters 5–7 to the miracle stories in chapters 8 and 9.

The cleansing of a person with leprosy[1] in Matthew 8:1–4 stands as the first of ten miracles performed by Jesus in chapters 8 and 9 that call forth memories of the ten miracles of Moses in Egypt (Exod. 7:8–11:10). This is just one of many ways the Gospel invites the reader to hear the stories of Jesus in the context of Moses and the First Testament Scriptures. Another Matthean technique that links Jesus to the tradition is demonstrated when the first three miracles (8:1–4, 5–13, 14–17) conclude with

---

1. The text of Matthew, following Mark, identifies the person as "a leper." The NRSV inserts a heading before the story: "Jesus Cleanses a Leper." Luke 5:12 identifies the person as "a man covered with leprosy." For purposes of interpretation, I choose to speak of "a person with leprosy," which first affirms one's personhood. See Kathy Black, *A Healing Homiletic* (Nashville: Abingdon Press, 1996), for more discussion about placing the emphasis on "person" and "with," never permitting the disability to be primary.

Homiletical Perspective

Until this point in the Gospel, the story of Jesus has been a lot of talk. Matthew begins with the genealogy of Jesus (1:1–17), gives his account of the Nativity (1:18–2:23), reports on the proclamation of John the Baptist and the beginning of the ministry of Jesus (3:1–4:25), and devotes three chapters to the Sermon on the Mount (5:1–7:29). Preaching on the first seven chapters of Matthew will inevitably include some of the most memorable teachings of Jesus, but very few actions.

In chapter 8, the Gospel shifts from word to deed. Matthew always gives precedence to words over works, a priority grounded in the creative power of the Word of God. From beginning to end, the Bible testifies to what God accomplishes through a word: Genesis reports that "God said, 'Let there be light'; and there was light" (Gen. 1:3), while the Gospel of John says God's "Word became flesh and lived among us" as Jesus (John 1:14). Although Christians are going to disagree about many theological points, there is wide agreement that God's Word has creative power. Preachers can highlight Matthew's shift from word to deed by reminding their congregations that words have true power, and that the Word of God is a creative force in the world.

In Matthew's telling, the transition from word to deed occurs quickly, when "Jesus had come down

Matthew 8:1–4

Theological Perspective

What do our bodies say about our beliefs? Many of us have learned to distance our bodies from our liturgies. No kneeling, no clapping, no gesturing, no turning, no twisting, no rising up. What is left to our bodies before God in our common liturgies? To sit and stand. Nothing else. Our bodies know very well what to do and, even more, what not to do in worship.

I was at a black church in Harlem, New York, and I saw something that moved me deeply. The choir was singing in the back mezzanine high above the pulpit. The more the choir sang, the more the congregation was fired up. All of sudden, a choir member started doing a solo with the accompaniment of the choir. He came down the aisle and walked all the way to the front door and left. The choir continued to sing. Then he came back, singing with full force, his lungs crying out to God as the choir continued to support him. At this point the congregation was ecstatic, and we were all praising God with the fullness of our minds, hearts, and bodies. The singer went back to his place with the choir, and they finished singing. A spirit of fullness was all over that space, and the pastor had to wait until it "dissipated" a little bit and we all could return to our normal breathing. The whole community had offered its praise to God, as if we were all bending our bodies, hearts, and minds to God.

It is said that theology is the loving of God with our minds. However, mind does not exist without bodies actually living off this love, giving contours and content to our faith. This leper came to Jesus with his mind bent to the assurance that if only Jesus wanted, Jesus could heal him, his body prostrated in respect and honor, and his heart filled with a hope that we could perhaps translate as love. For hope is a form of love.

The healing event here was not about the potentiality of Jesus' might, checking on Jesus' status as a prophet or a proper healer sent by God. Instead, the healing here was placed before God's freedom and Jesus' choice to heal. This is very far from the demands that the new theologies of prosperity make on God by saying, "If God is the owner of everything, God *must* give this and that to me, for I am a King's son/daughter and I must live out like a prince/princess." What matters here is not *our* desire but *Jesus'* desire, and whatever desire Jesus has for us, it will be for our best (Jer. 29:11–14a).

Then the text says that Jesus "stretched out his hand and touched him, saying, 'I do choose. Be made clean!' Immediately his leprosy was cleansed"

Pastoral Perspective

and showed me a tiny face hidden there. "Lady, I will get some for you after I finish this wedding." She then insisted with such a desperate look on her face that I held up the whole wedding to get her the milk.

Milk for a hungry baby is one thing, but how do you heal a leper? Some believe the story of the leper is a metaphor for the spiritual cleansing that all of us need before understanding the redemption the Savior brings. The leper represents those in pain who recognize the power of Christ to heal and restore. This was more than psoriasis. The leper had tried Head and Shoulders, but his scaly skin represented a deeper problem than something merely dermatological. He needed more than the world could give him. You can see it in Korea. Christians there attend worship more frequently than once a week or once a month; they go every day. When they worship, their devotion to God is a full-body thing. You see it written all over their faces, their upraised arms, the tears on their cheeks, their shouts of joy and praise when they pray and sing.

They are more than "suits" going through the motions of worship. They are hurting people whose love of Christ and what Christ can do with and through them shows not just at church but in their daily lives. These are people who understand at the very core of their being that Christ loves them. They know that, no matter how foul and awful your suffering may be, even if you are maimed and disfigured in body, mind, and soul, beaten down by addictions of every kind, Christ will never turn away from you, especially if you come to him in complete confidence and faith.

Notice the way the leper approaches Jesus that day as you think about how our communities might be led to Jesus by their deepest needs. Notice how quickly Jesus responds as you reflect on institutional religion's squabbles over who is included in God's love. There is no equivocation here, no looking the other way to avoid the immediate revulsion one naturally feels when confronted with a life so obviously scarred. Jesus does not say, "You should go to someone else for a second opinion." He simply touches, speaks, and heals. Theologically, this is incarnational ministry at its best. Jesus is not some angel come slumming or a puppet dropped from heaven. He is not some disembodied, gnostic ghost floating here and there. On the cross he says, "I thirst," and actually "feels the pain" of the leper by being strung up himself as an outcast on the city dump outside the city limits.

Notice the simplicity of Jesus' remedy as you reflect on the church's response to people in

one of the formula quotations Matthew used to show Jesus' ministry within the context of the scriptural tradition; "This was to fulfill what had been spoken through the prophet Isaiah" (see also 1:22–23; 2:5b–6; 2:15b; 2:17–18; 2:23b; 3:3; 4:14–16; 8:17; 12:17–21; 13:14–15; 13:35; 21:4–5; 26:56; 27:9–10).

Three miracles in Matthew 8:18–9:8 and four miracles in Matthew 9:18–34 conclude the section that begins here at Matthew 8:1. Each of these miracles shows Jesus interacting with persons who are marginalized by the social/religious culture in some way. Each of these miracles demonstrates Jesus' authority and affirms the diversity of early Christian communities.

Matthew has relied on the Mark 1:40–44 story of Jesus' cleansing a person with leprosy. However, Matthew's version of the story is more succinct than his Markan source. Matthew omits words he considers extraneous to his focus on Jesus and on the power of Jesus' word. Thus in Matthew, no omniscient narrator needs to describe Jesus as "moved with pity" as in Mark 1:40–41. Just watch the action, listen to Jesus' words, and be astounded!

In Matthew, as in Luke but not in Mark, the person with leprosy addresses Jesus as "Lord." While "lord" was used as a respectful address by an inferior to a superior, the term more likely reflects the later-first-century countercultural proclamation of the early church that "Jesus is Lord" (in contrast to the Rome-required "Caesar is Lord"). Even though the narrative presents the person with leprosy as addressing Jesus as "Lord," we do well to hear the early church claiming the title for Jesus, even from the beginning of his ministry. Note that "Lord" is used far more often in the later Gospels (Matthew, Luke, John) than in Mark, where Jesus is never addressed as "Lord" by disciples or by anyone approaching him for ministry.

The "cleansing of lepers" hereafter appears in litanies of Jesus' ministry. See also Matthew 10:8, where Jesus sends his disciples to "cure the sick, raise the dead, cleanse the lepers," and Matthew 11:5, where Jesus' ministry is summarized by "the blind receive their sight, the lame walk, the lepers are cleansed, the deaf hear, the dead are raised, and the poor have good news brought to them."

In Matthew, Jesus' word embodies Jesus' power. Nothing happens until Jesus speaks the word. Here Jesus reaches out his hand, touches the person with leprosy, and speaks the word, "Be made clean!" Jesus' touch affirms the person; the word heals him. By his touch Jesus includes the person in the

from the mountain," followed by "great crowds" (8:1). Jesus descended from the elevated place where he had offered the extraordinary words of the Sermon on the Mount. He came down to the valley, a location filled with the ordinary and messy challenges of life, specifically to the place where "there was a leper who came to him and knelt before him" (v. 2), and there Jesus performed his first miracle. At this turning point, a preacher could stress that in the ministry of Jesus there is no fissure between these two worlds: Mountains are not split from valleys, nor are teachings separated from deeds. They all hold together in the divine plan of God.

Here a sermon could touch on one of the most vexing issues facing church and culture today: the relationship between religion and science. The Christian community is often characterized as being divided into creationists and evolutionists, believers in miracles and skeptics about divine intervention. However, there is no reason that religion and science have to move on separate tracks.

Francis Collins, the scientist and medical doctor who oversaw the Human Genome Project and authored *The Language of God: A Scientist Presents Evidence for Belief*,[1] sees no contradiction in accepting that humans are the product of evolution and believing that God decided evolution would be the method by which humans would be created. As a scientist and a Christian, he has coined the term "BioLogos," from the Greek *bios*, "life," and *logos*, "word." This term, grounded in Collins's belief that God spoke life into being, offers the church a way to hold religion and science together.

Preachers can use BioLogos as an interpretive tool in Matthew's story of Jesus cleansing the leper. The disease afflicting this man was not necessarily Hansen's disease, a chronic illness caused by bacteria. "Leprosy" in biblical times referred to several different skin diseases, but the outcome for all those called "lepers" was the same: the leper was cut off from the community with a social death sentence, in accordance with the commandment of Leviticus, "The person who has the leprous disease . . . shall live alone; his dwelling shall be outside the camp" (Lev. 13:45–46). Here the leper trusts that Jesus has the power of BioLogos, the ability to speak life into being. Believing that a word from Jesus can heal his skin and restore him to community, the leper says, "Lord, if you choose, you can make me clean" (Matt. 8:2).

---

1. Francis Collins, *The Language of God: A Scientist Presents Evidence for Belief* (New York: Free Press, 2007).

Matthew 8:1–4

Theological Perspective

(v. 3). Jesus touches a leper. Going against the social/religious rules, he touches an unclean person. Jesus' touch summons the mind/body/heart of our faith. Jesus' touch shows that God's love comes to our skin/bodies as much as it comes to our ways of thinking and feeling. God's touch to an unclean, foreign, sick body changes the body/mind/heart of this man forever.

Verse 4 mentions Jesus telling this man not to say a word to anybody, but to go to the priest. With this move, Jesus is not hoping for any gesture of gratitude or reciprocity from this man but, rather, is making him engage the tradition of which they both are a part, namely, the Jewish faith. A testimony of God's healing is now due, to offer the "gift that Moses commanded," and the leper has to fulfill it. With every blessing comes a gift: a joyful worship, thanksgiving, a sacrifice of praise and gratitude.

With this passage we can consider:

1. How have we separated personal time and community time, and lost the sense that perhaps the fulfilling of our lives and ministries lies precisely in the thin/thick moments of these complex relations, in the *betweenness* of our breaths?

2. How is the body as fundamental to the living of this faith as our minds and hearts?

3. How much and when do we actually make a conscious use of our bodies to relate with, live for, and worship God?

4. How have our liturgies impinged theological arthritis into our body joints?

5. How often are our desires tied up with personal fulfillment, rather than with service to an other?

6. How much have we lost the possibility of giving testimonies in our churches as an offering of a gift of praise and thanksgiving to God who heals us and transforms our lives so often and so completely?

CLÁUDIO CARVALHAES

Pastoral Perspective

extremis. There is no fanfare here, no dramatic description of the healer's antics. There is no swoon that people see and hear watching some TV preacher. There is no wave of a magic wand, just the brief words and unpretentious action: "I do choose. Be made clean!" The action is as simple as the words—the touch of the Master's hand.

Physicians and nurses who care for the whole patient, not just the disease, understand the power of touch (that is, once they have washed their hands repeatedly so as to avoid passing on nosocomial or staph infections, the kind you can get in the hospital). Health-care providers who reach out to their patients and connect in appropriate physical ways are the ones who bring real healing. These are the ones who know that there is something more going on here than mere clinical improvement. I once heard a patient say, "I was so scared and out of sorts until the doctor spoke to me tenderly and grazed the stubble on my face. That simple touch made all the difference in the world."

Jesus touched the leper and in so doing turned the world upside down. Touching the unclean is on the one hand inappropriate, and on the other hand dangerous. After all, you might catch something! Jesus did not mind breaking religious codes that are not divinely inspired, especially regulations that not only exclude those who are different but give them no opportunity to be healed. The other way Jesus reorders the world is by removing the humiliation that lepers experienced at that time. So the one who died ignominiously as an outcast on a cross gives the key to the city and opens the door to an untouchable at the bottom of the social food chain. He does so by sending the leper to the priest, who certifies his healing and welcomes him as an accepted member of the community—which may be the real miracle in this story!

WILLIAM J. CARL III

community; by Jesus' word, immediately the leprosy was cleansed. No action is required of the person (or the leprosy), as in Mark 1:42 (and Luke 5:13) where "the leprosy left him."

Jesus then sends the person who previously had leprosy to show himself to the priest and to offer the gift that Moses commanded. (The instructions for cleansing or proving one is cleansed from leprosy are found in Leviticus 14.) "Leprosy" can refer to a number of diseases. Persons with leprosy were considered unclean and were denied access to the temple and to other social opportunities within the community. Matthew (following Mark) is clear that the priestly ritual does not affect the cleansing. Jesus has already accomplished that with his word. In this telling of the story, the directive accomplishes at least three things: (a) the action provides proof to the people that the cleansing is real and that Jesus' power is real; (b) Jesus is shown to honor the tradition and affirm the preservation of Mosaic law; (c) Jesus' ministry is linked with Moses, who was thought to have authored the entire Pentateuch and therefore to have written the instructions about confirming the cleansing of one with a leprous skin condition.

Matthew retains the Markan admonition, "See that you say nothing to anyone." Matthew's use of the instruction, however, is more related to expectation of an immediate appearance before the priest, rather than a prohibition against interacting with the crowd, as in Mark and Luke. Again, Matthew's succinct account keeps the focus on Jesus and his word, rather than on all the reactions and interactions of those around him.

Metaphorically, Jesus has begun his healing ministry with the cleansing of Israel and a reaffirmation of the Mosaic tradition. In the next story, Matthew will demonstrate how Jesus extends that ministry to the Gentiles as well.

JUDITH HOCH WRAY

"If you choose" is the homiletical hinge of this passage. If Jesus says no, the man remains unclean and isolated. If Jesus says yes, the leper is healed and restored to community. Preachers should grab this opportunity to confess that we continue to treat whole groups of people as lepers. We push many outside the mainstream of community life because of their immigration status, economic level, race, nationality, personal hygiene, sexual orientation, or extreme political views—left or right. As a church, we can choose to reach out and include those who are "outside the camp" (Lev. 13:46), or we can continue to label them unclean and exclude them. The choice is ours.

Notice that Jesus does not hesitate to include. He quickly stretches out his hand and touches the leper, saying, "I do choose. Be made clean!" (v. 3). Through the power of BioLogos—speaking life into being—the man's leprosy is cleansed, and he is restored to community. Church members should be reminded that our words have similar power when we reach out to a stranger and say, "Come sit at my table." Bridges are built when we ask a newcomer, "Tell me your story." Although some people complain that talk is cheap, we all know the value of a well-chosen word. Nothing can restore a fractured relationship better than the words "I forgive you." Nothing describes deep longing and commitment better than "I love you." In our world today, words continue to create reality.

Preachers should also acknowledge the deep respect that Jesus has for religious tradition when he instructs the man to go quickly to the priest "and offer the gift that Moses commanded, as a testimony to them" (v. 4). His guidance is in line with the teachings of Leviticus, which says that "the priest shall make an examination" of the leper (Lev. 14:3), and that offerings shall be made when the disease is healed. Sermons on Matthew should be grounded in the understanding that Jesus came "not to abolish but to fulfill" the law and the prophets (Matt. 5:17), and should make clear that the miraculous deeds of Jesus are confirmations of the truth of the Word of God. Through his words and actions, Jesus is practicing the ancient tradition of BioLogos, speaking life into being.

HENRY G. BRINTON

Matthew 8:5–13

⁵When he entered Capernaum, a centurion came to him, appealing to him ⁶and saying, "Lord, my servant is lying at home paralyzed, in terrible distress." ⁷And he said to him, "I will come and cure him." ⁸The centurion answered, "Lord, I am not worthy to have you come under my roof; but only speak the word, and my servant will be healed. ⁹For I also am a man under authority, with soldiers under me; and I say to one, 'Go,' and he goes, and to another, 'Come,' and he comes, and to my slave, 'Do this,' and the slave does it." ¹⁰When Jesus heard him, he was amazed and said to those who followed him, "Truly I tell you, in no one in Israel have I found such faith. ¹¹I tell you, many will come from east and west and will eat with Abraham and Isaac and Jacob in the kingdom of heaven, ¹²while the heirs of the kingdom will be thrown into the outer darkness, where there will be weeping and gnashing of teeth." ¹³And to the centurion Jesus said, "Go; let it be done for you according to your faith." And the servant was healed in that hour.

Theological Perspective

In this healing story, Jesus will not only heal the body of this person but use healing as a way of talking about our present and future. In this passage, the person is in such a bad shape that he cannot go to Jesus. He needs someone else to plead his case. What shocks us here is that his boss is the one who makes his way to Jesus and begs Jesus to heal his servant. For a moment, the structure of power is shifted upside down: the one who is to be served becomes the servant of his slave. Is not this story a parable of the kingdom of God, where people relate and live in equality? We are so used to people in power not caring for those they should be serving and always wanting to be served. We forget that Jesus' model, as set in the washing of the feet (John 13:1–14), is totally different: those who were to be served must serve.

This centurion has great power. He knows he can say whatever he wants, and his slaves will surely make it happen. The idea of a slave for us today is completely unacceptable, but if we can think of a man with that much power with ears to hear, eyes to see, and a heart filled with compassion that can feel for his servant, we can somewhat understand why Jesus is in awe of him. The centurion does not need to do anything like that. Why would he care? He could simply let his slave die and get another

Pastoral Perspective

Notice how Jesus keeps breaking through barriers and crossing into dangerous territory. What a risk-taker he is! First he touches a hideous-looking leper; now he gives audience to a Roman centurion, who is definitely the enemy. One of the many surprising things that happen in this story is that this powerful foreigner, like the leper, approaches Jesus in humility, faith, and trust. There is not even a hint of arrogance born of privilege. "I am not worthy," he says with head bowed.

What does he mean in saying he is not worthy? This is a man with authority, who rules over others. He is the conqueror, while Jesus represents the conquered. Jesus should be bowing and saying, "I am not worthy to approach you!" However, as in so many other stories about Jesus, the roles are reversed, and the world is turned sideways. Why does the centurion say he is not worthy? Because he knows that Jewish custom prohibits Jews from entering the houses of Gentiles. The centurion understands the culture in which he lives and is taking local tradition seriously. Jesus reads his heart immediately and relates to him personally.

From the bottom of the barrel (a leper) to the top of the heap (a centurion), Jesus is able to connect with everyone. Nevertheless he is surprised by the appearance and acquiescence of this powerful man.

Exegetical Perspective

The healing of the centurion's servant, the second of Jesus' miracles in this section (8:1–17) that follows immediately after the Sermon on the Mount (Matt. 5–7), is packed with information about the life and theology of the early church. In these few verses we find commentary on the inclusion of Gentiles in the community, on Jewish and Gentile Christian dynamics, on Jesus' authority, on the power of Jesus' word, on faith, and on the messianic banquet.

For this miracle story, Matthew has drawn on a tradition found in the lost sayings source (designated Q). Luke's version, based also on Q, is found in Luke 7:1–10. John 4:46b–54 shows that John had knowledge of a similar tradition but probably not direct access to the text used by Matthew and Luke.

Based on the multitude of references to Jewish traditions and Scripture in Matthew, we have concluded that the Matthean community was predominantly Jewish Christian. This community of displaced or Diaspora Jews, living under the control of the Roman Empire in the late first century, probably in Syria (but perhaps in Galilee), interacted regularly with the Gentile community. The Roman centurion is one of those Gentiles.

While Matthew 10:5–6 indicates that Jesus understood his mission to be to Israel, and Matthew 15:21–28 demonstrates how difficult making the shift

Homiletical Perspective

Although the word "Trinity" does not appear in the Bible, Matthew seems to have a strong affinity for the number three. He is the only Gospel writer who quotes Jesus using Trinitarian language in the commissioning of the disciples to baptize "in the name of the Father and of the Son and of the Holy Spirit" (28:19). His genealogy of Jesus is divided into three parts (1:1–17), as is his description of the temptation (4:1–11). The teachings of the Sermon on the Mount are delivered in three parts (5:1–7:29), as are the mighty acts of Jesus, which contain three sets of miracle stories (8:1–9:34). The healing of the Roman officer's servant is the second of three miracles in the first set, coming right after the healing of the leper.

As the story begins, Jesus enters Capernaum, where he had "made his home" after leaving Nazareth (4:13). It is a relatively safe place for Jesus after the arrest of John, but it also has an alien feel, located in "Galilee of the Gentiles" (4:15). Given this multicultural setting, the presence of a Roman centurion is not surprising. The shock comes when this military officer approaches Jesus and makes the appeal, "Lord, my servant is lying at home paralyzed, in terrible distress" (8:5–6). Sermons on this text could highlight this unorthodox request, comparing it to a captain in the United States Marine Corps

Matthew 8:5–13

one the next day. However, he does not. Moreover, the same pattern of concern and humbleness this man has with his slave are also shown in the way he approaches Jesus. He knows that a single word from Jesus can do the work. That is all that he needs from Jesus, a word. This man's faith is so strong that he is praised by Jesus.

Jesus is so surprised by this man's faith that he uses this event to talk about God's future for us. This man is a centurion working for the Roman army, thus not a friend of the Israelites. In spite of that, this man becomes part of Jesus' own people. The centurion does not need to have a proper nationality or a proper religious affiliation to receive Jesus' word. His compassion and humility are his entrance to the kingdom of God.

With this example, Jesus stretches the kingdom of God to all the earth: from the East and from the West people will come for the great banquet. Jesus' invocation of the eschatological banquet serves in two ways: to strengthen the faith of the people for a future that is held in God's hand and to say that this future banquet of joy and fullness is what shapes our lives here and now. This man, in that moment, is shifting the idea of belonging in the realm of God and shifting the criteria of who can come to the banquet. Not only Jews from East and West but also Roman people and others will be present.

The future banquet is a great and unforeseen expansion of the eucharistic banquet we have now, with people coming from all over the world. As Rubem Alves, a Brazilian theologian, says: Our tables are only "aperitif of the future."[1] With whom we will eat at this banquet has to do with the ways we live today and the eschatological future we are creating together under God's love.

This story is a constant call issued to us; our living together is transformed every time we eat at the Lord's Table, a present and eschatological feast. For every time we hear the call issued by Jesus and celebrate the great banquet of love, solidarity, and justice in the Lord's Supper, we both announce and incarnate the love of God among us, even when life is amid strife of all kinds, deeply hurt by signs of division, taken over by individualist desires and lack of compassion.

When we try, with our sinful divisions and exclusions, to undo the future of God's community of love, solidarity, and care as it is lived in heaven, we

1. See Rubem Alves, *I Believe in the Resurrection of the Body* (Eugene, OR: Wipf & Stock, 2003), 73–76.

It has to be something pretty special to surprise the Son of God, who would not normally be surprised by much of anything—but not this time. Jesus is amazed to see a Gentile power figure bowing before him to ask a favor. I thought God was supposed to surprise us, not the other way around!

What was it that got to Jesus that day? There are several things to notice in the text. First, the centurion's humility was not something Jesus expected. Perhaps Jesus had seen firsthand the cruelty of typical Roman centurions. He knew how much they were hated by his own people. He had heard his fellow Jews grumble under their breath, the way employees do behind the boss's back. This centurion was different. Jesus knew it from the moment he laid eyes on him. For starters, the man came alone to meet Jesus. He led no entourage of sycophants. Perhaps there was something about the way he looked at Jesus that might have helped Jesus see that the man meant him no harm. Maybe Jesus had never met a humble centurion, only arrogant, malicious, violent ones. No wonder he was surprised.

The second thing that surprised Jesus was that the centurion pleaded for help not for himself but for a lowly servant boy. Why was the kid so special to the soldier? It was almost as if this servant was an adopted son, someone the centurion had taken under his wing. Maybe he saw something of himself in the boy. Maybe the boy went out of his way to help the centurion, as any good administrative assistant would do for someone he trusted and admired. Matthew never tells us. All we know is that Jesus was surprised that the soldier wanted help for someone who was nothing more than a slave, something that could have been seen as a sign of weakness to the centurion's men. That in itself was unusual.

The centurion was not a typical leader, even by today's standards. He represented a man of sensitivity, a true servant leader, a responsible CEO. He cared for his servants. He cared for the people who worked for him. He even cared for the people who were different, in this case the Jews. Jesus was impressed by his love for an underdog and was not deterred by entering the centurion's house, although he never had to.

Finally, Jesus was surprised by the centurion's faith. Some, but not all, weak and poor people have faith in God because they have nothing and are completely dependent on God. On the other hand, persons of power, prestige, and financial security sometimes have more of a challenge believing in God because they assume they have gotten it all on

to include Gentiles may have been for the church, the Gospel as a whole makes it very clear that Gentiles were an integral part of the early Christian communities. Gentiles are included in the genealogy in Matthew 1 (Tamar and Ruth). The visit of the magi in Matthew 2 places Gentiles among the first to see and recognize Jesus as the Messiah. Now, in the healing of the centurion's servant, we see Jesus interacting with a Gentile.

When Jesus enters Capernaum (see Matt. 4:13), the centurion approaches Jesus directly, with no intermediary (cf. Luke 7:3–10). Like the leper in Matthew 8:2, the centurion addresses Jesus as "Lord" (see exegetical commentary on Matt. 8:1–4). The description of his servant "lying paralyzed at home, in terrible distress," explains why the servant could not be brought to Jesus.

"Authority" is a key word in this presentation of Jesus (7:29; 8:9). Jesus has authority. The interaction with the Roman centurion who commands 100 Roman foot soldiers, who defines himself as one under authority and as having authority, highlights the authority of Jesus and the results of recognizing Jesus' authority. Jesus' authority, clearly established earlier in his teaching and demonstrated in his cleansing of the leper (8:1–4), now becomes the occasion for establishing a relationship with the Gentile and a means to define faith in a fresh way. Understanding authority and making oneself available to divine authority, according to Jesus' response to the centurion, is faith!

Matthew 8:10–12 includes an affirmation of the faith of the centurion at the expense of the faith of others. What appears to be a polemic against Judaism must be read in context. Jesus was Jewish. Most of the early followers of Jesus were Jewish. The angry rhetoric of the early church, as it struggled to define itself over against rabbinic Judaism after the destruction of the temple in 70 CE, frequently gets placed in the mouth of Jesus. In the midst of this rhetoric we find Matthew's favorite saying designed to evoke the horror of the final punishment ("weeping and gnashing of teeth": Matt. 13:42, 50; 22:13; 24:51; 25:30; cf. Ps. 112:10). In the antagonistic struggle for honor and shame that marks Greco-Roman antiquity, as well as in today's interfaith relations, we see how easy (and unnecessary) it is to put down another person's faith in order to affirm one's own faith. That position, however, is inconsistent with the gospel, which graciously calls and affirms Jew and Gentile alike. To the extent to which we can hear these verses as political rhetoric, we can interpret this text more responsibly.

who was a Christian approaching a Muslim cleric in a remote tribal village and pleading for help with a personal problem. The fact that the officer calls Jesus "Lord"—a term reserved for superiors, including the Roman emperor—makes it even more surprising.

Jesus responds, "I will come and cure him" (v. 7)—or does he? There is no punctuation in the original biblical text, so a preacher could read the line as a question, "I will come and cure *him*?" Cure an outsider to the Jewish faith and community, a servant in an occupying military force? Make the line a question, and you wonder, "Why in the world would Jesus do *that*?" Preachers can explore a number of possible reactions, from hesitation to determination. Perhaps Jesus hesitated, remembering he had just reaffirmed his commitment to Jewish law after healing the leper (v. 4). Maybe he discovered a new determination to use his power to bring light to the Gentiles, "people who sat in darkness" (4:16). Whether his response is a hesitating question or a determined statement, Jesus sets the stage for the centurion to make a statement of faith.

The centurion answers, "Lord, I am not worthy to have you come under my roof; but only speak the word, and my servant will be healed" (v. 8). This line is the basis of a response in the Roman Catholic Mass, and the recent revision of this service gives preachers an opportunity to reflect on the importance of this verse from Matthew. In the service, the priest invites the congregation "to the supper of the Lamb," and the people respond, "Lord, I am not worthy that you should enter under my roof, but only say the word and my soul shall be healed." Catholics echo the words of the centurion when they offer this response, proclaiming his faith in what Jesus can do. We are reminded that although none of us is entitled to demand that Jesus come to us, each of us can be faithful enough to trust in the power of Jesus to heal us. At every mass, Roman Catholics remind us of the faith of the Roman centurion.

Like the leper before him (v. 2), the officer knows that a word from Jesus can create a new reality: "only speak the word, and my servant will be healed" (v. 8). He has deep respect for the power of Jesus' word and says, "For I also am a man under authority, with soldiers under me; and I say to one, 'Go,' and he goes, and to another, 'Come,' and he comes, and to my slave, 'Do this,' and the slave does it" (v. 9). Having both received and given orders—Go, Come, Do this, Do that—the centurion knows the force of a command, and trusts that Jesus has the authority to heal his servant with a single word.

Matthew 8:5–13

Theological Perspective

become "heirs of the kingdom [who] will be thrown into the outer darkness, where there will be weeping and gnashing of teeth" (v. 12). There is already so much weeping and gnashing of teeth in our world today that we must bear witness tó a kingdom of love and care that issues a call for all to be at God's table, where every tear will be wiped away and we will celebrate in joy and gladness.

Our task as Christians is to weep before God for the world, while announcing that the kingdom of God belongs to the poor. Our weeping together is our work under God's call to create a time and space of light and solidarity, an appetizer that gives people a foretaste of a world where none are in the outer darkness gnashing their teeth. Not paying attention to the cries of those around us, from whatever nationality they might be, is to become the antithesis of the centurion, those who are already thrown into outer darkness.

Our work is that of the centurion who used Jesus' model of service: pay attention to those we must serve, hear their cries, make ways to see their lives transformed, their bodies healed, their hearts filled with love, and their minds gathered in peace. Only then, when, by God's grace, all of us are seated at the table of Jesus Christ, we will be able, perhaps, to hear Jesus saying to us what he said to the centurion: *"Go; let it be done for you according to your faith."*

CLÁUDIO CARVALHAES

Pastoral Perspective

their own. That is why people are occasionally surprised when persons of fame and power demonstrate real faith, not for show but genuinely and authentically. Otherwise, Jesus would not have joked about it being easier for a camel to go through the eye of a needle than for a rich man to enter heaven.

This centurion was going to have no trouble entering heaven. In fact, he had a better shot at heaven, Jesus mused to the gathering crowd, than typical church people who thought they already had their room reserved. If Jesus was surprised by the centurion, you can be sure the Pharisees and Sadducees hanging around that day were taken off guard by Jesus' apparent slap in the face. He seemed to be saying that heaven would be filled with people you will be surprised to see there, and perhaps they will be surprised to see you. To add insult to injury, he seemed to indicate that those who think they are religious might not be there at all!

Jesus certainly is full of surprises. The biggest one of all is that because of the outsider's faith the young boy is healed instantly "from a distance." Greek mythology talks about the Greek god of healing, Asclepius, having this kind of telepathic power. Maybe Matthew had that in the back of his mind when he relayed this story. This is not, however, a normal, everyday magic trick. It is the sovereign power of the universe responding to the faith of a "resident alien" who has stepped forward in humility and trust. Maybe we are the ones who are surprised the most, for the real miracle here is the centurion's faith.

WILLIAM J. CARL III

Exegetical Perspective

Thus Jesus says to those who "followed him" (i.e., the church, 8:1) that the faith of Gentiles is acceptable and sometimes even more exemplary than their own. The challenge can be heard as given to the Jewish Christian church, rather than as a polemic against the Jewish people as a whole.

"Many will come from east and west"—this includes Gentiles and has already been fulfilled in 2:1 with the coming of the magi from the East—"and will eat with Abraham . . ." Gentiles are included at the future messianic banquet (cf. Matt. 22:1–14). The saying also probably reflects the diversity at the eucharistic tables of the early churches known to Matthew. Jesus' ministry focuses on the variously marginalized. All who demonstrate faith are welcome at the table.

The term "heirs of the kingdom" (*huioi tēs basileias,* v. 12) is found only here in the Gospel. The implication is that the Jewish community is still understood by Matthew and his community as "heirs of the kingdom." The polemic is ultimately intended to invite in, rather than to exclude, these sisters and brothers.

Note Matthew's preference for "kingdom of heaven," rather than the "kingdom of God" most frequently found in Mark and Luke. Matthew, following Jewish prohibitions against pronouncing the name of God, prefers "heaven" as an alternative way of pointing to God, without saying the name.

To the centurion Jesus speaks the word: "Go; let it be done for you according to your faith." Jesus' word embodies Jesus' authority. Matthew consistently avoids any actions that would imply Jesus' using some kind of magical manipulation to affect healing or other miracles. (Note, for example, that Matthew does not include a version of the Mark 8:22–26 healing of the blind man at Bethsaida, probably because Jesus' actions there might be construed as those of a magician.) This account highlights the power of Jesus' authority and word! He does not even have to name healing as the goal. Jesus' authoritative word confirms the centurion's faith, and the servant is healed in that hour. In the next story, Matthew will demonstrate Jesus' serving and healing within the community of disciples.

JUDITH HOCH WRAY

Homiletical Perspective

Matthew tells us that when Jesus hears him, he is amazed. Sermons should include reflection on Jesus' complete astonishment that a military officer would grasp a teacher's authority; that a Gentile would put his trust in a Jew; that an outsider from Rome could teach lessons to the insiders of Israel. Shaking his head in amazement, Jesus says, "In no one in Israel have I found such faith" (v. 10).

Exactly what is the faith that the centurion possesses? It is not belief in the Torah or adherence to religious customs. Instead, his faith is *trust in the power of Jesus.* Although ignorant of theology, he grasps the truth of what Martin Luther said: "Faith is a living, bold trust in God's grace."[1] The centurion has living willingness to put himself in the hands of a loving and graceful God, and bold trust in the power of Jesus. Seeing this, Jesus is amazed and says, "I tell you, many will come from east and west and will eat with Abraham and Isaac and Jacob in the kingdom of heaven, while the heirs of the kingdom will be thrown into the outer darkness" (vv. 11–12). Jesus concludes by saying to the centurion, "Go; let it be done for you according to your faith"—according to your living, bold trust. Matthew tells us that the servant was healed in that hour (v. 13).

A sermon on this text can explore how we often get lost in theology, debating questions such as how a Triune God can simultaneously be one God and three persons. There is a time for such conversations, and Matthew seems to invite them with his Trinitarian baptismal formula and triads of teachings and miracles. However, the healing of the centurion's servant reminds us that Jesus is less amazed by theological speculation than he is by the faith that is, quite simply, a bold and living trust in his power.

HENRY G. BRINTON

---

1. Johann K. Irmischer, *Dr. Martin Luther's Vermischte Deutsche Schriften* (Erlinger: Heyder und Zimmer, 1854), 63:125.

Matthew 8:14–17

¹⁴When Jesus entered Peter's house, he saw his mother-in-law lying in bed with a fever; ¹⁵he touched her hand, and the fever left her, and she got up and began to serve him. ¹⁶That evening they brought to him many who were possessed with demons; and he cast out the spirits with a word, and cured all who were sick. ¹⁷This was to fulfill what had been spoken through the prophet Isaiah, "He took our infirmities and bore our diseases."

Theological Perspective

This text has several stories of healing. Throughout this chapter we see Jesus engaging with different people in different ways. A social analysis of Jesus' behavior in this chapter alone would have a hard time finding any predictable ways of acting. Instead, for each situation a different approach, engagement, and answer. At the heart of these events, there is the body. The body in pain, the body prostrate, the body without strength, the body ill, the body burning, the body that cannot move, the body hurting in ways that take away the strength of the spirit, the tranquility of the mind, and the peace of the heart.

From these short stories of healing events, we are challenged to pay attention to the body and the ways in which we must incarnate our faith. Christianity is grounded in incarnation, from the theological movement of God becoming flesh, Emmanuel, God with us, one of us. It is from this perspective of Jesus' incarnation that we must look at our theological understandings, our liturgical actions, and our ethical life—in one word, our Christian faith.

Here is a question. What would happen to our understanding of faith if we looked at it from the perspective of our bodies? What does it mean if we say that the Holy Spirit acts in and through us by way of our bodies? Jaci Maraschin, a Brazilian artist and liturgical theologian, said once, "It is in the body

Pastoral Perspective

Craig Barnes talks in lectures to seminary students about developing one's pastoral identity, especially in hospital calls, where clergy often feel out of place. Physicians have white coats and stethoscopes. What do we have? Look at Jesus for the answer. In the first two healing stories in Matthew 8, the leper and the centurion come to him; but with Peter's mother-in-law Jesus initiates. Others ask for healing; this woman does not. Jesus sees the need and acts. Often we wait for people who are hurting to come to us, but some never come. We need to be on the watch for those we sense are hurting and waiting for us to make the first move. You know people like this; they never complain about anything until it is too late.

Another thing we can learn from Jesus about developing our pastoral identity is to enter unexpected places, places others might not go. Jesus' entry into Peter's lowly home is a way of saying, "I care enough about you to meet you where you are." He shows humility and love for everyone, whatever his or her station in life. Consider for a moment Dom Helder Camara, former archbishop of Olinda and Recife in Brazil, who was dubbed "Bishop of the Slums" because of his love and care for the poor. He shocked everyone in his archdiocese by moving out of the palatial residence dedicated to archbishops and into a small room next to a small church,

Exegetical Perspective

The healing of Peter's mother-in-law, the third of Jesus' miracles in this section (8:1–17) that follows immediately after the Sermon on the Mount (Matt. 5–7), can be understood to affirm Jesus' healing power within the community of disciples. Demonstration of Jesus' healing power on behalf of the Jewish community and on behalf of Gentiles has preceded this story. These healings are the first three of ten miracles designed to elicit comparison with the ten miracles of Moses in Egypt. Each recipient of Jesus' healing and/or cleansing power has in one way or another been marginalized from the community. Jesus' word restores them to health and to the community. The diversity represented among those who were healed by Jesus suggests an early church that includes a wide range of persons, previously excluded or marginalized, who now claim a testimony about the power of Jesus to heal and restore to community.

Peter is here identified as married, although information about his wife is nonexistent. In 1 Corinthians 9:5, Paul also says Peter/Cephas was married. The mother-in law's presence in Peter's home may indicate that she had moved in with her daughter, a practice in keeping with Jesus' concern that parents be honored and cared for by their children (15:1–10). Alternatively, the living arrangements may indicate

Homiletical Perspective

As Jesus enters the house of Peter in Capernaum, his ministry is about to reach its "tipping point." This term was made popular by journalist Malcolm Gladwell in *The Tipping Point*.[1] This phrase describes the moment when an idea, product, message, or social behavior catches on, takes off, and "tips"—becomes something big. Gladwell illustrates this epidemic-like behavior with descriptions of the rising sales of Hush Puppies shoes in the mid-1990s and the dramatic drop in the crime rate in New York City during the same decade.

In the preceding chapters of Matthew, Jesus has demonstrated a set of gifts that can create a tipping point. His Sermon on the Mount (Matt. 5–7) reveals that he has a powerful ability to link people with new information; Gladwell calls such teachers "mavens," information specialists. Jesus also has a special gift for bringing diverse people together, as he does when he reaches out to a leper (8:1–4) and a Roman centurion (8:5–13). In the world of *The Tipping Point,* such a person is a "connector" who can span a number of different worlds. Finally, in this third miracle after the Sermon on the Mount, Jesus heals a sick woman and many others (8:14–17). He shows that he has charisma, which is the Greek word for "divine gift,"

1. Malcolm Gladwell, *The Tipping Point: How Little Things Can Make a Big Difference* (New York: Back Bay Books, 2002).

Matthew 8:14–17

Theological Perspective

that we are spirits. When we speak about bodies we have to be aware that not only man is a body, but also woman and children. When I say that it is in the body that we are spirit I am thinking also in the body of the community."[1]

What Maraschin is saying here can help us interpret these texts. The healing of our bodies can only happen by way of the breath of the Holy Spirit in us. When Jesus heals the people, touching them and speaking a word, he is filled with the Spirit and gives life to people who are now gaining back the presence of the Spirit of life. Thus the healing of our bodies is the constant unfolding of God's Spirit in our body, of our becoming spirit in our bodies, thus becoming human, integrated, undivided body/spirit sons and daughters of God, a family of God in all its diversity and strangeness.

In these verses, Jesus offers himself fully to each occasion. The first story is about Peter's mother-in-law. The text says that this woman has a fever (v. 14). Verse 15 says that "he touched her hand, and the fever left her, and she got up and began to serve him." With her body healed, she got a new spirit and was able to get up and serve the people at her house. This is similar to what Maraschin said: "It is in the body that we are spirits" and we become a community.

Verse 16 mentions that on "that evening they brought to him many who were possessed by demons; and he cast out the spirits with a word, and cured all who were sick." Word incarnate, Jesus speech becoming flesh, life, Spirit! A broken community is now being mended, put together, re-membered. Bodies/minds/hearts acknowledged, remembered, cared for, healed, becoming spirits filled with life for one another. What a night that was!

Verse 17 says, "This was to fulfill what had been spoken through the prophet Isaiah, 'He took our infirmities and bore our diseases.'" Jesus' body was a mirror of our bodies: his body broken because of our brokenness, his body ill from our own sickness, his body infirm by our lack of spirit, his body sacrificed because of our social injustices and diseases.

It is against these agents of death that Jesus starts his ministry. Jesus' life and ministry are with the outcasts, with ill, infirm, injured, oppressed people, and for these people he devotes his full life, to the point of offering his body to heal our wounded bodies. That is also what we remember in our celebrations of

1. Jaci Maraschin, "The Transient Body: Sensibility and Spirituality," paper presented at the event "Liturgy and Body," Union Theological Seminary, New York, October 20, 2003.

Pastoral Perspective

because he wanted to live among the poor. Instead of being chauffeured here and there, he got rides with others or would walk wherever he needed to go. Think of Toyohiko Kagawa, Japanese Christian leader, who moved into the Kobe slum to be close to the poor. Like Jesus, Camara and Kagawa went in person where the need was the greatest.

Like Camara and Kagawa, Jesus was a man of few words. With Peter's mother-in-law, we are told that he simply "touched her hand," and she was healed. Often, during a prayer in a hospital room or by the bedside of someone on the point of death, clergy will hold the hand of the one lying there helpless. To be the recipient of that firm grip when you are the one in pain is like sensing a jolt of new life, or at least the comfort you need in that moment to get you to the next. A touch like this brings peace and oneness in a way you have never experienced before. We will never know how it worked that day; all we know is that it did and apparently immediately.

Evidence of how quickly the healing occurred can be seen by the patient's response. The woman practically leapt up and began serving Jesus. Here we see one of the resurrection words often used in the New Testament to describe Easter people who "get" what Jesus is really about, people who "get up" to new life and become "new persons altogether" in Christ. More is occurring here than simply planting your feet on the floor and standing up. The word used here is a metaphor for little resurrections that can happen to all of us when we respond to the touch of Christ in our lives. The Greek word for "get up" in this case is presented in passive construction. It means literally she "was raised." The same word is used in reference to Jesus in Matthew 28:6–7 and in some places is translated "He is risen!" (KJV, ASV).

Thus we see the profoundly spiritual response to Jesus' entry into our lives, "touching" us at our deepest points of pain. We become "new persons altogether" and find ourselves wanting to do something right then that shows our sincere appreciation. For Peter's mother-in-law it was service, which could be thought of *sacramentally*, as in preparing a table of food—Eucharist—or *spiritually*, as in diaconal service (the verb with the same root as "deacon" is used here)—discipleship.

It is little wonder people lined up at the door for healing. All his life, Jesus had gathered everyone in—from the ayatollahs from the East who followed the star to find him in the manger to the leper and the centurion who sought him out and the mother-in-law of the future rock of the church. Think of the

that when Peter left his parents' house, he became a part of his wife's family (cf. Gen. 2:24; Eph. 5:31), and thus Peter's domicile was indeed *her* home.

Again, Matthew's account is much more concise than that of his Markan source (see Mark 1:29–31 and Luke 4:38–39). Extraneous information about who may have been present is omitted from Matthew's account. The focus is on Jesus.

In Matthew's version, Jesus enters the house, sees Peter's mother-in-law lying sick with fever, and takes the initiative to heal her. Unlike in the accounts in both Mark and Luke, in Matthew no one brings her illness to Jesus' attention. He takes the lead and heals her without being asked or assisted in the process. In fact, this is the only healing in Matthew's Gospel where Jesus takes the initiative. Jesus sees the need and takes the initiative to serve, to tend to the needs of the community without being asked. In Matthew, the only ones identified as serving are Jesus (20:28) and women (8:15; 27:55–56). Jesus serves Peter's mother-in-law's needs; then she rises to the occasion and serves him. This account provides one of the rare occasions in Matthew where Jesus does not say a word. His authority is so great that he needs only to touch her hand and the healing is effected.

The evangelist reports that she rose and served (*diēkonei*, v. 15) him. The only other disciples reported by Matthew to serve (*diakoneō*, "provide for") Jesus are the many women who also stood by him at the cross (27:55–56). If we were to posit ecclesiastical connotations to the story, then Matthew has depicted the first deacon and noted the importance of women deacons in the early church. Even though Matthew is the only evangelist to name "the church" (*ekklēsia*, 16:18; 18:17) within the account of Jesus' life and ministry, he shows no interest in church offices such as elder and deacon. Whether the early church communities who heard Matthew's account would have recognized the affirmation of women's ministry as deacons cannot be confirmed. However one understands the ecclesiastical dynamics of this story, this woman, known to us only as "Peter's mother-in-law," serves, even as Jesus came to serve (*diakoneō*, 20:28). The Twelve are instructed to "serve" (*diakoneō*, 20:26–28) but are never shown doing so.

Both Mark and Luke report that Peter's mother-in-law served "them," presumably all of the men in the house. Matthew, however, keeps the focus on Jesus alone. She serves "him."

Matthew has focused on Jesus' healing/cleansing of three different individuals: a Jewish leper, a Roman centurion's servant, and Peter's mother-in-law. Jesus'

but his charisma is not the persuasive power of a salesperson. Instead, it is the healing gift of God.

A sermon on this healing can use *The Tipping Point* as a starting point, because Jesus clearly acts as a maven and a connector, and he shows the charisma needed to tip people toward the kingdom of God. Matthew tells us that when Jesus enters Peter's house, he sees Peter's mother-in-law lying in bed with a fever. He touches her hand, the fever leaves her, and she gets up and begins to serve him (vv. 14–15). Notice that Jesus makes an immediate personal connection with the sick woman, instead of being told about her illness by others, as is the case in Mark 1:30. He also reveals his charisma—his divine gift—by touching her hand and healing her. Unlike the two previous miracles, there is no information in this story about the faith of the person who receives the gift, no indication that the woman kneels before Jesus as the leper did (8:2) or that she expresses trust in the power of Jesus as the centurion did (8:8). Instead, the focus is on the initiative of Jesus to use his power to heal a sick woman and restore her to fullness of life.

How do we know that this healing creates a tipping point? Because of the woman's response. Matthew tells us that "she got up and began to serve him" (v. 15). Restored to complete vitality, Peter's mother-in-law responds by tipping toward the kingdom of God and serving Jesus as a disciple (or more literally as a deacon, since the Greek word used in this verse for "serve" is *diēkonei*). Clearly, the message and behavior of Jesus is catching on, taking off, and tipping—becoming something big. Then, like an epidemic, the word of Jesus' power spreads quickly, and Matthew says that on that same evening "they brought to him many who were possessed with demons; and he cast out the spirits with a word, and cured all who were sick" (v. 16). Preachers should stress that crowds are drawn to Jesus as we would be attracted to a magnetic figure today, although Jesus responds not by selling them a spiritual book or DVD, but by casting out their demons and curing their diseases.

Jesus heals. He is no charismatic salesperson, creating a sensation for his own profit or benefit. No, Jesus is a compassionate healer who exercises his divine gift for the benefit of others, using his power to overcome anything that can hurt or destroy people in body, mind, or spirit. All of his mighty acts are focused on overcoming evil, whether he is performing exorcisms or healings. Modern congregations need to understand that there was no

Matthew 8:14–17

Theological Perspective

the Eucharist. From death he is risen and offers himself to us as the bread of life and the cup of salvation! The epiclesis, or the eucharistic calling of the Spirit in many traditions, means the coming of the Spirit in our midst to anoint us, to heal us, Emmanuel making our bodies become the Spirit of God, as we all become the communal body of Christ in the world.

For us today we can think about the ways in which our bodies are related to what we believe. How do our faith, bodies, Spirit, and community intertwine? How much have we made our faith serve only the desires of our individual bodies, instead of the desires of our community? How can we use our faith and God's healing actions to help our bodies, individual and communal, engage with globalization and offer wholeness to compartmentalized versions of life where we keep the dichotomy between mind and body, flesh and spirit, faith and daily life? How can Jesus' stories help our bodies gain the Spirit of God when we interact with new formats of living around computers and virtual communities and virtual love?

Perhaps Jaci Maraschin can help us again: "It is in the body that we are spirit especially when our bodies are ready to recreate life. Let us, then, make of our bodies our main instrument of worship."[2]

Re-creating life: this is what Jesus was doing all along. Creating life where there was none and re-creating life when life was lost. It is in our bodies, our main instrument of worship, that we can, along with God, create and re-create life all around us and offer it to the world.

CLÁUDIO CARVALHAES

Pastoral Perspective

awful scenes of people cramming together, hoping to be helicoptered out of Vietnam, Cambodia, or Liberia, or praying to be on Schindler's list. In those terrifying and bloody moments, not everyone makes it, but when hurting folks come to Jesus, everyone makes the list! His inclusiveness is not just political correctness; it represents instead the universal scope of his reach. Amazingly, he heals them all with a single word.

I remember Walter Burghardt, talking about the power of words, once saying, "Three words—'Here I stand!'—rent Christendom asunder. Two words—'Sieg Heil!'—bloodied the face of Europe." If God, being the verbal deity, can speak creation into existence, then Jesus can mend a broken heart, heal an ailing body, and soothe a troubled soul with a single word.

For Jesus, the body and soul were one. His view of the mind-body equation was less the Hellenistic/Cartesian perspective, which separates mind and body and has doctors looking at patients as very uninteresting appendages to very interesting diseases. His view was more Hebraic; the Jewish word for soul, *nephesh*, means all of who you are—mind, body, heart, and soul. So healing for Jesus was never a quick fix for a physical ailment, but was "healing" at a much deeper level, the level of a person's separation from God and from the community. Physical sickness affects the whole person. True healing does the same. No wonder the word for salvation in Greek, *sōtēria*, means "health, healing, wholeness, peace, harmony, and oneness" for the whole person and the whole community. It is a synonym for *shalom* in Hebrew and *salaam* in Arabic. The one we call Jesus somehow knew all that, and "touches" us every day so that we might know it, be healed, and live new lives in his service.

WILLIAM J. CARL III

2. Ibid.

ministry began with Israel, extended to the Gentiles, and resides in the church. Jesus' power is not limited, however, to the healing of certain individuals. Matthew concludes this section with the report that "many" were brought to Jesus.

True to his Jesus-focused agenda, Matthew modifies the Markan source to highlight the power and authority of Jesus and to emphasize the power of Jesus' "word" to heal and to cleanse. For the "many who were possessed with demons" Jesus "cast out the spirits with a word." The text of neither Mark nor Luke includes "word" (*logos*, cf. Matt. 8:8). For Matthew, Jesus' word is sufficient. No other action is needed. No implication of magical manipulation is permitted. (Note, for example, that Matthew does not include a version of the Mark 8:22–26 healing of the blind man at Bethsaida, probably because Jesus' actions there might be construed as those of a magician.) The account concludes simply with the summary report that "he cured all who were sick" (see 4:23; 9:35; 10:1; 12:15; 15:29–31).

This section of three miracles (8:1–4, 5–13, 14–17) ends with one of Matthew's formula quotations: "This was to fulfill what had been spoken through the prophet Isaiah . . ." (See Isa. 53:4. Note that here and elsewhere, Matthew relies on or quotes from the Greek version of the Scriptures, i.e., the Septuagint.) This is the eighth of fourteen almost identical quotations by which Matthew reiterates his proclamation that Jesus is the Messiah who fulfills the law and the prophets. (See 1:22–23; 2:5b–6, 15b, 17–18, 23b; 3:3; 4:14–16; 8:17; 12:17–21; 13:14–15, 35; 21:4–5; 26:56; 27:9–10.)

The recital of the ten miracles performed by Jesus continues in the following verses of Matthew 8–9, interspersed with short teaching opportunities. Similar to this first section of three miracles, both the second section of three miracles (8:18–9:8) and the third section of four miracles (9:18–34) conclude with Jesus interacting with and healing crowds of people. These individual healings/miracles have put human faces to the many who experienced the power of Jesus' word.

JUDITH HOCH WRAY

distinction in biblical times between spiritual, physical, mental, and emotional afflictions. All were seen as destructive forces that undermined the health and wholeness of God's creatures. When Jesus casts out demons and heals, he is actively tipping people away from the kingdom of Satan and toward the kingdom of God.

Matthew tells us that this powerful and compassionate activity of Jesus is to fulfill the words of the prophet Isaiah, "He took our infirmities and bore our diseases" (v. 17). Although this line comes from Isaiah 53:4, a verse from one of the prophet's Suffering Servant passages, there is no sense in Matthew that Jesus is suffering as he removes our infirmities and diseases. No, he does his work in Galilee from a position of power, as a gifted maven, connector, and charismatic healer. He begins a spiritual battle that reaches a climax in Matthew 12, where he cures a demoniac and says to the Pharisees, "But if it is by the Spirit of God that I cast out demons, then the kingdom of God has come to you" (12:28). Jesus is determined to drive out a demonic kingdom and establish a holy kingdom at the center of human life.

A sermon on this healing story should reach back to the end of the Sermon on the Mount and reveal that the tip toward God's kingdom begins when Jesus says, "Everyone then who hears these words of mine and acts on them will be like a wise man who built his house on rock" (7:24). Jesus the maven has spoken in his Sermon, offering essential information. However, the tipping point of the kingdom of God comes when Jesus' Sermon is followed by mighty deeds that benefit people on the margins of society—lepers, centurions, sick women, and others. The same is true for us: it is not enough to be a person who "hears these words" of Jesus; we also need to be someone who "acts on them" (7:24). Only then can we participate fully in the kingdom of God, a realm that is experienced in both authoritative teachings and mighty acts.

HENRY G. BRINTON

Matthew 8:18–22

¹⁸Now when Jesus saw great crowds around him, he gave orders to go over to the other side. ¹⁹A scribe then approached and said, "Teacher, I will follow you wherever you go." ²⁰And Jesus said to him, "Foxes have holes, and birds of the air have nests; but the Son of Man has nowhere to lay his head." ²¹Another of his disciples said to him, "Lord, first let me go and bury my father." ²²But Jesus said to him, "Follow me, and let the dead bury their own dead."

Theological Perspective

Here are two sayings about the difficulty of discipleship. In both cases, Christ requires his followers to forsake something basic to life in the world: the security of shelter in the first instance, the bond of duty to parents in the second. The immediate question that meets us here is, what must Christians give up to be Christians? The deeper question that underlies the first concerns the nature of Christians' relationship to the social world around them. That relationship has always involved a tension between two strong impulses in Christian faith: (1) an impulse to separate ourselves from the rest of society—that is, from those outside our fellowship—on the basis of a pure obedience to Christ that excludes other obediences (see Luke 14:26); (2) an impulse of commitment and love toward the whole world, including human society, as God's beloved creation. The first moves us toward disconnection from the world, the second toward connection with it. Clearly the sayings here give expression to the first impulse. Nevertheless, can we read them in such a way as not to lose sight of the second, that is, not to let go of our love for the society from which we have separated ourselves?

Commentators on this passage have tended, if anything, to magnify its sense of separation from those who stand outside the fellowship of the

Pastoral Perspective

From beginning to end, Matthew's Gospel is a call to discipleship. Our brief passage makes clear what Dietrich Bonhoeffer names when he writes his great study *The Cost of Discipleship*. In this passage we get two vignettes about would-be disciples who, so far at least, are asking for discipleship but not bothering to count the cost.

The first would-be disciple is admirably eager but problematically ignorant: "Teacher, I will follow you wherever you go." The fact that this scribe calls Jesus "teacher" may indicate that he is not yet ready to be a disciple. If so, the second interlocutor has made some progress by his willingness to address Jesus as "Lord."

The scribe also reverses the usual order of discipleship in Matthew's Gospel. For Matthew, disciples are drawn by the call of Jesus; they are recruits rather than volunteers. In any case, it is clear that the scribe has not paid attention to the difficulties that the life of discipleship will entail: "Foxes have holes, and birds of the air have nests; but the Son of Man has nowhere to lay his head" (v. 20). The implication is clear; the servant is not greater than his master. If Jesus' faithfulness will require sacrifice and insecurity, so will the disciple's faithfulness.

What would make a person, like this scribe, willing to journey forward with no clue of what lies ahead? Our pastoral experience gives us some clues.

Exegetical Perspective

This is the first of three vignettes highlighting Jesus' authority, which calls for faith and commitment. The theme of discipleship is concretized by the journeying motif as Jesus leads his followers across the Sea of Galilee and back. The first incident occurs en route to the boat (8:18–22), the second over the water (8:23–27), and the third on the other side, after which Jesus returns to Galilee by crossing the lake again (8:28–9:1).

By this time in Matthew's narrative, Jesus has already called four disciples (4:18–22), but he has yet to name the Twelve (10:1–4). In chapter 8, the differentiation between people in the crowd and committed disciples is beginning to emerge. The verb to follow (*akoloutheō*) is used five times: first of the crowd in general (8:1, 10), then of two potential disciples (8:19, 22), and finally of a small group of disciples (8:23).

For Matthew, Jesus is in control. The author strengthens this impression by restating Jesus' words in Mark. Mark writes, "*Let us* go across to the other side" (Mark 4:35); Matthew writes, "[Jesus] *gave orders* to go over to the other side" (Matt. 8:18). The other side of the lake is the Gentile region of the Decapolis. The mention of a crossing to "the other side" anticipates the last vignette of the series of stories, which takes place across the lake (8:28–9:1).

Homiletical Perspective

Because these verses form the transitional section between accomplished words of wisdom spoken and approaching deeds of power anticipated, the first question that the preacher in today's interim period must ask him- or herself is, "How does one translate the gospel from a time so long ago to speak to the present circumstances of our lives?" The final editor of Matthew's Gospel had to ask himself the same question, even though he was closer to the original interlude portrayed. The situation in which that writer found himself differed from the circumstances of the first observers of Jesus' actions, but his goal was his Master's goal: to create a community of disciples. The words he chose to narrate the events of the past were intended to effect the same transformation of lives in his contemporary setting. Our task is the same: to create a community of disciples in a constantly changing world.

As preachers aim to interpret the worldview of the final, canonical document that we call the Gospel according to Matthew, at the same time being true to the original situation of the life we proclaim, we must first take into account the environment of the final redactor, before we begin to translate its meaning for today's listeners. Words take their meaning from other words, and contexts affect their interpretation. The fact that there are so many layers of

Matthew 8:18–22

Theological Perspective

disciples. Specifically, Christ has been pictured discouraging the outsider (the scribe, vv. 19–20) from joining, and admonishing the insider (the disciple, vv. 21–22) not to leave. In point of fact, Matthew says nothing about the scribe *except* that he was a scribe and that he desired to be a disciple.

Jerome (d. 420) framed the interchange between Christ and the scribe as a choice between the letter and the spirit, a contest between synagogue and church that dramatized Jewish rejection of the gospel. The scribe, says Jerome, did not recognize Christ's divinity, but rather saw him as only "a teacher, one among many"; had he instead addressed him as "Lord," he would have had a more inviting response. Moreover, the scribe "wanted to follow the savior in order to acquire a profit from the miraculous works. He was longing for the same thing that Simon Magus had also wanted to purchase from Peter."[1] Centuries later, John Calvin imagined the scribe as a man who believed that discipleship itself was reward enough and so inevitably stood outside the circle of true followers.

How much these commentators seem to know about this barely glimpsed scribe! The concern that underlies their imagining, at any rate, is to define what makes one an insider, thus also defining what makes one an outsider.

As for the saying addressed to the disciple—"let the dead bury their own dead" (v. 22)—commentators have typically rationalized it to make it more palatable, but here too the thrust is to clarify the distinction between the insider and the outsider. Ancient and medieval writers often took the noun "the dead" to mean, in the phrase of the eighth-century commentator Hrabanus Maurus, "whoever does not believe." This interpretation makes this a saying about the necessity for believers to separate themselves from nonbelievers.

Calvin later understood the saying similarly when he took it as hyperbole, as a way of underlining the importance of obedience over and against the example of those who "overlook God" and thus are "like dead folk." Again the central concern was to stake out the border between insiders and outsiders, between those who are committed Christians and those who are not.[2]

Of course that border is not unimportant, and the impulse to maintain the distinction between insider

1. Jerome, *Commentary on Matthew*, trans. T. Scheck (Washington, DC: Catholic University of America Press, 2008), 102.
2. Hrabanus Maurus, *Expositio in Matthaeum* (Turnhout: Brepols, 2000), 243; Calvin quoted on p. 255.

Pastoral Perspective

For one thing, the scribe probably has only a tiny glimmer of the level of commitment involved. Jesus makes clear that there is no rest for those who choose the life of discipleship, no juncture at which the disciple is allowed to say, "I am ready to turn back," or "I have had enough," or "Is it time to take a break?"

The tough word in this passage is that the disciple has to follow Jesus (the Son of Man). The comforting word in this passage is that, in deprivation as in triumph, Jesus leads the disciple on the way.

Perhaps there is a faint picture of the uncertainty of discipleship, the hazards of the journey of faith. Most of us know stories—or have lived through stories—of flights unexpectedly delayed, of a trip suddenly less comfortable than we had thought. During major storms television newscasts provide generous footage of travelers curled up with jackets or resting on luggage. They are awaiting word of when they will get home, while they remain at the mercy of the elements and the airlines.

Similarly, for both first-century disciples and twenty-first-century disciples, life is full of unexpected detours, demands, and delays. The disciple's agenda is always governed by the twofold command: "You shall love the Lord your God with all your heart, and with all your soul, and with all your mind. . . . You shall love your neighbor as yourself" (Matt. 22:37, 39). Sometimes the love of God sends us on braver journeys than we had imagined; often the love of the neighbor interrupts our careful agenda and our overly optimistic itinerary.

Too often as contemporary Christians we find our discipleship compromised by our goal-oriented culture and our goal-oriented personalities. Anyone who has gone on a long car trip with a child has heard the question, "Are we there yet?" Impatience causes joy to wither. We come to value outcomes and results so much that we undervalue the process, the journey. So either we fail to appreciate the tasks and gifts that come with discipleship, or we live with a kind of idolatrous devotion to delayed gratification: "When I get older, or when I get richer, or when I get married, or when I retire," then at last my life will be set right.

The wise pastor will find ways to assert the call of God in Jesus Christ in ways that make clear both its demand and its blessing. In sharing the administration of the church, in occasions of pastoral care and counseling, in times when the pastor leads prayer, he or she will want to affirm some version of the old saying: "I do not know exactly where I am going, but

Exegetical Perspective

Within this pericope, it provides an immediate opportunity for the two people who claim they want to follow Jesus to put their words into action. The implicit question is this: after knowing the costs and demands of discipleship, will they still follow Jesus to "the other side"?

Challenge to Radical Self-Denial. The first would-be disciple is a scribe. He approaches Jesus in the same way rabbinical students do when seeking out the rabbi under whom they want to study. Jesus' practice, however, is to recruit his own disciples (4:19, 21; 9:9). While nonbelievers and enemies are often shown to call Jesus "Teacher" in Matthew (12:38; 19:16; 22:16), there is no need to assume a hostile intent on the part of this man. By asking to follow Jesus, he shows a measure of goodwill. As a scribe, he already has had ample training, yet he finds something so compelling about Jesus—perhaps his teachings or his miracles (7:28)—that he wants to follow him *wherever* he goes (8:19).

Jesus' answer is a reality check for the scribe. It underscores not only the itinerant nature of Jesus' mission but also the prospect of rejection. Even birds and foxes fare better than he does in matters of shelter and security (cf. Ps. 84:3). Nests and lairs are home to these insignificant creatures, yet "the Son of Man has nowhere to lay his head" (8:20). While Jesus seems to have a home in Capernaum (Matt. 4:13; Mark 2:1), his itinerant lifestyle necessitates that he constantly depends on other people's hospitality, thereby creating a sense of homelessness. This indebtedness keeps him in a low status in a society governed by the values of honor and shame, patronage and reciprocity. Furthermore, homelessness also refers to a life of suffering and persecution, which in Jesus' case will culminate in death on a cross. Soon, in chapter 10, when Jesus sends his twelve disciples to preach the good news, they too will rely on other people's provision and encounter rejection along the way (10:16–42).

The second inquirer is already a disciple, since he addresses Jesus as "Lord" (cf. 8:2; 9:28; 15:22). The issue here is not whether he wants to become a follower, but the radical allegiance that Jesus demands of him, because the kingdom is near and time is short.

From the sound of the request, "First let me go and bury my father" (8:21), one may surmise that this disciple is male, perhaps even a firstborn son. When the father dies, ancient Jewish burial practices require that the family bury him the same day and

Homiletical Perspective

redaction evident in Matthew reminds us preachers that contexts serve as filters between writer(s) and readers, just as they do between preachers and hearers. Put another way, the world of a second-century Jewish Christian in Antioch not only looked different from the world of Jesus in his day, but also differs from the world of a twenty-first-century western European male or a black African woman standing on the same spot of land in Israel/Palestine today. What we comprehend is filtered and affected by the social arena in which we find ourselves.

As is evident in the verse that precedes this pericope (8:17), the writer is trying to preserve both the old and the new, both what he has inherited from Jewish tradition and what is being newly revealed. In this respect he has much in common with today's preacher: a person living with one foot firmly grounded in Scripture and the other poised to proclaim new birth for the emerging church. While the author stands firm in the belief that "this was to fulfill what had been spoken," he is also setting the stage for a new teaching by the Son of Man (v. 20), a title for Jesus that he uses here for the first of thirty times.

The Son of Man speaks this new teaching with authority. In Matthew, in contrast to the parallel account in the Gospel according to Mark, this Jesus gives orders (v. 18). What he proclaims is the theologically foundational story of the new church, a concept of discipleship that boldly acknowledges the cost of becoming a true disciple of Jesus' message. Expanding on his sources (Mark and the tradition known as *Quelle* or Q), the author clarifies and elaborates the meaning of discipleship with graphic antithetical parallelism: at the surface level, a Jewish scribe—the title given an opponent in this Gospel—makes what sounds like an overture to become one of this teacher's followers (v. 19). However, the true disciple addresses Jesus as "Lord" (v. 21). The scribe is, in a sense, asking permission to see the world in the way he has always seen it. Jesus says, in effect, "You do not choose the Way. I select my own followers and my own direction." The genuine disciple reverences this Son of Man whom he calls "Lord" and follows his orders, even when they defy conventional morality.

Whether or not this latter disciple was being asked to neglect familial duties to follow Jesus (v. 21) is not the point. Rather, the preacher's task is to ask in what regard we see God at work in the deeper questions of our own day. Just as the scribe is told that the old world is being replaced by the new, we are prodded by this passage to ask, What from the past is worth preserving? What is coming toward us

Matthew 8:18–22

Theological Perspective

and outsider is not to be denied, as though the faith made no basic difference in the life of believers. Perhaps, though, there is another way of reading these sayings that keeps them connected to that other impulse, love and commitment toward society itself. Francis of Assisi (d. 1226) provides a glimpse of such a reading. Francis separated himself from his social world by giving up possessions and social ties, yet simultaneously committed himself to the good of that social world through steadfast service. In one version of his Rule, he exhorted his friars to "let the dead bury their dead," as a provocative (if slightly imprecise) shorthand summary of the parable of the Sower, whereby the friars were to make themselves "good soil" for the "seed" of the gospel, rather than allow themselves to be the sort of persons who would let that seed fall on (i.e., be buried in) barren soil. For Francis, the saying therefore exhorts the reader to service, not separation.

Francis's early companions remembered how he would often also quote the saying, "Foxes have holes . . ." They associated this saying with his insistence that the cells in which he sometimes stayed not be called "his" cell, and that if this happened, he would afterward refuse to inhabit them. This was, they said, out of a concern to "safeguard poverty and humility,"[3] virtues that he saw not as ends in themselves, but rather as means by which to communicate the gospel to the society in which he lived. He cared deeply about how his actions would exemplify the gospel and affect the people who witnessed them. Though the refusal to have a "place to lay his head" set him decisively apart from his society, it actually expressed his love for that society. The impulse to disconnect oneself from others becomes, in this sense, a sign of that opposite impulse, the impulse to connect oneself to others.

JOHN W. COAKLEY

Pastoral Perspective

I am on my way." We want to affirm that we are on our way because Jesus has called us, and we want to affirm that Jesus goes with us on the way, all the way.

If we sometimes mar our discipleship by our obsession with goals, we sometimes try to evade discipleship by putting it off into the future; meanwhile, we think there are more important tasks to be done.

That is the situation of the disciple in the second vignette in our passage: "[Before I follow you,] Lord, first let me go and bury my father" (v. 21). Jesus' answer seems devoid of compassion: "Follow me, and let the dead bury their own dead." In Jesus' days as in ours, acknowledging the death of a loved one, especially a parent, claims precedence over everything else. Family members, friends, and coworkers are excused from work and school to attend memorial services. Police officers stop traffic for funeral processions. Jesus' acerbic tone seems out of place until we remember the depth and the exclusiveness of the demand to follow him. In the light of that primary allegiance, every other allegiance fades in importance; in the light of the relationship to him, every other relationship is relativized.

Still, amid all the uncertainties of discipleship comes reassurance, the promise of protection to those who join the Son of Man on his journey. The psalmist proclaims: "You who live in the shelter of the Most High, who abide in the shadow of the Almighty, will say to the LORD, 'My refuge and my fortress'" (Ps. 91:1–2a). Jesus himself vows to those who follow on his sometimes-wearying way: "Come to me, all you that are weary and are carrying heavy burdens, and I will give you rest" (Matt. 11:28).

ASHLEY COOK CLEERE

---

3. R. Armstrong et al., eds., *Francis of Assisi: Early Documents* (New York: New City Press, 1998–2001), I:80, II:59.

Exegetical Perspective

be in mourning at home for another six days. Then, after one year, the eldest son must return to his father's tomb, collect his bones, and rebury them in an ossuary. A proper burial epitomizes the children's obedience of the fifth commandment, to honor their father and mother (Exod. 20:12). The seriousness of this filial duty is well documented in the OT and in Jewish literature (Gen. 50:5–6; Tob. 4:3; 6:15; Sir. 38:19), so much so that the obligation to bury one's parent takes precedence even over the recital of the *Shema* and the Eighteen Benedictions (*b. Ber.* 31a).

While the disciple's request is legitimate, the word "first" in verse 21 is telling. It allows for possibilities ranging from a father who is near death to one who is still healthy but needs care in his old age. To fulfill the filial obligation to care for his father, including the burial requirements upon the latter's death, this disciple may take months or even years before he returns to follow Jesus.

At first glance, Jesus' response may seem odd and outrageous: "Follow me, and let the dead bury their own dead" (8:22). Does Jesus mean, "Let the spiritually dead bury their own spiritually dead," or "Let the spiritually dead bury their own physically dead"? Perhaps it is best not to split hairs, and let the idiom paint a general picture. Jesus is essentially saying, "Let these matters of familial obligation take care of themselves." Jesus is not against filial piety, for elsewhere he strongly advocates that one must honor one's parents (15:4; 19:19). Rather, following Jesus takes priority over even the most revered of human relationships. The "Lord-disciple" relationship demands an allegiance that is second only to that due God!

The readers are not privy to the outcome of these two encounters, yet Jesus' words provoke them to self-reflection. Is following Jesus worth all the risk and sacrifice? The answer lies in the identity and authority of Jesus, which will become clear in the next two stories.

DIANE G. CHEN

Homiletical Perspective

from the future that requires us to adapt? What is the theologically foundational story for the emerging church of the twenty-first century? What kind of community of disciples is God creating to address the questions of our time?

Two points in this passage are crystal clear: discipleship requires renunciation, and discipleship is costly. What are our communities of disciples being asked to renounce to meet the demands of today's world? The answers to that question will not be simple or easy, but this passage bids us ask that question every day. The needs of our world are no longer only occasionally broadcast. Layer upon layer of communications, like redaction, barrage us and threaten to overwhelm us—but no more than the threatening command of the Son of Man who has no place to lay his head. Dare we lay down our heads and ignore the desperate circumstances we know in pockets of poverty, environmental degradation, and spiritual anguish? The preservation of security—whether that security be physical, mental, or emotional satisfaction—is not the mission to which our Lord summons his disciples.

The preacher's task is to make that indictment clear. We are to stand on the boundary between our accustomed perceptions and those of a new world, to examine the ramifications of our lifestyle choices, and to ask about the impact they have on the very real needs of our brothers and sisters around the globe. Taking a stand on the issues of our day may involve risk; but Jesus, our judge, is challenging us to make a claim for his kingdom, now.

JUDITH M. MCDANIEL

Matthew 8:23–27

²³And when he got into the boat, his disciples followed him. ²⁴A windstorm arose on the sea, so great that the boat was being swamped by the waves; but he was asleep. ²⁵And they went and woke him up, saying, "Lord, save us! We are perishing!" ²⁶And he said to them, "Why are you afraid, you of little faith?" Then he got up and rebuked the winds and the sea; and there was a dead calm. ²⁷They were amazed, saying, "What sort of man is this, that even the winds and the sea obey him?"

Theological Perspective

For Matthew this is a story about faith, specifically faith as an existential condition rather than as a matter of chosen belief. We see this in the way he reworks Mark's version. In Mark, Christ awakens in the storm-tossed boat, immediately stills the winds and waves, and only then chides the disciples for having "still no faith" (Mark 4:40): the miracle stands therefore as a reason for having faith. It confronts them with the choice to believe.

In Matthew, Christ chides first, *before* he exercises his power ("why are you afraid, you of little faith?" v. 26a), and makes no comment afterward. The focus of the story has shifted from the action's consequence to its context, namely, the disciples' preexisting faith or lack of it. Faith here is an elemental attitude or disposition. It is more about what one brings to the moment of crisis or divine intervention, than about what one acquires from it.

To point out this notion of faith as an attitude or disposition is not to minimize the importance of that other notion of faith—the one in Mark's version—that makes it a response to divine power. The latter is to be found in stories throughout the Gospels and the Acts and in later accounts of rulers like Constantine and Clovis, who decided that the power of Christ exceeded that of other potential allies. It is a notion also embedded in many other conversion

Pastoral Perspective

It may seem unlikely that a discipline as recondite as redaction criticism might help us in seeing the pastoral implications of a text. However, in the case of Matthew 8:23–27, the study of the way in which Matthew as a redactor, or editor, uses his source can prove instructive as we seek to understand Matthew's particular perspective on this miraculous event.

The story on which Matthew bases his account is almost certainly found in Mark 4:35–41. In neither Mark's nor Matthew's version of this story do the disciples appear as paragons of faith, but there is a subtle difference between the two Gospels in the portrayal of those who are in the boat with Jesus.

The heart of the matter is summed up in the word that we think Matthew coined to describe the disciples, not only here but elsewhere in his Gospel: "You of little faith." In the Greek the accusatory description is all one noun: "You little-faiths!" (v. 26). What is striking is that Matthew is here softening Jesus' rebuke to the disciples in Mark's Gospel, where Jesus says instead, "Have you still no faith?" (Mark 4:40). For Mark the disciples have no faith at all. It seems as though in telling the story Mark wants to emphasize the disciples' fear, which implies a lack of faith. Matthew also wants us to notice that the disciples are able to cry out, "Lord, save us! We are perishing!"

Exegetical Perspective

The twin themes of Jesus' authority and discipleship continue in this pericope as the crowd is now left behind. A band of disciples accompanies Jesus, small enough for all to fit into one boat on the journey across the Sea of Galilee. By reworking the phrasing in Mark, "[The disciples] took him with them in the boat" (Mark 4:36), Matthew highlights Jesus' leadership: "When [Jesus] got into the boat, his disciples followed him" (Matt. 8:23). Having just overheard Jesus' answer to the scribe, that following Jesus would entail a life of insecurity (8:20), the disciples will soon receive an object lesson in a most dramatic and frightening way.

At 600 feet below sea level, the Sea of Galilee sits in a deep basin surrounded by ravine-marked hills. As strong winds rush down the gullies onto the surface of the lake, they intensify and generate sudden storms, often without warning. The size of these storms is substantial, judging from the fearful response of the disciples, among whom are seasoned fishermen like Simon, Andrew, James, and John. Matthew's description of the storm in verse 24 as a big earthquake (*seismos megas*) in the sea is apt; "the boat was being swamped by the waves" as though the seabed itself was shaking.

Because of their destructive potential to life and property, sea storms form a perfect metaphor in the

Homiletical Perspective

How does a preacher deal with miracles? One way is to ask what they represent. In this first in a series of three miracles, the author of Matthew is using a section of narrative inserted between sections of discourse to teach his own community the cost of discipleship. Most good preaching includes some teaching, and teaching normally involves logic. For example, a teacher can easily prove that if proposition A equals proposition B, and B equals C, then it follows that A equals C. This type of argument is rational, but the deliberative reflections of preachers with their listeners are not only rational. They are also reasonable. A reasonable argument is substantive, prudential, and practical; but its first principles or grounds are not self-evident, as are those of logic. They are temporal or circumstantial, generalized, and presumptive, because they are inferred from prior experience. As if recognizing that the difference between teaching and preaching is shared experience, Jesus now follows a lecture with a demonstration. Having just taught about discipleship, Jesus illustrates it symbolically by enacting a parable.

The crowd has been pressing, crushing in on him; so with his smaller group of disciples he gets into a boat to leave Capernaum and go to the other side of the lake. The lake is not named in the Gospel

Matthew 8:23–27

Theological Perspective

stories, ancient and modern, that hinge upon the power of God to rescue the potential believer from impending death or some other peril—an addiction, for instance. Such stories are not to be dismissed out of hand as though the conversions were somehow invalid.

However, we also find this other sensibility, this focus on faith as a disposition or orientation of the person, a notion that has had its own history in the Augustinian traditions of the West, where it underlies our modern idea of a "self" as a unique individual with an inner "landscape" of feeling. That perspective, though not properly understood as a biblical idea, finds a fertile response in this text nonetheless.

According to Matthew, the opposite, or foil, of faith is not *doubt* but rather *fear*—not the lack of belief per se, but the lack of a felt security. Faith is confidence in one's ultimate security, even in the face of events that call that security into question. Faith stands over against the fear that otherwise would be natural.

The problem here with the disciples' supposed faith is that what they actually display is fear, its very opposite. Since the disciples, after all, stand as the core of the church's tradition—apostolicity being its guarantee of authority—their lack of faith has worried readers of this story for centuries. The eighth-century monastic writer Hrabanus Maurus, for instance, gratuitously describes the disciples before the storm as "not feeble in their faith but rather firm and stable, being gentle and loyal men who were removing themselves from the world, not ambivalently but unreservedly." Hrabanus then says that Christ himself caused the storm to "put his disciples in fear, that they might ask his help and he might manifest his power."[1] In his reading, the event becomes a story of divine power and answered prayer, with the disciples playing a role otherwise out of character for them. The apparent cluelessness of the question in verse 27 ("What sort of man is this, that even winds and sea obey him?") has also weighed heavily on commentators, with many ancient and medieval writers denying that the disciples spoke those uncomprehending words, attributing them instead to other unidentified persons (perhaps sailors, says Jerome[2]).

Still, it is possible to take the disciples' fear seriously in its own right, as no mere expedient for

Pastoral Perspective

(v. 25). However, for Matthew, that cry implies at least the beginning of faith.

Much has been written about preaching to outsiders, those who are not part of the church or adherents to the Christian faith. We would do well to think about pastoral care for outsiders too. If a person is in trouble or is troubled, facing illness, or mourning loss, we do not begin with trying to find out whether that person is faithful enough to warrant God's care, Christ's kindness. Following Matthew, we learn that asking for help is the beginning of faith. Knowing that you want faith is a major step on the pilgrimage toward faith.

Whether in the traditional setting of the pastor's study, or at coffee hour, or after the annual choir concert, when someone says to the pastor, "I do not believe very much, but I need help," she believes more than she may know. She believes that her present distress is not the final word about her life, and she believes, most amazingly, that even the paid representative of the traditional church may have a word to say. Little faith is probably not finally enough faith, but it is almost always enough faith for *now*. Even that sometimes-annoying moment—when the person next to you on the airplane or the train or the bus notices that you are reading a book about religion and says, "I have never been much of a believer, but I have wondered . . ."—may be the moment when your attentive listening or your wise counsel can help the little-faith person touch the great faithfulness of Jesus.

Notice too that at the end of the story Matthew presents the punch line somewhat differently from Mark. In Mark, the disciples ask, "Who then is this, that even the wind and the sea obey him?" (Mark 4:41). In Matthew, they ask it slightly differently: "What sort of man is this, that even the winds and the sea obey him?" (8:27). Matthew writes his whole Gospel to tell his readers then and now what sort of man Jesus is. If people did not care, they would not ask. If they ask, they care: little faith on the way to becoming more.

Our passage also gives us some insight into the shape and the efficacy of prayer. Many of us spent long hours in seminary classes or drinking coffee with our friends pondering what counts as appropriate prayer. Should we really ask God to mess with the laws of nature? Probably for most of us the danger is not from a storm at sea but from more mundane storms: illness, the loss of a job, a sadness that simply never lifts. Illness has to do with the natural condition of our bodies and the drive of bacteria

---

1. Hrabanus Maurus, *Expositio in Mattheum* (Turnhout: Brepols, 2000), 246.
2. Jerome, *Commentary on Matthew*, trans. T. Scheck (Washington: Catholic University of America Press, 2008), 103.

minds of ancient people for chaos and evil (e.g., Ps. 69:2, 14–15). Since YHWH is the creator of all winds and waves, the divine power to control storms and subdue these dangerous natural forces is symbolic of God's saving grace (Pss. 65:7; 89:9; 106:8–9; 107:23–29). The disciples have yet to fathom how Jesus, a fellow human being whom they call Lord and rabbi, can manifest the same authoritative power as YHWH over the raging waters. They venture beyond their normal categories and ask, "Who sort of *man* is this, that even the winds and the sea obey him?" (v. 27).

Something Greater than Jonah. It is difficult to escape the comparison and contrast between this storm and the storm Jonah encounters on his way to Tarshish (Jonah 1). A fierce storm that can sink the boat rages in both incidents; Jesus and Jonah are both asleep in the boat while everyone else is terrified; and both of them are instrumental in causing the storm to cease.

The differences, however, are significant. Jonah sleeps, perhaps because he has worn himself out from running away from God. Jesus' sleep may be indicative of his trust in God's protection (Ps. 4:8; Prov. 3:23–26). The verb to sleep (*katheudō*) is in the imperfect tense, so not only has Jesus fallen asleep, he continues to sleep. Matthew deftly omits Mark's detail that Jesus is sleeping "on a cushion," to remind the reader that "the Son of Man has nowhere to lay his head" (Mark 4:38; Matt. 8:20).

Unlike Jonah, who ends up being thrown overboard for the storm to subside, Jesus rebukes the winds and the waves (v. 26). Later on in the narrative he also rebukes a demon (17:18). Indeed, someone greater than Jonah is here (12:41), someone far more authoritative, whose power is on par with that of God, the creator who commands heaven and earth, winds and seas!

From Fear to Faith. Again, omitting the complaint that the Markan disciples launch at Jesus, "Teacher, do you not care that we are perishing?" (4:38), Matthew gets to the heart of the matter. Three Greek words convey the urgency of the situation: "Lord, save us! We are perishing!" (*kyrie, sōson, apollymetha*, v. 25). They are desperate. There is no time for more words.

Despite their fear, the disciples know exactly to whom to turn for salvation. Inherent in their declaration of Jesus as "Lord" is the trust that he is also "Savior." Later on, Peter will encounter a similar situation where he falters in the midst of trying to walk

according to Matthew, suggesting that it is a representative body of water, perhaps symbolizing life itself.

We think we know water. Like those among the disciples who were fishermen, we use the sea for our own purposes. We chart its tides. We know how to exploit its bounty, and we approach much of the rest of our life in the same way. We deal with daily tasks. We chart our goals. We manage our resources carefully, until something interrupts us: Our employer lays off thousands of workers, and we lose our job. A significant relationship deteriorates and is broken. We are confronted with serious illness. The necessary losses of age force us to face our own death. In all of these events, when compelled to reimagine, reconfigure, or even redesign our lives, like Jonah we resist.

Although we may be challenged or may feel threatened by the prospect of discerning new directions, Christian self-understanding is enlightened by being tested in different contexts. Jesus seems intentionally to place his disciples in new contexts to expand their understanding of discipleship. They know the sea, but they do not know it from the perspective they are about to encounter.

Because of our own experiences with water, we know instinctively that the sea is symbolic of power. Sailing on the impressive expanse of what is known today as the Sea of Galilee can be serenely calming; but when a strong wind comes up, its waters can be terrifying. The verbal and structural parallels to the story of Jonah in Matthew's redaction are noticeable: a great storm, seismic in proportion, comes upon the sea. Is this storm meant to draw a comparison between the chaos present at creation or the floods of the Old Testament and the disciples' present experience? In any case, destruction seems imminent. The boat is not simply filling with water; it is swamped and threatening to break up. While all this is happening, the protagonist is asleep; but in this case, he is not sacrificed to the sea to save the rest of the crew. Rather, Jesus is greater than Jonah. Jesus commands the wind and the sea. Before he demonstrates his power over evil, he responds to a petition that recognizes his authority. More than a request of a teacher, or even a master, this is an anguished appeal for a savior: "Lord, save, us!" cry his followers; and he does.

This first miracle in a succession of three on the sea, or along the seashore, illustrates what it means to follow Jesus. In creating a community of disciples, Jesus calls upon his followers to renounce old ways of looking at the world and risk a new direction, exercising the faith they already have in order to

Theological Perspective

framing the miracle, but rather as an experience that somehow coexists with faith. A classic attempt at such a reading is demonstrated by John Calvin, who famously defined faith as "a firm and certain knowledge of God's benevolence toward us," yet recognized the persistence of fear in the hearts of believers and struggled to explain how this could be so without compromising faith's firmness and certainty. In reading this passage, he comments, "If we fear nothing, the idle apathy of the flesh is creeping in, then faith languishes, the mood for prayer turns drowsy and at last the very thought of God is extinguished." In other words, a little fear may be a good thing. The implied metaphor is quantitative; the danger would be to have *too much* fear, and thus *too* "*little* faith" (v. 26), of which the warning sign would be a loss of "tranquility."[3] One wonders whether, even on Calvin's own terms, a quantitative metaphor is adequate. Fear would seem by definition to upset tranquility, and conversely tranquility to rule out fear, and so both resist being thought of in complementary quantities. The implied problem anticipates the question that later preoccupied the Puritans: "*do* I have faith?"—a question that often has led precisely to *uncertainty*.

"Firm and certain knowledge of God's benevolence toward us" tends to elude us when we try to perceive it directly, like the blind spot on the retina, but this fact does not remove it from our interior landscape. Here, ironically, the absence of a modern notion of the self as a unique individual gives the text a certain power for those of us who simply assume it. Matthew does not try to sort out faith and fear, but leaves them together, which is, I suspect, how we, in our no doubt unique ways, tend to experience both.

JOHN W. COAKLEY

Pastoral Perspective

to flourish. Job loss has to do with the somewhat unpredictable variations of an economy beyond our control. Depression has to do with genetic proclivities and immovable difficulties. In such situations, are we right to pray?

Matthew's text suggests that Christ is far less concerned with the propriety of our prayers than we are. Even in Mark, Jesus may rebuke the disciples for their lack of faith, but he does calm the storm. In Matthew, a little faith and a great deal of grace make even seas and winds obey Christ's strong voice. Scholars who study the biblical examples of lament remind us that the heartfelt cry—"Lord, save us! We are perishing!" (v. 25)—may be the most honest and therefore the deepest prayer. How many of our prayers, individually or before our congregation, seek to protect God? When it comes to prayer, we are so wary of the prosperity gospel that we sometimes slight the powerful gospel.

A pastor friend visited a terminally ill parishioner in a hospital and sought to pray carefully and cautiously: "Grant comfort and strength to our brother as he lies here in his illness. Help him to know the kindness of your love." When she was about to leave, the patient said, "Will you please just pray for God to make me well?" The pastor did not know whether God would answer that prayer as the patient wished. The patient knew the pastor did not know. The question was, would their prayer be honest, and would they trust God to be God? Lack of faith or little faith, we are still invited to pray and to help our people pray, "Lord, save us! We are perishing!"

DAVID L. BARTLETT

---

3. John Calvin, *Institutes of the Christian Religion*, trans. F. Battles (Philadelphia: Westminster Press, 1960), 551; John Calvin, *A Harmony of the Gospels Matthew, Mark and Luke*, vol. 1, trans. A. Morrison (Grand Rapids: Eerdmans, 1972), 281.

Exegetical Perspective

on water. There he again cries out, "Lord, save me!" (*kyrie, sōson me*, 14:30). In both incidents, deliverance from drowning is but the beginning of a much greater salvation through Jesus, that is, salvation from eternal destruction.

While the Markan Jesus first calms the storm and only afterwards chides his disciples, "Why are you afraid? Have you still no faith?" (Mark 4:40), Matthew reverses the order and brings the issue of faith to the fore, even before Jesus rebukes the storm: "Why are you afraid, you of little faith?" (v. 26). In Matthew Jesus gives the disciples credit for having at least *some* measure of faith, albeit insufficient and in need of strengthening. In Mark, they are reprimanded for *still* having no faith, implying an expectation that they should have fared much better.

Throughout the Gospel of Matthew, every time Jesus identifies an individual or a group of persons as having little faith, he is referring to his disciples (6:30; 8:26; 14:31; 16:8; 17:20). By contrast, Gentiles and outcasts are commended for having faith: a centurion (8:10, 13), the friends of a paralytic (9:2), a woman suffering from a flow of blood (9:22), two blind men (9:29), and a Canaanite woman (15:28). While this does not mean that Jesus' own disciples will never have the same kind of faith as these supposed "nobodies," the contrast underscores that faith in Jesus transcends alleged social and religious qualifications.

Strong and true faith, in whatever measure it is needed, must be grounded in Jesus' identity as "Lord" and "Savior." In the OT, these titles are attributed to God. The disciples' question, "What sort of man is this, that even the winds and the sea obey him?" (v. 27), on the one hand expresses their bafflement, and on the other hand declares the status of Jesus as God's agent, himself a man, yet possessing God's power over nature. That life-threatening storm is actually an opportunity for the disciples to experience a theophany. Because they know to cry out to Jesus for salvation, they also experience what Jesus can do for them, both now and for eternity.

DIANE G. CHEN

Homiletical Perspective

grow. What happens? At first they appear to founder. Then, when they call out for help, they are set free from themselves to cooperate with Jesus. Their perspective on reality changes.

"What sort of man is this, that even winds and sea obey him?" they ask themselves. From what context does he come? Into what context will he thrust us? This cosmic upheaval is making a theological point about God's world, a world that differs markedly from our own. The author of Matthew is in the process of constructing a new community, laying the foundation of a new church based on God's coming kingdom. Then what is coming happens: God's future arrives in the present. Jesus, the end in person, strides into the picture; and everything is changed. The future and the present are one.

God made heaven and earth; and at the last God will remake them both and join them together forever—a "new Jerusalem coming down from heaven to earth, uniting the two in a lasting embrace."[1] For God loves the world God created and the people who have inhabited and will inhabit it, and in the end God will perfect them. Just as we pray in the Lord's Prayer—thy will be done on earth, as it is in heaven—so it will be. For heaven and earth are made for each other, and at certain points they intersect and interlock. Heaven is not a future destiny but the other, hidden dimension of our ordinary life: God's dimension and our miracle on which to take a stand.

This teaching on discipleship began with Jesus setting the direction and his disciples then following. Like them, we will not understand the risks and the blessings of discipleship by means of logic. Instead, we will look back at shared experience and recognize that grace was at work and can be trusted to take us through the future to our destination.

JUDITH M. MCDANIEL

---

1. N. T. Wright, *Surprised by Hope: Rethinking Heaven, the Resurrection, and the Mission of the Church* (New York: Harper One, 2008), 19.

Matthew 8:28–9:1

²⁸When he came to the other side, to the country of the Gadarenes, two demoniacs coming out of the tombs met him. They were so fierce that no one could pass that way. ²⁹Suddenly they shouted, "What have you to do with us, Son of God? Have you come here to torment us before the time?" ³⁰Now a large herd of swine was feeding at some distance from them. ³¹The demons begged him, "If you cast us out, send us into the herd of swine." ³²And he said to them, "Go!" So they came out and entered the swine; and suddenly, the whole herd rushed down the steep bank into the sea and perished in the water. ³³The swineherds ran off, and on going into the town, they told the whole story about what had happened to the demoniacs. ³⁴Then the whole town came out to meet Jesus; and when they saw him, they begged him to leave their neighborhood.
^{9:1}And after getting into a boat he crossed the sea and came to his own town.

Theological Perspective

Mark framed this exorcism account as a story about the faith of the possessed man, beginning with the details of his original condition and ending with his request to become Christ's disciple. Matthew removes that frame, and by adding a second possessed man to share the stage with the first one, he makes it even clearer that this is now *not* the story of a central character undergoing personal change through an encounter with Christ. Although the theme of how people respond to Christ does make an appearance at the end of the story, in the townspeople's plea to be left alone, Matthew's main focus is on the relationship between Christ and the demons themselves—and hence (so I suggest we read Matthew) on the relation between the power of God and the power of evil.

A word first about the townspeople's rejection of Christ: commentators have often read the whole story through the lens of that event, as a story about who will accept the gospel and who will not. For Hilary of Poitiers (d. 367/8), the townspeople signify the Jews, and the boat in which Christ then sailed off, leaving them behind, signifies the church. Just so then, the two demoniacs, who have been excluded by the townspeople (and thus are "outside the synagogue of the law and prophets") stand for the Gentiles (descendants of Ham and Japheth), whose

Pastoral Perspective

One could use a colorful array of adjectives to describe this scene in Matthew in which Jesus performs an exorcism that results in demons drowning in the Sea of Galilee with a herd of wild pigs. One could call the passage unfathomable, incredible, bizarre, fantastic, magical, imaginative, unimaginable, amusing, amazing, alarming, odd. Just as odd as the miracle is the reaction of the townspeople. When Jesus graciously protects the town from the threatening behavior of two demoniacs, the residents implore him to get out of town.

As pastors we wonder, why are the villagers so displeased with Jesus? While we do not talk much about demon possession or exorcism in most of our mainline churches, many of us know people whose psyche is so beyond their own control that we might almost say demons have them in thrall. Too many bad habits and destructive addictions take up housekeeping in people's formerly contented lives. Think what an addiction to gossip or gambling or smoking can do to the well-being of people entrusted to our care. Credit cards that look as if they might solve our financial problems end up only exacerbating them. Some of us hoard papers and some of us hoard grudges. Social networks that are supposed to enhance relationships become substitutes for real and fragile friendship.

Feasting on the Gospels

Exegetical Perspective

The exact location of this incident is debated. Between Mark's "Gerasenes" (Mark 5:1), Matthew's "Gadarenes" (Matt. 8:28), and other textual variants, proposals include Gadara, Gerasa, and Gergasa. Each suggestion has its merit, whether in terms of place name, location, or geographical feature, but none provides a perfect match for the scene described: a lakeside town with tombs and cliffs. The ambiguity remains, but the point is not lost: Jesus leads his disciples across the lake to the predominantly Gentile Decapolis, a region marked by its unclean places (tombs), unclean practices (herding swine), and unclean spirits (demoniacs).

The Hierarchy of Powers. In the ancient world, spiritual forces, whether good or evil, were thought to be more powerful than human beings. When evil spirits were suspected of taking up residence in people, they were thought to cause the victims to behave violently, threatening both their own well-being and that of their community. Peace and restoration were considered possible only when the evil spirits were expelled from the hosts by a more powerful force.

In this story, the hierarchy of powers is evident. The demons control the two men, causing them to be a menace to the community. They are "so fierce that no one could pass that way" (v. 28). Nevertheless these

Homiletical Perspective

There are at least three directions a preacher might take in interpreting the story of the Gadarene demoniacs, all of which overlap to some extent. First is the more straightforward approach, which examines the events in the passage in light of the literary context in which they are found. For example, in this second in a series of three miracles, Jesus is teaching about discipleship. Formerly, he has healed by words; now he heals by deeds. The implication is that if his disciples are faithful, they will be able to do likewise. Matthew's recounting of this miracle condenses Mark's account in order to focus the reader's attention on Jesus, emphasize his authority, and underscore Jesus' teaching on discipleship.

Jesus has led his disciples through a storm into Gentile country. While the other Synoptic Gospels tell of one demoniac coming from among the tombs, in Matthew's version there are two demoniacs. As this author has done in other stories—the healing of two blind men rather than one; the triumphal entry into Jerusalem on both an ass and a colt, the foal of an ass—he doubles the supernumeraries for effect: Jesus is the teacher and healer whom none can surpass.

Further comparisons with the other two Synoptic Gospels are beneficial: "What have you to do with me/us?" cry the possessed, recognizing his power

Theological Perspective

freeing from the demons signifies their conversion, while the newly possessed pigs represent that fresh group of outsiders, the heretics (of whom Hilary was a notable enemy). For the eighth-century Frankish monk Hrabanus Maurus, however, the townspeople represent not Jews but Gentiles, whose desire for Jesus' departure comes "not from pride, as many judge, but from humility," since they (perhaps like the ostensibly Christian common people of Hrabanus's time and place) "reckon themselves unworthy" of holiness when they encounter it. In yet another interpretation, John Calvin saw the townspeople rather as individuals than as a group—as the quintessential persons who lack faith, like some of those who heard the preaching of the Reformers in his own time but were "touched with no sense of the divine grace." All of these classic interpretations, for all their differences, in effect read the story backward and find the meaning of the exorcism through the ending, which serves then as the catalyst for sorting out responses to the gospel.[1]

If we instead read the story *forward*—that is, not using the ending as our interpretive lens for what comes before—Christ's encounter with the demons itself, rather than people's acceptance or rejection of him, becomes the focal point of the story. The key to that encounter is the demons' cry of recognition—"Have you come here to torment us before the time?"—by which they acknowledge Christ's power over them, even as they challenge its present scope on the grounds that his final victory has not yet come (and presumably will not come until the Last Judgment). This turns out to mean that Christ can *displace* them but cannot, or rather will not, *expel* them yet from the world; indeed he obliges their wishes (!) by sending them into the herd of pigs, where they continue their evildoing. So the paradox is that evil is both subject to God and permitted by God. Here, as throughout the Scriptures, evil does not appear as a power of its own, as though it could stand against God, but neither does it disappear.

The venerable tradition of Christian literature about demons, from New Testament times to the present, has always had as its great theme this simultaneous subjugation and persistence of evil. Athanasius of Alexandria (d. 373) gave it classic expression in his account of a speech about demons by the desert father Anthony of Egypt (d. 356). Demons were

---

1. Hilary of Poitiers, *Sur Matthieu* (Paris: Edition du Cerf, 1978), 1:197–99; Hrabanus Maurus, *Expositio in Matthaeum* (Turnhout: Brepols, 2000), 255; John Calvin, *A Harmony of the Gospels Matthew, Mark and Luke*, trans. A. Morrison (Grand Rapids: Eerdmans, 1972), 1:287.

Pastoral Perspective

Even people who acknowledge the harmfulness of such habits may be loathe to give them up because we are so identified with the addictions that drive us. A friend finally giving up smoking said of herself: "Now I finally know who I am; I am someone who smokes." She found a new identity free of nicotine, but not without a major reframing of her sense of herself. Those of us who love dessert may find not only pleasure but a kind of identity as chocoholics, and those of us who delight in living somewhat upscale have a hard time downscaling when our debts demand frugality.

Imagine the well-meaning family member who decides to clear out the crowded closets of a loved one. What seems like thoughtfulness on the part of the organizer can seem like inexcusable interference to the person who has saved all this stuff for all these years.

Sometimes racism and sexism are so embedded in our sense of humor that when we are called to account for our prejudices, we fear that we might lose our (entirely imaginary) charm. All of us are like the demoniacs, who are not only being destroyed but who know they are being destroyed and still cannot let go.

Congregations also have difficulty letting go of practices that stand in the way of their progress. During a Sunday service, established congregants rise to sing the Doxology or sit to recite the Lord's Prayer, not noticing that visitors know neither the proper posture nor the "familiar" words. If you do not know the Lord's Prayer and are handed a bulletin that simply says ("debts") at that point in the service, what clue have you about how to proceed?

What about the way in which our identity as church officers may so thoroughly shape who we are that we cannot imagine *not* being the head usher, or the treasurer, or the alto soloist?

The scandals of sexual abuse in Catholic and Protestant churches alike carry some of the danger signs of the demonic. Like the demoniacs of Jesus' time, church leaders of our time rush to defend our institution against the threat of publicity and—oddly enough—against the threat of justice and healing. We just wish it would all go away (as the demoniacs wished Jesus would just go away).

Sometimes it is not just the power of habit or resistance to change; sometimes we are kept in the thrall of our demons by the realization that healing demands too much effort or too much sacrifice. Astonishingly, though, in our passage it is not finally the effort of the demoniacs that is portrayed or even demanded. It is the word, the command of Jesus,

ferocious demons are no match against Jesus and will soon be reduced to begging for survival (v. 31).

Compared to Mark's rendering of the same incident (Mark 5:1–21), Matthew's account seems sparse. Less, however, is more. By omitting details that take the spotlight away from Jesus, Matthew sharpens the depiction of Jesus' superiority in this power struggle. For example, in Matthew the description of the men's madness is less elaborate, the verbal exchange between Jesus and the demons is minimal, and the number of demons ("Legion") is not mentioned. Also missing is Mark's reporting that the restored man wants to be with Jesus but is told to return to his own people instead.

The only addition that Matthew makes to Mark's account is his doubling of the demoniac from one man to two men. This is a distinctively Matthean literary feature. In another healing miracle Matthew presents two blind men instead of the one found in Mark (Matt. 20:30; Mark 10:46). Doubling the demoniacs may serve to compensate for Matthew's exclusion of Mark's first exorcism story (Mark 1:23–27). It may also represent Matthew's way of strengthening the credibility of the Gospel's witness about Jesus, since two witnesses are required in the Jewish court of law for testimonies to be valid (18:16; 26:60). Overall, in his redaction of Mark's account, Matthew keeps in clear focus the power of Jesus over the evil spirits. This is but the first of five specific exorcisms that the author has included in his narrative (see also 9:32–33; 12:22; 15:21–28; 17:14–18; and the summary statements in 4:24; 8:16).

"What Sort of Man Is This?" At the end of the previous story, the disciples ask, "What sort of man is this, that even the winds and the sea obey him?" (8:27). The correct answer is given here, ironically, by evil spirits speaking through two demon-possessed men. They address Jesus by his rightful title: "Son of God" (v. 29b). Even though the demons oppose God's purposes by torturing these men and their community, they can neither deny the true status of Jesus nor overcome the power differential between Jesus and themselves.

At first the demons are defiant. The demoniacs come out of the tomb to challenge Jesus, "What have you to do with us?" (v. 29a). This is a common idiom that signifies distancing, as if to say, "What do you want from us? We have nothing to do with you" (cf. 2 Sam. 19:22; 1 Kgs. 17:18; 2 Kgs. 3:13).

The second question betrays the demons' recognition of Jesus' superiority: "Have you come here to

and naming Jesus Son of God. Again, in all three Synoptics, the demons beg Jesus to send them into the (unclean to Jews) swine. Jesus does so, and they rush down a steep bank into the sea and perish. The herdsmen then flee to the city and tell what happened, whereupon the people of the city come out to see and beg Jesus to leave their neighborhood. These parallels to Mark and Luke highlight what the author of Matthew considers most important: demons recognize Jesus' power. Do his disciples? Do we? Here the preacher has an opportunity to speak of Jesus as the one who leads his followers through hostile territory and commands evil when he confronts it. All he has to do to take control is to say, "Go!" "Go!" is what he says to powers and principalities, to his disciples, and to us. Though we may encounter hunger, thirst, sickness, and imprisonment[1] of various kinds, he bids us to follow him into his kingdom with strengthened faith because of what we have seen.

A second approach to the passage focuses on what the author of Matthew may be telling us about his church, a new community of Jewish Christians that is open to a mission of evangelism to Gentiles. While Matthew's developing church exhibits both a negative attitude toward the rabbinical Judaism that is in the process of being formed and an especially combative mien in confronting the descendants of scribes and Pharisees, it still hopes for the repentance and salvation of Israel.

Observant of the law of Moses, Matthew's church had a special interest in the fulfillment of Old Testament prophecy and the book of Isaiah in particular. This first sign of triumph over all the powers of evil is reminiscent of Moses' leading the people of Israel through the Red Sea to safety as the Egyptian armies perished behind them in the waters of that same sea. Here is the one longed for through centuries of domination by foreign powers, destruction, and exile. However, the dominion from which God's people are being released is deeper and more lasting than that of mere mortals. This new Moses not only heals the sick; he banishes the hegemony of Satan in death itself.

A third approach to the passage considers the symbolic actions that it foregrounds. Whether or not one interprets what happened in the land of Gadara/Gerasa/Gergesa/Chorsia literally, the story points to truths that are deeper than a surface reading of the story allows. Having come to the other side, a symbolic transit to a symbolic locale, Jesus encounters

1. Matt. 25:31–46.

Matthew 8:28–9:1

Theological Perspective

created good, but "fell from heavenly wisdom" and now, with the Creator's permission, their job is to tempt us to sin. However, they have no real power; it is only our weakness and failure that gives them success. Our best lines of defense are to practice prayer and self-denial, and to call the demons' bluff, confronting them with their powerlessness. We must learn, Anthony says, to sense their presence in our emotions (fear being one indication) and to identify the differences among them and the variety of their strategies against us, such as appearing in various forms and inserting evil thoughts in our heads.[2] The fact that they embody evil in multiplicity allows us the possibility of separating, classifying, and ranking the manifestations of evil in order to subdue them more effectively.

The rest of the Christian tradition of demon stories ultimately makes the same point: that if we divide the war against evil into many battles, all are winnable, even though, as in Matthew's narrative, the enemy will persist and the war will continue. Over time, this body of insight has not been limited to the sphere of individual spirituality. For the "powers" evident in our social, economic, and political lives—the structures that oppress—may be successfully confronted but still retain great demonic potential; the message of Matthew's story applies.[3] To speak of demons is to speak of the encounter with evil—wherever we experience it—in practical and hopeful terms, yet with wariness and a fundamental conviction of its reality and persistence.

If then we read this story as a demon story, a story about God and evil, what do we say about the townspeople? Well, perhaps they are just townspeople, reasonably wanting to avoid losing any more pigs.

JOHN W. COAKLEY

Pastoral Perspective

that brings healing. "Go!" he says, and the demons go. The effort required is finally the effort of acquiescence; the work demanded is really not a work at all—it is the gift of trust.

The pigs rushing into the sea mirror the demons rushing through the souls of the possessed; and then they are destroyed. One little word shall fell them. Gentle Jesus meek and mild can turn quite fierce when confronted by the destructive powers of old habits and frightful addictions. Pastors need to know that, and cling to him and count on him. Certainly we turn to books and therapists and support groups, but we turn to Jesus too.

Of course this summary eviction is not what the townspeople had in mind. Jesus rearranged their world and did so at the behest of two demoniacs, rather than at the invitation of the upstanding citizens. They protest—as we often protest—because health can be more frightening than sickness, and liberation threatens the fragile truce required by every status quo.

Therapists tell us that families build family systems around the idiosyncrasies and even the illnesses of the members who seem most "possessed." The recovering alcoholic threatens to do in the whole system that has been built around his alcoholism. Social workers warn those escaping addiction that sometimes they should not go home again, because home is structured around the very habits that will destroy them. If we find a way out of our hypochondria, we can offend all those friends and family who are so devoted to being devoted. Healing always hurts, and it hurts not only the most obvious victim.

We are struck again by how much we humans cling to what can only harm us. We are struck again by how much we cling to what is harming the people we love. We are struck again by how much the power of Christ can heal.

ASHLEY COOK CLEERE

2. Athanasius of Alexandria, *Life of Anthony*, trans. R. Gregg (Mahwah, NJ: Paulist Press, 1980), 43–64.
3. Walter Wink, *Naming the Powers* (Philadelphia: Fortress Press, 1984).

torment us before the time?" (v. 29c). According to Jewish thought, demons expect their powers to cease at the end of time (1 En. 15:8–16:1; Jub. 10:5–11), but since the eschatological judgment has yet to come, they are complaining that Jesus has appeared too early to effect their demise.

The demons also know their protest is futile. As a last resort to avoid annihilation, they change their tone and beg for time, "If you cast us out, send us into the herd of swine" (v. 31). It is not a matter of "if" but "when." *When* Jesus casts them out from the men, they will need a replacement host (cf. 12:43–45).

To the Jews, unclean pigs were a natural abode for unclean spirits (Lev. 11:7; Deut. 14:8). Even so, the text does not satisfy our curiosities: Why the pigs? Is it because they happen to be there? Why does Jesus give consent? What are the moral and economic implications of destroying a large herd of swine that does not belong to him in the first place?

Matthew's account resists such distractions and keeps the focus squarely on Jesus' power. The Son of God speaks one authoritative word, "Go!" (v. 32), and the demons go. Their destructive power is immediately transferred from one host to another, for the entire herd of swine then plunges over the cliff to its death. Whether the demons are destroyed with the pigs is not clear, but there is no doubt that the two men are no longer possessed.

Recalling the disciples' frantic cry for help in the storm, "Lord, save us! We are perishing!" (8:25), these two men are also saved from perishing by Jesus, the Son of God, who demonstrates his power not only over nature but also over demonic forces. Sadly, the local people misinterpret Jesus' action. Perhaps they view him as a magician who can bring more harm than good. Like the demons begging to go into the pigs, they also beg Jesus to leave. So Jesus gets into the boat, crosses the lake again, and returns to Capernaum (9:1).

This story concludes the series of pericopes on the theme of discipleship, appropriately captured in Jesus' leading his followers across the lake and back (8:18–9:1). While the disciples encounter life-threatening danger and rejection, they also witness Jesus' supernatural authority. As the identity of Jesus is progressively revealed, will the disciples, and the readers, remain faithful to the one they call "Lord"?

DIANE G. CHEN

evil that is fierce as death: two men possessed by demons come "out of the tombs" (v. 28). *Out of the tombs*: is this image a precursor of what is to come? Could it be said that this episode presages Jesus' resurrection and our deliverance from sin and death?

What does it mean that the powers of death recognize him? Power knows power. Power senses the authority of another power, who confronts the power of evil and death without hesitation. The demons, the spiritual forces of evil, know power and sense it in the one who meets them. Moreover, the people of the city, when told the results of this confrontation, understand such power and fear rather than embrace it.

Here the author of Matthew, as he so often does, employs allusions to Isaiah. This passage echoes Isaiah 65:1–5, in which God extends himself to a faithless nation "who sit inside tombs, and spend the night in secret places; who eat swine's flesh" (Isa. 65:4). What are the tombs in which we sit, our secret hiding places, where we feed ourselves with practices that do not nourish? The term "herd," *agelē*, used only here and in the Synoptic parallels, commonly refers to livestock rather than pigs. "Herds" is used when referring to animals of one kind that are kept under control or to indistinguishable masses of people.

A herd mentality is one in which individuals are driven by outside forces rather than inner conviction. A person with a herd mentality might be said to be spiritually dead. Inner conviction characterizes the motivation of those who follow Jesus. They affirm their religious identity by abandoning the security of their comfortable hiding places; they exercise the faith they have to renounce the spiritual forces of wickedness that rebel against God, the evil powers of this world that corrupt and destroy the creatures of God. They do so empowered by the one who saves.

JUDITH M. MCDANIEL

Matthew 9:2–8

²And just then some people were carrying a paralyzed man lying on a bed. When Jesus saw their faith, he said to the paralytic, "Take heart, son; your sins are forgiven." ³Then some of the scribes said to themselves, "This man is blaspheming." ⁴But Jesus, perceiving their thoughts, said, "Why do you think evil in your hearts? ⁵For which is easier, to say, 'Your sins are forgiven,' or to say, 'Stand up and walk'? ⁶But so that you may know that the Son of Man has authority on earth to forgive sins"—he then said to the paralytic—"Stand up, take your bed and go to your home." ⁷And he stood up and went to his home. ⁸When the crowds saw it, they were filled with awe, and they glorified God, who had given such authority to human beings.

Theological Perspective

Matthew's story of the healing of the paralytic is preceded by numerous stories demonstrating Jesus' authority to heal, to teach, to calm the forces of nature, and to expel demons. Over and over again, people expressed awe at the authority with which he spoke and acted, an authority that they recognized as "not like that of the scribes." In Matthew 9:2–8, Jesus reveals the divine origin of his authority in the radical act of forgiving sin. He responds to the scribes' silent judgment by physically healing the paralytic, thus inspiring the crowds to glorify God, "who had given such authority to human beings" (v. 8). This story also reveals the power of faith *and* sin as communal realities. It demonstrates both the real power of evil and sin to thwart human life and freedom, and the real authority given human beings of faith to overcome and transcend that power, for themselves and for others.

The paralytic, while a real human being in need of healing, functions symbolically in this passage. We know nothing about him, but his being paralyzed evokes a paralysis in the human condition, a blockage of energy, a lack of dynamism and freedom. Though not dead, the paralytic on his mat is the symbolic antithesis of the aliveness and freedom befitting the children of God.

Pastoral Perspective

Something of the pastoral perspective inherent in this pericope is lost by many of our English translations. For example, the Gospel writer, Matthew, sets up a sharp encounter between Jesus and the scribes by beginning both verses 2 and 3 with the two Greek words *kai idou*, "and behold!" The latter is a "grab-you-by-the-shirt-collar" term, a "pay-attention-to-this!" command to the reader that most renderings do not capture.

That phrase provides an invaluable and arresting contrast between Jesus' response to the paralyzed man and the scribes' put-down of Jesus. Whereas the scribes simply call Jesus a blasphemer and say nothing to the poor man, Jesus tells him to have courage for the present time as he is going through this trial and names him "child" (v. 2, NRSV "son") before he announces to him the fact of the full forgiveness of his sins. Jesus' soothing choice of words focuses our pastoral care of so many people in our congregations who are suffering with long-term illnesses, chronic disabilities, lasting struggles. Sometimes all we have to offer them is an encouraging word to "hang in there through it," to endure what cannot quickly be changed, to wait through what might seem to be lasting "forever."

Many of us go through similar periods of waiting—through illnesses or handicaps or other trials.

Exegetical Perspective

For many centuries Christians assumed that Matthew's Gospel was the earliest of our Gospels. With the rise of historical criticism, in more recent centuries most New Testament scholars now believe that Mark's was the earliest Gospel and that Matthew and Luke were both written, not only using Mark's general outline, but using and revising a good many of Mark's words.

When we look at these verses from Matthew, we want to raise three questions.

What does this story tell us as we find it both in Mark and in Matthew? In the first century, miracle stories start with some description of the infirmity of the person who wants healing. Then there is a description of Jesus' reaction to this infirmity—sometimes a word, sometimes an action. Then there is a demonstration that Jesus is an effective miracle worker. Finally the onlookers in a kind of chorus praise God or Jesus for *what they have seen.*

As we find the story of the paralytic both in Matthew's Gospel and in its forerunner, Mark's Gospel, we find all these marks of a miracle story. In Mark and Matthew, however, there are some interesting variations on the traditional form. As is often the case in Gospel miracles, there is an emphasis on the importance of faith for this healing, but here in both Mark and Matthew the faith displayed is not the

Homiletical Perspective

There are a number of ways to preach on this story of Jesus' healing of a paralytic. It is one more healing story. It is one more testament to the power of Christ and the collective understanding of Jesus as the Son of Man. It is one more notch in the belt for those who have faith and for those who are thus rewarded in kind. These are always preachable themes, and the story of the paralytic in Matthew lends itself to exploring any or all of them. Congregations can never hear enough about God's omnipotence and Christ's ministry to those in need.

This text (and its parallel text in Luke 5:17–26) lends itself to some themes less visited in the pulpit, as well.

When I was fortunate enough to have Dr. Emilie Townes as a professor, she would begin each class with a prayer that ended in these words: "And those who were gathered, that were able, said Amen." While I am certain that there is a richer history to this language than the conclusions that I personally reached, I found these words to be a pastoral prayer. For those gathered who are able, by the joys in personal lives, success in the job market, health of those whom we love, let them lift up that word of affirmation used in the Christian tradition: "Amen."

Let us say "Amen" for those who are unable to say it as well. This is a foundational purpose of church:

Matthew 9:2–8

Theological Perspective

One thing we do know from the passage is that the paralytic's companions are carrying him toward healing. We may surmise that they are acting in response to their friend's desire to be brought to Jesus; we may also surmise that they are moved by compassion for and solidarity with their friend. Jesus' authority to teach, to heal, and to set free must have been known to them. Most likely, their immediate hope was for the paralytic's physical healing. Perhaps they were surprised by Jesus' initial pronouncement: "Take heart, son, your sins are forgiven" (v. 2c). Perhaps the deep Jewish entwinement of sin and physical suffering was so ingrained in them that they received these words as intrinsic to the process of healing.

The scribes, in contrast, watch in silent judgment. The power of forgiveness is a divine power; only God can forgive sin. The corollary would seem to be that only God can judge human actions, but this is lost on the scribes, who also function symbolically. "Why do you think evil in your hearts?" (v. 4b) Jesus asks. He could be speaking to any of us. Why do you harbor these thoughts that cast doubt and shadow upon agents of God's grace in the world? Why do you shore up systems that burden, constrict, and paralyze the children of God?

If sin is the thwarting of life, the fragmentation of community, the creation and deepening of division, then the passage casts the scribes as symbolic agents of sin. Authentic freedom challenges the scribes' constructs and unmasks the fear that gives rise to their negative judgments, which have real power to undermine community and diminish the flourishing of individuals. Jesus subverts such negative power. Having performed the "invisible" miracle of forgiving the paralytic's sin, he now performs the "visible" miracle of healing that is but its outer sign.

The life-giving faith of the paralytic's community of friends created the conditions that made Jesus' divine power to forgive efficacious and made Jesus' dramatic act of physical healing possible. By Jesus' authoritative word, the paralytic was liberated from the paralysis and affliction of spirit that is sin. By that same authoritative word, he was freed from his physical paralysis to become a new creation, in body as well as in spirit. Jesus' declaration that "the Son of Man has authority on earth to forgive sins" (v. 6a) is a declaration that he shares in God's original power to create, to author life. According to James Alison, God's gift of forgiveness is original and prior to the foundation of the world as we know it. "In this sense," he writes, "the 'foundation' of the Church is

Pastoral Perspective

What a comfort Jesus' words must have given the poor man, especially since some in his community may have blamed him for his infirmity! Of course we do not know what caused his paralysis, but the reaction of Jesus and his soothing greeting stand in bold distinction to the lack of compassion shown by the scribes.

Jesus underscores this difference by asking the scribes why they had such evil in their "hearts" (v. 4)—a word choice that demonstrates the Gospel writer Matthew's emphasis that their wills were involved more than just their feelings and/or thinking. This might suggest that they had no pity at all for the afflicted man.

All of these dissimilarities between the story's major characters enable us to go off in several different directions that are pastorally important. One is the piercing division between the scribes' lack of sympathy and Jesus' tender concern for the burdened man. The same thing happens in our day when acquaintances of those who are ill do not know what to say to those who are sick and wind up repeating hurtful sentiments, such as "Get well quickly" when there is no possibility for a swift cure in sight. The command to get well quickly leaves the sufferer only distressed that s/he has no way, in fact, to hurry. Any injunction that cannot be fulfilled is like a hammer over the injured person's psyche, rather than a word of motivation or inspiration.

Reflection on the universality of tragedy is another pastoral direction that we could explore. Many people endure hunger, are impaired with various diseases, or are suffering as a result of natural disasters. In what sense do churches bear witness to Jesus' mercy and power to heal as the communities act to alleviate their pain and hardship? In times of economic downturn, many agencies that work to address human suffering find themselves far short of sorely needed funds. Programs are cut, and needs are left unmet. Though the extensiveness of calamities is too great a subject to be treated comprehensively here, it is a pastoral concern to which the text points.

A third pastoral direction involves the healing power of God's forgiveness revealed in the actions of Jesus. Jesus asks us a tough question, whether it is easier to forgive sins or to enable a paralyzed person to walk. That is a puzzle we should all ponder. Do we believe that the Son of Man really has the power to forgive sin? Do we think it is easier for God to forgive us or to heal our bodies? In the story Jesus does not answer the question directly. He simply commands the disabled one to stand, walk, and go home.

faith of the paralytic but the faith of the friends who bring him to Jesus.

Almost uniquely in our Gospels the question of healing is explicitly linked to the question of the forgiveness of sins. In both Mark and Matthew, Jesus initially omits what seems the obvious response to the paralytic's need and pronounces him forgiven. It is only after Jesus has raised the puzzling question of whether it is "easier, to say, 'Your sins are forgiven,' or to say, 'Stand up and walk'" (v. 5) that he goes on to perform the more obvious, visible healing of the paralysis.

Also, in both Mark and Matthew (and sometimes in the other Gospels, including John) the miracle story is intertwined with a controversy between Jesus and his opponents about his authority. It is hard to know whether the emphasis in the story as we have it lies on the healing or on the dispute.

The way in which Jesus handles the dispute is fairly typical of the way he deals with his opponents in Matthew and Mark (and the other Gospels as well). He asks them a question that puts them on the defensive. One of the remarkable features of this story is that those of us who hear it are left puzzled in much the same way that Matthew's scribes are puzzled.

Which is easier? In one sense it is easy to *say* either, "Your sins are forgiven" or "Stand up and walk." What is difficult is to say those words and make them matter. The effect of the word about walking is more immediately visible, but the effect of the word about forgiveness is no less miraculous.

This reminds us that both Matthew and Mark presuppose a connection between sin and paralysis in this story. It does not mean that they thought that all physical afflictions were a result of sin, but in this case there is no way to read the double healing without acknowledging the complicated connection between the sense of sin and the paralysis. (For a quite different take on the connection between sin and affliction, see John 9:1–3.)

What editorial changes did Matthew make in the story and with what results? Much of the time Matthew seems to be condensing Markan material. In this rewriting of Mark, what is missing includes the tenacious way in which the paralytic's friends drag him to the roof and then dig a hole in the roof and lower him down. In both Gospels Jesus responds to the faith of the man's friends, but in Mark's Gospel it is particularly clear how much energy that faith requires.

In Mark's Gospel the charge of blasphemy against Jesus is made clearer: "Who can forgive sins but God alone?" (Mark 2:7).

to lift up those who struggle, to be present to those who are suffering, and to be witnesses to the love of God when that love is sometimes very difficult to see or feel.

When Matthew writes that Jesus notices their faith in verse 2, the exact identity of the recipients of this faith remains vague. It might include the paralytic himself, but then again it might not. What it certainly does include is the faith of those who carry the man on the bed and, in the Lukan parallel, push through a crowd, climb a roof, dig through it, and lower the man to Jesus. It includes those who surround the one who is suffering. The faith of those who lend their time, effort, and energy to comfort and care for their neighbors is recognized not just as a faith that Jesus admires but as a faith that is a catalyst for transformative healing.

We often find that our culture deems it our duty to care for our loved ones when they are ill or struggling, and sometimes we do so at great cost and sacrifice. Rarely does this sense of duty extend to the stranger who may sit only four pews away from us every Sunday morning. This particular message from Matthew 9:2–8 opens our eyes to the faith of those who surround the suffering and unstops our ears to those who say "Amen" on behalf of one another in times of crisis. The message of transformative healing, in and of itself, is essential to the life of Christ's church. A sermon on this text could certainly prove to be a starting point for honest evaluations of the strengths and needs of the church community.

Another path that the preacher could take would be to try and answer the question that Jesus poses to the scribes in verse 5: "Which is easier, to say, 'Your sins are forgiven,' or to say, 'Stand up and walk'?" Perhaps this is a familiar question, but there does not seem to be any easy answer to offer.

God's forgiveness of our sins through Jesus Christ is the greatest gift of Christian faith. It allows us to shout "Alleluia" every Easter morning, but does it resound within us and among us the rest of the year? Bogged down with guilt, we might not say with ease that our sins are forgiven or, in stronger terms, that grace is just. It might also be that as a forgiven people, we do not often live as though our daily lives are changed by the gift of atonement. If we find ourselves in these places, as sometimes we almost certainly must, it might be easier to point to the paralytic walking by and conclude that the miracle was no big deal.

Then again, we might notice how many paralytics there are all around us, even when we do not include

Matthew 9:2–8

Theological Perspective

nothing other than the efficacious revealing of the forgiveness of sin, which is itself our only way back into God's original plan for us."[1] God's original plan for us is our full flourishing as a new creation.

God's gratuitous gift of life is the means by which we receive our identity as God's children and come to know the freedom that that identity entails. "The way gratuity is experienced within a world such as ours can only be as the unlocking, unbinding, of the established order in order to be able to grow into that which we shall gratuitously become."[2] Jesus' forgiving and healing of the paralytic symbolically unlocks the established order of the scribes and unleashes the new creation. Matthew's story foregrounds the power of communal faith in relation to the divine authority at work in Jesus, even as it depicts the disintegration of the old order. The good news of this story for us today is encapsulated in the exhilarating effect of this event upon the crowds that "glorified God, who had given such authority to human beings."

The designation of Jesus as "Son of Man" is accurately rendered as "the Human One," that is, the fully and authentically Human One, the embodiment of the new creation and forerunner of all we are created by God to be. We are the human beings who by faith share in the divine authority of the fully Human One. We are the disciples authorized and obligated to forgive in God's name. In some of our churches, the tendency to bind such authority to ordained ministers mirrors the fearful control of Matthew's scribes and inhibits the flourishing of the new creation. Official sacramental action at its best ritualizes and celebrates the power already at work in the community of faith. "The authority given by Jesus to bind and loose, ritually focused in the ordained clergy, is given to all disciples."[3]

Matthew's story of the forgiving and healing of a paralytic calls contemporary Christian disciples to embrace and enact their own God-given authority to unbind, raise up, and set others free as a means of making visible the forgiveness already wrought in Christ, the new creation in whom we live.

KATHLEEN A. MCMANUS

Pastoral Perspective

What an amazing action of healing! When has God's forgiveness allowed us as individuals, or freed the church as a community, to stand, walk, and return to the life God has given us to pursue?

In this passage Jesus performs a holistic healing that foreshadows God's spiritual and consummate cure through Jesus' obedience, suffering, death, and resurrection. He will make available a full forgiveness for everyone's sin, even if we are not granted physical healing. We may need to discuss with our congregants the fact that some of us may not experience complete corporeal health or restoration this side of the grave. Sometimes God grants us other kinds of healing instead—providing us with emotional, social, or spiritual wholeness. God is to be thanked no matter what gifts are presented to us. Occasionally, we may receive some of what we envisioned, but not all. Still, whatever God accomplishes for, through, and in our bodies is extraordinary!

That leads us to the final point for our pastoral work on this pericope. Verse 8 proclaims that the people standing around were filled with awe at this miraculous healing of the afflicted man and praised God, glorifying God that Jesus had been granted such authority. Probably our world's worst affliction is that all the medical advances of the last few years have robbed us of our awe. We no longer stand (or bow or lie down) in wonder at the greatness of God and God's creation. That God forgives our sins is a stunning marvel, to be counted greater than all the wonders of the creation! What can we do in our pastoral care or what can the community of faith do in its practices to increase the awe that should reign in our midst? How can we recapture the utter reverence we felt as children at the overwhelming sublimity of God?

MARVA J. DAWN

---

1. James Alison, *The Joy of Being Wrong: Original Sin through Easter Eyes* (New York: Crossroad, 1998), 175.
2. Ibid., 174.
3. Ibid., 186.

Exegetical Perspective

In Matthew's Gospel the response of the crowd underlines the theme that Mark suggests but that Matthew frequently repeats: Jesus' special authority. "They glorified God, who had given such authority to human beings" (v. 8). Many scholars think that for both Matthew and Mark, the story is told to make a claim not only about Jesus but also about the church. Now in Jesus' name the church also declares forgiveness of sins—a claim that must have seemed at least as blasphemous as the claim Jesus makes in our story.

Where does this story fit into Matthew's larger narrative and its themes? Matthew's Gospel is fairly clearly divided into sections that contain lengthy sermons and related narrative material. The material from Matthew 4–9 is especially concerned with the issue of Jesus' authority.

In the temptation narrative of Matthew 4, Jesus makes clear—over against Satan's guile—both the range and the nature of his authority: it is God's authority and not his own. At the end of the Sermon on the Mount, Matthew and the crowds acknowledge, however, that Jesus is an appropriate, perhaps *the* appropriate, deputy of God's authority. Borrowing a line from Mark, Matthew says, "The crowds were astonished at his teaching, for he taught them as one having authority, and not as their scribes" (7:28b–29).

In Jesus' discussion with the centurion (8:5–13), the centurion acknowledges Jesus' authority to heal, and Jesus demonstrates it. Now in 9:6 Jesus claims even further authority, the authority to forgive sins.

When this Gospel draws to its close, Matthew will make clear where Jesus' authority comes from and also the depth and breadth of its power: "All authority in heaven and on earth has been given to me" (28:18).

DAVID L. BARTLETT

Homiletical Perspective

ourselves among their ranks. There are innumerable people throughout the world who are stuck in the mire of physical and mental illness, addiction, depression, economic hardship, discrimination, violence, and a litany of paralyses that is too long to rehearse here. With the earthly odds stacked against us, we think it easier to turn away from hope in the world than to affirm the transcendent gift of Christ's forgiveness.

The preacher would do well to hold up and share this puzzlement as one that is difficult for all Christians. Neither one of those claims is easy to make, and Matthew leaves us wondering just what it was that the scribes were supposed to say before the attention of the crowd and the Gospel writer turned to the man who had been cured.

The hope of Matthew's story, proclaimed to paralytics and their friends then and now, is that God's goodness does not rest on the hinges of a terribly difficult question of faith. Jesus does not wait for us to search for an answer before he both heals the paralytic and continues on toward Calvary. Our questions do not need to be answered nor our struggles understood before God begins working in our lives. With God's help that might be a message that will allow both those of us who come to preach the word and those of us who come to hear the word to pick up our beds and move a little bit further down the road.

JONAH BARTLETT

Matthew 9:9–13

⁹As Jesus was walking along, he saw a man called Matthew sitting at the tax booth; and he said to him, "Follow me." And he got up and followed him. ¹⁰And as he sat at dinner in the house, many tax collectors and sinners came and were sitting with him and his disciples. ¹¹When the Pharisees saw this, they said to his disciples, "Why does your teacher eat with tax collectors and sinners?" ¹²But when he heard this, he said, "Those who are well have no need of a physician, but those who are sick. ¹³Go and learn what this means, 'I desire mercy, not sacrifice.' For I have come to call not the righteous but sinners."

Theological Perspective

Questions arise from a desire to know, learn, or understand. They emerge from the questing spirit, which is distinctively human, which marks us as transcendent beings made for mystery, made in the image of God, stamped with the yearning to know and be one with God. In his transcendental anthropology, Karl Rahner has indicated that human beings are, in fact, constituted as a question to which God is the ultimate answer;[1] indeed, God's own spirit in our depths is the source of our questioning and longing, leading us into the fullness of the divine life. Of their nature, questions expand our individual and collective boundaries, opening up ever greater space for the divine and human mystery to inhabit.

The Pharisees pose a question to Jesus' disciples: "Why does your teacher eat with tax collectors and sinners?" (v. 11b). They acknowledge Jesus as "Teacher," but their question does not arise from curiosity, wonder, or a genuine desire to learn or understand. They are observing behavior that falls outside the boundaries of acceptability based on their conventional understanding. Their judgment has already been cast; the verdict is in. Those who are righteous according to the law do not break bread with those who are outside the law.

1. Karl Rahner, *Foundations of Christian Faith* (New York: Crossroad, 1987), intro., esp. 11.

Pastoral Perspective

It is wonderful when a lectionary text applies to everyone in our parish family, but it can also be treacherous when the text concerns each person differently. What is a pastor to do? She prays for wisdom, of course, but it is sometimes *very* difficult actually to believe that God will give us what we need. In chapter 9 Jesus says, "Follow me." The writer of Matthew puts Jesus' command in the present tense ("be following me") to emphasize that we need continually to pay attention to what the Son of Man asks of us. Our following takes many different forms, depending on our current state. In fact, discipleship might change by the day or hour!

For example, suppose a congregant is a busy executive in a company that formerly was hiring new workers at a rapid pace. Suddenly, given an economic downturn, he now must lay off several recent hires and deal with their resentment and anxiety. Of course, the pastor requires vastly different skills to care for the executive, mostly dexterity in shifting to a posture of compassion and sorrow, but also the ability to communicate encouragement and hope. Does Jesus give us models for communicating grace to this man? In verse 12 Jesus says that the well or strong have no need for a physician, but those who are ill; so that at least suggests care. Nevertheless, more than that wisdom alone will be required if the

Exegetical Perspective

Matthew probably writes his Gospel for a community composed mostly of Christians who have been raised in the synagogue. Sometime quite recently he and his fellow believers have broken away from their former community. Much of the purpose of Matthew's Gospel is to argue that Jesus is a better interpreter of the Torah than was Moses and that Matthew's community is closer to God's purposes for Israel than the synagogue they have left behind.

In this passage, as in the preceding passage, Matthew draws on distinctions Mark has already made between following Jesus and following other Jewish interpreters of the law. However, Matthew finds ways to make particularly clear that Jesus' new way is a fulfillment of the old way, that Jesus is the heir of Moses and the prophets.

Again, as in the verses of our previous reading, the material for this pericope is entirely an editing and shaping of material already found in Mark. Here again we can ask three questions of the passage.

What does this story tell us as we find it both in Mark and in Matthew? In both Mark and Matthew the first part of our passage—the calling of the tax collector—is a kind of continuation of the call narrative found in Mark 1:16–20 and Matthew 4:18–22. In both Gospels we have a further example of the power of the call to discipleship. As the fishermen

Homiletical Perspective

"Which side are you on?" It is an oversimplified question, but it is certainly at the heart of the matter for any congregation that hears the story of Matthew's call to discipleship and Jesus' subsequent fellowship with those cast to the margins of society. None of us wants to be pushed to the margins of society. That is no one's wish. However, neither do we want to feel as if we have been left off the invitation list when Christ comes calling for partners at the table.

It may be that we have reached the proper Christian mentality. Which side is the preacher on? Taking Jesus' side in the pulpit on Sunday morning, many of us try to emphasize that the love of Christ and the grace of God meet all people, regardless of their decisions, their lifestyles, or where they may be in their personal journey of faith. On the other six days of the week, that is not always the side we find ourselves on.

A number of years ago I went to see Joe Strummer perform. Once the front man for the Clash, Joe Strummer had disappeared from the music scene. I had unceasingly dedicated my musical life to all things Clash-related. I owned a multitude of Clash memorabilia and knew all sorts of Clash trivia. I had been waiting to see Joe Strummer perform for as long as I could remember.

Matthew 9:9–13

Theological Perspective

The people with whom Jesus associates are already relegated to categories of judgment: "tax collectors," instruments of both the Roman government and their own Jewish client kings, despised for exploiting their own people; and "sinners," all those others whose lives render them unrighteous in light of the Jewish law as the Pharisees understand it. Now Jesus and his disciples fall under suspicion for associating with these sinners. Indeed, the question posed by the Pharisees is not a question at all, except in the rhetorical sense.

In the face of the Pharisees' question, the disciples, perhaps stumped, remain silent. Jesus, the one being observed and judged, but not addressed, nevertheless hears and responds, with an injunction to "go and learn." The teacher bluntly explains, "Those who are well have no need of a physician, but those who are sick. Go and learn what this means, 'I desire mercy, not sacrifice.' For I have come to call not the righteous but sinners" (vv. 12b–13). Matthew the evangelist presents Jesus as an authoritative teacher who stands in contrast to the Pharisees, whom he depicts as false teachers. "They are," according to Pheme Perkins, "blind to what the Torah requires. . . . Jesus, by contrast, represents the perfect embodiment of God's love."[2]

The "perfect embodiment of God's love" must have been what Matthew the tax collector sensed as Jesus was walking along and saw him. Jesus "saw" him. How many others ever really "saw" this man, who was neither fish nor fowl, used by two layers of oppressors and despised by his own people? What drew—or forced—him to become a tax collector? What assaults to his self-worth must he have suffered as he lived out this profession? What despair might he have felt of ever being anything other than what, by trade, he was—a despised tax collector?

As Jesus was walking along, he "saw" Matthew, saw him in all his personal ambiguity and vulnerability. He saw him and addressed him with a personal call: "Follow me." Come with me. Enter into relationship with me. Join me in my relationships with others. Help me create a community that embodies and fosters God's rule on earth. Just be with me. We can only imagine the impact that Jesus' intimate, accepting, loving gaze had on Matthew. The Gospel simply states: "And he got up and followed him" (v. 9d).

In no time, Matthew and other tax collectors and sinners are sitting with Jesus and his disciples

Pastoral Perspective

pastor is truly to strengthen and inspire the miserable executive.

Imagine that the situation of another man has changed because of his failing health. He was not active in the community before, since he did not feel he needed it. Perhaps he thought his faith did not demand community support, but suddenly a fear of his own mortality has led him to return to the pew. How can a pastor respond to this man's vulnerability and take it as an opportunity to urge and inspire a renewal of faith? We might wish that he had not turned to faith as a "fire extinguisher." Nevertheless, God's providence has delivered him to the church that he may come to know the Great Physician in his time of need.

In both of these cases, pastoral care will require the kind of enormous love that comes only from God and empowers pastors to love the people whom they have been given to tend. They in turn may come to experience new life in Christ in the present tense and be given new hope for the future. Just so, Matthew invites us into a fresh and deeper pastoral love for all our congregants, as Jesus' command to *continue following* kindles in all of us new diligence as we seek to inspire in others a greater love for God and an increased capacity to experience God's enduring love for us.

The second word in this text to pastors is found in the model Jesus offers in verse 10, that in following him we will be known by the company we keep. In Jesus' time, that company included tax collectors and sinners. How many outcasts from our society find their home in our church communities? How well do we reach out to strangers beyond our walls? This will depend, of course, on where our church buildings are located and what opportunities are open to us or can be created by us.

Such dependence on location, however, does not point to the pastor as the only leader responsible for the outreach of any particular community. How might we enlist others in the faith community's involvement with neighbors? How do we rouse the gifts of those within the church to imitate Jesus' example to "eat with tax collectors and sinners" (v. 11)? That is, how do we inspire others to follow Jesus wherever he may lead?

A final pastoral directive comes from verse 13, Jesus' concluding guideline in our pericope: we should all go and learn what it means that God desires mercy and not sacrifice (see Hos. 6:6). We stumble on that command because in our day we *want* parishioners to give sacrifices of their financial

2. Pheme Perkins, *Introduction to the Synoptic Gospels* (Grand Rapids: Eerdmans, 2007), 192.

immediately leave their boats to follow Jesus in the earlier passages, so does the tax collector immediately leave his tax booth to follow Jesus in the passage.

In Matthew 9 we now see the range of the call. Jesus' call is not only to the relatively common people like fishermen; it also extends to a radically despised person—a tax collector. We remember that in Matthew's time tax collectors were twice despised. They were despised because they collected taxes, often exorbitantly and often to their own profit. They were also despised because they were hirelings of the Roman Empire. They collected taxes for the occupier. In both Mark and Matthew the call of the tax collector provides the transition to the story of Jesus eating not only with tax collectors but with other outcasts—with sinners.

In both Mark and Matthew this meal gives Jesus' opponents the opportunity to question him once again, though now they do so indirectly, by questioning the disciples. In the first section of this chapter they questioned Jesus for forgiving sins; now they question him for consorting with sinners.

In both Mark and Matthew Jesus responds to his opposition by citing first a proverb and then a pronouncement that move us back from the immediate context of the meal to the first issue of our passage, the call:

Proverb: "Those who are well have no need of a physician, but those who are sick" (v. 12)

Pronouncement: "For I have come to call not the righteous, but sinners" (v. 13).

What editorial changes did Matthew make in the story, and with what results? First, as in the earlier part of Matthew 9, Matthew simply shortens some of Mark's descriptions to make the story more dramatic and compact. Matthew also makes two substantive changes. First, he changes the name of the tax collector from "Levi son of Alphaeus" to "Matthew." Assuming that Matthew's Gospel uses Mark's Gospel as a source, we may wonder why it was that the first Gospel changes the tax collector's name. Ulrich Luz suggests persuasively that our evangelist is concerned to establish the authority of the Twelve as leaders of the first community and as model leaders for Matthew's own community. Levi is not known as one of the inner circle of Twelve; Matthew is. By choosing Matthew's name for this disciple, the evangelist guarantees the integrity and the limits of the

I arrived at the venue early and secured a spot front and center at the stage. By virtue of my height I could lean over the security railing and see the set list, those songs that Joe was going to perform. This must have prompted a woman behind me to ask me if he would be playing two particular songs. I informed her that Joe had neither written nor sung either of the songs that she inquired about. She then admitted that she had just come for the party anyway. I was horribly offended at that statement. Who was she to enjoy the same performance that I had dedicated years of my musical life to prepare for? I had done my homework. I had gone through the proper rituals of research, lyric memorization, and memorabilia purchase. I was furious that she was there next to me.

Preaching on this Gospel text requires honesty from the pulpit. It is far easier to look back at the apparent foolishness of this group of questioning Pharisees than it is to look around us and recognize that in religion, even more than popular music, we ask the very same questions that line us up on their side. Why them? More importantly, why not us? Why not the regular church attenders, the generous pledgers, the Sunday school teachers, and the mission-trip volunteers? Are we not the ones who have earned the love and attention of Jesus?

Then we notice that the disciple Matthew met no standards of faith that would separate him from the crowd. In fact, in the very brief story of his calling (a story that consists entirely of one verse), one almost gets the sense that Jesus beckons him, "Follow me," while casually walking by. Matthew simply has no reason to say no. He could have at least signed up to usher. He could have stayed for coffee hour. He could have come through the door on time before the first hymn began.

As if the story of Matthew's calling is not difficult enough for the "every Sunday" Christian, we soon see that Jesus shares fellowship with the sinners and outcasts of society. It is, in fact, his declared mission to attend to those who are wandering off the path, rather than to address directly those for whom religious piety and faithful reading of Scripture have become second nature. "Those who are well have no need of a physician, but those who are sick. Go and learn what this means, 'I desire mercy, not sacrifice.' For I have come to call not the righteous but sinners," says Jesus in verses 12 and 13. Christ's contemporary listeners would be familiar with the reference to Hosea 6:6, but modern hearers of the word are familiar only with the sentiment. Christ calls those

Matthew 9:9–13

Theological Perspective

at dinner—breaking bread, sharing in conversation, trusting one another, coming alive, dissolving boundaries of every kind—and entering into genuine communion. This evident communion is what threatened the Pharisees. The clean categories of the righteous and unrighteous were being flouted, and their secure world was being turned upside down.

The Gospel writer does not say that Jesus required the repentance and conversion of these sinners before he sat down to a meal with them. He called Matthew, so this tax collector was now a disciple, along with the other disciples. All the other tax collectors and sinners were potential disciples, called into Jesus' company without condition. Jesus, perfectly embodying God's love, knew that the source of genuine conversion is unconditional love. Any transformation that would occur among this colorful band of people would be the result of loving acceptance and trusting communion—the mysterious power of that genuine community that instantiates the reign of God.

In this colorful band around a table with Jesus, so colorful as to attract the notice of the Pharisees, who are the disciples? Who are the tax collectors and sinners? Is there really a distinction? Are not all embraced by the unconditional, transforming love of God in Jesus? Are not all invited to "follow" in the very experience of vulnerable and trusting communion? Are not all (including the Pharisees?) empowered by the loving gaze of Jesus to respond?

Why does your teacher eat with tax collectors and sinners? Because he is the enfleshed Word of a God who is known in mercy, not sacrifice, in communion, not separation, in healing acceptance, not judgment. Because he is the embodiment of the new creation hinted at in Hosea's unrelenting compassion and acceptance. Because he is the divine physician bent on healing and drawn to those most in need of it. "I have come to call sinners, not the righteous." What could be plainer than that? What could be more liberating?

KATHLEEN A. MCMANUS

Pastoral Perspective

means so that we can do the congregation's work! We choose to distinguish for our people a sacrifice that is merely an empty ritual from one given out of love and adoration. For many reasons today congregants may give meaningless duties as offerings and not out of mercy.

For example, think of the man cited before, who suddenly became involved in a church community out of awareness of his own fear of death. We desire not only that he learn to love God but that his love for God will make him a lover of his neighbors.

Similarly, our pastoral care causes us to be especially rigorous in ensuring that our congregation is not led to understand and respond to services of worship as "exciting" but superficial rites. Rather, we should foster worship that our congregants can experience as the true sacrifices of praise, lament, and intercession from the heart that they are intended to be. We all know that the temptation to turn worship into attraction or entertainment is especially strong these days. Nonetheless, the major duty for most of us is to make sure that worship is faithful to its purposes: to love and praise God first, and only then to equip the parish for loving each other and extending and expanding the community.[1]

We personally should be wary lest we get so caught up in the society's cult of "fame" that it threatens to turn our acts of mercy into demonstrations of our "accomplishments" and/or fodder for the next pastors' meeting. Being aware of this enticement may help us avoid the snare of putting our reputation over our pastoral work; but if our congregations are to be known for mercy and not for our display, it requires our constant vigilance and continual commitment and burden sharing with the parish.

MARVA J. DAWN

---

1. See Marva J. Dawn, *Reaching Out without Dumbing Down* (Grand Rapids: Eerdmans, 1995).

Exegetical Perspective

inner circle of leadership—in Jesus' time and perhaps in his own.[1]

Second, Matthew adds these verses: "Go and learn what this means, 'I desire mercy, not sacrifice.'" When Jesus speaks to his opponents and his disciples, commanding them to "go and learn," he uses the root for "learn" that is also the root of one of his favorite words, "disciple." He is here telling his opponents and his disciples what sort of learning, what sort of discipling, is required of them: to learn mercy and not sacrifice.

The very fact that Matthew includes in this passage the quotation from Hosea 6:6 in its Septuagint version reminds us how essential it is for Matthew to ground Jesus' ministry and Jesus' teaching in Old Testament precedents. Here, as is so often the case, Jesus acts out the predictions and the exhortations of the Old Testament. By quoting the passage from Hosea, Matthew makes clear that Jesus' behavior is in accord with God's desires as recorded in Scripture. Jesus becomes the right interpreter and enactor of the prophetic word.

In Hosea 6, the passage that Jesus quotes in our passage, God is declaring his judgment on his people's privileging of (cultic) sacrifice over mercy. Now Jesus, greater than the prophets, speaks the prophetic warning to the leaders of his own time.

Where does this story fit into Matthew's larger narrative and its themes? In Matthew's Gospel our passage becomes a further example of Jesus' particular authority. By his authority he calls disciples. By his authority he breaks down barriers between the outcast and the established. By his authority he is interpreter of Scripture. In Matthew 5–7 he interprets the Torah; in Matthew 9 he interprets the Prophets.

This quotation from Hosea of Matthew 9:13 is repeated in Matthew 12:7, where again Jesus confronts the Jewish leaders with the claim that he is a better interpreter of Scripture than they. In chapter 12 the issue is Sabbath breaking, while in chapter 9 it is table fellowship. In both cases Jesus claims that he (and by extension his disciples) are those who rightly interpret the Law and the Prophets. They are discipled in mercy.

DAVID L. BARTLETT

Homiletical Perspective

who have fallen short of the cultural laws of religious obligation. Christ desires to return them to the fold.

Of course one cannot just relate this text to the "good Christian" and the "nominal Christian." To truly understand what the text means, and to preach fairly on the central message of this Gospel, the preacher must also look to the marginalized in society, not only to those who are victims of economic disparity, but also to those who are victims of social injustice due to race, gender, sexuality, and ability. While some of our congregants may find that this seems to be more of a "foreign" message, it is certainly the focal point of the text. Consider those whom we, as a culture and society, have pushed away from places of dignity and respect. Christ has come to attend to those whom he calls "the sick." Ironically, it is our own sinfulness, not theirs, that continues to be the virus.

Whatever path the sermon takes, it is of great importance to recognize that the marginalized join the disciples at the table. They do not replace them. We must not be fearful to welcome new faces to the table, even if it means that we will need to squeeze together with some discomfort in order to do so. We must not be concerned but celebratory as we extend the body of Christ to all our sisters and brothers, regardless of their social position and regardless of their apparent religiosity. This is a text that, if addressed honestly, will certainly rattle the nerves of many gathered in our pews. It is also a text that, if addressed honestly, will end only in good news. We welcome those who have thus far been unable to join us at the table, and we celebrate the gifts, knowledge, and faithfulness that each one brings.

JONAH BARTLETT

---

1. See Ulrich Luz, *Matthew 8–20* (Minneapolis: Fortress Press, 1989), 32.

Matthew 9:14–17

[14]Then the disciples of John came to him, saying, "Why do we and the Pharisees fast often, but your disciples do not fast?" [15]And Jesus said to them, "The wedding guests cannot mourn as long as the bridegroom is with them, can they? The days will come when the bridegroom is taken away from them, and then they will fast. [16]No one sews a piece of unshrunk cloth on an old cloak, for the patch pulls away from the cloak, and a worse tear is made. [17]Neither is new wine put into old wineskins; otherwise, the skins burst, and the wine is spilled, and the skins are destroyed; but new wine is put into fresh wineskins, and so both are preserved."

Theological Perspective

In the twenty-first century, followers of Christ are marked by a diversity that goes far beyond the multiplicity of denominations to which they might belong. Individual Christians today occupy a continuum of conscious religious experience that stretches from a wide and deep embrace of the new cosmology (an ecologically based theology first explored in the writings of Thomas Berry) to a narrow focus on institutional practice and religious ritual. These extremes need not be mutually exclusive; in fact, Jesus' response to John's disciples in Matthew's Gospel calls us even today to the freedom that flows from dwelling in the mystery of the Christ in our midst. This passage invites disciples today to the transformation that prepares us both to receive and to become this mystery.

The disciples of John the Baptist approach Jesus directly to ask about a difference in religious practice. They, like the Pharisees, fast often, but the disciples of Jesus do not. This difference is of interest, since Jesus was himself at one time quite possibly a disciple of John. Indeed, some of John's disciples have changed teachers, going over to Jesus. While the Pharisees are often portrayed as standing in judgment of Jesus' practices, John's disciples seem to be genuinely questioning. Jesus responds, not with an analysis of the pros and cons of fasting, but with a series of startling images: "The wedding guests

Pastoral Perspective

This text has often been misused pastorally. For example, those in favor of "contemporary" worship music have cited the end of Jesus' discussion (v. 17) to say that the new wine of this "new attempt at evangelism" should be put in the new wine bottles of "new music" in order to "attract" new believers to the gospel. You can tell by all the quotation marks in the second sentence that I believe it contains several nonbiblical ideas that we must refute.[1]

In order to correct this misunderstanding, pastors would do well to broaden the congregation's perspective on this text in light of the whole subject of fasting. Notice that the question was raised by the disciples of *John*, not by the enemies of Jesus. This is not a "setup" situation in which adversaries of Jesus want to frame him so that they can get rid of him. This is, instead, a simple question between friends or colleagues to deepen their ministries. The call of John was to urge people to repent because the Messiah was coming, whereas Jesus *is* the Messiah and, according to Matthew, is the fulfillment of the prophecies.

Although Martin Luther divided these two witnesses between the law and the gospel, we might characterize the tension more generally as the

1. See Marva J. Dawn, *A Royal "Waste" of Time* (Grand Rapids: Eerdmans, 1999).

Feasting on the Gospels

Exegetical Perspective

The changes that Matthew makes in his Markan source are minimal. He omits Mark's introductory note that the disciples of John and of the Pharisees were fasting, perhaps in part to shorten the pericope. He omits the reference to the "disciples of the Pharisees" in verse 14 and speaks only of the disciples of John and the Pharisees, perhaps because he recognizes that the Pharisees did not have disciples.

At the end of our passage, Matthew writes of the new wine and the new wineskins and adds: "and so both are preserved." Since this may have some implications for the interpretation of the text, we shall look at it briefly below.

A look at the Matthean redaction of the Markan text does little to deepen our understanding of Matthew's passage, so we do better to look directly at how Matthew uses this passage and how it fits into the overall movement of his Gospel. We again note that the overall outline of Matthew 9:1–17 follows the overall outline of Mark 2:1–21.

Nonetheless we can see the function that 9:1–17, especially verses 14–17, serves in Matthew's Gospel and for Matthew's community. Matthew's Gospel is written for a community of Jewish Christians that has recently separated from the synagogue. The overall claim of the Gospel is that Jesus has authority greater than that of Moses and that his disciples

Homiletical Perspective

As with most texts, the preacher may approach Matthew 9:14–17 from many different homiletical angles. Inevitably, however, it must be seen as a passage that centers on the transition (explained in terms of cloaks, wineskins, and fasting) from an old way of traditional religious life to a new way of life, in the light and presence of Jesus Christ.

In the text, Jesus refers to himself as a bridegroom. When the disciples of John approach him and ask, "Why do we and the Pharisees fast often, but your disciples do not fast?" (v. 14), Jesus' reply is an uncomfortable one. The old traditions of our faith cannot easily, or perhaps not at all, sustain the inevitable transformation of a congregation's needs in the early years of a new century.

Almost all mainline churches are facing this problem. Our members are getting older and wiser, but few younger people, especially in the immediate postcollege years, are joining them in the pews. Many preachers and church leaders find great comfort and power in the familiar litanies, hymns, and homiletical themes. However, our language, steeped in religious traditionalism, may be on its way to quickly becoming a foreign language to those just outside the doors of our sanctuaries who are debating whether or not to enter. Like the disciples of John or the Pharisees, we may be the old cloak that cannot form a bond

Matthew 9:14–17

Theological Perspective

cannot mourn as long as the bridegroom is with them, can they? No one sews a piece of unshrunk cloth on an old cloak, do they? Neither do people put new wine into old skins, lest the wine be spilt and the skins destroyed. New wine needs new wine-skins" (vv. 15b, 16, 17, slightly reworded). Either positively or by contrast, each of these images opens up insight into the reality of God's inbreaking reign and the existential response it evokes.

Jesus does not jettison the practice of fasting. Rather, he puts it in its proper place. The impossibility of fasting while the bridegroom is present is juxtaposed with the acknowledgment that, when the bridegroom is taken away, then the disciples will fast. In the time of sorrow, which surely will come, people will naturally fast because their hearts are heavy; eating and imbibing then are existentially impossible. This represents an insight of the later Christian community who endured the absence of the person of Jesus after his death and resurrection, in spite of the fact that they were animated by his Spirit. Jesus himself announced the inbreaking of God's rule that his own disciples experienced in his person and presence. As Edward Schillebeeckx puts it, "Being sad in Jesus' presence is an existential impossibility: his disciples 'do not fast.'"[1] In the company of Jesus, the abundant life and joy of God's reign is at hand, it is existentially present. The disciples experience "the presence of salvation in the actual person of Jesus of Nazareth. The disciples being together with this Jesus is in essence a celebration of good fellowship, a meal prepared by Jesus himself and a fellowship in which there is salvation. . . . [T]hey simply adored him because they knew: in him we are aware of receiving a gift, a present from God to us."[2]

This divine gift was the experience of abundant freedom and well-being. It was the concrete and immanent experience of God's will for human flourishing and the flourishing of creation. In the presence of Jesus, the disciples knew their deepest identity as God's children. They experienced this freedom because they imbibed it from their friend and Master: Jesus was the truly living, truly free human being-from-God, and what he communicated by his presence was contagious. His freedom to do good and to be utterly himself in the service of others was the essence of his mysterious authority. It was precisely this freedom that posed a threat to the religious and secular institutions of Jesus' time.

1. Edward Schillebeeckx, *Jesus: An Experiment in Christology* (New York: Crossroad, 1987), 202.
2. Ibid., 203.

Pastoral Perspective

difference between judgment and grace, a contrast as large as that between night and day. Pastors need both in their daily work, but not at the same time. Some congregants yearn for gospel comfort and assurance that God loves them and forgives them, while other members of the community require rebukes and encouragement to change and to begin living in accordance with God's ways. Sometimes judgment is essential to arouse hunger for grace.

The contrast proves to be very apt for many pastoral situations. In fact, we find that numerous encounters require the exercise of both judgment and grace. Sometimes an entire counseling session will focus on judgment, but then the gospel hope is added at the end, so that the parishioner does not go away in total despair. At other times, the gospel promises remain the sole focus, because a congregant is so beaten by the forces of judgment in society. Our parishioners crave some good news somewhere, and we are pleased to pour out the solace and abundance of the gospel.

Luther himself urged that every sermon should contain both judgment and grace, in different measures according to the text. Present-day pastors should be very aware of this caveat as they prepare to preach or equip others to do so, because various societal forces tend toward overemphasis on one or the other. For example, I have heard too many sermons that were all judgment and no grace—repeatedly accenting such phrases as "should," "ought to," and "must" or a host of imperative verbs. The listeners become overwhelmed. They feel condemned because they cannot fulfill all the obligations. Where is the exhilaration of the gospel? If the church does not offer them God's grace, why belong?

Part of the problem also originates in a society that leaves people without hope. Where can anyone find hope, if not among God's people?

However, if a pastor imparts only grace, then the parishioners do not have enough motivation to obey laws. The situation becomes, "I like to sin; God likes to forgive. Isn't that a nice arrangement?" As you can tell, all of this requires an intricate dialectical balance between judgment and grace. Pastors will constantly need to entreat God for wisdom if they are to achieve the right balance, for with every preaching occasion the symmetry shifts.

Jesus refers to that shift in this pericope (v. 15) by telling John's disciples that there will come a time when the bridegroom is taken away, and then Jesus' disciples will fast. That is why the church practices two seasons (Lent and Advent) in which we mourn.

have authority greater than that of the scribes and Pharisees.

The opening three pericopes of Matthew 9 make clear three ways in which Jesus' authority exceeds that of Moses. First, Jesus—and in his name the church—can forgive sins. Second, Jesus—and by extension the church—offers the gospel to tax collectors and sinners, beyond the traditional bounds of the covenant. Third, in our text, Jesus and the church can redefine the function of fasting for a faithful community.

We cannot be sure exactly what that redefinition looks like. In responding to the complaint that his disciples do not fast, Jesus draws on the brief metaphor or parable of the bridegroom. Whatever this saying might have meant in the early teaching of Jesus, it is clear that for Matthew the meaning is allegorical. Jesus is himself the bridegroom who is present with the disciples and other followers—the wedding guests. (John's Gospel provides a version of the same metaphor in which Jesus is the bridegroom and John the Baptist is the best man [John 3:22–30]. In John there is no hint that John the Baptist would be fasting; he is rejoicing greatly.)

It is clear enough that Matthew thinks the disciples were not to fast during Jesus' earthly ministry; it is impossible to discern what appropriate church practice would be in Matthew's time. The little parable works against some of Matthew's own strongest claims. After the crucifixion and resurrection, is the bridegroom really taken away? That is hard to credit in the light of Matthew 18:20: "For where two or three are gathered in my name, I am there among them." It is almost impossible to credit in the light of Jesus' last words to his disciples: "And remember, I am with you always, to the end of the age" (Matt. 28:20).[1]

Perhaps the best way to understand this puzzle is to note that Matthew has taken over the metaphor from Mark without making the kind of editing adjustments we usually expect of him when he is shaping a text for his own purposes.

The NRSV, like most English translations, includes the twofold saying about the cloth and the wineskins in the paragraph on Jesus and fasting. The early Greek manuscripts of Matthew, of course, would not have had any paragraph breaks—much less chapters and verses. It seems at least equally plausible to read Matthew 9:16–17 as the conclusion to all the episodes of Matthew 9:1–15.

1. On this puzzle, see Ulrich Luz, *Matthew 8–20* (Minneapolis: Fortress Press, 1989), 37.

with the new patch. Our services and sermons may be old wineskins and the wine inside them, the good news of Jesus Christ, may explode and spill from our churches if we are not able to find new wineskins in which to carry it. To steal a buzzword from that old rival Darwin, perhaps we must evolve to survive. Drastically put, if a radical word needs to be spoken, we must change or die.

I count myself among the ministers who cringe slightly when we see an electric drum kit near the organ, the words "worship band" instead of "choir" in the bulletin, or a video screen dropping down with flashing PowerPoint presentations that suggest our seminary-trained oratorical skills are just not enough for the plethora of learning styles in our congregation. I understand the love of tradition, and I empathize with the disciples of John and the Pharisees who felt the same way.

I have had both the privilege of working in a church with a very strong youth group program and the challenge of working in a church that needed to develop youth services directed specifically at that target audience, an audience, unsurprisingly, rarely seen on a Sunday morning. We did pull out a number of the "new wineskin" tricks, including the worship team, PowerPoint presentation, and an emphasis on shorter, less difficult scriptural texts. I was also assigned the task of writing short homilies for these services, often in themes or patterns that I deemed to be relevant.

The services were successful, but in no way due to my hours of preparation. High school seniors had volunteered to be a part of these particular services and shared personal messages and stories that resonated with the common narrative of their peers. Even though I was not too far removed from their age and experience, this was a narrative that I was unable to offer them, even using the full force of whatever God-given gifts I could muster.

These youth did not hook on to the importance of Christ's ministry to the marginalized until it was pointed out that they knew the faces of the marginalized within the cruel cafeteria seating patterns of their school. They could not wrestle with sin until the seniors painted familiar, daily pictures of what it meant to fall short of God's expectations. They could not welcome grace until they were told in their common language that they never fell so far that God stopped caring for each and every one of them. If we had at one point grown attached to the form of many of our familiar liturgies, then the words of their calls to worship, the honesty of their prayers of

Matthew 9:14–17

Theological Perspective

Unlike the Pharisees, John's disciples seem not so much threatened as perplexed by the nonfasting of Jesus' disciples. John the Baptist, like Jesus, offered the possibility of salvation, and he offered it in terms that differed from the old institutions:

> Jesus was to take up the mantle and some of the content of John's preaching in his proclamation of the coming Kingdom of God. . . . [Both] offered the possibility of salvation. Neither Jesus nor John, though, offered a salvation connected with the salvific institutions of the Old Testament: the Temple, ritual, sacrifices; they offered something quite different: baptism in John's case, unconditional trust in Jesus' case, and true conversion in both.[1]

The difference in Jesus was that God's reign of freedom and love was palpably inaugurated in his person. So how are we to construe the unshrunk material patched onto the old cloak? Here it seems that Jesus is addressing the attempt to weave the utter newness of God's reign into old ways of being. On the one hand, Jesus is not rejecting the message of the Hebrew Scripture, with its plural expressions of God's promised reign; on the other, he is saying that it is not enough to graft the new onto the old. While ever faithful to the ancient promise to Israel, God is "doing a new thing" (see Isa. 43:19a), which requires a new consciousness, a new construct, a new way of being. This is a truly "new creation" requiring "new wineskins," new receptacles. To be prepared to receive the reign of God, to enter the new covenant, to imbibe the new wine, we need to undergo conversion, or *metanoia*. We need to become utterly new vessels. Paradoxically, the becoming is itself a gift imparted by the divine life that engenders our trust.

Twenty-first-century understanding of the cosmos expands the implications of our "becoming" a new creation, even as it enriches our consciousness of Christ. Although science cannot explain the mystery of Christ, it can open up new dimensions in our "seeing." In Jesus' time, something was changing radically, and he urged his disciples to perceive it. Do we, in our own time, perceive the radical paradigm shift? Will we trust the living Christ in our midst to transform our very being into the new wineskins that can hold this mysterious new creation?

KATHLEEN A. MCMANUS

Pastoral Perspective

The early saints realized that we do not appreciate the gift of the Messiah unless we recognize how desperate for Christ we are, by means of four weeks of Advent. Similarly, even earlier in history, the church fathers set up the forty days of Lent (minus the Sundays, when we celebrate the resurrection) to repent for the sins that made it necessary for Jesus to die. I do not mean that these two periods are the only times in which we fast and lament (some traditions invite people to pray psalms of repentance every Friday in honor of Jesus' death); rather, in these two seasons we especially concentrate on mourning.

Finally, how should we understand the parable of the New Patch on an old cloak (v. 16)? As editors Johannes Louw and Eugene Nida remind us in their *Greek-English Lexicon of the New Testament Based on Semantic Domains* (New York: United Bible Societies, 1988), many cultures in the world today cannot understand the parable as Jesus meant it, because in their societies sewing on patches is exactly what everybody does!

It is indispensable that pastors explain how, in Jesus' time, an unshrunk piece of cloth would pull away from an older piece of garment and make a worse tear. His message of God's love and grace was precisely gospel, instead of the judgment that John the Baptizer, his predecessor, taught. People were to find in him the reconciliation with God and forgiveness from God for which John's proclamation of impending judgment had made them thirst.

This does not mean that we have to use new music to make the Gospel relevant, although fresh, unprecedented forms and words are always desired. We do not, as pastors, have to throw out everything that is old, although some of it deserves to be discarded. We need to be thoughtful about the criteria we use to evaluate what is appropriate for our worship and what is more suited for campfires and children's programs. This pericope is not about that pastoral work, but about the disparity between judgment and gospel.

MARVA J. DAWN

---

1. Jon Sobrino, *Jesus the Liberator* (Maryknoll, NY: Orbis Books, 2001), 74.

Exegetical Perspective

Jesus' authority (and the church's authority) to forgive sins is new cloth and new wine. It will not fit the old cloth or the old wineskin. It is part of the newer dispensation of the community that has broken away.

The extension of the gospel to sinners (and soon to Gentiles) does not fit with the old cloth or remain in the old wineskin. It is part of a new community and a new covenant.

The appropriate practice of fasting (whatever that may be) does not fit the old requirements for fasting, nor would it find any place in the older communities of the Pharisees or John the Baptist. It is a new practice for a renewed people.

If this is correct, then the double metaphor of cloth and wineskin is related not only to the immediately preceding discussion of fasting, but to the material we have looked at from the beginning of Matthew 9 on. This would help make sense of the Matthean addition to Mark's material of the very end of Matthew 9:17: "new wine is put into fresh wineskins, *and so both are preserved.*" The gospel is manifest in the new community—the church—and so both gospel and church are preserved. The appropriate practices of the new covenant find their place in the renewed community, not in the old; so the practices and the community that undertakes those practices are both preserved.

A further note may be added, not germane to the overall thrust of our passage, but curious nonetheless. Ulrich Luz points out that here—as nowhere else in Matthew's Gospel—John the Baptist is included as a representative of the old era.[2] The practices of his disciples, like the practices of the Pharisees, were appropriate to the age that is passing away—old wine and old cloth. Elsewhere in this Gospel it is clear that John is the herald of the new age. He says exactly what Jesus says and promises new cloth and fresh wine:

John: "Repent, for the kingdom of heaven has come near" (Matt. 3:2).

Jesus: "Repent, for the kingdom of heaven has come near" (Matt. 4:17).

DAVID L. BARTLETT

Homiletical Perspective

confession, and the hopeful note of their words of assurance would be almost as difficult for many of us to grasp as were the original Greek words of the Gospel writer.

The goal of the preacher should certainly not be to inform her congregation of the inevitable generational disconnect and the Sisyphean task of permanently bridging the gap. It should be honestly to begin a conversation that will lead the congregation to recognize that the beloved old cloak will not last forever in its current form. It should be to offer the infinite hope of the bridegroom's presence to generations of wedding guests and churchgoers that have preceded us and generations yet to come. The language and presentation will continue to change, but as long as the church of Christ remains open to those who wish to enter, then the gospel will remain good for all those who hear it. As long as Christians are able to show love for one another by welcoming change and diversity in our worship of God, then we will do nothing but grow stronger as we celebrate with the multitude of those who long for the word of Jesus Christ.

In the context of today's Christian church, the cloaks and wineskins of Matthew's story are not so much Darwin as they are Auden, who said, "We must love one another or die."[1] Love is what Christ offers to the guests at the wedding, and love is what sustains Christ's church, even through the most trying times of change.

JONAH BARTLETT

---

2. Ibid., 36.

1. W. H. Auden, "September 1, 1939," in *Selected Poems*, ed. Edward Mendelson (New York: Random House, 1989), 86–89.

Matthew 9:18–26

[18]While he was saying these things to them, suddenly a leader of the synagogue came in and knelt before him, saying, "My daughter has just died; but come and lay your hand on her, and she will live." [19]And Jesus got up and followed him, with his disciples. [20]Then suddenly a woman who had been suffering from hemorrhages for twelve years came up behind him and touched the fringe of his cloak, [21]for she said to herself, "If I only touch his cloak, I will be made well." [22]Jesus turned, and seeing her he said, "Take heart, daughter; your faith has made you well." And instantly the woman was made well. [23]When Jesus came to the leader's house and saw the flute players and the crowd making a commotion, [24]he said, "Go away; for the girl is not dead but sleeping." And they laughed at him. [25]But when the crowd had been put outside, he went in and took her by the hand, and the girl got up. [26]And the report of this spread throughout that district.

Theological Perspective

Introduction. As the reader engages this passage, one must be ever aware of the two social constructs that defined the daily lives of first-century Palestinians. First, Roman imperialism informed every aspect of life: social, political, religious, ethical, and cultural. While the supposed intent of the *Pax Romana* was a benevolent peace for the subjects of Rome, it was often enacted by the very violence it was intended to subdue. The threat of physical violence was used to keep order, a condition that was in no way "peaceful."

Second, Matthew clearly sees the Pharisees as problematic in their imposition of the Law. As Leander Keck writes, "Matthew shows Jesus to be on the side of the Torah in such a way that the opponents are put in the position of misconstruing the will of God."[1] Jesus' acts of compassion and healing, along with his teachings, threaten the foundation of their authority; thus they contrive various verbal traps to discredit Jesus. In his interactions with the daughter of the ruler and the woman who suffered from twelve years of bleeding, Jesus reveals the fictions of the Romans and the Pharisees.

While there are many theological themes that can be mined from this brief but exceedingly rich

1. Leander E. Keck, "Ethics in the Gospel according to Matthew," *Iliff Review* 41 (1984): 49.

Pastoral Perspective

Illness is a leveler. It makes no difference whether we are rich or poor, whether we are at the center of power or on the margins. Illness causes great disruption in our lives, and with some long-term illnesses we lose hope that we will ever be healthy again. Sometimes we look around and see models of faith among us, people battling serious diseases who seem to have this inner peace, people who pray over those in pain and seem to ease their suffering, people who read passages of Scripture that give them strength in tough times, people who are simply present with the ill to give comfort or a cup of water when needed. What do we learn in this passage about the nature of illness and the place of faith and hope in healing?

We are told of two people battling illness: a leader of the synagogue who seeks out Jesus for his daughter, and a woman who has been bleeding for twelve years. These are two people who would not associate with each other, were they healthy. The male leader would be unlikely to associate with a female, let alone a female possibly made unclean by a bloody hemorrhage. Nevertheless, here their distress places them in the same story, even in the same crowd, seeking a healing miracle from Jesus. They seek a healer to do what they have no power to do for themselves.

Exegetical Perspective

Although this tightly told story of two miracles is presented here as a separate pericope, it is perhaps better to think of Matthew 9:18–34 as one unit. Those who are interested in literary structure identify this as the third set of miracle stories in chapters 8 and 9, which is itself a unit in between the two blocks of teaching material in chapters 5–7 and 10. In these stories, Jesus raises the dead and makes the blind see and the mute speak. Taken together, these stories can be read as fulfilling the messianic hope of Isaiah 35:5–6. They also set the stage for Jesus' response to the question sent by the imprisoned John the Baptist: "Go and tell John what you hear and see: the blind receive their sight, the lame walk, the lepers are cleansed, the deaf hear, the dead are raised" (11:4–5).

Matthew's version of this incident changes the setting and takes away many of the details of Mark's original. Jesus appears to be still at table eating with tax collectors and sinners (possibly at the home of Matthew; cf. 9:9–10). While he is responding to criticism, first from Pharisees and then from John's disciples, a man rushes to beg for Jesus' help. He is identified simply as a "leader" (the NRSV has added "of the synagogue"). He kneels at Jesus' feet in an act of supplication but also worship (the same language is used of the magi in 2:11). This is the second time

Homiletical Perspective

By the time we get to this point in Matthew's Gospel, a question is still hanging in the air. It is a question that will continue to puzzle many who will be listening to the preacher's sermon. Earlier in the Gospel, Jesus' own disciples were astonished at Jesus' ability to still the storm that had threatened their lives (8:23–27). After their jaws drop, they ask: "What sort of man is this, that even the winds and the sea obey him?"

No doubt some in your congregation who know their Bibles have a ready answer to that question: "Messiah," "King of the Jews," "Son of David," and "Son of God," to name just a few. There were those no doubt in Matthew's community who would have the same responses. Then as now, these titles for Jesus unsettle some, confound most, and comfort others. Peter has the answer that Matthew is looking for, and he will give it later (16:13–20). For now, Matthew wants the readers or hearers to have time to struggle with the question themselves. Who is Jesus? What sort of man is he? What is the nature of his authority? What is his claim upon the church? These are questions for all congregations to consider.

Matthew certainly did not think that he was writing for all time when putting together his Gospel, any more than any preacher thinks that her sermon will last forever. Matthew had his own congregation

Matthew 9:18–26

Theological Perspective

passage, three seem most important to the larger Gospel narrative. First, who has power, and what is the nature of that power? This is both a theological and a christological question. Second, how do we live as God's people? While we have the laws of our government and the laws of our religious community, what are the limits of those laws in the grand scheme of things? Third, how do we follow Jesus as faithful disciples? This question drives the miracle stories in Matthew 8–9 to their conclusion in Matthew 10 with the calling and commissioning of the Twelve.

A Question of Sovereignty, or Who Has Ultimate Authority? While Rome claims to provide the people with peace, and the Pharisees in Matthew adhere to an understanding of the Law that they believe embodies a right relationship with God, Jesus' acts of healing demonstrate a kind of sovereignty that is committed first and foremost to life. This is not the life of subjugation imposed by Rome; it is the life that Jesus encourages in earlier chapters (e.g., the Beatitudes, the call to "do unto others," the Lord's Prayer). While much can be made of Jesus' raising of the daughter as a foreshadowing of his resurrection, it is important to note that the healing stories not only restore but also transform life. Both the daughter and the woman in this passage are presumably ritually impure, yet touch is a part of their healing, despite the fact that touching them could potentially render Jesus ritually impure (Lev. 15, 21). It is noteworthy that no mention is made of this by Jesus or the narrator.

It is also noteworthy that the passage begins with a leader of the synagogue coming to Jesus (v. 18). This is a direct challenge to the authority of the religious leaders, a sign that their control is not as complete as they would hope. It also demonstrates a commitment, on the part of the leader, to a higher calling, to that of life itself. Who can imagine a parent looking at a dying daughter and not doing everything within one's power to save the child? The synagogue leader's action illustrates his theological conviction that this one who can heal people and calm storms must be one who is the very source of life itself.

A Question of Righteousness, or What Is the Role of the Law? The stories of the synagogue leader's daughter and the woman clearly illustrate that all is not right with the world. What then can make things right? What does righteousness look like for those represented in this passage, and accordingly for us?

Pastoral Perspective

How often have we sought help from a physician when we are ill? We may try our own home remedies at first, but at some point we realize that our knowledge and expertise is not enough, that we need someone with knowledge of the body and medicine who can guide our treatment. We must put our trust in this person, that she or he will be able to diagnose our illness and prescribe the correct treatment. We would like a healer who will listen to our distress and calmly suggest an appropriate and successful plan of treatment.

When the leader of the synagogue, known elsewhere as Jairus (Mark 5:21–43), approaches Jesus, all hope for a successful outcome seems lost. His daughter is already dead, yet this man is not hopeless. He asks Jesus to lay hands on her with the expectation that she will live again. The interruption of the woman does not seem to concern him. There is no record of Jairus interrupting the conversation between the woman and Jesus in order to get his miracle back on track, even though a man of power might expect Jesus to pay more attention to his need than to that of the woman. Perhaps at that moment he sees in the face of this woman a fellow sufferer. After twelve years, she has probably sought her share of assistance from others; but she too has not lost hope, saying, "If I only touch his cloak, I will be made well" (v. 21).

Such great faith from these two witnesses in Matthew! It almost feels too easy. "Suddenly" (vv. 18, 20) they are there before Jesus, and just as suddenly he has answered their requests. For the woman, he confirms that her faith has made her well; with the daughter, he simply takes her by the hand and she gets up. When we read these accounts, they may make our own faith seem weak and insignificant by comparison. When faced with a cold or flu, do we complain mightily or seek solace in Scripture and prayer? When faced with even more significant and perhaps life-threatening illness, where do we find the strength to carry on?

There is a great mystery here provoked by these healing stories. Why does Jesus respond to these people, among all those who are probably seeking his help? Do they have the greatest faith or the greatest need, or both? Why, when we pray for healing for ourselves and others, do some prayers seem to go unanswered? Is it because our faith is not strong enough?

These stories of miraculous healing follow on the heels of Jesus' words about placing new wine in new wineskins (9:17). If we try to measure our faith by

in this section that someone in a position of local authority has come to Jesus not only requesting help but expressing the conviction that Jesus is able to provide it (cf. the centurion in 8:5). Their confidence or faith in Jesus precedes his actions. In a notable change from Mark's version, the leader's daughter is not gravely ill but already dead.

Jesus responds by getting up and "following" the leader to his home. In Matthew's Gospel the verb, "to follow," and its nominal form, "follower," is the usual way the author refers to Jesus' disciples. Probably Matthew uses it here in the ordinary sense of accompaniment, but it is also possible that describing Jesus' action in this way suggests that he functions here as a model for the behavior of faithful followers: he goes immediately where he is needed to bring hope and healing.[1]

On the way, a woman suffering from hemorrhages comes up behind him and touches the fringe of his cloak. Once again, Matthew has trimmed back details from Mark's story: gone are the description of the severity of her illness, the press of the crowd, and Jesus' sense that power had gone out of him. By comparison, this version is quite straightforward. Matthew has also relocated the announcement of the healing. In Mark, the healing comes instantly when the woman touches the cloak. Here, perhaps to blunt any hint of magic, Jesus commends the woman for her faith, and then (instantly) she is healed.

Commentaries have made much of this woman's condition and the idea that she is "marginalized" because chronic bleeding makes her "unclean" according to purity codes. According to this reading, Jesus' action goes beyond healing and becomes a deliberate violation of the Law of Moses. Jewish New Testament scholar Amy-Jill Levine argues, however, that this interpretation requires bringing purity codes (not mentioned in the story) into the story and sets up a false antithesis between Jesus and Judaism. In this case in particular, she notes that the text itself does not include any mention that the woman is unclean (e.g., the people around do not react negatively to her). Further, she argues that the provision purported to cover this case (Lev. 15:25–30) in fact does not say that touching a menstruating woman makes the one who touches her unclean. Finally, she points out that the purity issue primarily relates to those who would be about to go to the temple;

---

1. See Amy-Jill Levine, "Discharging Responsibility: Matthean Jesus, Biblical Law, and Hemorrhaging Woman," in *A Feminist Companion to Matthew*, ed. Amy-Jill Levine with Marianne Blickenstaff (Sheffield, UK: Sheffield Academic Press, 2001), 84–85.

in mind, a congregation looking for answers in a time when the world was undergoing profound change. Pressed by cultural, political, and religious forces, Matthew's community steadied themselves by holding on to traditional stories, beliefs, and practices about God and their place in God's world, even as they entertained new interpretations. In this respect, Matthew's congregation faced challenges similar to our own.

What was at stake was learning to live a faith that honored tradition, welcomed new revelation and insight, and made a difference in their lives and in the world they inhabited. Theirs would be a community that embodied the radical grace they learned from "the sort of man" Jesus was and his presence among them as their risen Lord. Their community would be a habitation for their exalted Lord, where they would practice the mercy and compassion exhibited in these texts.

The text flows from an interruption. Jesus is in the midst of an oral examination, this time by disciples of John the Baptist. One wonders, What is the tone of their question about fasting (9:14)? Are they simply being curious? Is there a bit of hostility? After all, Jesus was baptized by their mentor, John! By what or whose authority does Jesus teach a different way of practicing faithfulness and fidelity to God than John taught? We might imagine the ensuing talk about what was old and what was new, whose patches were being put on what old cloth, and who was in possession of the "new wineskins" to be fraught with tension. Then a new situation arises. Human need often intrudes upon arguments over "right" faith and practice.

A desperate man comes in and assumes what is for him an unfamiliar posture. He is a "leader," yet he is kneeling before Jesus as if Jesus were the one in authority. Matthew's listeners have seen this posture before. Not only "wise ones," but a leper has acknowledged Jesus' authority in the same manner (2:11; 8:2). The text does not tell us who or what he leads. He is there, as Tom Long says, "as a representative of the community; he symbolizes the way things are."[1] Life happens. People sicken and die, no matter what their status or level of accomplishments. Death comes, even in the presence of the exalted Lord. A father coming to plead for his dead daughter is one way that Matthew shows the investment God's Christ has in human living and dying, celebrating

---

1. Thomas G. Long, *Matthew* (Louisville, KY: Westminster John Knox Press, 1997), 108.

Matthew 9:18–26

Theological Perspective

Is it legalistic adherence to the letter of the law or the completion of a religious checklist? For Matthew, Jesus comes to "fulfill all righteousness" (3:15) and "not . . . to abolish the law or the prophets . . . but to fulfill" (5:17).

By law, Jesus should be discouraged from touching the dead child or allowing himself to be touched by the bleeding woman, if he wants to remain ritually clean. However, it is through such touch that healing comes. For Matthew's Jesus, righteousness defies religion and reaches across the barriers constructed by human convention. Righteousness makes compassion real through the kind of faithful acts that transform suffering and grief. It is noteworthy that the word used in 9:22 to describe the woman's healing ("made well") is a form of the verb "to save." Righteousness is the work of salvation, enacted by God and made manifest in humanity: "Clearly the ethic of Jesus, as Matthew portrays it, is an ethic of the Torah but not of the scribes and Pharisees, even though they too claim the Torah."[2]

A Question of Discipleship, or How Shall We Serve?
These two miracles are included among a variety of actions that lead to Jesus' commissioning of the Twelve. These actions, therefore, are not provided solely as christological descriptions. They are also prescriptive, not so subtle calls to "go and do likewise." For example, note that in Mark (5:22–43) and Luke (8:41–56) Jesus is touched by the suffering woman and "the power went out of him." In Matthew, however, Jesus turns and sees her, sees her suffering, sees her faith. Jesus is not simply the source of healing power; through his recognition of the woman he embodies God's reconciling love. The healing comes as much through her faith as it has through Jesus' power.

The call is to reach across those barriers that once discouraged us from touching those at the margins, those deemed ritually unclean, and those for whom society has no hope, to assert the love of Jesus and our faith in his healing touch in ways that can transform all that we once knew. One needs only to peruse the daily news rapidly to construct a list of those whom, even now, we are being called to touch, to heal, and to offer Jesus' transforming love.

TRACE HAYTHORN

Pastoral Perspective

how many good deeds we have done or by the size of our contributions to the church, or if we ascribe our illness to sins we have committed, these thoughts belong with the old wineskins. Jesus is giving us signs of kingdom living in these passages. The same word the woman uses for "made well" also means "saved." Perhaps our hunger for salvation and the confidence that Jesus can right the wrongs in our lives has more to do with our wholeness than the healing of our physical symptoms.

Jesus does not just speak to these two daughters. He touches them. Both would potentially make him ritually unclean; one by the blood in her illness, the other by her death.[1] Still, Jesus allows himself to be touched and takes the young girl on her deathbed by the hand. He shows that this new wineskin is about breaking down the barriers that separate us. Illness and death are something we share. It is precisely at these times that we most long to be touched, even if our bodies are ugly and in pain.

As we think about the illnesses of others, we know that we too can be the hands of Jesus. We may not have the trained hands of a surgeon or nurse, but the touch we bring comes with hope. This hope contains our faith that Jesus Christ is still moving among us, suddenly making us well and saving the weak and weary in unexpected ways. Let us be bold in proclaiming the good news that Jesus Christ recognizes our suffering and our faith. He who died on a cross knows what it is to be in pain. He who is risen has the power to make us whole.

KATHY L. DAWSON

---

2. Ibid., 50.

1. Stanley P. Saunders, *Preaching the Gospel of Matthew: Proclaiming God's Presence* (Louisville, KY: Westminster John Knox Press, 2010), 82.

since this incident takes place in Galilee, the issue of ritual purity is moot.[2] Levine's argument is that these two healing stories are important instances of Jesus' power to heal. Bringing in a supposed conflict with Judaism of the time does not add anything to what is already a deeply memorable moment in his ministry.

The story then returns to the leader and his daughter. Jesus and his disciples arrive at the leader's home. The crowd of customary mourners and musicians has gathered. Jesus sends them away, saying that the girl is "sleeping." Once again, most of Mark's details are missing: no mention is made of specific disciples accompanying Jesus, of both parents being present, or of Jesus' words to the child. He simply goes into the house and takes her by the hand, and she gets up. The simplicity of the story focuses on Jesus' power to restore the child to life. The verb "get up" (also used in 8:15 to describe the healing of Peter's mother-in-law) is closely associated with resurrection. The faith of the leader that Jesus could make his dead child live has been fulfilled.

These two powerful and familiar stories, told in Matthew's spare and straightforward style, emphasize the power of Jesus not only to heal but to bring the dead back to life. Thus they also point to Jesus' own resurrection and the promise that through him all who believe will share in his power over death. The stories emphasize as well the power of faith: the faith of the father and of the woman who suffers from hemorrhages. They seek out Jesus; he sees their faith and fulfills it.

CYNTHIA M. CAMPBELL

and mourning. Death is a hard reality that even Jesus will have to face. In the face of that reality, the father "leads" us in a body prayer of hope—that death is not the end of life in God's grace.

On the way to the funeral there is another interruption. A woman who has been suffering from internal bleeding for twelve years moves up behind Jesus and touches the fringe of his robe. Somewhere there is an old wineskin marked with a teaching from Leviticus—"if a woman has a discharge . . . beyond the time of her impurity, all the days of the discharge she shall continue in uncleanness," as will the one who touches her things (Lev. 15:25–27). Jesus' word affirming her act of faith bursts the old wineskin to release a healing flow of new, life-giving wine.

Whenever the women in Matthew's community faced old cultural norms, customs, and political pressure that threatened to marginalize them, they had stories like this one to remember. In God's eyes, as revealed through Jesus, women were fully deserving of God's healing attention. To underscore the positive status of women in God's eyes, there is the following account of a young woman "rising up" to new life in Jesus' ministry.

Now it is Jesus' turn to interrupt what is going on. By the time that he arrives on the scene, the funeral service is well underway. Someone has followed the customary way to regard the dead. Musicians are setting the mood, and professional mourners are offering models of appropriate behavior. There is no denying that death is the master of ceremonies— that is, until Jesus arrives. When he does, things turn upside down. A "bridegroom" has arrived at a funeral; now that he is present, there is to be no mourning (v. 15). There is laughter, but it comes from those who do not understand how reality is changing before their eyes. A young woman's death has actually become the occasion for the gift of new life, denying death's right to pronounce the benediction. It is no time for a benediction in Matthew, anyway. There is far more to the story.

RICHARD F. WARD

---

2. Amy-Jill Levine, *The Misunderstood Jew: The Church and the Scandal of the Jewish Jesus* (San Francisco: Harper, 2006), 173–74; see also Levine, "Discharging Responsibility."

Matthew 9:27–34

²⁷As Jesus went on from there, two blind men followed him, crying loudly, "Have mercy on us, Son of David!" ²⁸When he entered the house, the blind men came to him; and Jesus said to them, "Do you believe that I am able to do this?" They said to him, "Yes, Lord." ²⁹Then he touched their eyes and said, "According to your faith let it be done to you." ³⁰And their eyes were opened. Then Jesus sternly ordered them, "See that no one knows of this." ³¹But they went away and spread the news about him throughout that district.

³²After they had gone away, a demoniac who was mute was brought to him. ³³And when the demon had been cast out, the one who had been mute spoke; and the crowds were amazed and said, "Never has anything like this been seen in Israel." ³⁴But the Pharisees said, "By the ruler of the demons he casts out the demons."

Theological Perspective

Introduction. The healings contained within these two brief pericopes complete a series of healings that began in chapter 8. Over the course of chapters 8–9, Matthew crafts a christological argument about the nature and breadth of Jesus' power. Through a series of brief stories, Matthew illustrates that Jesus has power over the physical world and over the spiritual world. Jesus is Lord over all creation: over the forces of weather, over the sea and the land, over illness, and ultimately over life. Matthew does not try to give a rational or sacramental explanation of how healing happens; instead, he asserts that healing comes through Jesus Christ.

Matthew also develops a theological argument about the nature of discipleship (with multiple illustrations of human shortcomings in heeding God's call). As Jesus' disciples, we are called to be agents and enactors of life, a life that is rooted in compassion, a life that touches and heals those who were once marginalized by our communities but in Christ are restored to wholeness.

Healing and the Life of Faith. Beginning in chapter 8, Matthew walks the reader through a series of Jesus' healings, physical (of leprosy, paralysis, fever, hemorrhages, blindness, and deafness) as well as spiritual (exorcisms). Jesus calms a storm (8:23–27)

Pastoral Perspective

If the last passage challenged our thinking about the relationship between illness and faith, this passage presents even more difficulties as we consider those with differing measures of faith. The people to be healed in these stories are not given names. They are simply identified by their condition. We have two blind men and a mute demoniac. We know little more about these individuals than their disabilities. To our modern sensitivities, this seems somehow wrong or inhumane.

We live in an age when blindness, physical limitations, and varying abilities to communicate are not linked to the faith that one has or does not have. Instead, we turn to science to explain why things are so. In the church, when we address disabilities, we are currently more concerned about making the life of the church accessible to all than the root cause behind particular physical issues, and rightly so. Kathleen O'Connor sets this essay in its proper light by telling us that biblical scholars have called the majority of us "temporarily abled," rather than labeling those who are "disabled" as somehow distinct from the norm. We all will deal with some lessening of ability in body, mind, and spirit at some point in our lives.

If this is so, then one can place oneself in these stories as the blind or the mute, the crowds or the

Exegetical Perspective

These two healing stories are the final miracles in this section of Matthew (8:1–9:34), which focuses on Jesus' deeds of power. Eugene Boring notes that Matthew records more healing miracle stories than any other Gospel and that each story points in some way to the meaning or purpose of God made known in the saving life, death, and resurrection of Jesus: "Each one shows some aspect of human need, symbolizing human separation from God, authentic life and the need for salvation (from hunger, sickness, meaninglessness, subjection to demonic powers and the accidents of nature, sin, death)." Even when the faith of the person or persons being healed is part of the story, the focus is always on the power of God through Jesus to restore or make whole.[1]

Here, the first two in need of healing are blind; the next is both demon possessed and mute. Together with the story of reviving the dead child (9:25), these stories both fulfill the prophecy in Isaiah 35:5 and set up Jesus' response to the disciples of John in 11:5. In Jesus' ministry, the signs of God's power are on display for all to see. This heightens the irony of the concluding charge that Jesus casts out demons using demonic power (v. 34).

1. Eugene Boring, "The Gospel of Matthew," in *The New Interpreter's Bible* (Nashville: Abingdon Press, 1995), 8:245.

Homiletical Perspective

Ask a parent how the child got his or her name and you are likely to get a good story. A name can serve as a living memorial to an ancestor. It can show respect for a family tradition or simply honor a family friend. Sometimes given names are amended through the course of the child's life to include nicknames that catch other dimensions of the child's personality: "We named her Martha but we always call her Trixie!" Names speak of origins and connections, express how one is experienced among family and friends, and give scope and depth to one's identity.

This text offers the preacher the chance to explore one of Jesus' names. When we pray "in Jesus' name," what do we mean? What are some of the names for Jesus that your community calls out? Lord? Master? Son of God? Matthew recalls one of his favorite names for Jesus in this story. He places "Son of David" on the tongues of two blind men, echoing the very first words of Matthew's Gospel. You can spend some time in your sermon exploring what it meant in Matthew's community to call Jesus "son of David" and what it means for your community today.

In the ancient context of the Gospels, to be the son of David meant that you were the fulfillment of a dream that God's people had had for generations. The son of David would "deliver the needy when they call, the poor and those who have no helper."

Matthew 9:27–34

Theological Perspective

and raises a little girl from her deathbed (9:18–26). Jesus is no mere magician: "Never has anything like this been seen in Israel" (9:33b).

For many of the healing stories in Matthew, faith plays a central role. In 9:27–29, Jesus claims that it is the faith of those once blind that has opened their eyes. In 9:32–33, the demoniac is brought to him, which may lead the reader to infer faith on the part of those who brought him (though no explicit reference is made to their belief). These descriptions offer grace to the contemporary reader, disrupting any notion that there is a formula one must follow for such healing to occur. In some cases, it appears to be about Jesus' recognition of the faith of the believer. In others, it seems to be about the faith of those who care for the one who suffers. In others, it is simply an act of compassion on the part of Jesus. The common theme within all of the stories is a key christological assertion in Matthew: that healing is made manifest through Jesus.

The Disciplined Life of Faith. Scattered along the path of the wonders cited above, Matthew drops in brief stories of the challenges of discipleship. In 8:18–23, Jesus gives difficult responses to those who profess their desire to follow him. In 9:9, Matthew is called as a disciple, not exactly the model citizen among the Israelites. In 9:30, Jesus offers a different call, one that sounds more like Mark's messianic secret. In healing the two blind men, he "sternly ordered them, 'See that no one knows of this.'" However, they simply cannot contain themselves. The healing they receive compels them—a striking result in that while they profess faith that Jesus can restore their sight, they are not *disciplined* followers of Jesus. Discipleship is not simply the sharing of the good news as we know it; it is our obedience to the Christ who calls us, who heals us, who invites us into the fullness of life with God. While their sight is restored, they do not yet share in the vision of Jesus.

Dependence, Independence, and Interdependence. In the best of circumstances, such healings offer a deeper relationship with the healer, for both those who experience physical transformation and the witnesses (who have the potential of spiritual healing in such moments). The healing is thus a change not only for an individual body but also for the body of Christ. Too often we assume that the goal of such a healing is to move an individual from a place of dependence to independence. In our society, we presume the greatest goal is one's ability to move by

Pastoral Perspective

Pharisees, and listen for the wisdom and hope each perspective can offer for this day. The two blind men approach Jesus and somehow recognize that he is greater than those who surround him. They are certainly not basing this on any physical attributes he may have. They call him the son of a king and ask for mercy. Notice that they do not ask for healing, but for mercy. It is Jesus who interprets their request and restores their sight. When we approach God in prayer, what do we ask? Does God offer something we need even more in place of our request? When we pray to God, do we acknowledge that God is greater than we are, or do we send our requests to God the way a child would make a wish list for Santa Claus? With this passage about the healing of the blind men we have an opportunity to focus on our relationship with Jesus Christ. The blind are not named, but they name Jesus. The focus is on the power of Jesus Christ rather than on those asking for mercy. It is not so much about being made whole as it is about the person who heals and brings mercy.

There is a danger in putting too much emphasis on seeking relief. The danger is that the church will become a therapeutic community where we come expecting to be made whole, rather than come seeking the one who may shake us up and disrupt our lives as much as he will make them smooth. When the gospel reaches us in our brokenness, we emerge transformed for new missions in the realm of God on earth. Think of Saul on the road to Damascus. Blindness was not taken away but given, so that ultimately the good news could be carried into the world.

From the two blind men we now put our feet in the shoes of the mute demoniac. This may be an even more difficult place for us to imagine ourselves. Demons are not something that many people talk about in polite conversation. Some people equate them with mythological creatures like giants and ogres, the product of premodern minds searching for meaning. However, if we dismiss demons—as we do in some Western cultures—we also make taboo the conversation about the nature of evil in our world. This, in turn, mutes our awareness of the presence of evil in certain situations. So let us look at this mute demoniac on his own terms.

Unlike the two blind men, the mute demoniac does not come to Jesus of his own accord. He is brought to Jesus. Because he is mute, he is not able to address Jesus as son of David or by any other name. I wonder if he came willingly or if he was carried to Jesus against his will by someone who cared

Matthew seems to have based the healing of the blind in verse 27–31 on Mark 10:46–52, but he has both simplified the story and added to it. On the one hand, these men have no names; on the other hand, there are now two of them, just as there are two when Matthew essentially repeats this story in 20:29–34. Where Mark had one story of one blind man, Matthew now has two stories of two blind men. (Matthew has already employed this technique of "doubling" in the story of the demoniacs in 8:28.) Perhaps Matthew is concerned to emphasize Jesus' power to open blind eyes. Physical blindness often stands in for spiritual blindness, an affliction that affects not only Jesus' enemies but insiders or disciples. This may be the point of the note that these blind men were "following" Jesus. In Matthew, a "follower" is synonymous with a disciple.

The most prominent link between Matthew and Mark's version is the phrase "Have mercy on us, Son of David." This may be another indication that the two men are part of the extended Jesus community, since they use this rather specific title, which links Jesus to one form of messianic hope, namely, that the Messiah would restore the people of Israel in their own land. The Messiah's role as the one who shows mercy or compassion again echoes Isaiah and is explicitly repeated in 9:36. Jesus' healing ministry is not primarily about demonstrating divine power; it is, rather, an exercise in compassion to those in need.

The interchange between the blind men and Jesus is intriguing. They do not ask for healing, specifically; they ask for "mercy." To which Jesus responds, "Do you believe that I am able to do this?" The question is: *What* is Jesus referring to? Is he asking whether they believe he is able to have mercy or to heal them? Perhaps the reason that the two are not differentiated is to underscore the relationship between Jesus' compassion and his power to heal. Jesus commends their faith or trust, but the healing still depends on him. Their eyes are opened *after* he speaks.

The story ends with a note more characteristic of Mark than Matthew. Jesus orders the men not to speak of this to anyone, but they go out and do just the opposite. Matthew does not have the same concern for the so-called "messianic secret" that is characteristic of Mark. So why introduce that element here? Boring contends that Matthew is making a point about the importance of obedience to Jesus' commands; thus the healed men stand for people within the Matthean church who are not always

When he was revealed, the son of David would "save the lives of the needy" and "redeem their lives . . . from oppression and violence" (Ps. 72:12–14). For the blind, deaf, and mute, that meant receiving sight, hearing, and speech. Matthew names Jesus as this long-awaited leader who has come to set up God's reign in opposition to that of an oppressive empire. Jesus is God's promised agent of justice and compassion. He has come to bring gifts of mercy for "the least of these" (Matt. 25:45)—like the blind and the mute in this story. A sermon that takes up this challenge of naming Jesus as the "son of David" would identify who "the least of these" are in our world and would state God's longing to show them mercy. The preacher can help the congregation see what the blind men "saw" in this story: that ministry in the name of the "son of David" is the embodiment of God's mercy and compassion.

The preacher might also develop an image of discipleship that appears in this part of the story. Two individuals are "following" Jesus (v. 27) in the manner of disciples, with a partial understanding of who Jesus is. They have cried out for mercy and have acknowledged dependence on God's grace for their very lives. Only in this story, Jesus is not the one doing the calling! He does not say, "Follow me," as he did to Simon and Andrew or James and John (4:18–22). These two are already present in his entourage. Sometimes disciples need to follow the example of these two—to call out for God to act and to make oneself available to show mercy in Jesus' name. What happens when God's mercy is released? As you will see in this text, the gospel gains momentum that not even Jesus can control!

Look at how the story takes an odd turn. The action steps out of the public eye and into the relative intimacy of a house (v. 28). First, there is an interview about the content of their faith: "Do you believe that I am able to do this?" The candidates for discipleship seem to have less trouble answering that question than many do today: "Yes, Lord." It is their faith in Jesus' authority and power to heal a situation that brings about a transformation.

Suppose the preacher turns to the congregation to ask a similar question: "What do you believe Jesus has the power to do in our world? To what extent can Jesus' power make a difference in our world? How might that power be realized through our community?" In the story, Jesus' stern command to "see that no one knows of this" (v. 30) goes unheeded. Even Jesus does not have the power to control the spread of the good news! There is no stopping the

Matthew 9:27–34

Theological Perspective

oneself, unfettered by either the world or personal constraint. Perhaps our assumption is not so different from the experience of the two blind men who were healed as they scrambled back to their homes to share their amazing news. No longer would they have to rely on the support of family and friends; they could now make their own way in the world.

Even as we might hope for such a transformation for ourselves or for one we love, it is not out of a desire to free one another from relationship. While the men can now see, they are not free from worry, hurt, concern, pain, loneliness, or alienation. They may have the gift of sight, but they are still weak and vulnerable, just like the rest of us.

The faithful response to such a healing is one of interdependence. From this place we can claim not only our abilities but also our vulnerabilities as creatures of our God. Thomas Reynolds quotes Jean Vanier: "'Weakness carries within it a secret power. The cry and the trust that flow from weakness can open up hearts.' The vulnerability of another is a window into our own vulnerability, evoking a sympathetic relation that eludes the tyranny of the normal, sweeping under the radar of conventional economies of value exchange. In this way, Vanier suggests that those who embody weakness and are considered 'nobodies' in a society—i.e., people who exhibit disabilities—'have profound lessons to teach us.' They invite us to move out from behind closed walls of false security and exclusion to acknowledge and accept our vulnerability."[1]

Jesus invites us as vulnerable disciples, aware of our weakness even in the wake of the healing we may find in him. It is from such a place that the interdependence of the body of Christ finds its wholeness.

TRACE HAYTHORN

Pastoral Perspective

about him. From the passage we know not who brought him, only that he was brought.

Here the emphasis is even less on the healing itself, and more on the reactions of others to this event. We do not get a step-by-step exorcism, nor do we hear the first words of the man. The focus is on what the observers will conclude about Jesus in light of what they have seen. The crowd apparently responds in awe and wonder, saying, "Never has anything like this been seen in Israel" (9:33). The synagogue/church officials respond in a different way, equating Jesus to the king of the demons rather than the son of King David. Who is disabled in spirit in this passage?

When we speak of Jesus Christ, who will we say he is? Is he a cosmic therapist who swoops in to address our requests, or does Jesus meet us where we are, whether we can call him great or are brought to him mute in our distress? Can we place ourselves among the crowd in this latter story and with awe and wonder exclaim that the signs performed by Jesus have left us amazed? As we continue to wrestle with the difficult issues that pertain to faith in those times when we are not temporarily abled, let us be alert for the signs around us that Jesus Christ is indeed with us in whatever place we find ourselves. We may approach him with confidence as the two blind men did, or others may bring us when we cannot or will not bring ourselves. Either way, Jesus Christ is already there waiting.

KATHY L. DAWSON

---

1. Thomas E. Reynolds, 2007, "Vulnerable Humanity: Disability and Community beyond 'Normalcy'" (Faith Seeking Understanding: Being Human, Hastings College), http://tinyurl.com/4s238e5; accessed June 13, 2012.

Exegetical Perspective

obedient.[2] This, frankly, seems like a stretch. Surely people who were blind and are suddenly able to see would want everyone to know of the amazing good fortune (grace) they have received. It is more likely that Jesus' statement sets up the reference to "the crowds" that occurs in the transition passage that follows. The crowds were in all likelihood drawn both to Jesus' teaching *and* to the signs and healings that he performed. The testimony of the formerly blind makes this dramatically plausible.

The healing of the man who cannot speak is so very brief as to be almost an afterthought. Primarily what this incident does is set up the amazement of the crowds and the response of the Pharisees. On the one hand, the contrast is between those who come to Jesus believing that he can make them whole and those who scoff. On the other hand, the deeper conflict is between those who see his power as coming from God and those who think his power is demonic. Once again, Matthew foreshadows what comes next. In chapter 10 Jesus gives instructions to his followers about how to deal with those who will reject their ministry, and in chapter 12 the charge of being under demonic authority is made once again (12:24). This time Jesus does not answer the charge but goes out even more broadly (into "all the cities and villages") in his ministry of teaching and healing.

What do we make of the healing miracles that figure so prominently in (especially) this Gospel? Some will argue that they must be taken literally, because to fail to do so undercuts not only the divinity of Jesus but the authority of the Bible. Others are nervous about the supernatural element and want to read these stories as symbolic of God's desire for healing and wholeness in human life. Another approach is to read these stories as theological statements that point both to Jesus' true identity as the Son of God and to the eschatological promise that when God comes to make all things new, there will be no pain or suffering or crying or death, for all of those powerfully destructive things will have passed away.

CYNTHIA M. CAMPBELL

Homiletical Perspective

flow of new wine, once it bursts forth from old wineskins! Perhaps the good news of God's mercy is spreading even today, defying attempts to obstruct or control it! We catch a glimpse of the dynamism of God's gospel in what follows.

While the two are out spreading the news about Jesus, against Jesus' wishes, a person who is mute is brought to Jesus, his inability to speak attributed to the power of a demon (v. 32). Those in the grip of evil are not outside the reach of God's mercy. The "Son of David" releases him from that grip, and his speech flows freely. This may call to mind someone you know who has been released from the grip of addiction, sorrow, or a cycle of violence and is now able to speak of it. You might respond to such good news in the manner the crowd does in the text. They "marvel" and exclaim, "Never has anything like this been seen" (v. 33).

The sermon can now step back and take a look at the characters who have recently received mercy from the Son of David. A bleeding woman, a young girl, two blind men, and a person who is mute have all joined the ranks of those who are drinking deeply of the "new wine." This is Matthew's way of showing his own diverse community just how inclusive this movement of God really is.

Then a shadow falls across the movement. Opposition and misunderstanding also find a voice in this text. "By the ruler of the demons he casts out the demons," it says (v. 34). Elites who find themselves threatened when God's grace moves to the margins will attempt to demonize God's agents and control the flow of God's favor. That is part of the story too.

RICHARD F. WARD

2. Ibid., 239.

Matthew 9:35–10:4

35Then Jesus went about all the cities and villages, teaching in their synagogues, and proclaiming the good news of the kingdom, and curing every disease and every sickness. 36When he saw the crowds, he had compassion for them, because they were harassed and helpless, like sheep without a shepherd. 37Then he said to his disciples, "The harvest is plentiful, but the laborers are few; 38therefore ask the Lord of the harvest to send out laborers into his harvest."

10:1Then Jesus summoned his twelve disciples and gave them authority over unclean spirits, to cast them out, and to cure every disease and every sickness. 2These are the names of the twelve apostles: first, Simon, also known as Peter, and his brother Andrew; James son of Zebedee, and his brother John; 3Philip and Bartholomew; Thomas and Matthew the tax collector; James son of Alphaeus, and Thaddaeus; 4Simon the Cananaean, and Judas Iscariot, the one who betrayed him.

Theological Perspective

After two chapters of miraculous healings, Matthew draws to a close this section, which summarizes the substance of Christian ministry: teaching the faithful, proclaiming the good news, and showing compassion to the "harassed and helpless." While the unit begins at 9:35, the preceding verse is noteworthy. There Matthew does little more than report the accusation of the Pharisees that Jesus is acting on behalf of "the ruler of the demons." As Jack Kingsbury writes,

> Matthew says nary a word to the effect that the religious authorities conspire to destroy Jesus (cf. Mark 3:6). The absence of this kind of narrative remark at the end of chapter 9 is highly conspicuous, for it discloses that Matthew has not yet invited the reader to construe Jesus' conflict with the authorities as "to the death."[1]

The result is a sharp contrast between the embittered response of the Pharisees to the exorcism Jesus performs and the qualities of faithful ministry outlined in 9:35–36.

Jesus is the model for ministry. While many people often come together seeking Jesus' assistance,

[1.]Jack Dean Kingsbury, "The Significance of the Earthly Jesus in the Gospel of Matthew," *Ex Auditu* 14 (1998): 63.

Pastoral Perspective

The church is always searching for leaders. This is true whether the leader occupies an actual governing office or is a volunteer nursery worker or sexton. How does the church's nurture of leadership lead the church's officers and volunteers to a better understanding of what it means to be a disciple of Jesus Christ?

Some churches have elaborate training regimens for those who are called to be leaders. For instance, The Presbyterian Church in East Africa has a lay training school, where all leaders, regardless of their role, attend specific classes taught by denominational leaders and undertake a curriculum that is prescribed across all of Kenya. There are many different ways of preparing leaders for their part in the ministry of God.

In this passage, we will consider four movements of leadership that may prompt our own reconsideration of how leaders are formed: (1) modeling leadership, (2) viewing the world compassionately, (3) making a timely response, and (4) sending out empowered leaders.

Modeling Leadership (9:35). In this one verse, Matthew summarizes all that has happened in Jesus' ministry thus far. He has traveled to communities large and small. He has taught in the houses of worship and healed any who have sought him out. As

Exegetical Perspective

This passage serves as a transition between chapters 8 and 9 (in which Jesus demonstrates the good news through various healings) and chapter 10 (one of the five blocks of teaching material in Matthew). Nevertheless, even as a literary transition, this passage presents important themes for this Gospel, including the portrayal of Jesus as shepherd, the *eschaton* as harvest, and the commissioning of disciples who are to carry the mission forward.

The transition begins with a summary statement: "Jesus went about all the cities and villages, teaching in their synagogues, and proclaiming the good news of the kingdom, and curing every disease and sickness" (9:35). This repeats almost exactly what we read in 4:23, the transition verse that ends the first section of this Gospel. Thus these two passages act as bookends for the chapters that set out, first, Jesus' teaching ministry (chaps. 5–7) and then his healing ministry (chaps. 8–9). Teaching, proclaiming, and healing are all of a piece—the same thing in different modes. First, Jesus describes the reign of God; then he demonstrates it. This is the ministry to which he will commission his disciples. It is also the mission to which he calls the church today.

When Jesus sees the crowd in 5:1, he goes up the mountain to teach. This time the crowd seems to him like "sheep without a shepherd" (9:36b). John's

Homiletical Perspective

We come now to a way station in the plot of Matthew's Gospel. It gives us the chance to look back through the story to see that Jesus has been boldly practicing what he preached in the Sermon on the Mount (5:1–7:28). Through his speech and actions Jesus has been blessing the poor in spirit, the mourners, the meek, and the persecuted. His ministry is evoking faith in the recipients of God's mercy and care. He is fulfilling "the law and the prophets" (5:17). We have witnessed how Jesus has the power to heal and to command the natural order, yet cannot control the spread of the good news. The gospel seems to have a power of its own! So does the rising opposition. These two centers of power are on a collision course, and the tension between them is rising.

The text tells us that Jesus' ministry of healing, teaching, and preaching (9:35) will continue, but now we are going to see the disciples get into the act. Up to this point, they have blended into the crowd. We have barely heard mention of them since he first called Simon, Andrew, James, and John (4:18–22), and then Matthew (9:9). Now Jesus is ready to make the transition from model of faithful ministry to mentor. The response to God's grace is overwhelming, but so is the need for an expanded invasion of God's mercy. Jesus needs help to carry out his mission. His "one-man show" is about to become an ensemble of care.

Matthew 9:35–10:4

Theological Perspective

they do not come together as a community. They do not come together as a collective; they amass as a crowd, driven by their individual needs. In many ways, they embody the heart of the call in Matthew. James Bailey writes, "In Matthew's narrative, the crowds are depicted as needy in search of food and healing; in contrast, the discipleship community is enabled to move beyond its own needs to be in ministry for others. For Matthew, the church exists to identify with needy people (all people)."[2] The faithful leader of a community of believers is like a shepherd, often meeting them as a crowd and leading them into a community of compassion.

Leadership of this sort in first-century Palestine, however, is a precious commodity. The harvest, a common biblical reference for the final judgment, is plentiful, but the workers are few. After demonstrating many acts of compassion in the presence of the disciples, Matthew has Jesus name the Twelve, the apostles who will be entrusted with "authority over unclean spirits, to cast them out, and to cure every disease and every sickness" (10:1b). These practical acts of compassion are not new ministries; they are the very acts in which Jesus has been engaged throughout his ministry (4:23; 9:35). No longer are the disciples observers of Jesus' mighty acts; they are now cohealers, literally the "sent ones." Jesus' ministry is now their ministry, and in this transaction their ministry becomes the ministry of the church. Jesus, however, complicates matters, beginning in 10:5.

There is a great deal of contemporary publishing dedicated to the exploration and development of leadership. Academic programs, professional conferences, and consulting services abound for those seeking to develop their abilities and capacities for leadership. Much of that, however, falls within the sociological or psychological realm (or even within specific disciplines such as business, medicine, or politics). The leadership called for in this pericope is a theological construct: Who is God calling these people to be? How is God calling them to live? Jesus grants the authority to heal and perform exorcisms to the Twelve who have been following him, watching as he has performed these same acts. They have undergone an intentional formation process under Jesus' leadership, learning to live, lead, and do as God would have them do. As with Jesus, such leadership is not in contrast to the Law; it is the fulfillment of the Law. With all due respect to the writer and

Pastoral Perspective

he has been doing these things, his disciples/learners have been watching him work. They have seen him in his triumphs and when he is tired. They have listened to his teaching and have heard him confronted by the religious establishment. They have sacrificed a home and stability for the opportunity to be a part of a movement that will usher in a new way of being in relationship with God.

What might this look like in our churches and ministries of today? It could be the recovery of an apprenticeship model of leadership. In this model a less experienced worker is paired with someone who has already learned the craft or acquired the necessary leadership skills. In asking someone to teach church school for the first time, one would pair that person with an experienced teacher. When choosing a church treasurer, one would want this person to have time to observe another who has been holding this position for a time. Walking alongside does not mean dominating; it means guiding and coaching the person in the tasks that he or she will need to do. We hope that, in the process, friendships are formed and faith continues to grow for both parties.

In following the leadership of others, we cannot help but become attuned to the needs of those to whom we minister.

Viewing the World Compassionately (9:36). In this verse Jesus looks on the crowds who have been following him with compassion and concern. He sees that those who should be helping the people are not doing so. Why else would there be so many seeking knowledge and healing? He likens their plight to that of a herd of sheep without a shepherd, wandering around aimlessly, not knowing where they are headed or where they might find nourishment. He calls them "harassed and helpless." They are powerless to change their own lot, and there is no one who will step up and show them the way.

Think about the powerless in your own congregation and community. Who are without a voice? Where is their need? It may be the youngest or the oldest in your midst. It may be those who are ill or lonely. It may be those who are jobless or in financial distress. It may be those who are in destructive relationships and see no way out. Who are the "harassed and helpless" in your community? The needs are great, but as Jesus points out in our next verse, the leaders are few who will minister to those who are in need.

Making a Timely Response (9:37–38). In the face of so much need, it is easy to shut down or be confused

---

2. James L. Bailey, "Church as Embodiment of Jesus' Mission," *Currents in Theology and Mission* 30, no. 3 (June 2003): 190.

Gospel reflects at length on the image of Jesus as the good shepherd, but even in this brief passage, the rich OT metaphor for God's relationship to Israel comes into play (see esp. Ezek. 34:8). Eugene Boring points out that the phrase is taken from Numbers 27:17, a story about transition in leadership. Moses asks God to select a leader to follow him so that Israel may not be "like sheep without a shepherd." Just as Moses will pass the mantle to Joshua, so Jesus is about to commission his followers to take up and continue his ministry.[1]

Matthew calls attention to the heightened emotion in the scene in two ways. First, the people are "harassed and helpless" (or "torn apart," 9:36b). Their situation is dire. Second, Jesus' response is very strong; "compassion" literally means a "stirring in the bowels." He reacts the same way to the hunger of the crowd in both accounts of the feeding in the wilderness (14:14 and 15:32). Jesus' deeds of power ("miracles") are not simply displays of divine authority. Rather, they well up from a deep sense of care for the needs of people. Once again, Jesus provides a model for the ministry that is to be done in his name.

Then the metaphor shifts. The primary image with which Matthew now works is that of the harvest. This is a thematic eschatological image that stresses the urgency of the time. Whenever the crop is ready, the farmer or grower needs to mobilize people and equipment to bring the crop in as quickly as possible. Just as Jesus sees a flock of sheep needing the care and direction of a shepherd, so now he sees a large crop waiting in the field for farm workers to complete the harvest. Tom Long points out that these are words Jesus is always speaking to the church. "[This] is a mission that cannot wait for a more opportune time—when the church is stronger, richer, or more confident. The harvest time has come, and laborers are needed in the fields *today*."[2]

In direct response to this teaching, Jesus then gathers "his twelve disciples" (10:1). This is the first time that we have heard that there are twelve. The number appears to be symbolic for the twelve tribes of Israel. While this could be read as a supersessionist text, it is better to read it as a sign of Jesus' ministry to renew and restore Israel rather than replace it. Interestingly enough, this Gospel has told us about the calling only of Peter, Andrew, James, John, and

Perhaps it is because Jesus senses the presence of the opposition, or perhaps it is because he has not been able to control the progress of the good news, but Jesus' relationship to "the crowds" changes. He *sees* them differently. They are not simply the chorus that responds with puzzlement and wonder to his miraculous deeds. Look between the lines of this brief text and imagine Jesus walking through those towns and villages (v. 35); imagine seeing the faces of those he encounters. Do they look like anyone from our world? Imagine him listening to what they have to say and attending to their afflictions. See him teaching in the synagogue. Consider how the tone of a question might strike his ear or how children might react to his stories. What might Jesus say to a congregation like that?

Jesus' experiences among the crowds have trained his eyes to see them as "sheep without a shepherd" (9:36b). It is dangerous to leave sheep unattended; they are "helpless" and "harassed" by predators (9:36b). What arises in Jesus is compassion. This is not some idle sentiment. Jesus' feeling for the crowds comes from the seat of his emotions and prompts him to act. Jesus sees the crowds as God sees them. So deep is the compassion and concern that God has for Israel that God has sent Jesus to shepherd them. However, there is not enough time for Jesus to do the shepherding all by himself.

The next part of the story strikes a note of urgency with a shift in imagery. The crowds are fields ripe for harvest. Laborers are needed immediately to reap a bumper crop. A question is implied: who is available to become one of God's harvesters? Your sermon could explore what it takes to become one of God's harvesters. Matthew's text suggests that one need only believe that Jesus embodies God's love and follow his lead. God's harvesters see the crowds as God sees them and respond with compassion to their expressions of need. The sermon should carry the note of urgency in the text. The needs of the crowds we see are immediate. God's harvesters cannot wait until they get their doctrine straight, their budgets adjusted, or all their questions answered. They act early and often to expand the parameters of God's Realm.

Jesus' vision of the crowds ends with a prayer request: "Ask the Lord of the harvest to send out laborers into his harvest" (9:38). In the flow of the narrative, it does not take much time for that prayer to be answered! Matthew presents a list of twelve disciples who are authorized and empowered to expand the reach of the ministry Jesus has been doing,

1. Eugene Boring, "Matthew," in *The New Interpreter's Bible* (Nashville: Abingdon Press, 1995), 8:252.
2. Thomas G. Long, *Matthew* (Louisville, KY: Westminster John Knox Press, 1997), 113, emphasis added.

Theological Perspective

leadership guru Robert Greenleaf, this collection of folks is, in many ways, called to demonstrate the original model of servant leadership.

However, their model is also not entirely new. In 10:2–4, the disciples are identified in four different ways. First, three are identified by the names of their fathers: James and John, sons of Zebedee, and James son of Alphaeus. At one level this formulation simply distinguishes the two disciples named James from one another; on another level, this traditional Jewish formulation sets them within their context, not apart from it. Second, Matthew, the only disciple in this passage singled out for his occupation, is identified as the tax collector. The Gospel makes an important point about the role of one's past in one's ministry: when we follow Jesus, we are defined by what we are becoming, rather than by what we once were. Third, Simon (not Peter) is identified as the Cananaean. Traditionally, interpreters have understood this name to be related to the Aramaic term for Zealot. Unlike Matthew, who is identified by his occupation, Simon is identified by his political (and perhaps revolutionary) activity. Perhaps this is Matthew's way of signaling that the gospel of Jesus is not "nice" or innocuous but has the power to transform the community, the nation, even the world. Finally, Judas Iscariot is introduced as "the one who betrayed Jesus." Not only does this label presuppose knowledge of the larger narrative of Jesus' death; it also colors Judas's role among the disciples from this point forward.

Here are two notes in conclusion. While the terms and labels of the Twelve represent a certain diversity, this is an essentially homogenous apostolic core: all male, all Jewish residents of first-century Palestine, all working or lower class (there are no elites in the group). There are no women, foreigners, or political or religious leaders in the mix. Therefore one should be cautious in characterizing this group as the model of Christian leadership, given the many other examples of faithful discipleship throughout the text. Second, the diversity that is present within the group, the occupational and vocational distinctiveness of several apostles, is an important critique for those who seek only a certain type of pastor. In Jesus Christ, God called a group together that would likely not make it past most of our discernment/qualification/selection processes in today's denominations. Who might God be calling even now to ministry in our midst who is nothing like the pastors we have known or imagined for our communities of faith?

TRACE HAYTHORN

Pastoral Perspective

about where to begin as we try to address these problems. Jesus impels us toward action with his claim that the harvest is upon us. Now is the time that laborers are needed. The harvest is ripe. Everyone should go into the fields, cities, and towns and get to work. For Jesus this is not the time to sit around and shake our heads at the problems of the world; it is time for action, with plenty of work to go around.

Sometimes the church seems to work at a snail's pace. We work through committee structures, we talk endlessly about action, and eventually we may get around to doing something. The emergent church/house church movement has prophetically challenged the institutional church to think about other models for doing the mission of Jesus Christ. From small groups blending Bible study with hands-on outreach, many young adults go out into the fields (as it were) while traditional churches are still weighing alternatives. Perhaps we should think about supporting the work that is being done already by individuals within the church community and inviting others to join the harvest.

Sending Out Empowered Leaders (10:1–4). Jesus chooses his twelve disciples/learners to be laborers in the harvest. He gives them a new designation that is not used elsewhere in Matthew. They are "apostles," those who are sent out. They are named in pairs; so apparently they are not sent out alone. They are given authority to do what they have seen Jesus do.

There comes a time in the life of every teacher when "letting go" needs to happen. New leaders need to be given authority and permission to be human. As they observed the humanness of their teacher when the teacher was their model, so they will make mistakes. In letting go, the teacher must trust that the teaching has been sufficient, that God will supply the needed answers and strength, and that the One who teaches all of us will sustain us as we continue to labor on behalf of those in need.

KATHY L. DAWSON

Exegetical Perspective

Matthew. How the other seven were selected out of the larger group of followers, we do not know.

These twelve are then called "apostles" (10:2a). This is the only time Matthew uses this term. While it becomes a formal title (almost an office) for Luke and Paul, here it seems to function in the literal meaning of "those who are sent out." The lists of the Twelve are not the same among the Synoptic Gospels; John never lists the Twelve and cites at least one (Nathanael) not named in the Synoptics. Paul adds others as apostles (including James, the brother of Jesus). All of this suggests a certain fluidity of leadership in the early years of the Christian movement. The transformative nature of Jesus' ministry can be seen even in this list, however. The title "the Cananaean" after Simon's name suggests that he was part of a group committed to the overthrow of the Roman occupation. Matthew, the former tax collector, made his living off the occupation. Nevertheless here they are together in a very new kind of community.

One of the most memorable passages in the Gospel of Matthew is the Great Commission, when the risen Jesus sends out his followers into all the world. Here, in this transitional passage, Jesus commissions his disciples and sends them out. Even during his lifetime, there was more than enough ministry to go around. While he was instructing them, Jesus gave his followers amazing power to demonstrate the good news of the reign of God. Surely this is a reminder to us today that ministry—proclaiming and teaching and healing—is the gift and responsibility God continually gives to the church.

CYNTHIA M. CAMPBELL

Homiletical Perspective

casting out demons and healing those who are ill. In what particular ways might we be an answer to Jesus' prayer? If we do not have the power to "cast out demons" or to heal with a miraculous touch, what power do we have to release sufferers from the mysterious grip of evil?

Matthew dubs these twelve "apostles," which carries a different connotation from "disciples." Just as someone in authority might send an envoy or ambassador, Jesus commissions his "apostles" or "ones sent." Here Matthew is giving the term more freight. He signifies that these are "the Twelve," that is, they are guardians of a tradition that is still in flux and in danger of being eclipsed by "false teachers."[1]

As with any list, the preacher may be tempted to skip past this roll call in order to get to the next section. Before you do, take note of two things. First, note the juxtaposition of "Matthew the tax collector" (v. 3), a minion of Rome, and "Simon the Cananaean" or "Zealot" (v. 4), an enemy of Rome.[2] This is a new community indeed, where old animosities and hatreds are overcome in favor of God's mission!

Second, note one more thing about this list that still haunts the church. No women are authorized to be "apostles"! Women are full recipients of God's mercy in Matthew's Gospel (8:14–15; 9:18–26; 15:21–28) and will be witnesses to his death and his resurrection (27:55–56; 28:1–10). Not to name women as apostles who are recognized as bearers, guardians, and envoys of Jesus' saving work unsettles the authority of this list. Fortunately, God's gospel spreads beyond the control of men or any other group that tries to limit its reach. Note this omission in Matthew's list, and add to it by naming women who have faithfully served as God's envoys.

RICHARD F. WARD

---

1. John P. Meier, *Matthew* (Wilmington, DE: Michael Glazier, 1980), 104.
2. Ibid., 105.

Matthew 10:5–15

⁵These twelve Jesus sent out with the following instructions: "Go nowhere among the Gentiles, and enter no town of the Samaritans, ⁶but go rather to the lost sheep of the house of Israel. ⁷As you go, proclaim the good news, 'The kingdom of heaven has come near.' ⁸Cure the sick, raise the dead, cleanse the lepers, cast out demons. You received without payment; give without payment. ⁹Take no gold, or silver, or copper in your belts, ¹⁰no bag for your journey, or two tunics, or sandals, or a staff; for laborers deserve their food. ¹¹Whatever town or village you enter, find out who in it is worthy, and stay there until you leave. ¹²As you enter the house, greet it. ¹³If the house is worthy, let your peace come upon it; but if it is not worthy, let your peace return to you. ¹⁴If anyone will not welcome you or listen to your words, shake off the dust from your feet as you leave that house or town. ¹⁵Truly I tell you, it will be more tolerable for the land of Sodom and Gomorrah on the day of judgment than for that town."

Theological Perspective

The Gospel according to Matthew blends five discursive segments into its larger narrative about the birth, life, death, and resurrection of Jesus of Nazareth. The first—and most familiar—is the Sermon on the Mount. Matthew 10:5–11:1, the second of these segments, focuses on the mission that Jesus gives to his disciples (or, as in 10:2, his "apostles" or "sent-out ones"). The third, fourth, and fifth segments are about the kingdom of heaven (chap. 13), the shape of Christian community (chap. 18), and the coming *eschaton* (chaps. 24–25). The ordering of the five segments ought not be ignored by those who would preach or teach from Matthew 10, for each segment answers important questions about the shape of Christian life and thought and builds on previous segments. This makes the content of Matthew 10 especially provocative, as it (1) describes the work of discipleship, (2) closely joins that work to the ministry of Jesus, and (3) addresses both the benefits and costs of pursuing the kind of discipleship that links one to Jesus' ministry. Think of it as the teaching that Jesus does before sending his disciples out on their first internships.

How does Jesus convey and nuance these ideas in his pre-internship "lecture"? For the sake of convenience, it is helpful to divide Matthew 10 into parts: verses 5–15, in which Jesus describes their

Pastoral Perspective

Preacher Joanna Adams tells the story of a woman who faithfully traveled to church conferences at Montreat, North Carolina, every summer. When Joanna asked about her regular attendance, the woman explained that she had been there as a girl when the preacher for the day was handed a message as he ascended the pulpit, opened the note, and announced that World War II had ended. Ever since, she explained, she had come to the gatherings hoping for news as good as that.

In the church our good news is often shrouded in conditions, caveats, scholarship, somberness, and "shoulds." Buried beneath is the simple gospel Jesus instructed his disciples to proclaim: "The kingdom of heaven is at hand." To believe that the reign of God is at hand should lift the spirit of every service of worship, sermon, song, and prayer—and yes, even our business and polity! Often we are so busy parsing God's unconditional love that the sick get sicker, the dead prefer the status quo, lepers are excluded, and the demons of dysfunction have a field day in congregations and at regional and national church gatherings!

Sometimes we fail to focus on our own families and congregations as we impose on the world "the new order" implied by the reign of God—what Jesus may have been warning his disciples about when he

Exegetical Perspective

If you are a Gentile (I suspect most of the readers of this essay are), Matthew 10:5–15 does not get off to a promising start: "Go nowhere among the Gentiles and enter no town of the Samaritans." The discipleship envisioned in Matthew 10 applies to Jews who are following the Jew Jesus, whose mission is first to "the lost sheep of the house of Israel" (see Ezek. 34:16, 23). As one commentator observes, "It is not clear whether this means all of Israel that is lost, or the lost amongst Israel, or even the northern tribes who were thought to be lost, that is, the Galileans."[1] Here, the geographical limitations on mission described by Jesus are consistent with the way Matthew tells the gospel story. Only after Easter (Matt. 28:19) will the risen Jesus unequivocally expand the horizon of mission for his disciples to include "all nations" (*panta ta ethnē*). Fortunately for all Gentiles, then and now, Matthew 10:5–15 is not the final word from Jesus about who is to be on the receiving end of God's good news.

In this text, Jesus' disciples are sent out (*apostellō*) to do what Jesus does. They are to preach, heal the sick, exorcise demons, raise the dead, and cure the lepers. They are to carry out this mission wherever

1. Ben Witherington III, *Matthew,* Smyth & Helwys Bible Commentary (Macon, GA: Smyth & Helwys, 2006), 218.

Homiletical Perspective

A minister friend of mine once bought a new robe. It was a souped-up version of the black Geneva gown that is worn in my tradition—it was, in fact, a black Geneva gown on steroids. It featured multiple colors, with red piping around velvet panels that stretched across the front and down the length of the robe. It boasted embroidered symbols of the church stitched on either side of its lapel. It had three chevrons on each arm that called attention to my friend's newly earned doctorate, and they too were surrounded by the red piping. When supplemented with a clerical collar, Geneva tabs, and the various stoles of the liturgical year, the whole ensemble featured everything except blinking lights and tires with white sidewalls. I asked my friend, "What possessed you to buy this?" After looking a bit sheepish, he replied, "It gives me more authority."

Those of us who serve the church for a living often rely, in moments of anxiety, upon all manner of ecclesial bling that we expect will enhance our pastoral authority: fancy robes, impressive titles, purple shirts, a string of degrees following our names, anything that eases our professional insecurities and yearnings for power.

A text like this one—a set of instructions Jesus is giving his disciples as they are sent out to serve as missionaries of the kingdom of heaven—shows up

Matthew 10:5–15

Theological Perspective

impending tasks; verses 16–23, in which he names the implications of those tasks for those who would pursue them; verses 24–33, in which he places those tasks in their larger cosmic context; and verses 34–42, which include Jesus' paradoxical and profoundly theological claim, "Those who find their life will lose it, and those who lose their life for my sake will find it" (v. 39), and in which he reiterates and nuances the earlier sections. The remainder of this essay focuses on verses 5–15; the next two essays focus on verses 16–23 and verses 24–33.

Perhaps the single most remarkable verses in 10:5–15 are verses 7–8, which constitute far more than a commissioning of the disciples as they go off on their internships. The tasks they are charged with (proclaiming the kingdom of heaven, healing the sick, raising the dead, cleansing lepers, and driving out demons) are remarkable, not primarily in their ambitiousness—though they are certainly that—but because these are the very actions that Jesus has performed in the preceding chapters. Doing these things, then, constitutes more than being obedient to the charge that Jesus has given them. Doing these things becomes a way of participating in Jesus' ministry and life.

It is one thing to be obedient. Servants obey. Soldiers obey. Trained animals obey. Obedience has its value. It maintains order, wins battles, and makes many forms of work possible. However, obedience is also dangerous. It reveals and reinforces differentials in power and authority, reifies traditional hierarchies, and can be an excuse for perpetrating horrors.

Jesus' instructions to the Twelve, on the other hand, disrupt those hierarchies and therein begin to reveal the true source of all power. By charging the disciples to perform the same tasks that he has performed, Jesus invites the disciples into his ministry, so that they may better understand his life. There are some things that he alone will do, some qualities that he alone has. Nevertheless, the things that make him unique do not prevent Christians from participating in at least some of what he does and is. A kind of *imitatio Christi* (or, more accurately, an *imitatio Jesu*) shapes the life of believers and reveals the democratization of the power of God for the good of the world.

Conventional wisdom argues that Matthew's focus is not on Jesus so much as it is on the kingdom of heaven that Jesus inaugurates and to which he points. This conventional wisdom is not wrong: Matthew's Gospel really is different from hagiography. However, the conventional wisdom is incomplete, because it misses just how tightly the kingdom of

Pastoral Perspective

charged them to go first to "the lost sheep" of their own house or tribe. This exclusive focus on "the house of Israel" may have been Matthew's concern more than that of Jesus. The mission of Matthew's Gospel is to proclaim the good news to one's own. Who better than our own might listen to us?

Regardless of the focus, Jesus urges us to trust the gospel. How often Christians resist taking risks to proclaim our good news, fearing loss of church members and donors, expecting support for endorsing the way things are, losing sight of the way things should be! How did the disciples take to trusting the people to whom they were sent, carrying "no gold, or silver, or copper"—not even a bag with a change of clothes? Did they at least come to trust that God would return the peace they visited on households or towns whose inhabitants turned out to be unwelcoming and thus unworthy?

It must feel good to "shake the dust off your feet as you leave that house or town" (v. 14b), expecting like Jonah to witness the Ninevites' much deserved punishment from the heavens, or feeling no little satisfaction as Sodom and Gomorrah were destroyed for their inhospitality.

What if we, the church, are Sodom and Gomorrah? In workshops, biblical scholar James Sanders would say that if we read Scripture and identify with the "good guys" in the story, we may have missed its point. What if *we* are the unreceptive household or village that refuses to hear, "The kingdom of heaven is at hand"? What if Jesus' disciples now are the very people we resist listening to and attending to: the vulnerable, the dying, contemporary "lepers," the demonized? What if *we* are the ones who cannot be trusted to welcome them into our household of faith and hear their cries about God's inbreaking realm? What if the peace *they* offer *us* returns to them and leaves us shouting a panicked "Heads up!" for the fire and brimstone of Sodom and Gomorrah, rather than announcing the good news of God's reign?

A rabbinic teaching has it that Sodom was destroyed, not simply for being unwelcoming of strangers, but because it codified its inhospitality, adding to its polity a requirement that every household and congregation refuse hospitality to strangers, lest the town be overrun. How often has the church done the same, literally and metaphorically?

The kingdom of heaven, the reign of God, changes everything. How we view the world. How we look upon one another. How we understand ourselves. How we experience God. God's realm is awesome, beyond imagination, a place of healing

they are sent, but in Matthew that will be most often in the "city" (*polis,* a favorite locale for the mission of Jesus, appears more than twenty-five times in this Gospel), rather than in the village/country that serves as the setting for most of Mark's Gospel. It is quite likely that the intended audience for Matthew is the church trying to understand and negotiate discipleship in an urban setting.

There is no public/private distinction in Jesus' mission instructions to his disciples. They are to bring the transforming power of the gospel to bear against every force—public, private, political, or social—that diminishes or demeans human life. Matthew's community could not have missed the implication that Jesus' mission instructions to his disciples were now mission instructions to the emerging church. Those overhearing this Gospel, whether in the early church or today, should take comfort that Jesus not only sends but also equips those he sends to carry out his mission.

Why leave the comfort of home or company with Jesus to head out to the rigors of a mission in unfamiliar environs and with unfamiliar people? Matthew's Jesus will answer that query in one statement: "You received without payment; give without payment" (v. 8). This is a reminder that all disciples and all apostles (those sent out), are recipients of the grace of God, freely given. This conviction, found not just in Matthew, reverberates throughout the New Testament (see 2 Cor. 11:7; 1 Cor. 9:3–18; Mark 6:8–9).

Jesus does *not* equip his own disciples, and by implication Matthew's church, with lots of discipleship accoutrements. In fact, the recurring rhetorical note in this text is "take no" sandals, cash, or extra tunic. To follow Jesus is not so much a matter of honor or prestige; it is a radical call not to hedge our bets, but to trust in the one who awaits us wherever we travel. Eugene Boring argues: "For both Jesus and his disciples, proceeding on a mission without even the basic equipment for sustenance and self-defense was a prophetic sign, an acting out of the presence of the kingdom similar to the symbolic actions performed by the biblical prophets."[2]

Boring is right, but one can go even further. The disciples' mission was more than a prophetic sign; it was *kerygmatic* in nature. They were to announce what Jesus himself had declared, namely, that the kingdom of heaven, the reign of God, was near (*ēngiken).* The disciples and then Matthew's church saw nothing less than the reign of God embodied in

2. M. Eugene Boring, "The Gospel of Matthew," in *The New Interpreter's Bible* (Nashville: Abingdon Press, 1995), 8:256.

right on time to challenge our conjured-up symbols of authority in the name of the only real authority we have. This text is like the charge to the new pastor at his or her ordination. While it is addressed to Jesus' disciples, I believe Matthew intends for his church—and now ours—to overhear these instructions, because, in fact, they are timeless.

After all, the mission of the church—its pastors and its members—is a continuation, through the ages, of Jesus' ministry. To the extent that we add our own energies to his ongoing ministry, that ministry itself is the greatest source of our authority. It is not our bling, our pulpit voices, our records of measurable success, our growing budgets. It is rather the evidence of how we join Jesus in the work he continues to do in the world. To care for our people, the community, and the world around us—in all the forms that such caring takes—is to participate in the always unfolding, always emerging kingdom of God.

Years ago, during my early ministry in a particular parish, an incoming pastor was being examined by my judicatory. An urban parish was interested in his going there to lead them in some creative new ministries designed to address its changing context. It had been a church of some wealth, but the times—and the neighborhood—had changed, and the church knew it had to change too. A graduate of one of our denominational seminaries, this man superbly sustained his examination on all points—theology, Scripture, church history, polity, the works. The rub came when he insisted on the judicatory's approval of dramatic changes in his salary. He did not want to accept the salary and terms the church was offering. He wanted that salary to be dramatically *reduced* so he could qualify to live more simply in nearby public housing. His reasoning was that this move would enable him and his church to relate better to the new demographics of the area he would be serving.

The judicatory responded by suspending the examination and eventual approval of that man's call until he could be examined by a team of psychologists.

I wish someone at that judicatory meeting had thought to read this text out loud: "Take no gold, or silver, or copper in your belts, no bag for your journey, or two tunics, or sandals, or a staff; for laborers deserve their food" (vv. 9–10). It is a text, after all, that encourages us never to claim the implied authority of our own possessions or substantial giftedness, but rather the authority of Jesus Christ our Lord.

Tom Long, professor of homiletics at Candler School of Theology of Emory University, in his

Theological Perspective

heaven is bound to Jesus' life, death, and resurrection. To observe the kingdom is to observe the work of Jesus; to participate in the kingdom is to participate in the life of Jesus; to understand the kingdom is to know Jesus and, through him, God.

In observing and participating and knowing, Christians discover the actual nature of their own lives. They will be reminded that they have "received without cost" and so ought to "give without charge" (v. 8b). They can neither make claims about the merit of their own work apart from the prior grace of God nor demand recompense for that work, as if they had earned participation in the divine life. They will realize that the sent-out life is inherently relational, as they rely on others rather than their own power and devices (vv. 9–12). They will learn the difficult task of making wise judgments, rather than either refusing to act in discerning ways or damning all who are not like themselves (vv. 13–14). They will come to know that the divine economy shaped by grace, dependence, and discernment is also a just economy, which is both threat and promise (v. 15).

Recognizing the centrality of grace, dependence, and discernment, all bound together in the divine economy, helps mitigate some of the more bruising interpretations of verses 5–6. Being commissioned to go not to the Gentiles but only "to the lost sheep of the house of Israel" need indicate neither an ontological ordering between different people groups nor a setup for the rejection of those Jews who do not respond to the disciples' proclamations even after being specially targeted. Neither seeming (but only seeming) natural differences nor vengeful rejection follows logically from such a center. This is not to dismiss the peculiar specificity of Jesus' charge: the relation between Jews and Gentiles in the New Testament—and certainly in Matthew—is convoluted. It is, though, to try to keep the major theological claim major and the minor one minor.[1]

MARK DOUGLAS

Pastoral Perspective

and a place of trust for those who are sent and for those who welcome them, a spiritual commonwealth of which we are, every one of us, fellow citizens and heirs with Christ as beloved children of God. Jesus knew that. He sent his disciples out to their own people to learn—not just teach—that gospel firsthand.

That is why the vantage point of a pulpit or pew is inadequate to see the kingdom of heaven. That is why the privileged view of a theologian, dogmatist, or ethicist is not enough. That is why orthodoxy and legalism reach no more effectively into God's heaven than the building blocks of Babel. We too must be sent. We must focus. We must take risks. We must do so without expecting a personal return. We must offer the peace of Christ as we proclaim, "The kingdom of heaven has come near!"

In 1473, Catherine of Genoa, a lay woman, had a powerful experience of God's love for her. She gave up a privileged life to care for the sick and poor at a hospital. No doubt that firsthand experience of God's reign inspired her to write:

> As for heaven, I guess you've noticed, God put no
>   doors there.
> No, God didn't. And don't you wonder why?
> It's because whoever wants to enter heaven, does.
> That's how God's love works.
> All-merciful, standing there with [God's] arms wide
>   open,
> God's waiting—this very moment—
> to embrace us and take us into [God's] splendid
>   beauty
> and kindnesses.[1]

This is the good news that we come to gatherings of the faithful to hear. This is the good news that we deliver when helping others. This, according to religion historian Elaine Pagels in her book *Beyond Belief*, is what attracted people to the early Christian movement: "Such generosity, which ordinarily could be expected only from one's own family, attracted crowds of newcomers to Christian groups, despite the risks."[2]

CHRIS GLASER

---

1. Though I hesitate to offer such a naive interpretation, I wonder whether it is at least worth imagining that Jesus sends the disciples to Jews first for the same reason that seminaries send interns to familiar churches: they have a better sense of what they will be getting into.

1. Catherine of Genoa, in *A Little Daily Wisdom: Christian Women Mystics*, ed. Carmen Acevedo Butcher (Brewster, MA: Paraclete Press, 2009), 253.
2. Elaine Pagels, *Beyond Belief: The Secret Gospel of Thomas* (New York: Vintage Books, 2003), 8.

the person, healing, preaching, death, and resurrection of Jesus. The time of advent, of active waiting for God to send the promised one to Israel, was over. To follow Jesus, according to Matthew, is to live into the transforming reality of the reign of God.

One faithful response to the imminent reign of God is the practice of radical discipleship. The disciples of Jesus were to head out on their mission by traveling lightly, trusting in the sure provisions of God. They were also to trust in the radical hospitality of the community to which they had been sent. As apostles for Jesus, they were to expect to be received, fed, and housed by members within each community they visited. They were to stay in one home in each city, to prevent their exhausting time and energy looking for a new place to stay each night and worrying how they would cover the cost.

Ben Witherington provides some cultural context behind this exchange between Jesus and his disciples:

> In that [ancient Near Eastern] culture . . . one was honor-bound to do all one could to make the guest, even a stranger, feel comfortable throughout the visit. One was to provide for, care for, and protect the guest (cf. the actual stories about Sodom and Gomorrah in Gen 19—even at the risk of one's own family and property).[3]

Those who refused to practice hospitality were guilty not just of poor manners; they were guilty of missing the reign of God that had come near through the mission of the disciples of Jesus.

It would be hard for Matthew's church to miss the implication that Christian discipleship involves radical trust in God, simplicity in living, and also the practice of radical hospitality. No doubt, the early church would have appreciated a more detailed operating manual for how to practice such radical discipleship and hospitality, but at its core Matthew 10:5–15 outlines, in both theology and practice, what it means to follow Jesus in any time and in any place.

GARY W. CHARLES

commentary on Matthew's Gospel, states: "Ministers of mercy are to carry themselves humbly; they are to be vulnerable, depending on the providence of God. Evangelists who show up in a Ferrari with a suitcase full of designer clothes cannot expect to have their gospel call taken seriously."[1]

This does not mean that we accept nothing in the carrying out of our work. "Laborers," after all, "deserve their food." At a recent meeting of our seminary's board, one of our graduating seniors—an enormously faithful and talented young man who has a bright future of ministry ahead of him—gave a report on student life in which he detailed the rhythms of study and classes and worship and community. As his report came to an end, he shared with the board his hopes for the future, beyond his graduation—how he wanted to find a meaningful place to serve, anywhere in this wide world to which God might choose to call him.

Like so many in his young generation, he expressed an astonishing lack of interest in "a career path": first, a gig in a small church, then a gig in a larger church, finally a gig in a "destination church" (frankly, the sort of path I envisioned for myself). He was not interested in any of that. He simply expressed the strong and faithful desire to go wherever God might be calling him to go—anywhere on the planet! The board was riveted by the conclusion of his report: "Here's the nub of it: I just want to serve Jesus, and, if possible, I'd like a paycheck."

Our authority as servants of our Lord is not in the perks of our ministry. Our authority is in serving the One who first brought the joyful announcement that "the kingdom of heaven has come near," and in our participation in the ways in which that announcement is forever expressing itself in the midst of the people with whom we serve.

THEODORE J. WARDLAW

---

1. Thomas G. Long, *Matthew* (Louisville, KY: Westminster John Knox Press, 1997), 117.

3. Witherington, *Matthew*, 222.

Matthew 10:16–23

16"See, I am sending you out like sheep into the midst of wolves; so be wise as serpents and innocent as doves. 17Beware of them, for they will hand you over to councils and flog you in their synagogues; 18and you will be dragged before governors and kings because of me, as a testimony to them and the Gentiles. 19When they hand you over, do not worry about how you are to speak or what you are to say; for what you are to say will be given to you at that time; 20for it is not you who speak, but the Spirit of your Father speaking through you. 21Brother will betray brother to death, and a father his child, and children will rise against parents and have them put to death; 22and you will be hated by all because of my name. But the one who endures to the end will be saved. 23When they persecute you in one town, flee to the next; for truly I tell you, you will not have gone through all the towns of Israel before the Son of Man comes."

Theological Perspective

Participation in the life and ministry of Jesus comes at a cost. How could it not, given the cost of Jesus' own life? If the life of discipleship is shaped by grace, dependence, and theological discernment, then those who would attempt to live lives shaped by merit, autonomy, and worldly wisdom will see the actions of the sent-out ones as eccentric or a threat. Matthew 10:16–23 begins to lay out the implications that come with participating in the ministry and life of Jesus, even as it reinforces many of the lessons of verses 5–15.

The passage begins on a peculiar and formative note: "Be wise as serpents and innocent as doves" (v. 16b). Given that the first half of the verse contains an implicit warning, and that the verses that follow describe lives of extraordinary hardship, one wonders what advantage can be served in being wise and innocent.

Nevertheless wisdom and innocence shape the sent-out life. In the public sphere, displaying wisdom—regardless of whether others agree with it or not—reveals that such a life is shaped by neither madness nor foolishness. Wise words are hard to easily ignore or passively deny and, as such, reveal that there is at least an argument being made that needs to be worked through. In that same sphere, retaining innocence—regardless of whether others

Pastoral Perspective

Jesus' ancient warning of persecution from authorities would not mean as much to us in our context, were it not for our ability within the church to persecute one another. The punitive measures to which communities of faith sometimes turn to resolve differences over belief and practice—betrayal, hatred, even what we may deem to be forms of persecution—are cause for being wary of "wolves" among us. Those who have held unpopular convictions within the church know firsthand the need to be "wise as serpents and innocent as doves." Though today we rarely try people for heresy, we do hold trials for ordination by which we determine what is orthodox in belief and practice.

An old joke told in many denominations focuses on a candidate for ordination who is being grilled by an ordaining body for a very long time. When finally asked, "Are you willing to be damned for the glory of God?" the would-be ordinand famously responds, "I am willing for this entire body to be damned for the glory of God!"

In a discussion on the ordination of gay men and lesbians before a governing body, a woman quoted Paul's purported opposition to homosexuality in Romans 1. A response putting Paul in context reminded the woman that Paul would not have allowed her to voice her opposition in the first place,

Exegetical Perspective

Matthew 10 narrates the intimate and intense mission instruction that Jesus gives to his disciples and that, by inference, Matthew shares with the church. Matthew 10:16–23 is best understood then within the context of instruction given within the first fifteen verses of this chapter. Jesus reminds those who would follow him that Christian discipleship necessarily involves hostility and conflict (see 1 Pet. 4:12). These realities of discipleship are not optional for the Christian life. They are inevitable, and how those who are sent in the name of Jesus engage that hostility and conflict will provide—or fail to provide—a powerful witness to the reign of God alive in the world.

Jesus' instructions to his disciples are a far cry from the more familiar mentality of "get them before they get you." Instead, he says that they are to imagine themselves as sheep being sent out among wolves—not a very romantic picture of human nature and not a very triumphal view of the church. Their response to these wolves is not to defeat them through cunning, but to rise above their violent and vitriolic ways through faithfulness and devoted commitment to Jesus.

In the twentieth-century civil rights movement in America, Matthew 10:16 provided biblical wisdom for Christians who were encountering hostile and often violent resistance. Tom Long reflects:

Homiletical Perspective

Being a representative of Jesus Christ and the gospel is never as simple as proclaiming a word that is universally and joyfully received. Rather, the gospel, and certainly the gospel ministry, always makes its way amid high stakes and competing faith claims, both within and beyond the church. We will not be able to succeed in this ministry unless we live under a big enough view of God and of what God is doing in the world—not just from day to day, where it is sometimes so hard to discern what God is doing, but ultimately.

The warning in this text from Jesus to his disciples takes into account such a big view and sees our work with just the right kind of eyesight—eschatological eyesight. Jesus looks off to the horizon and sees not only grateful churches hanging on to the words of faithful pastors and thereby doing all manner of good in the world. Jesus also sees what he calls "wolves"—forces that act to deter the daring and risk-taking ventures to which he calls us. He is candid about the dangers involved. We who are sent out in his name are to be "like sheep among wolves," practicing wisdom and discernment in the face of these dangers.

Jack L. Stotts, a theologian and ethicist who for years was president of Austin Presbyterian Theological Seminary, used to offer an annual charge to

Matthew 10:16–23

Theological Perspective

know what to do with it or not—lends credibility and authenticity to the personal testimonies that help to constitute those arguments. There are advantages related to both political persuasiveness and individual integrity that come with being this strange snake-bird hybrid.

Were that the whole case, though, the sent-out ones might imagine that their ministries might mirror the easy conceits of the prosperity gospel: the wiser and more innocent they are, the more likely that their ministries will have their intended and generally beneficial effects. As the following verses make clear, however, general beneficence is unlikely to follow the missions to which these interns have been called.

Arguments and actions that are absurd, foolish, or obviously hypocritical are easily ignored, but arguments and actions that must be engaged seriously—especially when those arguments and actions are disruptive to established ways of thinking and acting in the world—can be threatening. When the sent-out ones preach about the coming kingdom of God, heal the sick, and raise the dead, they disrupt established ways of thinking and acting by proclaiming that this is not as good as it gets, that health rather than disease is God's intent, that death does not get the last word. Those with vested interests in maintaining the status quo may not be pleased. Like strong medicine, that which is best for the hearers will still be heard as a threat to them. The sent-out ones will be challenged by the "powers that be" because their lives challenge the solidity of those powers.

Worse, the sent-out ones' ministries will lead to conflicts within families. Families, after all, have as much interest in maintaining the status quo as any other collection of persons, no less in Jesus' day than in ours (though the need to protect the customary standing of the family in Jesus' day had to do with the significance of the family as a political unit, whereas in our day it has more to do with the significance of the family as a haven from political life). Brother will betray brother; parents and children will oppose each other (v. 21).

There is no easy way through all this, especially when the very virtues that help disciples move forward influence the opposition that disciples face. However, there is a promise to be claimed along this difficult path: by participating in the mission (and, therein, the life) of Jesus, the disciples are caught up into the life (and, therein, the mission) of Jesus. There are qualities about Jesus that make him unique (not the least of which is his relation to the

Pastoral Perspective

given his belief that women should not speak in church. A pastor who was present dismissed the latter speaker's entire perspective with the judgment, "He is going to have to lose that bitter streak."

Jesus' counseling of wisdom and gentleness has been needed—but not always received—in all the divisive church debates that Christianity has seen over topics such as military service, war, usury, celibacy, marriage, slavery, civil rights, women's rights, interracial marriage, divorce, foreign policy—and, more recently, abortion, gay rights, and transgender concerns. The advice toward wisdom and gentleness has nearly always been applied to the *underdog* facing the suspicion and opposition of powerful and privileged religious and political authorities. So in the course of time we have recognized the wisdom and gentleness of people like Sojourner Truth, Elizabeth Cady Stanton, Margaret Sanger, Martin Luther King Jr., Cesar Chavez, Maggie Kuhn, Oscar Romero, Mother Teresa, and Desmond Tutu.

Why are those who oppose such movements of the Spirit often not similarly counseled to wisdom and gentleness? Why are they allowed to get away with ignorance and harshness? Like Daniel in the lions' den and Shadrach, Meshach, and Abednego in the fiery furnace, the vulnerable need protection from those who would devour them or burn them with fiery rhetoric. Just as the body of Christ shielded the woman accused of adultery, surely the body of Christ, the church, is called to shield those that the self-righteous want to stone. A seminarian once explained that she did not quite "get" the psalmist's references to "enemies" until she came out as a lesbian in the church. In her book *Leaving Church*, Episcopal priest Barbara Brown Taylor despaired that positions on divisive issues were now being used as litmus tests for belonging to a church. Her denomination was better known as the church of common prayer, not common beliefs![1]

In his early writing, Henri Nouwen, a Roman Catholic priest, described the minister, that is, *every* Christian, as *a wounded healer*. In *The Inner Voice of Love,* the book published on the day of his death, he still found it necessary to warn: "People will constantly try to hook your wounded self. They will point out your needs, your character defects, your limitations and sins. That is how they attempt to dismiss what God, through you, is saying to them."[2]

1. Barbara Brown Taylor, *Leaving Church: A Memoir of Faith* (New York: HarperCollins, 2006), 111.
2. Henri J. M. Nouwen, *The Inner Voice of Love: A Journey through Anguish to Freedom* (New York: Doubleday, 1996), 100.

Exegetical Perspective

One thinks of the nonviolent approach of the civil rights movement in the American South. Drawing upon the resources of the gospel, the movement, in terms of submitting to the violent actions of the hostile culture, was "innocent as doves," but, in terms of being effective against the evil of segregation, the movement was "wise as serpents."[1]

In Matthew 10:16–23, apocalyptic overtones of Mark 13:9–13 can be clearly heard, especially as it relates to persecution. Ben Witherington comments:

> This is perhaps not only because he [Matthew] knew there was rejection of the witness of disciples during the lifetime of Jesus, but also because persecution and even prosecution was an ongoing problem for the minority sect of Jewish Christians in the Holy Land. . . . There is nothing here about finding a friendly homogenous target audience or taking the path of least resistance![2]

Scholars differ as to the real persecution experienced by the Matthean church and the extent of that persecution, but even the threat of persecution can threaten faithful discipleship and lead anxious disciples to exhibit profound theological doubt about the sovereign reign of God. These verses in Matthew 10 anticipate at least the potential for persecution and the assurance that persecution is not a sign of the absence of God, but will be an occasion to experience the intimate presence of God.

Early on in this text, disciples of Jesus are dissuaded from any naive notion of their calling. Just as Jesus was "handed over" (*paradidōmi*) to the authorities, so also will the faithful disciples of Jesus (see Isa. 53:6 in the LXX). No longer as in Mark will disciples be beaten in synagogues (Mark 13:9), but in Matthew Christian disciples will be flogged in "their" (Jewish) synagogues. By the time Matthew is written, Christians are experiencing conflict not only with Rome but with former kin ("their" synagogue), from whom they are now estranged. Matthew will not have the church lulled into the false confidence that if they are just faithful enough, they will be spared trial and persecution and estrangement.

While assuring them of hostility and resistance to their mission work, Jesus also assures the disciples that they will be accompanied by the Spirit of God in the midst of conflict. They will not be abandoned by God or left tongue-tied before the harsh rhetoric or

Homiletical Perspective

graduating students. One year he based his charge upon this text and dwelt upon the various wolves that threaten faithful ministry:

> In the churches which have suffered loss of membership . . . there is the wolf of uneasiness and discomfort that invites us to focus on what will add numbers without counting the cost to the full-voiced gospel. In a market-driven religious environment, there is the temptation to offer what will please rather than what will stir. For a church that struggles with its identity, there is a temptation to settle on the lowest common denominator, one that will hold people together at all costs. And there is the equally corrupting temptation to provide a formula-faith that invests authority in what is *pen*ultimate: our experience, the Scripture, the church, or a creed, rather than what is ultimate— the God who calls us in Jesus Christ. There is the alluring temptation in an unstable environment to long for and to seek a risk-free world, or at least an enclave of assurance and comfort. And thus there arises in the church a culture of intimidation that works against standing up for the right and seeking the truth, no matter what. This culture is one of defensiveness and fear, discouraging or avoiding struggle, of denying the wolves of ignorance and greed, of poverty and constriction of spirit, the wolves that prowl around us and within us, ravenous beasts of prey.
>
> But listen, "I send you out like sheep among wolves." It is not a threat. It is a charge worthy of your gifts, your faith, your knowledge. It is a word not to douse your enthusiasm but to elevate it. It is a word not to discourage you but to encourage you. It is a word not to make the task of ministry threatening, but to affirm its noble and ennobling dimensions. . . . And I send you out not armed with automatic weapons to kill the wolves, but as a bearer of love that will overcome them. This love confronts the beasts that devour our spirits and others' bodies. This love rests on the love of God that has in Jesus Christ overcome the wolves of the world, rebuking the untruthful, urging thinking and acting that frightens even its proponents, and having the courage to risk one's own comfort and security for the sake of the gospel. It is a love which never fails in times of need.[1]

This is how things in our world—even the terrible things—look from the perspective of eschatological eyesight, and it is with this particular eyesight that we are called to be representatives of the gospel. We are equipped for this work not simply with the right

1. Thomas G. Long, *Matthew*, Westminster Bible Companion (Louisville, KY: Westminster John Knox Press, 1997), 120.

2. Ben Witherington III, *Matthew*, Smyth & Helwys Bible Commentary (Macon, GA: Smyth & Helwys, 2006), 222–23.

1. Jack L. Stotts, *A God to Glorify* (Austin: Austin Presbyterian Theological Seminary, 1996), 49–51.

Matthew 10:16–23

Theological Perspective

Father); it is these very qualities that Jesus lends to his sent-out ones: the "Spirit of your Father" (v. 20) will speak through them when they face the persecutions that come with a sent-out life, so they need not worry about what they will say. The adequacy of one's speech turns on neither wisdom (who could be so wise in such a setting, when one's wisdom helped shape the problem?) nor innocence (who could be so innocent in such a setting, when one's desires would certainly include flight, fright, or fight in the mix?). Instead, Jesus' unique qualities are imputed onto the disciples as they participate in his work.

The promise then bears some of its fruit in the present. Like many of God's promises, though, its full fruition is in the future. In the concluding verses of the passage there are twin promises: salvation for the ones who endure to the end, and the (seemingly) imminent arrival of the Son of Man. It is tempting to read a developed eschatology into the passage. Resist the temptation. Eschatology is not especially well developed within Matthew. Rather, part of Matthew's theology is precisely to resist an overly developed eschatological perspective that risks, on the one hand, gnostic-like reification of some secret wisdom about the future and, on the other hand, undermining the significance of Jesus' life, work, death, and resurrection—the very center of the Gospel story.

This is not to say that the promises in the text ought to be ignored. Instead, it suggests that they should be treated as *promises*, things that are not yet, but that can nevertheless motivate current ministries. The goal of the sent-out ones' mission is neither some final individual salvation nor the opportunity eventually to rub the errors of those who persecute the disciples in their faces. After all, the mission that Jesus sends them out on earlier in the passage says nothing explicit about promising future salvation or karmic justice as an expression of the kingdom of heaven. Instead, the works that Jesus commissions the sent-out ones to do are (or ought to be) more than adequate revelations of what God is actually doing in the world. Matthew need not couch his portrayal of their ministries in claims about what God will do.

MARK DOUGLAS

Pastoral Perspective

Thus it is hard to embrace Jesus' confidence in the Spirit inspiring just the right thing to say: "When they hand you over, do not worry about how you are to speak or what you are to say" (v. 19a). These days one almost needs a lawyer or focus group to vet every word one speaks, in order to avoid misunderstanding or advance a cause. Nevertheless, Henri Nouwen once chided this writer to "trust the Spirit more."

Prayerful preparation is key to gaining the confidence to speak, even in the Spirit. Jesus himself took time to go out to lonely places to pray. Preparing for any given day—whether attending a committee meeting, addressing city council, preaching a sermon, or engaging in simple dinner conversation with one's spouse or family—best includes time in prayer when each context and constituency may be lifted up to God. That brings to the day's agenda what Buddhists call *mindfulness* and what is more broadly named *intentionality*. It also allows one to accept with greater equanimity the interruptions to the day's agenda.

Nouwen's advice about trusting the Spirit echoed the guidance his own spiritual director had once given him. He had observed Nouwen's tendency to do everything as if his "whole identity [were] at stake," when it was rather a life of prayer and meditation that could give him true security in his identity. As Henri later noted, "The monk, more than anyone else, realizes that God dwells only where man [*sic*] steps back to give him room."[3] Making room for the Spirit is key. As Jesus said, "What you are to say will be given to you at that time; for it is not you who speak, but the Spirit of your [God] speaking through you" (vv. 19b–20).

Finally, Jesus told his disciples, "The one who endures to the end will be saved." Stamina is one of the most undervalued spiritual gifts, but it is absolutely necessary, because in the spiritual life, there is no finish line. When you feel that you have spiritually "arrived" is when you may be in the most spiritual danger.

CHRIS GLASER

---

3. Henri J. M. Nouwen, *The Genesee Diary: Report from a Trappist Monastery* (New York: Doubleday, 1976), 148–49.

Feasting on the Gospels

rigorous examination of political and religious councils. God will use even persecution as an occasion for the gospel to be spoken and expressed. Specifically in verses 19–20, Matthew highlights

> a word of encouragement for Christians who find themselves on trial. They will not need to depend on their own resources, but will be inspired by the Holy Spirit ("the Spirit of your Father," a uniquely Matthean expression) to speak words of witness. The Holy Spirit is an eschatological gift (see 3:11). "Do not be anxious" reminds the reader of 6:25, where the same words are used.[3]

Borrowing from a verse found later in Matthew 10, Jesus expresses confidence that his disciples have no real cause for fear, "for nothing is covered up that will not be uncovered, and nothing secret that will not become known" (v. 26). Jesus recognizes that fear is the greatest threat to faithful discipleship, often leading disciples to give political and religious authorities ultimate authority over life when they never have more than penultimate authority.

Anyone who reads Matthew 10:21–22 will not mistake Christianity for anything other than the ultimate call of God on a person's life, even at the expense of division and separation within families and the sting of being hated simply for being Christian. These verses echo the prophetic warning and instruction found in Micah 7:6–7:

> For the son treats the father with contempt,
>   the daughter rises up against her mother,
> the daughter-in-law against her mother-in-law;
>   your enemies are members of your own
>   household.
> But as for me, I will look to the LORD,
>   I will wait for the God of my salvation;
>   my God will hear me.

Jesus takes these old prophetic words and imbues them with the promise of the presence of God's Spirit, even in the most extreme turmoil.

Verse 23 reminds the sheep that they are to witness to the reign of God among the wolves, but they are not called to martyr themselves. They are to be "wise as serpents and innocent as doves" (v. 16b). Faithful disciples are to be wise and resourceful, to know when the effectiveness of their witness is over or threatened, and to flee to where they can bear a continued witness to the power of the reign of God.

GARY W. CHARLES

kind of eyesight. We are also equipped with the abiding companionship of the Holy Spirit, who will not desert us, even when times are hard.

Precisely because the gospel message is the good news, it will be met with hostility from those other forces advancing truth claims that are ultimately destined by God to crumble and fall, but none of this hostility will have the final word.

Kinky Friedman, that eccentric musician and philosopher and Texas icon, once wrote an essay about the Texas hill country—that peaceful, bucolic expanse of rolling hills, green valleys, wooded canyons, and sparkling creeks that stretches across central and west Texas. Friedman laments, though, the way in which this scenic region is increasingly imperiled by the arrival of tourists and folks from the big city seeking second homes. It is so bad at times, says Friedman, that one can encounter, in front of some old country store, a Volvo with out-of-state tags and a bumper sticker that says, "Free Tibet." Friedman cites an old-timer named Earl Buckelew, who recently showed some hill country acreage to a man from the city who wanted to know if the land was any good for farming or livestock. "No," said Earl. "All it's good for is holding the world together."[2]

With the right kind of eyesight, we get a certain take on the church of Jesus Christ in all of its various expressions. It is not always much to look at—often polarized, embattled, and timid in the face of the wolves of our time. All it is really good for is holding the world together. So there is a message that continues to be proclaimed, and Jesus Christ continues to lead people like us out there to be the church in the world. He sends us with a warning, with encouragement, and with the promise of the Holy Spirit to stand beside us every step of the way.

THEODORE J. WARDLAW

---

3. M. Eugene Boring, "The Gospel of Matthew," in *The New Interpreter's Bible* (Nashville: Abingdon Press, 1995), 8:259.

2. Kinky Friedman, "Change, Pardners," *Texas Monthly* (April 2003): 204.

Matthew 10:24–33

24"A disciple is not above the teacher, nor a slave above the master; 25it is enough for the disciple to be like the teacher, and the slave like the master. If they have called the master of the house Beelzebul, how much more will they malign those of his household!

26"So have no fear of them; for nothing is covered up that will not be uncovered, and nothing secret that will not become known. 27What I say to you in the dark, tell in the light; and what you hear whispered, proclaim from the housetops. 28Do not fear those who kill the body but cannot kill the soul; rather fear him who can destroy both soul and body in hell. 29Are not two sparrows sold for a penny? Yet not one of them will fall to the ground apart from your Father. 30And even the hairs of your head are all counted. 31So do not be afraid; you are of more value than many sparrows.

32"Everyone therefore who acknowledges me before others, I also will acknowledge before my Father in heaven; 33but whoever denies me before others, I also will deny before my Father in heaven."

Theological Perspective

If Matthew 10:5–15 outlines the nature of the missionary project on which Jesus is sending the disciples and 10:16–23 explores the implications of that project, we might read 10:24–33 as filling out the context in which that project takes place. The passage reveals the complexity of this context in four overlapping ways. First, it clarifies the relation of the work of the sent-out ones to that of their master/teacher: they remain slaves/disciples while doing their work. Second, they live in and bear witness to a world in which things that have been unknown are becoming known: the world—or at least our understanding of it—is undergoing change. Third, all this is happening within the context of God's continued care, knowledge, and power: the world is changing through the work of divine, not demonic, forces. Fourth, the centrality of Jesus to that changing world, the mission of the disciples to reveal the changing world, and the graceful work of God in changing the world are all bound together, such that no part of this context can be understood apart from the other parts: "Everyone, therefore, who acknowledges me before others, I also will acknowledge before my Father in heaven; but whoever denies me before others, I also will deny before my Father in heaven" (vv. 32–33).

Disciples remain disciples, but what is the nature of such discipleship? Jesus' mention of Beelzebul is

Pastoral Perspective

If Jesus was ignored, maligned, misjudged, abandoned, betrayed, tortured, and crucified, then those who follow him ("disciples") and those who belong to him ("slaves") should not expect better treatment. That was especially true for the early proclaimers of his gospel, who announced, "The kingdom of God is at hand." It has also been true for Christians ever since, given "the powers that be."

A Jewish friend asked me to accompany her in seeing the Mel Gibson film *The Passion of the Christ,* a brutal depiction of the torture and crucifixion of Jesus. We both had heard the "anti-Semitic" buzz around the movie, and that was one of the reasons she wanted to see it with a Christian. I had avoided it because of its extreme violence, though I had also felt some professional obligation to see it. As it turned out, we both could appreciate the story in our own way. In the portrayal of Jesus' suffering for who he was and what he believed, I recognized the violent abuse of people all around the world who still suffer for who they are and what they believe. Later I would write of the crucifixion as a Roman hate crime meant to intimidate the Jews.[1]

"So have no fear of them" (v. 26). In the context of the risks his disciples will face, Jesus reiterates

1. Chris Glaser, *Progressive Christian Reflections,* www.chrisglaser.blogspot .com, April 20, 2011.

Exegetical Perspective

In Matthew 10:24–33 Jesus' recurring refrain to his newly commissioned disciples is: "Do not fear."[1] One way the disciples can allay their understandable fear of living out the mission instructions that Jesus gave them is by keeping the proper perspective on their relationship to Jesus. The disciples are called to be like Jesus, to follow him faithfully, to heal, to exorcise, and to preach what they have come to know as the gospel, but they are never to confuse imitating Jesus with becoming, themselves, the head of the household (*oikodespotēs*) of faith. That is a position reserved for God and Jesus, acting as God's representative. The disciples are called to serve and speak in the name of God, but never to assume that they are on a parallel footing with God. This is a critical perspective on discipleship that bears relevance for the church in any age.

Another way to allay the natural fear of living out Jesus' mission instructions in a hostile environment is to trust that God is at work to accomplish God's good purposes, whatever challenges are present. In Matthew 10, Jesus' disciples are to see themselves as a part of a divine "apocalyptic" movement, a public

---

1. "The speech is directed to disciple-missioners who experience such rejection and persecution, and who may be afraid to speak out boldly for their new faith. Thus this section continues with a twice-repeated command not to be afraid (vv. 26, 31)" (M. Eugene Boring, "The Gospel of Matthew," in *The New Interpreter's Bible* [Nashville: Abingdon Press, 1995], 8:259).

Homiletical Perspective

The history of the last two millennia testifies to the attempt—on the part of rulers or whole cultures—to silence the gospel's proclamation among the faithful. During the Cultural Revolution in China, for example, there was the persistent concern among many of the world's Christians, in the absence of much information, about how the church was surviving in the midst of official hostility. As such official hostility began to lessen and China began to move toward greater transparency, there was much rejoicing that the church had somehow—remarkably—been sustained and had developed its own unique character in a kind of hiding for all those years. The church in China has become a contemporary parable, one among many, of how the world is not able to destroy God's activity amid God's people. In the words of Jesus in this text from Matthew's Gospel, "nothing is covered up that will not be uncovered, and nothing secret that will not become known. What I say to you in the dark, tell in the light; and what you hear whispered, proclaim from the housetops" (vv. 26–27).

Even if messengers of the gospel are killed by tyrants, their message endures. After all, the power of tyrants is limited to what they can do to the body, for only God has power over the soul. On the Sunday after the atrocities of 9/11, the sanctuary of the congregation I was then serving was packed, like

Matthew 10:24–33

Theological Perspective

doubly significant. On the one hand, it is a reminder of the opposition that Jesus and his disciples face—an opposition so great that his enemies would rather refer to him as Beelzebul than open themselves up to an interpretation of his acts and words as coming from God. If Jesus is Beelzebul, then the disciples are not only evil but, in their wickedness, comparatively weak. However, since Jesus is *not* Beelzebul, his disciples need not think of themselves as either weak or evil. They stay disciples, but in an order that affirms both their goodness and their power. They are not divinized, but neither are they diminished in their work: better to be a doorkeeper in the house of God than to live in the tents of wickedness (Ps. 84:10). Their power is wide reaching.

Their power shapes the insight and courage that helps them in their mission. They see what has been covered and know what has been secret; in seeing and knowing, they are emboldened to proclaim from the rooftops what has only been whispered in secret. The world is being changed; in that changed world, they need not fear those who would malign them, for such malignancy is part of the old world.

Instead, in the world being changed, the only one worthy of fear is the one who is changing it—the one who is aware of each sparrow and knows the number of hairs on all their heads. The verses reiterate portions of Jesus' Sermon on the Mount (esp. 6:25–33), which the hearers of Matthew's Gospel would certainly have remembered. Thus, in a crafty rhetorical move, the writer of Matthew is able to use the allusion to that speech to help shape the vision of what the world is being changed into: the world that, among other things, the meek will inherit.

These are both bracing and encouraging words, especially given how early in the book Jesus says them and how new the disciples are to the mission on which he is sending them out. Another writer might move this section—indeed, all of chapter 10—until later in the narrative, as if to clarify that Christians need to understand the coming kingdom and the shape of Christian community before setting out to share their faith; another writer might let the disciples take all the classes Jesus has taught before "graduating" and being sent out. The writer of Matthew, however, joins learning to doing, with both the practical and theological implications that follow.

The practical implications are that (a) the Christian life does not separate belief from practice or thought from action; and (b) the practices of Christian belief are, necessarily and from very early stages, focused outward into the world. Christians do not

Pastoral Perspective

the same providence of God he illustrates earlier in the Sermon on the Mount (6:25–34): "Are not two sparrows sold for a penny? Yet not one of them will fall to the ground apart from your Father. And even the hairs of your head are all counted. So do not be afraid; you are of more value than many sparrows" (10:29–31).

Complete openness is the context for this reminder: "Nothing is covered up that will not be uncovered. . . . What you hear whispered, proclaim from the housetops" (vv. 26b, 27b). Jesus has no intention of starting a cult, an exclusive religious club with secret wisdom and rituals in which only an elite hierarchy will rule and be saved. Many who read this will smugly take pride in the assumption that our church is nothing like that. Experience, though, teaches that some churches are very much like that: an exclusive religious club with secret wisdom and rituals in which only an elite hierarchy rule and are thus "saved." Church leaders hold on to their power by refusing to be "up front" about things, from agendas to relationships to intrachurch dynamics. Only those deemed "worthy" are allowed full participation, and usually only by conforming to unspoken (thus hidden) rules and expectations. Full participation in a church should never be determined by the largesse of so-called gatekeepers, but by the absolute grace of Jesus' unconditional love. Furthermore, it is not only "secret wisdom" that interferes with full participation. It is often just the plain old "secrets" kept from newcomers that are at the root of dysfunctional behavior within a church.

"Do not fear those who kill the body but cannot kill the soul; rather fear him who can destroy both soul and body in hell" (v. 28). "Hell" is Gehenna, the valley outside the walls of Jerusalem, where trash continually burned; thus it is a metaphor rather than a doctrine. One way to interpret the metaphor is to recognize that the only one we have to fear is ourselves, because only we can destroy both soul and body in the fires of our own making. If this is so, then when we pray, "Deliver us from evil," in the Lord's Prayer, we pray to be delivered from our own evil, which we experience as more toxic to our spiritual well-being than anything anyone can do to us. Another way to interpret the metaphor is to think of Gehenna as God's amnesiac fire, which burns the dross of our lives so that what is of value may be preserved.

"Everyone therefore who acknowledges me before others, I also will acknowledge before my Father in heaven; but whoever denies me before others, I also

revealing of what God is accomplishing through and beyond their witness. The disciples need not fear what to say when confronted by hostile authorities; they need only speak with courage what has been spoken to them in private, trusting that the one they call Lord will not desert them or leave them speechless in their hour of crisis ("What I say to you in the dark, tell in the light; and what you hear whispered, proclaim from the housetops," v. 27; see also Matt. 10:19–20 and 28:20b).

In times of hostility and controversy, disciples are tempted to lie low, to take the path of least resistance, to accommodate to the prevailing powers, and to silence the witness of the gospel. Matthew 10 warns reluctant disciples not to expect better reception to their message or better treatment than their teacher received. This text also calls disciples to move out from their fearful temerity in the face of public ridicule and scorn, to bear a clear public witness to the gospel, and to remember that ultimate authority resides not with public or religious officials in any country or any era, but with God alone.

Tom Long wisely observes,

> There is nothing that the world can do that is able to eradicate the gospel or destroy God's loving and watchful care over the faithful. The world can forbid missionary activity and enforce it by throwing those who bear witness to the kingdom in jail, but "nothing is covered up that will not be uncovered, and nothing secret that will not become known" (Matt. 10:26). The world can even kill those who serve the gospel, but the murders are not to be ultimately feared. They may have momentary power over bodily life, but they have no power over the soul. Only God has that. Only God is to be feared, and God, who counts the hairs on our heads and who does not fail to note even the falling of a single common sparrow, can be trusted to reassure those who serve the kingdom (Matt. 10:28–31).[2]

Thus throughout this passage a breathtaking theological intimacy is expressed. The God whom Jesus reveals is unlike any sovereign in Rome or any other sovereign at any other time of history. This "God of the sparrows" is a God who not only numbers all our days but numbers the hairs on our head. The God we meet in Matthew 10 is not the God of the deists, a distant deity who set the world in motion only to withdraw from any active engagement with

so many other sanctuaries across America on that particular weekend. Our service on that occasion proceeded pretty much as we had planned it on the day before planes flew into the World Trade Center towers, the Pentagon, and a Pennsylvania hillside. We celebrated the baptism of a baby, the commissioning of a new staff member, and all of the other events planned for that day. One thing was changed intentionally: the opening hymn. In the wake of 9/11, we decided to strike the first hymn and to replace it with that majestic hymn of the church "A Mighty Fortress Is Our God." Like so many others, I knew the first verse by heart, but on that particular Sunday, I noticed for the first time the power of its third verse:

> And though this world, with devils filled, should
>   threaten to undo us;
> We will not fear, for God hath willed His truth to
>   triumph through us.
> The prince of darkness grim, we tremble not for him;
> His rage we can endure, for lo! his doom is sure,
> One little word shall fell him.[1]

This text from Matthew assures us of the same thing. "Do not fear those who kill the body but cannot kill the soul" (Matt. 10:28a).

In our privileged First-World settings, those of us who serve as messengers of the gospel rarely if ever experience the mortal dangers imagined in this text. We may be tempted, therefore, to spiritualize these dangers or to reduce them to metaphor. In that sense, we might express quiet prayers of thanksgiving, but we also need to acknowledge the profound ways in which our relative safety limits us.

A few years ago, I taught liturgics for a month-long intensive course in a sister seminary of the one I serve, in sub-Saharan Africa. Because I was required to prepare my syllabus in advance of my traveling there, I was doing all of my planning (I realized later) in a context markedly different from the one in which I would do my teaching. This disconnect became painfully clear to me during the last week of my teaching assignment in that African nation. The day arrived when, according to my syllabus, I would teach my class of some forty African students all about music. In the familiarity of my home context, I had planned for this particular day a survey lecture covering the Hebrew psalms, the earliest known music of the infant church, the polyphony

---

2. Thomas G. Long, *Matthew*, Westminster Bible Companion (Louisville, KY: Westminster John Knox Press, 1997), 121.

1. *The Presbyterian Hymnal* (Louisville, KY: Westminster/John Knox Press, 1990), #260.

Matthew 10:24–33

Theological Perspective

order their ideas before testing them in conversations with others, nor do they nurture their practices within communities of the like minded, so as to get them right before acting them out in front of others. For the writer of Matthew, the shape of Christian life is not primarily about orthodoxy or orthopraxis; it is, rather, about gradually joining thought/belief (*doxa*) and action (*praxis*) into a life that can become more properly lived (*orthōs*) only in an extended project of outward engagement and transformation. So disciples are sent out early, practicing at proclaiming, healing, raising, cleansing (10:7–8), not only as a way of revealing or sharing their faith, but also as a way of discovering and growing in it.

The theological implications follow from this. To live such a life is to find oneself regularly vulnerable and off balance. It would, after all, be far easier to know correctly and act purely before engaging others—secure in the buffering protection of one's uprightness from the threats and challenges of the world. However, as Jesus' teachings in Matthew 10 make clear, this is not the life that his sent-out ones will lead. They will be vulnerable (indeed, they must be vulnerable), and so they must rely on the hospitality of others. They will be challenged (indeed, they must accept challenges), and so they must learn to put their trust in their master/teacher. In doing so, they will discover not only that they are participating in his life and work but also that by participating in his life and work, they will find genuine security and life in the love and presence of God.

MARK DOUGLAS

Pastoral Perspective

will deny before my Father in heaven" (vv. 32–33). This is the "bottom line" of Jesus' instructions to his disciples in Matthew 10. Contemporary and privileged readers may think that the first disciples and the early Christians for whom this was written needed to hear this more than we do, as do those Christians who endure today as religious minorities or political outcasts in other countries. The truth, however, is that "persecution" of Christians—and of all people of faith—exists today even in the privileged world of religious freedom.

The persecution is just more subtle, more often expressed in apathy than antipathy. Religion has become a private matter, often banned, along with politics, from discussion. Despite Stephen Carter's well-argued case for bringing religion into the public square in *The Culture of Disbelief*; Glenn Tinder's contention in *The Political Meaning of Christianity* that religious values need to critique the public sphere; and Christian Iosso and Elizabeth Hinson-Hasty's powerful collection of *Prayers for the New Social Awakening*; the church's shaping of public policy is too frequently left to Christians with a politically confining agenda. No Christian should check Jesus' values at the door when exiting the church and entering the public sphere: Jesus' compassion for the poor, the sick, the imprisoned, the vulnerable, and the demonized may shape public policy just as much as the Enlightenment values of equality, liberty, and the pursuit of happiness. In this way as well, we "proclaim the good news that 'The kingdom of heaven has come near.'" In the United States, the revivals of the two Great Awakenings led the way to the social reforms that followed.

There is another way that acknowledging Christ speaks to our times. Some Christians place conditions on God's unconditional and extravagant love in Jesus Christ, resisting a gospel of grace. Other Christians, in deference to our multicultural and multifaith world, avoid talking about Jesus and resist a gospel of particularity. Each is a way of denying both Jesus and his gospel proclamation that the realm of God is at hand.

CHRIS GLASER

the created world. Jesus speaks of a God who is to be trusted and feared, precisely because God does not disengage from the world. Jesus calls his disciples to overcome their fear in order to engage the world with confidence, to speak boldly, and to live out the gospel.

Matthew 10:26–31 is a preview of the kingdom parable in Matthew 25:31–46, a dire warning to disciples to avoid the way of the "goats" (25:32) that is oblivious to human need, a way that gives far more power to ruling authorities than they warrant. Matthew warns that misplaced fear often results in a timid church and a resulting meager public witness that is not worthy of the claims of the gospel.

One cannot read the urgent appeal to confess faith in Jesus publicly and the accompanying warning found in verses 32–33 without thinking ahead to the poignant and tragic denial of Jesus by Peter (see Matt. 26:33–75). Jesus' teaching about the positive and negative consequences of acknowledging or denying Jesus follows directly upon his assurance to the disciples that they need never fear the removal of God's supportive and inspiring presence. Jesus' call for a public witness is rooted in his confidence that God will provide Jesus' disciples abiding attention ("every hair on your head has been counted," v. 30 NJB) and tender affection ("So do not be afraid; you are of more value than many sparrows," v. 31).

For preachers and congregations who fear the daunting tyranny of secularization and who refuse to equate Christianity with capitalism, this passage can elicit the courage to speak gospel truth into public arenas that find Christianity boring, irrelevant, or a direct challenge to the prevailing gods of society.

GARY W. CHARLES

of medieval plainsong, the stout hymns of the Reformation era, the romanticism of nineteenth-century American hymns, the modern dissonance of many hymns from the mid-twentieth century, ending up with contemporary Western composers and their new hymnody. By now, though, I had spent several weeks in Africa participating daily in chapel services where the most heartbreakingly beautiful native harmonies and instrumentation had joyously delivered often-familiar hymn texts to my ears in astonishing new melodies.

Now far less confident in what I could possibly teach them about music, I changed my lecture at the last minute and instead spent the three hours of that particular class inviting my students to share their music with me. By the grace of God, I was no longer teacher but student, introduced by patient and eager new teachers to the great tradition of their own lively hymns and songs. At the end of that time, I asked, "What does this music mean to you?"

There was silence for awhile, and finally one student—the student body president—stood up and said, "Abusa, for us here, it has often been hard." He was a master of understatement. What I heard beneath that simple sentence was a mental list of the perils of ministry there: a government rife with corruption and graft, a poor infrastructure, grinding poverty, the omnipresence of AIDS, few hospitals, economic colonialism that stripped their natural resources, one cardiologist in the whole country, the ever-present threat in any village of the witch doctor, a neighboring country ruled by a ruthless dictator. Ministry in such a setting was not easy, in other words. "Abusa, for us here, it has often been hard." Then he continued: "It has often been our music that has sustained us in spite of it all."

It is the "music" of the gospel that sustains us all. It reminds us that our mighty God has already settled the results of our labors. All we have to do, in the face of any danger, is to proclaim that music from the housetops. It is what sustains us in spite of it all, "and even the hairs of [our] head are all counted" (10:30).

THEODORE J. WARDLAW

Matthew 10:34–39

³⁴"Do not think that I have come to bring peace to the earth; I have not come to bring peace, but a sword.
³⁵ For I have come to set a man against his father,
   and a daughter against her mother,
   and a daughter-in-law against her mother-in-law;
³⁶ and one's foes will be members of one's own household.
³⁷Whoever loves father or mother more than me is not worthy of me; and whoever loves son or daughter more than me is not worthy of me; ³⁸and whoever does not take up the cross and follow me is not worthy of me. ³⁹Those who find their life will lose it, and those who lose their life for my sake will find it."

Theological Perspective

Jesus' words in Matthew 10:34 are chilling: "Do not think that I have come to bring peace to the earth; I have not come to bring peace, but a sword." How do we make sense of this verse, given Jesus' command to Peter in Gethsemane to put away his sword (Matt. 26:52) and his statement before Pilate: "My kingdom is not from this world. If my kingdom were from this world, my followers would be fighting" (John 18:36)?

Earlier, Jesus warned that his disciples will be "flog[ged] . . . in their synagogues" and "dragged before governors and kings" and "hated by all because of my name" (Matt. 10:17a, 18b, 22). In fact, conflict is so central to Jesus' mission that he predicted it would run down the middle of believers' families: "I have come to set a man against his father, and a daughter against her mother, . . . and one's foes will be members of one's own household" (vv. 35–36). This claim echoes Jesus' earlier statement in verse 21: "Brother will betray brother to death . . . and children will rise against parents and have them put to death." Indeed, given these verses, a sword of persecution is pointed *at* Jesus' disciples, not wielded by them.

Are persecution, division, and conflict what Matthew means by the word "sword" in verse 34? Are persecution, division, and conflict a result, rather, of the type of sword that Jesus brings? Though Jesus affirms throughout chapter 10 that believers can

Pastoral Perspective

This Matthean text is part of the missionary instruction (9:35–10:42) given to those who had answered Jesus' call and were being rejected by their families and persecuted by religious and civil authorities. The first listeners to this text would likely have heard echoes of the prophet Micah (Mic. 7:6) and associated Jesus with the prophetic tradition that warned against those who say, "Peace, peace," when there is no true peace (see Jer. 6:14; 8:11; Ezek. 13:10). Jesus refused to endorse a false peace that simply covered up domination or exploitation. Like the prophets, he called his followers to find their life in loving mercy and doing justice—even if it meant losing their life.

What does this mean to people who are not being persecuted for their faith? What does it mean for us to lose our lives? Perhaps we might be invited to examine our lives for places where we are complicit in systems that need to be divided by the sword of truth for the sake of justice and peace.

After all, if a public relations expert had reviewed Matthew's Gospel before it went to print, surely this disturbing sound bite, "I have not come to bring peace, but a sword" (v. 34b), would have been reworded if not omitted. It offends our sensibilities for these words to be on the lips of Jesus, whom Christians call the Prince of Peace, after all. Even those who have been marginally exposed to the Bible

Exegetical Perspective

The Jesus sayings that are gathered in these few verses are as difficult and controversial as anything else in the Gospels. Each saying, on its own, challenges a traditional and cherished human value. Together, they undo normal conceptions of what constitutes a good life. Jesus seems to be attacking our core beliefs about who we are and who we should be. It is not surprising that Christians have pursued readings of these sayings that soften their terror, making them somehow cohere with our accepted values and beliefs.

The opening saying introduces the problem because Jesus, famous for his message of peace, declares, "I have not come to bring [Greek "throw"] peace, but a sword" (v. 34). Responses to this seeming affirmation of "a sword" range from seeing this as evidence of Jesus' revolutionary politics to seeing this as a call to spiritual warfare within one's self. However, in the context of Matthew 10, the saying can also be read more as an announcement of the violence that occurs when the Messiah arrives. The entire chapter details the conflict and violence that results from disciples proclaiming the good news (10:7). Understood in the context of Matthew's narrative, the sword does not arrive because Jesus or his disciples bring it, but because governors and kings draw it, in response to the words and deeds of the disciples.

Homiletical Perspective

It is important for preachers to keep the contemporary cultural mind-set before them as they approach this radically countercultural saying of Jesus. That mind-set is that in spite of the dysfunctional state of many families in North America, the family is still viewed as the solution to what is wrong with this country. As the popular view goes, if the family can become healthy, society will make major strides toward drastically reducing poverty, crime, and drug and alcohol problems and increasing the health of the communities in which we live. Therapists often turn to a person's family history as the fountain from which a multitude of problems flow. Politicians play up their family values to win votes and disparage the family values of their opponents. Even businesses present themselves as "family owned and operated." The family is idolized, turned into a cultural measuring stick and the panacea for all social chaos. When we do this, we place on the family a burden that it cannot bear.

A preacher might consider how the church has succumbed to this same mind-set. Think of the popular adage, "If Christianity does not work at home, it does not work." Does that mean that if a person is divorced or if parents have a rebellious child or if a husband and wife have a strained relationship, they are not Christians? Does it imply that if Christian

Matthew 10:34–39

Theological Perspective

expect suffering, what does Jesus mean when he says that he brings a sword?

According to a variety of New Testament texts, the only "sword" Jesus brings is "the sword of the Spirit, which is the word of God" (Eph. 6:17). In Revelation, this sword materializes and issues from the mouth of the resurrected Christ and strikes down his enemies (Rev. 1:16; 19:15–21). Second Timothy 3:16 describes the written word as coming from God's breath *(theopneustos)*. This sword is designed to penetrate the human heart, to conquer sin and all of our affections for it. Hebrews 4:12 teaches: "The word of God is living and active, sharper than any two-edged sword, piercing until it divides soul from spirit, joints from marrow; it is able to judge the thoughts and intentions of the heart." When God's word wins the battle for the human heart, there are always social consequences, and the one Jesus warns his followers about in this text is family conflict.

Familial conflict created by following God's word is not the kind of division a therapist's couch can overcome. It results from the nature and power of the word itself, bringing personal transformation to a believer. It is a consequence of something being created, a new order of things where Christ himself is the head so "that in everything he might be pre-eminent" (Col. 1:18 RSV; NRSV "have first place"). In our text, Christ prepares his disciples for this conflict, saying that this sword will bring them affliction even from their homes.

These divisions in believers' personal relationships are actually generated by their union with Christ. When earthly bonds are not elastic enough to accommodate the exclusive claims of the lordship of Jesus Christ, then the family's social fabric is ruptured, and old wineskins can no longer contain the new wine. The bond of our union with Christ is underscored by a question Jesus asks his disciples in Matthew 12:48–50: "'Who is my mother, and who are my brothers?' And pointing to his disciples, he said, 'Here are my mother and my brothers! For whoever does the will of my Father in heaven is my brother and sister and mother.'" The spiritual union between believers surpasses all biological ones, and Jesus makes it known that this is true even for him.

Jesus knows that union with him is fraught with temptation. He understands one's social and familial bonds may tempt us to deny him. The passage under study clarifies: "Whoever loves father or mother more than me is not worthy of me; and whoever loves son or daughter more than me is not worthy of me" (Matt. 10:37). This is not a seeker-sensitive

Pastoral Perspective

will likely remember hearing at a Christian funeral the comforting words of Jesus from the Gospel of John, "My peace I give to you" (John 14:27); or recall the voice of a young child at Christmas proclaiming the announcement of the heavenly hosts from Luke, "Glory to God in the highest heaven, and on earth peace"(Luke 2:14). Even if they could not tell you that it was in Matthew's Gospel just five chapters back from this troubling sword verse, most people in our pews likely have some recollection that Jesus declared peacemakers to be blessed (Matt. 5:9).

The first pastoral task in teaching and preaching this passage, then, is to acknowledge how troublesome it is and to reassure those who cringe at its reading that everyday disciples as well as biblical scholars have wrestled with its interpretation since early on in the life of the church. Verses like this bring to the forefront issues of biblical authority and biblical interpretation. As church leaders, we learn to use principles of biblical exegesis and are warned of the dangers of sound-bite theology. Nevertheless many, perhaps most, parishioners have never been exposed to such concepts.

Those of us who take such concepts for granted should not underestimate the need for church leaders to teach such principles. It is quite likely that at one time or another most of our congregants have had the uncomfortable experience of being in conversation with coworkers or neighbors when someone has announced, "Well, the Bible says . . . ," and then quoted a verse that effectively shut down further discussion. I know elders in the church who have gone away from such experiences with their confidence in the trustworthiness of Scripture undermined or have vowed to avoid talking about the Bible in public. What might have happened if they had heard not only, "Well, the Bible says . . . ," but also how William Sloane Coffin used this very text to preach a 1972 sermon calling for nuclear disarmament, referring to verse 34 as "a wonderfully honest statement about the need for the sword of truth, Christ's sword of truth, that heals the wounds it inflicts."[1]

Many of our parishioners have conflicted feelings about Scripture. We are quick to bemoan the fact of biblical illiteracy in mainline congregations, but many congregants are not sure they want to know the Bible any better than they do, because they are not sure of its value when they read verses like this.

1. William Sloane Coffin, "Not to Bring Peace, But a Sword," on 30good minutes.org, program #3519, first broadcast February 16, 1992. http://30good minutes.net/index.php/component/content/article/23–member–archives/693 –william–sloane–coffin–program–3519?highlight=YToxOntpOjA7aTozNT E5O3O=; accessed on October 28, 2012.

Exegetical Perspective

In this passage, however, the messianic terror destroys families. Historians have long noted that the list in verse 35, which is taken from Micah 7:6, of man [*sic*] against father, daughter against mother, and daughter-in-law against mother-in-law, names the core relationships in the ancient household. There is no group in the ancient world that would not see terror in this saying, since the family's health is the ground of a good life. This threat repeats the one in 10:21, wherein these family members have each other killed. All of this is set in the context of messianic arrival. The "I have come" syntax evokes this arrival, and the infinitives that follow, in both Greek and English, suggest purpose. Understood in the context of messianic arrival, the Messiah has come in order to throw a sword in our midst, to destroy our families, and to provoke daughters to have their mothers killed. It is no wonder that readers have long puzzled with how to understand these sayings!

The warning against loving father or mother or son or daughter "more than me" has usually been read as creating a hierarchy of love wherein we are called to love God more than we love our children. Matthew, it appears, softened the original Jesus command to "hate" every single member of our family (Luke 14:26) with a command to love them less. However, Jesus does not really say that. Instead he warns against a hierarchy wherein we love our family "more than" him. The saying claims that in order to be "worthy" of the Messiah we must love him as much as we love our children. This seems closer to the nature of love. Hierarchies of love work only on paper. When we love our daughters and sons, we love them absolutely. We do not rank them on a descending list.

While it is the case that our absolute love for one child can be in tension with our absolute love for another child, to include the Messiah in this familial love installs a more threatening tension, a messianic terror, into the very center of the family. To love the Messiah is to endanger all our other loves. The danger comes not because we will love our children less. The danger comes because the Messiah and the kingdom of God threaten (and even reverse) the political and social orders of the world, including those of each and every family.

Into the midst of these threats to the family, the passage introduces the image and politics of the cross. To be "worthy" of the Messiah we must "take up" our "cross and follow" (v. 38). In the nearly endless and magnificent Christian readings of this passage, the cross becomes a metaphor for all kinds of

Homiletical Perspective

families are flawed, then Christianity or the church must be flawed too? We have gotten our priorities mixed up, like the college president who said a few years ago, "I would like to have a university that our football team can be proud of." The church has fallen into the same frame of mind: "We would like to have a church our families can be proud of." The tail wags the dog.

Preachers, however, need to take care not to over-simplify the relationship between church and family. It is a systemic relationship in which each is called on to serve the other.

A sermon on this text will develop the stark contrast between the way society and even the church view family and the way Jesus views it. On this occasion, Jesus gives missionary instructions to the Twelve. Through this discourse, Jesus seeks to shape the lives of the disciples as they carry forth his work. He warns them about the cost involved in following him and the conflict it will create. Of all things, the Prince of Peace tells the disciples that he has "not come to bring peace, but a sword" (v. 34). He declares that he has come to set family members against one another, son against father and daughter against mother (v. 35).

Jesus' words are so radical. They appear to go against Scripture and even his own teaching (see Gen. 2:18, 24; Exod. 20:12; Mark 7:9–13; 10:19). However, Jesus' values are first and foremost kingdom values, not family values. The individual and the family are of less concern than the ushering in of God's kingdom through the preaching of the gospel. When Jesus speaks of bringing a sword, he is not speaking literally (see 5:21–26, 38–39; 26:52). Rather, he speaks of the division that occurs within relationships as a result of allegiance to Christ (v. 35). The sword severs what naturally holds things together, including the intimate ties between family members. What Jesus calls his followers to do is to put loyalty to God above every other relationship, including family.

The task of preachers and of the church is to help families set the right priorities in their lives. The church can turn the family into an idolatrous institution. The moment it becomes its own god, the family is destroyed. For Christians, life is not about focusing on the family. Rather, life is about focusing wholeheartedly on God. Establishing such a priority may create division in some situations. In other situations, seeking first the kingdom of God may strengthen the family, giving it a purpose greater than itself that holds its members together and

Matthew 10:34–39

Theological Perspective

message. Bearing the rejection of family because of Christ is a cross all its own. The full impact of these words may not be fully appreciated in the secular West, where many families lie fractured, but in those Islamic cultures where religious convictions are socially enforced, division over the exclusive claims of God's word, being faithful to Christ alone, is especially difficult for believers with an Islamic background.

Jesus' sobering statement in verses 38–39 reveals that our union with Christ extends all the way to the cross. Five centuries ago, Luther taught a constellation of ideas that scholars have come to call his "theology of the cross." Luther observed that God's knowledge is hidden under opposites; thus reason on its own cannot make sense of what God has revealed without faith in the cross as its starting point. He claimed we see a paradox in the cross—God's power displayed in weakness, God's wisdom hidden under foolishness, grace under judgment, sovereignty under humble submission, and life under the death of the crucified Christ. On the other hand, to "theologians of glory," as Luther claims, the cross makes no sense. These people seek the accolades of self-righteousness and the power, glory, and honor of this world—all leading to death. Furthermore, suffering is a nonsensical intrusion into their world.

To a "theologian of the cross," however, suffering is one's most precious treasure, because the living God is revealed and yet hidden in such sufferings.[1] As 2 Corinthians 12:9 states, God's "power is made perfect in weakness." Therefore suffering is able to challenge the myth of self-reliance and disclose our need for God, while creating a hunger and thirst for God's word. It is here, through Scripture, that God personally draws near and true life is found for those who pick up their cross and follow. Thus Jesus may proclaim in the Beatitudes that the poor, the mournful, the hungry, the thirsty, and the persecuted are blessed (Matt. 5:1–11).

BONNIE L. PATTISON

Pastoral Perspective

Preachers and teachers will want to seize this teachable moment, to explore theologies of the Word, definitions of biblical authority, and principles of faithful interpretation (e.g., use the Bible to interpret itself; view all of Scripture through christological lenses; the authority of Scripture should neither supersede faith in God nor be conflated with the way we express faith in God).

How might religious public discourse in our country change if the people in our pews developed a working vocabulary that empowered them to speak candidly about how their interpretation of the Bible has informed their political, social, and religious convictions? In-depth exploration of such issues must be done in formal and informal educational settings. Sunday school classes are obvious places for this, but what about as part of a devotional time at the beginning of a meeting of church leaders? When visiting parishioners who feel trapped between the faith convictions they are growing into and the claims they hear authoritatively pronounced on television? Even as a part of devotional materials sent out with our short-term mission groups?

A reading for multiple voices juxtaposing texts like "I have not come to bring peace, but a sword" (Matt. 10:34) with texts like "All who take the sword will perish by the sword" (Matt. 26:52) could serve to heighten awareness of, and perhaps even increase anxiety about, the incongruous passages of Scripture, laying the groundwork for exploring a theology of the Word and the high calling of the people of God to faithfully interpret Scripture in its literary, historical, canonical, political, and social contexts—and in light of our own contexts.

Another approach to the text could be to acknowledge the tendency in American culture to reduce Christianity to a different kind of sound bite. Ministers can be tempted to reduce their communications to memorable, pithy summaries of the gospel that fail to communicate God's strong claim on us. Perhaps we rarely hear sermons on this verse precisely because we have been reticent to proclaim the cost of discipleship in as bold a manner as twentieth-century martyr Dietrich Bonhoeffer did in his book of the same name.

PAM DRIESELL

---

1. Alister E. McGrath, *Luther's Theology of the Cross* (Oxford: Blackwell, 1985), 151.

difficulties. To take up your cross is read as dealing with the hard things in life. However, such a softening of the shame and terror of the cross would make little sense to early Christians. Everyone, Christian or not, has difficulties that must be faced. The image of the cross should not become simply a reminder that life is hard. The cross belongs, first of all, to messianic politics. To follow the Messiah is to face a particular kind of terror; it is to provoke kings and governors to draw their swords.

In some ways, the final verse both intensifies and justifies what precedes. The imagery of finding one's life and losing one's life has, like every other image in this passage, been regularly spiritualized in Christian readings. Such spiritualized readings are not wrong or inappropriate, but they soften too quickly the political and social terrors of these sayings. In Matthew, to "find" your life is to become a good and respected citizen in the ancient world; and to "lose" (Greek "destroy") your life is to lose your social and political position. We are called to destroy our public lives and endanger our families for the sake of the Messiah.

However, there is a promise. We are not called to quit loving our families; we are not called to unsheathe our swords; we are not called simply to destroy our lives; we are called to love and follow the Messiah. We are promised that, if we "destroy" our life "for the sake of" the Messiah, we will find it. While Christian readings have tended to see the life we destroy as our life on earth and the life we find as life in heaven, there is nothing in the saying that requires such a distinction. The blessings of following the Messiah can and do occur on earth. Jesus does not bring only sword and discord; Jesus also brings peace and love. We risk following this Messiah because we believe the disruptions and terrors of his arrival belong to the good blessings of God's kingdom.

LEWIS R. DONELSON

causes them to love one another. Whatever the consequences are to the family, the command to follow Jesus is supreme.

It will be important for preachers to provide specific images or examples of how Jesus' perspective plays out in life. Here is one from my own experience. When I was in seminary, I knew a fellow student whose father disowned him when he became a Christian. His father, who was not a Christian, had offered to pay his way through law school. Instead, the son, after he became a Christian, enrolled in seminary. The father turned his back on his son. He would not even speak to his son. The student paid his way through seminary by working at fast-food restaurants. About a year into seminary, he began receiving anonymous checks in the mail. He never knew the identity of his donor, but the checks kept coming on a regular basis. My friend graduated and later began teaching at a well-respected seminary. When I visited with him a few years ago, he told me that a couple of years after he graduated, he discovered who had been sending him the checks. It had been his dad. The father never became a Christian, but he learned to appreciate his son's decision. I know this kind of positive outcome is not typical, and some families remain estranged, but the story does illustrate the profound power, for better or worse, of the decision to take up the cross of Christ and follow him.

As difficult as it is to put God and God's kingdom above family, that is what Jesus calls us to do. In God's family, as William Willimon points out, "water is thicker than blood."[1] The waters of baptism create a new family and invite all kinds of people from diverse families to join. To be a Christian is not to belong to a family that revolves around itself, but to discover a new family composed of those who have discovered that their ultimate commitment is to God. In God's family, water is thicker than blood.

DAVE BLAND

---

1. William Willimon, *Peculiar Speech: Preaching to the Baptized* (Grand Rapids: Eerdmans, 1992), 122.

Matthew 10:40–11:1

40"Whoever welcomes you welcomes me, and whoever welcomes me welcomes the one who sent me. 41Whoever welcomes a prophet in the name of a prophet will receive a prophet's reward; and whoever welcomes a righteous person in the name of a righteous person will receive the reward of the righteous; 42and whoever gives even a cup of cold water to one of these little ones in the name of a disciple—truly I tell you, none of these will lose their reward."

11:1Now when Jesus had finished instructing his twelve disciples, he went on from there to teach and proclaim his message in their cities.

Theological Perspective

In Matthew 10:40, we read Christ's teaching on the divine implications of welcoming his disciples: "Whoever welcomes you welcomes me, and whoever welcomes me welcomes the one who sent me." Something as simple as extending hospitality to a follower of Christ has a profound implication: God is the ultimate recipient.

Jesus' comments illuminate two New Testament doctrines, the first being our union with Christ. We are personally united to Christ through faith and the indwelling gift of the Holy Spirit; in fact, our union is so complete that Paul routinely refers to this relationship as being "in Christ" (e.g., 2 Cor. 12:2). When Christ appeared on the Damascus road, he confronted Saul with the words, "I am Jesus, whom you are persecuting" (Acts 9:5b). In saying this, Jesus was fully identifying with those believers Saul was throwing into prison. In the same way, Matthew 10:40 declares that when a believer is welcomed, Christ considers himself welcomed.

Second, Matthew 10:40 helps express the *perichoretic* love relationship between the members of the Trinity—that is, the eternal coinherence or oneness of the Father, Son, and Holy Spirit, defined by 1 John 4:16 as "love," the very essence of divinity itself. Due to this mutually shared divine nature—because Christ is "in the Father" and the Father is

Pastoral Perspective

"We have it in us to be Christs to each other . . . to work miracles of love and healing as well as to have them worked upon us."[1] This bold assertion by Frederick Buechner could well have been written as commentary on Matthew 10:40–11:1. These are the closing words of Jesus' missionary discourse, a series of instructions and warnings given to those being sent out like "sheep into the midst of wolves" (10:16). This passage contains the heart of Matthew's Gospel: a timeless call for the church to go out into the world in Christ's name, as well as to receive and welcome the "little ones" of the world in Christ's name.

The term "little ones" (*mikros*) refers not only to children but to those considered inferior and vulnerable. These little ones foreshadow the reference to "the least of these" in Matthew 25:31–46, the vulnerable ones who are, indeed, Christ in need. In Matthew 25, we get a clue as to what the reward is for those who indiscriminately meet human needs: they inherit the kingdom. The ones who have given food and drink to the hungry and thirsty, clothed the naked, cared for the sick, and visited prisoners are the ones who will know blessing, who will have both encountered Christ and embodied Christ.

1. Frederick Buechner, *A Room Called Remember: Uncollected Pieces* (San Francisco: Harper Collins e–books, 1992), 136.

Feasting on the Gospels

Exegetical Perspective

The brief set of blessings in this passage comes as a conclusion to the series of blessings and curses—promises of rewards and punishments—that are detailed in Jesus' speech to the Twelve as he sends them to proclaim the gospel. In Matthew 10, the disciples are not simply going forth to announce the good news; they are being sent by Jesus. This sending creates a peculiar intimacy between Jesus and his disciples. The blessings and terrors of Jesus' own ministry belong to and define the ministry of his disciples: "A disciple is not above the teacher" (10:24). While much of the chapter focuses upon the fate of the disciples themselves, this passage addresses the fate of those who hear the gospel and show hospitality to those whom Jesus sends.

Jesus has already indicated that how people receive the disciples determines their eschatological fate. Jesus instructs the disciples to "let your peace come upon" any house that welcomes "you" and to "shake off the dust from your feet" against any house or town than does not welcome "you" (10:13–14). "It will be more tolerable for the land of Sodom and Gomorrah on the day of judgment than for that town" (10:15).

However, in this passage, the violence and divisions that frequent the ministry of Jesus and those he sends are set aside. This passage emphasizes the

Homiletical Perspective

During the eighteenth century, a group of missionaries influenced by Anthony Norris Groves (1795–1853) opposed organized missionary societies, organizations that aided local congregations in pooling resources financially to support missionaries. In stark contrast, the faith-missions movement—or faith missionaries, as they came to be called—believed that cooperation among churches demonstrated a fundamental lack of trust in God. They believed missionaries must trust that God would provide the resources necessary for their work.

Missionaries must depend completely on the hospitality and care of others along the way. Therefore, missionaries should not go out raising money or worrying about salaries. Instead, they should simply launch out, believing that someone will respond with aid. Such a missionary, for example, might head to the train station or the shipyard and wait until the locals hear about his or her presence and willingly pay the fare. Trust in God meant relying unconditionally on the goodness and hospitality of others.

Such a practice does seem to have biblical precedent as we listen to Jesus' words in the missionary discourse to his disciples. Jesus instructs the Twelve to proclaim the good news of the kingdom of heaven, exhorting them to trust God to provide for their basic needs (vv. 5–15). Like the faith

Theological Perspective

"in Christ"—our union with Christ brings us into a mediated union (through Christ) with the Father as well (John 14:10–20). Consequently, any hospitality given to a believer is also received by God the Father.

Jesus goes on to address in verse 41 the reward for those who extend hospitality to believers: "Whoever welcomes a prophet in the name of a prophet will receive a prophet's reward; and whoever welcomes a righteous person in the name of a righteous person will receive the reward of the righteous." A prophet is one who *proclaims* God's word. A righteous person *embodies* God's word. When Jesus uses the phrases "in the name of a prophet" or "in the name of a righteous person," he clarifies that the hospitality offered is *because* they are a prophet or righteous person. This implies that "whoever" offers hospitality will "receive the reward of the prophet" or the "righteous." Taken together with Christ's words in verse 40, such extensions of hospitality are acts of service to Christ as well as the Father. Thus believers assume a christological role as priestly mediators to God for whoever serves or welcomes them. Furthermore, when acts of hospitality are directed toward a believer, this brings those who extend a welcome into communion with God, God's work, and, hence, God's reward.

Verse 42 shows how low the bar is set for someone to receive a divine reward: "Whoever gives even a cup of cold water to one of these little ones in the name of a disciple—truly I tell you, none of these will lose their reward." The phrase "one of these little ones" is best understood to mean "one of the least of these" and applies to any ordinary Christian, including a child. The phrase "in the name of a disciple" highlights that the giver of cold water recognizes the person to be a follower of Christ.

Jesus mentions a "cup of *cold* water" (emphasis added) to indicate not only hospitality but sacrifice: to offer cold water required drawing water from a deep well and often carrying it uphill in a heavy jar to the family home. Who would want to drink room-temperature water if new, cold well water was available? The simple act of giving "a cup of cold water" to an ordinary believer was a sacrificial act, a generous gift that might require another arduous trip downhill to the village well to draw up more cold water for the household. Jesus' words reveal that no act of service or personal sacrifice toward "the least of these," who belong to Christ, will go unnoticed or unrewarded by God. As Jesus also promises in Matthew 25:40, "As you did it to one of the least of these who are members of my family, you did it to me."

Pastoral Perspective

Mother Teresa reminds us that every day we encounter Christ in "distressing disguise" in those "hungry not only for bread, but hungry for love; naked not only for clothing, but naked of human dignity and respect; homeless not only for want of a room of bricks, but homeless because of rejection."[2] As we explore the meaning of this passage for the church today, we are confronted with the inherent identity of the church as those who are "sent out" into the world with the gospel. Although our context is vastly different from the Matthean community's context, the church's call remains the same: in spite of any and all opposition, we are to go out into the world, to alleviate human suffering and meet real needs, to work miracles of love and healing by hospitable acts equivalent to offering a cup of cold water to the lowliest in Matthew's community. We go as those open to having the miracle of hospitality "worked upon us."

The preacher or teacher must not limit interpretation to one side of this equation: we are all "sent ones" who are called to receive the hospitality of the stranger, as well as the ones who welcome and receive the stranger who comes to us. This passage reminds us of the human capacity to "be Christs to each other." We can—in fact we are called both to *represent Christ to* the stranger and to *encounter Christ in* the stranger.

Five times in Matthew's Gospel the writer announces the end of a major discourse and indicates geographical movement, as is done here in verse 11:1: "Now when Jesus had finished instructing his twelve disciples, he went on from there to teach and proclaim his message in their cities." This marks the end of the missionary discourse of chapter 10, which is packed with action verbs: Jesus summons, gives authority to, and sends out the disciples, charging them to go, cast out, cure, proclaim, raise, cleanse, and ultimately lose their lives for his sake.

These are the verbs that still define the mission of the church. Teaching and preaching this passage will involve asking what it means for our congregations, both as individuals and as communities of faith, to do these things. In the last several decades, the language of "missional church" and "missional ecclesiology" has emerged among scholars and clergy seeking to describe a new way of being church in post-Christendom Western culture. Church of Scotland Bishop Lesslie Newbigin's *The Other Side of*

2. Mother Teresa, *Words to Love By* (Notre Dame, IN: Ave Maria Press, 1983), 80.

intimacy and mutual blessings among Jesus, the disciples, and those who welcome them. It begins with a declaration that sounds like the Gospel of John: "Whoever welcomes you welcomes me, and whoever welcomes me welcomes the one who sent me" (v. 40). In John, this unity occurs through seeing and believing, in Matthew through hospitality. The divine implications of hospitality are a pervasive theme throughout the ancient Mediterranean world. To Jews, Christians, Greeks, Romans, and perhaps everyone else, when you welcome a stranger into your house, you may be welcoming the God of Israel (or the Messiah) or one of the many gods and goddesses of the ancient world. When a stranger knocks at your door, it is a dangerous and potentially wonderful moment.

The blessings of hospitality are then articulated with three somewhat curious examples. The first two follow the same syntax: "Whoever welcomes a prophet/righteous person in the name of a prophet/righteous person will receive a prophet's/righteous person's reward" (v. 41). There are several puzzles here. It is not clear in the Greek or the English what the phrase "in the name of" means. Some translations render the Greek as "because," meaning that one welcomes a prophet because he or she is a prophet. More likely is the rendering "as," meaning that one welcomes a prophet with all the honors and authority due to a prophet. It is also not clear what a "prophet's reward" might be. Most readers assume some sort of reward from God, either in the present or the future. Finally, it is not clear what is meant by "a righteous person" and how a righteous person connects to the sending of the Twelve in the rest of the chapter. Do the terms "prophet" and "righteous person" apply to every disciple sent by Jesus? Are prophets and the righteous subsets within the disciples?

The third example is a bit different. The person is no longer someone with obvious social status, but rather "one of these little ones." The unspecific "welcome" becomes even more evocative with "gives even a cup of cold water." The giving of the cup is done "in the name of a disciple." The reward is not, as we might expect, "a disciple's reward," but "their reward." Some readers suggest that these examples assume classes of reward, with prophet the highest and the little ones the lowest. However, this seems contrary to the way Jesus speaks elsewhere in Matthew. In fact, the judgment scene in Matthew 25:31–46 suggests, if anything, that the reward for giving a cup of water to a little one would be the highest reward. As

missionaries, the disciples should demonstrate complete trust in God. Such a disposition, however, can easily take a subtle turn toward misuse. Trusting in others to practice hospitality and provide for one's welfare can turn from a gracious gift one may receive to a right one deserves, an entitlement. Preachers still face this temptation, whether it comes in the intangible form of unique standing in the community or more concretely in the form of special tax rules. Because we serve as God's spokespersons, we may come to believe that we are entitled to special privileges from our congregations and society. Every preacher must continually assess where his or her trust really resides.

The flipside of this burden for ministers is that Christians at large all have a responsibility to practice generosity toward those God has called to serve as missionaries and ministers. In Matthew 10, Jesus speaks of the suffering and hardship the disciples will experience. He calls them to take up their crosses and follow him (v. 38). Jesus ends the teaching, however, by shifting the weight of responsibility from the missionary disciples to those who practice hospitality toward them (vv. 40–42). Despite the difficulties the disciples will face, some along their way will encourage them and welcome them into their homes. These acts of hospitality toward the disciples, however, have nothing to do with any sense of entitlement but with others' commitment to provide for the disciples' well-being. It takes more than missionaries and ministers to accomplish Jesus' mission. The whole faith community takes ownership.

When one receives Jesus' messengers, one receives Jesus (v. 40). Jesus calls the church to practice hospitality toward those who serve as God's ambassadors, be they missionaries, righteous people, or prophets. Notably the hospitality he calls us to practice does not involve unusual heroic deeds. Instead, it involves ordinary acts of kindness, like giving a simple cup of cold water (v. 42). When one gives the least that courtesy demands, it will not go unrewarded. Foreshadowing a later theme in his ministry (25:31–46), Jesus reminds all Christians that our most ordinary gestures carry some of the most profound meanings.

A number of years ago, my wife Nancy was driving down a busy street in Portland, Oregon, with our five-year-old son. Out of the corner of her eye, she saw an elderly man on the sidewalk collapse to the ground. She turned the car around, called 911, and waited until the ambulance arrived to take him to the hospital. She visited him in the hospital the next day and continued to keep in touch over the

Matthew 10:40–11:1

Theological Perspective

Jesus' comments in Matthew 10:40–42 seem to bestow salvation and divine reward to "whoever" gives hospitality to a believer. However, this appears to conflict with Reformation theology built on passages like Ephesians 2:8: "For by grace you have been saved through faith, and this is not your own doing; it is the gift of God."

One way theologically to make sense of Jesus' comments in Matthew 10:40–42 is to examine Rahab's act of hospitality toward the Jewish spies, mentioned in James 2:25. For James, the story of Rahab illustrates his point that good works *reveal* faith and *complete* it (vv. 18, 22); therefore, Rahab was justified by her works and not by her faith alone (vv. 24–25). In Joshua 2 we learn that Rahab was a harlot, a Canaanite, and a very good liar. In short, Rahab was a sinner. However, Rahab chose to extend her hospitality to the spies because she and her people had heard the forty-year-old story of the way "the LORD dried up the water of the Red Sea," and the more recent news of "what [Israel] did to the two kings of the Amorites that were beyond the Jordan" (Josh. 2:10). From this knowledge Rahab makes an amazing confession to the spies: "The LORD your God is indeed God in heaven above and on earth below" (Josh. 2:11), confirming Moses' prophecy (Deut. 2:25; 4:39).

Rahab did not know the Mosaic law or offer a ram for her sins, yet, her confession of Israel's God was a mustard seed of faith revealed by her act of hospitality, which resulted in her salvation and that of her family. Furthermore, Rahab could never have fathomed God's great reward, part of which was making her—at least according to Matthew's genealogy—one of King David's great-grandmothers and thereby including her in the lineage of God's Son, Jesus Christ, through whom God's salvation would come to the world. Such is one example from Scripture of Jesus' promise to his disciples in Matthew 10:40–42, of God's great reward to those who offer hospitality to God's people, and how a simple welcome may reveal a mustard seed of faith.

BONNIE L. PATTISON

Pastoral Perspective

1984: Questions of the Churches, published by both the British Council of Churches and the United States National Council of Churches, is often cited as one of the catalysts of this movement. Darrell Guder notes that Newbigin brought into public discussion the missiological consensus that "'mission' means sending and it is the central biblical theme describing the purpose of God's actions in human history." In many ways this amorphous "movement" has been prophetic for the institutional church, confronting the Western church's tendency to see itself as "the purpose of the gospel, rather than its witness."[3]

Inasmuch as the church has been preoccupied with institutional survival, rather than being God's witnesses sent into the world to bless all people, we have essentially *not* been the church. The term itself, though, is simply redundant: there is no such thing as a church that is not a missional church. When we cease to be missional, we are no longer the church; we are simply one more cultural organization serving consumerist needs as if there were nothing more significant than consumption.

The fact is that most people today shop for a community of faith in the way they shop for a pair of jeans, asking themselves when they visit our congregations, "Is this church a good fit for me, for us? Do I like it?" Perhaps we should warn those in our new-member classes that it matters far less to us whether they like it here than that they think of themselves as sent out into the world: to be Christs and to meet Christs; to risk—for the sake of love and justice—reputation, persecution, and irreparable family rifts; to face the wolves of insatiable greed, rugged individualism, and exploitive power; to lose their life and find it; indeed, to inherit the kingdom. Then we are being Christ to them, and they can become Christs to us.

PAM DRIESELL

3. Darrell Guder, *Missional Church: A Vision for the Sending of the Church in North America* (Grand Rapids: Eerdmans, 1998), 4 and 5.

with the "prophet" and the "righteous person," it is not clear who the "little ones" are meant to be.

Perhaps the best guess is that Jesus (or Matthew) begins with the two examples of the prophets and righteous because everyone knows that showing hospitality to people of such status (or to angels from heaven) results in divine reward. To these examples of giving hospitality to people of high status, Jesus attaches the more difficult admonition to show hospitality to those of low status. In focusing on the gentle kindness of giving a cup of cold water to a little one, Jesus stands, of course, at the center of Hebrew prophecy. Moreover, the saying evokes echoes from all over the Gospel of Matthew. Readers have often noted connections to the radical love of the Sermon on the Mount and to the claim in 25:31–46 that the hungry and thirsty, those who are naked and in prison, and even the stranger are actually Jesus himself.

For all the intimacy between Jesus and the Twelve, the passage concludes with a physical separation. Jesus goes on "from there to teach and proclaim his message in their cities." The Twelve do the same, but they do so without Jesus in their company, even though, as we have seen, Jesus is also in their midst. When disciples engage in mission, Jesus is with them. Furthermore, disciples encounter him whenever they encounter any of the "lost sheep of the house of Israel" (10:6).

We might note, in conclusion, how this passage keeps changing the role of the reader. In some moments, we the readers are the disciples whom Jesus is sending. We proclaim and teach and heal and bless. In some moments, we are the ones to whom the disciples are preaching and teaching. We are the ones called to give a cup of water to the little ones. We are the little ones to whom the water is given. This sounds like classic Christian theology. We who need to hear the gospel spoken to us every day are called every day to speak the gospel to others.

LEWIS R. DONELSON

next few months. Sometime later, he invited us to his downtown apartment for dinner. As we talked that evening, I learned he was a retired pastor from a little church in Fort Collins, Colorado. I was intrigued, since I had grown up in that area. When I asked what church he served in, he responded, "It was just a little church there in town. You wouldn't know it." Out of curiosity I pushed him for further details. "It was," he answered, "just a little Church of Christ church on Shields Street. I distinctly remember a teenager with thick glasses leading songs." Caught by complete surprise, I exclaimed, "That was my dad! You knew my dad as a teenager!"

As I later reflected on this, I thought to myself, "You just never know who it is you are helping." Then Jesus immediately reminded me, "Oh yes, you do. You always know. Inasmuch as you have done it to the least of these, you have done it unto me."

This incident, and the many that others could report, do not illustrate this text only because the hospitality extended was to a minister. Clearly hospitality to missionary disciples provides the immediate context for Jesus' teaching, but it is irresponsible to limit his message to this select group. Jesus' exhortation to the faith community should extend beyond evangelists to the homeless, the disenfranchised, and the displaced people—in other words, to the "little ones" who are vulnerable and weak in any culture (v. 42).

Jesus calls Christians to make hospitality a practice, a natural routine of life as we extend a cup of cold water to a stranger or a person in need (v. 42). Such hospitality calls us to use our homes not as places of retreat, where we shut the doors against the needs and demands of others, but as places where hospitality is offered to the world. Ours is not the hospitality our society celebrates; it has nothing to do with proper etiquette, gourmet cooking, elegant dinnerware, or a spotless house. It is about an open heart that welcomes others, especially the "little ones." Hospitality harbors no hidden agenda and expects no reciprocity. This hospitality flows out of the routine activities of life. It means inhabiting ordinary patterns of behavior that welcome others. This kind of hospitality is a practice, a spiritual discipline.

DAVE BLAND

Matthew 11:2–19

²When John heard in prison what the Messiah was doing, he sent word by his disciples ³and said to him, "Are you the one who is to come, or are we to wait for another?" ⁴Jesus answered them, "Go and tell John what you hear and see: ⁵the blind receive their sight, the lame walk, the lepers are cleansed, the deaf hear, the dead are raised, and the poor have good news brought to them. ⁶And blessed is anyone who takes no offense at me."

⁷As they went away, Jesus began to speak to the crowds about John: "What did you go out into the wilderness to look at? A reed shaken by the wind? ⁸What then did you go out to see? Someone dressed in soft robes? Look, those who wear soft robes are in royal palaces. ⁹What then did you go out to see? A prophet? Yes, I tell you, and more than a prophet. ¹⁰This is the one about whom it is written,

'See, I am sending my messenger ahead of you,
who will prepare your way before you.'

Theological Perspective

While John the Baptist languished in prison, his soul languished in doubt. Matthew writes, "When John heard in prison what the Messiah was doing, he sent word by his disciples and said to him, 'Are you the one who is to come, or are we to wait for another?'" (vv. 2–3).

How could this be? John *saw* the Spirit descend upon Jesus at his baptism (John 1:32); he *heard* the voice from heaven declare, "This is my Son, the Beloved, with whom I am well pleased" (Matt. 3:17). John preached that the Messiah would "baptize with . . . fire," that his "winnowing fork" was "in his hand," and he would "gather his wheat into the granary; but the chaff he will burn with unquenchable fire" (3:11–12). Certainly, John must have had great expectations of Jesus.

John's doubt probably took root while he was imprisoned for preaching against Herod's illicit marriage to Herodias, and Jesus did not come to his rescue. Instead, Jesus "withdrew to Galilee" (4:12). Why did Jesus not begin to claim David's throne by overthrowing Herod? Whatever theological assumptions may have cradled John's doubt, the text indicates he was not having a *crisis of faith*; rather, he was seeking *clarification for his faith*.

Circumstances have a way of thrusting themselves into our theological paradigms, challenging our

Pastoral Perspective

In pondering the pastoral implications of this complicated text, it is tempting to concentrate on verses 16–19 and to reflect on the fickleness of the faithful. If we are honest about the challenges of pastoral leadership, we will acknowledge that while God is hard to serve, God's people are often hard to please. Time after time a congregation calls a pastor who will help overcome the idiosyncrasies of her predecessor, only to discover that the people wish the new pastor were more like the old. "For John came neither eating nor drinking, and they say, 'He has a demon'; the Son of Man came eating and drinking, and they say, 'Look, a glutton and a drunkard, a friend of tax collectors and sinners!'"

One can read the text more positively. We can be thankful that God does not provide a standard job description for the faithful leader—ordained or lay. The occasional attempts of seminaries to define the perfect product or of denominations to describe the excellent pastor are mercifully thwarted by God's capacity to surprise. Likewise, the ambition of many a pastor to fill the session or the vestry or the diaconate with the properly pliable is confounded by God's astonishing capacity to use the stubborn and annoying for the sake of God's reign.

In Matthew's Gospel, there is an even deeper way to understand the significance of the distinction

¹¹Truly I tell you, among those born of women no one has arisen greater than John the Baptist; yet the least in the kingdom of heaven is greater than he. ¹²From the days of John the Baptist until now the kingdom of heaven has suffered violence, and the violent take it by force. ¹³For all the prophets and the law prophesied until John came; ¹⁴and if you are willing to accept it, he is Elijah who is to come. ¹⁵Let anyone with ears listen!

¹⁶"But to what will I compare this generation? It is like children sitting in the marketplaces and calling to one another,

¹⁷ 'We played the flute for you, and you did not dance;
  we wailed, and you did not mourn.'

¹⁸For John came neither eating nor drinking, and they say, 'He has a demon'; ¹⁹the Son of Man came eating and drinking, and they say, 'Look, a glutton and a drunkard, a friend of tax collectors and sinners!' Yet wisdom is vindicated by her deeds."

Exegetical Perspective

Hanging over this wonderful, complex series of sayings is John the Baptist's question to Jesus: "Are you the one who is to come, or are we to wait for another?" (11:3). Part of Jesus' response to John's question is to explore the status of John himself. It is the relationship between the overlapping identities of John and Jesus that creates unity in this diverse passage. John, as forerunner, helps to define the messianic roles of Jesus.

Despite John's seeming recognition of Jesus' status in Matthew 3:14, in this passage he appears to ask an honest question: Are you the one who is to come, or not? Jesus' rather famous answer points to his fulfillment of certain prophetic promises in Isaiah. The indirectness of Jesus' answer shows the difficulty of the question. It is not the case, despite what was once claimed in academic literature, that all or even most first-century Jews were waiting for a military Messiah, a son of David to drive out the Romans. Some Jews were looking for a Messiah; some were not. Furthermore, those who were did not agree on the profile of the Messiah. John is not simply asking if Jesus is the one. He is also asking what the profile of the Messiah is supposed to be.

Jesus' answer is not that he has fulfilled the agreed-upon messianic requirements and thus is the Messiah. Rather, Jesus points to some of his deeds

Homiletical Perspective

A few years ago, a friend of mine was having outpatient surgery that required anesthesia. He could go home after the surgery but had to have someone drive him. I volunteered to do so, knowing I had to sign papers agreeing actually to do it. My friend insisted, "Just sign the papers, and when we get to my car, I'll go ahead and drive home. It will save you an hour of driving time. I don't want to inconvenience you more than I have to." I insisted that, ethically, I could not let him drive if I had signed the papers and reassured him it was no inconvenience. We argued and in the end, out of stubbornness, he opted not to have the surgery because he refused to accept my help.

Refusing the help of others can result in serious consequences. Not only is this true when it relates to one's physical health; it is also true when it comes to one's spiritual well-being. It is most frustrating, for example, to witness a married couple resisting the advice of a therapist, a youth refusing to listen to the wisdom of a parent, or a student defying the guidance of a teacher. Still it happens regularly. All kinds of reasons are offered to explain the resistance.

Matthew 11:2–19 describes the resistance Jesus and John the Baptist face as they announce God's redemptive aid extending to all humanity and creation in the coming of the kingdom. These verses

Matthew 11:2–19

Theological Perspective

basic assumptions. Such was the case with John. Like Anselm with his "faith seeking understanding,"[1] John came to Jesus fully believing what the prophets had written but seeking clarification concerning whether those writings pointed to Jesus.

Jesus instructed John's disciples to report what they "hear and see" (v. 4), and then paraphrased Isaiah 35:5–6 and 61:1: "The blind receive their sight, the lame walk, the lepers are cleansed, the deaf hear, the dead are raised, and the poor have good news brought to them" (v. 5). John would have noticed what was missing. Jesus' paraphrase of Isaiah 61:1 leaves out the phrase "He has sent me . . . to proclaim liberty to the captives, and release to the prisoners." This "now and not yet" tension in Jesus' answer affirmed he is the Messiah while clarifying that he would not rescue John from Herod's prison. This royal Son of David would not overthrow the wicked human rulers over Israel. Knowing John could be personally disillusioned by Jesus' reply and lack of action, Jesus offered him a gentle word in the form of a blessing: "Blessed is anyone who takes no offense at me" (v. 6).

Jesus did not rebuke John for his doubt or his inadequate theology of the kingdom and its Messiah. In fact, Jesus praised John to the crowd! Through his questions, Jesus led them to conclude that John was no faithless "reed shaken by the wind" or person of power and privilege (vv. 7–8). Though John might have questions about Jesus' identity, Jesus had no doubt who John was: "Among those born of women no one has arisen greater than John the Baptist . . . and if you are willing to accept it, he is Elijah who is to come" (vv. 11, 14). Indeed, John is "more than a prophet" (v. 9); he is an object of biblical prophecy (vv. 10, 14). Not even Moses or Daniel holds that honor. Even so, Jesus offered the kingdom perspective: "The least in the kingdom of heaven is greater than he" (v. 11). In the kingdom, the least are greater than John—the greatest man in all human history.

Jesus then gave this puzzling statement: "From the days of John the Baptist until now the kingdom of heaven has suffered violence, and the violent take it by force" (v. 12). John's arrest and decapitation showcased Jesus' point: the profile of God's kingdom on earth is cruciform. God's kingdom does not come in the power, splendor, and glory of human achievement (or what Luther would call a "theology of glory") but, according to a "theology of the cross," in

1. See Karl Barth, *Anselm, Fides quarens intellectum: Anselm's Proof of the Existence of God in the Context of His Theological Scheme* (Pittsburgh: Pickwick Press, 1960).

Pastoral Perspective

between John the Baptist and Jesus. "Yet wisdom is vindicated by her deeds" (v. 19). John is the representative of God's wisdom as proclaimed by the prophets. He is himself a prophet and more, and his life fulfills the prophecy of Exodus and Malachi (see v. 10). Jesus is not only proclaimer of God's wisdom; he is that wisdom incarnate. At the end of this chapter Matthew has Jesus declare what Matthew's Gospel has proclaimed: that Jesus is the divine wisdom that gives rest to the weary and direction to the confused (see 11:28–30).

As pastors, we are invited to invite people to partake of God's wisdom. Among all the competing claims to knowledge about how the world works, the church proclaims time and again that the prophets point us to the way the world works, and that the life of Jesus is the way the world works. To see rightly what's what is to see our lives and human history through the lens of Jesus, who is God's own wisdom among us.

Our pastorates and our congregations will also acknowledge that Christian wisdom has enormous consequences. When Jesus says that wisdom is justified (proved, enacted, vindicated) by her deeds, he points back to the beginning of our passage. John the Baptist declares that wisdom is visible in his courage and his clarity—even unto death. That Jesus is wisdom is evident in his compassion and his obedience—even unto death.

To live as people who trace our histories to John and ground our lives in Jesus is to be deeply concerned with consequences. When John's disciples come to ask whether Jesus is the expected wisdom from on high, Jesus responds first not by citing his teachings but by citing his mighty deeds: "The blind receive their sight, the lame walk, the lepers are cleansed, the deaf hear, the dead are raised" (11:5).

As followers of Christ who seek to live out divine wisdom, we are under the mandate to follow him, not only in what we know, but by how we act. It is much too simple to say that we need to practice what we preach. God's wisdom is not first studied and then enacted. God's wisdom is embodied wisdom. Christ does what Christ says, and the church's discipleship always includes action.

When we think about the ways in which we structure our congregational life, we might think about eliminating the distinction between "mission" committees and "nurture" committees, or between "education" and "action." If wisdom is justified by her deeds, our nurturing includes enabling our people to serve others, and our educating includes educating for action, educating by acting.

that fulfill some, but not all, prophetic promises. In fact, these promises are not necessarily messianic. In his answer, Jesus is defining the character of the Messiah as a compassionate and healing Messiah who enables the blind to see and the lame to walk. At the same time, Jesus is evoking a classic Christian claim: to know what the Messiah should be like, look at Jesus. The blessing on those who take no offense at Jesus becomes quite complex. No one can decide the identity of the Messiah based purely on evidence, because the data can always be disputed. A decision to see Jesus as Messiah comes not only from analyzing messianic data but also from the leap of faith.

In the second part of this passage, Jesus makes a claim about the messianic roles of John and himself. Jesus notes that the people who went to see John sought neither the asceticism of the desert nor the comfort of soft clothing, but the hard voice of a prophet. Jesus, by connecting John to the coming Messiah, argues that the category of prophet is not sufficient for John. Jesus quotes Malachi 3:1: "I am sending my messenger ahead of you." John's greatest role is to announce and prepare for the coming of "you." Jesus will claim in 11:14 that John is the Elijah who is predicted in Malachi 4:5 to arrive "before the great and terrible day of the Lord." Furthermore, the syntax of "you" in the Malachi quote becomes a veiled messianic confession on Jesus' part. God is speaking to Jesus in this text; Jesus is the "you." Thus, in applying this text to John, Jesus makes a claim about himself.

The announcement that, even though no one "born of women" is greater than John the Baptist, "the least in the kingdom of heaven is greater than he" has created difficulties for many Christians who want to include John in the kingdom. Jesus' comment belongs in the context of the messianic arrival. John's role as the one who announces and prepares for the Messiah precedes the arrival of the kingdom. Thus John, as forerunner, does not act within the time frame of the kingdom itself. However, this does not mean that John could not be included in the kingdom as a believer. Early Christian theology typically included in the kingdom not just John the Baptist but also the patriarchs, the matriarchs, the prophets, and even Socrates.

Various translation and interpretation issues surround the phrase "has suffered violence" (v. 12). Some readers have suggested the violence is positive, since it may come from people's desire to enter the kingdom. It is more likely this violence is negative and comes from people's opposition to the kingdom

revolve around the issue of the identities of John and Jesus and the ultimate rejection they experienced from their contemporaries. Verses 2–6 focus on Jesus' identity. Verses 7–15 shift attention to the identity of the Baptist. The identities of Jesus and John are intertwined. John is part of the answer to Jesus' identity, and Jesus defines who John is. Both meet with resistance, in part due to misunderstandings about who they are and in part due to stubbornness in refusing to accept help from another source.

That is how Matthew rounds out this unit in verses 16–19. He describes the response of the crowd to the arrival of Jesus and John with a parable about the childish games "this generation" (v. 16, a pejorative term for Matthew) plays in order to avoid responding to God's kingdom offer. Jesus describes his contemporaries as spoiled brats who constantly complain that others will not live up to their desires and expectations.

John the Baptist came demanding repentance, but they were not ready to hear that message. They were playing a delightful tune and wanting him to celebrate (v. 17). Then Jesus came proclaiming the good news of the kingdom of heaven and entering into festive fellowship with others, but the people demanded he fast and eliminate the riffraff from his company (v. 19).[1] Charles Siburt observes, "These domineering, hard-to-please children are angry with the other children" because they will not play by their rules. As passive spectators, they "prefer the less strenuous guise of flute players and dirge singers, leaving to their playmates the more demanding exercises."[2]

What an amazing picture this is! John came and they accused him of being an ascetic, too gloomy. Jesus came and they accused him of being a glutton, too worldly. John was too serious; Jesus was not serious enough! They hated the preaching of repentance, and they hated the proclamation of the gospel. Regardless of what is done, they are not satisfied. The Messiah had arrived, and they did not recognize him because they were too busy quarreling about childish games. In reality their criticisms and games were ways of refusing God's gracious help.

The parable provides remarkable insight into the way people resist God.[3] The childish games people continue to play are legion and provide excuses in order to elude responsibility. Consider the game of

1. W. D. Davies and Dale C. Allison, *The Gospel according to Saint Matthew*, International Critical Commentary (London: T. & T. Clark, 2004), 2:262.
2. Charles Siburt, "The Game of Rejecting God: Luke 7:31–35," *Restoration Quarterly* 19, no. 4 (1976): 208.
3. Ibid., 209.

Matthew 11:2–19

Theological Perspective

humility, poverty, suffering, and the lack of worldly power. As John Calvin taught the persecuted French church:

> Let us remember that the outward aspect of the Church is so contemptible that its beauty may shine within; that it is so tossed about on earth that it may have a permanent dwelling place in heaven; that it lies so wounded and broken in the eyes of the world that it may stand vigorous and whole, in the presence of God and his angels; that it is so wretched in the flesh that its happiness may nevertheless be restored in the spirit. In the same way, when Christ lay despised in a stable multitudes of angels were singing his excellence; . . . when the sun failed, it was proclaiming him—hanging on the cross—King of the world; and the tombs opened were acknowledging him Lord of death and life.[2]

What the Reformers understood, and what was not grasped by many religious leaders of Jesus' day or even John the Baptist, was that God's revelation in Christ is paradoxical, hidden under the sign of its opposite, and hence offensive.

In closing, Jesus noted that "this generation" are like stubborn children dithering in the market over whether they should play wedding or funeral (vv. 16–17). John's countercultural life was offensive to them. Thus, unable to hear God's call to repentance through his ministry, they dismissed John as a demoniac (v. 18). Similarly, Jesus was offensive because he extended fellowship, communion, and grace to sinners, eating with whoever invited him to dinner. Thus Jesus was dismissed as a glutton and a drunkard (v. 19). Therefore, the same word Jesus spoke to John applied to John's "generation" as well as to ourselves: "Blessed is anyone who takes no offense at me" (v. 6).

BONNIE L. PATTISON

Pastoral Perspective

A longtime pastor commented that he was tired of all the reference to the "social gospel." For him there was only "the gospel." For Jesus in Matthew's Gospel, church is not a matter of faith followed by deeds; church is thoughtful deeds and active faith.

We cannot avoid looking briefly at the most troublesome verse in our text: "From the days of John the Baptist until now the kingdom of heaven has suffered violence, and the violent take it by force" (v. 12). The commentaries make clear how difficult it is to translate this obscure verse, but however we translate it, we find it troubling. Is violence an inescapable part of human history, perhaps even an inescapable aspect of the coming of God's reign?[1]

Perhaps the most suggestive way to interpret the text is to interpret it as part of Matthew's narrative. Remember that the passage begins with John in prison; the prophet of God's wisdom has suffered violence. Jesus, wisdom incarnate, may be gentle and lowly of heart, as the rest of chapter 11 assures us, but he is also the victim of cruel and calculated evil.

Pastoral care and Christian education are bound to come up against some variation of the question, why do the good so often suffer violence? Reading Matthew's Gospel we are bound to suggest that the presence of good often stirs up the resistance of evil. Herod slays the innocent. The demons cry out against Jesus. John the Baptist is imprisoned and will be executed. Jesus will be betrayed, arrested, tried, and executed too.

Pastoral wisdom will acknowledge that, in ways beyond our understanding, grace meets resistance; good and evil struggle. The wisest pastoral care will also know that the line between good and evil does not run between you and me or between us and them; the line runs through every human heart. When we proclaim that grace always meets with resistance, we are bound to acknowledge that often we have met the resisters, and they are us. Faithful pastoral care will still believe that grace is stronger than resistance, and goodness greater than evil.

DAVID L. BARTLETT

---

2. John Calvin, *Concerning Scandals*, trans. John W. Fraser (Grand Rapids: Eerdmans, 1978), 29–30.

1. The richest literary interpretation of the text is Flannery O'Connor's novel *The Violent Bear It Away*.

of heaven. In this reading, the violence suffered by the kingdom echoes the violence of chapter 10 and anticipates the conflict in verses 16–19.

While there is much debate about the origin of the images in verses 16–19, the point of these verses is fairly clear. The children in the market are the people who reject Jesus and his understanding of the kingdom of heaven. They demand that Jesus and John conform to their expectations of Messiahs, either dancing or mourning, as they prefer. Of course, beneath the rhetoric of children's fickleness lurks the horrible violence of chapter 10 and the crucifixion of Jesus.

Historians see the contrasting critiques of John and Jesus as being largely accurate. The Gospels portray John's ministry as focused on Jewish repentance and preparation. If the Messiah is coming tomorrow, we should repent today. By contrast, the Gospels note that Jesus is frequently criticized much as he is in these verses. He is "a glutton and a drunkard, a friend of tax collectors and sinners" (v. 19a). John's moment belongs to repentance, but messianic time is for celebration.

The passage concludes with a rather eloquent image: "Wisdom is vindicated [or made righteous] by her deeds" (v. 19b). The meaning of the saying seems clear enough. In the deed we see the value of a thought. However, the context here is messianic recognition. In a way, Jesus returns to the argument he used with John the Baptist in 11:4–5: Judge me by what I do.

So how can anyone know if a deed or person belongs to the kingdom of God? There is no way to prove someone is the Messiah, because the Messiah's profile is always contested. In these verses Jesus cannot prove his case; he can only respond by pointing to what he has said and done. This passage makes two arguments. First, Jesus and his ministry fall within the traditional range of messianic images and prophecies. Second, beyond any authenticating data, Jesus is the true Messiah and thus defines who the Messiah is.

LEWIS R. DONELSON

hypocrisy: "Christians are just a bunch of hypocrites. I don't want any part of that." The game of critiquing worship is also a favorite: "The worship is too boring." "The worship is too much about performance and entertainment." Of course, anyone who desires can always find fault with the preacher: "I just don't like his (or her) preaching style." A trump card is, "I was treated unfairly." "They mistreated my spouse or my mother." "I never felt welcomed." If someone wants to go the doctrine route, they can always find a theological stance of the church with which they disagree. The possibilities are endless. Any of these can be turned into a game that takes longer than Monopoly! While the criticism goes on, however, what really matters is pushed aside.

Churches can also play childish games. When called to minister outside their comfort zones, they offer convenient reasons for not responding: "We do not have the financial resources." "We do not have enough human power." "We do not have the space." "It is dangerous for our members to work in the inner city."

We preachers need to hear a strong word of warning as well. We too can play childish games. We proclaim the good news of the gospel and hear people accuse us of dishing up soft scoops of grace. We call for repentance, and they say we are harsh and judgmental. Then we turn these criticisms into childish games in order to take the path of least resistance in our preaching. We find ways to blame others for our failures. We can be just as stubborn and resistant to help as anyone else. All childish games are costly. They take a heavy toll on individuals, churches, and preachers alike. They deprive everyone of the rich spiritual blessings God holds out to those who humbly repent and actively participate in the coming of God's kingdom.

DAVE BLAND

Matthew 11:20–24

²⁰Then he began to reproach the cities in which most of his deeds of power had been done, because they did not repent. ²¹"Woe to you, Chorazin! Woe to you, Bethsaida! For if the deeds of power done in you had been done in Tyre and Sidon, they would have repented long ago in sackcloth and ashes. ²²But I tell you, on the day of judgment it will be more tolerable for Tyre and Sidon than for you. ²³And you, Capernaum,
   will you be exalted to heaven?
   No, you will be brought down to Hades.
For if the deeds of power done in you had been done in Sodom, it would have remained until this day. ²⁴But I tell you that on the day of judgment it will be more tolerable for the land of Sodom than for you."

Theological Perspective

This passage consists of a series of judgments against those towns that have witnessed Jesus' "deeds of power" yet have not repented. Biblical writers used the word "woe" to introduce prophetic oracles of lament or condemnation, but here the "woes" introduce judgment. Comparing two Galilean Jewish towns (Chorazin and Bethsaida) with two Gentile cities on the Mediterranean coast (Tyre and Sidon), Jesus says that if his deeds of power had been performed in those cities, they would have repented long ago in the "sackcloth and ashes" (v. 21). In turn, Jesus compares Capernaum (the town where he began his ministry) with Sodom, the proverbially wicked city that, along with Gomorrah, was destroyed by judgment fire (v. 23). Described in a preceding passage, Jesus' deeds of power refer to what people can actually see and hear: the blind receive sight, the lame walk, lepers are cleansed, the deaf hear, the dead are raised, and the poor have good news brought to them (vv. 4–5). What is the theological significance of these words of judgment and references to Jesus' deeds of power?

First, we should note that these woes are set within the context of depictions of Jesus not just as a teacher of wisdom, but also as the embodiment and personification of God's Wisdom. Prior to this passage, Jesus is presented as the one anticipated by the

Pastoral Perspective

This series of woes in chapter 11 of Matthew makes it easy to give in to the temptation to snicker at the poor fortune of Chorazin and Bethsaida. We read that they are being scolded, and perhaps we slip unknowingly into a state of relief, like what we felt when the Joneses down the street were told that their new fence, previously the object of so much envy, does not quite match neighborhood-association guidelines. Like the Pharisee described in Luke, we may not say so aloud, but in some dark corner we think, "God, I thank you that I am not like other people: thieves, rogues, adulterers" (Luke 18:11). We are grateful that, unlike the simpletons of these maligned cities in Matthew 11, we enlightened ones understand.

Chorazin gets no mention elsewhere in Scripture, with the exception of Luke's version of this same passage (Luke 10:13). Bethsaida receives a bit more credit, as one of the places in Galilee where Jesus ministered (Mark 6:45; 8:22) and as the home of Andrew, Peter, and Philip (John 1:44). While we may not have heard or read too much about either city, Jesus lets it be known up front that both places have seen plenty of examples of his holy power. Surely, we read with quiet delight, they have experienced enough of his healing and teaching prowess to turn from their wicked ways. Just as Tyre and Sidon

Exegetical Perspective

As Jesus travels throughout the region with his disciples to "teach and proclaim his message" (11:1), he speaks to the crowds and cities about their expectations, perceptions, and response toward both John the Baptist and himself. In a series of short passages (vv. 2–6, 7–15, 16–19) that culminates here in verses 20–24, Matthew underscores that it is not enough simply to encounter Jesus. What the gospel requires of those who would follow Jesus is true seeing, the kind that signals understanding and inspires human activity that embodies the way of the kingdom of heaven. However, both misplaced messianic expectations and arbitrary interests (vv. 16–17) blunt the capacity to grasp who Jesus and John are. Matthew casts the tragic repercussions of such narrow vision in the characteristically apocalyptic imagery that permeates Matthew's Gospel narrative.

Following on the heels of the reproach that Jesus utters in the previous scene, verses 20–24 open with Jesus' indictment of "the cities in which most of his deeds of power [*dynameis*] had been done," specifically Chorazin, Bethsaida, and Capernaum, "because they did not repent" (v. 20). All three Galilean "cities" were fairly close to one another. Capernaum, a center of Jesus' ministry, sat on the northwestern shore of the Sea of Galilee about two and a half miles from the point where the Jordan River reaches the

Homiletical Perspective

"Familiarity breeds contempt." Many of us have been led to believe that the guru we admire at a distance is more significant than a person with the same gifts who serves our community. Like the people of Chorazin, Bethsaida, and Capernaum, we would like to have an appreciation for the miraculous in our daily lives, but there is something within that causes us to take the blessings in our lives for granted.

In what appears to be an act of pastoral frustration, Jesus rebukes the communities of Chorazin, Bethsaida, and Capernaum because the people of those cities did not repent after witnessing the miracles of Jesus, which happened with regularity. In the Gospels, more than thirty-five wonders of Jesus are recorded. Surveying all four Gospels, twelve of those miracles occurred in Capernaum alone. Jesus rebuked that community, along with the others, because he knew what he had given them. He chided them because even a place as wretched as Sodom would have repented, had it witnessed all Jesus had to give.

Jesus treated Capernaum as home; it is no wonder that so many of his miracles are recorded to have occurred in Capernaum. To take one example from another Gospel, it was in Capernaum that Jesus directed the future disciples to experience the miraculous catch of fish. After teaching the crowds from Simon Peter's boat, he urged the disciples to sail into

Matthew 11:20–24

Theological Perspective

law and the prophets. Just as the people had rejected the "funeral games"—that is, the wailing and mourning—identified with John's ministry, so now they reject the "wedding games" identified with Jesus' ministry, calling him a "drunkard" and "glutton," a "friend of tax collectors and sinners." In identifying Jesus with the personification of Wisdom in the Scriptures, Matthew asserts that "wisdom is vindicated by her deeds" (vv. 18–19; cf. Prov. 8–9, Wis. 7:22–8:21). Right after this passage, the theme of Jesus as Wisdom is reiterated. Because of the uniqueness of his relationship with God, which has the full intimacy of a child and a parent, Jesus is God's embodied Wisdom, who calls to us: "Come to me, all you that . . . are carrying heavy burdens, and I will give you rest" (vv. 26–28).

Why are these woes and references to Jesus' deeds of power set within the context of passages about Jesus as Wisdom? Jesus' deeds of power are the tangible manifestation of God's kingdom; they fulfill the law and the prophets. Through Jesus—his life, his person, and his activity—God's reign of justice and mercy is being enacted in our midst. Matthew in particular places great emphasis on how Jesus does not abolish but fulfills the law (God's Torah or covenant with Israel). Jesus is the Wisdom of God whose yoke embodies and personifies what the law requires (v. 30). In his own person and in the fullness of the intimacy and transparency he has with God, Jesus is the means by which God's will and purpose are realized and perfected in the concrete circumstances of our lives.

Another way to speak of Jesus as God's Wisdom is to notice how Jesus embodies God's creative righteousness. If righteousness is a central theme for Matthew, then that righteousness is present within us not simply as an external command—an imposed mandate—but rather as a reality that is continually created within and around us through Jesus' presence. This is why Jesus' deeds of power are not merely accessories to Matthew's Gospel, ornaments to its long passages on Jesus' teaching. They are part and parcel of Jesus' message about the kingdom of God. They embody what happens when God's reign is enacted among us: the sick are healed, the blind see, the deaf hear, and the poor have good news brought to them. This is not a righteousness that we muster up, drawing on our highest ideals; this is what God creates through Jesus' presence within and among us.

Why the harsh judgment? Because when we reject God's creative righteousness—the reality of God's just and merciful activity being created within and

Pastoral Perspective

received their comeuppance as Philistine strongholds so many years ago, we know that these cities are in trouble—and we are secretly pleased to live in a better place.

When we reach verse 23, things shift from self-righteousness past disbelief to outright giddiness as Capernaum is dragged into the mess. The city that Jesus made his home, this city that made those in his hometown of Nazareth envious, is mentioned in the same breath with Hades and Sodom. The mighty are about to fall spectacularly, and front row seats are available.

This dynamic in human affairs is so common that we often fail to notice that we are caught up in it. It can feel as harmless as chuckling around the water cooler over the hyped downfall of a rival team's slugger, and it usually gets passed around unchallenged when it comes our way as a bit of gossip. In local churches, we may sigh and roll our eyes at a story about "that congregation" or "their pastor." Deeper and darker still, we may relish the fact that our budget and our music program are not theirs.

This is usually when we learn painfully about what is described in James 3:5–10 as the power of the tongue to bless the Lord out of one side of our mouths while cursing a neighbor, a rival, or even an enemy out of the other. This ugly potency of the tongue is the antithesis of God's power to bring us together with healing love; our foul words the antithesis of those Jesus is calling us to use. In Matthew 11, Jesus reminds us that holy power is both most tangible and most transformative when it surfaces as deeds that unify and heal.

True redemption cannot be found through the demise of a perceived enemy. When we delight in the downfall or suffering of another, we reveal our own need for healing. Godly cities, congregations, and individual lives are built on reconciling grace that comes from God and comes to life in our own deeds of power. Since early in the biblical narrative, a pattern has emerged wherein human sins are followed not by godly gloating but by God's invitation back into wholeness. For Christians, this healing work culminates in the desire of God in Jesus to bring us home. Jesus does not enter into these Gospel cities of Chorazin and Bethsaida in order to shift bragging rights around the Mediterranean. He comes with divine love in order to melt hardened hearts and bring us to our senses. He comes because he wants nothing more than what God wants: a cosmic remembrance of God's love and a massive homecoming return to its Source.

lake. Chorazin was a small village in the hills over-looking the northern shore of the Sea of Galilee, about two miles north of Capernaum. Bethsaida was a fishing village east of Capernaum, on the northern shore of the Sea of Galilee. From chapter 4 on, Matthew has focused his readers' attention on Galilee and its prominent place in Jesus' ministry. Having left Nazareth, Jesus returns to Galilee from the wilderness and relocates to Capernaum at the start of his ministry (4:13). Galilee remains the primary locus of his work, with Capernaum serving as the setting of Jesus' healing of the centurion's servant (8:5–13), Peter's mother-in-law (8:14–17), and a paralytic (9:1–7). These environs provide the general context for the stories that unfold throughout chapter 9, up to the point when Jesus goes "about all the cities and villages, teaching in their synagogues, and proclaiming the good news of the kingdom, and curing every disease and every sickness" (9:35).

Thus the passage's reference to the cities of Chorazin, Bethsaida, and Capernaum brings into bold relief Matthew's way of framing the beginning of Jesus' ministry. Matthew clearly sees in Jesus' relocation to Capernaum "by the sea, in the territory of Zebulun and Naphtali" (4:13) the purposeful fulfillment of Isaiah 9:1–2: "Land of Zebulun, land of Naphtali, / on the road by the sea, across the Jordan, Galilee of the Gentiles— / the people who sat in darkness have seen a great light, / and for those who sat in the region and shadow of death, / light has dawned" (4:15–16, adapted from Isa. 9:1–2). For Matthew, that light is the dawning kingdom of heaven that Jesus evidences in word and deed, proclamation and person.

The irony is that here in 11:20–24 Chorazin, Bethsaida, and Capernaum are cast in unfavorable contrast to the Gentile cities of Tyre, Sidon, and Sodom. The light has come, and in deeds of power. The cities have responded with excitement (9:8) and seemingly en masse, but they have not responded adequately, that is, with deeds "worthy of repentance" (cf. Matt. 3:8). Through an obvious inversion, and perhaps playing on cultural stereotypes to underscore the irony of his point, Jesus asserts that the Gentile cities of Tyre and Sidon would have been more responsive to his mission and ministry than Chorazin, Bethsaida, and Capernaum have been. The ensuing allusion to Isaiah 14:12–15 draws a jarring parallel between Capernaum and fallen Babylon: "And you, Capernaum, will you be exalted to heaven? No, you will be brought down to Hades" (v. 23). Those who have directly encountered

deeper water and let down their nets. Though the fishermen doubted his instructions, they obeyed the Lord and caught so many fish that the net was about to break, and they had to call on friends to help them secure the bounty (Luke 5:1–11).

Returning to Matthew, it was near Capernaum that Jesus gave the Sermon on the Mount, a life-changing message so powerful "the crowds were astounded at his teaching, for he taught them as one having authority, and not as their scribes" (Matt. 7:28–29). It was there that Peter's mother-in-law, who was sick, was healed by Jesus' just touching her hand (Matt. 8:14–15). Later that evening, many other people came for healing and to have demons cast out of them.

It was in Capernaum that Jesus healed a paralytic. The man was carried to Jesus on a bed. When Jesus forgave the man's sin, scribes were present who accused him of blasphemy. Then Jesus told the man to stand up and walk, so that the people may know he had authority to forgive sins. The crowds were filled with awe (Matt. 9:1–8).

That night, still in Capernaum, a leader of the synagogue approached Jesus and said his daughter had just died (Matt. 9:18ff). On the way to the man's house and as Jesus was surrounded by a crowd, a woman who had been hemorrhaging for twelve years touched the fringe of his cloak. Jesus turned and, seeing her, declared that her faith had made her well. When Jesus finally arrived at the synagogue leader's house, he said that the girl was not dead but sleeping. The crowd that had already gathered to mourn laughed at him. Jesus went into the house, took the girl by the hand, and she got up.

Another day in Capernaum, two blind men started following the Lord, asking for mercy. Jesus asked the blind men if they believed; when they said that they did, he healed them (Matt. 9:27–31). That same day, Jesus ran into a man who was mute and demon-possessed. When Jesus cast out the demon, the man was able to speak. The people saw he had been healed and marveled at the healing (Matt. 9:32–34).

One Sabbath in Capernaum, there was a man with a withered hand in the synagogue. The religious leaders tried to trick Jesus and asked if it was lawful to heal on the day of rest. Jesus asked if they would save a lost sheep on the Sabbath; then he told the man to stretch out his hand, and the man was healed (Matt. 12:9–13). On the seashore near Capernaum, Jesus fed thousands of people with five loaves and two fish (Matt. 14:13–21). Matthew records that there were

Matthew 11:20–24

Theological Perspective

among us—we lose out. When we see Jesus creating something new within and around us—right before our very eyes—and consistently reject or negate it (with our cynicism or preconceived notions about how God acts), we miss out on its creative potential for us and for others. Indeed, we condemn ourselves to Hades, the Greek equivalent to the Jewish Sheol, the realm of the dead.

It is significant that Matthew compares supposedly righteous towns with supposedly condemned towns. Matthew's harsh language is always directed against those who presume they are righteous; it is never directed against the "least of these" (25:45). Unfortunately Christians have often interpreted Matthew's harsh judgments in anti-Semitic terms. Although a text like this was forged during a time when the Christian movement was defining itself as something other than a sect within Judaism—and thus as a movement that could include both Jews and Gentiles—we miss its point when we fail to see how their judgment continues to speak to us today, especially to those of us who consider ourselves righteous.

The fundamental issue here has to do with whether we are open to the ways Jesus, the Wisdom of God, is embodying the kingdom of God's deeds of power in our time. Where is God's Wisdom, God's creative righteousness, being enacted in our midst? Where are the lame walking? Where are the blind seeing? Where are the deaf hearing? Where are the poor having good news preached to them? Where do we see Jesus manifest among us—among the hungry, the thirsty, the stranger, the naked, the sick, and those in prison (25:31–45)? How are we discerning and participating in God's Wisdom, the fullness of Jesus' deeds of power, as it is being enacted within and around us, not only for us (and those who are as righteous as we think we are), but for everyone, including the "least of these"?

LOIS MALCOLM

Pastoral Perspective

It is fitting for those of us caught up in the daily work of parish life to wonder what part we play in this reconciling drama on any given day. Surely we work at least on some level to bring souls to Christ, to mend the fabric of creation, to build the kingdom—but are such things often measured in budgets and attendance figures? Do we rejoice when a neighboring congregation celebrates their own revival or milestone, or do we wonder why it was not us?

One of the themes running through this portion of Matthew is what Jesus names in three separate places as "deeds of power" (vv. 20, 21, and 23). The failure of folks to recognize these deeds draws wrath from Jesus, and it is not, I think, an ire that comes from their failure to notice Jesus. He is mad or disappointed in them and us because these works of God are unfolding all around us all the time, and we fail even to take notice, let alone offer thanks and praise.

Additionally, we miss opportunities to live out our baptismal birthright and participate in these life-changing works. As Jesus promises in John 14:12, "the one who believes in me will also do the works that I do and, in fact, will do greater works than these, because I am going to the Father."

How are the ministries and programs of our parishes reflecting or even building upon these works and this power of which Jesus speaks? How are we involved in healing and hope, particularly for people on the margins? How does our life as church give flesh to God's vision of reconciliation and resurrection power? Maybe what Christ is seeking most as he comes into our cities and our churches and our lives is to know that we are using all that we have—tongues, hands, minds, everything—in our own displays of loving power in God's name.

ERICK R. OLSEN

and witnessed Jesus' powerful embodiment of the kingdom of heaven will be held accountable for not responding adequately. They compare unfavorably to even Sodom, the biblical emblem of the inhospitable and reprobate (vv. 23–24).

The significance of verses 20–24 is further illumined by its particular placement in the Gospel and its relationship to the preceding chapters. Throughout chapters 8 and 9, Jesus has repeatedly demonstrated great power in a series of healings and exorcisms. Indeed, it is because of such power that the crowds bring to Jesus "many who were possessed with demons; and he cast out the spirits with a word, and cured all who were sick" (8:16). Moreover, it is to these same crowds that Jesus "proclaims the good news of the kingdom" and shows great compassion (9:35–36). Thus Matthew illustrates a compelling relationship between Jesus and those to whom he ministers in the Galilee.

With the relationship between Jesus and the people and the prominence of the Galilean cities, particularly Capernaum, firmly established in the narrative, Jesus' rebuke in verses 20–24 is therefore especially striking. Jesus condemns Chorazin, Bethsaida, and Capernaum because they have not repented. The operative concept here, repentance, emerges from the very heart of Jesus' central message ("From that time Jesus began to proclaim, 'Repent, for the kingdom of heaven has come near,'" 4:17). Matthew's use of the metaphor of fruit-bearing trees ("Bear fruit worthy of repentance," 3:8; and "every good tree bears good fruit, but the bad tree bears bad fruit," 7:17) underscores that repentance is less about belief and much more about embodying in one's actions the way of the kingdom. In other words, repentance in Matthew's Gospel is comprehensive. It signals the reception of, commitment to, and realization of Jesus' primary message and vision of the kingdom of heaven. Any response short of true repentance is unworthy of the kingdom of heaven.

MARY F. FOSKETT

five thousand men present for that miracle, besides the women and children. After the people were fed, Jesus had the disciples row their boat to the other side of the lake while he prayed. That night there was a storm and Jesus walked on water (Matt. 14:23–27). Another day, the temple tax collectors, looking for a way to accuse Jesus, asked if he paid the temple tax. Jesus paid the tax by asking Peter to go catch a fish; inside the fish's mouth was a coin that was worth enough to pay both his and Peter's taxes (Matt. 17:24–27).

Given the abundance of miracles Jesus performed in and around Capernaum, it is not surprising that so many of the people of Capernaum had heard of the miracles; however, compared with the people in non-Israelite cities along the coast, they did not understand or believe. The words Jesus said as he sent the disciples out to preach and heal in these towns come to mind: "Truly I tell you, it will be more tolerable for the land of Sodom and Gomorrah on the day of judgment than for that town" (Matt. 10:15).

Jesus urged the people of Capernaum, Chorazin, and Bethsaida to turn away from their sins and devote themselves to the way of faith. He knew they were unrepentant, not because of ignorance, but because of indifference. In Capernaum they had received the very best he had to give to transform their hearts; yet it seemed their familiarity with the miracles bred contempt rather than conversion.

Two thousand years later, Jesus calls each of us to believe in his healing power and respond in faith to his miraculous ministry. We are being called to move out of indifference into active faith. The miraculous power of Jesus is all around us, just as it was around the people of Capernaum.

SHELLEY D. BEST

Matthew 11:25–30

²⁵At that time Jesus said, "I thank you, Father, Lord of heaven and earth, because you have hidden these things from the wise and the intelligent and have revealed them to infants; ²⁶yes, Father, for such was your gracious will. ²⁷All things have been handed over to me by my Father; and no one knows the Son except the Father, and no one knows the Father except the Son and anyone to whom the Son chooses to reveal him.

²⁸"Come to me, all you that are weary and are carrying heavy burdens, and I will give you rest. ²⁹Take my yoke upon you, and learn from me; for I am gentle and humble in heart, and you will find rest for your souls. ³⁰For my yoke is easy, and my burden is light."

Theological Perspective

This passage is an important source of later Trinitarian formulations, along with other related texts (cf. John 3:35; 10:14–15; 17:25). In this text, we see that Jesus is not only a teacher, prophet, and miracle worker; he is the Son of God, which the early church later would identify with the second person of the Trinity: the Word and Wisdom of God, who was God and was with God at the beginning of creation (John 1:1–4; cf. Prov. 8–9). Not only is Jesus a son of God in the sense that Israel or individuals within Israel were sons of God—as those who kept God's covenant with them—but Jesus is also the Son of God in a unique sense. First, he has everything that God has: the one Jesus calls "Father" (what the tradition would later identify with the first person of the Trinity) has handed everything over to him, thus giving him the fullness of divine life. Second, Jesus as Son and the one he calls Father stand in a unique relationship of unity and intimacy with each other: only the Father truly knows the Son, and only the Son knows the Father.

Matthew embeds this passage about the unique relationship between the Father and the Son within surrounding texts that depict Jesus as God's Wisdom.[1] Jesus as Wisdom is "vindicated by her deeds"

1. For more on Jesus as God's Wisdom, see Elizabeth A. Johnson, *She Who Is: The Mystery of God in Feminist Theological Discourse* (New York: Crossroad, 2002).

Pastoral Perspective

Some readers of this essay undoubtedly will have paid many dear dollars to institutions of higher learning in order to gain the education and earn the credentials that seem to be required for certain types of service in the church. However, here is Jesus thanking God for hiding "these things from the wise and the intelligent" (v. 25). If we consider ourselves to be anything like wise or intelligent, we can hardly wait to discover just what "these things" might be. The Lord has our attention—and perhaps a bit of our consternation.

We wonder if truth would be withheld from those who seek to know God more fully and serve God more faithfully. This is particularly or even painfully true for those who believe God still has messages to deliver. We do well, of course, to remember that Jesus rarely presents truths to us in simple black-and-white formulations. Reflection upon these verses in that light yields some good fruit. This passage is not about a secretive God or a sneaky Jesus; it is, rather, about seeking prayerful access to God's truths through Christ and striving to keep our humility through the process.

While we may not know in fullness just exactly what "these things" are all about, we do know with some security that God hopes for us to continue to grow and blossom. God wants us to be better than

Exegetical Perspective

Jesus' emphatic indictment of those who have encountered his powerful witness to the kingdom of heaven, but whose own lives have not reflected what they have seen and heard, leads to a passage that takes aim at another cultural assumption, namely, the expectation that wisdom belongs to the conventionally wise (*sophoi*) and intelligent. Not so, asserts Jesus, who prays, "I thank you, Father, Lord of heaven and earth, because you have hidden these things from the wise and the intelligent and have revealed them to infants; yes, Father, for such was your gracious will" (vv. 25–26). Jesus upholds the biblical valuation of wisdom, but in a manner similar to 1 Corinthians 1:18–31 and Isaiah 29:14, he turns the identification of both wisdom and the wise on end. True wisdom is lived out in right response. Echoing Matthew 11:19 ("wisdom [*sophia*] is justified by her deeds [*erga*]") as well as Matthew 11:20–24, Jesus underscores that the wise are those who live according to the way of the kingdom that Jesus reveals.

Because Matthew's Jesus outlines key teachings about the nature of the kingdom in his Sermon on the Mount, wisdom is an important motif that underlies both Matthew 11:20–24 and Jesus' extended discourse in Matthew 5–7. Throughout the Sermon on the Mount, Jesus offers paradigms that point to the values, attitudes, perceptions, and

Homiletical Perspective

According to the National Sleep Foundation, citing studies conducted from 1999 to 2004, on any given night more than forty million Americans did not get enough sleep.[1] When you meet people who are a bit distracted or cranky, have mercy on them. Each day, more of them than you realize are so sleep deprived that their daily activities are impacted.

Peaceful slumber should be natural. The human body was divinely designed to require six to eight hours of rest for renewal. Unfortunately many of us live lives that limit our ability to unplug. Some of us stay connected around the clock to cell phones and our office e-mail. Our brains are so stimulated by the constant electronic glare of computer and television screens that we chase away the experience of rest.

Many of our friends and neighbors find sleep a challenge because of the emotional difficulties of daily life and the enormous pressures of the job. With job cuts, downsizing, and restructuring, those left behind are required to do the work of multiple people, all in a forty-hour work week. We are tired from the increased work load and struggle to sleep because of an ever-expanding to-do list.

1. American Psychological Association, "Importance of Sleep." http://www.apa.org/topics/sleep/why.aspx; accessed October 2, 2012.

Matthew 11:25–30

Theological Perspective

(11:19) and Jesus as Wisdom beckons "all you that are weary and are carrying heavy burdens" to take "my yoke upon you" and "find rest for your souls" (vv. 28–29). From texts like these, the early church concluded that Jesus as the Christ or Messiah is not only equal to God (who has handed everything over to him), but that from all eternity there has been a distinction within God between God as the source of divine life and God as the Word and Wisdom who embodies that divine life in incarnate form (see John 1:1–18). As the Christ or the Messiah, Jesus is the Word and Wisdom of God (i.e., God's self-expression), through whom God has not only freely created the world but also redeemed it, thus "summing up" and completing or fulfilling God's purposes for all of nature and history.[2]

Moreover, this passage tells us something about how Jesus, as God's Wisdom, reveals who God is. The Jewish Scriptures had already identified the Torah (God's covenant with Israel) with God's Wisdom, the means by which all could discern and enact God's design for their lives and the world in concrete circumstances. The Gospel of Matthew presupposes this connection between the Torah and Wisdom and uses it to interpret the significance of Jesus' identity. In Matthew, Jesus is the Wisdom of God whose deeds of power enact God's reign of justice and mercy and thus fulfill the law and prophets. Through Jesus, the embodied Torah, we are not only able to perceive—to see and to hear—who God is to us. We are also enabled to enact—to obey—God's will and purpose for our lives.[3]

Thus, as God's Wisdom, Jesus beckons all those who "are weary and are carrying heavy burdens" to "come to me" (v. 28). As the rabbis had used the metaphor of a "yoke" to describe the arduous but delightful task of living out of the Torah, so Matthew has Jesus call to us to "take my yoke upon you, and learn from me" (v. 29). Unlike the "burden" of religious or ethical ideals, which can at times stand over and against our deepest desires, Wisdom's yoke does not burden us or impose on us an alien set of demands that we cannot fulfill or that alienate us from ourselves. Rather, Wisdom's yoke is easy and her burden is light, for she is gentle and humble in heart. In Jesus, as God's Wisdom, we "find rest for [our] souls" (v. 29).

In other words, as Wisdom, Jesus becomes a yoke—a way of life—whose life-giving power

Pastoral Perspective

we presently are, and this includes the growth of our minds. Congregations and denominations have fittingly rich connections with public and private education, and churches often house libraries. Clergy surely are expected to attain and maintain particular standards of learning, and congregants surely seek in worship to have their heads engaged along with their hearts and spirits. God is a fan of intellectual vitality.

However, if we continue this guessing game about the mind of God, it is correct to say that God does not want us to become so obsessed with scholastic achievement and intellectual prowess that they become objects of worship. Perhaps Jesus is pushing us here to consider our priorities. It is worthwhile, if unsettling, to consider the charges on our monthly credit card statements and how they express our values: What portion of a family's budget is allocated to education, compared to gifts to a local church? Are we nearly as passionate about spiritual pursuits as we are about academic achievement? Of course, we ideally seek growth of our spiritual muscles along with our bodies and brains.

Jesus lifts up infants as a model at the end of verse 25, because he wants wonder to remain central to our relationship with God. If our classroom time feels as if it is filled with grueling attempts to bury mystery with data, then one perilous side effect can be the loss of a sense of awe. Our hope should be that our life in the academy stirs up within us a desire to engage deeper questions, a yearning for more profound knowing. There is another push here from Jesus: Do maturation and the formal training that comes with it require us to leave behind that part of ourselves that finds pure joy in watching a butterfly emerge from a chrysalis? Do we need permission to sit and watch such a thing, even if it means we are not engaged in productive work or serious study?

In verses 28–30, Jesus paraphrases from the Deuterocanonical book of the Wisdom genre commonly called Sirach. In Sirach 51:26, we read, "Put your neck under her yoke, and let your souls receive instruction; it is to be found close by." In our focus passage from Matthew 11, it is curious that Jesus pairs "yoke" and "rest," since one conjures an image of oxen bound for work and the other invites the reader into a state of peace for one's soul. Perhaps we are being challenged to consider that the most fruitful and productive of all labors is precisely that which brings our souls closest to God. One tenet of the Wisdom tradition is that we may never fully know God's mind but that we are called to try. We

---

2. We find a classic expression of this in Irenaeus, *Against the Heretics*.
3. On Jesus as embodied Torah, see Robert Jenson, "Toward a Christian Theology of Judaism," in *Jews and Christians: People of God*, ed. Carl Braaten and Robert Jenson (Grand Rapids: Eerdmans, 2003), 1–13.

orientation that enable his listeners to envision what the kingdom of heaven, or the way of God, is like. Jesus' central message, "Repent, for the kingdom of heaven has come near" (Matt. 4:17), is a call to acknowledge God's sovereignty over all creation and to live life accordingly. Each of the lessons in the Sermon on the Mount, whether about anger and reconciliation (5:21–26) or wealth and accumulation (6:19–34), points to life lived in a new key, that is, to life lived according to the kingdom that Jesus announces. The Sermon on the Mount teaches a particular way of seeing, being, and living in the world. Jesus instructs his disciples to "strive first for the kingdom of God and its righteousness" (6:33), because it is the wisdom of the kingdom that provides the very context and ground for how Jesus' followers ought to live. Though people from Capernaum and its environs had flocked to Jesus to witness the healings he would perform, they were without such wisdom (11:20–24). What they needed to grasp was the wisdom that had given rise to Jesus' activity in the first place and that would engender in them right action and the bearing of worthy fruit.

Not only does Jesus' teaching point to the nature of true wisdom; his prayer in verses 25–26 emphasizes that wisdom has been given to a group other than the conventionally wise. Just as he asserted a striking and surprising contrast between the Galilean and Gentile cities identified in verses 20–24, so does Jesus upend expectations here. In language recalling the "little ones" upheld in 10:42 and anticipating the elevation of the "humble" children in 18:1–5 and the "little children" in 19:13–15, Jesus declares that it is the "infants" to whom divine wisdom has been revealed. The point is clear: those who follow Jesus and practice his countercultural vision of the kingdom with humility are blessed with true wisdom. Like the kingdom of heaven itself, those who participate in its reality defy conventional norms and expectations.

Jesus grounds his authority in his identity as God's Son. The term "Father," rendered familiar by its frequent appearance in the Sermon on the Mount (5:48; 6:1, 4, 6, 8, 9, 14, 15, 18 [twice], 26, 32; 7:11, 21), occurs five times in verses 25–27. Thus it lends shape to Matthew's portrayal of both God and Jesus. Reference to Jesus as "Son" appears three times in verse 27. Jesus' identity as the Son of God is central to the entire Gospel narrative. It appears very early in Matthew's Gospel (2:15; 3:17), serves as the theme of Jesus' encounter with the devil in the wilderness (4:3, 5), and relates directly to the Gospel's opening

The stresses on the modern adult are daunting. Everyone is confronted with a variety of trials, challenges, and temptations that far exceed our capacity to deal with them by ourselves. However, we are not meant to live as isolated individuals who are in complete control. The lesson God desires us to understand is the requirement that we surrender our independent "know-it-all-adult" point of view and become vulnerable and dependent on God, much as children are vulnerable and depend on adults. We will find Jesus there, ready and willing to help us each carry our burdens.

In verses 28–30 of our text, Jesus beseeches us, "Come to me, all you that are weary and are carrying heavy burdens, and I will give you rest. Take my yoke upon you, and learn from me; for I am gentle and humble in heart, and you will find rest for your souls. For my yoke is easy, and my burden is light."

At first glance, the call is appealing, for Jesus beseeches those who are worn out from carrying a heavy load of spiritual, physical, and emotional burdens to come and rest. Given the struggles most of us are facing, this is appealing, for when people find themselves weighed down with things that are troubling, they deeply desire relief. It too is only natural.

However, Jesus does not offer to help us in the way most of us want. After all, when we are carrying a heavy weight, our desire may be for Jesus simply to take the weight away; but what we desire and what we need may not be the same thing, and God's concern is for our needs. In this, we are once again shown that God's ways are not our ways. So in counterintuitive fashion, we are not promised that the load will be removed; we are, instead, urged to trust Jesus and place a different weight on our shoulders: his yoke. With faith in a God who knows our needs and helps carry our loads, we end up with a benefit that lightens our heavy loads and refreshes our souls.

We do not see many yokes around these days. Indeed, we may forget that a yoke—a wooden bar or frame that joins two animals together so they can pull a heavy load—is not only something that is meant for two, but something that was used by farmers to train inexperienced animals for their work. Less experienced beasts of burden would be teamed with more experienced ones so that the neophyte could learn how to pull the weight of the plow.

Jesus knows our yoke. Through him, we learn how to do our own work—and of the rest that comes when we work with him. Through faith, we are partnered with Jesus and taught how to balance and maneuver what is at hand, with the help of one

Matthew 11:25–30

Theological Perspective

transforms our deepest desires into passion for God's just and merciful reign in the world. As Wisdom, Jesus provides us with a yoke that is neither an absolutist claim, standing over and against us as an abstract universal, nor a relativist acquiescence to our own or other people's whims and desires. Rather, as Wisdom, Jesus provides us with a yoke that, when we take it upon ourselves, heals our deepest hurts and pains so that our lives can embody in all their concrete circumstances the creative deeds of power identified with God's wise and just reign in the world. In this way, Jesus, as God's Wisdom, brings rest—wholeness and completeness—to our lives.

This text may surprise some readers, especially when they discover that Matthew (along with other biblical writers and those in the early church) had no difficulty identifying Jesus with the personified female figure of Wisdom (e.g., in Prov. 8 or Wis. 7). Indeed, the early church's understanding of Christ's identity as both divine and human drew heavily on NT passages like this, which linked Jesus with the figure of Wisdom. The more profound challenge of this passage has to do with the tangible way in which Jesus is, in fact, God's Wisdom for us, here and now in our lives even today. As we take on Jesus' yoke, we not only become more fully united with Jesus, God's tangible Wisdom in and for our lives; we also enter more fully into the intimacy Jesus had with the one he called Father. In this way, Jesus truly is God's Wisdom for us, whose yoke embodies a new way of being in the world, not as a set of standards we need to live up to (or a new set of ideals), but rather as God's incarnate—if easy and light—presence within our lives.

LOIS MALCOLM

Pastoral Perspective

are created to seek deeper understanding. Jesus was steeped in this tradition and this quest. He reminds us of this need here, lest we try to delude ourselves into thinking we already know what is worth knowing of God.

We are invited into a deep humility here, and Jesus knows now, as he knew then, that such an invitation will not always be eagerly or consistently embraced. Accepting this invitation means we have work to do, even if there are an easy yoke and a light burden awaiting us. It means that we are admitting up front that we are not, truth be told, self-made women or men. It means that if we agree to walk this walk with Jesus, we must recognize that we do not have all the answers, in spite of our countless diplomas.

As we read in Proverbs 1:7, "The fear of the LORD is the beginning of knowledge; fools despise wisdom and instruction." Sadly, it is fear of seeming weak and needy that often keeps us from entering more fully into an open and vulnerable state of formation before God, into the humility noted above. The fear of the Lord is not about cowering in terror. It is about approaching God with fitting reverence and in an attitude of anticipation that we are about to become something better than we were before we entered in, someone more complete than we could ever become on our own.

Can we demonstrate and celebrate wonder, and still claim to be intelligent, growing beings? Indeed, part of the message of Jesus here is that the two are inseparable. A desire for greater knowing goes hand in hand with our recognition that God's world still holds in store for us marvelous new insights and discoveries and myriad encounters with unfolding truth. If being humble is knowing more fully our true selves, then perhaps some of our most precious learning about God will come to light as we look within.

ERICK R. OLSEN

announcement of Jesus' messianic identity ("An account of the genealogy of Jesus the Messiah, the son of David, the son of Abraham," 1:1). Matthew wants his readers to make no mistake: Jesus relates to God as a beloved Son, and God acts as Father to Jesus. What is most compelling about Matthew's use of kinship language here is not its mere occurrence; it is the intimacy that defines Jesus' relationship to God: "and no one knows the Son except the Father, and no one knows the Father except the Son and anyone to whom the Son chooses to reveal him" (v. 27).

His words underscore a theme befitting this Gospel, for Matthew places much emphasis on establishing and nurturing the kind of interpersonal and social relations that express the presence and ruling of God in our midst. Jesus, who in his ministry and person reveals that "God is with us" (1:23), extends to his followers the intimate knowledge of God that he enjoys.

Jesus' intimacy with God and the authority that he claims ("All things have been handed over to me by my Father," v. 27) lead him to offer his concluding invitation: "Come to me, all you that are weary and are carrying heavy burdens, and I will give you rest. . . . For my yoke is easy, and my burden is light" (vv. 28, 30). Ancient Jewish tradition referred to "yoke" as teaching and instruction in wisdom (Sir. 51:26–27). Here again, Jesus' pronouncement thwarts expectations. Participation in the kingdom and the righteousness that "exceeds that of the scribes and the Pharisees" (5:20) is easier to bear than the status quo (cf. 23:4), not more difficult. Wisdom born of enlightenment, renewal, and reorientation lightens, rather than burdens, the soul.

MARY F. FOSKETT

who is more seasoned in the tasks associated with living. At first, the appeal to take on something more (like spending time in prayer or Bible study or other spiritual disciplines) in order to walk closer to Jesus seems impossible—or at least a step in the wrong direction. Jesus promises that by walking closer to him, our encumbrances will be lessened and we will find repose in the midst of what would otherwise be an onerous and lonely journey.

The lesson of the yoke is learning how to get in sync with Jesus, whose presence balances the weight of our pressures. Through loving-kindness and gentleness, carrying the yoke of Jesus, we learn to navigate our challenges and walk in wisdom. The burdens we carry in our lives are meant not to crush us but to make us stronger. The purpose of the struggles in life is always to bring us into a deeper relationship with the One who knows us better than we know ourselves.

When what we are going through seems beyond our ability to carry, that is exactly the time when faith is calling us to surrender our way and trust God's way. Perhaps our burdens seem too much for us because we were never meant to carry them alone. The struggle is meant not to crush us but to build us up and lead us in the paths we might not ordinarily choose on our own. "Trust in the LORD with all your heart, and do not rely on your own insight. In all your ways acknowledge him, and he will make straight your paths" (Prov. 3:5–6). Trust Jesus to help us carry our load and find rest.

SHELLEY D. BEST

Matthew 12:1–8

¹At that time Jesus went through the grainfields on the sabbath; his disciples were hungry, and they began to pluck heads of grain and to eat. ²When the Pharisees saw it, they said to him, "Look, your disciples are doing what is not lawful to do on the sabbath." ³He said to them, "Have you not read what David did when he and his companions were hungry? ⁴He entered the house of God and ate the bread of the Presence, which it was not lawful for him or his companions to eat, but only for the priests. ⁵Or have you not read in the law that on the sabbath the priests in the temple break the sabbath and yet are guiltless? ⁶I tell you, something greater than the temple is here. ⁷But if you had known what this means, 'I desire mercy and not sacrifice,' you would not have condemned the guiltless. ⁸For the Son of Man is lord of the sabbath."

Theological Perspective

Jesus' disciples are hungry on a Sabbath day and begin plucking heads of grain in a field and eating them. Some Pharisees see this and ask Jesus why his disciples are doing what is not lawful to do on the Sabbath. Jesus responds with three biblical allusions. First, he appeals to a story about David, recalling how David and his companions entered the temple one day when they were hungry and ate the consecrated loaves intended for sacrifice that were set out weekly (1 Sam. 21:1–6). Second, he appeals to priestly ritual, pointing out that priests perform their duties of offering sacrifices on the Sabbath, yet they remain guiltless (Num. 28:9–10). Third, he appeals to a quote from the prophet Hosea: "I desire mercy and not sacrifice" (Hos. 6:6).

Why these allusions? The first indicates that human need—in this case, hunger—is greater than sacrifice. The second allusion indicates that sacrifice is more important than Sabbath observance. Finally, the quote from Hosea—"I desire mercy and not sacrifice"—reiterates the point of the first allusion to David and his companions: mercy, which always responds to specific human needs (like hunger), must be greater than the Sabbath. Something is also being said here about Jesus' identity, because the final quote from Hosea is embedded between two statements about Jesus: "something greater than the

Pastoral Perspective

The Pharisees do not have a question for Jesus. They have a statement that we have heard or said too often: "We have never done it that way before"—which is another form of "We have always done it like this." Taken together, these two gripes are probably heard more regularly than any quote from sacred texts within any given faith community, and this says something about our bonds with the Pharisees.

The Pharisees in this story wish only to find fault rather than to achieve understanding. Consequently there is little or no chance for developing any kind of relationship. We can imagine how things might have gone differently, had they opened our story with a question: "Jesus, can you please explain why your disciples feel that they may pluck grain on the Sabbath?" This at least implies that they are willing to give Jesus credit for being able to see what is unfolding right in front of him. It establishes their own willingness actually to hear what he thinks. Further still, it implies that they are willing to entertain even a remote chance that they could learn from him. When we approach another with openness rather than judgment, we demonstrate that we know we are not perfect and that God may teach us and form us through another as we enter into relationship.

Change is unsettling. The rules and norms of our lives help to maintain a sense of stability and safety.

Exegetical Perspective

This scene follows Jesus and his disciples as they continue their ministry and mission throughout the region, proclaiming in word and deed the good news of the kingdom of heaven. Matthew 12:1–8 develops at least two themes found in the previous chapter. It probes further the kind of response that Jesus encounters in Matthew 11:2–24, and it underscores how Jesus' ministry and vision signal both the affirmation and reinterpretation of Torah tradition. That the Torah tradition occupies a significant role in the passage is made evident by the opening verse's succinct juxtaposition of three conditions that set the scene: it is the Sabbath; the disciples are hungry; they pluck heads of grain in the fields through which they are walking, so that they may have something to eat (v. 1).

The Pharisees, with their quickly voiced objection, are exemplars of those who oppose Jesus, but their stance is hardly remarkable. The suggestion that Jesus' disciples are violating Sabbath law resonates with Exodus 34:21: "Six days you shall work, but on the seventh day you shall rest; even in plowing time and in harvest time you shall rest" (cf. Exod. 35:2–3). Clearly, Sabbath observance was practiced by first-century-CE Jews, and Jesus was no exception. Rabbinic and New Testament texts alike provide ample evidence that pious Jews strove to interpret Sabbath teaching with integrity and fidelity.

Homiletical Perspective

When someone acknowledges the inner call to service, God has a seductive way of drawing that person nearer. With pure love and acceptance, the One who knows you better than you know yourself welcomes you and invites you to make a difference in the world exactly as you are. Through this compelling faith, followers come to understand that they have the power to live bigger as they give their lives toward healing the world.

This journey of spiritual formation is daunting. Those who choose to respond to this divine urging miraculously follow God into the great yet generous unknown. Fortunately, the One who calls with loving-kindness also prepares and sustains us and knows exactly the gifts we possess and the difference we can make in the lives of others.

Called into community, the community also affirms this call—albeit in the halting and faulty ways in which communities always operate. Thus the process of being accepted as a spiritual leader by the people of God can be likened to a pledging process. Most religious contexts have a number of authentication tests, written and unwritten. The culture of spiritual formation can appear to be that of scrutiny rather than embrace, all in the name of "educating" the novices and preserving the traditions.

Matthew 12:1–8

Theological Perspective

temple is here" and "the Son of Man is lord of the sabbath" (vv. 6, 8). What is the theological significance of this story and its biblical allusions? This story brings home the point that in Jesus' presence Sabbath law is fulfilled.

First, we must note that this story is not about Jesus abolishing Sabbath law. In the Gospel of Matthew, Jesus always fulfills, but does not abolish the law (5:17–20). Indeed, the law and the prophets, and biblical teachings about wisdom, serve as the interpretive frame Matthew uses to understand the significance of Jesus' life and ministry. Matthew presupposes what the Jewish Scriptures teach: that the Torah (God's law or covenant with Israel) is given in direct response to human need—specifically, the human need to perceive and respond to life in ways that are life giving and not self-destructive or destructive to others. Matthew presupposes that the Torah is God's gift to Israel, a gift that enables them, as God's chosen people, to choose life and not death in all that they do. Thus he presupposes that the Torah's deontological character, its mode as a demand that stands over and against us, can never be severed from its teleological purposes—the way that it wholly completes and fulfills our deepest needs and yearnings. In sum, this story is not about Jesus negating the Sabbath—God's provision of regular periods of rest and renewal—but about how Sabbath rest is truly fulfilled or enacted.

In line with these assumptions about the Torah, Matthew also presupposes in this story—and throughout his Gospel—the great themes of the biblical prophets. The theme in the quote from Hosea— "I desire mercy and not sacrifice" (Hos. 6:6)—is reiterated throughout Matthew's Gospel. Religious observance and practice that is severed from the just and merciful treatment of others (especially those who have the least power) is a blasphemy. In chapter 23, for example, Matthew will denounce—again in the tradition of the prophets—religious leaders whose practice is not in line with their teaching: who put heavy burdens on others without lifting a finger to remove them; who love to be seen performing religious acts in public but neglect the weightier demands of justice, mercy, and faith; who outwardly appear to be beautiful and righteous but inside are full "of the bones of the dead and of all kinds of filth . . . [and] hypocrisy and lawlessness" (23:27–28). For Matthew, the weightier demands of justice and mercy—especially toward those who are most in need (the hungry, the thirsty, the stranger, the naked, the sick, and those imprisoned, etc.)—can never

Pastoral Perspective

When they are threatened, so are we. This happens within local church discussions about inclusive language in the Doxology, praise music versus traditional hymns, even changing curtain colors. It holds true in our homes when a child ages to the point where "Because I told you so" ceases to be viewed as a valid answer to life's timeless question of "Why?" Being in any kind of relationship requires an ability to maintain the delicate balance between safeguarding traditions and accommodating growth and new insights. Both are important, and disregard of either usually results in hurt feelings or worse.

There are too many stories of church people who have turned away from decades or even generations within a particular fellowship because of a perceived slight. For faith communities willing to wrestle with some thorny questions, there is opportunity here for fruitful learning around the importance of covenant. Can we rise above petty squabbles, in light of our identity as interdependent members of Christ's body? On a wider scale still, this balancing work— and let us be clear that a balancing "act" will not suffice here, for work is mandated—presents people of faith with an opportunity to learn and understand one another in the context of ecumenical and inter-faith relationships.

Returning to our passage, we find Jesus working against the temptation to uphold the law at all costs. Where relationship with God is undermined due to legalism or zeal for adherence to the smallest details of the legal code, Jesus reminds us that the ultimate purpose of the law is to safeguard access for all to God's love. The law is not meant to be swept aside or supplanted but, rather, reminds us of our covenants with each other and with God. He makes this point in verse 3 by invoking the blessed memory of David and the story from 1 Samuel 21:1–6, of how the king worked around the law in order to secure food from the priest Ahimelech. Reaching further back still, he reminds them of the offering rules given directly to Moses, codes that allowed the priests to make sacrificial offerings on the Sabbath.

If we are not flexible in this life, parts of us will break as we encounter and endure the countless changes that will come our way. Life within faith communities requires suppleness and an ability to accommodate varying and often passionate perspectives. Those who cling with tenacity to deep tradition might lessen their grip in order to be led into new ways of being faithful, just as outspoken advocates for change might lower their voices and listen more for the wisdom of ancient customs.

Exegetical Perspective

As with all codified legislation, interpreters of the tradition had to discuss and sometimes debate the finer points of the law. They would ask, What constitutes work, precisely? Does assisting a sick or injured animal or person on the Sabbath count as the kind of activity that violates Sabbath observance? In the case of the situation that Matthew describes here, plucking grain certainly resembles the work of harvesting. Is it lawful or unlawful on the Sabbath? Jesus himself declared that he had, in fact, not come "to abolish the law or the prophets; I have come not to abolish but to fulfill. For truly I tell you, until heaven and earth pass away, not one letter, not one stroke of a letter, will pass from the law until all is accomplished" (5:17–18). He had also added, rather emphatically, "Whoever breaks one of the least of these commandments, and teaches others to do the same, will be called least in the kingdom of heaven" (5:19). Therefore both the Pharisees' objection and Jesus' decision to engage them should strike readers as unremarkable when read in light of ancient Jewish practice and concern.

Jesus' response, however, is unanticipated, for the precedent he cites does not actually concern Sabbath law at all. Rather than addressing the topic the Pharisees have introduced, Jesus changes the subject to focus instead on the relative value of cultic observance. The story of David feeding his men the ritual bread used only by the priests in temple (1 Sam. 21:1–6) exemplifies the hospitality and compassion shown by the priest Ahimelech toward the men and his willingness to depart from ritual practice in order to do so. The lesson Jesus is offering is that of placing compassion above individual sacred practices and ordinances. Thus he quotes Hosea 6:6, "I desire mercy and not sacrifice," for the second time in Matthew's Gospel. The first instance occurred after the Pharisees questioned him about his eating "with tax collectors and sinners" (9:11–13). What God seeks and values is acts of mercy and compassion.

Before the scene concludes, Jesus goes a step further. He asserts his authority to counter the Pharisees' interpretation of Sabbath observance. When he cites the Torah legislation that allows priests to perform ritual practices on the Sabbath (Lev. 24:8; Num. 28:9–10), he draws a parallel between their sacred authority and his own. By adding, "I tell you, something greater than the temple is here," Jesus expresses a sense of authority that surpasses even his oft-repeated "But I say to you" in the Sermon on the Mount (5:22, 28, 32, 34, 39, 44). The capstone assertion, "For the Son of Man is lord of the sabbath"

Homiletical Perspective

In our text, Jesus is traveling with his disciples on the Sabbath. It is important to remember that the followers of Christ are not men who come from affluent families that can provide financial support for their sons' rabbinic education. Jesus offers the opportunity to men of modest means who, by their station in life, can relate to service as the poor. When the Twelve decide to follow the Lord, they do so—mostly—with reverence and humility. Given where they each come from, the opportunity to seek a vocation of "life transformation" is far beyond anything they could have hoped for. Perhaps this is why they embrace Jesus' unorthodox curriculum with passion. Jesus offers everyday men from the "wrong" social position the chance to become something more to themselves, their families, and the community.

Ministry training for the disciples is on-the-job training. Their lessons in healing come from hands-on experiences. The texts they would write are the eyewitness epistles of real-life miracles. Their education happens on roadsides and among wheat harvests; it was, quite literally, a field education! The gifts of social acceptance and self-esteem came from the community formed around Jesus.

The Pharisees in this passage are members of the religious elite, empowered by their recognized positions. When the Pharisees see whom Jesus has called—an unofficial ragtag group of bootleg scholars—they take it upon themselves to correct Jesus and the disciples; to put them in their places. The Pharisees may believe that Jesus and his students are not properly following the rules of the unordained. They most likely believe that Jesus' crew of everyday people in service is making a mockery of their sacred profession by their apparent ignorance of what they should do or not do on the Sabbath. As people with the authority to accept and reject those who claim to be faithful, they seize the opportunity to call attention to what is wrong with Jesus and the disciples.

To their surprise, Jesus retorts with complete confidence, reminding them of David and his companions eating the actual "bread of the Presence" when they were hungry. Further, he reminds them that priests work on the Sabbath. The priests seemingly do what is unlawful but are not guilty of breaking the law. Jesus the rabbi gives the Pharisees the opportunity to delve into deeper self-examination rather than condemnation.

The disciples observe the teachable moment between the Pharisees and Jesus as a messianic paradigm shift when they hear Jesus say, "I tell you,

Matthew 12:1–8

Theological Perspective

be severed from religious observance or practice (25:31–46).

Nonetheless, Matthew appeals to the law and the prophets in his Gospel as a whole—and alludes to David, priestly activity, and the prophet Hosea in this passage—in order to make a christological point about who Jesus is and what happens when Jesus is present in the midst of our lives. As noted, the story concludes with the statements "something here is greater than the sabbath" and "the Son of Man is lord of the sabbath" (vv. 6, 8). It is preceded by a passage linking Jesus with the biblical figure of Wisdom, who calls out: "My yoke is easy, and my burden is light" (v. 30), and it is followed by another story about the Sabbath—about how Jesus heals a man with a withered hand on the Sabbath (12:9–14). What follows that story is a general description of Jesus' healing ministry and a quotation about the "Servant" in Isaiah. God will pour out God's Spirit on him so that he can proclaim justice and hope to the Gentiles—not breaking "a bruised reed" or quenching "a smoldering wick" until he "brings justice to victory" (12:15–21; cf. Isa. 42:1–4).

What point is Matthew making here about Jesus? The "something greater than the temple" that is "here" in their midst is Jesus, the Wisdom of God, who embodies the Torah, God's covenant with God's people. Jesus embodies the Torah by enacting the reign of God among all those he comes into contact with—curing the sick, enabling the blind to see and the deaf to hear, bringing good news to the poor, and so on. It is in this way that Jesus (as "the Son of Man") is the "lord of the sabbath." Why? Because in his presence—and in all that he does for us—everything that God requires and promises in the Torah is fulfilled or realized within and among us. Not only are God's wise and just intentions for our lives wholly realized in and through Jesus' presence, but our deepest yearnings and needs are also satisfied. Thus it is "here"—in and though Jesus, God's embodied Wisdom for us—that, we "find rest" (11:29).

LOIS MALCOLM

Pastoral Perspective

This is why Jesus brings David and Moses into the picture: tradition is our bedrock as we seek to keep building the kingdom in new ways. The rituals that we have embraced for decades or millennia bring us some constancy and contact with the timeless nature of God. Jesus challenges us in verse 6 with his reminder that there is indeed something greater here than our local church. Whether we find ourselves closest to God through high technology or through quiet labyrinth walks, nothing should supplant our Lord as the center of our worship. Jesus wants to remind us in these verses that there is nothing either old or new that may be so important as to harm our relationships with each other or with God.

As an exclamation point in verse 7, Jesus cites Hosea 6:6 and its call for steadfast love rather than sacrifice. Do our congregations enforce norms around the "how" of worship that are so alien or exclusive that some of our fellow worshipers fail to feel the love of the faithful, let alone of God? Are we so caught up in programs and meetings that Sunday morning feels more like a workout than worship, again resulting in guests and visitors feeling left out? Maybe Jesus is reminding us that we need to take a careful look at what is most important in the life of our local church. Whether we have the latest hymnal in use each week or we still proudly do it the way we always have, do our faith practices proclaim with joy that Jesus is, as he says in our last verse, "lord of the sabbath"?

ERICK R. OLSEN

(12:8), removes any ambiguity about Jesus' perspective. As God's Messiah, Jesus has the full authority to interpret and teach the true meaning of Torah. Not only does his teaching surpass that of even Moses; Jesus stands as lord over the Sabbath. It is Jesus alone, then, who is able to interpret the law both in part and in whole. He teaches the meaning of specific legislation, as he did in Matthew 5–7, but he also reveals the very purpose of the law itself.

Jesus' response to the Pharisees underscores again the degree to which Jesus' overarching vision of the kingdom shapes what he does and what he teaches. Jesus continually seeks to reorient the characters in the Gospel narrative, as well as the readers and hearers of the Gospel, to a way of being that is both old and new. It is old because it is grounded in the Torah that Jesus upholds and by which he lives. It is new because it is reinterpreted by Jesus in ways that appear to run counter to conventional wisdom and teaching. The summary expression of Jesus' perspective on the law occurs later in the Gospel when a Pharisee asks him to identify the greatest commandment. Jesus replies, "'You shall love the Lord your God with all your heart, and with all your soul, and with all your mind.' This is the greatest and first commandment. And a second is like it: 'You shall love your neighbor as yourself.' On these two commandments hang all the law and the prophets" (22:34–40).

As the Son of God, Jesus claims the authority to interpret the meaning of particular laws. As Immanuel ("God is with us"), Jesus teaches and embodies in his person the very meaning of the law as a whole, which is to engender love of God and neighbor. In this sense Jesus' call to repentance and participation in the kingdom of heaven is a call to renewal and a reminder of what had been intended for God's people all along.

MARY F. FOSKETT

something greater than the temple is here" (v. 6). The temple is created by human hands, but the disciples are men created by the hands of God. The followers of modest means who have given up everything to serve God and make the world a better place are much more significant than the buildings or a list of rules and regulations. Jesus continues by saying, "But if you had known what this means, 'I desire mercy and not sacrifice,' you would not have condemned the guiltless. For the Son of Man is lord of the sabbath" (vv. 7–8).

Jesus urges the Pharisees to let go of a way of rigidly engaging religious rules and regulations without attending to the One who has given those rules and calls them to have compassion for those of low estate—those who serve without the privileges of affluence. The Pharisees in most cases come from upper-class families and have always known lives of comfort and contentment. It is because of their station in life they have the time, health, and security to critique those they see as so clearly "below them." Jesus urges them to release themselves from that way of thinking in order to have mercy on those who have never known privilege. Jesus wants them to realize that a relationship and fellowship with "Immanuel," God who is with us, far outweighs a rigid adherence to the very rules that ought to shape a covenant relationship.

Socrates taught that the unexamined life is not worth living. As people of faith we might reframe the phrase: "The unexamined religious life is not worth living." With almost two thousand years of church history behind us, we have the benefit of looking back to see policies, procedures, and activities that have harmed some of God's people and the reputation of the church. Not everything done in the name of religion had the blessing of God. Human attachments to power, control, and exclusion continue to exist in this generation. Even with historic examples of atrocities against individuals because of race, ethnicity, and gender, people of faith continue to fall into similar traps. With the benefit of hindsight, we must pray to make the church a place with a heart for service that welcomes all. If God calls and draws individuals to join in the cocreation of our world, let us welcome them as blessings of a new Sabbath.

SHELLEY D. BEST

Matthew 12:9–14

⁹He left that place and entered their synagogue; ¹⁰a man was there with a withered hand, and they asked him, "Is it lawful to cure on the sabbath?" so that they might accuse him. ¹¹He said to them, "Suppose one of you has only one sheep and it falls into a pit on the sabbath; will you not lay hold of it and lift it out? ¹²How much more valuable is a human being than a sheep! So it is lawful to do good on the sabbath." ¹³Then he said to the man, "Stretch out your hand." He stretched it out, and it was restored, as sound as the other. ¹⁴But the Pharisees went out and conspired against him, how to destroy him.

Theological Perspective

Having finished yet another debate with the Pharisees—this one on grain eating and Sabbath keeping—Jesus goes on from there, and so does his running conflict with the religious leaders. He walks right into their synagogue, the place of their authority, and almost dares them to confront him with the question: "Is it lawful to heal on the Sabbath?"

Is it perhaps the other way around? Are they setting a trap for Jesus? Perhaps they know he is coming to the synagogue, so they place the one who needs healing directly in his path, just to put him in a bind. Are they daring Jesus to defy them? We do not know. Neither do we know if those who ask Jesus the question had passed by the one with the deformed hand before, on Sabbaths and ordinary days alike, and done nothing to heal him. All we know is that this one who needs healing seems like little more than a prop in an ethical debate.

Once the action starts, Jesus seems to be completely unwilling to compromise. The situation facing him is a classic dilemma. He can heal someone who needs his help. However, healing, unless a person's life is in danger, is a kind of work, and work is not permitted on the Sabbath. He can do something good, but only by breaking the rules. At least on the face of it, this is a standard undergraduate ethics debate over ends versus means.

Pastoral Perspective

A congregation in Minnesota once drastically changed their Sabbath practice when, on consecutive Sundays, they intentionally canceled their worship services. Both Sundays, church members went out in groups with the desire to better understand their community. Members spoke to business owners and residents. They lent a hand to people working in their yards. They struck up conversations with dog walkers and people waiting at the bus stop. The point, the church leaders explained, was less to advertise their congregation than to become better acquainted with their neighbors.

The *New York Times* has published an occasional series, "Sunday Routine," describing weekend rituals. The stories, reflecting New York's diversity, are quite varied. One well-known New Yorker said that he enjoyed taking a long walk and buying a bag of mini-bagels. An artist for Marvel Comics reported receiving fewer work e-mails on Sundays and spending the uninterrupted time drawing comic book covers. The series also included a hard rocker who sleeps in, several people who have brunch out, and a comedian who spends his day off playing video games and watching TV. Churchgoers may find it easy to scoff at these stories of Sabbath days bereft of worship attendance, but the "Sunday Routine" series sounds a helpful theme for Christians, as it encourages reflection

Exegetical Perspective

This Sabbath healing and the accompanying controversy dialogue have parallels in the other Synoptic Gospels, and it clearly is related to the Sabbath controversy that immediately precedes it. Looking at this pericope on its own, however, we discover a neatly balanced chiastic structure. This story is not, at its heart, a miracle story, but a controversy story. The healing is occasion for the dialogue, and the focus is on the surpassing nature of Jesus' statement.

Here is the chiastic structure:

A: he entered their synagogue
    B: man with a withered hand
        C: "Is it lawful to cure on the sabbath?"
            D: Jesus' pronouncement: "how much
                more . . . "
        C': "It is lawful to do good on the sabbath."
    B': withered hand is restored
A': they (the Pharisees) went out

The story begins when Jesus enters "their" synagogue, although there is no further indication that this synagogue is a particularly Pharisaic one; it is apparently simply a Jewish synagogue. Historically the reference to "their" synagogue likely signals distance between Matthew's community and the synagogue(s) from which they are estranged. In the narrative, Jesus' entering "their" synagogue signals

Homiletical Perspective

Whenever preaching texts include an account of one of Jesus' miracles, it is almost inevitable that at least one congregant will comment afterward about the whole notion of Jesus' miracles. For some, the main struggle of miracle stories is their apparent defiance of science or logic. For others, it is that all the miracle stories in the Gospels seem to be just more of the same—making no differentiation between the healings of the one born blind, the woman who touched the cloak of Jesus, the paralytic lowered from the roof, and, here, the man with the withered hand who was healed by Jesus on the Sabbath. Each of these miracles of Jesus offer new ways to understand the dynamics of faith in a world like ours. Here, Jesus' command to the man, "Stretch out your hand," offers such an opportunity.

In a world that shrinks each day through technological contact, we can be hemmed in by a surprisingly rigid imagination about life in God's world. For Jesus, that rigidity included the expectation of whom and what Sabbath was for, and what could and could not be undertaken. In our day, this rigidity includes a deep skepticism about how God's love really can work in a world of strife as well as an agnosticism toward the vital hope of God's future. In this context, "Stretch out your hand" is not just a procedural instruction. It is a deep, bold statement of faith that

Matthew 12:9–14

Theological Perspective

As an ethics case, however, this is not difficult. There is an easy way out here, a simple solution for Jesus to keep everybody happy, if that is what he wants to do. Most of us probably would just say to the one waiting for healing, "Wait a little longer, my friend. The sun will go down in a few hours, and the Sabbath will end. You can have your healing, the authorities can have their rules, and I can please everyone."

Jesus says no such thing. He challenges them. Is it right to suspend the rules for a greater good? Many of his hearers would agree that sheep may be rescued on the Sabbath. If so, then surely a human being may be healed. So a good end justifies questionable means? Well, not exactly. Here it seems to justify an exception to the rules or at least a suspension of the calendar.

Is that really the point here? Deep down, is this just another story about competing ethical theories? Does Jesus argue with them in order to persuade them to agree with his interpretation of the law, or to expose their true motivations? Of course, the story does seem to support the view that sometimes rules have to be tempered by compassion and calendars reordered by crises. Yes, the story warns us not to let rules become excuses for doing nothing to help. Is the point of the story that Jesus is some sort of ethical consequentialist and his opponents just rule-bound, incorrigible deontologists?

If that is the conflict, does it really make sense that they would "take counsel against him, how to destroy him"? Debates about ethical theories usually do not arouse such passions. It would be closer to the truth to say that the central conflict is theological much more than ethical. The confrontation is between two views of God. More precisely, it is a confrontation between the inbreaking action of the living God and the guardians of the commands spoken earlier by this same God.

In a way, the story really is all about timing, not in the sense of a day too holy for healing, but in the more profound sense of failing to recognize the new when it is in front of you breaking up the old. It is not that the religious authorities are wrong about obedience to God. They just do not know God's timing. They think it is the day to rest, not the day to welcome the future. For them it is enough to rest in what God has done. In fact, they see rest on the Sabbath as mandatory, because they cannot imagine God doing something new through Jesus. We know what our God has done, they say to themselves, and

Pastoral Perspective

on one's own Sunday routines.[1] This passage from Matthew serves as a helpful teaching aid for all of us making a similar self-assessment.

Many Sabbaths ago, Jesus met one of his neighbors in a synagogue. The Pharisees, who had already challenged Jesus' behavior on the Sabbath (vv. 1–8), quickly asked him, "Is it lawful to cure on the sabbath?" (v. 10). Jesus' answer, as was his practice, included both telling and showing.

In the passage Jesus teaches, questions the status quo, and heals a man with an injured hand. Answering the Pharisees' dangerous question about curing on the Sabbath, Jesus concludes, "It is lawful to do good on the sabbath" (v. 12). Jesus' action supports his teaching, and the man's hand is healed. Healing is permissible because it is good.

The Pharisees spend this particular Sabbath day attempting to trap Jesus, "so that they might accuse him" (v. 10). While Jesus' actions heal and are good, Matthew describes the Pharisees as leaving the scene only to continue conspiring against Jesus, plotting "how to destroy him" (v. 14). Matthew leaves no question as to whose Sunday routine is preferable. Ironically, in the Pharisees' honest attempts to uphold the Sabbath, they become bitter and angry as Jesus does good.

Though the story appears in three Gospels (also in Mark 3:1–6; Luke 6:6–11), Matthew is the only Gospel in which the Pharisees begin the exchange with a question to Jesus about lawful Sabbath keeping. Perhaps we who study this story could ask ourselves questions like:

Do we spend our Sabbath days doing good or plotting against others?
Are the Sunday rituals we enjoy about loving God and neighbor, or do we simply stick to our Sabbath traditions because they are traditions?
Are Sundays in our congregations (and homes) marked by doing good, healing, and showing that every human being is valuable in God's sight?

Today, it is difficult for churchgoers to consider Sundays without bemoaning the multitude of activities competing with church obligations. Gone are the days when stores were closed or youth sporting events finished. Indeed, no generation is immune. Grandparents attend their grandchildren's sports tournaments or shuttle them to practices. Parents check their smartphones on sidelines, or stay home from church to catch up on work with TV Sunday talk shows blaring in the background. Youth,

1. *New York Times* Topics: Sunday Routine: http://topics.nytimes.com/top/features/timestopics/series/sunday_routine/index.html; accessed May 18, 2012.

that Jesus is not on his home turf. Jesus and the disciples are the visitors; the synagogue is the opponents' stadium. A victory here would be an advantage for Jesus and an embarrassment for the home team.

The text is ungrammatically blunt: "Look! A man with a withered hand" (my trans.). He appears as if from nowhere for the sole purpose of igniting Sabbath controversy. The man's hand is stiff, shriveled, withered. It is useless, so it is unlikely the man would have been a successful manual laborer, the occupation of most of Jesus' audience. An otherwise capable man may well have been reduced to beggary by such a condition.

The Pharisees ask, "Is it permitted to cure on the Sabbath?" (v. 10). For most Pharisees this question would be the opening gambit in a protracted debate. The saving of human life, Pharisees apparently agreed, overrode Sabbath regulations. Even if it was not clear whether a person was in mortal danger, rabbinic tradition indicates that Sabbath laws could be suspended in order to protect life (e.g., by dropping medicine into the mouth of a man in pain[1]). However, how should Sabbath laws be weighed against less urgent medical conditions? The question might have made for lively Pharisaic debate.

Jesus, though, will have none of these deliberations. In the statement that forms the center of this story, Jesus shifts to another area of Sabbath law, but also shifts the question away from theoretical debate: "Which *of you*, having one sheep, if it falls into a pit on the Sabbath, will not grasp it and lift it out?" (my trans. and emphasis). His question is provocatively phrased, deliberately avoiding the compromise position of providing padding or a ramp so that the trapped animal could escape on its own.[2] A man with only one sheep would be unlikely to resort to such time-consuming measures, and a poor peasant might not have bulky material to spare, or a board to make a ramp. Such a person would not hesitate to rescue such an important asset, Sabbath or no Sabbath.

Jesus' words have other resonances as well. Describing a man who has only one sheep could hardly fail to bring to mind Nathan's parable in 2 Samuel 12:1–4, a story that has nothing to do with ritual observance but everything to do with the callous regard of the well off for those whose existence is precarious, and a story that brings home the ethical responsibility of compassion. Nathan's parable is also a story told in a context of entrapment:

confronted the powers that be and their withered imaginations. Opportunities for people of faith to stretch likewise present themselves every day.

A preacher might want to explore with a congregation how we limit ourselves in the face of God's bold promises. While the opportunities to stretch present themselves to people of faith, there are plenty of voices that seek to diminish or hold back that opportunity. What are those experiences in our everyday lives in light of this text? Beyond that, there are many in our pews (and in our pulpits) who have had quite enough stretching in their lives, thank you very much. How can the invitation to stretch still be seen as opportunity in the wake of painful experience?

In his book *In the Neighborhood: The Search for Community on an American Street, One Sleepover at a Time,* Peter Lovenheim relates how he experienced stretching, even as he was reeling from a horrific tragedy of domestic violence and the murder of two small children and their mother in his neighborhood. Struck by the isolation of neighbor from neighbor, he asked his neighbors to do something totally unnatural in the suburban world: he asked each of them if he could spend the night at their house. The book offers a multifaced examination of what happens when the rigid, staid rules of suburbia are opened by one person having one sleepover after another with his neighbors.

Inside the tidy houses fronted by neat, well-kept lawns, there are marriages coming apart, terminal illnesses being wrestled with in quiet suffering, and a subtle desperation in many of those who think they are just "living by the rules" that were passed down to them. The neighborhood's rules of how you lived and worked and related constituted "business as usual," until Lovenheim started stretching the norms of their rigid, constrained lives beyond usual convention. These sleepovers became acts that broke loose new possibilities for relationship and community.[1]

While not all preachers will have that dramatic an example of suffocating societal expectations so desperately in need of stretching, pastoral work does present a multitude of opportunities to see how God works in defying convention, breaking down walls of fear and apprehension, and even stretching through abject pain to a new reality.

In the fields where the disciples are challenged about Sabbath, Jesus engages the powers of the day

---

1. Mishnah *Yoma* 8.6; an online translation is available at emishnah.com.
2. Babylonian Talmud; translation is available online at halakah.com.

1. Lillian Daniel, "Suburban Search for Meaning," *Christian Century*, August 9, 2011, 26–27, citing Peter Lovenheim, *In the Neighborhood: The Search for Community on an American Street, One Sleepover at a Time* (New York: Perigee Books, 2010).

Matthew 12:9–14

Theological Perspective

our job is to protect God's legacy, to safeguard the memory and enforce the rules.

Their timing is off, way off. They condemn healing on the wrong day. Why? Because they are looking the wrong way. They reject what God is doing in the name of what God has done. If we take this story at face value, we can only conclude that the religious authorities are so determined to protect the God who has come to them that they take counsel together on how to destroy the God who is coming. In the name of God, they would destroy God's own incarnate presence. They are so right about their theology that they are completely wrong about God.

Is it too much to wonder whether it is the religious leaders who most need healing? Their theology is what needs to be restored and made whole. It is almost as if Jesus wants to say to them: "Stretch out your theology."

Here we see the profound irony that lies at the core of this simple story. Where Jesus acts to restore the withered hand, the religious leaders act to destroy Jesus. In its simple narrative structure, the text captures the gracious asymmetry of restoring and destroying, offering and refusing, stretching out and circling up. By these contrasts, the text reveals grace as disruptive, healing and yet provoking, wanted and yet resisted. The Gospel story includes it all, the restoring and the resisting.

When we see ourselves in the full mirror of this text, we wonder what it is about Jesus that evokes our deepest longings and provokes our most frightening hatred. More to the point, what is it in us that desperately needs salvation and even more desperately wants to destroy it? We see this in ourselves through the grace of our savior Jesus Christ, who offers us healing and whose gift in us is already achieved in part when we see that we do not want it.

RONALD COLE-TURNER

Pastoral Perspective

in addition to sports and other extracurriculars, squeeze in one last play date before tackling homework due Monday. Professional sports demand our Sunday attention, luring many to the couch for rituals of channel surfing and beer drinking. The busyness seems a far cry from the commandment to honor the Sabbath and keep it holy.

Before congregational leaders rail against the degradation of the Sabbath, we should consider our own Sunday schedules. Several pastors I know have assessed their own Sunday agendas and begun to question their congregation's Sabbath practices. With church school, church potlucks, children's choir practice, council meetings, youth group, hospital visits—not to mention worship—some congregations have made Sundays as overscheduled as the rest of the week.

With Jesus' teaching in mind, consider two questions. First, are our church's tasks of Sabbath keeping doing good? Jesus challenged the notion of Sabbath as upholding the status quo. For some people—perhaps pastors—this will mean spending less time telling congregations to be in church on Sunday and more time asking them how their Sabbath practices honor God and help others. Approaching the question of church attendance through a lens of honoring God and serving others invites believers to make their own decisions about whom to serve and how to serve. The leisure activities many enjoy on the Sabbath take on a different hue alongside the obligation to use the day to do good. Ultimately, followers of the one who healed on the Sabbath should make certain their Sundays promote health and wellness not just for themselves but for all.

Second, if families do insist on partaking of the smorgasbord of Sunday options available, should church leaders consider new Sabbath practices? If a family insists on being away for a sports tournament one weekend, the church could provide a rubric for a simple family prayer service. Following Jesus' example, we should not become so cemented in a particular way of Sunday worship that we lose focus on the broader task of serving God in all that we do.

Jesus' interpretation of Sabbath laws did not throw out Sabbath keeping entirely; rather, it expanded a narrow interpretation of ancient Sabbath laws. By healing the man with the withered hand, Jesus showed what he meant by his words. If we are to carry on Jesus' message, congregations and individuals must both teach and show how to follow the lord of the Sabbath.

ADAM J. COPELAND

Exegetical Perspective

Nathan's purpose is to convict David of his sin in taking Bathsheba. In the present situation it is the Pharisees who are hoping to entrap Jesus; his reference to Nathan's parable subtly communicates his perception of the Pharisees' intent and his plan to turn their scheme against them.

Jesus' *qal wahomer* ("light and heavy") reasoning is likewise a classic tactic of Pharisaic (and later rabbinic) argument: if the lesser ("light") case is true, how much truer is the greater ("heavy") case? The comparison is focused on the relative value of a sheep and a person. Jesus elides differences between the cases of the only sheep and the handicapped man, making moot the matter of urgency, which would have fueled the debate about the relative weight of Sabbath observance and compassionate practice.

Having established its central point, the story now progresses back through its chiasm. Jesus transforms the Pharisees' original debate-opening gambit into an ethical statement: "It is lawful to *do good* on the sabbath" (v. 12). The point, in Matthew's view, is not debatable. The Pharisees are given no chance to respond. Jesus has the last word.

Jesus' healing miracle is narrated briefly. Jesus commands, the man responds, and he is healed. The only elaboration is the emphasis that the man's once-useless hand is now "as sound as the other." Jesus' act is fully sufficient.

"The Pharisees went out . . ." The competition has become a rout. Not only is the home team defeated; they flee the arena. "Their" synagogue is now occupied by Jesus, a newly healed man, and a transformed understanding of the duty of compassion and "doing good."

Two elements of this story do not conform to the tidy chiastic structure. Rhetorically, they jar us twice: once through their peculiar placement in the pericope and once through their disturbing content. These are the two statements (vv. 10b and 14b) that reveal the dangerous and ultimately murderous nature of the Pharisees' plot against Jesus. As has often been noted, the absolute antagonism of the Pharisees, as a group, to everything that Jesus did and stood for is a function of Matthew's narrative plot (and perhaps of the growing tension between the Matthean church and the developing rabbinic tradition), rather than a reflection of historical reality. As plot development, however, these comments signal a turning point, a point of no return for Jesus' ministry and the opposition to it. These somber comments set up the summarizing pericope that follows.

SANDRA HACK POLASKI

Homiletical Perspective

by stretching their understanding of godly practice and priority. Then, in the synagogue, when met with human need, Jesus continues the stretching. "It is lawful to do good on the sabbath" (v. 12) is a stretch to common practice. As the world conspires to shrink and make rigid, Jesus acts in a way to stretch and open up the possibilities of God's hopeful future. Christian discipleship calls followers of Jesus not only to understand the law, but to stretch our full understanding of God's law to radically new acts of obedience. Jesus lived in a way that stretched previously settled customs and controlled imagination.

"Stretch out your hand," Jesus said to the man with the withered hand. "He stretched it out, and it was restored" (v. 13). Why not just heal him? Why make the man go through the painful process of stretching out a withered hand—a hand rigid and shrunken from years of lack of use—rather than simply easing the pain and restoring the hand directly? There is something in the stretching that Jesus deemed important in relation to God's healing and wholeness. There is no time, no circumstance, no condition, no spiritual outlook that can be whole without stretching. Jesus' command to the man is an invitation to life and to faith.

Finally, we are told that in this act, the powers that be "went out and conspired against him, how to destroy him" (v. 14). Stretching may be healthy, it may lead to wholeness, it may be Jesus' way and God's intention. Nevertheless, the world will summon its power to resist it. A world of controlled imagination and rigid expectations will work against a world where stretching is God's way to a whole, faithful life. The way to God's whole, faithful life is led by the one who was stretched out on a cross and whose love refuses to be contained in the diminished expectations of business as usual.

MARK RAMSEY

Matthew 12:15–21

¹⁵When Jesus became aware of this, he departed. Many crowds followed him, and he cured all of them, ¹⁶and he ordered them not to make him known. ¹⁷This was to fulfill what had been spoken through the prophet Isaiah:
18 "Here is my servant, whom I have chosen,
my beloved, with whom my soul is well pleased.
I will put my Spirit upon him,
and he will proclaim justice to the Gentiles.
19 He will not wrangle or cry aloud,
nor will anyone hear his voice in the streets.
20 He will not break a bruised reed
or quench a smoldering wick
until he brings justice to victory.
21 And in his name the Gentiles will hope."

Theological Perspective

This text begins with a brief narrative that makes five statements: Jesus knows the plot against him. He gets away. Many follow. He heals all of them. He orders them not to make him known. Then follows a long quote from Isaiah 42:1–4, attached without much connection to the action that precedes it.

Begin with the five statements. What do they tell us about Jesus, and how do they challenge some of our ideas about Christ—in other words, our Christology? What do they suggest about us?

That Jesus is aware of the plot is a bit of an understatement. He seems to have provoked it deliberately, or at least not taken a path of compromise to avoid it. His action prompts the religious leaders to want to destroy him.

We do not quite want to say that Jesus causes his critics to reject him. It is their free choice, or at least that is what we feel most comfortable saying. They alone are responsible for their hate and their plots. We know it really is not that simple. Jesus does not only beckon. In this text at least, Jesus is a complicated figure, complex in ways that are not fully captured in our theories about him. Here Christ is not just the accommodating friend who invites everyone to come. He attracts and repels, draws near and withdraws, invites and offends. We can hope we are the ones invited. In the larger story of Matthew 12, Jesus confronts and

Pastoral Perspective

Good pastors know paradox. Consider the practical paradox associated with leading a church: pastors who work fewer hours but empower other people get more accomplished. Another: once attendance at a worship service nears the capacity of the room, prospective members who visit are less likely to join the church, since they can see plenty of people are already involved. Finally, Jesus spoke about the paradoxical nature of the kingdom of heaven: "The last will be first, and the first will be last" (Matt. 20:16). Paradox.

Pastors on the lookout for paradox will find this passage from Matthew's Gospel full of beautiful—and sometimes maddening—paradoxes of faith. Though paradox, by its nature, defies easy categorization, the passage addresses at least the paradoxes of power, popularity, and the cross.

The Paradox of Power. When I was in seminary, one of my favorite professors was known for seldom answering questions directly. Students would ask fairly straightforward questions, and this professor's answers would immediately strike us as either rambling or missing the point entirely. Later and upon further reflection, I would recall a morsel of this professor's answer and realize the wisdom of the response. Rather than avoiding answering our

Exegetical Perspective

Hard on the heels of the announcement of the Pharisees' murderous plot, Matthew returns to a formula quotation, the third since the infancy narrative and the longest in the entire Gospel.[1] These statements usually follow specific details about Jesus' life and demonstrate how otherwise trivial elements corroborate messianic prophecies in Scripture (e.g., to explain why Joseph and Mary settle in Nazareth [2:23] or why Jesus chooses Capernaum as his adult home [4:13–16]). The presence of these quotations in Matthew's Gospel may signal that there circulated among early Christians a collection of prophecies that they understood as having been fulfilled in Jesus. In this instance, however, the quotation is much more expansive than the single detail to which it is tied in context, and it provides an overview of Jesus' ministry.

The setting Matthew gives the saying is fairly general, but somewhat curious. That Jesus leaves the scene of danger is not surprising, particularly since he has already instructed his disciples to flee when persecuted (10:23). Nor is the comment that "many crowds followed him." The statement that he healed "all of them," though, may give the reader pause.

Homiletical Perspective

Expectations. In Matthew's Gospel, Jesus is portrayed as the "new Moses," the offspring of King David, the heir of God's promise to Abraham, and the Messiah. Now, in the middle section of the Gospel of Matthew, there is a tension between the expectations of Jesus' identity when placed alongside Jesus' instruction in this text "not to make him known" (v. 16). While the reasons for Jesus' order of secrecy are well debated in commentaries, a preacher facing this text may want to consider a focus on the expectations we put on God, on Jesus' work, and on ourselves as followers of Jesus.

In W. H. Auden's "For the Time Being: A Christmas Oratorio," Herod the king, symbolizing the practical, reasonable nature of many of us in our time, begins to argue for a less majestic, less powerful, and more ordinary figure. Auden has Herod begging Jesus to "become our uncle . . . escort Madam to the Opera, help . . . with homework." Later, in exasperation Herod explains:

> The God I want and intend to get
> must be someone I can recognize immediately
> without having to wait and see
> what this God says or does.[1]

---

1. Fulfillment quotations in Matthew appear in 1:22–23; 2:15, 17–18, 23; 4:14–16; 8:17; 12:17–21; 13:14–15, 35; 21:4–5; and 27:9–10.

1. W. H. Auden, *Collected Poems* (New York: Vintage International, 1991), 392–93.

Matthew 12:15–21

Theological Perspective

provokes and condemns. In any case, the Christ we worship and the God he reveals are more complex than our flattened theology would suggest.

Aware of the conflict he has provoked, he leaves. He goes quietly enough to avoid a showdown with the opposition, but not so secretly that the people could not find him. Surrounded by a friendly crowd, he is safe for the moment. Notice, however, that at this moment in our text, Jesus is not *coming*. He is *leaving*. If people want to be with Jesus, they have to keep up with him. They have to pay attention to his movements and be ready to move with him.

Here again, the movements of Jesus of Nazareth do not square too easily with the generalizations of our Christology. We speak of Jesus coming to us, coming into our world, coming into our lives, or coming again in glory. We do not speak very often of Jesus leaving. We like to emphasize the grace of his coming to us more than the grace by which we are able to watch his movements, acknowledge our fear of being left alone, and follow him.

In our story, the religious leaders who reject Jesus and the crowds that follow him are all actors whose movements are critical to the story. The gospel is the whole action, theirs along with his. By whatever mysterious promptings of grace stirring within them, they do not just sit there watching and waiting for the end of the story. They do not wait to see what happened and then sit down to discuss what it all means. They do not sit until Jesus comes to them. They take a position. They are either drawn to him or threatened by him. Their decisiveness is part of the gospel, part of the Christ event.

Those who are drawn and who follow are healed. "Many crowds followed him," Matthew tells us, "and he cured all of them" (v. 15b). In itself, this is a pretty startling statement. All of them need physical healing? Is it, rather, healing in the broader sense that we all need healing? Whatever the text means, we get the clear sense that because they chase down Jesus, their lives are changed in dramatic ways.

Next comes the puzzler: "He ordered them not to make him known" (v. 16). Talk about timing. These may be the words of Jesus, but this is clearly not a general rule for Christians. We are to make Christ known, to proclaim the good news, to share what we have heard. In fact, Matthew is writing this Gospel expressly to violate this specific instruction—but not yet, not at this point in this story. It is not yet time to trigger the impending confrontation.

So while Jesus is ready to provoke conflict, he is also eager to contain it for the moment. More than

Pastoral Perspective

questions, our professor used them for the greater good of learning, teaching us how to think critically and broadly. I came to understand his approach as savvy and intentional. In actuality, by holding back and not answering directly, our professor taught in such a way that we were led to arrive, on our own, at a more complete understanding.

Like my professor, Jesus must have held back a lot of knowledge to teach a broader point. For instance, prior to this text, Matthew reports the Pharisees plotted to destroy him. Surely Jesus could have pursued them and continued to teach them, just as he clarified and expanded the meaning of the Sabbath laws (12:1–14). Instead, Jesus chose to hold his power close to his chest and not patronize the Pharisees at that point.

In a similar way, through his public speaking ability—not to mention his healing skills—Jesus revealed his ability to gain followers and the political power that accompanied them. Jesus was surely a great leader, but his leadership included the paradoxical instruction not to make him known.

In verses 18–21 Matthew quotes from Isaiah 42 to place Jesus in the tradition of the Servant of the Lord. Again, power is portrayed in characteristic paradoxical fashion. Power is about holding back one's voice, restraining the desire to break even a weakened reed, and bringing justice in a quiet, peaceful fashion unimaginable to most rulers.

The Paradox of Popularity. Everywhere one looks these days, new forms of media have arrived to communicate the latest trends, news, and controversies. Social networks and other avenues for new media make broadcasting one's opinions—or what one ate for breakfast—as easy as a few clicks. Some parents purchase Internet domain names for their children as soon as they are born, or even before. Surely this world of new media and its possibilities is a far cry from Jesus' time; even so, it is helpful to note that Jesus eschewed several means of popularity available to him.

In Matthew's Gospel, Jesus is always traveling from place to place. Rather than staying put and letting his popularity grow, Jesus plants a seed and moves on to let it germinate without his physical presence. Even though it would spread his message, Jesus asks the crowds not to speak of his miracles and speeches. (Of course, perhaps by doing so, Jesus only increased the inclination of the crowds to spread the word—gossip is certainly a cross-cultural pastime—but there is no hint of that in the text.)

Exegetical Perspective

Earlier (8:16) Jesus is said to have healed all the sick that were among the crowds following him, which already is a claim about Jesus' authority. We may simply assume that "all" here must obviously mean all the sick ones. Who else could it mean? Still, we are right to take note of the hyperbole of the phrase as it is stated: Jesus is Healer of all.

In general, the author of Matthew shows little interest in Mark's messianic secret motif; theologically the messianic secret does not fit with Matthew's understanding of who Jesus is.[2] Here, however, he utilizes the theme of secrecy to connect the quotation that follows. While the quotation is only tangentially related to the theme of keeping Jesus' identity quiet, it does provide a summary of sorts of Jesus' ministry to the present, beginning with a clear echo of the divine voice at Jesus' baptism and stressing the role of the Holy Spirit in Jesus' ministry.

Matthew's representation of Isaiah 42:1–4 hints at a complicated text history for this passage. The Septuagint (Greek) version, as we have it today, is not a straight translation of the Masoretic Text (Hebrew); Matthew's version sometimes looks like a direct translation from the Masoretic Text, sometimes follows the Septuagint, and sometimes is closer to the Targum (Aramaic translation used in the synagogues). Either Matthew was working with a Greek translation that is completely unknown to us today, or—as scholars suggest is more likely—he was making or using a redacted reworking of this passage that brought out the resonances of the text to Christian readers.

To represent the Hebrew word meaning "servant," instead of the more common Greek translation *doulos,* Matthew (or his source) chooses *pais,* which can mean "servant" but more commonly means "child." Since the words "beloved" and "well pleased" also appear in the first part of this passage, by using *pais* Matthew draws a close connection between the Isaiah passage and the divine voice at Jesus' baptism (although there he is claimed as *huios,* "son"). Where the Septuagint reads, "I have given my spirit," Matthew's translation instead follows the Targum, "I will put my spirit," making the passage more clearly a prediction of future divine action. Again following the Targum, Matthew represents Hebrew words that could be translated more neutrally as "cry out" and "raise one's voice" to say that "he will not wrangle or cry aloud." In Matthew's handling, this passage presents Jesus not simply as quiet but as a peacemaker

---

2. The idea that Mark espouses a theology of a messianic secret has been widely discussed for over a century; see, for example, Heikki Räisänen, *The 'Messianic Secret' in Mark's Gospel* (Edinburgh: T. & T. Clark, 2000).

Homiletical Perspective

There is no easy answer to why, when Jesus had the synagogue officials on the run after their verbal sparring over Sabbath practice, he did not pursue them further. There is no simple explanation why, as the crowds followed him, Jesus cured them and ordered them not to "make him known." Always, those who seek to follow in the way of discipleship need to be careful about the expectations we have for Jesus.

Our world is filled with many gospel interpretations. A prosperity gospel, a gospel of success, and a gospel of liberation are some that may be present in a congregation that hears this text. Each of these "gospels" carries with it its own expectations. How close to or far from the Jesus that Matthew presents are these gospels? This question can provoke lively and provocative reactions as a congregation engages this text. Jesus had a mission, yet his power and presence led others to try to attach their own agendas to his. In a world where cries for justice often are met with the crushing power of vested interests, where even the cries themselves can be expressions of vested interests, it far outstrips our own imagination to put our trust in One who will set things right with a voice that cannot be heard in the streets, who will not break a bruised reed or quench a smoldering wick. Who is this Jesus, giving hope to the hopeless, who does not act or speak in all the ways we have come to expect (and reject)?

There are many implications for the practice of discipleship. One of them is that we are called to pay attention—both to Jesus' voice and to what it means for our lives. The God Matthew seeks to proclaim comes in ways and from places we do not expect. God gives Jesus to the world, but the world does not expect a Messiah who looks, acts, and is like this. We have to pay attention. That this text includes the longest quote from Isaiah in the Gospel of Matthew seems to indicate that the Gospel writer is pulling out all the stops to convince the reader that something unprecedented is happening in the ministry of Jesus. Matthew is both connecting Jesus to the long history of God's promise and possibility with God's people through the Isaiah text and at the same time serving notice that these texts, promises, and possibilities always must be refocused and reimagined through the Jesus who is before them now.

The same can be said of every congregation that gathers to hear this word proclaimed. Jesus will not be captured by others' agendas. Followers can never be too sure they have Jesus' message or purpose neatly managed and understood. Jesus commanded

Matthew 12:15–21

Theological Perspective

eager, he is insistent. He provokes and withdraws, comes and goes, heals and silences. What is going on here? More profoundly, is there anything in the coming and going that is of significance for us today in our experience of Jesus Christ? Is this merely narrative clutter, or is it essential to the identity of the incarnate Christ and the God revealed in Christ?

We might wonder whether Jesus is still ordering us not to make him known, healing us but refusing to be pinned down in definitions and dogmas. To what extent does he still reveal himself by hiding the full weight of his identity, giving but also withholding, always insisting that he is much more than we can think or know or dare to imagine?

Perhaps to make the point more clearly, our text quotes Isaiah 42:1–4, a text that does not really fit the action and sparks more questions than answers. This much seems clear: there is a connection between God's chosen Servant and Jesus. The power of God—specifically the Spirit of God—is with Jesus. He proclaims justice, but he does not break or destroy in order to achieve it.

Jesus is a shepherd, not a wrangler. If there is a connection here between the Isaiah quotation and the narrative portion of our text, it may lie in the way that Jesus withdraws from the confrontation and keeps his identity quiet. He is provocative but not coercive, always ready to heal and even to confront but not to bruise or destroy.

RONALD COLE-TURNER

Pastoral Perspective

Whereas in most congregations leaders attempt to drum up support for any significant changes to the church, in verses 15–21 Jesus seeks no public approval. Jesus looks at all times to be obedient to God, not to bow to the crowds' latest whim.

The Paradox of the Cross. A recent study of religious "deconversion" (those who were once Christian but have since left the faith) revealed that a main reason for deconversion was related to human suffering.[1] Those surveyed wondered, if God were really all-loving and compassionate, why would God allow disease, famine, hardship, and all the other sobering challenges of our day? In the passage, Jesus addresses the problem of disease quickly and decisively: he cures "all of them" (v. 15).

For many believers, stories of Jesus' healing have lost much of their effect. For others, though, such as "deconverts," these stories of healing only highlight the healing needed today in our own congregations, the nation, and the world. Rather than ignoring these issues, pastors would do well to note the challenges and speak a word of hope.

Jesus' life, death, and resurrection get to the heart of the matter, for they demonstrate that despite his many miraculous healings, more needed to be accomplished for the whole world. In life, Jesus healed many bodies, but through his death and resurrection, bodies and souls, minds and hearts are shown the power of a love beyond the capabilities of any medical doctor. This all points to the greatest paradox of all: Jesus, though he saved so many others, did not save himself.

A hymn by Sylvia Dunstan, originally named "Christus Paradox," addresses many of the paradoxical issues of Christ's life and death.[2] Christ is both "lamb and shepherd . . . prince and slave . . . peacemaker and sword-bringer." He is the one we both "scorn and crave," who is "gift and cost." While he preaches a way that is narrow, he has "a love that reaches wide." Good pastors embrace paradox: it is essential to their pastoral duties and exemplified by their Lord.

ADAM J. COPELAND

---

1. Bradley Wright, "Why Do Christians Leave the Faith? Breaking-up with a God Who Failed Them," http://www.patheos.com/blogs/blackwhiteandgray/2011/11/why–do–christians–leave–the–faith–breaking–up–with–a–god–who–failed–them/; accessed November 24, 2011.
2. Sylvia G. Dunstan, "You, Lord, Are Both Lamb and Shepherd," in *Sing the Faith* (Louisville, KY: Geneva Press, 2003), #2102.

in the positive sense, neither seeking confrontation on his own nor instigating a popular rebellion to demand justice.

The images of the Servant who will "not break a bruised reed or quench a smoldering wick" (v. 20) may seem strange to contemporary readers. A crushed reed is useless—why not break it off? If a wick is smoking, is it not time either to trim it or extinguish it? It is perhaps unsurprising that interpreters have looked for "secret" meanings in these odd images, but they are neither allegories nor fixed metaphors. Instead, what this passage seems to mean is that this figure is so compassionate as to refuse to destroy what is clearly imperfect, even what appears useless. These odd images, then, vividly emphasize the Servant's kindness, mercy, and love.

The most important feature of this quotation, though, is the twice-mentioned emphasis on the goal of Jesus' ministry as bringing justice (or judgment) to the Gentiles. Most modern translations choose "justice" to translate *krisis*, and this translation fits well in the context of the passage: the Servant does not seek to obtain justice for himself, but rather brings justice to those who hope in him. Matthew elsewhere uses *krisis* to speak of the final judgment, and we should probably seek to hear both meanings. The justice the Servant brings is ultimate justice, final judgment.

This justice/judgment is brought to the *ethnē*, "nations," namely, the Gentiles. Although Matthew is often thought of as the most Jewish of the four Gospels, Gentiles appear in the story at several key points to anticipate Jesus' significance to the whole world (the most familiar example being the wise men from "the East" that come to worship Jesus at his birth). Still, thus far in the story Matthew is telling, God's salvific activity through Jesus has been limited to Israel, with hints that the nations also will receive the blessing (see 8:11–12; 10:18). This passage, both summarizing Jesus' ministry to this point and anticipating what is to come, is the clearest statement thus far that Jesus' lordship extends both to Jews and to Gentiles.

SANDRA HACK POLASKI

those gathered that day "not to make him known" (v. 16). We see Matthew's words echoed in the imagery of Isaiah linking power and gentleness, justice and meekness. Those of Matthew's day—and we, as well—are challenged again by Jesus to pay attention to the labels, agendas, and shallow expectations that run counter to faithful living.

In 1987, the Irish rock band U2 brought out their album *The Joshua Tree*. Lead singer Bono talked about his experience as a child growing up in a very divided country, referencing the first song on *Joshua Tree*, "Where the Streets Have No Name."

"I was trying to sketch a location—maybe a spiritual location," Bono said.

> I often have the feeling of wanting to go somewhere where the values of our society don't hold you down. In Belfast, by what street somebody lives on—you can tell not only their religion, but tell how much money they're making—literally by which side of the road they live on. . . . that said something to me, and so I started writing about a place of grace—a place where things are right, you know? A place where the streets have no name.[2]

After expressing his dis-ease with a world around him that is so confining and leaves him yearning for something more true and real and authentic, Bono sings, "I want to reach out and touch the flame where the streets have no name."[3]

When Jesus became aware of the threats against him, he departed. Where did he go? Perhaps to the place of God's justice: a place of no names, no labels. A place where the most unexpected among us bring God's truth and show God's love. Surely, it was not a place, as in Auden's poem, where we find "a God who should be as like me as possible." Rather, it is the place where God's hope and Jesus' faithful purpose and power change the world and bring hope and justice to life.

MARK RAMSEY

2. "Bono: The Beliefnet Interview" http://www.beliefnet.com/Entertainment/Music/2001/02/Bono–The–Beliefnet–Interview.aspx?p=1; accessed August 28, 2012.
3. U2, *The Joshua Tree* (Island Records, 1987).

Matthew 12:22–32

²²Then they brought to him a demoniac who was blind and mute; and he cured him, so that the one who had been mute could speak and see. ²³All the crowds were amazed and said, "Can this be the Son of David?" ²⁴But when the Pharisees heard it, they said, "It is only by Beelzebul, the ruler of the demons, that this fellow casts out the demons." ²⁵He knew what they were thinking and said to them, "Every kingdom divided against itself is laid waste, and no city or house divided against itself will stand. ²⁶If Satan casts out Satan, he is divided against himself; how then will his kingdom stand? ²⁷ If I cast out demons by Beelzebul, by whom do your own exorcists cast them out? Therefore they will be your judges. ²⁸But if it is by the Spirit of God that I cast out demons, then the kingdom of God has come to you. ²⁹Or how can one enter a strong man's house and plunder his property, without first tying up the strong man? Then indeed the house can be plundered. ³⁰Whoever is not with me is against me, and whoever does not gather with me scatters. ³¹Therefore I tell you, people will be forgiven for every sin and blasphemy, but blasphemy against the Spirit will not be forgiven. ³²Whoever speaks a word against the Son of Man will be forgiven, but whoever speaks against the Holy Spirit will not be forgiven, either in this age or in the age to come."

Theological Perspective

The conflict that runs through Matthew 12 now explodes. The religious authorities who oppose Jesus reveal the full weight of their condemnation. It is not just that Jesus heals on the Sabbath and violates the rules. According to his critics, Jesus is in league with Satan. His power is great because it comes from the ultimate personification of evil itself. He only pretends to be the enemy of the demons. In truth he is merely redeploying the demons, moving them around from one poor soul to another while amassing his own power. Stop him before it is too late.

To which Jesus responds: Satan casting out Satan? You mean he is divided against himself? Satan is too smart to adopt a losing strategy.

Really? Maybe Satan is divided against himself, feigning weakness for strategic advantage. Maybe the religious authorities are onto something. What better way is there for evil to get the upper hand than by persuading the crowd to trust someone who has the power to control evil? When you worry about demons, you trust the exorcist. Maybe the exorcist is a double agent.

The religious leaders have a good argument—maybe even the better argument. After all, what evidence supports the claim Jesus is making? Any evidence he can point to can also be construed as making the case against him. The decision for or

Pastoral Perspective

Part of mainline congregational life—at least when things are going well—includes making space for people's questions. Rather than ignoring the deep and sometimes confusing questions of faith and culture, many congregations thrive by embracing new, sometimes difficult, questions. For example, church women's groups are asking questions about their structure and purpose, now that women work outside the home at much higher rates. Church worship committees ask questions about what hymns and songs best give voice to the faith and what instruments best fit. Congregations are asking questions about whether older practices should continue, be reworked, or simply be left behind. Lest we think our tough questions are the first to cause upheaval among the faithful, Matthew 12:22–32 tells us of Jesus' own experience.

After healing a demoniac, Matthew reports that the crowds, in amazement, asked Jesus, "Can this be the Son of David?" (v. 23). Another translation notes the tentative nature of the question: "This man couldn't be the Son of David, could he?" (CEB). It remains unclear why healing the demoniac finally brought about this question, rather than the previous instance, when Jesus "cured all of them" in the crowds (v. 15), but whatever the reason, the man who once could not, now can both speak and see.

Exegetical Perspective

In this passage, the themes of the Pharisees' opposition (12:14) and the role of the Spirit in Jesus' ministry (12:18) come together, so that opposition to Jesus is clearly shown to be opposition to the Spirit of God. The occasion of the controversy is the healing of a man who is mute and blind by casting out the demon that possesses him. (A very similar story is told in Matt. 9:32–34.) While contemporary readers may want to probe the connection between demonic possession and the loss of faculties, this story shows no interest in the topic. Jesus is able to cast out the evil spirit and restore the man to wholeness. What matters, rather, is the controversy dialogue that follows.

As in the earlier Sabbath miracles, the reactions of "the people" and "the Pharisees" are diametrically opposed. The people are even more astounded than before, and start to ask whether Jesus might possibly be "the Son of David." First-century Jews did not necessarily expect the Davidic Messiah to be a healer, but their response connects Jesus with Jewish history and tradition, and so provokes the Pharisees (who, in Matthew's telling of the story, are the primary opposition to Jesus and anything he says or does).

The Pharisees' interpretation of the healing both demonstrates their understanding of power and reveals the reason they find Jesus' actions so

Homiletical Perspective

Some texts appear to both preacher and listener as new, fresh, or unfamiliar. Others, like this one, come to our hearing with echoes of other uses. This text deals with a continuation of Jesus' sparring with the powers that be. It involves an appeal to the crowds that had been increasingly drawn to Jesus' words and actions. This text involves a demonstration and a controversy around power. Perhaps it should not be surprising, then, that the memorable rhetoric of at least two American presidents can be traced to these few verses. In June 1858, Abraham Lincoln accepted the nomination of his party to run for the U.S. Senate with a speech that, in its fifth sentence, declared, "'A house divided against itself cannot stand.' I believe this government cannot endure, permanently half slave and half free."[1] It was a controversial statement at the time, one that many historians believe contributed to Lincoln's electoral defeat in that race, even as he was admired for his moral stand. On September 20, 2001, President Bush appeared before a joint session of Congress and, in light of the 9/11 attacks, said: "Either you are with us, or you are with the terrorists."[2] Lincoln and Bush are joined by leaders of many different stripes in invoking parts

---

1. http://www.historyplace.com/lincoln/divided.htm; accessed May 25, 2012.
2. http://quotes.liberty–tree.ca/quote_blog/George.Bush.Quote.6634; accessed June 3, 2012.

Theological Perspective

against Jesus does not seem to hang on the weight of evidence.

So it is all on the line now for Jesus. Everyone agrees that he has unimagined spiritual power. The big question is, Whose power? Satan's or God's? The tough question is, How can we tell?

Our world may often seem to be a grayish mix of light and dark, but here things are sorted out. There is no middle ground. We are with Jesus or against him. His power comes from the Spirit or from Satan. If the options are that stark, the only choice is to say this: The Spirit of God is upon Jesus, and Jesus does the work of God by the power of God.

What is most striking about this text, however, is the way in which the question about the Spirit in Jesus immediately becomes a question about the Spirit in his followers. Jesus does the work of God by the Spirit of God. How do his followers know? How do they know he is not Satan's puppet? Because the Spirit in Jesus is also in them. In the text, this point is made through the language of warning: Do not speak against the Spirit. Blasphemy against the Spirit will not be forgiven.

These are harsh words, of course, and it is no wonder we wince at the thought of blaspheming the Spirit or the possibility of an "unforgivable sin." We argue with the text. Murder is forgiven, but speaking against the Holy Spirit is not? We debate the relative seriousness of possible sins and whether anything limits God's forgiveness—all the while missing the key point in this text. Denying the Spirit is damnably serious.

We never speak against the Holy Spirit, we tell ourselves, and we have a point. We do not speak *against* the Spirit. We do not speak of the Spirit very much at all, at least not enough to run much risk of blasphemy.

So we try to comfort ourselves by claiming that we are not nearly as bad as the religious leaders described in this text. After all, they ascribed the works of Jesus to Satan. That is explicit blasphemy, speaking against God. Our sin is more like a silent blasphemy that speaks of Jesus without saying much about the Spirit. We talk freely about the work of Christ in our lives without reference to the power of the Spirit within. Yes, the religious authorities in the text denied the Spirit, while we merely neglect to speak of the Spirit. Is the space between denying and neglecting really so great? Can we blaspheme by silence?

The part of the text that really makes us squirm is when Jesus warns that speaking "against the Holy Spirit will not be forgiven, either in this age or in the age to come" (v. 32). This does not sit well with

Pastoral Perspective

Such hesitant questioning may be familiar to many in the church. We hear them when we host free meals after worship for the community or when we mark foreheads with water and the sign of the cross, speaking the words, "You are Christ's own forever." There is something about faith in Jesus Christ that causes us to stop short and wonder if, really, this miraculous grace is true.

Many, including those in our churches, find Jesus' message difficult to grasp. Likewise, the Pharisees cannot explain how Jesus has the power to heal, and they are not comfortable with letting bygones be bygones, or letting a good deed go unanalyzed. We surely know many with the sort of personality (perhaps including ourselves) for whom it is difficult to enjoy a piece of music unless they can analyze the chord progressions, or who cannot be grateful for a hefty Sunday offering unless it fully gets them back on budget.

One Sunday, an elementary school–age boy and his friend attended church together. For one of the boys, this was a normal occurrence. The other, however, had stayed over as a guest at the first boy's house the night before, and his parents had elected to pick him up after worship. When it came time for the Eucharist, both boys went up to receive the sacrament. The boy who regularly attended church went first, receiving the bread and wine. The second boy imitated the first, but when the presider handed him a piece of bread and said, "The body of Christ broken for you," the boy's eyes widened. Loud enough for several rows to hear, the boy exclaimed, "Wow! Really?" Let there be no doubt: this was not the appropriate moment to explain the ins and outs of transubstantiation. Amazement can quickly lead to questioning, and pastors must carefully discern when best to respond.

After the Pharisees accuse Jesus of healing in the name of Beelzebul, Jesus gives several logical reasons they are mistaken. First, Jesus argues that if he were Satan, there would be no reason for him to cast out the demon from the man; it would be counterproductive! Second, Jesus notes that the Pharisees support other exorcists, so they already give credence to some healings. Third, Jesus implies that through the healings he is "tying up the strong man" of Satan, showing Jesus' own power over him (v. 29). Jesus does not stop at strict logic; instead, he expands his reply to include labeling those who are with him or against him and suggests the troubling notion that one who sins against the Holy Spirit will not be forgiven.

threatening. They claim that Jesus has power over the evil spirits because he is in league with Beelzebul, the demons' acknowledged authority. New Testament scholar Daniel Patte says this line of thinking is in keeping with the Pharisees' understanding of power: in order to wield power, one must be recognized as an authority by the ones over whom power is exercised.[1] The Pharisees' deepest fears about Jesus lie here as well. If the people were to change their allegiance and no longer recognize the Pharisees' authority, their source of power would evaporate.

Jesus' response devastates the Pharisees' claim and demonstrates an altogether different understanding of power and authority. Divine power, as Jesus claims to exercise it, does not depend on human acknowledgment of divine authority. It is an invasive force, destroying the forces of evil, whether or not human beings choose to recognize it. Jesus' actions weaken Beelzebul; therefore, Jesus' authority is from God.

From verse 25 on, Jesus' statements are phrased either as synonymous ("both this and that") or antithetical ("not this but that") parallelisms. The effect is of Jesus hammering home his point again and again, by repetition or contrast.

The first two verses (vv. 25–26) frame a logical argument that the Pharisees might well concede. Division within any social or political entity weakens it from within. It follows, then, that if satanic authority were used to cast out demons, Satan would be working against his own kingdom.

Jesus' next words are more challenging. Jesus takes for granted that others can also perform exorcism successfully. However, he knows that the Pharisees will angrily reject any insinuation that their associates are minions of Satan. So he provocatively poses a rhetorical question that he knows the Pharisees cannot satisfactorily answer.

The only possible answer, as Jesus demonstrates, is to reject the hypothesis: Jesus does not cast out demons by Beelzebul. The opposite hypothesis, that Jesus casts out demons by the Spirit of God, leads to the inevitable conclusion that "the kingdom of God has come to you" (v. 28b). Matthew, who usually substitutes the phrase "kingdom of heaven" in keeping with Jewish piety, pointedly does not do so here. The kingdom of God, established by the Spirit of God, stands in bold opposition to Satan's kingdom.

The image of the strong man bound by robbers (v. 29) is an odd one; the language of "plundering" is used elsewhere in Matthew's Gospel to speak of

1. Daniel Patte, *The Gospel according to Matthew: A Structural Commentary on Matthew's Faith* (Philadelphia: Fortress Press, 1987), 175–77.

of these verses, including Vladimir Lenin, George Orwell, Benito Mussolini, and Hillary Clinton. With this text, controversy abounds generation to generation.

To avoid being caught up in categories that take us far beyond Matthew's text, as well as diminishing Jesus' mission and ministry, care must be taken to understand what sort of "controversial Jesus" we are proclaiming here. The disruption Jesus presents in this text is not rooted in exorcisms or unauthorized healings that Jesus performed. Rather, it is based in the radical claims of discipleship, of life's priorities, of faithful devotion to Jesus and his emerging ministry in Matthew.

The division Jesus references is not because of an honest disagreement about religious practices. It is because Jesus is overturning long-established loyalties and insisting on a deeper loyalty to God. Jesus is not only the one we serve but also the one we attempt to emulate. A potential follower of Jesus is led to a place of decision: Are you for God or not? Are you going to follow Jesus and the radical nature of his claim on your whole life, or will you claim your life for your own agenda? Anyone may reach this point of challenge again and again in life, yet no one can go forward divided on these competing claims. Such a house cannot stand.

Before Ernest Campbell was pastor of Riverside Church in New York City, he was a pastor in Ann Arbor, Michigan. Following the assassination of President Kennedy, a church member called Campbell to suggest that the one thing the church might do to partially redeem the tragedy would be to provide Marina Oswald with an opportunity to improve her English. The widow of the accused assassin, Lee Harvey Oswald, she was Russian by birth, had been in the United States for only a short time, and, given what had happened, was universally reviled for her husband's deeds. With the cooperation of the FBI and others, Marina Oswald came to Ann Arbor. She slipped into the community at night by train. She lived with a modest family that took seriously its devotion to God and neighbor.

The church was pressed and finally issued a small press release. Some immediately reacted, proclaiming how unpatriotic this action was. Others called the church foolish and stupid. Still others suggested that this was a profoundly unwise action. One woman called it unfair: "I have been a member of a church for forty years, and in that time, all that the church has done for me I could write on the back of a postage stamp; yet you do this for the wife of that

Theological Perspective

our view of Jesus. Over the centuries, Christians have struggled to interpret these words. They sound ominous, but their meaning is more theologically profound than we often think.

If the meaning is profound, the logic is quite simple. How do we know God? Through Jesus Christ. How do we know that Jesus Christ is acting on God's behalf and not some deceiver? Through the Holy Spirit. Without the Spirit, we are not joined with Christ and therefore cannot know God. Refusing the Spirit is "unforgivable" in the sense that it is the one thing we can do that cuts us off from saving grace.

Basil of Caesarea (ca. 329–379), one of the greatest theologians of the early church, put it this way: "It is impossible to believe in the Father and the Son without the presence of the Spirit. He who rejects the Spirit rejects the Son, and he who rejects the Son rejects the Father. . . . It is impossible to worship the Son except in the Holy Spirit; it is impossible to call upon the Father except in the Spirit of adoption."[1] John Calvin agrees: "We cannot come to Christ unless we be drawn by the Spirit of God." He says, in fact, that Scripture itself "cannot penetrate into our minds unless the Spirit, as the inner teacher, through his illumination makes entry for it."[2]

Whether the denial of the Holy Spirit is best seen as an unforgivable sin or an impossible barrier, it is the ultimate cutoff. Without the Spirit it is impossible to be joined with Christ. No wonder it is dangerous to reject or neglect the Spirit.

RONALD COLE-TURNER

Pastoral Perspective

For some, the concept of the "unforgivable sin" is a familiar one, perhaps an idea with which they have wrestled for many years. For others, an unforgivable sin will simply not fit into a belief system heavily biased toward God's grace. All, however, would benefit from further consideration of Jesus' puzzling claim.

In context, Jesus' words are directed to the Pharisees who have accused him of blasphemy. Jesus, in return, presents the possibility that the Pharisees are in danger of committing the same offense. By contrasting those who speak against the Son of Man and those who speak against the Holy Spirit, Jesus is suggesting two different types of blasphemy. On the one hand, identifying the Son of Man is a difficult task. John the Baptist and Jesus' own disciples question his identity. So blaspheming against the Son of Man, while not ideal, is forgivable. On the other hand, speaking against the Holy Spirit is more serious. In the fullness of time it will be made clear who Jesus is and by whose power Jesus lived, died, and was raised. To know and believe, to truly understand God and all God's purposes, and still to blaspheme against the Holy Spirit, Jesus presents as another matter. As R. T. France writes, "This saying is a wake-up call to the arrogant, not a bogey to frighten those of tender conscience."[1] As many have calmed a worried soul: if you are worried you have committed the unforgivable sin, it is certain that you have not. The verse should not be used to frighten or accuse.

In this passage, Jesus answers the Pharisees with words that are important and necessary. Jesus' logical explanations should not be underestimated, but they all stem from the crowd's hesitant question, "Can this be the Son of David?" (v. 23). To lose sight of what instigates the question—Jesus' miraculously healing *another*, this time a demoniac—would be missing the forest for the trees. Ultimately, Jesus' words, for all their beauty, logic, and faithfulness, are further clarified by his deeds of healing and love. Any lingering questions, logical or otherwise, are answered in his ultimate deed on the cross.

ADAM J. COPELAND

1. Saint Basil the Great, *On the Holy Spirit*, trans. David Anderson (Crestwood, NY: St. Vladimir's Seminary Press, 1980), chap. 11, par. 27, p. 48.
2. John Calvin, *Institutes of the Christian Religion* 3.2.35, ed. John T. McNeill, trans. Ford Lewis Battles, Library of Christian Classics (Philadelphia: Westminster Press, 1960), 20:582.

1. R. T. France, *The Gospel of Matthew* (Grand Rapids: Eerdmans, 2007), 482–83.

the work of evil powers. It is clear that here Satan is the strong man who is bound and whose property is ransacked, the startlingly violent language reinforcing Jesus' depiction of divine power as an invasive force.

The final section of this pericope has arguably caused as much distress and division in the church as any passage in the Gospels. The claim that "whoever is not with me is against me, and whoever does not gather with me scatters" (v. 30) has been interpreted to mean that opposition to the church (often meaning, of course, the interpreter's own branch of the church) is by definition opposition to Christ. However, in narrative context, the saying is not about Jesus' legacy but about Jesus himself. It is language that will be recalled just before Jesus' crucifixion, when he tells his disciples that "it is written, 'I will strike the shepherd, and the sheep of the flock will be scattered'" (Matt. 26:31, quoting Zech. 13:7). Opponents of Jesus will not have the final word. The very last words of Matthew's Gospel promise the disciples that Jesus will be with them "always, to the end of the age" (28:20).

Another, even thornier set of problems attends Jesus' proclamation that a word against the "Son of Man" can be forgiven, but that blasphemy against the Holy Spirit is unforgivable sin. The application to the narrative context is clear: Jesus' Pharisaic opponents have already decided to destroy him (12:14) and, in so doing, have attributed God's work to Satan. In the world of the story, this is a permanent hardening of heart, so questions about the possibility of repentance are moot. Even less does this story address the question of whether Christian believers can commit unforgivable sin, debates about which have unfortunately dogged the church for much of its history. Instead, in its context, this saying of Jesus reinforces the belief that was crucial to Matthew's community: when it comes to Jesus, neutrality is impossible. Either one believes and commits oneself to a life of discipleship, or one turns away and in so doing denies the work of the Holy Spirit.

SANDRA HACK POLASKI

monster?" The church answered every letter, no matter how harsh. In every case, for every letter, their response was the same: "The one thing that you have not shown us is that what we have done is unlike Jesus Christ."[3]

Almost any cause attracts an array of people whose varying investment in the cause ranges from mere admirers to devoted followers. Matthew records that "all the crowds were amazed." This provoked those who were most threatened by Jesus' actions to get busy disputing Sabbath rituals, healing practices, and the power to cast out demons. For followers of Jesus, those were secondary issues. Jesus had placed a claim on their whole life: how they thought, what they said, how they acted, what they valued. Either people responded to Jesus' claim and followed, or they moved their admiration off to a safer distance.

In confirmation classes I have taught, the young people gathered to inquire about faith have speculated on the identity of the sin that can never be forgiven. Is it murder? Something worse? Is it some act that harmed a large group of people? The reference within this passage, that "blasphemy against the Holy Spirit will not be forgiven," always provokes uncertainty. What is that? How does that happen? These sincere questions—from any potential follower—can provide a deeper encounter with God. Well intended as they are, these apprehensive questions forget the essential attribute of God. It is God who ceaselessly takes initiative with us in our lives. At the fork in the road of our life's journey we are faced with a choice: between living by our own agenda and acknowledging the claim Jesus has put on our life. We are not alone, however, as we stand at that fork in the road. The Holy Spirit, against which we must not blaspheme, is working in us and through us and for us, shaping every part of our life and helping us in every moment to act like Christ.

MARK RAMSEY

3. Ernest T. Campbell, "Follow Me," in *A Chorus of Witnesses*, ed. Thomas G. Long and Cornelius Plantinga (Grand Rapids: Eerdmans, 1994), 169.

Matthew 12:33–37

³³"Either make the tree good, and its fruit good; or make the tree bad, and its fruit bad; for the tree is known by its fruit. ³⁴You brood of vipers! How can you speak good things, when you are evil? For out of the abundance of the heart the mouth speaks. ³⁵The good person brings good things out of a good treasure, and the evil person brings evil things out of an evil treasure. ³⁶I tell you, on the day of judgment you will have to give an account for every careless word you utter; ³⁷for by your words you will be justified, and by your words you will be condemned."

Theological Perspective

Matthew gathers Jesus' short lessons on the tree and its fruit, treasures, heart and speech, and the last judgment. These lessons guide reflections on the interconnections between inner thoughts, spoken words, actions, and their impact on others.

Jesus interprets a commonsensical "good tree-good fruit, bad tree-bad fruit" lesson morally (vv. 33–34). The tree represents the heart that is either good or bad, and the fruit is whatever spills out of the heart in one's speech. The word *kardia* (heart) has multiple meanings: inner self, mind, volition, desire, and intent. Jesus also explains the same correlation between inner self and its outward manifestation using the metaphor of treasures. Is this simple formula, "the good person brings good things out of a good treasure, and the evil person brings evil things out of an evil treasure" (v. 35), workable in the complex working of the human psyche? A modern person is well aware that there is a close connection between what is stored up in one's heart and what is communicated out of one's mouth. One's thoughts and feelings may be consigned to temporary oblivion or the subconscious, whether they are passions, concerns, angers, or resentments. Eventually, though, one's words and body language betray the foul smell of a rotten core.

We may also see societal expressions of our collective hearts. In the U.S. South, one recalls Billie

Pastoral Perspective

A child came home from school one day, upset because he had said something that made a girl cry. "I tried to take it back," he explained. "I told her, 'I take it back! I take it back!'" She had not stopped crying, and he got his first lesson on the difficulty of taking back painful words.

Words that devastate, damage, or violate cannot be unsaid; they can never fully be undone. Words do not just *say* something; they *do* something. They are a kind of action: they can build up or tear down, encourage or manipulate, illuminate or deceive. Words are so little, just a tiny push of air through the vocal cords, molded by the tongue and lips, cut off with the teeth. Just a puff, and then the word is gone. That is part of their power: once they are out of our mouths, we have no more control over them. Once loosed, our words are out there, creating or destroying, doing good or doing harm.

Jay Asher's best-selling young-adult novel *Thirteen Reasons Why* is the story of a teenage suicide told in the voice of the deceased. Before her death, Hannah Baker records a series of tapes as a sort of audio suicide note. In the tapes she holds people responsible for the things they said and did that damaged her reputation and her sense of self. She takes responsibility for her decision to end her life, but she wants to explain how other people's words

Exegetical Perspective

The immediate context of this harsh reply from Jesus to the religious authorities is his curing of a man who is demon possessed, mute, and blind. Stunned and amazed by the miraculous healing, the crowds wonder aloud whether this man might indeed be the "Son of David." The Pharisees, troubled by this near profession of faith, reissue a familiar charge (see Matt. 9:34): Jesus must be using the power of Beelzebul, the ruler of demons, to cast out demons. The accusation of Matthew 12:24 is the occasion for Jesus' severe reply in the following verses, which is both a defense of his divine power (vv. 25–29) and an indictment of the religious leaders who have raised the issue (vv. 30–37).

In his final reply, Jesus makes two analogies to illustrate the difference between himself and the Pharisees. The first is that of trees and fruit. Though the opening expression is awkwardly phrased in the Greek text (probably best translated, "take for example"), the point could not be clearer: a tree is either good or bad (v. 33). Good trees produce good fruit and bad trees produce bad fruit. There is an inevitability to the result. The direct address of verse 34 makes explicit what has been implied before: the Pharisees are bad trees and, by accusing Jesus of using demonic power, have borne bad fruit. They are condemned for the words that they have

Homiletical Perspective

The homiletical perspective of the Revised Common Lectionary on Matthew 12 is clear: "Do not bother preaching these texts." Matthew 12 occurs nowhere in the RCL, so churches that follow the RCL will miss this pivotal chapter in the Gospel according to Matthew. In chapter 12, Jesus feeds the hungry, heals the sick, and casts out demons, while the religious authorities question his identity and the religious propriety of his work. Chapter 12 offers important and challenging spiritual reflection on particular types of healing that people and institutions continually need.

A good biblical sermon on Matthew 12:33–37 will attend to its historical and social contexts. Matthew writes to Jewish followers of Jesus, probably in Antioch, who have experienced intense sources of distress: the destruction of the temple, oppression at the hands of the Romans, and marginalization in the synagogue for their beliefs about Jesus. To the ears of marginalized hearers, this sharp critique of a particular group of Pharisees, representing authority and power, can be understood as Jesus' challenge to the oppressive forces of the times. To modern ears, Jesus' words also represent the hope of a divine challenge to the oppressive forces of today.

Matthew's first hearers were also wounded, responding to crises and interpersonal divisions. They

Matthew 12:33–37

Theological Perspective

Holiday's haunting song of the strange fruit hanging in the air, which showed the evil heart of the segregationalist culture that produced lynching. Nevertheless, from the same region during the same period, numerous missionaries went out to preach the gospel of Jesus Christ in Asia, Africa, and the Americas, which bear much fruit in today's global Christian movements.

It is to the religious teachers that Jesus warned of the destructive power of spoken words: that on the day of judgment one is to "give an account for every careless word" (v. 36). This warning reverberates with Jesus' reinterpretation in Matthew 5:21–25 of the sixth commandment, "You shall not murder." Jesus says that angry, insulting, demeaning, and unjust words, hurled toward a brother or a sister, deserve condemnation as murder. Whenever we speak damaging words to our brothers and sisters, it is as if these hurtful words were said to the Holy Spirit (v. 32). If one is to be "justified" or "condemned" by one's words/reasoning (*logos*), is it better to remain silent? Who keeps account of all the words one utters? If we successfully control our speech, do we not need to similarly worry about our actions?

Modern Protestants tend to reduce Luther's message of justification by faith alone into a gospel of laziness. Despite his reluctant acceptance of the letter of James, Luther never despised all works. His criticism was against the misguided reliance upon ceremonial works for justification. In *On Christian Liberty* (1520), Luther defined Christian identity this way: "A Christian is the most free lord of all, and subject to none; a Christian is the most dutiful servant of all, and subject to everyone."[1] Then he discussed the good works of love that Christians do for their neighbors because faith given by God in one's heart overflows as good words and works toward others.

In my classroom, I often hear self-righteous words against the supposed "works-righteous Catholics." Not so. Catholic teachings do not require the believers to do good works in order for them to gain entrance to heaven. They would agree that it is God's love that moves Christians to freely share their good fruit, good treasures, good heart, good words, and good works with their neighbors in everyday living.

In the long history of catechetical tradition, Christians observed the works of mercy in words and actions. Seven spiritual works of mercy are to admonish those in error; instruct the ignorant;

Pastoral Perspective

and actions have contributed to her pain. The story, though heavy-handed, is compelling, and its moral is that, since none of us fully knows what the impact of our words and actions might be, we had better take care. One of the teenage readers of the novel wrote the author to say that the book made her want to "be wonderful to everyone."[1]

In Matthew 12:36–37 Jesus himself sounds heavy-handed. "I tell you, on the day of judgment you will have to give an account for every careless word you utter; for by your words you will be justified, and by your words you will be condemned." The adjective translated here as "careless" (*argon*)—rendered in other versions as "idle" (KJV), "thoughtless" (REB), and "useless" (TEV)—literally means "not working." This is not to say that such words are nonfunctional, but that they do not function usefully or toward good ends. Unlike God's creating word, such words at best do nothing constructive and at worst are actively destructive. How many hundreds of thousands of words each day come flying out of our mouths, or from our fingertips onto a computer screen, or into our ears and minds? Do we stop to consider how the words are working, or how many may not be working at all for good purpose—just filling up space?

The issue of useless words takes on further weight for those of us whose work is words. "You can't order a poem like a taco / Walk up to the counter and say 'I'll take two,' / and expect it to be handed back to you ," poet Naomi Shihab Nye writes in "Valentine for Ernest Mann."[2] It sometimes feels as if pastors are called on to do nearly that, with sermons, prayers, and pastoral words for all occasions. Week by week, our words are ordered up, and we must deliver. How do we keep from losing our mindfulness about the importance of words and our sacred duty to tend them with care?

One of the great tasks of the church is the care of words. We give special attention to the words we say about God (what we call "theology"), but it is clear that Jesus commands us to give care to *all* our words. Throughout the Sermon on the Mount, he returns to the issue of our speech, addressing matters of anger (Matt. 5:22), oath taking (5:34), truthfulness and reliability (5:37), empty prayers (6:7), judgment and hypocrisy (7:15), and confessions of faith that are not backed up by faithful living (7:21–22). Later in

---

1. See the full text online via the Wittenberg Project at http://www.iclnet.org/pub/resources/text/wittenberg/luther/web/cclib-2.html; accessed October 1, 2012.

1. Jay Asher. "Knowing That Someone Understands," posted on November 21, 2008. http://www.myspace.com/jay_asher/blog/450767376; accessed February 9, 2012.
2. Naomi Shihab Nye, "Valentine for Ernest Mann," in *The Red Suitcase* (Rochester, NY: BOA Editions, Ltd., 1994), 70, lines 1–4.

spoken, which give witness to the substance of their hearts (v. 34b).

In response, Jesus repeats the words of John the Baptist from Matthew 3:7: "You brood of vipers!" (v. 34a). In chapter 3 the insult comes when the Pharisees and Sadducees approach John for baptism without bearing fruit "worthy of repentance." John goes on to state that "every tree therefore that does not bear good fruit is cut down and thrown into the fire" (3:10). Jesus' charge against the Pharisees and the language he uses pick up where John left off. The analogy of trees is also a clear reference to Jesus' earlier words in the Sermon on the Mount describing false prophets as wolves in sheep's clothing (7:15–20). That description ends with a pithy phrase that might summarize our passage as well: "Thus you will know them by their fruits" (7:20).

In verse 34, Jesus' vocabulary shifts from "bad" fruit (*karpos*) and trees to "evil" (*ponēros*) persons. The latter is a morally loaded term and gives further weight to the accusation against the Pharisees, perhaps recalling Jesus' words in Matthew 5:37, where speaking falsely is linked to the evil one. Thus Jesus here turns the Pharisees' claim against him in 12:24 back on them. They might sound pious and righteous, but the fruits they bear demonstrate that they are in fact evil, rotten to the core. The final clause of verse 34 is a summary statement of the passage and appears verbatim in Luke 6:45: the contents of one's heart are made manifest in the words that one speaks.

Verse 35 shifts the image from trees to treasure, but the message is the same: one's actions (or words) consistently, even if unintentionally, reveal the deepest values of the heart. The Pharisees are the owners of only bad treasure; so when they open their mouths, only false gold is released. The accusation against Jesus is the prime example for the readers of Matthew, who might also find a parallel to this second analogy in the Sermon on the Mount, Matthew 6:21: "where your treasure is, there your heart will be also." Indeed, the ethical themes of this passage resonate with the tone set in the Sermon on the Mount, emphasizing actions rather than words, as the best indicator of a person's convictions and character.

The concluding comments in verses 36–37 follow an introductory phrase of emphasis, "for I say to you that . . . " (*legō de hymin hoti*); a similar phrase introduced an earlier claim in 12:31. The term "careless word" (*rhēma argon*) is a bit enigmatic in the context. The adjective does not seem to describe accurately the Pharisaic response to Jesus' curing of the man possessed by a demon. These verses also shift

surely carried troubled hearts, and since "the mouth speaks out of an abundance of the heart," they too would have a propensity to speak harshly. So while Jesus here is correcting the wronghearted speech of mistrustful religious authorities, the teaching applies to all who carry wounds and weights in their hearts. We all need to tend to what we say, and to heal the places from which our caustic words come.

The literary context in which this text appears also assists its preaching. The Gospel of Matthew calls for rightheartedness in all aspects of life, which pours out of hearts and into the world by offering mercy wherever there is suffering, as exemplified by Jesus himself. Then, in the antecedent text, readers encounter the mercy and the challenge of Jesus. He heals a demoniac and rebukes the Pharisees who are more concerned with religiosity than healing. Embodying mercy and healing is the primary business of God's Spirit in Jesus, who has come to show us this way and cast out all that steers us off track. The reign of God has come to those who understand this (12:28).

Speech should be understood, according to this text, as fruit of the tree, or the product of a person's heart. As trees are known for their fruit, people are known for what they say. The command of the passage, "make the tree good, and its fruit good" (v. 33a), implies that good and evil are potentially shifting forces in the delicate ecosystem of a person, and that care for this ecosystem can help determine which fruit sprouts forth. This text, like the entire Gospel, is concerned with having a right heart so that everything we produce is righteous.

By drawing the connection between speech and the heart, the text does far more than encourage us to "watch what we say"—and so should the preacher. Since speech is a reflection of the heart of a person, speech can be understood as a tool for spiritual diagnosis. If, as Jesus says, "the mouth speaks out of the abundance of the heart," what does our speech say about the health of our hearts? Pastors, especially those who have had clinical education, may have their own experiences of self-diagnosis to offer as illustration. Give the congregation permission and space to consider this text's convicting connection between our speech and our hearts.

Jesus goes on to say that good people bring good things out of a good treasure, suggesting that in our speech we have an opportunity to choose what we draw from, either good treasure or bad treasure. When we draw upon good treasure, understood in Matthew's Gospel as the spirit of mercy and

Matthew 12:33–37

Theological Perspective

counsel the doubtful; comfort the sorrowful; bear wrongs patiently; forgive injuries; and pray for the living and the dead. Seven corporal works of mercy are based on Matthew 25:35–36: to feed the hungry; give drink to the thirsty; clothe the naked; shelter the homeless; visit the sick; visit those in prison; and give proper burial to the dead, especially those poor who cannot afford it.

My favorite model in this is Justa of Nagasaki, a new convert in the Jesuit Japan mission in the 1570s.[2] On her own initiative, Justa organized and led a consorority of married women to practice these works of mercy. Justa and her women admonished men who drank too much and disturbed the peace. They helped many destitute persons during the period of civil war there. They ran nursing homes for old men, women, and the terminally ill. Justa guided old women, who felt useless, to pray for the salvation of the people in the whole world. Because their good fruit was widely appreciated, the Japanese government that had already banned Christianity in 1587 did not stop these works of mercy until the last moment of persecution. Even after they destroyed the institutions in 1614, the members took the old, sick, and dying into their homes, bearing a strong testimony of Christian love to the anti-Christian society.

This returns me to the lesson on the good tree and its fruit. The cursed tree becomes a life-giving cross when Christ is hung on it to liberate humanity from the curse of the law (Gal. 3:13). If Christians, who are freed by this Christ, abide in Christ, the true vine, they bear good fruit, even to the point of giving up their lives for the sake of others (John 15:1–17). Christian freedom is not for self-congratulation and stagnation. It is the freedom to strive to love God, neighbors, and even enemies with all energy. If the church is practicing its faith daily, or living by the Spirit, it offers good fruit of love, joy, peace, patience, kindness, generosity, faithfulness, gentleness, and self-control (Gal. 5:22–23) to be enjoyed by many in this world who hunger for them.

HARUKO NAWATA WARD

Pastoral Perspective

Matthew, Jesus will make the shocking (and, to the Pharisees, offensive) claim that "it is not what goes into the mouth that defiles a person, but it is what comes out of the mouth that defiles" (15:11).

Jesus sets the notion of words in the context of character. "Out of the abundance of the heart the mouth speaks" (v. 34). Words reveal the heart; they are like doors that open, showing the world what is inside us and letting it out, for good or for ill. If the tree is good, the fruit—words and deeds—will be good. If the tree is bad, the fruit—words and deeds—will be bad (v. 33). Jesus is responding to men who, on seeing his healings and exorcisms (good fruit!), have declared it the work of Beelzebul (bad tree!). Such twisted words are sick fruit from sick trees. Their problem is not only their saying, but their seeing. They look at good and see it wrong, so they say it wrong, calling it evil. From Matthew's point of view, this shows that they are the ones who are evil.

However, the world is not as simple as Matthew's dualistic portrayal of it. Like weeds and wheat, good and evil are all mixed together in us; even our best intentions are bent. When Jesus says, "Make the tree good," we are left to wonder, "But how?" We cannot make a tree good; we can only nurture good conditions for its health and growth. Is it not also central to our faith that we can never make ourselves good? What we *can* do is confess our faith in the One who is good. If our confession of faith is more than a careless, idle, unworking word, then God's own word will take root in our hearts, grow in our lives, and bear good fruit.

STACEY SIMPSON DUKE

---

2. See Haruko Nawata Ward, *Women Religious Leaders in Japan's Christian Century, 1549–1650* (Hampshire, England: Ashgate, 2009), 295 ff.

from third-person to second-person language, giving rise to the supposition that their content is proverbial. Matthew has previously used "day of judgment" language in 10:15; 11:22; and 11:24, always to describe punishment for sin. Verse 37 brings Jesus' response to a clear ending and provides a fitting summary: spoken words are a faithful indicator of the nature of a person's heart, and therefore provide an appropriate basis for character judgment. The accusation of the Pharisees against Jesus provides an occasion for him to make clear the power of words to do far more damage than "sticks and stones." A similar perspective is offered later in the New Testament, in James 3:1–12.

In addition to echoing themes from Matthew's Sermon on the Mount, elements of this passage also appear in the so-called Sermon on the Plain in Luke 6. There they serve as general exhortation and instruction. In Matthew's telling, however, these words are placed in the context of clear confrontation with the Pharisees. In Matthew 9:34, when the Pharisees accuse Jesus of healing a demoniac by the power of demons, no words of self-defense are recorded. In chapter 12 his defense is vigorous and his charges against the Pharisees are forceful. Jesus here asserts that words matter because they reveal much about the heart of the speaker. The Pharisees' accusations against Jesus reveal the substance of their own character, for a person is known by the words and actions that flow from the heart. The concluding verses expand this teaching from the particularity of Jesus' encounter with the Pharisees to the universality of the coming day of judgment.

At that time, we will all be called to account for the fruit of our trees and the content of our treasure chests. By these words, we will be justified or condemned. The Pharisees have demonstrated the substance of their hearts to be evil by their words of condemnation against Jesus. Readers of Matthew's Gospel are given the opportunity and the charge to demonstrate our faith in Jesus Christ, the fruit of good trees, and the substance of hearts filled with the right things.

CHRISTOPHER A. HENRY

righteousness shown in Jesus Christ, our words contain goodness. When our words draw instead on our own sense of self, they risk being defined by our own reactions, wounds, and prejudices. Our self-reliant speech is uninspired, unreliable, and a broken treasure.

Take care in your words, says Jesus, because they reveal who you are. Draw your words from the good treasure of the merciful heart revealed for us in Jesus. Do not utter careless or lazy words, but be thoughtful and compassionate in all speech. The preacher can easily cite examples of careless and lazy speech from the arenas of politics or celebrity, but a more efficacious sermon will take on dangerous kinds of speech that fly under our usual radar, and maybe even emanate from our own lips.

One important arena of modern life to which this passage speaks is our digital life. Online technologies have expanded the scope and stakes of our words, increasing the capacity of our words for love or harm. The ease of publishing public words also encourages us to be lazy and careless about what we write. In all contexts, do we thoughtlessly use commonly accepted and casual words that are potentially offensive to other races, other religions, other classes, or other sexualities? Are our words thoughtless and careless, or are they drawing upon the treasure that is good, full of mercy, gentle, and open? The difference matters, and it is worth our attention.

This passage takes seriously the power of our words to destroy or to help save. Encourage the weary and divided people gathered before you to watch their mouths and the tender places in the heart from which our words come. We are called to carry forward the mercy given and shown to us by Jesus. If we embody this mercy, in action and in speech, we participate in God's growing reign in the world, and therein lies our salvation.

DAVID LOWER

Matthew 12:38–42

³⁸Then some of the scribes and Pharisees said to him, "Teacher, we wish to see a sign from you." ³⁹But he answered them, "An evil and adulterous generation asks for a sign, but no sign will be given to it except the sign of the prophet Jonah. ⁴⁰For just as Jonah was three days and three nights in the belly of the sea monster, so for three days and three nights the Son of Man will be in the heart of the earth. ⁴¹The people of Nineveh will rise up at the judgment with this generation and condemn it, because they repented at the proclamation of Jonah, and see, something greater than Jonah is here! ⁴²The queen of the South will rise up at the judgment with this generation and condemn it, because she came from the ends of the earth to listen to the wisdom of Solomon, and see, something greater than Solomon is here!"

Theological Perspective

Some religious leaders ask to see a sign or supernatural proof from Jesus the rabbi, who calls them harshly "an evil and adulterous generation" (v. 39a). According to Kaufmann Kohler, the rabbis did discuss the miraculous signs recorded in the Hebrew Scripture and the place of these in the Jewish faith, but always remained cautious about them, due to the Torah's warnings against "diviners by dreams" who promise "omens or portents" (Deut. 13:2–4). He claims that sign seeking "is certainly not true of the representatives and exponents of Judaism. Miracles, which occupy so conspicuous a place in the New Testament and in the history of Christianity, are viewed as matters of secondary importance throughout the rabbinical literature."[1] He was correct in detecting early Christian skepticism toward "the wonder-seeking Jews" (1 Cor. 1:22), as historically the church has often dismissed Jewish scholars' questions, simplistically repeating Jesus' and Paul's disapproval as its own. Here Jesus does not deny the possibility of signs, and he reminds the Pharisees of the familiar story of the prophet Jonah.

Jesus interprets the story of Jonah quite humorously. He equates Jonah's time in the fish's belly with

Pastoral Perspective

The popular atheist Web site "God Is Imaginary" lists fifty "proofs" that God is not real. The proofs focus on matters like prayer, miracles, heaven, science, and the Bible; the creator of the Web site has a big problem with Jesus too. "Jesus could have made his message so clear," the author writes, "and the proof of his godliness so obvious, that all six billion people on the planet would have aligned with him."[1] For some, the primary obstacle to following Jesus is a distinct lack of evidence that he was who the New Testament says he was.

Modern-day skeptics are not the first to have this problem with Jesus; they stand in a line in which many of us have also stood, with our own questions for him. The difference between us and the people who stood at the front of that line is that they got to approach him face to face. They did not ask for evidence; they demanded it (v. 38). One has to wonder what sort of sign might have satisfied them. They had already witnessed any number of miracles, but miracles were not what they were looking for. They were looking for unambiguous proof that Jesus was from God. The kingdom of heaven had drawn near in dramatic, visible ways, but the Pharisees had failed

1. See Kaufmann Kohler, "MIRACLE," in *Jewish Encyclopedia*, http://www.jewishencyclopedia.com/articles/10869–miracle; accessed on September 28, 2012.

1. "Proof #35—Notice Jesus' myopia." *God Is Imaginary*. http://godisimaginary.com/i35.htm; accessed February 9, 2011.

Exegetical Perspective

Jesus' contentious interaction with the religious authorities continues in Matthew 12:38–42, as the Pharisees and scribes demand to see some proof of his identity. The introduction of scribes into the scene may pick up the thread from 9:3, as their inclusion has no parallel in Mark or Luke. Regardless, the shared article ("the scribes and Pharisees," v. 38) suggests that Matthew refers to scribes of Pharisaic persuasion. The earlier narrative unambiguously identifies the collection of religious leaders as Jesus' opponents and makes readers aware that their motives are evil and their hearts filled with the wrong things (12:34–35).

Still, their request for a sign from Jesus could be taken as a concession on their part, an openness to accept his divine power if they see it for themselves. Without the context, their request could be read as an acknowledgment of Jesus' power to heal and a desire to see some manifestation of it. As it is, the request is further proof of the escalating tension between Jesus and the Pharisees.

It is also an opportunity for Matthew to portray ironically the willful ignorance (or denial) of the religious authorities. Clearly the Pharisees have already seen Jesus' miraculous healings in a variety of forms. Still they request a sign, a miraculous confirmation of Jesus' credibility and identity. The scribes and

Homiletical Perspective

As the rivalry between religious legalists and Jesus intensifies, the scribes and Pharisees want Jesus to prove himself. Apparently, their skepticism went unsatisfied by the preceding teachings, healings, and demon castings. Signs often speak to the legitimacy of the divine agent in question. The skeptics, however, consider Jesus illegitimate because he claims divine authority but does not conform to their interpretation of the religious traditions they uphold.

The request for a sign offers the preacher an opportunity to explore the difference between doubt, which can be a healthy attribute in a life of inquisitive faith, and distrust, which can operate as a form of spiritual blindness. Many faith communities will be full of good and faithful doubters on Sunday morning, persons who come to hear and wrestle and ask questions in their hearts. Preachers should be careful not to lump healthy doubting into the same category as what is exhibited by the religiously righteous scribes and Pharisees. Doubting people who look for or ask for signs of divine agency in the world are open to what might be signified.

Preacher Fred Craddock tells a story about the time he almost met Albert Schweitzer, the great German-French theologian, organist, doctor, and humanitarian. Craddock had just finished reading Schweitzer's controversial book *The Quest of*

Theological Perspective

the Son of Man's descent into the heart of the earth. One imagines Jonah and the Son of Man in dismay in these dark, warm, slimy, smelly places that can melt down their bodies. This passage inspired the early church iconography of Jonah's exodus from the Leviathan's mouth as Jesus' resurrection from death. Medieval Christians continued to speculate what Jesus was doing between the time of his death and resurrection, and what hell was like, especially in the light of the creed that says, "He descended to hell." In his Easter sermon in Torgou in 1533, Luther preached that Christ was already triumphant when he descended to Hades. Having destroyed the gates of Hades, Christ completes his mission by proclaiming salvation to the people of God and rescuing them from the power of death. In contrast, Calvin, in the *Geneva Catechism,* interpreted Jesus' suffering in hell as "excruciating agony of conscience" that he was forsaken by God. Calvin also taught that Christ "subdued and crushed" the power of hell for humanity's sake.

The important point that Jesus makes on "the sign of Jonah," though, was not about his trip to hell, but about voices of witness arising from unexpected peoples, pointing to Jesus as the sign. His first example is the Ninevites, who, upon hearing God's message from Jonah, immediately repented. Nineveh was "wicked," unlike "the cities in which most of [Jesus'] deeds of power had been done" (11:20–23). Jonah, an unwilling Israelite preacher, crossed over religious and cultural barriers and reached the hearts of the ancestors of today's Iraqis.

Jesus then brings up the queen of the South as another unexpected witness of God (v. 42), even though Jesus has just said that only the sign of Jonah is given, which he repeats later in 16:4. In this retelling of the story of queen of Sheba (1 Kgs. 10:1–13 and 2 Chr. 9:1–12), the aspect of her eagerness to come "from the ends of the earth to listen to the wisdom of Solomon" is highlighted. Having witnessed the wisdom of the wisest man, the queen also acknowledges the true wisdom, God the Sophia, Jesus.

With the people of Nineveh, the queen will "rise up at the judgment with this generation and condemn it" (v. 42). Matthew depicts something like a court scene, where the Ninevites and the queen of the South stand up as star witnesses as if to say, "Jesus Christ, right here in front of your eyes, is the one who is greater than Jonah and Solomon." The incarnation of God in Jesus Christ is greater than these signs. In the proclamation of the resurrection and divine wisdom beyond human understanding, there is good news.

Pastoral Perspective

to see; perhaps they had *refused* to see. What about us? What already-given signs have we failed to see?

Jesus did not take a pastoral tone with the Pharisees, but called them an evil and adulterous generation (v. 39). The implication was that their stance was not one of openness, even if they were to receive what they were asking for, but of hard-hearted argumentativeness. Matthew does not intend for us to sympathize with the Pharisees, but we can relate to their question. We might wish to see a sign too. Who of us has not wanted more evidence about Jesus?

Jesus told them they would get no sign except the sign of Jonah, an answer that hardly makes things easier for us. The story of Jonah in the belly of the sea monster may be as difficult to swallow as the story of Jesus being raised from the heart of the earth. Still, the comparison is instructive. Jesus did not deconstruct the "sign of Jonah" for them; he simply offered the promise of his death and resurrection in relation to that sign. Jonah became a sign to the Ninevites of God's mercy and compassion for them; the resurrection of Jesus will become a sign of God's mercy and compassion for all.

The Ninevites repented and called on the mercy of God, whom they did not know; Jonah, who did know God, decided he would rather die than live in a world governed by that mercy. The queen of Sheba came from the South to receive the wisdom of Solomon; his own sons refused to live by that wisdom. The sign of Jonah upends old assumptions and old patterns. Those who think they are on the inside find themselves cast out; those on the periphery find themselves brought to the very center of God's care. The sign of Jonah flips all the old powers and structures.

Is this not what Christ's death and resurrection finally did for us all? This is what Jesus said the sign of Jonah is: three days and three nights Jonah spent in the belly of the fish; for three days and three nights the Son of Man would be in the heart of the earth. (There is no sense in quibbling over Matthew's math; the point is that just as Jonah was swallowed up and spewed out, Jesus will be buried and raised.) Under this sign, the powerful will be brought down, the lowly will be lifted up, the hungry will be filled, the rich will be sent away, and in the final reversal, death itself will be swallowed up.

Not to embrace and live according to that sign is to face an inevitable judgment. Jesus puts it this way: the Ninevites, who responded and repented at the preaching of a prophet, will rise up at the judgment and condemn "this generation," who, when

Pharisees address Jesus as "teacher," a common title given him by opponents in Matthew's Gospel (see 9:11; 17:24; 19:16). The title is one of respect and is not incorrect, but it is incomplete.

We cannot determine what kind of sign the religious leaders request, but there is precedent for the validation of a prophet through the performing of miraculous signs. We find examples in OT figures such as Moses (Exod. 3–4), Saul (1 Sam. 10:1–9), Elijah (1 Kgs. 18:17–40), and Isaiah (Isa. 7:11–14).

Jesus' response in verse 39 destroys any possibility of softening his conflict with the Pharisees, which began with the healing of a demoniac in verse 22. For the first time, these opponents are taken as representatives of their generation, one that Jesus labels "evil and adulterous" and to whom he offers only the "sign of the prophet Jonah" (v. 39). Jesus' description of his generation, his refusal to comply with the request, and the introduction of the sign of Jonah all demand further exploration and provide interesting avenues of interpretation and proclamation.

When Jesus describes his opponents as "evil," he refers to their own accusation in 12:24 that his healing power comes from Beelzebul, the ruler of demons. As he has previously implied, the words of the Pharisees are evil and give voice to *their* association with Beelzebul. The adjective "adulterous" is unique to Matthew's account of this interaction. Relevant OT models for this usage appear in the prophets Ezekiel (16:38 and 23:45) and Hosea (3:1, whose LXX translation "evil and adulterous" is precisely Matthew's language), where Jerusalem, Israel, and Judah are all compared to an adulterous woman. Thus the generation of whom Jesus speaks (through their representatives the Pharisees and scribes) resembles the unrighteous generation sent into exile in Babylon.

Jesus' labeling of the generation leads to his refusal to grant a sign. Why would he refuse the request? The most apparent reason is that the religious authorities have proven themselves unwilling or unable to acknowledge the myriad signs that they have already witnessed. In describing the generation as "adulterous," Jesus uses the Hebrew Bible's metaphoric description of unfaithfulness. If both evil and unfaithfulness are at the heart of the request of the scribes and Pharisees, then they deserve no response from Jesus. Further, the use of the passive voice in verse 39 ("no sign will be given") indicates that the refusal of a sign comes directly from God.

Still, Jesus does offer a sign to the religious leaders, albeit one that they would not have expected or understood. As a sign to them, he describes the story

the Historical Jesus and had a legal pad filled with critiques of the author's work. In particular, Craddock thought Schweitzer's search for the Jesus of history left the reader with no reason to worship. "Not enough Jesus to believe in," he wrote on his pad, and he went to a Schweitzer concert to confront Schweitzer and his watered-down pseudointellectual theology. Craddock was prepared to take Schweitzer to task for his paper-thin Jesus during the postconcert discussion.

Then Schweitzer stepped to the podium: "I appreciate the hospitality of you all and of this church. I'd like to stay longer and take questions, but I can't. My patients in Africa need me. They are dying, children and their mothers and fathers, dying at home. I have to go. But if you have the love of Jesus in your heart, maybe you will come with me?" With that, Schweitzer walked out of the room. Craddock looked down at his legal pad, filled to the margins with criticism. "In that moment I was changed. I knew what it was to be a Christian, and I hoped someday I would be."[1] Doubt can be persuaded by signs of truth.

Doubt functions differently from distrust, which is a more accurate description of the character exhibited by the religious authorities in their encounter with Jesus. Doubt keeps the door open with questions and wondering, while distrust seeks to keep the door closed, causing an inability to see or hear the truth from anywhere except oneself.

Preachers who can illustrate the way that distrust operates destructively in our times and in our hearts will bring the problem of Jesus' rivals to life. Distrust is a plague upon our nations, our politics, and our churches. Distrust prohibits openness, respect, mutuality, and compromise. A few months ago, I had an experience of distrust when a different-minded Christian asked me, during an intense theological conversation, "Pastor, forgive me, but are you saved?" Our mutual distrust was crippling to the experience, the relationship, and any possibility of redemption in the moment. This passage provides an opportunity to explore the ways that members of the assembly may distrust "other-minded Christians" and what limitations that places on the Christian community that we are called to be together.

The point of the opening verse is that while we all want signs of divine presence and power to assuage our healthy doubts, there is no sign that can satisfy distrust. Only sustained mutual relationship has the power to heal the blindness of distrust. While Jesus

1. Fred Craddock, *Craddock Stories* (Atlanta: Chalice Press, 2001), 125–26.

Matthew 12:38–42

Theological Perspective

Amy-Jill Levine, a New Testament and Jewish studies scholar, comments that Matthew uses examples of autonomous women who "assume positive, active roles in the Gospel."[2] In the example of the queen of the South she also sees Matthew elevating "those who do not exploit the position of power" and condemning "attitudes of complacency."

With Matthew, we may want to ask: At which point and in what places does our church today remain complacent? The witnesses again may rise from forgotten or unexpected places. One witness comes from one of the three women Nobel Peace Prize laureates of 2011, Tawakkol Karman. In her acceptance lecture, she calls for the witness of the queens of Sheba, named Arwa and Bilqis, in her Yemeni Arab Muslim tradition:[3]

> Here I am, in this unique moment, one of the most important moments of human history, coming from the land of the Arab Orient, coming from the land of Yemen, the Yemen of wisdom and ancient civilizations, the Yemen of more than five thousand years of long history, the great Kingdom of Sheba, the Yemen of the two queens Bilqis and Arwa.

Referring to the wise rule of her beloved queens, whose reigns were devoted to the peace and welfare of their people, Tawakkol condemns the current situation of bloodshed, caused by the powerful dictators, which is overlooked by the world leaders, and upholds her vision of "true globalization of peace and equity" for all.

This reading from Matthew, which names some witnesses from Israel, Iraq, and Yemen, can provide a starting point for interreligious and ecumenical dialogue, in the light of the signs of the Spirit of God at work today in unexpected places, and help Christians move out of our complacency.

HARUKO NAWATA WARD

Pastoral Perspective

confronted by someone far greater than Jonah, did not repent. We do not typically think of the day of judgment in those terms, one group of people rising up to condemn another. Still, the image has relevance, especially if we think less of what happens in the future and more of what is already happening in the present.

Whose faith would shame our own? Often the most faithful people we know are those on the edges—the poor, the elderly, the sick, the children. Like the Ninevites, their faith is not propped up by a system that puts them in the center or in control. The strength and vitality of their faith seems to come from a willingness to respond to God out of need, not demand; out of powerlessness, not presumption; out of readiness, not refusal. Truly their faith is a kind of judgment on ours; and as judgment, it becomes for us both a question and an invitation. Might our faith grow toward a faith like theirs—and, if so, how?

It will not be with the help of hard evidence. We will never get that kind of proof. Jesus says the only sign we get is the sign of Jonah. The only sign we get is Christ crucified, Christ raised. The sign we get is the one we need: old powers and principalities have been overthrown, sin and death have been undone, love has been unleashed, and God is on the loose. The proof we need is the one we live: lives remade by God's grace, our repentance, and Christ's compassion born in us, a compassion that will know no boundaries. We do not need more evidence; we are the evidence. We do not need another sign; we, Christ's church, broken and blundering as we are, are becoming the sign. Our regenerated lives are the sign of Jonah: Christ crucified and raised.

STACEY SIMPSON DUKE

---

2. Amy-Jill Levine, "Matthew," in *Women's Bible Commentary*, ed. Carol A. Newsom and Sharon H. Ringe (Louisville, KY: Westminster John Knox Press, 1998), 252–53.

3. See "Tawakkol Karman – Nobel Lecture: In the name of God the Compassionate the Merciful" (Nobelprize.org. 15 Dec. 2011) via http://www.nobelprize .org/nobel_prizes/peace/laureates/2011/karman–lecture_en.html. See http:// www.wisemuslimwomen.org/muslimwomen/bio/queen_arwa_al–sulayhi on Yemeni Queens of Sheba; both accessed on October 3, 2012.

of Jonah. The emphasis of this sign falls not on the miraculous deeds of Jesus but on his death and resurrection, still to come. Using the language of Jonah 1:17, Jesus suggests that just as the prophet was in the belly of the sea monster for three days and three nights, so the Son of Man will be in the heart of the earth for that length of time. Although the accounting does not match (Jesus was "in the heart of the earth" only two nights), the implication is quite clear: just as his time in the belly of the sea monster confirmed Jonah's role as a preacher of judgment, so Jesus' death and resurrection will confirm his identity as righteous judge. The sign of Jonah, Jesus' death and resurrection, is not a "sign" in the sense that the Pharisees and scribes have requested, but it does serve as a confirmation of his role as judge achieved through rejection and suffering.

Verses 41 and 42 give two examples, one prophetic and one royal, that continue the theme of judgment and elevate Jesus and his ministry, while also expanding the reach of his reign. In these verses, Jesus is described as both "something greater than Jonah" (v. 41) and "something greater than Solomon" (v. 42). In the first example, the people of Nineveh are given the place of judge over the present generation, because of their repentance through the proclamation of Jonah. The scene described is the final judgment, and the people of Nineveh are sharply contrasted with the people of Jesus' generation. In the second example, "the queen of the South," unnamed but clearly a reference to the queen of Sheba and her visit to Solomon (1 Kgs. 10:1–13), also rises at the judgment to condemn this generation, and is praised for her acceptance of the wisdom of Solomon.

Both the people of Nineveh and the queen of Sheba represent Gentiles who are receptive to God's purposes, a possible reference to Jesus' words to the centurion in Matthew 8:10–13. As the encounter between Jesus and his religious opponents moves toward conclusion, there is an expansion of scope. The Pharisees and scribes have become representatives for an entire generation of faithless evildoers, and Jesus' reign, confirmed in his death and resurrection, takes in Gentiles as well as his own people.

CHRISTOPHER A. HENRY

says no new sign will be given, he points out that the sign has already been given through the prophet Jonah. The sign is old and familiar, in the story of Jonah and right under their religious noses. Jesus relates the time span of Jonah's deadly jump and deliverance to the time span of the coming death and raising of the Son of Man. Jonah's deliverance foreshadows Jesus' deliverance. The things of old point to the things yet to come.

While the true sign of Jesus' divine agency and power, the resurrection, is yet to come, in the meantime, the sign is repentant people who have witnessed deliverance. The people of Nineveh, who turned back from their wickedness, and the queen of Sheba, who turned toward the wisdom of Solomon, are historical figures of repentance, who stand in contrast to the present unrepentant generation. The preacher should clarify the word "repentance" (*metanoia*), better translated as a wholesale change of mind and heart to faith in God. Those who repent and turn to God, even those witnesses to us from the ancient past, are redeemed and shine a revealing light on those who do not! The characters on the witness stand cast extra judgment on the reigning religious establishment, for the Assyrian Ninevites and the Egyptian queen, although outsiders, demonstrate the very transformation asked of Jews and Christians.

Wisdom is another theme the preacher may choose to draw out of the text. Jesus links the revelation in his death and resurrection to the divine wisdom tradition, and even suggests it is greater. Perhaps the wisdom revealed in Jesus is greater because it is embodied more than spoken, or because it is more articulate about the risky self-giving to which all are called, or because Christ's wisdom is given for all and not just the religious few. This is the full culmination of the wisdom of God, an ancient wisdom that can be attested by the repentant. When we grasp the depths to which God will go to bring us back from chaos and despair, we come to understand the fullness of God's love, which will wash away our doubt and distrust, and leave us standing convicted and redeemed.

DAVID LOWER

Matthew 12:43–45

⁴³"When the unclean spirit has gone out of a person, it wanders through waterless regions looking for a resting place, but it finds none. ⁴⁴Then it says, 'I will return to my house from which I came.' When it comes, it finds it empty, swept, and put in order. ⁴⁵Then it goes and brings along seven other spirits more evil than itself, and they enter and live there; and the last state of that person is worse than the first. So will it be also with this evil generation."

Theological Perspective

These words of Jesus, an exorcist, refer back to his curing a blind and mute demoniac and the subsequent discussion of the power by which Jesus exorcised (12:22–32). To call the mentally ill or communicatively handicapped demon possessed is offensive to our sensitivity. On the one hand, we sympathize with many who suffer from illnesses that modern medicine and science cannot cure and who seek healing in religious miracles. On the other hand, we remain skeptical of religious healers, especially when we hear of their abuse of power for personal gains. While ritual exorcism has mostly disappeared from mainline Protestant denominations, in various churches in North America and in other parts of the world, it continues to provide an important ministry of healing. The church is still charged to exorcise the power of evil and exercise the power of the Spirit for the healing of those who suffer.

We receive some wisdom from Christian history. Just as we read here that the expelled spirit roams through the waterless regions, the image of the desert as a demon-haunted place became a shared symbol in monastic spirituality. In the early church period, ascetic monks went out of the cities into the desert to wrestle with the demons. In the *Sayings of the Desert Fathers and Mothers* one finds interesting stories in which these wise women and men encounter demons

Pastoral Perspective

If you visit the self-help section of any bookstore, you will find a multitude of books that will show you how to get your house, your waistline, your finances, and your life in order. The allure of these books is the manageability of their programs: solutions exist in a matter of steps, days, or weeks. You can conquer clutter with three steps, beat depression with six steps, cultivate success with seven habits, achieve optimum health in eight weeks, find financial freedom in nine steps, gain self-esteem in ten days, and unlock your creativity in twelve weeks. The implied promise of all of these programs is the sense that with the help of tools, tips, and techniques, we can wrestle our lives into some sort of order. Many of us long for the stability and peace that we assume come with such a tidy life.

We may not think of purity and cleanliness in the same way that people of faith did in Jesus' day, but we can understand the desire for it. We may not resonate with the notion of demons, but we can understand the sense of chaos, powerlessness, and mess that comes with feeling in the grip of something beyond our control. There are forces at work in the world and within us—unclean spirits, you could call them—that stand in opposition to what is holy and healthy and loving and good. To find ourselves released from such a "possession" is the work of

Exegetical Perspective

This latest episode in the dispute between Jesus and the religious officials begins when Jesus casts out a demon and heals a man who is both blind and mute, drawing accusations from the Pharisees that his power comes through Beelzebul, the ruler of demons. In his final words to the Pharisees and scribes, Jesus reframes this exorcism as a dire warning to the people of his generation, using a parable quite likely drawn from tradition. The demon he has cast out, he explains, goes in search of a new dwelling place, eventually returning to the empty vessel that it has left behind.

These verses fit well within the overall context of Jesus' healing of the demoniac and his harsh words toward the Pharisees, though the break between verses 42 and 43 seems quite abrupt until the final sentence of verse 45, in which the reference to "this evil generation" returns. These comments from Jesus are best understood as a parable, using the particular exorcism as context for a more universal moral story and warning.

Perhaps referring to the demon expelled in 12:22, Jesus now labels it an "unclean spirit," a term also used to describe demon possession in 10:1, where the disciples are given the authority to perform exorcisms. Here, however, the text gives no specific reason for the unclean spirit's exit. The emphasis is

Homiletical Perspective

Jesus has just taken up the subject of repentance or *metanoia*, which includes letting the gospel of God's love deliver us from the depths. However, submitting ourselves to God, letting ourselves be delivered, and changing our orientation toward God, is vulnerable and risky business. Unclean spirits do not leave forever, according to these words of Jesus. They multiply, return, and haunt.

This passage has the spooky feel of an Edgar Allan Poe story, with spirits ganging up to ruin a person. While most preachers cannot cast out demons, we can cast out modern demonizing. Unclean spirits are not to be understood as the stuff of a Bram Stoker fantasy novel. They are real forces at work upon us and through us that turn us away from the ways of God. Also, unclean spirits are to be understood not as dirty but as unholy.

We have modern frameworks through which to understand unclean spirits, thanks to psychology and spiritual direction. We know the things that drive us away from our authentic self are usually shaped by experiences like wounds, fears, and grief; or sometimes by unrefined characteristics like apathy, pride, and self-righteousness. While psychological approaches to naming and understanding the unholy issues that bind us up are helpful and therapeutic, the spirit-world framework also has wisdom

Matthew 12:43–45

Theological Perspective

within and without. From the desert, voices of the prophets also rose against the evils of the dominant society. Social historians such as Peter Brown interpret some demons as manifestations of racism, sexism, and classism in the Roman Empire.[1]

Such feelings of social and ecclesiastical marginalization and voices of resistance appear often in the writings of medieval visionary women. Psychological historians such as Rudolph Bell explain these women's refusal of food as psychosomatic illness.[2] Theological historians such as Caroline Walker Bynum see these women's acts as deeply rooted in their eucharistic theology.[3] Forbidden by the church to be priests, Catherine of Siena and numerous other women refused to eat but gave away food to the poor and served the sick, like Jesus, while they received communion directly from Christ in their visions. In sixteenth-century Spain, Teresa of Ávila regarded her monastery as the desert in the city, where she taught ways of prayer in a time of spiritual aridness. She used the traditional rhetoric "mere woman" subversively to combat the evil spirits that possessed the church of her time, which was plagued by incompetent male leadership and which criminalized people of Jewish and Muslim lineage. The monastic tradition has continued to provide a desert where monks face internal and external demons in prayer and work and send out the spirit of protest and healing to the world.

Note that the exorcised evil spirits never leave us alone. The unclean spirit comes back to repossess its "home," now that it is "empty, swept, and put in order" (v. 44b). It brings a company of seven friends "more evil than itself," with the result that "the last state of that person is worse than the first" (v. 45). Does this mean that even though a person is cleaned up, she or he can again become possessed and defiled? Can we prevent these spirits from coming back?

During the late Middle Ages, sudden death was very possible due to plague, war, and famine. Even more terrifying was spiritual death. Preachers encouraged Christians to examine their conscience frequently. The doctrine of seven mortal sins became popular in these *ars moriendi* (art of dying) sermons. These seven (wrath, envy, greed, gluttony, sloth, lust,

1. See Peter Brown, *The Body and Society: Men, Women and Sexual Renunciation in Early Christianity* (New York: Columbia University Press, 1988).

2. See Rudolph M. Bell, *Holy Anorexia* (Chicago: University of Chicago Press, 1985).

3. See Caroline Walker Bynum, *Holy Feast and Holy Fast: The Religious Significance of Food to Medieval Women* (Berkeley: University of California Press, 1987).

Pastoral Perspective

grace (and grace can surely come at times through working the steps, the habits, or the weeks of a program). The question is, what happens next?

Following the healing and the exorcism of a blind and mute demoniac, Jesus speaks of how an unclean spirit, having gone out of a person, wanders through waterless regions looking for a resting place. When it cannot find a place to go, it returns to the house (the person) from which it came and finds that house "empty, swept, and put in order" (v. 44b). What might be an appealing image, to those of us searching for a sense of order in our lives, is used here by Jesus to show what happens when we get rid of a mess and allow the space it claimed in our lives to lie empty. That emptiness is an invitation for the problem (or obsession, habit, addiction, or sickness) to return eightfold.

In her essay "Settling for Less," a meditation on Luke 4:13 and the meaning of Lent, Barbara Brown Taylor writes, "I am convinced that 99 percent of us are addicted to something, whether it is eating, shopping, blaming or taking care of other people. The simplest definition of an addiction is anything we use to fill the empty place inside of us that belongs to God alone."[1] That hollow place is meant to be a holy place, a dwelling place for God.

When we have been released from whatever else has possessed, obsessed, or defined us, what do we do with the gap that is left? We can leave it untended and empty, vulnerable to whatever else seeks to take hold. We can fill it up with more things that do not satisfy. On the other hand, we can yield it to God, who in Christ "fills all in all" (Eph. 1:23). When the writer of Ephesians speaks of Christ filling all things, he is speaking not of individuals but of the church, noting that the church is the body of Christ, "the fullness of him who fills all in all" (Eph. 1:23). Likewise, the implications of this parable move from personal to communal. What is true for the individual—the empty space will become occupied—is also true for the community of faith. If the church is not occupied with the pursuit of God and the fullness of Christ, then it is an empty house susceptible to occupation by dangerous substitutes.

Linguist Geoff Nunberg declared the word "occupy" to be the 2011 "Word of the Year."[2] After the Occupy Wall Street movement, the word "occupy" became shorthand for the concept of

1. Barbara Brown Taylor, "Settling for Less," *The Christian Century*, February 18, 1998, 169.

2. Geoff Nunberg, "'Occupy': Geoff Nunberg's 2011 Word of the Year," Fresh Air from WHYY, posted December 7, 2011. http://www.npr.org/2011/12/07/143265669/occupy–geoff–nunbergs–2011–word–of–the–year.

Exegetical Perspective

clearly *not* on exorcism as such, but rather on the demon's departure and search for a "resting place." A number of commentators suggest that the parable draws on a traditional and well-known story, pointing to another potential reference in 2 Peter 2:17–20. There too those who "escape the defilements of the world" are "again entangled in them and overpowered"; thus "the last state has become worse for them than the first." There are clear parallels in the two accounts, though the immediate context in 2 Peter is the danger of false teaching rather than demon possession. It is, of course, plausible that the latter would give rise to the former, just as Jesus has earlier described, "By your words you will be condemned" (Matt. 12:37).

After exiting a person, the unclean spirit is described as wandering through "waterless regions" or deserts, a common home of demons in Old Testament texts and the place of the devil's temptations of Jesus in 4:1–11. Still, the specific term finds no easy parallels in other New Testament texts and is probably best understood as a more generic description of areas where humans are most vulnerable and often fail to thrive.

The brief soliloquy from the unclean spirit shifts the focus from aimless wandering to a directed attack on "the house from which it came," that is, the person who was formerly possessed. In Mark 9:25, Jesus explicitly forbids an unclean spirit from reentering the body of a young boy after he performs an exorcism. Here no such command is given. The emphasis is not on exorcism or repossession, but on the emptiness of formerly possessed persons. Here we find a commentary on the emptiness, and therefore vulnerability to evil, of the current generation. The unclean spirit finds an empty space in the body of its former host. To make matters worse for the one who has been possessed, the single unclean spirit gathers others "more evil than itself" (v. 45), who also make a home in the person. The conclusion is a statement of the obvious: "the last state of that person is worse than the first." Jesus closes the encounter by making the implications of the parable quite apparent and concrete, linking the story to the "evil generation" represented by his religious opponents in 12:39.

This odd parable comes at the end of Jesus' contentious interaction with Pharisees who accuse him of being possessed by evil demons. In this context, it serves as a sharp warning of the danger that awaits those who refuse to accept the signs that Jesus offers and instead accuse him of evil. A demon is cast out

Homiletical Perspective

and value, because unclean spirits like old wounds often behave more like demons than they do like conditions. Unclean spirits can function like beings that possess us more than like psychological issues that harm us.

Unholy spirits are possessive and personal because they are rooted in particular experiences and perspectives. They cannot find another resting place because they are born and bred in people, and thus are unique to them. Unholy spirits persist, and we should beware of their return.

As a boy, I remember attending a living room memorial service during which a pastor, who did not know the deceased or her family very well, offered kind words of prayer about her life and achievements and acknowledged the solace that she now rests in heaven. At that point a man angrily interrupted the prayer: "You are speaking lies! I do not even know who you are talking about. That old woman was wicked and abusive and poisonous. And I'm not the only one who's glad she's dead! If there's a hell, that's where she is!" The man of the astonishing and inappropriate outburst was her son, who had suffered at her hands. Although he had put those wounds in a closet of his heart, they multiplied and returned as an uncontrollable and venomous force prompted by the pastor's prayer, a prayer that might have been chastened by a pastoral visit to the family prior to the service.

We should all be wary of the unclean spirits at work upon us. Pastors know full well how unholy spirits can possess communities too, and may find an opportunity to let this text shed light on the spirits at work in a particular community. Family-systems theory illumines the deep and lasting power that unclean spirits can have. Families, communities, and churches can sweep themselves clean and maintain an appearance of order and tidiness on the surface, while on the inside they are empty and driven by fear. This text may present an important opportunity to name, carefully, the oft-hidden damaging spirits that persist in the community, like patriarchy, classism, racism, and religious discrimination.

The preacher must also make explicit the solution Jesus implies: keep evil spirits out of your house by filling it up! The word Matthew uses that is translated "empty" is an unusual word, a participle meaning "having leisure."[1] The empty house is unoccupied and at leisure, not inhabited with good words and

---

1. Douglas R. A. Hare, *Matthew*, Interpretation series (Louisville, KY: Westminster/John Knox Press, 1993), 144–45.

Matthew 12:43–45

Theological Perspective

and pride) lead to the destruction of individuals' spirits and do harm to those around them.

What if the power of the evil spirits becomes too overwhelming, even for Christians who are vigilantly trying to keep their conscience clean? Jesus' concluding remark against "this evil generation" again points more toward the collective conscience than the individual one. Evil resides in the generation of the religious leadership that prefers to maintain the status quo, even after they witness Jesus' healing exorcism.

During the Reformations period, while religious and civil leaders were busy defining who the worthy poor were, laypersons and monks networked across their confessional divide and provided nursing and other charitable care for all persons in need. Their love for their neighbors moved them to act. Today we need to examine our conscience to see if we demonize others while we ignore the evil spirits within us. Are spirits of wrath, envy, greed, gluttony, sloth, lust, and pride dwelling in us and leading to the destruction of our own lives, families, and communities? Are we tempted to acquire cheap goods made by the hands of the global poor who are forced into slave labor? Are these spirits leading us to wage wars that produce a massive population of injured and displaced? Are they leading us to abuse the environment and hurt ecosystems that sustain all of life? With present-day monks such as Sister Simone Campbell and the Nuns on the Bus, we might ask how the church cares for the neighbors who are suffering from numerous systemic social evils.

In the earlier discourse, we learned that it is "by the Spirit of God" that Jesus "cast out demons" (12:28). Jesus also gave the twelve apostles "authority over unclean spirits, to cast them out, and to cure every disease and every sickness" (10:1). We pray that the same Spirit fills and empowers the church for the task of discerning evil spirits and delivering those who suffer under their bondage.

HARUKO NAWATA WARD

Pastoral Perspective

working to overturn power, simply by the act of habitation. "Occupation" is a Jesus word too; he comes to cleanse but, much more, to inhabit, to give life, and to give it in abundance.

A practice of *lectio divina* could help a person explore this text in a meaningful way. Let the text ask intimate questions: What unclean spirits have taken hold of my life? Have I been released? How have I attempted to keep my life clean, orderly, and controlled? How have I kept even God at a distance? What harmful habits, obsessions, drives, or addictions might be lying in wait for me, if I do not tend to my soul? What kind of invitation or commitment might I need to make, in order to allow God to dwell more deeply in me, to move into my empty spaces? This could be an illuminative passage to explore as part of a Lenten practice or in a retreat setting. It could be used as part of communal practice as well, for inviting a congregation to consider what occupies center place in its life together.

The flipside of this text cannot be neglected. We will not likely be filled with the Spirit's new presence apart from having been cleansed of assumptions, attitudes, and behaviors that oppose and crowd out newness. There are necessary exorcisms to be undergone and new purities to be yearned for and claimed. Being cleansed is never the goal; rather, the goal is making way for the fuller reign of God within us and among us. As Thomas G. Long writes, "The Christian life is not merely the absence of bad things; it is the presence of good things. The life of faith is not a vacant lot where sin used to be; it is an active neighborhood where justice, mercy, and peace live together."[3]

STACEY SIMPSON DUKE

---

3. Thomas G. Long, *Matthew* (Louisville, KY: Westminster John Knox Press, 1997), 143.

Exegetical Perspective

at the beginning of the encounter, but unless the vacated space is filled with the clean spirits and good intentions, matters will become even worse. Within the parable, the conclusion is a proliferation of unclean spirits, resulting in an aggregation of evil.

Outside of the parable, the encounter ends with Jesus' dire warning to "this evil generation" (v. 45). The multiplication of evil described in the parable is also taking place within the community of those who refuse to accept Jesus' divine power and instead accuse him of demon possession and evil intention. Their "houses" are empty of God's Spirit and are therefore susceptible to unclean and evil spirits. The specific punishment warned against is unclear, but likely refers to the scenarios described in 12:41–42, in which Gentiles rise up at the judgment to condemn those who have failed to believe the multitude of signs offered in the life and ministry of Jesus.

It is not surprising that these difficult verses do not appear as part of any lectionary readings. Still, they provide a helpful and appropriate summary of the encounter between Jesus and the Pharisees that begins in 12:22 with the healing of a demoniac. Each side accuses the other of evil power and intentions throughout the confrontation, but Jesus has the final word. Again, the Pharisees serve as representatives for their generation, which has become an empty vessel filled with faithlessness and evil. Though they have been given every opportunity to see, hear, and accept the power of God at work in the life and ministry of Jesus, this "evil and adulterous generation" has chosen the path of faithlessness.

Their refusal to hear and believe Jesus is not merely a rejection of God; it is an invitation to the powers of evil. The parable makes it clear that the life of faith is not merely the absence of unclean spirits but the presence of God's Spirit. It is not only the absence of bad fruit but the presence of good fruit. The language may be harsh and grim, but the warning is as clear and necessary in the contemporary context as it was when first delivered.

CHRISTOPHER A. HENRY

Homiletical Perspective

works. Fill the house with God's Word through worship and study, and with God's living Spirit through community and mission work. The empty, swept, and tidy house will eventually be filled with something. So fill it with the good things of the gospel-inspired life: mercy and righteousness. This is the true wisdom, fully revealed in Jesus Christ, who has come to save us all from our unholy, obsessive, and purposeless involvements, so that we may have our lives filled with the right things.

A man named Charlie told me his story a few years ago at a dinner party.

> Two years ago, I lost my job at a chemical plant. I was depressed and felt worthless to the world. I took a job as a custodian at a local high school to try to make ends meet, and the ridicule and hurt those kids put on me every day was intolerable. At the end of my rope, I was angry, scared, and frustrated. But something deep inside me helped me realize that those nasty kids were angry and scared too, like me.
>
> I decided I would try to do what I could to help those kids earlier in their lives, so I transferred to a job cleaning up at the local elementary school. I see the makings of all those mean kids there; they live in the ghetto and they're mad and they don't know why they're mad. When I see them out of line, I call them out and talk to them. I've been there, I tell them, and they should be angry about being poor, getting bullied by gangs, and watching the school and community just sit there while it happens. But I tell them God knows it doesn't have to be this way, that they don't have to be this way.

Charlie cleaned out the old unclean spirits and, instead, filled his house and his community with new spirits inspired by God's love and hope.

Beware of unclean spirits and their return. Be vigilant. The God-filled life requires constant attention to what resides in you and in the communities of which you are a part. Fill yourself up, and fill your communities up with the merciful, compassionate, and loving activity of God, and the unholy things that possess you will eventually run out of room.

DAVID LOWER

Matthew 12:46–50

⁴⁶While he was still speaking to the crowds, his mother and his brothers were standing outside, wanting to speak to him. ⁴⁷Someone told him, "Look, your mother and your brothers are standing outside, wanting to speak to you." ⁴⁸But to the one who had told him this, Jesus replied, "Who is my mother, and who are my brothers?" ⁴⁹And pointing to his disciples, he said, "Here are my mother and my brothers! ⁵⁰For whoever does the will of my Father in heaven is my brother and sister and mother."

Theological Perspective

In Matthew, Jesus is not a "family values" preacher. While he does quote Genesis in response to a question about divorce, saying, "a man shall leave his father and mother and be joined to his wife" (Matt. 19:5), he nowhere speaks of procreation as the principal end of these relationships. He does not hold up the nuclear family as the root of moral and ethical decency. He certainly does not provide an ideal model of filial piety.

Relativizing Family. The renunciation of families is not uncommon in the world's religious traditions. In the Hindu tradition defined by the *Laws of Manu*, the renouncer (*sannyasin*) stage of life follows three earlier stages: student, householder, and retiree. Severing ties with community frees the renouncer from attachments that may stand in the way of spiritual liberation. Ordinarily one renounces family only after one has fulfilled one's responsibilities to it. There are important exceptions to this rule, however. The great teacher Sankara became a *sannyasin* during his studenthood, and Siddhartha Gautama (the Buddha) left behind a wife and a newborn baby. In each case, men severed ties with their families in order to seek enlightenment.

Matthew emphasizes the potential for faith in Jesus to drive a wedge between family members; for him,

Pastoral Perspective

Idolatry of the Family. We have all seen them—on billboards, four-color mailers, the cover of church-related catalogs, and congregational Web sites—the perfect "family," featuring a smiling father, mother, and 2.2 children. They may not look like most of the people in our local parish, but we know them all the same.

Idolatry is a strong word but perhaps the most appropriate one here: idolatry of the narrow, limited way our culture in the United States defines family; idolatry of the so-called nuclear family as the one true form of family, which ultimately must be protected at any cost. Janet Fishburn writes:

> Family idolatry is a tragically misdirected form of religious devotion. It involves a preference for the familiar over the unknown, the local over the universal, and treats the familiar and local as if they were absolute. When Christians direct reverence toward love of family without acknowledging the source of that love, they may imagine they are expressing reverence for Christ when they are, in fact, engaging in idolatry.[1]

Consciously or unconsciously most churches and preachers have bought into this "American Dream"

1. Janet Fishburn, *Confronting the Idolatry of the Family: A New Vision for the Household of God* (Nashville: Abingdon Press, 1991), 107.

Exegetical Perspective

Jesus' work as a traveling preacher took him away from his birth family. He left Nazareth, the village where he had grown up, and returned there only occasionally (13:54–58). For a while, it seems, Simon Peter's lakeside home in Capernaum, twenty miles away, became a base for some of his work. Although Matthew does not mention this "second home" as clearly and often as Mark does (cf., e.g., Matt. 9:2 with Mark 2:1), he does appear to set this particular episode in Capernaum, for we hear in the very next verse (13:1) of Jesus leaving "the house" and going down to the shore. Earlier Jesus had warned his friends that his mission and message would strain and divide families (10:35–37). Now we see something of this in his own experience.

Jesus' birth family has not appeared in this Gospel since the infancy material in the early chapters (1:17–2:23). Now they come back onto the stage (12:46). Joseph is not involved; perhaps he has died by this time. Mary is here, although the Gospel does not name her at this point, as it did in the first chapter. There are four brothers too and at least two sisters (13:55–56), and some of the brothers have traveled to Capernaum with Mary.

Incidentally, it seems natural to many readers to think of these brothers and sisters as younger sons and daughters of Joseph and Mary. However, many

Homiletical Perspective

Today's text provides an opportunity for preachers to wade into the swirling waters of contemporary family life. This is a topic that some preachers fear—and with good reason. "Family" is a complicated subject. In our culture the notion of family is sentimentalized in various ways: dim memories of fifties sitcoms, lavish weddings, extravagant baby showers, stereotypes of what constitutes normative family life.[1] Our sentimental ideas about family set people up with unrealistic notions of what it takes to make a life together. These images especially pervade ecclesial contexts. It can be difficult in some pulpits to admit the decidedly unsentimental truth that families are messy configurations that can disappoint and hurt as well as give us joy.

How important it is for people to hear this very truth from their preachers! The grief and loss of family life are too often hidden in churches, causing people to experience this pain as a failure of their faith. Faith should be a resource for people struggling with family life, not a battering ram. While this text does not offer solutions to the messiness of family life, it does offer reassurance. It reminds us that the stresses and strains of family life are yet another aspect of human life that God experiences in the person of

1. The examples I use here reference Euro–American culture in the United States. Other cultures will have their own experiences of what constitutes normative family life.

Matthew 12:46–50

family relations are relatively unimportant (see 10:34–39; 19:18–21, 29–30). He mentions Mary and Jesus' brothers only one other time (13:54–57). Here, when Jesus' mother and brothers request a word with him (v. 46), he seizes the opportunity to redefine family—his true "brother and sister and mother"—as "whoever does the will of [his] Father in heaven" (v. 50).

Does Jesus actually abandon his family? We do not know whether Jesus' mother and brothers are part of the crowd that has been following him through "all the cities and villages" (9:35). Perhaps they too are counted as persons who do the will of the heavenly Parent. The passage also does not state that Jesus turns his family away, or that he refuses to speak with them. Elsewhere in Matthew, Jesus explicitly denounces persons who refuse support and honor to their parents (15:4–7).

Even if Jesus does retain ties with his mother and brothers, he significantly reorients the nature of these commitments. Attachments to mothers and siblings are not inherently debilitating, but Jesus subordinates these relationships to the concerns of ministry, that is, to seeking and doing God's will. As Jesus takes up an itinerant teaching lifestyle, and as Matthew exhorts the missionaries going out from his movement, the primary nexus of support shifts to the religious community.

Alternative Community. Matthew presents the community of faith as an alternative family. When religious dissention tears families apart, as happened frequently in Matthew's context, the loss of original relation is difficult to bear. One wonders about the audience that first heard Jesus' statement about his true family. We read that "someone told him" his mother and brothers were waiting (v. 47), and that "to the one who had told him this," Jesus issues his reply (v. 48). Is the messenger a person caught in the middle of familial strife over her decision to follow Jesus? In the context of competing ideas about how to be a Jew, does she feel torn between these alternatives? Are Jesus' words a salve for the messenger's deep wound of loss?

Such persons can find it liberating to designate religious community as their new family. The reader must ask, however, what model of authority Matthew envisions. What is "the will of my Father in heaven" (v. 50), and how is it mediated? Does it reinscribe patriarchal patterns of religious authority? Amy-Jill Levine notes that the Mosaic law and the injunction to serve others provide the parameters for discerning the divine will in Matthew's Gospel. Following the

concept of family. Who wants to stand in the pulpit on a Sunday and attack the family as an idol?

In all three Synoptic Gospels, Jesus steps forward and does exactly that! In Matthew, Jesus is concluding a tough couple of chapters where he has faced challenges and opposition from both friend (John the Baptist) and foe (the scribes and Pharisees). Now his family is "standing outside" (v. 46) the house—a posture conceivably signaling only half-hearted support of his ministry.

In response, Jesus puts his hands out over his disciples and radically alters our notion of family, calling them and the gathered crowd his new "brother and sister and mother" (v. 49). Of course, we should have seen this coming back in 10:34–37, when Jesus questions the worthiness of one who loves a parent or child more than him.

The powerful, countercultural nature of this text is illustrated in a story NT scholar Luke Timothy Johnson tells of being asked by a local parish to preach on the subject of families. He sent them the title of the sermon: "God Doesn't Like Families." However, when he arrived at the church and opened the bulletin, the title had been changed and now read "Godlike Families."

So what is at stake here pastorally? As Jesus no doubt perceived in his own time and culture, an "idolatrous posture" toward the family can lead to the belief that the family is not only *necessary* but also *sufficient* for faith. The narrow bonds of our nuclear family become so strong and entrenched that the gospel call to find our true family in the larger body of Christ becomes almost impossible.

Extended Family. A couple of strategies for the preacher come to mind. First, it may be helpful to remind the congregation that the nuclear family as we know it is a fairly recent development, dating from the Industrial Revolution. Nevertheless, we have been deeply formed by a powerful narrative of the "family pew"—one filled by a father, mother, and several children—that has its roots in the Victorian period. Shaped by this narrative, rarely do we question the assumption that the most intimate and formative ties are in the *biological* or *adopting* family and not in the *faith* community. Rarely do we notice that those who are not part of a nuclear-family unit can easily be marginalized in a congregation.

The invitation here is to reconsider how our cultural notion of family was formed and what practices in the life of the church undergird those familiar, comfortable, yet distorted images. Who can we

Christians over the years have wondered about other possibilities—either that these are Joseph's children by an earlier marriage, or that they are actually Jesus' cousins. We simply do not know enough to be sure about these matters.

Mark indicates that the family is anxious about Jesus; they come "to restrain him" (Mark 3:21) and to bring him back under their influence and control. In comparison, Matthew's version of the episode is briefer, and the tension is a little less obvious. Nonetheless, in Matthew's Gospel too there is a clear contrast between Jesus' birth family and the company of disciples around him. By the end of the paragraph the focus is firmly on this second group; they have become his new family.

"Mother and brothers" is the chorus line of the paragraph. These two nouns appear in every verse. Only in verse 50 does the formula expand to "brother and sister and mother." Relationships matter, and these—according to the text—are shaped more solidly by lifestyle than by location. Birthplace and biology are incidental; the vital thing is to follow Jesus' way and word. Those who shape their lives by his teaching are the people he regards as true family. These are the ones who do "the will of my Father in heaven" (v. 50). As so often in Matthew's Gospel, lifestyle is the key issue—putting the word into practice (7:21, 24; 13:23). This is the fullest kind of family likeness, and it creates the strongest sort of kinship bond.

So when we see Jesus' natural family "standing outside" (vv. 46, 47), the language works at two levels. They are outside the house where he is speaking. They are outside the circle of his followers too, beyond the reach of his teaching and leadership. Later on, things will change, and they will come to trust him. So we see Mary standing at the cross (John 19:25), and she and Jesus' brothers sit with the apostles in the upper room (Acts 1:14). In time James will lead the Jerusalem church (Acts 15:13–21), and both he and Jude will contribute letters to the New Testament; but all this is ahead. For the moment the family seems estranged, out of touch and out of tune, as Jesus gathers followers to himself and his cause.

The new family over which Jesus "stretches his hand" (v. 49, my trans.) is the focal point of this short episode. As Matthew portrays Jesus' ministry, response has been patchy (11:20), and we see Jesus complaining about "this generation" (12:42, 45). In the parable of the Sower (13:1–9) he goes on to speak of some varied reactions to the seed that he spreads. Then gradually, in the chapters that follow, we see a definite community coming into view. Jesus

Jesus Christ. It makes clear that Jesus did not have a perfect family. He had a human family, as do we, and we can infer from this text that as we struggle with the misunderstandings or resentments or tensions in our own families, Jesus joins us. He is not only to be found in the goodness of family life; he is even more readily found in its stresses and strains. We are not alone in the troubling family moments when we may need God the most. God in Christ is with us, and that is great, good news.

Taking the opportunity to engage incarnational themes and complicated family life is but one way to approach this text. Another option for preachers is to tackle the primary theme of the text: discipleship. Here Jesus uses the metaphor of family life to talk about what it means to follow him.

Jesus says that his mother, brother, and sister are those who do the will of the Father. This statement is suggestive in a number of ways. It is, first, a statement of intimacy and belonging. By using the metaphor of his family to talk about his followers, Jesus brings us close; we are not here characterized as followers, who could be imagined as tagging along at a distance; we are not spoken of as servants, whose status may be unequal to his; we are not referred to as friends. We are mothers, brothers, sisters, part of an intimate circle bound by familial ties. We are part of Jesus' own family.

This is a statement of belonging, but it is not a sentimental one. Juxtaposed as it is with Jesus' apparent resistance to his family of origin—Mary and his siblings—it broadens our notion of family without forgetting that every family is a mixed experience of happiness and frustration. This is not an occasion to say, "Our church is one big, happy family," and leave it at that. In discipleship we belong to one another and to Christ, as if we were born into the same complicated family. What might that mean for the church as a community of faith? How might this text speak to us of the commitments we have to each other that transcend the everyday bickering and competitiveness that sometimes attend family life? What is the bloodline that ties us together as sisters, brothers, mothers of Christ?[1]

What does it mean for us as individuals to participate in this family of faith? This text additionally gives us an opportunity to extend our metaphors of personal discipleship to include mothering, sistering, and brothering.

---

2. I am grateful to Veronica Johnson, who first raised this question for me, in a sermon on a parallel text.

Matthew 12:46–50

Theological Perspective

prophetic tradition, God's word, not special insider status, is the criterion for belonging. This "new ethnically mixed movement" is open to Gentile membership. Men and women—mothers, brothers, and sisters—contribute to it. "The only 'father' is the one in heaven; no earthly father is mentioned in the context of this new social experiment."[1] The community is radically inclusive.

Jesus' pronouncement lends support to the feminist preference for the language of "kin-dom" rather than the prevalent, monarchical language of the "kingdom of heaven" (*basileia tou ouranou*). Jesus' metaphors of mother, brother, and sister (vv. 49–50) bend discipleship toward mutuality and reciprocity. Jesus' disciples are not only on the receiving end of his word. Discipleship is a two-way street. The members of the community of faith are family to one another, and they are family to Christ as well. When Jesus looks at the women and men surrounding him, eager for his enlightening word and his healing touch, he sees people who enrich and touch him as well. The body of Christ takes shape through the influence of those who love him—who give birth to it, grow with it, and forge new bonds of fidelity within it.

The family metaphor captures the nurturing capacity of the church. Many in the Christian tradition have envisioned the church as a woman breastfeeding the community through teaching and the sacraments. The metaphor also captures the church's potential for dissent. Close bonds raise the stakes of any argument. As anyone who has ever been a member in one of the institutional churches will recognize, the divine will is not always easy to discern, especially when all of the voices of the community count. Because the danger of injury and loss is present in the reconstituted Christian family, as well as in families of origin, Christ must repeatedly point the way: "*Here* are my mother and my brothers!" (v. 49).

Jesus' family values encompass families insofar as they discern and carry out the divine will together. However, Jesus' family values also replace the rationale of "natural" bonds with a radically inclusive norm that extends beyond blood, nation, and conventional notions of authority. This extended family, this kin-dom, is always *becoming* mother and sister and brother—with all that entails—to one another.

MICHELLE VOSS ROBERTS

Pastoral Perspective

imagine is being left out when bounds of the family are too tightly drawn?

Second, the preacher can lift up a vision of new, extended family. For example, we can learn an important lesson from Hispanic Christians about "family life" in the church. Justo L. González notes: "Significantly, one of the values most cherished by nuclear families in the dominant culture is privacy—a word that does not even exist in Spanish. When they come to church, most white middle class families wish to preserve their privacy. When they come to church, most Hispanic nuclear families come to be part of the one extended family of the church."[2]

The "extended family" that Jesus envisions is not based on biological ties or our need for privacy but instead is made up of those who do the will of God (v. 50). To be Jesus' disciples means that we have no "unmediated relationships," as Bonheoffer put it. Instead, Christ stands as the mediator of all human attachments—between parent and child, between husband and wife, in the midst of all relationships.

Again, our imaginations are fired by Jesus' radical challenge in this text: to live out this new, reconstituted family we call the church. The preacher can invite the congregation to explore more deeply its commitment to and involvement in the local community in light of our new understanding of family. How might our local mission look if we understood that the young woman staying in the women's shelter is indeed our "sister"? How is our outreach to a neighbor school transformed when we embrace the students as our "daughters and sons" in Jesus?

Let us be honest. "God Doesn't Like Families" is not an easy sermon for anyone to preach! Nevertheless, our first allegiance as Christians is with the particular story and practice of our "Jesus family." Especially in a culture of extreme individualism and broken relationships, the good news of Christ as the center and foundation of all families and relationships is a message we must proclaim and live out. This new Jesus family is most evocatively visible at the baptismal font. Swimming together in the watery grace and mercy of God, we rise as members of a new family whose kinship is both *with* and *in* Christ.

MARK R. BURNHAM

---

1. Amy-Jill Levine, "Matthew," in *Women's Bible Commentary with Apocrypha*, ed. Carol A. Newsom and Sharon H. Ringe, expanded edition (Louisville, KY: Westminster John Knox Press, 1998), 339–40, 344.

2. Justo L. González, *Santa Biblia: The Bible through Hispanic Eyes* (Nashville: Abingdon Press, 1996), 109–10.

Exegetical Perspective

feeds his people (14:13–21; 15:32–39), builds them up (16:18), and teaches them how to order their common life (18:1–35). He still speaks to Israel as a whole—to crowds, opponents, and passersby—but he shapes in a special way the life of the inner company around him. Perhaps he saw them as a new core, a fresh center, for the nation's faithful response to God. He called them his family.

Certainly Jesus sometimes spoke very positively about commitments in home and marriage (19:3–12). He did not like the thought of people using religion as a cover, to avoid their proper duty to relatives (15:4–9). He also was keen to shape a community that would reflect his values, embody his teaching in their living, and eventually pass on to others the commands he had given (28:20). Such a community was, for him, a family of faith and of faithful practice.

As we read Matthew's Gospel, we sense that this is the kind of church Matthew wanted to belong to and the kind of church life that he hoped his Gospel would nurture. Such a people would take obedience seriously; they would be attentive to the teaching that had come to them from Jesus; they would take one another seriously too. For the "Father in heaven" (v. 50) would give the group its identity and make it a company of equals, without rank or deference (23:9). Women would belong, as fully and truly as men, to him who calls his friends "sister" as well as "brother" (v. 50). In such a community Christians would learn to be family. They would practise a kinship that was defined by deeds rather than by DNA, by heaven rather than earth.

JOHN PROCTOR

Homiletical Perspective

What might it mean to mother the gospel? Despite its gendered possibilities and limitations, this is a multifaceted and rich metaphor that opens up as we consider what mothers do. On their good days, mothers act in ways that are life giving and life supporting. Mothers carry new life; they raise up and nurture that new life. They create safe and hospitable spaces in which vulnerable people can grow and develop as God intended them to do. Some mothers—Moses' mother, for example—exercise subversive strategies to preserve and protect life. Other mothers do the routine, everyday work that keeps us going: they feed and direct us; they bear with us; they are resilient and loyal and patient. Mothering is a lens through which we can think about discipleship: the work of carrying the gospel, bearing God's truth, and giving and supporting life, especially on behalf of the most vulnerable in our midst.

Sistering and brothering are also lenses through which we can apprehend particular aspects of discipleship. These sibling metaphors are egalitarian ones that invite us to think about aspects of faithful living that contribute to our mutual maturity, our growing up together. Again, let us think about what sisters and brothers do. They share everyday life and common memories, they know each other intimately. As family members, they are not really themselves without the other; it is impossible to be a sister or brother by oneself. The inescapably communal and collaborative reality of discipleship is embodied in these metaphors.

Of course, no one is ever a perfect mother or sister or brother. Everybody makes mistakes in human relationships. These are not metaphors to be romanticized. Rather, they are metaphors that can help us put flesh on what it means to be a disciple and what it might mean to do God's will together as a family of faith and as followers of Christ.

DEBORAH J. KAPP

Matthew 13:1–9

¹That same day Jesus went out of the house and sat beside the sea. ²Such great crowds gathered around him that he got into a boat and sat there, while the whole crowd stood on the beach. ³And he told them many things in parables, saying; "Listen! A sower went out to sow. ⁴And as he sowed, some seeds fell on the path, and the birds came and ate them up. ⁵Other seeds fell on rocky ground, where they did not have much soil, and they sprang up quickly, since they had no depth of soil. ⁶But when the sun rose, they were scorched; and since they had no root, they withered away. ⁷Other seeds fell among thorns, and the thorns grew up and choked them. ⁸Other seeds fell on good soil and brought forth grain, some a hundredfold, some sixty, some thirty. ⁹Let anyone with ears listen!"

Theological Perspective

The parable of the Sower comes first in a series three parables about seeds, followed by the parables of the Wheat and the Tares (vv. 24–30) and the Mustard Seed (vv. 31–32). Unlike most of Jesus' parables, it is followed by a passage in which he provides an interpretation for his disciples. Most commentators agree that this interpretation belongs to early Christian tradition rather than to Jesus himself. We consider this interpretation in a later entry (13:18–23, below); here, we offer a theological perspective for the contemporary context.

Jesus speaks the parable of the Sower out of his experience as a preacher, in which his words sometimes fail to take root in the hearers. Rejection is a strong theme in Matthew's Gospel. Its audience has experienced intrareligious conflict. The community's missionaries need a theological perspective to frame their failure and disappointment. In the traditional interpretation, the different sorts of soil correspond to different sorts of hearers. The quality of each determines their reception of the gospel: the path corresponds to hearers upon whom the seed is wasted, or from whom it is stolen by "the evil one" (v. 19); the rocky ground to shallow people, whose commitment fades under persecution; the thorny soil to people distracted by the cares of this world;

Pastoral Perspective

Chapter 13 of Matthew marks a significant shift in the Gospel narrative. Jesus is now "out of the house" (v. 1) and about to embark on his third great teaching discourse. The preacher or teacher must not, however, leave behind the claim of the previous pericope (12:46–50) that those who do God's will are brother, sister, and mother to Jesus, the Son of God. From a pastoral perspective, Jesus has prepared us for a rigorous lesson in living the reality of our new, extended family—the church.

Stanley Hauerwas makes this connection clear when he writes that the parable of the Sower is "crucial for the church to imagine the kind of community that we must be in order to survive in a world that assumes that biological kinship is more determinative than our kinship in Christ. The boat on which Jesus sits to deliver his parabolic sermon on the parable is the church that the parables bring into being."[1]

This parable (and others following) also consists of Jesus' response to the increasing opposition and rejection he is experiencing from the religious leaders and from "this generation" (12:38–45). The dichotomy of inside/outside and true/false family

1. Stanley Hauerwas, *Matthew* (Grand Rapids: Brazos Press, 2006), 126.

Feasting on the Gospels

Exegetical Perspective

Matthew's Gospel presents the bulk of Jesus' teaching in five long discourses. The third of these, which starts here, fills most of chapter 13, up through verse 53. It is all about parables—what they are, how they operate, and what they accomplish—and includes eight parables altogether. Most of these eight start with a little preface: "The kingdom is like . . ." (e.g., v. 31), but this first of the group plunges directly in. "Listen!" says Jesus (v. 3). "A sower went out."

Like the sower, Jesus too "goes out of the house," down to the shore (v. 1). As crowds gather, he takes a boat to serve as a makeshift pulpit. Then he sits to teach, as he did on the mountain (5:1) and as a rabbi would do in a synagogue (Luke 4:20). Floating a few yards offshore, he is audible to the people on the beach, but just out of their grasp and touch. This seems to be the way that parables work too—easy to hear, but a little harder to get hold of.

This is not the first parable in Matthew, but it is the first time the word "parable" is used (v. 3). The word had quite a broad range of use—proverb, riddle, maxim, analogy, illustrative story. All of these have one feature in common: a parable is "an utterance which does not carry its meaning on the surface, and which thus demands thought and

Homiletical Perspective

Recently a friend and I bought a share in a local community supported agriculture (CSA) farm, which meant that from April through December we shared a box of vegetables that was delivered weekly by an organic farmer who works in downstate Illinois. Vicky, the farmer, is a strong woman who loves her work. In her weekly e-mail reminders about our veggie delivery schedule, she told us about the farm. In the spring she wrote about planting and reflected eloquently about the first green shoots, the early lettuces, the warming soil, and lengthening days. In the summer she told us about the ripening crops, the grief of losing all the tomatoes to a huge rainstorm, and the relentlessness of the year's summer heat. In the fall she told stories of bumper crops and rich harvests, and then she brought us kohlrabi, kohlrabi, and more kohlrabi. Really, it seemed like thirtyfold and a hundredfold kohlrabi.

For us as urban dwellers, these vegetables and weekly e-mails are the closest my friend and I ever get to a farm. Participating in our CSA reminded us of the rhythms, routines, and realities of agricultural life, which is the setting for this text. Like Vicky, the protagonist of the parable is a farmer who knows all about the unpredictability, disappointments, and bumper-crop delights of farming. It is clear from this text that farming is not for the faint of heart.

Theological Perspective

and the good soil to persons who receive, understand, and reproduce the word.

Unlike the church of the time when the text was written, Christianity today enjoys the status of a dominant world religion. To be sure, Christian missionaries still encounter various degrees of response to their work, and Christians themselves can be hard-hearted, shallow, distracted, or productive to various degrees. The shift from Christianity's early minority status to one of frequent complicity with political and economic hegemony across the globe, however, invites reconsideration from another angle.

Let us consider not primarily the soil, but the seed. A seed contains forces of life and transformation. It encapsulates potential; but as potential, its actual future is open. It unfolds relationally, for it depends upon its own potential, the potential within the soil, and the quality of their interaction. Like a parable.

A parable is a story that speaks, not directly or abstractly, but parabolically, curving in from the side. The early Christian scribe nails down the identity of the seeds as "the word of the kingdom" (v. 19), but may we not view the seeds as the very parables Jesus sows in this passage? "He got into a boat . . . and he told them many things in parables, saying: 'Listen! A sower went out to sow'" (vv. 2–3). The tale of the sower and the seeds can be read as a parable about parables, about how these compact kernels of insight unfold according to the potential both within the story and within the recipient. Someone other than the direct audience may become the beneficiary of a parable, as when birds receive nourishment from seeds that fall on the path. The kernel may generate immediate enthusiasm but soon be forgotten. Its message can get lost in life's busy chatter. Sometimes a story so captivates an audience that they in turn become storytellers, who capture the imaginations of others.

Following biblical scholar John Dominic Crossan, theologian Catherine Keller reads Jesus himself as a parable: "The master teller of parables becomes, for those who have ears to hear and eyes to see, the parable of God."[1] Too often, she observes, Christians clamp down Jesus' significance with christological titles and claims of his unique salvific nature. Christ, the icon of God, is instead treated as a mirror or a transparent window—in short, as an idol.[2]

Pastoral Perspective

is brought to the fore as the audience is made to choose if they are for or against Jesus and the kingdom he proclaims. No equivocation allowed!

The parable has three "actions" that invite our pastoral reflection: *sowing, growing,* and *listening.*

Sowing. First, we discover that the farmer in the tale sows the seed with wild abandon and unfocused aim. The seed goes everywhere—on the path and in the thorny patch, on rocky ground and into rich topsoil. Tom Long sees great promise here: "Keep on spreading the seed; keep on preaching the gospel and showing the compassion of the kingdom. In ways we do not always know and in places we cannot always see, . . . even now the great harvest of God is growing rich and full in the fields."[2]

For the early church this must have been a story of great encouragement. They needed to know the hard truth that not *all* of their efforts would bear fruit. Some seed would land on fertile ground, and others would be lost. They needed to be prepared for the reality of the same opposition that Jesus faced.

The church today needs to hear this message: You will not always succeed. Failure is part of ministry. Remember that only one out of four succeeded in the parable! So try many different things; throw out lots of seed, and see what happens. A church not failing at anything is perhaps one not risking enough.

Henry David Thoreau once wrote, "I have great faith in a seed. Convince me that you have a seed there, and I am prepared to expect wonders."[3] Perhaps this is a good time for the preacher to remind the congregation that they too are called to sow with wild abandon and to expect wonders in their fields.

Growing. My father is a lifelong gardener in upstate New York, and I am amazed at the work involved. Every spring the garden plot must be tilled; large rocks and stones must be removed. Tomatoes are carefully planted in the basement under a heat lamp and nurtured until ready to be moved outside. Even then, they face the threat of frost and bugs, or can be eaten by deer or rabbits. Getting a ripe, juicy tomato at the end of the summer is almost a miracle when you understand the care and protection required.

Jesus' parable echoes this same process—except that his version is a more realistic view of life. Not

1. Catherine Keller, *On the Mystery: Discerning Divinity in Process* (Minneapolis: Fortress Press, 2008), 155. Cf. John Dominic Crossan, *Dark Interval: Towards a Theology of Story* (Allen: Argus, 1975), 124.
2. Keller, *On the Mystery,* 124.

2. Thomas G. Long, *Matthew* (Louisville, KY: Westminster John Knox Press, 1997), 147.
3. Henry D. Thoreau, *Faith in a Seed: The Dispersion of Seeds and Other Late Natural History Writings* (Washington, DC: Island Press, 1993), vii.

perception if the hearer is to benefit from it."[1] So listening to a parable draws the hearer into a conversation with the story. Insight, patience, and perhaps even effort are needed to grasp the point. It matters to get beneath the surface, to the substance.

It is hard to tell if this description of a sower's work is meant to be realistic. Some of Jesus' parables certainly do seem offbeat and incongruous, and this one may be too. Would a sower really scatter seed on barren soil or among thistles and thorns? Is Jesus making the straightforward point that the farmer's task always has a random and unpredictable aspect? You must use the land you have; good and bad soils lie side by side, and you cannot avoid strewing some of the grain on ground where it will not flourish.

Certainly the seeds in the parable have very different life spans, which increase steadily in the course of the story. Those on the path last no time at all; the birds gobble them up (v. 4). On the rocky ground, destruction comes pretty quickly too; there is no root or deep moisture to sustain the young corn, and it shrivels in the midday heat (vv. 5–6). The thorns take longer to do their work; if these had been plowed in after a previous harvest, they would grow up with the sown seed until they choked the life from it (v. 7). Finally comes the good soil, with growing corn and generous yield (v. 8). Thirty, sixty, and a hundred grains on a stalk are by no means incredible figures. This crop is realistic, not a fantasy.

There are many suggestions about the parable's original meaning. One reading relates it to issues of land and wealth. The birds, rocks, and thorns may well remind Jesus' hearers that much of the farmer's yield is claimed by rent, tithes, and taxes. However ably you sow, much of your land will never benefit you. The wealth will be drained out of it and diverted to people who have plenty already. By this reading, Jesus is speaking of the sufficiency of God's creative goodness in an unjust world. Despite demands and depredations, grace will have the last word. The land still has wealth enough to feed God's people.

Another approach looks for echoes of the Hebrew Scriptures and points to Isaiah's prophecy that God's word shall not return to heaven void. As surely as rain causes seed to grow, the word will be effective (Isa. 55:10–11). As an ancient curse once brought thistles and toil to the earth (Gen. 3:17–19), now God sows a new covenant in the land, of hope and trust and pardon (Jer. 31:27–34).

---

1. Richard T. France, *The Gospel of Matthew*, New International Commentary on the New Testament (Grand Rapids: Eerdmans, 2007), 502.

Farming is, of course, a metaphor for discipleship. Apart from being a ready-at-hand comparison that Jesus could use in a culture that was familiar with agricultural rhythms and routines, farming is an apt comparison for discipleship. What does farming have to tell us, as a metaphor? If we opt for the explanation that Matthew offers in verses 18–23, we read the story in a rather passive manner. In this reading of the text, the sower is Jesus, the seed is God's word, and the soils are different kinds of disciples and their readiness to receive the word. Unfortunately most disciples in this explanation are reception challenged, apparently unable to change or grow, and they fall short for a variety of reasons. From this perspective, it seems that very few of us are effective disciples who are able to hear, understand, bear fruit, and produce.

A more active reading of this text puts disciples into the shoes of the sower. We believers are charged with the responsibility of farming God's word. It turns out that such a task is easier said than done. Discipleship is no more for the faint of heart than is farming.

Discipleship is not susceptible to careful planning. One would think—and hope—that the farmer could map out her land, determine where the best soil was, and plant there, but the story emphasizes something different from this orderly approach. The story emphasizes disorder and reminds us that even the best farmers cannot control the world around them. Birds have minds of their own, as do storms, cold spells, heat waves, droughts, weeds, and pests. Good farming, like good discipleship, is found somewhere in between orderly planning and things we cannot control.

Discipleship is no stranger to risk and failure. It is, by its very nature, open to risk, loss, and adventure. How different this sounds from many churches I know, faithful institutions that do their best to minimize risk, avoid failure, and guarantee success! Our ecclesiastical carefulness can make us cautious, like the servant in another of Matthew's parables who chose to bury his talent instead of invest it. The farmer in today's parable is not so careful: he invests; he takes the risk and scatters his seed, chances failure, and experiences it. Crops fail sometimes; this is a reality of agricultural life. Vicky one year lost all her tomatoes to unfriendly weather, and the farmer in this parable loses crops to rocky soil, hot sun, and thorns. Sometimes disciples lose their investments too: a program goes bust, a church closes, a church is a bad match for a new minister. Stuff happens, as the

Matthew 13:1–9

Theological Perspective

Reclaiming Jesus as a parable has implications for Christian relations to other religious traditions. In imitation of Jesus' preaching, Christian mission might take on parabolic form. Expressive action and rich narrative may open possibilities where hard doctrines and fixed propositions shut them down. One never knows where or how the Jesus parable will take root. This parabolic relation will also be open to the possibility of hearing parables of divine presence in other religious traditions. The hard, rocky, thorny soil of Christian dominance may become fertile in new ways, as *all* people who bear fruit come to scatter new seed as parables of the Divine.

Matthew 13:1–9 carries a fundamental tension between oneness and difference. On the one hand, seeds ordinarily produce one plant, with its own roots and foliage. On the other hand, although a packet of seeds is expected to produce similar plants, the produce is not entirely predictable. Whenever I plant seeds, I learn this lesson anew. Some of my seeds never sprout. Others do, but local conditions and my tendency to overwater cause them to die. The plants that establish strong roots flourish; a few even produce beans or lettuce for my table. Sometimes, mysteriously, a squash blossoms amid the strawberries, or an errant sprig of mint pops up amid the parsley. Rhizomatic bulbs and tubers defy the "one seed–one plant" rule and branch off in unpredictable directions. Gardening is a parable of difference.

Though Jesus' parable values the capacity of good soil to bring forth grain, it acknowledges diverse manners of doing so, "some a hundredfold, some sixty, some thirty" (v. 8). There is nothing particularly miraculous about this manifold yield, as some readings of the parable imply. A single plant generates many seeds. We may follow this thread of diversity in our context of religious pluralism: Jesus as parable may harvest a genuine variety of responses. Who is to say that no one benefits when the birds eat the seed? That the quickly springing shoots did not delight the sower? That an injunction to thorn removal is not an important implication of this tale? "Let anyone with ears listen!" (v. 9).

MICHELLE VOSS ROBERTS

Pastoral Perspective

every seed receives the loving care that my father gives his tomatoes. The message from this story is clear: even though presumably the seeds were all equally able to grow into plants and bear fruit, the surroundings in which they are nurtured make all the difference.

Jesus knew what all farmers and gardeners know: Good environments yield healthy plants; bad environments yield little or nothing. It is not much of a leap to see this as a lesson of faith for us as Jesus' new family. Those in good soil hear the word of God and hold it fast, thus bearing the fruit and returning plentiful harvest. Others fall victim to weeds and rocks, and end up dormant or dead. To provide the good soil of love and joy as we nurture faith in our midst—that is what Jesus expects of the church.

Listening. Critical to understanding this parable is the final command: "Let anyone with ears listen!" (v. 9). The key lesson here is *listening* to Jesus' words. As many commentators have said, our ears are the soil of a faithful life. In the context of this parable, to lean in closely enough to the text to find "dirt in our ears" is a good thing! It means that we are attentively tuned to the words that Jesus speaks.

The teacher can invite reflection on listening as a spiritual practice. In our busy 24/7, social-media-dominated world, we are often distracted, unaware, or even resistant to the words of Christ. Are we so occupied by worldly concerns that the weeds of our culture choke out the gospel for us? Do we listen too closely to peer pressure and turn aside from our faith?

To live without listening—to be unfocused and inattentive—is an absurd way of life (the root in Latin is *surdus*, which means "deaf" or "dull, indistinct"), because we do not hear the voice of the One who calls us to new life. The listening life is one that is spiritually mature because it clearly hears and follows the voice of God's Spirit both within us and among us. In this new extended family, it is a necessary discipline to listen both to God and to one another.

MARK R. BURNHAM

Exegetical Perspective

Both of these interpretations raise interesting lines of thought, and of course we cannot be sure what Jesus' audience made of the story. Many a good parable is versatile enough to carry more than one message. For me, however, the most natural readings of this story set it against the background of the previous chapters. Throughout Matthew 11 and 12, people have responded to Jesus and his teaching in some varied ways. Many welcomed his word; others reacted with caution or challenge. His work was proving difficult, and the results were only patchy and partial; this matches the sower's experience. People heard Jesus in different ways, and some corners of the field proved more receptive than others.

Still, the parable has a strong positive climax. The lavish success of the final batch of seed justifies all the effort and disappointment, all the watching and waiting, all the misery of hopes that withered and failed. The reign of God will finally prosper. Despite struggles and setbacks, God will fulfil his purpose. Jesus lived in faith, and looked forward with confidence.

So this is also a parable about hearing. "Listen!" says Jesus (vv. 3, 9). He frames the parable, at start and finish, with an echo of God's ancient command, "Hear, O Israel." For just as Israel's creed merited attentive listening and frequent repetition (Deut. 6:4–9), so the new word of the kingdom deserves to be heard with a keen and open mind. It matters, says Jesus, to retain the word, to draw it deep into the heart, and to nurture it until fruit is borne. In this sense the sower is a parable about parables. They do not carry their meaning on the surface. Thought and care are needed to get to the marrow of the message. Only those who "listen" can truly gain what God gives.

JOHN PROCTOR

Homiletical Perspective

saying goes. Discipleship is honest about failure and not afraid to live into it.

Discipleship requires hope and resiliency. It is a marvel to me that people choose to farm; it is hard work, you cannot take vacation, and lots of farmers live at the edge of sustainability. Nevertheless year after year people plant, grow, and harvest crops. They sow and tend their fields. They labor in literal and figurative vineyards. Vicky is already looking forward to next spring's planting and potential crop. Although realistic, she is also excited and hopeful, focused more on the possibilities than on the memory of last year's losses.

Discipleship delights in God's abundance. At the heart of any farmer's optimism is the experience of bounty. We may have lost the tomatoes, but this year's kohlrabi crop was abundant, the cabbages were plentiful, and the squashes grew and grew and grew. There is so much to be thankful for, and, truth be told, it all came by God's abundant grace.

Paul says this well in 1 Corinthians 3, where he adjudicates a dispute between his followers and followers of Apollos, who are arguing with each other about which group should have precedence. Paul encourages them to work together; using the metaphor of farming, he reminds them who is really responsible for their church's growth: "I planted, Apollos watered, but God made it grow. Because of this, neither the one who plants nor the one who waters is anything, but the only one who is anything is God who makes it grow" (1 Cor. 3:6–7 CEB).

Discipleship is a wonderful adventure that invites us to share God's word as a farmer plants her crops: with a clear vision of the world's fickleness, a willingness to fail, hope, resilience, and the deep trust that by God's grace at least some of our work will bear fruit. We just have to get things started; it is God who will make them grow.

DEBORAH J. KAPP

Matthew 13:10–17

¹⁰Then the disciples came and asked him, "Why do you speak to them in parables?" ¹¹He answered, "To you it has been given to know the secrets of the kingdom of heaven, but to them it has not been given. ¹²For to those who have, more will be given, and they will have an abundance; but from those who have nothing, even what they have will be taken away. ¹³The reason I speak to them in parables is that 'seeing they do not perceive, and hearing they do not listen, nor do they understand.' ¹⁴With them indeed is fulfilled the prophecy of Isaiah that says:

'You will indeed listen, but never understand,
and you will indeed look, but never perceive.
¹⁵ For this people's heart has grown dull,
and their ears are hard of hearing,
and they have shut their eyes;
so that they might not look with their eyes,
and listen with their ears,
and understand with their heart and turn—
and I would heal them.'

¹⁶But blessed are your eyes, for they see, and your ears, for they hear. ¹⁷Truly I tell you, many prophets and righteous people longed to see what you see, but did not see it, and to hear what you hear, but did not hear it."

Theological Perspective

After Jesus relates the parable of the Sower, his disciples question him about his teaching methods: "Why do you speak to them in parables?" (v. 10). Opaque stories do not strike them as the most effective evangelism technique. As in many other places in Matthew's Gospel, the answer is that Jesus' actions fulfill Scripture. Isaiah prophesied that the people would "listen, but never understand . . . look, but never perceive" (v. 14, cf. Isa. 6:9). Indeed, the crowds cannot seem to make heads or tails of Jesus' strange words.

Jesus' answer, which likely belongs not to Jesus himself but to an early strand of tradition, contains a number of troubling statements: "For to those who have, more will be given, and they will have an abundance; but from those who have nothing, even what they have will be taken away" (v. 12). This pronouncement grates against contemporary democratic sensibilities, even as it reflects with remarkable accuracy the material situation of late-stage liberal capitalism. From a theological perspective, however, Jesus' language of secrecy is especially problematic: "To you it has been given to know the secrets of the kingdom of heaven, but to them it has not been given" (v. 11). Gnostic Christians in the first centuries took such statements to mean that salvation comes through esoteric knowledge (gnosis) available only to a select few, the "spiritual" believers. The

Pastoral Perspective

"The Great Aside" is what Dale Bruner appropriately calls this section of chapter 13. In a behind-the-scenes view that the Revised Common Lectionary prefers to omit, the disciples corner Jesus and demand to know what is going on. Bruner translates the disciples' question in verse 10 this way: "Why in the world are you talking to them in parables?"[1]

After all, this does appear to be a squandered opportunity. Jesus has a huge crowd gathered at the lakeside to hear him preach and teach. In response, though, Jesus implies that he is using the parables to intentionally confound the people. His performance, at least according to his closest followers, is both confusing and deeply disappointing.

The best place to start may be with the honest observation that this is a difficult passage to understand and to preach. To suggest that Jesus uses parables to deliberately *conceal* the good news from the people runs counter to everything we know of the gospel.

We also find here what some view as a disturbing insider/outsider dynamic, as Jesus' disciples are granted the special privilege of knowing the mysteries and secrets of the kingdom. This appears to reinforce an already-troubling trend in the church, for

1. Frederick Dale Bruner, *Matthew: A Commentary*, vol. 2: *The Churchbook*, rev. and exp. ed. (Grand Rapids: Eerdmans, 2004), 9.

Exegetical Perspective

These verses of Matthew appear to be a little interlude. Jesus has finished telling the parable of the
Sower (vv. 3–9), but has not yet started to explain
it (vv. 18–23). At first glance this section breaks an
important continuity and divides two pieces of text
that belong together. Matthew includes this pause
for a reason. This middle section helps to show why
parables and explanations will not always go side by
side. Indeed, parables may do their best work when
they are not explained immediately (or at all).

Much of the material in this passage is found in
Mark and Luke too, but Matthew's version is longer
than the others. In Mark the corresponding section
has only three verses (Mark 4:10–12), and Luke is
briefer still (Luke 8:9–10). Matthew, by contrast,
includes all the material that is in Mark, along with
three other components. The parallels are as follows:

Matthew 13:10, 11, and 13	match Mark 4:10–12
Matthew 13:12	matches Mark 4:25
Matthew 13:14–15	quote from Isaiah 6:9–10
Matthew 13:16–17	match Luke 10:23–24

Asking how this body of text was brought together
would lead us quickly on to complex questions about
Matthew's sources and the ways that he used them.
Much clearer, however, is the effect of this lengthy
interlude between parable and interpretation. It makes

Homiletical Perspective

This text brings people face to face with a troublesome truth: God is ultimately incomprehensible to
human hearts and minds. The fullness and beauty
and goodness and power of God are beyond our
knowing. God's depth and grandeur are shrouded in
mystery. God interrogates Job:

> In your lifetime have you commanded the morning,
>   informed the dawn of its place
> so it would take hold of the earth by its edges
>   and shake the wicked out of it?
> Do you turn it over like clay for a seal,
>   so it stands out like a colorful garment?
>   (Job 38:12–14 CEB)

Of course we do none of these things; we are human
beings, not divine. We see but a fraction of God and
the work of God's hands.

The Bible bears repeated witness to the human
experience of being unable to understand God. The
text before us today, in which Jesus talks about why
many people cannot understand him when he speaks
in parables, is one such example. A preacher could
take at least three different approaches in explicating
this text.

God chooses to be hidden from human beings.
Some biblical texts, including this one, seem to suggest that God decides to be obscure. Jesus says that

Matthew 13:10–17

Theological Perspective

writings of Irenaeus of Lyons (ca. 130–ca. 200) did much to establish an emerging orthodoxy that ruled against such an understanding of the faith: the apostolic tradition is publicly available through creeds and writings that have been faithfully handed down to the entire church.

Scripture does, however, contain many passages that are difficult to understand. The great Christian exegete Origen of Alexandria (ca. 185–254) proposed an enduring solution. The difficulties, contradictions, and even impossibilities in Scripture are meant to impel readers to search for a deeper meaning. By the Middle Ages, theologians regularly referred to the fourfold sense of Scripture (*quadriga*): beyond the literal meaning, the text can be read allegorically (as conveying symbols of key doctrines), morally (as providing ethical guidance), and anagogically (as pointing to future fulfillment). Believers grow in understanding as they learn to read Scripture on a variety of levels. What Isaiah demands—that the people "understand with their heart and turn" (v. 15, cf. Isa. 6:10)—happens developmentally, over a lifetime. Scripture's teachings hold something for everyone, beginners and deeply spiritual persons alike.

The parable form, in particular, simultaneously reveals and conceals. So parables nicely illustrate the analogical nature of theological language. An analogy sets up a comparison, a similarity-in-difference, with dimensions of both "is" and "is not." For example, when Christians refer to God as "Father," they employ a concept that both does and does not describe God. "Father" evokes certain aspects of God's relationship with the world but falls short insofar as it occludes other aspects. Theological speech becomes an idol when we forget the "is not" dimension of the analogy, as when the authority of fallible human fathers is equated with that of God. A parable preserves the analogical nature of theological language by speaking sideways, or parabolically, about its subject matter. It raises questions that invite theological inquiry: Is God the sower, or is Jesus? How is the divine sower like or unlike a human sower? Are other functions (watering, tending, weeding, and harvesting) also entailed in the analogy? What precisely is the seed?

Theological language must be analogical, or parabolic, because of its subject matter. Whether one views God as radically transcendent or as sacramentally immanent to the world, divinity remains a holy mystery. The mystics in various religious traditions understand best that to "see" and "hear," as the disciples have done (v. 16), is only to enter more deeply

Pastoral Perspective

some group or sect to claim special, secret knowledge that is hidden from the rest of us.

Rather than jumping over these eight verses, however, the preacher or teacher is challenged to bring forth this "messy" text for the congregation to wrestle with and ponder. After all, the writers of the three Synoptic Gospels found this "aside" important enough to include in the telling of the parable of the Sower. Perhaps we fall into the trap of making things too easy in preaching and strive for the "right answer," instead of presenting the demanding words of the unedited Gospel.

So, rather than *explaining* the parable (which, of course, defeats the purpose of using a parable in the first place), the preacher or teacher is invited to walk alongside the congregation in their struggle to understand and comprehend it. Like much of the prophetic literature, the parable can act as an invitation to faithful self-examination by both the individual and the congregation.

Mark Achtemeier suggests "that Jesus' aim is not to *cause* blindness in his hearers but rather to *illumine* a previously existing condition of blindness of which they are unaware. By deliberately obscuring his message in parables, Jesus seeks to alert his listeners to their present inability to profit from his teaching."[2] The reference to Isaiah, who knew something of obdurate people, seeks to support the prophetic nature of Jesus' teachings.

For example, one could ask what it means when our best effort to live an authentic life of faith falls short and does not yield the desired results. How do we remain faithful when Jesus' teachings do not match our own personal experiences in the world? What is standing in the way of truly hearing, understanding, and responding appropriately to the message of Jesus?

Another approach is to recognize that in this pericope Jesus is now speaking directly to the disciples and not to the whole crowd. He is acknowledging and explaining to his closest confidants what has become clear in the past few chapters: that some will be receptive to the Word while many others will resist it. In the context of the parable, Jesus clarifies why some seeds fail to flourish and produce a bountiful harvest.

Still another pastoral theme addressed here is loss and disappointment. While there is great hope and expectation as Jesus reveals the kingdom, we also discover in the parable (and in much of this

---

2. P. Mark Achtemeier, "Matthew 13:1–23," *Interpretation* 44, no. 1 (1990): 62.

Jesus' answer to the disciples' question in verse 10 both emphatic and elaborate. As we follow the conversation through, it moves in three stages. First we hear about the reason Jesus teaches in parables, and the divisions that this method both reflects and causes (vv. 10–12). Then comes an account of why some people fail to understand and respond (vv. 13–15). Finally there is a word about the blessing that comes to those who do receive the message (vv. 16–17).

"Why do you speak to them in parables?" The disciples are puzzled (v. 10). Jesus tells them why. The NRSV reads the Greek conjunction *hoti* at the start of his reply simply as a switch into direct speech; but it might well mean, "[I do this] *because* it has been given to you" (v. 11). He teaches in parables because people vary, and this method discriminates between those who accept the message and those who resist. It offers an interactive style of learning, testing attitudes and dividing people. In this, Jesus traces the hand of God.

The disciples, he says, have been "given to know the secrets of the kingdom" (v. 11). The word translated "secrets" literally means "mysteries"—insight that is hidden for a while, but that God will unveil, at the right time and with a providential purpose. The same word is used in the Septuagint (the Greek version of Hebrew Scripture) of Daniel 2 about the content and meaning of a royal dream. In that situation, understanding is definitely a gift of God. The kingdom, says Jesus, works in a similar way. The disciples are privileged. They grasp the message, while others do not. Parables deepen that division. This style of teaching gives fuller insight to people who have started to understand; yet it may seem deeply obscure to any who are still in the dark (v. 12).

The next lines (vv. 13–15) speak about those hearers who remain outside the secret. An Old Testament text (Isa. 6:9–10), summarized in verse 13 and then quoted more fully in verses 14–15, helps to explain their situation. For Isaiah himself, these verses predicted an unhappy ministry. His words would not move people to insight and repentance, but would leave many ignorant, obdurate, and distant from God. That will also be the effect of Jesus' parables. The text then goes on to consider why this is so.

Just as verse 11 ("to you it has been given") pointed to divine sovereignty, so verse 15 opens up the theme of human responsibility. The lines of Isaiah that Matthew quotes (from the Septuagint) emphasize the role of the human will. Attitudes shape responses, even to God's word. People's "hearts, ears, and eyes" are insensitive, because they make them so

the secrets of the kingdom of heaven have been given to some people and not others. He quotes a text from Isaiah, in which the prophet makes it clear that God deliberately makes people spiritually deaf and blind as a consequence of their sin. This text in Matthew lacks the sense of punishment that we read in Isaiah, but it nonetheless indicates that divine secrets have been unfolded only to some, and Jesus seems at least comfortable with the fact that a lot of people simply do not get what he is talking about. The interpretation that God in Christ chooses to be misunderstood by people raises significant theological questions that probably cannot be answered (because, of course, God's ways are not our ways), but nonetheless we ask them: Why be so deliberately obscure? Why make it more difficult for people to understand who you are? Why not make it easier for people?

Human hearts are calloused. The second approach that a preacher could take basically argues that God's obscurity is the fault of humanity. People's hearts are calloused, and that callousness deafens and blinds them to spiritual truth. In preparing this reflection I discovered that the Greek and Hebrew translations of "calloused" are "grown fat." Human hearts, it seems, are calloused with cholesterol. Rich eating and fatty foods have clogged people's arteries and made them sluggish. Creature comforts have turned people away from God; though humans hear, they can no longer understand; though they see, they can no longer comprehend. The distance between humanity and God is fashioned by human hands; people have only themselves to blame. A Calvinist preacher could even suggest that genetic disposition to heart disease is in our spiritual DNA; people pass it down from generation to generation.

Although there are plenty of biblical texts to back up either of these interpretations, both of them have their difficulties. The first depicts a God who puts people at a distance out of anger, or who selectively chooses only some individuals to receive the secrets of the kingdom of heaven. Preachers who opt for this interpretation will need to wrestle with knotty questions about God's character and the degree to which God cares for human beings. Preachers who choose the second interpretation, which depicts the fruits of human sinfulness, have a different set of challenges, not the least of which is that human sinfulness is not exactly a user-friendly sermon topic for worshipers.

It is a fact of the human condition that God is incomprehensible; yet human beings yearn for God, and believers trust that God yearns for humanity. How then shall we live? A third option for the

Theological Perspective

into that mystery. Thus Marguerite Porete writes that "everything one can say or write about God, or think about Him . . . is thus more like lying than speaking the truth."[1] Human understanding lacks the full capacity to know God; and beside God's truth, human language is but a lie.

Jesus speaks in parables because *all* theological speech is parable. Even so, the longing of the prophet for the reception of his message remains an important part of this passage. Isaiah laments that the dull of heart, the "hard of hearing," and those who "have shut their eyes" (v. 15, cf. Isa. 6:10) will not turn to God for healing. The frustrated prophet cannot coerce his audience (as Jesus does not), but he does not cease to cry out. Sandwiched between the parable of the Sower (13:1–9) and its interpretation (13:18–23), this passage assures both the disciples and Matthew's audience that the resistance they meet as they proclaim the gospel is simply to be expected. The "kingdom of heaven" (*basileia tou ouranou*) is an eschatological reality—already breaking through, but not yet fully present.

When the disciples ask why Jesus speaks in parables, he answers, "*The reason I speak to them in parables* is that 'seeing they do not perceive, and hearing they do not listen, nor do they understand'" (v. 13, emphasis added). The paradox of this statement does *not* boil down to a tautology: that because Jesus knows that people will not understand him, he chooses not to be understood. Jesus is not deliberately obfuscating the gospel. Parables conceal holy mystery, but they also reveal it with a subtlety lacking in other forms of communication. Jesus plants parables in the imaginations of his hearers to do the work that Scripture and theological language are supposed to do: take root, mature, and bear fruit. He does not promise results, for much depends on the recipient; but the parable is sown with the spirit of hope that undergirds all of Christian proclamation.

MICHELLE VOSS ROBERTS

Pastoral Perspective

section of the Gospel) that quite often seeds fail to grow, families do not always support us, and harmful weeds show up in the midst of the grain. Especially for the followers of Christ, knowing the true nature of discipleship and kingdom work is essential.

So, how do we deal with disappointment? How do we react when people and situations let us down? While perhaps not the main point of the text, these questions point to a pastoral issue that often comes up in the life of a congregation.

Our first reaction may be to put forth more effort and to exhort others to do more in order to increase the harvest. However, this response is based in anxiety, not in faith. The parable reminds us that God's work is most often hidden, mysterious, and silent. As heirs to the ones "blessed with eyes to see and ears to hear," we must look more deeply, exercise patience, and resist the temptation to assume that human action can bring our salvation. The sowing and harvesting are ultimately God's work, not dependent on human effort.

What appears now to be disappointment and failure is instead a "picture of temporary and provisional pessimism but ultimate optimism."[3] Is not the tension between pessimism and optimism often played out in the life of a congregation? For many churches this *is* a difficult time; economic stress, shrinking membership, and cultural exile can cultivate not just pessimism but even hopelessness and despair.

The preacher would do well *not* to ignore these signs with a falsely Pollyanna-like attitude. The church's liminal reality in our chaotic world must be acknowledged. At the same time, our call is to "ultimate optimism" in that we are people—the family—of the resurrected Christ, who already know the outcome of the harvest. Perhaps that is one interpretation of the "mysteries and secrets" that Matthew wanted the early church community to remember.

The Great Aside offers the preacher an opportunity to delve deeply into the messy issue of disappointment and loss. This can be dangerous territory for some, but can also produce an abundant harvest for those willing to follow Jesus' risky call to vigorous and renewed discipleship.

MARK R. BURNHAM

1. Marguerite Porete, *The Mirror of Simple Souls*, trans. Ellen L. Babinsky (New York: Paulist Press, 1993), 194–95.

3. M. Eugene Boring, "The Gospel of Matthew: Reflections," in *The New Interpreter's Bible* (Nashville: Abingdon Press, 1996), 8:306.

(v. 15), and they do this out of reluctance to "turn" their lives toward God. In turning they might find new wholeness. Instead, they hold at arm's length the word that calls them to this wholeness.

Among such people, Jesus teaches in parables. He does not confront the crowds with claims that require instant acceptance or rejection. Rather, he teases their minds and beckons them to grow into understanding. Many, he knows, will not go to the trouble that is necessary if they are to change. He has already spoken of the frustrations and resistance around his ministry (10:16; 11:20; 12:39). Others will "seek and find" (7:7), and they will surely be richly blessed in their finding.

The interlude ends with an emphatic and confident word of blessing. The disciples, says Jesus, are at a hinge point of history, a moment of unprecedented light and hope. They "see and hear" (v. 16)—not only formally and outwardly but inwardly too. They have begun to find Jesus' message clear and credible. This sets them apart from two other groups: the outsiders, who do not perceive; and the "prophets and righteous" of ages past (v. 17), who heeded God in their own time and would have loved to hear the fresh and present word of the kingdom. As elsewhere in the New Testament (John 8:56; Heb. 11:13; 1 Pet. 1:10–12), we see the faithful of the Old Testament as a people looking forward to the greater light that has now appeared in Jesus. This places the disciples in a company to be envied. They stand at the pinnacle and center of God's revelation.

Enviable though their place in time may be, these disciples still flounder between insight and failure. While Mark tends to highlight their ignorance and mistakes, Matthew will say more about their growth in understanding. Matthew will also acknowledge that they can be faithless and inadequate (16:22–23; 17:20). Their journey involves both progress and stumbling. Matthew writes as a wise pastor. Even a church that knows the gospel must learn—sometimes slowly and painfully—to live by it.

JOHN PROCTOR

preacher is to forget trying to explain why people cannot fathom the mystery of God, and explore instead how we might live with that reality.

Rabbi Abraham Joshua Heschel, a twentieth-century scholar and teacher known for his wisdom, his spirituality, and his concern for social justice and interfaith dialogue, suggests that prayer is a practice that helps believers live in the uncomfortable space between God's mystery and their own rough callousness.[1] Although Heschel writes from a Jewish perspective, he has profound insight to offer Christians. He understands prayer as an event, rather than a thought process, and as an action that allows people to perceive things that senses alone cannot discern. When lived into and practiced deeply, prayer can be an occasion in which—even for a moment—God draws near, or human callousness softens, or people see human and divine truths. Heschel writes, "To pray is to open a door, where both God and soul may enter. Prayer is arrival, for Him and for us. To pray is to overcome distance, to shatter screens, to render obliquities straight."[2]

As Christians we affirm that, in the person of Jesus Christ, God overcame the distance between God's mysterious grandeur and human sinfulness. Still, even in the fullness of salvation we sometimes hear without understanding and see without perceiving. We continue to be blind and deaf to the gospel. We are at times singularly obtuse, and at its best our theologizing falls short of fully embracing God's wondrous goodness.

In prayer we stop trying to figure things out and admit that we will never fully understand. Instead, we open the doors of our hearts and trust ourselves to the mystery and grandeur of God. Sometimes that is enough.

> We put our hope in the LORD.
> He is our help and our shield.
> Our heart rejoices in God
> because we trust his holy name.
> LORD, let your faithful love surround us,
> because we wait for you. (Ps. 33:20–22 CEB)

DEBORAH J. KAPP

1. Abraham Joshua Heschel, "On Prayer," *Conservative Judaism* 25, no. 1 (Fall 1970), reprinted with permission at http://www.notredamedesion.org/en/dialogue_sidicView.php?id=417; accessed December 31, 2011.
2. Ibid. I cannot do justice to Heschel's broad and multifaceted understandings of prayer in a few, short paragraphs. I refer interested readers to his books and other writings.

Matthew 13:18–23

¹⁸"Hear then the parable of the sower. ¹⁹When anyone hears the word of the kingdom and does not understand it, the evil one comes and snatches away what is sown in the heart; this is what was sown on the path. ²⁰As for what was sown on rocky ground, this is the one who hears the word and immediately receives it with joy; ²¹yet such a person has no root, but endures only for a while, and when trouble or persecution arises on account of the word, that person immediately falls away. ²²As for what was sown among thorns, this is the one who hears the word, but the cares of the world and the lure of wealth choke the word, and it yields nothing. ²³But as for what was sown on good soil, this is the one who hears the word and understands it, who indeed bears fruit and yields, in one case a hundredfold, in another sixty, and in another thirty."

Theological Perspective

In this text the hermeneutical problems confronting contemporary readers of the Bible emerge into open view. This parable acknowledges that the gap between the message and the meaning cannot be crossed without the intentional interpretive work of building a hermeneutical bridge. Whereas some other parables are left without explanation, with the assumption that both the materials and the blueprint for building the bridge are obviously present to the hearers, the need for an explicit statement of the parable's meaning highlights the alienation of the hearers from the interpretive traditions on which the parable depends. The interpretation of the parable in this case nearly overshadows the telling of the parable itself.

The interpretation of the parable being placed here following the parable itself is an admission that the primary issue for the hearers is an inability to bridge the gap between the message and the meaning. Therefore the interpretation not only attempts to explain the parable; it also attempts to show why the process of reaching understanding is fraught with difficulty. The interpretation itself lays out three hermeneutical snares that warrant the attention of the serious reader.

The first hermeneutical snare is suggested by the symbol of the seed sown along the path. The path is

Pastoral Perspective

In Matthew's presentation of the parable of the Sower, three categories emerge that in some way describe the reactions of real people, both ancient and contemporary, who either cannot accept Jesus' good news or who for various reasons are not able to sustain their faith in the Word. Jesus' explanation of this parable may not exhaustively describe how people understand the Word of the kingdom, and the three failed attempts in themselves may not form the main point of the parable or its explanation. Nevertheless, the explanation provided by Matthew's Jesus invites pastoral consideration of how and why the Word of the kingdom is received or not received in a variety of circumstances.

Besides the seed sown in fertile soil, the parable and its explication offer for our consideration the Word sown among those who do not understand, those for whom trouble and persecution outweigh their initial enthusiasm, and those whose belief is compromised by the cares and seductions of the world. In Matthew's Gospel alone, Jesus himself encounters enemies and friends who reflect these dispositions toward the Word. A number of scholars indicate that persecution and an attraction to worldliness were particular experiences of early Christian communities. This is no less true today. New Testament scholar M. Eugene Boring suggests

Exegetical Perspective

Jesus' parable of the Sower becomes the parable of the Soils in this allegorical interpretation of it. The focus shifts from the remarkable sower who can reap a miraculous harvest from an unimpressive planting—even though three-fourths of the seed is lost, he gathers a hundredfold—to the various locations where the seeds fall. Mark's interpretation of the parable has already done that, of course (Mark 4:13–20), but Matthew further draws our attention to the four kinds of soil by a series of small editorial changes. First, he emphasizes the personal character of the seed: "when anyone hears the word" in Matthew 13:19 is literally, "when *each* one hears." Matthew specifies that the "word" the sower scatters in his field is "the word of the kingdom" (v. 18). He further describes the one who hears "and does not understand," and says that the word is sown "in the heart" (v. 19). This is for Matthew not a story about Jesus or his preaching but about people's existential responses to that preaching, whatever the original parable may have said about Jesus' ministry.[1] Furthermore, this interpretation is addressed to Jesus' disciples alone, not to the crowd that hears the parable, which reinforces the impression that

1. For a perceptive discussion of how the parable may have sounded in Jesus' ministry, see Nils A. Dahl, "The Parables of Growth," in *Jesus in the Memory of the Early Church* (Minneapolis: Augsburg, 1976), 141–66.

Homiletical Perspective

Promise and danger await the preacher in Jesus' explanation of the parable of the Sower in the Gospel of Matthew. The promise is this text's organic relationship to the parables that follow it: the Wheat and Weeds, and the Mustard Seed. Should the preacher wish, this provides a natural arc for a sermon series, something along the lines of "seeds, weeds, and needs."

The generative nature—the "seeds" of the kingdom, grace—could ground the first sermon, while "weeds" could evoke both "seasonal" (circumstantial, situational) and "perennial" resistance to the gospel, whatever its form, source, or motive. The third sermon could speak to the power of growth despite resistance, as well as the image and purpose of the planting: fruitfulness, harvest, shelter.

There is danger, however. Without careful critical and self-reflective study, preachers can lapse into easy exposition of the obvious, a clichéd retelling of already-assumed meanings, and the self-congratulations of thriving Christians.

Preachers and interpreters of Scripture do their work inside what has been called the "hermeneutical circle": we come to the text with a nascent or even well-developed sense of what it means, even before we read it. After all, we have heard these texts read, taught, and preached; they have generated meaning

Matthew 13:18–23

the site of the encounter with the evil one or the one whose goal is to frustrate comprehension. What is it that makes the path so inhospitable to understanding? One possibility is that the seed sown along the path is seed sown before its time. The meaning of the parable in this sense concerns a journey toward true understanding. The seed—that is, the Word—will take root only at the journey's end or destination. It must be incubated until fertile ground is reached. A second possibility is that the path represents ground that has been tramped down under the futile foot traffic of failure. In the third place, the path may represent an avenue to truth that has been carved out by others. The Word does not take root along the beaten path, but only as fresh trails are cut and new avenues are discovered. The hermeneutical insight suggested here brings to mind the thought of reformer Martin Luther.[1] One's understanding of the text is not the simple acceptance of previous interpretations, but happens along new boulevards of belief. Interpretations that are authentic require a kind of obedience to the radical invitation of the Word.

The second hermeneutical snare is symbolized by the seed sown on rocky ground. Rocky ground is associated with a joyful but superficial reception of the Word. The problem is that this superficial emotional reception does not provide the opportunity for putting down roots. Roots grounded in something other than superficial emotionalism are required to endure trouble or persecution. When there are no roots, the result is a falling away. Here the text suggests that a true understanding of the Word cannot gain sufficient depth amid the rugged realities of human existence if it is planted in the shallow soil of emotionalism. When trials and tribulations are encountered, this kind of understanding has no staying power. The hermeneutical insight suggested here is one that emerged during the Enlightenment, especially in the writing of Giambattisto Vico.[2] Interpreting texts involves a particular self-understanding. One cannot understand the text without taking into consideration the experiential context of the interpreter. Understanding requires attention to our historical context. Interpretations that are authentic require a kind of self-examination.

the kingdom of heaven refers not only to past and future realities but also to our communities in the present that are entrusted with God's Word and the responsibility to do God's will.[1] This parable and Jesus' explanation speaks directly to the contemporary challenges before Christians responsible for communicating the Word and responding to the Word today.

In particular, because Jesus refers to people hearing the Word of the kingdom for the first time or who are still struggling to discover its meaning, this parable and its explanation have the potential to address the context of our youth and young adults. Some of them are grappling for the first time with, and growing in their understanding of, what this kingdom of heaven may be about. They are wrestling with what it means to live in response to God's Word in their daily lives. It goes without saying that today's youth grow up in very complex contexts and are tempted to listen to many words other than God's. Some may feel little obligation to listen to the Word, to try to understand it, to make sacrifices for it, to reprioritize their lives for its sake, or to participate actively in the kingdom now.

The good news contained in this parable may be that the Word of the kingdom may appeal to young people by the very way it is scattered. The sower scandalizes some because of his inefficient broadcast, almost indiscriminate in his willingness for the seeds to fall where they may, in the different soils and on the path. Episcopal priest Robert Farrar Capon notes that, in parables such as this one, God uses what Luther described as left-handed power. God does not force or use coercion but, instead, relies on the freedom of those in the parables (and those listening) to participate freely.[2]

Such an approach may appeal to young people because it respects and resonates with their yearning to make up their own minds about how to receive the Word, as opposed to being pressured to conform or to accept unquestioningly a Word that raises as many questions as it answers. Such an approach does not, however, remove the threats of trouble or persecution; it does not eliminate the cares of the world or the influence of greed from the lives of young people who accept God's kingdom and its responsibilities. It simply gives them space and time and freedom to respond.

---

1. Luther's confession of faith and his refusal to recant his interpretation of the Bible at the Diet of Worms in 1520 was based in his understanding of the authority of Scripture. He refused to accept the authority of any interpretation of Scripture save his own.
2. In Vico's influential work *The New Science* (1725), the noted philosopher and jurist argues that meaning and truth are created or made, that interpretation takes place within the context of history.

1. M. Eugene Boring, "Matthew," in *New Interpreter's Bible* (Nashville: Abingdon Press, 1995), 8:291.
2. Robert F. Capon, *The Parables of the Kingdom* (Grand Rapids: Zondervan, 1993), 20.

Exegetical Perspective

we are invited by this text to reflect on our own discipleship.

Discipleship is a major concern in Matthew's Gospel. A disciple follows Jesus, of course (4:20, 22; 8:18–22; 9:9, 27; 10:38; 12:15; 14:13; 16:24; 19:2, 21, 27–28; 20:29, 34; 21:9; 26:58; 27:55), but mere adherence is not enough. "Not everyone who says to me, 'Lord, Lord,' will enter the kingdom of heaven, but only the one who does the will of my Father in heaven" (7:21; cf. also 12:50; 21:31). To do God's will is to bear the fruit of righteousness (3:8, 10; 7:15–20; 12:33; 13:8, 26) and to offer a response worthy of the kingdom of heaven, as the parable of the Wedding Garment demonstrates so graphically (22:11–14). A disciple is not simply one who listens to Jesus' teaching (the word for "disciple" in Greek is derived from the verb "I learn"), but one who obeys him, who understands the radical implications of his interpretation of God's law (5:17–48), and who engages in Jesus' own ministry of exorcism, healing, and preaching (chap. 10).

Matthew sees three threats to one's hearing the word sown in the heart, understanding it, and bearing the fruits of discipleship. The first is cosmic in nature: the evil one might come and snatch away the word (v. 19). Satan is a minor character in Matthew's Gospel, but a powerful one. He appears first as Jesus' tempter in 4:1–11, where his three challenges and Jesus' responses interpret passages of Deuteronomy to describe Jesus' identity as God's Son and his work as God's Messiah.[2] Jesus calls Peter "Satan" at 16:23, when Peter rebukes Jesus for talking about his crucifixion. The devil will appear again shortly in chapter 13, when he is named as the "enemy" who sows weeds among the wheat (13:39). The inbreaking of the empire of heaven in Jesus' ministry is a threat not only to the Roman Empire but also to the reign of Satan. Although he will ultimately be defeated, he continues to wage war against the saints.

A second danger to discipleship is a superficial or insincere response to the gospel (13:21). Although this disciple initially welcomes the word "with joy" (v. 20), the world's hostile response is too much to bear, and in the face of persecution he or she abandons the faith. The word the NRSV translates as "trouble" refers to a good deal more than difficult life situations. The older translation was "tribulation," and Matthew's use of the word (see 24:9, 21, 29) accords with that of other apocalyptic Jews and Christians who speak of the heavenly and terrestrial

2. John P. Meier, *Matthew* (Wilmington, DE: Michael Glazier, 1980), 28–31.

Homiletical Perspective

in and among us. That said, some experience or reality outside the text—the lectionary, say, or a crisis in the congregation—brings us back to it, looking for insight, clarification, help. That conversation is ongoing.

Responsible readers—and those who read these texts in communities of faith—do not create their own subjective meaning, irrespective of the author or text's priority. Scripture is not a Rorschach blot. Neither, however, should preachers be content to mimic prior interpretations, as if a text's meaning is defined by past engagements.

The text before us is a prime example. It may be that Matthew has Jesus "explain" the parable of the Sower in light of his congregation's mystified and frustrated experience of preaching the kingdom in the world. We may find resonance in that explanation, but the Gospels remind us that Jesus said "many things in parables." That to say, the parables are polyvalent: the conversation continues, and meaning is never exhausted by one interpretation.

Alongside a historic reading, it may help preachers to interpret these parables (indeed, any text) through three additional lenses: the personal, the congregational, and the anti-self-congratulatory. It is most likely that if we read a text and identify with the good guys, we will have missed the point. That will be especially evident in the Wheat and the Weeds.

The parable of the Sower is present in all the Synoptic Gospels. Of interest: the sower is barely mentioned in any telling of the parable; and in Matthew and Luke, the sower is not mentioned at all in the explanation. The focus is on the seed, then the ground.

Mark tells us that the "sower" is the one who "sows the word," and while it is a natural impulse to identify the sower with Jesus, one could suggest that the sower is God, or the Spirit, or, indeed, anyone who speaks the word, "sows the seeds" of the kingdom.

If Matthew has in mind the early church and its evangelistic efforts, the four soils represent four prevailing reactions to the church's preaching (and most assuredly the experience of Matthew's church). Some do not, perhaps cannot, hear or receive the message at all; their hearts, minds, souls, like a path walked on so many times and hardened by experience or predisposition, have not the slightest crack into which a seed might fall. Others quickly receive or embrace "the word," but the growth is deceptive; when trouble or persecution comes, these wither away just as quickly. There are those who would welcome and

Matthew 13:18–23

Theological Perspective

The third hermeneutical snare is symbolized by the seed sown among the thorns. The thorns are associated with worries of life (existential anxieties) and the deceitfulness of wealth. The result is that the Word is made unfruitful. The text suggests that there is a relationship between existential anxieties, material deceptions, and interpretation. The hermeneutical challenge suggested by this third image is one addressed by Friedrich Nietzsche and Karl Marx. Both Nietzsche and Marx represent a kind of frustration, resignation, and despair regarding the possibility of fruitful interpretation. Nietzsche, despairing of the possibility of meaning, concludes that the message of theistic faith is absurd. The absurdity of the message is, in his view, a byproduct of the irrelevance of the idea of God. Thus we are left with the interminable anxieties of life.

Marx, convinced that meaning hides within the material crevices of life, declares that the message is simply a site for the manufacture of meaning. The meaning is simply the output of the means of production. Those who own the means of production in material terms also exercise hegemonic control over the production of meaning. Therefore the accumulation of wealth, in his view, constitutes a barrier to true understanding. The older view of wealth as a sign of God's blessing is thereby demystified. Wealth now reveals nothing about the character of humanity or the will of God. Wealth, in this sense, is deceitful. Faith is the name of the act of resisting the worries of life and the deceit of wealth and is the sine qua non of true understanding. Interpretations that are authentic require a kind of confession.

This passage ends with an affirmation: the seed that falls on good ground yields a crop (of interpretations) thirty, sixty, or a hundred times more than what was sown. What is noteworthy is that a fruitful interpretation or a successful hermeneutic is known as such because of its generative character: fruitful interpretations yield subsequent fruitful interpretations. This implies that the value of any interpretation is found, not in its finality or hegemonic claims, but in the fact that it continually gives birth to subsequent interpretations.

JAMES H. EVANS

Pastoral Perspective

Faith-community leaders have a role to play in embodying the grace of the kingdom with our youth as they shepherd young people through the pitfalls that may challenge their reception or seduce them away from their initial embrace of the Word. Here we need to consider the unintended consequences of our teaching and preaching. How do we communicate to youth in our preaching and teaching without sacrificing substance? We can keep our preaching simple, but in the process will we sound like proponents of cheap grace, or will we insult the intelligence of our young people? How do we learn to trust the wisdom of our young, whose reception of the Word may enhance our understanding as well?

Moreover, our presentation of the Word of the kingdom has to take into account the myriad other words being peddled to youth within the culture. Do we try to compete with those other voices and kingdoms vying for their attention? Will discipleship become one more activity in their overscheduled lives, choked out by competing priorities? Given the great variety of influences that cry out for their attention and offer promises from the moment our children are born, is it ever too early to introduce our young to the Word of the kingdom?

Attending to the proclamation of God's kingdom with an eye to where it does not grow, as well as with openness to new ways to facilitate growth, is an effective pastoral strategy. It challenges us to incarnate God's realm in our daily interactions and to invite others to shape their lives in similar ways in response to the Word. Offering options of how to live faithfully in response to the Word of the kingdom may aid others who face the seductions, anxieties, and persecutions that obstruct fruitful and abundant harvests. To live in response to the Word with integrity and embodied authenticity may be close to what Jesus meant when he spoke in this parable of the Word that is sown among those who receive it and respond with a fruitful enthusiasm.

ADAM E. ECKHART

cataclysms that will attend the last days. For Matthew, the realm of God not only evokes demonic hostility; it also causes cosmic disruption. Christian discipleship is not for the faint of heart.

Finally, "the cares of the world and the lure of wealth" easily derail Christian discipleship (v. 22). This, even more than the other two threats, is familiar to contemporary Christians. When Jesus calls you to leave your family (4:22; 8:22), sell your possessions and give to the poor (19:21), and to pick up your cross to follow him (10:38), the cost can seem far too great. The rich man in 19:16–22 is one such disciple, and Judas is another (26:47–50), but the rest of the Twelve are not so different once Jesus is arrested, and they flee in fear.

Stanley Saunders argues that Matthew's parables are deliberately ambiguous; they always offer more than one way of being heard. This interpretation of the parable of the Sower functions much as the parables themselves do. It confronts the listener with multiple images of how one might respond to Jesus. The disciples—and Matthew's listeners—are invited to wonder what kind of soil they are. Jesus has already told them they have been granted "the mysteries of the kingdom of heaven" (13:11, even more than the single "mystery" in Mark 4:11!); so perhaps they think of themselves as the good soil that produces a miraculous harvest. The greatest attention in the story, though, is paid to the road, the rocky patches, and the thorn bushes where seeds fall fruitlessly. Could the disciples instead be superficial followers of Jesus, who are easily deterred by hostile forces or seduced by comfortable lives? Saunders observes:

> We may be tempted to construe knowledge of the kingdom's secrets as an absolute gift, always ours once given. But the fate of seeds that fall on the road, spring up in rocky soil, or are choked by thorns warns us that knowledge will wither and dissolve when it is not sustained in faithful practice.[3]

E. ELIZABETH JOHNSON

embrace the word, and those who in fact do receive it, but their soil is already oversown and overgrown, and the late-arriving word is choked and proves unfruitful. There are those who are good soil for the good seed; there is growth and fruitfulness.

Does this allegorical interpretation "fit" the parable, either form or content? Scholars have debated. Whether or not, there is little question that the explanation both aptly describes what we can know about the reaction of the original audience to Jesus' preaching, and also what we may surmise about the experience of Matthew's congregation and our own.

It is precisely here, however, that we must be the most careful. It is so easy to self-identify with the good soil, and if we do, our preaching becomes self-congratulations. An honest "personal or pietistic" sermon could well ask, Are not all of these four soils present in each heart? Confession could play an important role: "my" spiritual acreage so hardened, so shallow, so overcommitted that the seed's fate in me is analogous to the seed in the parable. Still, there is some good soil too. How might that soil be tilled or cultivated to produce fruit?

A congregational lens might let us say, yes, we see how "they in the world" respond to the gospel, but how might these soils help us understand our congregation's response? A fascinating study would be to read Revelation 2 and 3 by means of the parable of the Sower: the "hard" church in Ephesus, the "shallow" church in Sardis, the "overgrown" churches in Pergamum or Thyatira, the "fruitful" churches in Smyrna and Philadelphia.

When discussing the parable of the Sower, C. H. Dodd suggested that the "various interpretations (in the explanation) meet the preoccupations of the early church, both in encouraging the hearing of the word and in accounting for lack of belief in it."[1] Yes, and that is not a bad thing. Our concerns and preoccupations—wider issues of the day in theology, nation, or world, and matters of the moment in homes, congregations, ministry—invite us to put on our corrective lenses in order to read these texts responsibly and authentically inside the hermeneutical circle.

THOMAS R. STEAGALD

3. Stanley P. Saunders, *Preaching the Gospel of Matthew: Proclaiming God's Presence* (Louisville, KY: Westminster John Knox Press, 2010), 120–27.

1. C. H. Dodd, *The Parables of the Kingdom* (New York: Charles Scribners' Sons, 1961), 145, cited in Bernard Brandon Scott, *Hear Then the Parable* (Minneapolis: Fortress Press, 1989), 344.

Matthew 13:24–30

²⁴He put before them another parable: "The kingdom of heaven may be compared to someone who sowed good seed in his field; ²⁵but while everybody was asleep, an enemy came and sowed weeds among the wheat, and then went away. ²⁶So when the plants came up and bore grain, then the weeds appeared as well. ²⁷And the slaves of the householder came and said to him, 'Master, did you not sow good seed in your field? Where, then, did these weeds come from?' ²⁸He answered, 'An enemy has done this.' The slaves said to him, 'Then do you want us to go and gather them?' ²⁹But he replied, 'No; for in gathering the weeds you would uproot the wheat along with them. ³⁰Let both of them grow together until the harvest; and at harvest time I will tell the reapers, Collect the weeds first and bind them in bundles to be burned, but gather the wheat into my barn.'"

Theological Perspective

This parable is one of the most familiar ones in the New Testament. Its importance is evident in the way that Christian writers have employed it to illustrate and support certain theological convictions. For example, Augustine referred to the parable as an analogy for the church, arguing that within the body of Christ reside wheat and tares: "I tell you of a truth, my Beloved, even in these high seats there is both wheat, and tares, and among the laity there is wheat, and tares. Let the good tolerate the bad; let the bad change themselves, and imitate the good."[1] Martin Luther cited the parable to argue that true believers and heretics must coexist until the eschatological harvest: "From this observe what raging and furious people we have been these many years, in that we desired to force others to believe; the Turks with the sword, heretics with fire, the Jews with death, and thus outroot the tares by our own power, as if we were the ones who could reign over hearts and spirits, and make them pious and right, which God's Word alone must do."[2] Roger Williams, Baptist

1. Augustine, "Sermon 23 on the New Testament," trans. R. G. MacMullen, in *Nicene and Post-Nicene Fathers, First Series*, vol. 6, ed. Philip Schaff (Buffalo, NY: Christian Literature Publishing Co., 1888), revised and edited for New Advent by Kevin Knight; http://www.newadvent.org/fathers/160323.htm.

2. *The Sermons of Martin Luther* (Grand Rapids: Baker Book House, 1906), 2:100–106; http://homepage.mac.com/shanerosenthal/reformationink/mltares.htm.

Pastoral Perspective

Congregations seeking to uphold God's justice may be confronted with complications that parallel those of the householder, slaves, the wheat and weeds.

If we hear the parable of the Weeds while experiencing injustice or evil, we may be stirred by the servants' questions: "Master, did you not sow good seed in your field? Where, then, did these weeds come from?" (v. 27). Variations of these questions are posed to God in prayer, to a pastor in her office, or to fellow Christians during coffee hour. We feel the grip of evil threaten our welfare and faith in God. Can we find hope from the householder's response that an enemy has done this, or that the weeds will remain until the harvest and in the meanwhile the wheat must persevere? Can those in the midst of suffering find much comfort in the fact that the servants do not protest? Would the civil rights movement, for instance, have made any difference if Martin Luther King Jr. and his colleagues waited for justice, as some white clergy suggested, rather than resist?

As unsatisfying as the householder's answers may be to suffering people, they pose other dilemmas for those compelled to separate goodness from evil. When the slaves ask the householder about pulling weeds, we can imagine their eagerness to help. However, the householder, representing God, cautions the

Exegetical Perspective

While some people accept the inevitability of having to weed their gardens, others in frustration may be tempted to invoke a line from this parable: "An enemy has done this!" For people who know well the vicissitudes of agriculture, there is something humorous about a farmer who blames an outsider—an enemy, even—for the weeds that invade his crop.

This particular farmer, though, is not paranoid or delusional. There really is nefarious activity afoot. "While everybody was asleep," Jesus says, "an enemy came and sowed weeds among the wheat, and then went away" (v. 25). Other farmers may deal with weeds as a fact of farming life; this farmer has a real enemy. The field hands too are surprised when darnel or rye grass springs up among the wheat (v. 27), because this is no ordinary nuisance. It is a plant that often carries a poisonous fungus that can contaminate a whole crop, particularly dangerous because it looks so much like the wheat.[1] Despite the fact that everyone has slept through the invasion, this farmer knows what has happened: "An enemy has done this" (v. 28). The dark humor of the situation suggests that Matthew intends the story to carry some kind of metaphorical meaning, as did the preceding

Homiletical Perspective

That ancient texts can speak in the present moment to contemporary circumstances is miraculous. That preachers can manipulate the texts to suit personal purpose or grind an ax is dangerous.

When texts are read carefully, they are at once generative and regenerative, confirming and correcting. However, sometimes we are so familiar with them—and this seems especially the case with the parables of Jesus—that we assume their "once and always" meaning, or rush to the "obvious" application that disrespects nuance, circumstance, and situation.

It was H. L. Mencken who said that for every complex problem there is an answer that is "neat, plausible and wrong."[1] He was not talking about biblical exegesis, but he might have been. The challenge for responsible preaching is, as it were, to "suspend belief," set aside presumed clear and simple (and often wrong!) meanings, at least until the text should, if it does, teach us that particular meaning again. Of course, it may not.

As we do with texts, then, we must also look beyond the obvious "presenting" issues that may preoccupy us in a moment, in order to discover what

1. Stanley P. Saunders, *Preaching the Gospel of Matthew: Proclaiming God's Presence* (Louisville, KY: Westminster John Knox Press, 2010), 128–29.

1. H. L. Mencken, "The Divine Afflatus," *New York Evening Mail*, November 16, 1917, reprinted in *Prejudices: Second Series* (New York: Alfred A. Knopf, 1920), 158.

Matthew 13:24–30

Theological Perspective

theologian and founder of Rhode Island, used the parable to support his views on religious tolerance.[3] Although this parable has been both useful and appropriate in these contexts, I want to suggest that there is a deeper and often unnoticed meaning to this passage.

Of the three seed parables that comprise this chapter, this one is not immediately accompanied by explanation or interpretation. It stands as spoken or received. The parable raises the question of what happens when the Word of God comes forth and its meaning is not readily apparent. Put another way, the mix of wheat and tares suggests that on occasion the hermeneutic task is stymied by the inexplicable. What happens when the message and the meaning are separated by an opaque veil? What is the relationship between the possibility of authentic understanding and the presence of evil? What is the relationship between the problem of theodicy and the hermeneutical problem? Matthew, the only one of the Gospels that includes this parable, provides an explication of the parable, but only later and at the insistence of the disciples. Rather than an interpretation, the explication turns out to be simply a transliteration, rendering, or rendition of the parable. It is symbolic, figurative, and allegorical.

The text suggests the economy of evil. First, good seed is planted in the field, which implies that the intention of the one whose Word goes forth is benevolent. Immediately, an enemy is introduced, who plants the weeds by night. The identification of the nighttime sower with the enemy exposes the intentionality of evil, rather than the presence of an unavoidable fact of life. The wheat initially blossoms, but afterwards the weeds appear. The goodness inherent in the good seed manifests itself initially. At the outset, it appears that the benevolence of the good seed will fulfill its destiny, but just as hopes are at the highest for the harvest, the weeds appear.

The question of the servant offers two insights. "Did you not sow good seed?" (v. 27b) raises the question of divine intentionality. "Where, then, did these weeds come from?" (v. 27c) raises the question of the origin of evil. These questions form the two poles of the theodicy question in Christian thought. Is evil part of God's plan? Is evil the evidence of another creative power? Both of these questions contain a challenge to the traditional affirmations of the goodness and power of God. However, the response

3. This parable lent further support to Williams's biblical philosophy of a wall of separation between church and state as described in his 1644 book *The Bloody Tenent of Persecution*.

Pastoral Perspective

servants that pulling the weeds will harm the wheat as well.

A church fires a pastor over misconduct but discovers that the termination affects not only the pastor but also the pastor's family. Missiles intended to strike enemy forces kill innocent civilians instead—so-called collateral damage. Wheat and weed coexist too closely to be dealt with separately.

Resemblance can also thwart efforts to separate good and evil. In less mature stages, weed and wheat will not be recognizable as a "fruit" or by easily discernible features. So too, motives, particularly in early stages, cannot be ascertained. When a wealthy parishioner donates a large sum to the church's benevolence fund, it may be to aid people in need or to elevate his or her position in church politics. Good and evil intentions can resemble each other so closely that only God can tell them apart.

The householder's reluctance to pull the weeds points out what American twentieth-century Protestant theologian Reinhold Niebuhr described as a fundamental dilemma in U.S. political history and a vexing problem of all human agency: ironic, unintended consequences.[1] When local churches send clothes to an overseas earthquake zone, could they know that instead of generously providing victims with vital supplies, they undermine an already-fragile textile market by flooding it with free clothes? Perhaps the people could not have known where their actions would lead. They have limited knowledge and power to control the ripple effects of their actions. On the other hand, how much research would it take to uncover the likely impact of the charity? Our good intentions can become as hurtful as those of the enemy, who swoops in at night, sows weeds, and departs as quickly as he came.

Unintended consequences point both to human powerlessness and to inherent moral ambiguity. In times of military action, for example, nations like to believe that they can eradicate evil or wage a war to end all wars, while claiming God is on their side. Such hubris assuredly leads to failure. We may want to serve as the householder's assistants—God's right-hand people—but the parable implies we are also God's plants, a complicated mixture of good and evil that cannot be fully pulled apart in history. God does not rely on our actions; we rely on God's merciful, steadfast patience to leave us in the field, intertwined until harvest time, rather than be pulled out early.

1. Paul Elie, "A Man for All Reasons," *Atlantic*, November 2007; http://www.theatlantic.com/magazine/print/2007/11/a-man-for-all-reasons/6337/.

explanation of the parable of the Sower in 13:18–23; again, differing options present themselves.

One way to think about this parable is to hear it as a description of the mixed character of the church. The parable of the Dragnet in 13:47–50 will similarly describe both "good" and "bad" fish that God will separate at "the end of the age" (v. 49), a phrase that recalls the harvest in the parable of the Weeds among the Wheat (v. 30). The harvest is a familiar metaphor for the Day of the Lord (9:37–38; 13:19), and the burning of the tares sounds for all the world like the fires of hell (cf. 3:12). Matthew later tells a highly allegorized version of the parable of the Wedding Feast (22:1–10; cf. Luke 14:16–24), to which substitute guests "both good and bad" are brought in (22:10; cf. 5:45; 13:48).

He then extends that parable with the story of one guest who has been hauled off the street of the destroyed city into the king's party to replace those on the invitation list who have been judged unworthy. He has no wedding garment and is therefore unworthy himself (22:11–14). So perhaps we are to see the wheat in chapter 13 as faithful disciples and the weeds as unfaithful. We are therefore, as the landowner says, to refrain from exercising judgment in the church before God executes it at the end of time: "Let both of them grow together until the harvest" (v. 30). If that is the case, though, what are we to make of Matthew's rather explicit instructions concerning church discipline in 18:15–20? There, the church is instead granted authority to bind and to loose (cf. 16:19).

On the other hand, perhaps the field in this parable is a metaphor not for the church as much as for the world. The farmer then might stand not for God but for the prevailing social and economic structures of Jesus' day, even the Roman Empire itself, and the "enemy" is instead Jesus, whose preaching, teaching, and healing are God's invasion of the old world with the empire of heaven. If so, Jesus is here, as in the Beelzebul controversy, the one who is stronger than Satan and ties him up in order to plunder his house (12:29), and the farmer represents the social, political, and economic forces that oppress God's people. Although the world opposes the church, it will not be destroyed. God will save it and judge its enemies.

Matthew's concern with the divided response to Jesus' ministry recurs throughout his Gospel. From the very start, he pairs the magi, who rightly discern Jesus' identity and worship him, with Herod's murderous treachery (2:1–18). Both John and Jesus preach about impending judgment using the

might be the deeper and more telling issues in ourselves and our circumstances—and thereby the more fertile ground for faithful cultivation. This deep "dialogue" is crucial (see 1 Tim. 4:16). Should we prove hermeneutically lazy on the one hand, or too bored, afraid, or distracted on the other, we will become what Edmund Steimle often called "expositors of the obvious": assuming meaning and borrowing application. This kind of obvious exposition is almost invariably self-congratulatory.

With that warning in mind, we turn to the parable before us, which is unique to Matthew: the Wheat and the Weeds. This parable is a prime example of a text that can provide surprising and interesting conversation if we do not assume too much at first about what it says, or too quickly imagine we understand what it says about us!

Very often this parable is preached and taught in a way that (a) lets preachers and hearers self-identify with the wheat; (b) gives the supposed faithful permission to identify not only the weeds but the source of the weeds and their certain doom; and (c) gives palliative counsel to "patience" by means of self-satisfied certainty: we will be saved, and they will be burned.

This traditional and typical allegorizing may in fact have been what Matthew wanted to say to his congregation: Yes, there are weeds among us, and "we" know who they are. We cannot do anything about it right now, but their day—and ours—is coming!

Still, there is enough ambiguity in the terms of the parable to produce real and healthy dissonance when attempting an interpretation. In other words, this parable, somewhat unlike the parable of the Sower, resists an easy allegorizing.

Is the man Jesus (or God) or someone else? Is the seed the gospel or believers, or something else? Does the field represent the world, or the church, or something else? Who is the enemy? Who are the servants of the householder? How shall we read and preach this parable? If it is an allegory at all, then it is an allegory in at least three ways.

One way to read this parable is as follows. God has generated, by Jesus and the seed of the gospel, the church. The church would be growing nicely, but an enemy has planted weeds among the wheat, to stunt growth, drain resources, and blight the field. We the servants might wish to root them out, but we are not allowed, indeed are unable. God assures us that when the time is right, the harvest will come. We will be gathered to heaven, and the

Matthew 13:24–30

Theological Perspective

to this question, "The enemy did this" (v. 28a), provides a productive detour around the traditional responses to the theodicy question. One traditional claim is that evil does not really exist; therefore, there is no personal manifestation of evil, that is, Satan. The identification of the enemy as the source of the evil runs counter to this.

However, the purpose of this parable is not to resolve the debates on theodicy, but to demystify evil in the experience of the listeners and readers. The point of this parable is not philosophical but ethical. The question is, what should be done in the face of the presence of evil in the world? Ethics is the point of the servants' question. They ask if they should pull up the weeds. This question reveals that the servants' understanding of the problem of the weeds (evil) is elementary. The presence of the weeds with the wheat means that the wheat must now compete in a field with plant life that provides no nourishment, feeds no souls, but uses precious resources. The planter responds that the good seed (the Word), while planted with pure intentions, must always contend with the impure. What is apparently good may also appear with evil. The wheat appears first, but as it reaches maturity, the weeds appear. In the world of the parable, soon after its appearance, the Word of God will be accompanied by error, falsehoods, and untruth.

At the end of the parable, the weeds seem to share a parasitic or symbiotic relationship with the wheat. It is impossible to separate them before the destiny of the good seed has been accomplished. This text suggests that the hermeneutical task may not be able to avoid the problem of evil. We must simply live with the weeds among the Word. Put another way, until the harvest, we may be compelled to interpret and hear the Word against the backdrop of negation.

JAMES H. EVANS

Pastoral Perspective

Reinhold's brother and fellow theologian H. Richard Niebuhr suggested that Christians are called to repent of their own wrongdoing before or instead of intervening in conflict, so that their actions do not judge their own sin. If God is active in human history, working toward the kingdom, then H. Richard Niebuhr believed that doing nothing could be an expression of faith in God's ultimate redemption of history.[2] This consideration, however, leads us back to the initial dilemma of deferring justice (and our complicity in injustice if we are not willing to intervene).

As those faced with opportunities for justice and service in history, we can appreciate how the parable itself calls both for discernment (seeing the difference between weed and wheat) and merciful withholding of judgment (especially in the face of unintended consequences). When serving at a local charity or on an overseas mission trip, listening to the wisdom of those whom we serve lifts up our common identity as God's children and gives voice to those who may otherwise feel neglected. Listening helps discern God's will as God's family and not as superior and inferior people.

Within congregations, our task is no different. Christ invites us to listen for God's direction and to each other, keeping the best interests of the community and God at heart, so that we are neither frozen in fear of doing wrong nor emboldened to act self-righteously.

A grown son took his mother to Christmas Eve worship. She was a teetotaler who did not approve of anyone drinking alcohol. As they sat down, the son noticed a disheveled man sitting in front of them whose head jerked back every few seconds. Initially the son presumed the man had a nervous tic—until he discerned the flask in the man's hand! The son was horrified, worrying that his mother might also notice the man drinking and demand the ushers escort him out; but when she did notice, the mother whispered into her son's ear, "That man is exactly where he needs to be tonight."

God calls the church to form and reform a faithful community of discerning people who persevere in hope of God's ultimate justice through Jesus Christ. At its best, the church is exactly where we need to be, because it is where we are seen for who we are—part weed, part wheat, and wholly reliant on God's grace.

ADAM E. ECKHART

---

2. "The Grace of Doing Nothing," *Christian Century*, March 23, 1932, http://www.ucc.org/beliefs/theology/the-grace-of-doing-nothing.html.

image of a tree that bears good or bad fruit (3:8–10; 7:15–19). The story of the paralyzed man in 9:1–8 contrasts the faith of his friends with the grumbling of the scribes.

Matthew himself will later offer another, allegorical reading of the parable of the Weeds and the Wheat (13:36–43) that also says the field is the world, but instead identifies the farmer as God, the wheat seeds as "the heirs of the kingdom,"[2] and the weeds as "the heirs of the evil one" (v. 38). The enemy is Satan, who plants the church's adversaries in God's field in an attempt to thwart the inbreaking of God's realm. This interpretation also assures the church of its eventual rescue from evil forces and its vindication at the judgment, but focuses on the church's opponents specifically. The characters in the parable with whom we identify make all the difference in the way we hear it.[3]

For the most part, Matthew's chapter of parables follows Mark's. This parable, though, stands in place of Mark's parable of the Seed Growing Secretly (Mark 4:26–29). Matthew's substitution focuses not so much on the surprising fruitfulness of Jesus and his ministry, which is what Mark's parables chapter underscores, but instead on the context of conflict within which Matthew's church lives. Although much of his Gospel reflects this conflict, it is perhaps clearest in the woes Jesus addresses to the scribes and Pharisees (chap. 23). Particularly in 23:13–15 we hear how fierce the competition is between Matthew and his Christian scribes "trained for the kingdom" (13:52) and their neighboring synagogues that do not believe in Jesus:

> You lock people out of the kingdom of heaven. For you do not go in yourselves, and when others are going in, you stop them. Woe to you, scribes and Pharisees, hypocrites! For you cross sea and land to make a single convert, and you make the new convert twice as much a child of hell as yourselves.

E. ELIZABETH JOHNSON

weeds will be burned (presumably, along with the one who sowed them.)

This particular interpretation is familiar to those raised in revival traditions or the Bible Belt, where evangelists regularly thundered that even those who imagined they were wheat were really weeds, and the time for judgment was coming! More authentically, though, this reading gains real traction where the church is infiltrated, oppressed, or even endangered for the faith. Read that way, the parable is a message of justice, of patience, of hope (see Rev. 1:9). Most of us in the United States are not in such a locus, though, and we must avoid the temptation to associate ourselves exclusively with the wheat.

A second reading, accordingly, might involve asking ourselves whether we are, individually or collectively, wheat or weeds. In other words, God indeed is planting, sowing, and the kingdom is trying to grow, straining toward a harvest of righteousness. Am I or are we—by attitudes and actions—stunting that growth, draining resources, blighting that good crop? Preachers need humbly to ask that question of themselves before they dare suggest it of others.

One interesting feature here is that it is the owner who demands patience of the servants, quite unlike the situation in "A Man Planted a Fig Tree" in Luke 13. Still, in both parables, the hortatory message is that "the time is surely coming."

A third option is more of a reach exegetically and certainly not in keeping with the allegorical interpretation of Matthew's Jesus later in the chapter (though somewhat in keeping with Luke's version of the Mustard Seed!). One could read the parable as a critique of "the System": the owner, the crop, the servants represent the economic, political, military status quo, while the church and even individual Christians are sown as subversive "weeds" in that field.

Absent the apocalyptic ending, there might even be a fourth way to read this parable. In each heart are both weeds and wheat, and we are not wise enough to know what, in fact, is what. Better to let God and the angels do their work.

THOMAS R. STEAGALD

---

2. The NRSV translates the phrase "children of the kingdom."
3. Saunders, *Preaching*, 128–30.

Matthew 13:31–32

³¹He put before them another parable: "The kingdom of heaven is like a mustard seed that someone took and sowed in his field; ³²it is the smallest of all the seeds, but when it has grown it is the greatest of shrubs and becomes a tree, so that the birds of the air come and make nests in its branches."

Theological Perspective

In this parable the seed can be understood as the Word of God upon which the kingdom of heaven is founded. The parables immediately preceding this one raise questions of interpretation. Prior parables in this chapter have drawn the reader's attention to the problems of interpreting the Word. The parable of the Seeds sown in various locales provides an entry into the hermeneutical problems that must have faced the hearers and later the readers of this parable. The parable of the Wheat and the Tares raises the issue of evil as a hermeneutical problem and suggests ways to address the interpretive challenges that surely must have faced its hearers and readers. The background questions here appear to be threefold. Where can we find the kingdom of heaven? How can we recognize its origins? What is the character of the kingdom in its fullness?

In this parable the kingdom of heaven is, as in previous parables, compared to a seed. This seed can be understood as a trope for the Word of God. Therefore, as noted above, it is out of this Word that the kingdom of heaven germinates. There is in this parable an inner tension that reflects the dynamic emergence of a kingdom consciousness among its hearers and readers. This inner tension is symbolized by the assertion that the seeds in question are planted *in a field* and the subsequent assertion that it

Pastoral Perspective

The parable of the Mustard Seed invites considerations of how we measure success. When we assess our work and aspirations with the kingdom of heaven in mind, it challenges the expectations of our consumerist culture. It is this kingdom, with its inauspicious inbreaking in the life and ministry of Jesus, that inspires reflections on this "smallest of all the seeds," which when full grown is "the greatest of shrubs" (v. 32)

Contemporary mores encourage ever-expanding consumerism and privilege grand achievement. Children are conditioned to expect they will continually grow out of everything, from clothes to each new round of electronics. Our young are often told that they are destined to grow up to do great and awesome things. Upwardly mobile parents expect from their children the best grades possible, in order to be accepted into the best colleges possible, in order to find the best job possible, so that they will accumulate the most lasting legacy possible. The gods of sport exhort athletes to "go big or go home." In many areas of our lives, contemporary culture sends the message, "the bigger, the better."

From this perspective, it would seem that the largest of plant life can come only from the largest of seeds and be known by the flashiest fruit. What happens to those who cannot compete, or those who

Exegetical Perspective

Few of Jesus' parables are as brief as the one-sentence parable of the Mustard Seed, and few as evocative: "The kingdom of heaven is like a mustard seed that someone took and sowed in his field; it is the smallest of all the seeds, but when it has grown it is the greatest of shrubs and becomes a tree, so that the birds of the air come and make nests in its branches." The image provokes a number of questions.

Why would someone deliberately sow mustard seed in a field? Although mustard could be a useful shrub, it had a reputation in antiquity for spreading like wildfire, much like the kudzu that was brought to the United States from Japan in the nineteenth century. It was meant to treat soil erosion and has now become an invasive nuisance throughout the Southeast, difficult to control and nearly impossible to destroy. This mustard of which Jesus speaks is particularly out of control: it is as large as a tree!

The claim that mustard is "the smallest of seeds" is something of an exaggeration; other seeds are smaller. The contrast between the size of the seed and the size of the mustard shrub seems to be the point of the parable, though. The image recurs at 17:20, where Jesus uses it again as a measure of smallness: "If you have faith the size of a mustard seed, you will say to this mountain, 'Move from here to there,' and it will move; and nothing will be

Homiletical Perspective

There is in the parable of the Mustard Seed both humor and hope. We find the parable in four versions (the three Synoptics and *Thomas*).

An intertextual observation: in Luke the parable has a discernibly countercultural message. How so? No (Jewish) person would intentionally sow mustard seeds in a garden—not only because the plant was wild and hardy, fecund and aggressive, but also because it violated the principle of "diverse kinds" that was so prominent in rabbinic discussion.[1] The Romans, however, (as evidenced by Pliny's *Natural History*) had an appreciation for the "pungent properties" of mustard and considered it beneficial for a host of gastrointestinal and other processes.[2]

Commentators will sometimes conclude that Luke either was unfamiliar with rabbinic concerns and added "garden" without realizing the problem, or was familiar enough with Roman custom to be undisturbed by the setting. More interesting is the notion that Luke, especially in light of his concern for reversals, is showing us how subversive the kingdom of God really is. God plants this weed in the world on purpose.

1. Bernard Brandon Scott, *Hear Then the Parable* (Minneapolis: Fortress Press, 1989), 374.
2. Ibid., 380.

Matthew 13:31–32

Theological Perspective

is the largest of *garden plants* (NIV) or *herbs* (KJV) or *shrubs/trees* (NRSV).

Some scholars have noted that the particular tree in question is quite invasive, and therefore listeners in Palestine would understand why it would not normally be planted in a garden. Pliny the Elder, writing around 78 CE, notes that the mustard tree, most likely the one referred to in this parable, was more like a malignant weed than desirable flora. He writes that "mustard . . . is extremely beneficial for the health. It grows entirely wild, though it is improved by being transplanted: but on the other hand when it has once been sown it is scarcely possible to get the place free of it, as the seed when it falls germinates at once."[1] On the other hand, if the parable is told to listeners who are outside of Palestine, then this detail would not be as important.

As told in Luke, the parable explicitly mentions that the seeds are planted in a garden, and in Mark the reader is left to assume that it is in a garden. Matthew, however, plants the seed in the field and suggests that the resulting plant turns out to be something other than a wild weed, introducing a theological tension in the minds of the listeners and readers.

Read intertextually, the reality to which the seed (Word) gives rise may be understood as a lovely tree in a well-manicured garden or as welcome refuge in an untended field. This suggests the presence of the Divine may be encountered in those moments and places where our lives are orderly, yielding an aesthetic appreciation. The kingdom of heaven may come in the form of glory and beauty. However, the presence of the Divine may also be encountered in those moments and places where our lives are chaotic, yielding an ethical comprehension of its challenges. The kingdom of heaven may come in the form of suffering and survival.

This parable is among the shortest of the parables of Jesus, and in its very structure suggests another hermeneutical challenge. The brevity of the parable is not just a feature of its formal structure; it is also part of the message of the parable. It has the literary form of a proverb. The seed is the smallest of seeds, yet its size is no indicator of its transformative potential. Another biblical reference compares this seed to the amount of faith needed to move mountains. This small seed can be understood as a little word. The parable is not just *about* a small word; it is itself the small word to which it refers.

Pastoral Perspective

discover the world really does not revolve around celebrity, or those who are overwhelmed by the pressures to consume and achieve? What happens when "going big" is understood in destructive terms? The words of poet Gwendolyn Brooks contain a haunting caution: "I shall create! If not a note, a hole. / If not an overture, a desecration."[1] Delusional promises of grandeur that suggest "the ever bigger will inevitably be better" eventually fall short, leaving those who ascribed to these misleading messages to face disappointment, emptiness, or even despair.

The kingdom of heaven does not hold out promises of fame or accomplishment, and does not see the signs of a bigger and better future in an unending stream of new technologies and unprecedented wealth. The ongoing inbreaking of the kingdom of heaven confounds our wildest imaginations, defies our best predictions, and continues to grow from seemingly small seeds. In some ways this is not new. One needs only to pay attention to significant movements in our world that sprouted from seemingly small seeds. Rosa Parks's refusal to change seats helps to launch the civil rights movement. Strangers in a San Francisco storefront decide to memorialize friends who died from HIV/AIDS with a quilt, and thereby initiate the world's largest participatory community art exhibit, which also generates awareness and compassion. For decades Muhammad Yunus revolutionizes the phenomenon of microcredit. By giving small loans, mostly to women who could not otherwise afford or qualify for credit, he in effect provides the seeds for thousands to start and sustain their own businesses. This initiative has a ripple effect economically, impacting families and communities across Bangladesh and spreading from there to the rest of the world, The so-called Arab Spring that results in the toppling of repressive governments in Tunisia and Egypt was spurred by the death of one young Tunisian man, Muhammed Bouazizi, who opposed his authoritarian government's unjust treatment of its people. Sometimes, as these examples demonstrate, the apparently smallest of seeds may prove surprisingly fruitful.

The small seeds are present in our own seemingly mundane, daily lives as well. The ongoing inbreaking of the kingdom of God continues in the ordinary: when a child reluctant to go to church camp experiences God's love in the activities and companions encountered during his week away; when a youth

1. Pliny the Elder, *Natural History*, trans. H. Rackham (London: W. Heinemann, 1938), 529–30. http://archive.org/stream/naturalhistory05plinuoft#page/528/mode/2up.

1. Gwendolyn Brooks, "Boy Breaking Glass," in *The Essential Gwendolyn Brooks*, ed. Elizabeth Alexander (New York: Library of America, 2005), 88–89.

impossible for you." In Mark, Jesus says of the mustard bush that "the birds of the air can make nests in its shade" (Mark 4:32). In Matthew, though, the shrub "becomes a tree, so that the birds of the air come and make nests in its branches" (Matt. 13:32). This is one large mustard plant, larger than any mustard plant Jesus' listeners would ever have seen. In addition to the exaggeration about how small the mustard seed is, Matthew increases the size of the plant that grows from it. Why?

Matthew 13 contains three parables about growing things: the Sower (vv. 1–9), the Weeds and the Wheat (vv. 24–30), and the Leaven (v. 33). This is not simply because Jesus' listeners are peasants who know about growing things, but because growth is itself mysterious; even the most experienced gardener marvels at the miracle of germination and the development of life. These are parables about the kingdom of God, which is also mysterious. What does growth say about God's mysterious realm? Is this parable intended to describe the invasive character of God's realm? Both the mustard seed and the leaven can be seen as stealthy, contagious, or invasive.

Does the parable instead attempt to explain why some people refuse to accept Jesus and his message? Some may have hard hearts, lack courage, or be subject to the devil's wiles (13:18–23). Others may resist "because of the strange and hidden manner in which God's empire is present" in Jesus' preaching, teaching, and healing.[1]

Warren Carter argues that the key to the parable is Matthew's exaggeration of the size of the bush become tree, because there are several passages in Scripture that similarly use trees in which birds make nests as symbols for empires.[2] In Judges 9:7–15, Jotham tells a parable against Abimelech in which a worthless bramble attempts to be king while an olive tree, a fig tree, and a grapevine refuse to do so. The bramble says, "Come and take refuge in my shade" (Judg. 9:15), rather than being useful to "gods and mortals" (vv. 9, 13), and thus is made a laughing-stock. In Ezekiel 17:1–10, the prophet portrays two competing monarchs, Nebuchadnezzar and Pharaoh Psammetichus II, as eagles that attempt fruitlessly to plant trees from a cedar from which they have taken pieces. Then the cedar that God transplants becomes so large that "in the shade of its branches will nest

1. Warren Carter, *Matthew and the Margins: A Sociopolitical and Religious Reading* (Maryknoll, NY: Orbis Books, 2000), 289.

2. Warren Carter, "Matthew's Gospel, Rome's Empire, and the Parable of the Mustard Seed," in *Hermeneutik der Gleichnisse Jesu: Methodische Neuansätze zum Verstehen urchristlicher Parabeltexte*, ed. Ruben Zimmermann and Gabriele Kern (Tübingen: Mohr Siebeck, 2008), 181–201.

What is not so obvious, but may be just as true, is that Matthew may be offering his version of the parable as a kind of countercultural word, just more subtly. The seed is planted not in a garden—though many in his presumably more affluent congregation might have had a garden—but in a field. If Matthew's hearers are not suspicious until it is too late, they are the more thoroughly "punked," as we might say. In other words, one way to read and preach this parable is as a joke—a joke on us!

Years ago I attended a preaching conference where the leader put on the video screen a large picture of Joel Osteen, and then another of Joel and his wife, both of them flashing megawatt smiles, as the conference leader quoted relevant passages from one or two of Joel's books: the prosperity God promises believers the obvious and even predictable evidence of God's favor, the material beauty of a life lived in faith. Then the leader put another picture on the screen: an aged Karl Barth. The place exploded in laughter.

When he put Joel and Karl side by side and left them there for a few moments, the laughter gave way to deep silence that suggests, in light of these two parables, an unspoken question: whose word will produce manifold growth for the sake of the kingdom of heaven?

To all appearances, given his own theological perspective, the man in the sharp suit and alligator shoes is already proof of the abiding fecundity of a prosperity gospel. This is what faith produces—for us! It is a peculiarly American perspective on the gospel.

Is the essence of the gospel what it does for us? Is it not, rather, what God provides for others and in really surprising ways?

We were seeing a kind of parable; the unlikely juxtaposition of those three pictures was worth several thousand words. Like many parables, and many good jokes, the effect was pungent, indeed. No further explanation was necessary.

The effect of the parable before us is also pungent. Mustard? MUSTARD?

Those who live in the southern United States may liken the mustard bush to kudzu. Once you get the stuff in your yard, there is no getting rid of it. Ever! Hear the laughter? The laughter is cleansing: an occasion for the faithful to laugh (as Abraham and Sarah did) at both the purposes of God and the instruments that serve God's purposes.

Weeds? Runaway shrubs? That signifies the kingdom? Yes, as does leaven or yeast, both of which carry a connotation of ferment or decay, qualities

Matthew 13:31–32

Theological Perspective

Thus the parable presents the hearer and the reader with a question. Is it possible for a small word to conceal a massive message? The power of a small word was central to the theological affirmation made by Martin Luther in his great hymn "A Mighty Fortress Is Our God." One verse points to the power of this little word when it speaks of the "one little word" that shall fell the prince of darkness grim.

In the popular interpretations, the parable is said to speak of the potential for the kingdom of heaven. Although God's dominion begins as a small seed, it grows large enough to encompass all. It is from small seeds and small deeds that the kingdom is born. This parable must have become a source of encouragement to early followers of Christ, because it recognized that they were a tiny sect that had been called to become a great movement.

The final image of the parable is of a tree that emerges from this smallest of seeds to become a shelter for the birds. This ending does nothing to resolve the textual tension in this story. Certainly, one interpretive trajectory holds that the expansive kingdom of heaven is embodied in the universal and worldwide reach of the church. In this sense, the church becomes the shelter that provides sanctuary for any and all seeking refuge in its branches. On the other hand, some scholars note that the mustard tree has never been particularly hospitable to birds and therefore would not normally attract them for nesting.

What does this say about the kingdom of heaven? Is the kingdom of heaven a beautiful and accommodating place that welcomes all into its open spaces? Is the kingdom of heaven a thorny and prickly place that tests, through suffering and discomfort, one's ethical resolve? The proverbial structure of this parable, like that of proverbs found in many cultures, embodies a deep experiential tension. The fact is that the parable points to the inner dynamic and tension within all talk about the kingdom.

JAMES H. EVANS

Pastoral Perspective

sees God in her neighbors during an Appalachian mission trip; when an estranged sibling's forgiveness reunites a family long torn apart. We participate when we teach Sunday school, share bags of groceries with our neighbors in need, accompany and pray for/with those who are sick. We participate in the ongoing inbreaking of the kingdom of heaven through our daily ministries, even though we may never really know if what we do or say makes a difference in the lives of others.

The parable of the Mustard Seed fuels our hope that indeed the seemingly insignificant not only matters but makes a difference and contributes in some way to the manifestation of the inbreaking of God's kingdom in our midst. It fuels our hope that God works at least as much through ministry as through majesty. We live in mustard-seed hope whenever we humbly engage in ministry in Christ's name, doing what may seem to be something really little for our neighbor, rather than something really big for ourselves. Such hope confounds those who seek the seeds of the kingdom of heaven among the grand; such hope challenges impulses to consume, especially at the expense of those among us in need; such hope both humbles and encourages.

If we presume that in our actions we have the potential to further God's will, then we may recognize in our ministries and interactions the significance of our service, even in the most mundane of circumstances. Just as God worked in the singular, humble life of Jesus Christ, God works still today through us, in apparently small and insignificant ways, to alter the course of history as well as the course of ordinary daily lives.

The parable of the Mustard Seed challenges us to evaluate critically those messages that advocate bigger as the source for better. The parable invites us to entertain the possibility that God intends for us not to be filled with big things, but to participate fully in God's kingdom here and now as well as eternally. If by God's grace we ground our ministry in hopeful humility, perhaps we may be able to pray in an embodied way the words of Jesus: "Your kingdom come. Your will be done, on earth as it is in heaven" (6:10).

ADAM E. ECKHART

Exegetical Perspective

winged creatures of every kind" and all nations will thereby know that "I [God] bring low the high tree, I make high the low tree" (Ezek. 17:23–24). Again in chapter 31, Ezekiel returns to the image of the Assyrian Empire as a cedar tree, this time so large that "all the birds of the air made their nests in its boughs" (Ezek. 31:6). In Nebuchanezzar's second dream in Daniel 4:10–12, "the birds of the air nested in [the] branches" of the tree that represents his empire. This biblical tradition of portraying empires as trees with nesting birds has influenced Matthew's retelling of the parable of the Mustard Seed. With it, he assures his people that, however much they are forced to accommodate the Roman Empire of their own day, God's empire will defeat it. Even though God's realm at present appears small and Rome appears to tower over the world, God's empire is mightier.

Stanley Saunders notes that Matthew's parables frequently point in more than one direction at a time. Although that might be said to be the very nature of parabolic or symbolic speech, Matthew seems to intensify the ambiguity of Jesus' parables and invite his listeners to work at interpretation. The parable of the Mustard Seed is a good example. Matthew exaggerates Mark's parable, uses language that points to familiar themes in the Bible, and, as Saunders's questions suggest, invites listeners to ponder what God is doing:

> Why does Jesus replace the mighty cedar tree, a symbol of power, arrogance, and empire, with the invasive mustard plant, a weed? Would the crowds have understood God's mustard-seed empire to be like Jack's beanstalk, reaching against all expectation, up to heaven and bringing the nations low? Is the kingdom of heaven a surprise that brings redemption, or a threat that must be eradicated, or both?[3]

E. ELIZABETH JOHNSON

Homiletical Perspective

that in large measure disqualified "leavened bread" from use in worship.

Little seed, big bush, a bush, not a tree, a shrub? Crabgrass! The kingdom of God is crabgrass. It is polk salad. It is dandelions. It is a flock of starlings. The kingdom of God is zebra mussels, invasive and (to some things) destructive and wildly, uncontrollably fecund.

More somberly, one can read the parable as Pauline. After all, God did choose what was weak in the world to shame the strong. God chose what is foolish in the world to shame the wise. God chose what is not to shame what is (see 1 Cor. 1).

What is it that God chose? Mustard, which Pliny says cleanses the bowels! God is determined to give the constipated world an enema! Of all things, mustard, a little seed, a shrubbish weed, for the sake of real need?

There is hope too, as well as humor, in this parable—for congregations and for preachers, who often feel like tiny seeds in a world that trades only in big, who feel insignificant in a world that trades in glamour and power, who feel like ugly failures in a world that is interested only in beautiful success. The hope is this: that from God's perspective the kingdom of God does not look only like big glass churches or former sports arenas, but like scruffy shrubs here and there—unattractive and unappealing, except to those birds that need shelter and shade. Mustard shrubs may be unwelcome to those cultivating a different kind of field, but they are celebrated by those who need just what they have to offer—room in their branches.

Preachers, abidingly, and congregations, increasingly, wonder whether who they are and what they are doing make any difference at all—or any lasting difference. Who would not want to be a mighty oak or a cedar of Lebanon? Who would rather be a small, scruffy bush with birds in our branches?

Jesus says the kingdom of heaven is like the scruffy bush, the leaven hidden. That same kingdom is glimpsed, even now, in the one with no form or comeliness who is telling the parable! When the kingdom does come, it will look a lot like a mustard bush: unimpressive, except to the one who sowed the seed, and those who find in it both shade and a place to raise their young.

A comforting word, and funny besides.

THOMAS R. STEAGALD

---

3. Stanley P. Saunders, *Preaching the Gospel of Matthew: Proclaiming God's Presence* (Louisville, KY: Westminster John Knox Press, 2010), 130.

Matthew 13:33–35

³³He told them another parable: "The kingdom of heaven is like yeast that a woman took and mixed in with three measures of flour until all of it was leavened."

³⁴Jesus told the crowds all these things in parables; without a parable he told them nothing. ³⁵This was to fulfill what had been spoken through the prophet:

"I will open my mouth to speak in parables;
I will proclaim what has been hidden from the foundation of the world."

Theological Perspective

The parables of Matthew 13 present readers with wonderful crosscurrents that trouble any attempt to derive a simple or moralistic meaning. As Augustine suggested, when we find difficulties in Scripture, we are being called to explore deeper levels of meaning. This is the great gift of Scripture, to call us into relationship with the Divine rather than to deliver pat answers. Before turning to reflect on this passage, let us first look at the practice of speaking in parables itself.

The narrator tells us that Jesus' parables fulfill the words of the prophet but alludes to Psalm 78:2–4:

I will open my mouth in a parable;
I will utter dark sayings from of old,
things that we have heard and known,
that our ancestors have told us.
We will not hide them from their children;
we will tell to the coming generation
the glorious deeds of the LORD, and his might,
and the wonders that he has done.

Speaking in parables conveys the wonders that our Beloved works in our lives and in history, so these works will not be hidden. However, the speaking is dark, opaque, indirect. The disciples do not understand (13:36). The parables themselves refer to things hidden—tiny mustard seeds, leaven hidden in

Pastoral Perspective

The question sounds simple: What is going on? This is one of the most important questions to ask, even if it is also one of the most difficult questions to answer. We ask the question when we are trying to discern the most caring response to a pastoral crisis. We ask it when we are trying to find our bearings or another's in a moral crisis. The difficulty is that asking questions sometimes gets in the way of figuring out what is going on. Who, what, when, where, why, and how are essential when gathering the details of a situation; but if we are seeking a deeper understanding, we are often impeded by a barrage of detail-oriented questions.

One key to figuring out "what is going on" involves being disrupted by the suspicion that something is going on in the first place. After all, empathy, or human understanding, is about being disrupted by another's crisis and uncertainty, being present with them when answers are not readily available. Parables invite readers to ask, "What is going on?" They disrupt our expectations and give us an opportunity to practice the kind of attention required for understanding.

We sense in these verses that Jesus has deep regard for the unexpected in the fabric of our everyday lives. We tend to think we understand well the images we see, the words we say and hear, and the

Exegetical Perspective

This segment of Matthew's parable discourse contains the parable of the Leaven (v. 33) and an explanation of the reason Jesus speaks in parables to the crowds (vv. 34–35).

Parable of the Leaven (v. 33). The parable of the Leaven is one of a group of "kingdom parables" in Matthew that begin with a set formula, "The kingdom of heaven is like . . . ," followed by a brief explanatory metaphor or vignette (see Matt. 13:31, 44, 45, 47; similarly 13:24). Matthew appears to draw this parable from one of his major sources, Q (see Luke 13:20–21). The "kingdom of heaven" (Matthew's characteristic designation rather than "kingdom of *God*") is compared to yeast that a woman mixes into three measures of flour. Ultimately the yeast leavens the entire amount of the flour.

There are several details that call for attention. The Greek term *zymē* for yeast is a loanword from Hebrew. In most metaphorical references to yeast in the Bible, it is considered a corrupting influence. The Passover ritual, for example, requires the casting out of old leaven (see Exod. 12:15). Paul uses the term in this same fashion: "Do you not know that a little yeast leavens the whole batch of dough? Clean out the old yeast so that you may be a new batch, as you really are unleavened" (1 Cor. 5:6–7; see also Gal.

Homiletical Perspective

The realm of God is like the yeast that a baker woman kneaded into a triple recipe until it permeated the whole batch. When it was ready, the bread was enough to feed the whole neighborhood.

It takes work to make bread. It takes the force of strong arms that can smash and squeeze and shape the dough. The leaven is distributed throughout the whole amount of flour. In the process the yeast is alive, pervasive, and hidden. After the work of kneading is the rest. The dough rests from the pulling and punching. The evidence of the yeast's power is revealed when the dough rises.

The parables rise up in us with new perspective. We are invited to see the world from a different angle. God-transforming moments can be hidden in the simplest of deeds. We may not see the effect of the power of the small and the hidden until there is a rising.

Leaven as Something Within. Years ago I was in my mother's kitchen. My two preschool children were happily playing on the floor. My mother and I were making biscuits. It was a recipe handed down to us from my mother's mother. My grandmother never used a recipe, but at our urging she gave us a handwritten card with estimates of the ingredients. Her method had been to scoop up a handful of this and

Theological Perspective

Pastoral Perspective

dough, seeds that mix weeds with wheat, a tale of a sower whose meaning is mediated, a treasure hidden in the earth. The Beloved longs to proclaim the kingdom of God, but his language can only indirectly evoke this glorious reign. Hidden and revealed, a treasure but one in the ground, a weed but one that shelters all creatures or grows up among wheat.

This riptide of hiding and revelation tells us something about how to wrestle with the parables. When we think of their meaning as comparable to Aesop's morality tales or fact-packed Wikipedia entries, we may be reducing our relationship with Scripture to a one-dimensional source of information or moralistic nuggets. Parables speak to us as spiritual creatures. They touch the mysterious depth where the divine image has not been darkened by despair or self-forgetfulness. Our reasoning mind tries to suck out of them a moral lesson, but the wonders that the Beloved has wrought elide this effort. They remind us that relationship is the most wonderful of the Beloved's work. They tangle us up in the mind of Christ, where nothing makes sense and yet we are consoled by his presence.

Parables open what is hidden in plain sight, something the Beloved relentlessly tries to expose, and yet even his closest disciples have trouble understanding. As we meditate on the parables, it is important to remember that they are speech that utters dark words, hiding even as they uncover. Nevertheless they are words spoken to crowds, written in Scripture so that they can be broadcast as widely as possible. Seeking a meaning that evades us, we fall into the mysterious depth of the Divine.

Like many parables, this offers a homely and humble image: the kingdom is like a woman kneading dough (v. 33). Jesus is working to convey to the crowd gathered around him the astonishingly old and breathtakingly new awareness that intoxicates him. He is lit but not exactly with knowledge; he is shot through with the immediate nearness, intoxicating loveliness of the divine presence. He walks in Paradise wherever he is. Dusty and hungry, he travels country roads where peasants have been dislocated by imperial economics, where fisherman are losing their livelihood, where artisans like his own father are driven from poverty to desperation and women suffer the predations of a society dissolving into military rule. Here, amid this suffering, horror, and confusion he roams: a light, a radiance. Crowds follow him everywhere. They exhaust him with their importunities. They beg for healing and food. They are dying of thirst, parched for a word.

things we do day after day. However, Jesus' parables invite new interpretations of the familiar. In this parable, Jesus evokes the image of a woman adding yeast to flour—but listen again: she is adding yeast to fifty pounds of flour! Matthew's readers might catch the similarity between the amount of flour in the first parable and the amount Sarah used to prepare cakes for the unexpected visitors (Gen. 18). This is no ordinary recipe for a simple loaf of bread. Something is going on here.

Jesus invites us to pay attention to the leaven that is hidden. As long as it is alive, yeast hidden will be found out in the rising and baking. For this reason, yeast has come to symbolize moral corruption—invisible yet infectious, hidden for now but soon followed by visible results.[1] The familiar reference to leavening, as analogous to a tangible threat of moral corruption so infectious that it impacts the whole heap of us, is upended. Yes, this leavening is infectious, but instead of a symbol of moral corruption, Jesus likens hidden leaven to the kingdom of heaven. Something is going on here.

Jesus invites us to pay attention to the image of a woman not as someone removed from the most important tasks of discipleship, but as the character necessary for the leaven to be mixed with the flour. Many of Matthew's readers and some readers today consider the work of women to be hidden inside kitchens, at home, away from public leadership. In this parable the manifestation of the kingdom of heaven could not happen without the action of the woman. The kingdom of heaven requires embodied human participation in preparing and kneading the bread of life. Here this woman's work is highly valued: it brings the bread of life to the world.[2] Something is going on here.

After disrupting our expectations with leaven mixed in an enormous amount of flour and with a woman as an agent of the kingdom's manifestation, Matthew turns our attention to the parable as the way Jesus "tells" the crowd. In parables, Jesus proclaims what has always been present yet continues to be perceived as hidden. How paradoxical! The parables themselves reveal the truth that has been hidden from the foundation of all creation. We remember that creation is founded in the deep (Gen. 1), the creative context of all of life as understood in Christian and Jewish traditions. Hidden in the ordinary

1. Bernard Brandon Scott, *Re-imagine the World: An Introduction to the Parables of Jesus* (Santa Rosa, CA: Polebridge Press, 2001), 21–34.
2. Amy-Jill Levine, "Matthew," in *The Women's Bible Commentary*, ed. Carol A. Newsom and Sharon H. Ringe (Louisville, KY: Westminster John Knox Press, 1992), 258.

5:9). Matthew's Gospel will also use "yeast" in a negative sense, as in 16:6, where he warns his disciples of the "yeast of the Pharisees and Sadducees."

In the parable of Leaven, however, yeast seems to be viewed as a dynamic and positive force, one that at the outset seems insignificant and inert but soon transforms all of the flour. Does Matthew choose the ambiguous sense of yeast here because the religious leaders have accused Jesus of being a corrupting influence? One whom in the preceding chapters they termed a "glutton and a drunkard" (11:19) and in league with Satan (12:24)?

The proportions of the ingredients are also something of a puzzle. "Three measures of flour" is a large amount. Although estimates vary, most commentators believe that this is more than fifty pounds of flour, which, once leavened into dough, is capable of yielding enough bread to feed more than a hundred people. Is this extraordinary amount to be seen as one of the typically fantastic features of Jesus' parables—something that is meant, in the words of the great British exegete C. H. Dodd, to "tease the mind into active thought about its meaning"?[1] Would Jesus' contemporaries find such an amount to be a startling exaggeration? Was bread making perhaps a collaborative village task, so that such amounts would not be exceptional?

In any case, there remains the stark contrast between the rather humble beginnings of the process (yeast placed in three measures of flour) and the ultimate outcome, when the yeast leavens all of the ingredients and completely transforms it from meal to dough. It is this transformation that seems to be the point of the parable, one that harmonizes with the message of several of the kingdom parables. What may appear to the human eye to be insignificant and fragile turns out to be triumphant and grand (fragile seeds yield a hundredfold, a mustard seed becomes a tree) as well as inevitable (the weeds unable to choke the wheat, the treasure that will be discovered, the pearl of great price bought, the good fish salvaged).

The pervasive transforming power of the yeast and its ability to touch all of the abundant flour may also suggest something about the irrepressible mission of Jesus in Matthew's perspective. Despite fragile and even threatened beginnings, highlighted in the infancy narrative with Herod's threats and the flight of the Holy Family and continuing in the Gospel narrative with the unbridled opposition to Jesus

a pinch of that. Since she used baking powder as the leavening agent, so did we. As we sifted and mixed and shaped the biscuits, my mother and I carried on conversation.

Kitchen time was our best time for heart talk. I remember the ache of my words as I sighed, "Mother, I don't know if I can do it. Being a wife, a mother, and a pastor is too much for me. I never thought it would be this hard." Silently my mother continued to gently fold over in her hands the biscuit dough. She reached one hand into the flour bin and sprinkled the white dust over the sticky batch to make it the right consistency. With her eyes steady on her work she said, "It is hard for you, but you are doing it with all that is within you, and it is a better road than allowing that *something* inside of you to die."

She knew about the *something*. She had longed to be a religious writer, but the activating agents for her rising up to meet her dreams were never available to her. Circumstances, social norms, and weariness were too strong for her to overcome alone. She did not complain of her plight, but instead nurtured the *something* in her own soul through countless acts of goodness and mercy. She kneaded the awareness of the *something* into the lives of her children. She made us aware of the inward happening of the Spirit that activated our lives.

Thomas Kelly poetically named the something with these words:

Deep within us all there is an amazing inner sanctuary of the soul, a holy place, a Divine Center, a speaking Voice, to which we may continually return. Eternity is at our hearts, pressing upon our time-torn lives, warming us with intimations of an astounding destiny, calling us home unto Itself. Yielding to these persuasions, gladly committing ourselves in body and soul, utterly and completely, to the Light Within, is the beginning of true life. It is a dynamic center, a creative Life that presses to birth within us. It is a Light Within that illumines the face of God and casts new shadows and new glories upon the human face. It is a seed stirring to life if we do not choke it. It is the Shekinah of the soul, the Presence in the midst. Here is the Slumbering Christ, stirring to be awakened, to become the soul we clothe in earthly form and action. And He is within us all.[1]

Leaven as Moral Outrage. Leymah Gbowee won the Noble Peace Prize in 2011. It all started with

1. C. H. Dodd, *The Parables of the Kingdom*, rev. ed. (New York: Scribner's, 1961), 5.

1. Thomas Kelly, *A Testament of Devotion* (New York: Harper and Row, 1941), 29.

Matthew 13:33–35

Theological Perspective

He touches them and feeds them. He tries to find words that let them share the inebriation in which he dwells: God with us. He looks at their drawn faces, hungry and dusty. Why are they not working? Why are they wandering around listening to him? Where are their homes and families? Why are there so many women without husbands to care for them? He is looking at the dregs and remnants of a society blasted by war, economic deprivation, and violence. He tells them stories of things they know, in order to uncover for them the treasure they have not recognized.

This kingdom of which they are unknowing citizens is not like the kingdom that rules through soldiers, taxes, and crosses. This kingdom is like tiny seeds that become a shelter for all beings. It is like a farmer sowing seeds. The kingdom of divine nearness is more like an old woman kneading dough than a great king on a throne. The kingdom is like all of those women who fold the dough over and over, slap it on a wooden slab, turn it over with work-hardened hands. The kingdom is an old woman kneading dough, but inside the dough she is hiding something precious. She is not making hard biscuits, food of the poor. She is making light and soft bread; hidden within the bread is something almost invisible, tiny, insignificant. As she folds the bread over and over, the agent of change is broken into the dough, and soon the dough rises. Its featureless flatness becomes soft, pliable, warm, and delicious.

The kingdom of divine nearness is an old woman. An image like this issues a challenge that is as radical today as it was two thousand years ago. We are invited into a logic, a way of life, that is utterly present here on earth, in this world, and yet utterly alien to the dynamics of power that structure our nations, our families, and even our churches. If we allowed this image of an old woman to enter us, it might be like a small and invisible agent of change breaking down our resistance and raising us up nourished and nourishing.

WENDY FARLEY

Pastoral Perspective

details of daily life is the truth that we are rooted and grounded in a Love that has been with us and for us from the very foundation of creation. Likewise the promised kingdom of heaven is glimpsed in the parables as a kingdom that is already and not yet here in the midst of the familiar. Something is going on here.

What is the something that might be going on in these verses? The leaven, the enormous amount of flour, and the woman mixing one with the other invite us to expect the kingdom of heaven will involve more than the familiar faces around the kitchen table or the well-known contours of Wednesday night church suppers. The kind of yeast that Jesus names affects all of the flour, moving from the hidden depths, indiscernible in the mixing and kneading, but unmistakable when the entire mass of dough has risen. Previously overlooked spaces and oppressed peoples are included in the kind of kingdom that Jesus promises: all classes, especially the poor; all people, especially those who have been discounted; all ages, especially children and those treated as children. What if the kingdom of heaven is like leaven being mixed, even now, into the raw materials of every human life? Imagine countless individuals who otherwise were as good as dead to the world rising; imagine each being kneaded into a whole whose size will astonish all who have eyes to see what has been hidden since the foundation of the world. Something pastoral is going on here!

Parables invite our deeper attention to what is going on in the midst of creation. Parables provoke us to notice the kingdom that has been hiding in the familiar from the beginning. Parables disrupt our expectations and give us an opportunity to practice the kind of attention required for understanding the person before us. Parables teach us to be present when answers are not readily available. "What is going on?" We might be surprised that the answer hidden from the foundation of the world has been present all along in the one who is telling the parable!

MELINDA MCGARRAH SHARP

that would result in his passion, the mission of Jesus would be triumphant. Matthew's Gospel concludes with the mountaintop scene in Galilee where the triumphant Son of Man returns and sends his disciples out into the entire world to make disciples of all nations (28:16–20).

The Fulfillment Quotation (vv. 34–35). The concluding portion of this segment picks up an earlier refrain of the discourse, namely, the reason that Jesus speaks in parables (see 13:10–17). Matthew stresses that Jesus is speaking to the "crowds" (see 13:1–3, 10), anticipating a significant turning away from the crowds, and to the disciples alone that will take place in the next verse (13:36). As Jesus' earlier explanation implies, the parables, like all metaphorical language, both mask and reveal meaning. For those who either reject Jesus or are indifferent to him, the parables are opaque and yield no meaning. For the disciples, however, who are gifted with understanding, the parables of Jesus reveal the mysteries of the kingdom of heaven.

Matthew seals this section with a so-called formula quotation, a device characteristic of his Gospel as a whole. Beginning with the infancy narrative and periodically throughout the Gospel story into the passion narrative itself, Matthew uses explicit quotations from the OT, introduced with a similar "fulfillment formula" to underscore that every aspect of the person and mission of Jesus "fulfills" the Hebrew Scriptures. As the keynote verse of 5:17 makes clear, Matthew understands the term "fulfill" (*plērosai*) not in the sense that Israel is now superfluous or discarded, but in the sense that all of the promises made to Israel now find their completion in Jesus and his mission: "Do not think that I have come to abolish the law or the prophets; I have come not to abolish but to fulfill."

The fulfillment quotation in 13:35 is taken from Psalm 78:2. As is often the case in Matthew, the quotations are a unique form, a mix of the Hebrew and the Greek (Septuagint) versions. The application of the quotation here reinforces the fact that Jesus' ultimate purpose is to reveal God and God's will to the people. Jesus' message, his ministry, indeed his very person reveal the reign of God to the world (see Matt. 11:2–6). The parables, as characteristic expressions of Jesus' teaching, are part of this mission of revelation. The responsibility to open one's heart to their message falls on those who encounter Jesus.

DONALD SENIOR

the leavening agent of moral outrage. In her native country of Liberia young boys were trained to be killers. Women and children were raped and beaten. Gbowee was overcome with the horror that was happening in the civil war in her homeland. She found other women who were equally outraged, but who also felt powerless in the face of so much violence.

The Women's Peacemaking Movement was formed with hundreds and hundreds of Muslim and Christian women. The women sat together in a soccer field in the heart of the capital city of Monrovia. Each and every day the women gathered to pray. They prayed for an end to the killings and the cruelty. They prayed for a safe land for their children.

For two years the women met together. Their seemingly small efforts worked the leaven of hope into their lives. With the leadership of Gbowee the women mobilized their strength. They had no power granted to them through position or money, but they had something else. They had a holy and divine spirit of justice and mercy. It pervaded their lives, enabling them to rise up with courage. It was a spirit that was alive and active in their gatherings. Their presence day after day eventually created an end to the war and the beginning of healing for their nation.

> Bread-baking God . . .
> as you nourish us
> with the bread of life
> and the milk of your Word,
> let your Spirit hang an apron
> around our necks,
> fashioned and patterned
> like that worn by our
> Lord-become-friend, Jesus.
>
> Instruct us,
> here in the halls
> of your kitchen-kingdom,
> with the recipes of mercy
> and forgiveness,
> of compassion and redemption.
>
> Leaven our lives
> 'til they rise in praise:
> Offered, blessed and broken
> For the healing of the nations.[2]

God is in her kitchen, and hope is still rising in the world.

NANCY HASTINGS SEHESTED

---

2. Kenneth L. Sehested, *In the Land of the Living: Prayers Personal and Public* (Raleigh: Publications Unltd.), 70–71.

Matthew 13:36–43

36Then he left the crowds and went into the house. And his disciples approached him, saying, "Explain to us the parable of the weeds of the field." 37He answered, "The one who sows the good seed is the Son of Man; 38the field is the world, and the good seed are the children of the kingdom; the weeds are the children of the evil one, 39and the enemy who sowed them is the devil; the harvest is the end of the age, and the reapers are angels. 40Just as the weeds are collected and burned up with fire, so will it be at the end of the age. 41The Son of Man will send his angels, and they will collect out of his kingdom all causes of sin and all evildoers, 42and they will throw them into the furnace of fire, where there will be weeping and gnashing of teeth. 43Then the righteous will shine like the sun in the kingdom of their Father. Let anyone with ears listen!"

Theological Perspective

The neat allegory the narrator inserts here seems at odds with the fusillade of parables in which it is embedded. The stories entice us with a depth or mystery, an uncanniness that belies the ordinary images. The images combine a familiar scene with a trace of the divine life. Jesus is invoking a divine kingdom through images of seeds, dough, treasure lost and found. Something about these images incites and assuages our thirst for the divine nearness, but the author of Matthew seems not entirely to trust these images. They must be brought back to earth, reduced to our expectations. In ordinary kingdoms, good people are rewarded by the monarch for their obedience and loyalty. Bad ones are punished for failing to cooperate with the system. Subjects will be even more fabulously rewarded and more horribly punished when the monarch is a divine one.

The parables and the allegorical interpretation of the parables suggest entirely different models for how we might participate in the kingdom of divine nearness; entirely different hopes are laid out before us. Many of these parables invite us to eschew images of monarchy and power, reward and punishment, in favor of the extraordinary, nourishing significance of insignificant things. We enter a kind of crazy world where news of divine nearness is carried by the things hidden from or despised by the

Pastoral Perspective

Do you really want justice? There is an enormous amount of inequality in the world in local communities, among nations, and indeed throughout the global village. Along with the other Gospel writers, Matthew affirms the value of righteousness deeply embedded in the Hebrew Scriptures. The righteous participate justly in a world in need of repair from the consequences of sin and suffering. In the midst of the constant risk of estrangement from self, others, and God, growing in righteousness through study and action brings people together in just and mutual regard. What might we learn about justice and righteousness from this passage that speaks of eternal divisions?

The disciples must have been tired after listening to this series of mind-bending stories, for they not only are hearers of stories but also will become the lead storytellers. They will be sent out to open depths of understanding in all people as they spread the stories of Jesus across communities. To people accustomed to the rabbinic practice of storytelling as moral discernment, the parables must have evoked feelings of excitement, restlessness, self-examination, and even exhaustion. Maybe Jesus is leading them inside to rest awhile, to continue the kind of conversation that, in a more informal atmosphere, effortlessly spills into the sharing of food and drink.

Feasting on the Gospels

Exegetical Perspective

The discourse now turns to Jesus' explanation of the parable of the Weeds and the Wheat (13:24–30). This segment begins with a notation that Jesus "left the crowds and went into the house," where his disciples approach him to ask about the meaning of the parable (v. 36). Some commentators see this move from the crowds to a focus on the disciples signaling a significant turning point in the Gospel as a whole. Following upon the conflicts and rejection by his opponents experienced in chapters 11–12, Jesus will concentrate on instruction for his own disciples.

This segment has two interlocking parts. The first is an allegorical explanation of each detail of the parable (vv. 37–40), and the second is a brief vignette describing the final judgment (vv. 41–43). The vocabulary and motifs throughout this passage are very characteristic of Matthew; this fact leads many commentators to conclude that this section of the discourse was composed by the evangelist himself.

The allegorical section moves in rapid fashion through each detail of the parable. The sower of the good seed is the "Son of Man." Matthew depicts the triumphant Jesus who comes at the end of time as the Son of Man (16:27–28; 19:28; 24:30, 37, 39; 25:31; 26:64). This enigmatic title, probably drawn from the book of Daniel, is applied in the Synoptics both to the suffering and humiliation of Jesus

Homiletical Perspective

"Tell us about the weeds!" Jesus' disciples exclaimed. They wanted more explanation about the parable of the Weeds in the Field. Could it be that the disciples wanted a detailed list of the enemies who were sowing weeds among the wheat? Could it be that they wanted a plan for how to uproot the sources of harm and horror in the land?

"Tell us about the weeds!"

Jesus knew weeds. He was a poor Jew who grew up among a powerless minority group. He saw life from the vulnerable land of injustice and suffering, not from a manicured garden of privilege and power. The Jewish people were living in occupied territory. Their lives were being choked by the "weedy" Roman rule that had control over most aspects of their lives. Many were losing land that had been in their families for generations. Some were losing their means of work. It was a time of economic upheaval. People were hurting, and they were afraid. How would they survive?

Perhaps there is no true entry into this passage until we stand with the disciples in their field, threatened with destruction by powerful forces of persecution. The Jewish people were looking for a Messiah, or someone, who could overthrow the Roman regime. The question was, how could it be done? As with all efforts to weed out injustice, there were

Matthew 13:36–43

Theological Perspective

world. A root sense conveyed by the parables is this divine nearness. Jesus seems to try everything under the sun to convey the radical and imminent love of a divine *abba* or *amma*. He dwells with outcasts, soldiers, women, somewhat narrow-minded religious leaders and those despised by them, poor people, wealthy people, collaborators, workers, displaced people. He heals, he tells odd stories. He is like a prism that breaks the invisible light of the Divine into colors so we can see it. We see in him what the divine nearness is like.

This is only one contradiction present in this chapter. In verse 34 the allusion to Psalm 78 indicates that parables are intended to bring to another generation the awareness of God's glorious wonders. However, in verse 15 an allusion to Isaiah suggests that parables are told to prevent people from understanding or being healed.

In the allegory of the parable, as in the desire to prevent people from being healed (!), we return to the logic of domination in which punishment and suffering triumph in the end, at least for the great majority of a human race we thought was cherished and beloved by their creator. It is a way of thinking that has been rife in Christianity: violence and hostility to others on earth, confident that God will torture them endlessly while we enjoy heaven. The innovation of the gospel seems to promise more than this, and continuing to wrestle with Scripture may reveal treasures hidden in plain sight.

This clash of paradigms within Scripture, within Matthew, within these few verses, invites us to consider what we are doing when we read Scripture. If we are faced with contradictions and alternative visions of divine nearness, we might consider that we are not here being offered a straightforward set of beliefs to be held. We are not privy to the fate of the unrighteous upon their demise. We are being invited into the divine life. Perhaps Scripture is more like love songs or caresses than explanations. If this is the case, we might enter Scripture as a living document. Until the Enlightenment and the triumph of secular, scientific, and more one-dimensional models of meaning and truth, Scripture was explored like a thousand-room mansion into which we roamed ever more deeply, our infinitely desiring heart seeking the infinite love of the Divine.

Where do we discover ourselves and our relationship to the Beloved in a story like this? What parts of us are wounding and distorting? In each of us there are seeds lying on rocky ground, seeds of anger, intolerance, harsh words, factionalism, selfishness,

Pastoral Perspective

Like a playwright adapting a novel for the stage, Jesus assigns parts: the field is the world. There are two kinds of sowers: one good, one evil. Both bear children, as both are credited with productivity and creative potential. Like wheat and weeds, the good and bad children grow together toward the sun, intertwined roots grounded in the same field. The harvest is not yet here. Jesus does at least some of the sowing, promising to send the angels at the appointed time. Only then will the angelic reapers separate weed from wheat. Their stage instructions will be this: to gather the weed that chokes out life, to bind it together, and to throw the whole bunch into a place of weeping and gnashing of teeth. The wheat that feeds is righteous and will be outside, shining like the very sun required for growth. At the end of Jesus' retelling, we have come full circle to a key element required for growth. The story starts with earth and ends with sun. Do you now understand God's justice?

Jesus explains the parable of the Weeds and the Wheat (13:24–30) with the image of a world split into discernibly good and bad, right and wrong, where roles are assigned and consequences are grave. In a highly individualistic world, any of us may be tempted to assign our own roles. Among the available options for human beings in the above passage, we ask, Am I a good child? Am I righteous? If so, how did I get that way? How do I stay that way? If not, what can I do to inherit the kingdom? Where did I get it wrong?

On the surface, there are a lot of people to blame for anything and everything, starting with bad parents and powerful reapers, who are ultimately the ones to do the sowing and the sorting. We may even blame the Son of God, the one who sends the angels to do the reaping. This kind of blame game leads quickly to fatalistic thinking: I am not now and never will be accountable for anything, because the choices of others have gotten me into this. I am good and must continually prove my goodness over against you who are bad. I am bad and can do nothing about it but rail against all of creation while I wither and die. When do you find yourself embracing these fatalistic interpretations of the meaning of life? Though familiar and human, all of these interpretations are deeply problematic if the goal is to be righteous, and if being righteous is to be as sun to all that grows from the field.

We humans have a destructive tendency: we claim the good for ourselves and project the bad onto others, to justify our hatred of them. At our worst, we

(17:12, 22; 20:18) and to his triumphant return at the Parousia.

The allegory continues, defining the "field" as the "world" (*kosmos*, v. 38). This is an important detail in determining the overall meaning of the parable. Matthew is not presenting the drama of the parable as an intrachurch struggle. Instead, the arena is cosmic in scope, with the seed being sown by the Son of Man in the world itself, with the "good seed" being the "children of the kingdom"—no doubt those who have faith in Jesus and, important for Matthew, follow through with righteous deeds—and the weeds being "the children of the evil one." Given the context of Matthew's Jewish Christian community and its experience of tension with the dominant majority of Judaism, the mixture of weeds and wheat undoubtedly refers in part to this intra-Jewish strife. However, the term "the world" and the contrast between the "children of the kingdom" and the "children of the evil one" imply that Matthew is grappling with the problem of evil in even broader terms. The final judgment scene in 25:31–46 foresees a gathering of "all the nations" (25:32), including Jew and Gentile alike, who will have to be accountable to the Son of Man.

The "enemy" who sows the weeds is the "devil"—the polar opposite of the Son of Man, who plants the good seed. Throughout his Gospel, Matthew pays respect to the seductive and deadly power of evil. Jesus himself is tested by the same devil in the desert immediately after his baptism at the Jordan (4:1–11). Several of his healings involve a confrontation with the demonic (see 8:16, 28–34; 9:32–33). Jesus warns his disciples of the threat of evil, and they are instructed to pray to be delivered from "the evil one" (6:13). At the same time, the disciples are empowered by Jesus to perform exorcisms, just as their Master does (10:1). The opponents of Jesus reveal the depths of their hardness of heart and their lack of comprehension when they accuse Jesus himself of being in league with Satan (12:24–32).

The conclusion of the allegorical explanation turns to the final judgment. The "harvest" is in fact the "end of the age." This is stock imagery for the consummation of the world found in the Old Testament (e.g., Joel 3:13; Hos. 6:11; Jer. 51:33) and in the book of Revelation (14:15–16). Those who gather the harvest are the "angels"; Matthew's eschatological scenarios include the Son of Man coming in judgment "with his angels," who will be sent to gather the "elect" (see 24:31) or the "nations" (25:32). In the explanation of the parable, the task of angels is to focus on those who have succumbed to evil (v. 41).

factions. The Zealots were the freedom fighters. The Essenes were the separatists living in the desert. The Sadducees sought accommodation with the "powers that be." The Pharisees were the gradual reformers. The disciples were followers looking for some show of force from Jesus. They were standing ready to start a weed-destroying program to eradicate the evils of their day.

Jesus answered as if he were setting up a melodrama on a theatrical stage. He used hyperbole. His over-the-top language is vivid with metaphor about the good seed and the weeds, the devil and angels, bonfires and harvests. The struggle was placed in the present. A life-and-death drama was being played out on the "field" of the world stage. It was the age-old battle between good and evil.

Jesus sounded like a doomsday prophet, but Jesus was not sentencing people to hell. He was inviting his disciples to attend to the holy work of tending the garden. He invited a long-range view of the mission at hand.

The first garden had the tree of the knowledge of good and evil. Since we first ate of it, choosing to know good and evil instead of God, we have been choking on that fruit with equal portions of horror and delight. Though we have always lived in the brutal consequences of this choice, we do not always know how to talk about it. How do we adequately describe "sin" and "evil"?

"We have all sinned and fallen short of the glory of God." This may indeed be true, but it hardly excuses the colossal scope of sin and violence that has plagued human history. "You have seen one sin, you have seen them all" does not begin to account for the unspeakable horrors of war, for example.

"Tell us about the weeds." What are the "weeds," the obstacles and the destructive forces that threaten God's harvest? If we see with God's vision, perhaps we can see what needs to thrive and what needs to be tossed, but discernment is required. The work of disentangling the cruel weeds from the life-giving wheat remains an ongoing process year after year, place after place, situation after situation. The daily drama in the midst of ordinary circumstances requires our attention and care. Jesus did not give a detailed list of the evildoers. Naming the harmful forces at work in our field, whether personal or global, is the responsibility of each generation.

The church has a long and tragic history of camouflaging evil with religious justifications. The church has been known to bless war as holy, bless violence as redemptive, hide sexual abuse to protect

Matthew 13:36–43   **389**

Matthew 13:36–43

Theological Perspective

fear, anxiety, judgmentalism, failures of nerve: works of the flesh, as Paul calls them. In each of us there is also the seed of divine intimacy that makes us shine like the sun. We are invited by the parables to embrace that part of us that is divine, that illuminates our own life and the lives of those around us. The weeds within us, those things that hurt us and alienate us from one another and from the Beloved we trust, are being burned away. Our divine Abba/Amma, who sent the Beloved to us to show us the great love always raining down on us, can be trusted to heal those things that separate us. Catherine of Genoa describes purgatory as a great joy, because it removes everything that separates us from the Beloved.[1] Protestants do not have to embrace her particular view of the afterlife to entrust our imperfections and obstacles to the divine goodness, knowing that the seeds sown by "the evil one" cannot survive the searing flame of love that embraces us.

For others it might be reassuring that the evil that triumphs in this world is not ultimate. We see so much evil that remains unhealed: greed and hostility that ruin lives, violence that is never healed, trauma that simply repeats itself in psyches and in history. Stories of the divine kingdom allow us to see beyond the finalities of history to a divine goodness that preserves the ultimate truth of reality in which the goodness of the good and the nothingness of evil is finally allowed to assert itself. In this world, acts of kindness or courage seem to fall on hard ground and die, but in the divine kingdom, they shine like the sun. In the kingdom, the destitute of history flourish a hundredfold, and evil is overcome.

If this allegory nourishes hatred, we might suspect seeds sowed by "the devil" are still flourishing in us. We can, though, turn this story one way and then another, seeing different aspects of the kingdom. Whether we need meat or milk, we can find something to nourish us.

WENDY FARLEY

Pastoral Perspective

take demonic joy in the imminent or eternal demise of other people. Poetically, the Hebrew Scriptures describe this kind of human-on-human destructiveness as weeping and gnashing our teeth on each other through words and deeds (Pss. 37; 112). When do you find yourself turning against the world, yourself, other people? Where are you temped to take on the role of angelic reaper, to sound the alarm for the harvest, to claim the role of the adjudicator of God's justice and mercy?

Recently, I asked a group of young adults the following question: Do you really want justice? The first response was another question: What do you mean by justice? Nearly all in the group eventually responded in terms of the criminal justice system. Every person assumed the role of bestower of justice upon the masses. Thankfully, we can take a deep breath when we read this passage from Matthew, because we are not assigned the role of justice bestower; nor are humans given the responsibility for sorting, plucking, or proclaiming harvesttime. Rather, we are simply to grow in the field with everybody else.

This interpretation of the parable places our moral discernment in the context of a complex world where good and evil are often indistinguishable and where our lack of understanding leads us to confuse them (Rom. 7). This passage speaks of the eternal threat of division between the bearers of righteousness and those who will be surrounded by weeping and gnashing of teeth. The harvest has not yet come, but this field we share bears the marks of hatred and divisiveness alongside beacons of hope and the creative potential for justice-love. When asked to clarify the meaning of life and death in the world, Jesus assigns to human beings the role of children whose allegiance is either to the kingdom or to the evil one. Therefore, our task is to strive to grow in this field we share with all of creation as children who seek the kingdom of justice-love, joy, and righteousness.

MELINDA MCGARRAH SHARP

---

1. Robert Ellsberg, *All Saints: Daily Reflections on Saints, Prophets, and Witnesses for Our Time* (New York: Crossroads Publishing, 1999), 402.

Exegetical Perspective

The final three verses of this passage present a brief but vivid judgment scene. The triumphant Son of Man sends his angels to collect the evildoers for their punishment, being thrown into the "furnace of fire"—a dire image perhaps drawn from the story of the fiery furnace in chapter 3 of Daniel. The desolate image of "weeping and gnashing of teeth" is found elsewhere in Matthew as an expression of torment and ultimate rejection (see 8:12; 13:50; 22:13; 24:51; 25:30). The righteous, on the other hand, will "shine like the sun in the kingdom of their Father" (v. 43). This image too may be drawn from Daniel, who speaks of the "wise" dead rising to "shine like the brightness of the sky" (Dan. 12:3). Matthew may also be recalling the moment of the transfiguration, in which Jesus' countenance "shines like the sun" (17:2). The passage concludes with Jesus' word of warning: "Let anyone with ears listen" (v. 43; see also 13:9).

The parable of the Weeds and the Wheat and its explanation counsel patience and tolerance in the face of a mixed world of good and evil; God will provide a final reckoning of justice at the end of the world. Matthew's Gospel displays a realistic view of the human condition. The disciples are called to profound holiness, yet they are "weak in faith" (14:31; 17:20). The religious leaders have positions of authentic authority, yet they are also hypocritical (23:2–3). The community itself endures conflicts and must seek reconciliation and have an infinite capacity for forgiveness (18:15–35). Although the presence of evil in the world is disturbing, the disciples are to trust God's providence and, in the meantime, be faithful to Jesus' teaching and thereby strive to be complete as the heavenly Father is complete (5:48).

DONALD SENIOR

Homiletical Perspective

the institution, and sanction hatred as ordained by God. The devil has taken up residence in God's garden of paradise.

This old destructive force can appear with confusing disguises. The noxious weed that Jesus describes is zizania, a plant that looks all too similar to wheat, until it is close to harvesttime. It is a relief that God's angels are the ones who do the final winnowing work. In the meantime, we are tenders of God's garden of justice and mercy, wisdom and truth. We muster all the courage we dare to discern within us and around us what is harming God's good life among us.

We cannot savor the good without sampling the evil. Sometimes we do not even have to reach for either one. It happens. "The banality of evil" was Hannah Arendt's characterization of the undramatic way that we can live with the absurd and call it normal. From all appearances, evil is as common as kudzu and as predictable as the evening news.

Still, surely it is the mystery of goodness that baffles and amazes us. It is the incredulity of good that astonishes our life together. Goodness still happens. Wheat finally prevails!

In Billie Letts's book *Where the Heart Is,* Lexie asks her friend Novalee how she will ever explain the sexual abuse done to her kids by her boyfriend. She wonders what to tell her kids about this evil visited upon them. Novalee answers,

> Tell them that our lives can change with each breath we take.... Tell them to let go of what's gone because men like Roger never win. And tell them to hold on like hell to what they've got—each other, and a mother who would die for them.... Tell them we've all got meanness in us ... but tell them that we have some good in us, too. And the only thing worth living for is the good. That's why we've got to make sure we pass it on.[1]

Those who have the ability to tend to God's goodness in the field alongside so much badness are the ones shining like the sun.

NANCY HASTINGS SEHESTED

---

1. Billie Letts, *Where the Heart Is* (New York: Warner Books, 1995), 291.

Matthew 13:44–46

⁴⁴"The kingdom of heaven is like treasure hidden in a field, which someone found and hid; then in his joy he goes and sells all that he has and buys that field.

⁴⁵"Again, the kingdom of heaven is like a merchant in search of fine pearls; ⁴⁶on finding one pearl of great value, he went and sold all that he had and bought it."

Theological Perspective

These verses are familiar ones to me because a Plexiglas octagon with a pearl and the words "Jesus is the pearl of great price" that belonged to my grandmother sits on my dresser. Matthew does not say this: *the kingdom of heaven* is a pearl of great price, and his barrage of images conveying what this kingdom is like offers strange twists.

One level of meaning might be the superiority of spiritual over material treasures. Certainly practices of voluntary simplicity are important to our own and the earth's well-being. The treasure in these parables cuts the cord with economic survival; it no longer circulates as wealth but is possessed for the joy it brings. When this joy becomes the basis of our economic life, we find that the urgency of possession eases and we are less driven by consumer addictions and insecurities. We live and work in the world but do so more like undocumented immigrants, hiding our identity, passing; but we have a secret treasure that makes our simpler life blessed.

The kingdom of heaven, whatever it is, would be a highly dangerous one to first-century Christians. It is not exactly dangerous to contemporary Americans, but its countercultural values make it extremely difficult to embrace. Nevertheless, it is worth spending all our means on it. The whole of the Gospels tries to paint a picture of this alternative universe, a universe

Pastoral Perspective

I have tried to like these parables. In each, someone happens to find, or is so focused on searching for, something valuable that, upon glimpsing it, he or she readily surrenders all worldly possessions. We could run with this interpretation in several directions. Focusing on a life of searching, the parable is about what persons do who find that for which they deliberately and carefully search. Focusing on the depths of joy, the parable reveals how beholding something of ultimate value evokes an intensely emotional response. Outlining an ethics of response in the face of divine surprise, the parable speaks to the theme of voluntary dispossession. After all, both finders in these parables about a treasure and a pearl immediately act by selling all material belongings. The text only partially supports each of these worthy areas of study.

I want these verses to connect a purposeful seeker, who can be any of us, with the paradox of a treasure so unexpected that it can surface anywhere. I want these verses to depict the ground of all creation as rich, fertile soil in which such a valuable treasure can be discovered and then enjoyed by all kinds of human identities and abilities. Mostly, I want this treasure or this pearl to be shared among all people and all of creation. As worthy as these desires may be, they all depart from the text. The text reveals a troubling underside of humanity.

Exegetical Perspective

The parables of the Treasure, the Pearl, and the Net bring the parable discourse to a conclusion. Unique to Matthew, they may have been drawn from special material available to the evangelist and his community and are concerned with commitment to the kingdom here and now.

The Parable of the Treasure in the Field (v. 44). The parable of the Treasure begins with a formula similar to previous parables: "The kingdom of heaven is like . . ." (see 13:24, 31). The emphasis falls on the exceeding value of the kingdom, which commands a radical change of life and full commitment. Here the compelling value of the kingdom is compared to a "treasure hidden in a field." Each detail is important. Earlier in the Gospel, Jesus had warned the disciples not to store up for themselves "treasures" (the identical Greek word is used: *thēsauros*) on earth "where moth and rust consume and where thieves break in and steal" but, rather, to "store up for yourselves treasures in heaven" (6:19–20). Indeed, Jesus observes, "For where your treasure is, there your heart will be also" (6:21), a commentary on commitment that fits well with the parable itself.

The treasure is "hidden," recalling the emphasis in the preceding parables of the Mustard Seed (13:31–32) and of the Leaven (13:33) on the hidden

Homiletical Perspective

Just when we thought the kingdom of God was to be found in the small seeds and hidden yeast, we are spun around to the surprise of God's reign popping up in hidden treasures and rare pearls. Once again we are struck with mystery. We cannot pinpoint on a map the vastness of God's holy happenings.

These two parables remind us that there is a cost to discipleship. Discovering God's treasure takes effort. We invest all that we have to offer. We give up what is less valuable, in order to invest in what is most valuable. With all the daily distractions of our lives, we seek what is hidden just beneath the surface of our lives. It is the costly path of discipleship.

"The God Movement." This was the way Clarence Jordan translated the hard-to-define biblical phrase "the kingdom of heaven." He believed that Jesus' teachings on the kingdom of God were more about perspiration than inspiration! His own life glistened with perspiration. Jordan was a Greek New Testament scholar who helped to found Koinonia Farm in the 1940s in south Georgia. A Baptist preacher from the South, he used the language of rural people to animate the gospel story. The *Cotton Patch Version of the Gospels* was written in a small shed in the midst of an experiment of interracial communal living and working.

Theological Perspective

hidden in the midst of our world, that operates by the logic of love. The costliness of Christianity is often put in terms of the cross, but here it is the sacrifice of our wealth that is figured.

If this saying is too hard, we might consider the senses in which Christians are called to a recalibration of desire. The treasure, after all, is not a penitential, gloomy sacrifice of our pleasures, but the great joy that arises as we dwell more transparently in the kingdom of divine love and presence. These images help us to work with the idea that transformation of desire is joyous and that a shift toward simplicity and nonattachment is not renunciation as much as liberation.

The treasure, in contrast to the pearl, is hidden; in fact it is reburied by a somewhat unscrupulous merchant, so he can buy it at a more affordable price. The merchant is something of a trickster. It is not entirely honest to find a treasure on a piece of land, hide it, and then buy the land to get the treasure. The Gospels have a decidedly antinomian strain. There is something a little amoral about love.

Why do we bury the treasure, hide our citizenship in the kingdom? This burying of a hidden treasure suggests something fragile; it cannot bear up under the calculating eye of the landowner. We hide it deep in the ground, we bury it deep in our heart, we seek it in secret (Matt. 6:6). There is a tension between citizenship in any worldly empire and citizenship in the kingdom of heaven. We do not have to literalize the New Testament's depiction of Satan as the "ruler of this world" to acknowledge that the dynamics of power and wealth, the psychological satisfactions of privilege, oppressive identities imposed by stereotypes or poverty, and the finality of death remain intransigent aspects of our experience. News of the kingdom pierces this totality of meaning: hidden in the midst of these realities is another way to be, another path to joy. It is in the field of our awareness unrecognized. So when, in our joy, we discover it we are directed to hide it more thoroughly.

There are many passages that indicate that we live in the kingdom through acts of love, mercy, compassion, and justice. Living out this truth is to inhabit the kingdom of divine nearness. In this passage the merchant is guided not by good works but by joy.

Christians can be very busy people—doing good (and evil) in God's name. These passages point us in a different direction. The world is intolerant of the kingdom. It crucifies its messengers, literally and figuratively. There are aspects of our faith that are to be kept secret, held closely to our breast, treasured

Pastoral Perspective

In three verses, we read parallel stories in which the kingdom of heaven is likened to something that happens to an individual with considerable means. We read of a kingdom that is like a treasure hidden in a field or a pearl of great price that requires an enormous economic investment. The end result—personal ownership—is troubling. Read in this way, these parables can foster dangerous practices of exclusion and entitlement. Picture the kingdom likened to an invitation-only, black-tie affair reserved for those who can afford to buy the finest pearls. Those of us educated in and shaped by post-Enlightenment modernity know this well: knowledge can be acquired with hard work and determination; success is credited to individual effort; money goes to those who want it badly enough. So it seems.

On the surface, the message of these two parables is this: know what you want; seek it out single-mindedly; once you have found it, hide it or keep it for yourself. There is no mention of sharing or doing anything communal with such valuable private property. Where is the good news in not one, but two stories of individualistic acquisition? What kinds of exclusion and oppression afford these two individuals such an expensive, joy-filled treasure?

We know that this cannot be the truth hidden in the parable, because we are still on the surface. Remarkably, these three verses invite us to greater depths in two ways: their form as parables invites us to find deeper understanding, and they tell a story about finding deeper understanding. Scholars think it not by chance that in the rabbinic literature of the time, wisdom gained through Torah study was referred to as a pearl.[1] So we also must dig beyond the surface ourselves for the pearl.

If the gospel is the pearl, the treasure, then as Christians invest time and money for the sake of that treasure, what kind of kingdom images do we present? Do we offer a gospel so precious and individualistic that only those who have "found" it have access to it? We ought to worry about the kind of confidence embraced by the one-sided—albeit often well-meaning—joy of believers. Parables are nothing if not reminders of how much all of us have to keep learning.

Over the past fifty years, theological images of pastoral care have become more oriented toward the communal dimensions of care and less focused on approaches that favor individualistic responses. Good care is understood in terms of what empowers

1. Amy-Jill Levine and Marc Zvi Brettler, eds., *The Jewish Annotated New Testament* (Oxford: Oxford University Press, 2011), Kindle edition.

or apparently insignificant impact of the kingdom for those who are not attuned to its reality. What appears to be hidden and insignificant will explode into bountiful life, as the parable of the Sower had proclaimed (13:23).

This treasure is hidden in a "field." Is the word "field" (*agros*) simply a necessary detail of the story, or does Matthew invite us to think of the same word used in the explanation of the parable of the Wheat and the Weeds? There Jesus explains that "the field [*agros*] is the *world*" (13:38). The implication for the parable may be that this hidden treasure is in the midst of the world, of everyday life, available to all who are fortunate enough to discover it.

An interesting feature of this parable is that it shows no concern about the legal or moral issues one might find here and ones actually discussed in ancient Jewish legal traditions. To whom does this treasure belong? It was not uncommon for people to bury valuables in times of threat or uncertainty, as many recent archaeological discoveries of hoards of coins and valuables attest. Does the parable mean to shock the hearer to attention by casually asserting something that was in fact illegal and immoral? More likely, is this whole aspect simply submerged in the parable's focus on the discovery of treasure and the response demanded by such a bounty?

The response of the character in the parable is clear: he reburies the treasure and then "with joy" sells all that he has to buy the field and gain its hidden treasure! The note of the joy of discovery occurs elsewhere in Matthew's Gospel. The magi who seek Jesus are "overwhelmed with joy" when the star leads them to the place where the child is to be found (2:10) and the women who discover the empty tomb and learn of Jesus' resurrection from the "angel of the Lord" leave the tomb "with great joy" to bring the news to the disciples (28:8).

To acquire the field—and therefore the treasure—the man must "sell all that he has" (v. 44). The totality of the commitment required, including the leaving behind of possessions, is a recurring motif of the Synoptic Gospels and is found at several points in Matthew. The focus is not on asceticism as such but on the freedom from entangling alliances that are an obstacle to full commitment to the kingdom of heaven. The first disciples who are called immediately leave their nets, their boats, and their father behind in order to follow Jesus (4:18–22), and Matthew leaves behind his toll booth (9:9). In contrast, the rich young man who is invited to dispose of his possessions and follow Jesus turns away sad

Jordan and a tiny band of treasure hunters found a gem hidden in the red clay dirt of Georgia. They spent all they had to buy the plot of land that they could farm. The treasure was the beauty of God's beloved community, hidden in an unlikely field of their lives in the segregated South. It was not easily unearthed in that place, but the treasure hunters were compelled by joy to invest all that they had in the vision of God's community of dignity and equality. Jordan said that all who joined their community entered with the same condition of being "flat broke."

The times were dangerous. Their roadside market was bombed. Gunshots riddled the sides of their homes as well as the farm's gas tanks. Their fences were cut. Their crops were stolen from the fields. There was a boycott of all Koinonia Farm products. The Georgia Bureau of Investigation spent a year deciding whether the community was involved in "subversive activities," or whether they were engaged in a plot to overthrow the government. The community still bravely carried on their mission in the God Movement.

Through all the persecution, Jordan found reminders of the hidden treasure and the pearl of great price in his study of the New Testament. His life and teachings called the church to follow the Jesus who shifts our allegiances and lays claim to the whole of our lives. He challenged the church's misguided material investments. On one of Jordan's preaching excursions the church pastor proudly pointed to the new cross atop the steeple. "That cross alone cost us ten thousand dollars." Jordan looked at the cross before saying to the pastor, "Brother, you got gypped. The time was you could get them for nothing." As he traveled to preach around the country, Jordan encouraged the church, "You ought to spend at least as much trying to house your brothers and sisters whom you have seen as you do trying to house God whom you have never seen" (cf. 1 John 4:20b). Jordan invested in this treasure trove of the God Movement. Koinonia Farm became a parable of racial reconciliation.[1]

What is the treasure for us? What is the pearl of great price that drains our bank account with delight?

Dr. Holmes was the pastor of our sister church. He grew up in Mississippi at a time when his family picked cotton. He was a man full of grace and truth. As a young pastor I sought his counsel on troublesome issues in the church. "Dr. Holmes, there

1. See Joyce Hollyday on Clarence Jordan in her introduction to *Clarence Jordan: Essential Writings* (Maryknoll, NY: Orbis Books, 2003), 15–36.

Matthew 13:44–46

Matthew 13:44–46

Theological Perspective

for their fragile beauty. Good fortune and bad fortune define us in the eyes of the world; but this identity is really nothing compared to the kingdom. Inside of us is a treasure that testifies to a different identity, a different set of values. First, we are lovers of Christ, devotees of the divine nearness. This treasure we guard and hide. When we speak it too much, too crassly, it becomes another element in the world; it is subsumed into the logic of prestige, of insiders and outsiders, of strife and factionalism and hostility. There is something in this treasure to be protected, an intimacy that demands discretion. The language of the marketplace is not the language of the bedchamber, as Simone Weil says.[1]

The joy of the kingdom puts us at odds with our ordinary citizenship. The Gospels consistently reject the values of wealth acquisition and consumer culture. The rich are sent empty away; they have had their reward. That Christian desire is formed more by the marketplace than by the gospel simply attests to the fact that we live in this world. However, Matthew's long series of teachings from the Beatitudes to these parables is a gentle and stern invitation to *metanoia*: to turn in a different direction, toward the transformation of desire that allows us to dwell in the divine kingdom, even as we live here in this world.

It is right to live out our Christian identity in the world in our ordinary activities: what we buy; how we engage the political process; how we treat our children, neighbors, strangers, and enemies; how we honor creation. These images of hidden treasure direct us to another way to cherish creation. As we preserve this treasure hidden in the field of our inner being, cherishing a pearl that is no longer merchandise but joy, the circulation of love from the Beloved to us and to the world refreshes everything we do.

WENDY FARLEY

Pastoral Perspective

or liberates those caught in webs of suffering, violence, and impoverishment. These are noble goals; yet the risk of adopting the role of liberator in relation to the world's suffering people is one-directional church mission whereby Christians alone think they are the ones who empower. When we glimpse the subtle dehumanizing tendencies in our own mission-minded orientations, we know that our best intentions have fallen prey to the illusion that we already know and own the story (the treasure, the pearl) and know how to share it and what empowerment looks like. What kinds of exclusion and oppression afford those inside this space such an expensive, joy-filled treasure?

Digging into these parables for greater understanding yields a surprising insight. These parables turn ownership on its head. The treasure in the first parable does not complete the finder's private estate or fund a better one. Rather, finding the treasure accompanies selling all other possessions. In the second parable, the pearl is not the crown jewel the merchant has been waiting for to set in an old imperial heirloom and wear for all to see. The moment of glimpsing and appreciating the value of the pearl is the same moment of releasing ownership of all other possessions to find meaning in a greater joy.

Who owns the kingdom? If detachment rather than ownership brings joy in the very moment that one glimpses the kingdom, then Christian communities have an opportunity to rethink traditional ways of doing mission by inviting *others* to share *our* vision. What if the kingdom of heaven is like the process of collaborative learning where knowledge leads directly to detachment from any one person or way of being church? What if the kingdom of heaven means that no one perspective owns the good news, the story of liberation and empowerment? This understanding certainly would make more space for the breaking in of divine surprises.

On the surface of our lives, who of us is good at detachment? However, digging into these parables leads to greater understanding of joy that comes with a kingdom that any and all may enter and that none of us owns.

MELINDA MCGARRAH SHARP

---

1. Simone Weil, *Waiting for God* (New York: Harper Perennial Modern Classics, 2001), 35.

Exegetical Perspective

(19:16–22). These stories illustrate Jesus' call for radical discipleship, found at several places in the Gospel (10:37–39; 16:24–26; 19:23–26, 27–30).

The Parable of the Pearl (vv. 45–46). This parable has a similar message to that of the Treasure and is linked with the preceding by the simple formula: "Again, the kingdom of heaven is like . . ." (v. 45; see also v. 47). There are, however, subtle but important differences between the two parables. In this instance the main character is "a merchant in search of fine pearls." Pearls were greatly valued in antiquity, perhaps even on a par with gold or diamonds. The book of Revelation observes that the Roman merchants will be desolate when their costly cargoes of "gold, silver, jewels and pearls" will no longer be sought (Rev. 18:11–12). This is implied in Matthew 7:6, where Jesus warns his disciples not to throw "your pearls before swine," equivalent to "what is holy" in the preceding parallel. In the parable of the Treasure, the man who discovers it seems not to have anticipated his good fortune—not unlike the first disciples when Jesus comes to them unexpectedly (4:18–19; 9:9). By contrast, the pearl merchant is "in *search* of fine pearls," and his active search is rewarded with the discovery of an exceptionally fine pearl. One thinks of the magi who seek out the Messiah (2:1–12). Even more proximate, the Matthean Jesus tells his disciples that in encountering him and his message they see and hear what many prophets and righteous people longed to see (13:16–17). Such an active search for the kingdom of heaven compels one to "sell all" in order to gain it.

In these two parables, John Dominic Crossan finds a fundamental pattern: (1) "advent" (i.e., the radical discovery of the compelling nature of the reign of God); (2) "reversal" (i.e., the call for conversion of life, whereby one subordinates everything to the demands of God's reign); (3) "action" (i.e., full commitment to the reign of God in all of one's life).[1] With short, vivid strokes these two parables describe the dynamics of Christian discipleship.

DONALD SENIOR

Homiletical Perspective

is so little commitment in our leadership. Even our church leaders are not willing to sacrifice for what really matters. Just last week seven of our twelve deacons did not even show up for the deacon's meeting. What would you do?" Dr. Holmes leaned back in his chair and smiled. "Why, I would lift up a prayer of thanksgiving." Still smiling, he added, "I used to be like you when I was young. But then I realized I was trying to build the church of W. D. Holmes and not the church of Jesus Christ."

What is the treasure of the church of Jesus Christ? What does the church have to give to the world? Perhaps the treasure and the pearl that we would give everything to possess begin with questions: What do we long to see or experience? Where do we say, "I would give anything to see that"? Could we say that we would give anything to see enemies befriended, racial divisions erased, family squabbles ended, hungry people fed, eroded land restored, and war ended? Would we give anything to see children educated, religious people united, humane programs funded? When we are swept up with the longing for an end to enmity, suffering, and destruction, we may find ourselves giving up everything to experience redemption. When we find others ready to relinquish whatever holds us back from participating in God's Movement, we find church.

What is the treasure that the church could sell all *in joy* to possess? Not doctrines, not creeds, not choirs, not preachers, not buildings. The pearl of great price shimmers through Jesus and his redemptive story. Jesus, who was born on the outside to outsiders. Jesus, who lived by grace for all those left behind from Love's embrace. Jesus, who challenged the powers in place and placed himself among the powerless. Jesus, who chose to live by the Spirit that was within him, a holy Presence that would not forsake him. Jesus, who was killed by the powers of this world and resurrected by the Power of all the world.

It is this Jesus who joyfully invites us to give our all to discover the treasures awaiting us in the God Movement.

NANCY HASTINGS SEHESTED

---

1. John Dominic Crossan, *In Parables: The Challenge of the Historical Jesus* (Sonoma, CA: Polebridge Press, 1992), 34.

⁴⁷"Again, the kingdom of heaven is like a net that was thrown into the sea and caught fish of every kind; ⁴⁸when it was full, they drew it ashore, sat down, and put the good into baskets but threw out the bad. ⁴⁹So it will be at the end of the age. The angels will come out and separate the evil from the righteous ⁵⁰and throw them into the furnace of fire, where there will be weeping and gnashing of teeth.

⁵¹"Have you understood all this?" They answered, "Yes." ⁵²And he said to them, "Therefore every scribe who has been trained for the kingdom of heaven is like the master of a household who brings out of his treasure what is new and what is old." ⁵³When Jesus had finished these parables, he left that place.

Theological Perspective

Even though this section of Matthew's Gospel seems to consist of three rather disparate elements (a parable, a conversation, an allegory), there is in fact a key theological theme that not only binds those three parts together, but locates them right in the focal point of Matthew's proclamation of the good news. This key theme is encapsulated with a uniquely Matthean term, *hē basileia tōn ouranōn*—the kingdom of heaven. Its preeminence in Matthew and in the Synoptic Gospels (with the equivalent term *basileia tou theou*—kingdom of God) leads us directly to the heart of *Jesus'* own proclamation, person, and ministry.

No wonder, then, that the term "kingdom of heaven" has occupied theologians from the beginning of the church, and that it is still a hotly debated issue, particularly in our day, for its apparently imperial language. Given the problems and dangers of such language, I have chosen the translation "God's reign," in order to indicate that however the metaphor *basileia* is understood and interpreted, the essential determination of this phrase occurs through its possessive case: it is *God's* reign we are talking about, not a human reign, and the metaphor in itself therefore critiques all destructive and oppressing uses.

Focusing on Jesus' metaphor of the *basileia tōn ouranōn*, these verses can only be contemplated and

Pastoral Perspective

Often the most difficult part of addressing the parables is that they are not clear teachings but, rather, stories through which we must go to encounter revelation. At its best, teaching can have an immediate return. Revelation is, by definition, hidden and takes a lifetime to grasp. In all the talk of the kingdom of heaven, Jesus gives no description of the world transformed, nor is there a picture of some celestial state. Instead, we are left with images, riddles, and puzzles that tease us and force our minds to wrap themselves around a new, expanded, undefined parameter of God at work in the world about us. Some parables are references to how God works; others tell of humankind's response to God. Let there be no mistake: there is no one absolute takeaway to the parables. Parables are a little bit like the kaleidoscope I had as a child. I could twist it and shine it in the light and I would always get a new vision. I could never see all the way through the colored glass reflecting the light. No matter how hard I tried, I could never make the vision stay the same.

Jesus asks his disciples, "Have you understood all this?" They answer, "Yes" (v. 51). It is a wildly bold and, dare I suggest, foolish response. Jesus spent countless hours speaking to his inner circle in obscure language. In chapter 13, he bundled together five parables that would make anyone's head spin, yet

Exegetical Perspective

"The kingdom of the heavens is like" doing (or being) *the right(eous) thing.* Our pericope is set in a semi-private domestic space where Jesus teaches his disciples in parables (13:36; cf. Mark 4:34). Part one (vv. 47–48) is the third in a trilogy of "the kingdom of the heavens is like" parables peculiar to Matthew. All three focus on appropriate action in particular circumstances: searching, finding, and buying hidden treasure; finding, selling, and purchasing a precious pearl; catching and separating good fish from bad fish. Part two (vv. 49–50) offers an eschatological interpretation of this third parable. Section three (vv. 51–53) includes a metaparable symbolizing the teaching relationship between Jesus and his disciples.

The Ins and Outs of the Kingdom of the Heavens (vv. 47–48). The Greek word translated "heaven" in the NRSV is actually the plural *ouranoi,* meaning "heavens" (see 3:2; 4:17; 5:3, 10, 12, 16, 45; 6:1, 9; 7:21; 22:2; cf. 21:31, 43; 24:31; Ps. 18:2 LXX). The singular "heaven" *(ouranos)* occurs in phrases like "angels in heaven" (22:30; cf. 24:36; 28:2, 18) or "whatever you loose on earth will be loosed in heaven" (18:18). The literal phrase "kingdom of the heavens" may reflect the transcendence and imminence of the kingdom, which is both beyond earth and on the earth. The kingdom of the heavens has come near

Homiletical Perspective

Upon reading this gospel story, anyone who has spent much time fishing would promptly observe that this is not how it works. Fish of every kind do not simply jump into the net. Seaweed? Yes. Debris? Probably. A few fish of mediocre size and quality, perhaps; but never fish of every kind. It is an exceedingly fortunate fisherman who has the luxury of separating out the good catch from the bad.

This is more than an anecdotal observation. It is a relevant point as we begin consideration of this passage, because it highlights one of the key possibilities for preaching this text. Like the string of parables that precede it in the thirteenth chapter of Matthew's Gospel, this is a parable of remarkable abundance and generosity. Just as the sower at the beginning of the chapter tosses seeds indiscriminately over the soil and the path and the thorns, so too does the fisherman gather from the seemingly unlimited bounty of the sea. This extraordinary catch—a net overflowing with fish of every size and variety—is every bit as rare and valued as a pearl of great price or a treasure hidden in a field.

This interpretation centers on God's abundant grace, a theme that preaches well in many contexts. A preacher might particularly emphasize the indiscriminate nature of the catch, implying that the kingdom of heaven is similarly unbounded in its abundance

Matthew 13:47–53

Theological Perspective

interpreted adequately with a perspective that is genuinely *eschatological*, concerned with the ultimate destiny of humankind and the creation. That is to say, from an eschatological perspective, the starting point for all considerations is God's reign: as it has already begun in Christ's ministry; as it is not yet wholly revealed, but prayed for; and as it is encountered in the present work of the Holy Spirit. Eschatology does not deal with some sort of otherworldly, after-life refuge (or, alternatively, an eternal hell), but with God's transcending and transforming, just and merciful presence here and now.

Considering its rather drastic and apocalyptic language, how does this eschatological perspective inform our understanding of the parable of the Dragnet? How does it help us comprehend the reign of God as *God's presence* here and now? What are the implications of God's reign for faith and life? It is important to note first that this parable is not primarily an *ecclesiological* one, that is, a parable on the church, as it has been understood quite often in the history of exegesis and theology. It is not first of all about the church as a mixed body of good and evil, classically termed the *corpus permixtum*; it is not a call for the church to remain patient and endure this mixed body. Likewise it does not threaten us with eternal torment in hell and the Last Judgment, nor is it meant to make the "good fish" (usually the true believers) feel morally superior, complacent, and self-righteous. It is instead a clarion call to act.

To whom does Jesus address this call? He is not talking here to the world in general; he is not even speaking to the crowds interested in his message. He is addressing the inner circle of his disciples. They are the ones who are to hear and act in response to the reign of God. To be sure, this message includes judgment on those who do evil, who do not act according to God's law, but Jesus does not condemn the evil deeds in order to frighten and paralyze his followers into nonaction. Within the world of the parable, he invites them to inhabit or glimpse the reign of God, where the bad is discarded and the good is gathered up. Contemporary readers may be offended by his choice of words, but Jesus' strong and apocalyptic language and imagery "is a reminder that Jesus has come to call us to a way of life commensurate with his reign."[1]

It would be a misinterpretation, though, to focus exclusively on God's divine wrath (on those "others," the bad fish), while ignoring or contradicting the

Pastoral Perspective

his followers claimed to understand. Time and time again in Matthew, the disciples prove themselves to be bold, but not always wise. Therefore this response should come as no surprise. It is hard not to wonder if the disciples fell into a mode of reductionism, an attempt to boil down mysterious questions to practical, tangible answers. In the realm of religion, reductionism can be treacherous, because, in many cases, it means to wipe away the need for mystery.

If this is where the disciples were going with their yes answer, then they were running the risk of limiting in their own minds what God could do and what might be possible in the kingdom of God. The same is true for us. When we say yes, we understand the mysterious, we comprehend the obscure, we do not leave room to constantly grow, to be open to mystery, to be surprised by revelation. We limit what we may grasp of the kingdom of heaven that is hiding, even now, in the ordinary details of our human existence.

The act of casting nets into the sea to collect the good and the bad fish without distinction begins with very ordinary details that are always a part of the parables. Fishermen are fishing. What is revealed of the kingdom of heaven in this ordinary scene? At the outset, perhaps casting the nets into the sea is a reference to the grace of God. In the kingdom of God, the net is cast far and wide, and all kinds are welcomed. Once ashore, however, another ordinary detail—the separation of good and bad fish—has always been where the church gets into trouble with itself and the world beyond. In the parable, this judgment at the end of time is left to the angels, implying that we should do the same.

As Jesus ends this series, he offers one more obscure comment; the kingdom of heaven is "like the master of a household who brings out of his treasure what is new and what is old" (v. 52). We have to wonder, after five parables about the separation of good and bad, the judgment and the grace that is to come, is this last statement simply another shot at the disciples? Is it just another way of Jesus teaching them to include in the church the believers you have been given, good and bad, old and new? Let God be the judge. Let Jesus offer salvation and forgiveness.

Dennis Covington's "Salvation on Sand Mountain" is the story of a journalist who left the big city to research this strange clan of religious snake handlers.[1] He entered into the assignment with all sorts of preconceived judgments. By immersing himself in

---

1. Stanley Hauerwas, *Matthew* (Grand Rapids: Brazos Press, 2006), 127.

1. Dennis Covington, *Salvation on Sand Mountain: Snake Handling and Salvation in Southern Appalachia* (Reading, MA: Addison-Wesley, 1995).

(cf. Mark 1:14, 15; Luke 4:43; 10:9). This imminent kingdom has suffered violence, beginning with John's imprisonment and death (11:12). Additionally, Jesus declared that "heaven and earth will pass away, but my words will not pass away" (24:35). This declaration likely does not refer to "heaven" as the space where God resides (23:22).

The two preceding parables compare the kingdom of the heavens with a person who has found and purchased hidden treasure (after selling everything) and who discovered and acquired a precious pearl (13:44–46; see also 6:33; cf. 20:1–9; 22:1–14; 25:1–13; Acts 12). Hidden treasure and pearls can both be associated with the sea. In our parable, the kingdom of the heavens is like a fishing net that is cast into the sea, filled, drawn in; then the catch is separated. All three parables may reflect the cultural and economic reality of many, including Jesus' disciples, who lived in cities surrounding the Sea of Galilee (4:12, 18–21). The first two parables may reflect the average hard-working fisherman's dreams to discover treasures that would allow him to escape the hardships of a fisherman's occupation. The parables metaphorically represent the character of the kingdom participant who willingly relinquishes all for the kingdom. Our third parable demonstrates the committed kingdom participant's ultimate vindication for relinquishing everything for the kingdom.

The third parable deviates from the previous two; what is drawn from the sea is not cherished in its entirety (cf. *Gos. Thom.* 8). A distinction is made among the fish. "Fishermen in the Sea of Galilee would have had to separate kosher and nonkosher fish from their nets."[1] A strict dichotomy is observed. Things are mostly black and white, in or out, which does not necessarily reflect reality. Good trees bear good fruit, and bad trees yield bad fruit (7:17–18). However, not everything is so black and white: "Our Father in the heavens" causes the sun to shine on the evil (*ponēros*) and the good (*agathos*), the rain to fall on the just (*dikaios*) and unjust (*adikos*) (5:45).

Ultimately One Is Either Evil or Just (vv. 49–50).
The good and bad fish represent just and evil people. The act of sorting the bad fish from the good represents the final judgment, when those people who are determined to be evil are cast into a fire. It is unclear whether the "weeping and gnashing of teeth" occurs just prior to, after, or both before and after

and invitation. The safe approach would be to stop there, but more daring preachers may wish to look at the parable's conclusion and confront the persistently troubling image of separation—the good from the bad, the righteous from the evil. By this point in Matthew's Gospel we have heard repeatedly about the weeping and gnashing of teeth that await those who do not see or hear or accept the gift of the kingdom. It is a harsh warning and a dangerous refrain—dangerous because the tempting (mis)interpretation is to divide ourselves and those around us into these very camps. We become the good and righteous, and they over there—whoever they may be—are the ones destined for the furnace of fire.

Needless to say, this interpretation can lead to much harm. It also does not square with the parable's emphasis on abundance, nor with the fact that angels and not human beings are charged with the tasking of sorting out at the end of time Thus it seems that a more responsible and holistic approach is to consider the conclusion of the parable in light of the beginning. To restate it, the initial thrust is one of invitation and inclusion—a net brimming full with fish of every kind. The trajectory of the parable at that point is not toward separation but, rather, the gathering in of as many as possible.

With that in mind, perhaps those who risk the furnace of fire are those who do not recognize or appreciate the simultaneous rarity and abundance of this kingdom. In that sense, they have distanced themselves from God's grace long before any future moment of judgment and separation arrives. They have ignored the treasured gift that God has placed in their midst, and perhaps the consequence is as much immediate as it is eternal. The kingdom described in this and the preceding parables is one that is present and available in this earthly life. "The kingdom of heaven *is*," Jesus says, not "will be." It follows that those who fail to respond to God's generosity are subject to weeping and gnashing of teeth today, as they face the trials of life without the mindful assurance of God's unbounded love and grace.

These considerations raise the question, though, of how any of us can recognize this kingdom. It is a fair question and one that presents further preaching possibilities. Where is the kingdom of heaven today? How does one access it or discover it or accept it as gift? Barbara Brown Taylor, an Episcopal priest and author who is brilliant in her ability to locate the Holy in daily life, discusses these questions in *The Seeds of Heaven: Sermons on the Gospel of Matthew*. First, she notes that the parables in this thirteenth

---

1. Aaron Gale, "The Gospel according to Matthew," in *The Jewish Annotated New Testament. NRSV*, ed. Amy-Jill Levine and Marc Avi Brettler (New York: Oxford University Press, 2011), 65n45.

Theological Perspective

good news of God's just mercy and merciful justice. God's judgment can rightly be understood only when seen in the light of God's faithful covenant with God's beloved daughters and sons. In addition, these offensive words may provide a word of comfort to those who suffer from the consequences of unrighteous, sinful actions: "Evil, whether of empires or individual, does not have the final word!"[2]

While understanding the theological substance of "all this" heaven talk (v. 51) is important, the parable calls hearers to incorporate their eschatology fully into their personal ethics, as well as into the way they order their lives in community. Jesus' message of God's reign rightly understood cannot remain a passive property to be stowed away, but becomes a motivating and transforming force and vocation.

The church must become a parable of hope to the world. In order to do so, Christian communities need the help and support of what Jesus describes as a "scribe trained for the kingdom of heaven" (v. 52) with an allegory that remains valid and useful throughout the centuries. This allegory, which I like to think of as a kind of "job description" for (academic and pastoral!) theologians, is translated by Elaine Wainwright, a feminist theologian from New Zealand: "A scribe trained for the implementation of the inclusive *basileia* vision of Jesus draws out of a treasure of past and present, the new and the old toward a rereading of the Jesus story for a particular historical situation."[3]

The parable, the conversation, the allegory: all three draw us into the center of Jesus' proclamation of the *basileia tōn ouranōn*, enabling us to live in response to God's present and coming reign for our life, church, and world.

MARGIT ERNST-HABIB

Pastoral Perspective

everything that seemed so foreign, he began to realize that these people, who seemed so very different, were in fact not foreign at all. Covington uncovered his own family connection to them and came to understand their faith. He was not necessarily a part of their world, nor did he endorse snake handling as a faithful Christian practice, but he came to see things through a different lens. Had he learned the snake handlers' history in a classroom, he likely would have held them at a distance; instead, understanding came through time and relationship and engagement with mystery, obscurity. The strangeness of parables requires the same of us. Unless we enter the world of the parable, unless we let go of our preconceived notions of the parable's "teaching," we will miss the glimpse we are given of the kingdom in its familiar and strange details.

Sometimes in the life of faith, we need to make a distinction between what we are supposed to learn in a traditional manner (a+b=c) and how we risk the known world for the sake of the truth that awaits us in the world of the parable. Do we give ourselves time and space for that to happen? Do we give ourselves space to lean into God and be open to God, rather than studying and knowing something definitively?

There is value in being stumped in these parables. There is value in humbly admitting we are not entirely sure what they mean. Most of the time, truth lies in mystery. Oftentimes truth comes in paradoxes; the challenges mired in conflict are the places where, if we dare to come close, truth reveals itself. When it comes to parables, truth lies in our ability to be open to the humanly unimaginable, inconceivable possibility. We have to sit with these stories to realize that the kingdom of heaven cannot be taught or analyzed. It has no permanent boundaries or structure. It is a sphere in which one enters both the earthly and the celestial, and it has no limits.

MARYETTA M. ANSCHUTZ

---

2. Warren Carter, *Matthew and the Margins: A Socio-Political and Religious Reading* (Maryknoll, NY: Orbis Books, 2000), 296.
3. Elisabeth Schüssler Fiorenza, ed., *Searching the Scriptures. A Feminist Commentary* (New York: Crossroad, 1995), 2:635.

they are thrown into the fire. Does "weeping and gnashing of teeth" signify remorse, guilt, or tortuous suffering? Elsewhere "weeping and gnashing of teeth" is connected with being cast into "outer darkness," reserved for "heirs of the kingdom" who lack great faith (8:5–12) and for a "worthless slave" (25:30). Similarly, a tree that does not bear good fruit is chopped down and cast into the fire (3:10). People or things considered evil or bad are dispensable. In order to escape the eschatological fires, participants in the kingdom of the heavens must act appropriately or be judged righteous. This focus fits within the broader Matthean theme of hearing and acting on Jesus' words, doing the will of the Father, and the eschatological reward based on just praxis (7:21, 26; 16:27; cf. 17:14–20). A participant in the kingdom who acts appropriately is righteous or just. This is finally delineated in social justice acts like clothing the naked, caring for the sick, visiting the incarcerated, feeding the hungry, providing water for the thirsty, and welcoming the stranger (25:35–46). All nations and peoples, not just the "heirs of the kingdom" who have heard the good news but do not act on it, will suffer the final judgment (25:31). Ultimately, the angels execute the separation of the good from the evil (24:31; 25:31; cf. 1:20; 2:13).

The Metaparable: The Master-Teacher Trains His Own Scribes (vv. 51–53). Matthew resorts to absolutes again: "*Every* scribe trained for the kingdom of the heavens is like the master of the household" (v. 52, my trans.). Jesus evokes, as a parable or extended metaphor, the image of the master of the patriarchal household who utilizes both old and new items stored in his treasury. This "kingdom of the heavens is like" metaphor signifies the narrative event of Jesus teaching his disciples in parables. It is a metaparable, a parable about parables. Jesus trained his disciples by attaching new interpretations to old images. The disciples understood (cf. Mark 4:34). Jesus' disciples are the scribes of the kingdom. A scribe in the kingdom of the heavens differs from the ones that oppose Jesus (2:4; 20:17–19). This opposition does not mean that John the Baptist's scribes or other Jewish scribes are mutually exclusive from those who participate in the kingdom (see 8:19). Jesus demonstrates a hermeneutical authority superior to the scribes and their teachers because he is the ultimate teacher (7:29).

MITZI J. SMITH

chapter of Matthew are tied together by the hiddenness of the kingdom. The treasure is hidden in a field, the pearl of great value is hidden among many others, and the net of fish is hidden under the surface of the sea.[1] This may seem to imply that finding or experiencing this kingdom is limited to those possessing great skill or luck, Taylor writes, but upon further reflection the things these stories describe as hidden are actually objects that appear in plain view nearly every day:

> If we want to speak of heavenly things, [Jesus] seems to say, we may begin by speaking about earthly things, and if we want to describe that which is beyond all words, we may begin with words we know, words such as: man, woman, field, seed, bird, air, yeast, bread; words such as: pearl, net, sea, fish, joy. These are the places to dig for the kingdom of heaven; these are the places to look for the will and rule and presence of God. If we cannot find them here we will never find them anywhere else, for earth is where the seeds of heaven are sown, and their treasure is the only one worth having.[2]

The seeds of heaven are here, in the midst of our earthly lives. Perhaps, in approaching this passage and all of the images and questions it conjures, this is the place to both start and end. God is here, and glimpses of heaven surround us, if only we will open our eyes and our hearts to receive the gift.

JOHN D. ROHRS

---

1. Barbara Brown Taylor, *The Seeds of Heaven: Sermons on the Gospel of Matthew* (Louisville, KY: Westminster John Knox Press, 2004), 42.
2. Ibid., 44–45.

Matthew 13:54–58

⁵⁴He came to his hometown and began to teach the people in their synagogue, so that they were astounded and said, "Where did this man get this wisdom and these deeds of power? ⁵⁵Is not this the carpenter's son? Is not his mother called Mary? And are not his brothers James and Joseph and Simon and Judas? ⁵⁶And are not all his sisters with us? Where then did this man get all this?" ⁵⁷And they took offense at him. But Jesus said to them, "Prophets are not without honor except in their own country and in their own house." ⁵⁸And he did not do many deeds of power there, because of their unbelief.

Theological Perspective

No, the Nazarenes are not extraordinarily obstinate and malicious people, intentionally ignoring Christ's powerful words and deeds, and willfully rejecting the God-sent prophet. First of all, they are regular people confronted with the irregular appearance and disturbing claim of one of their own: their neighbor Jesus, son of Mary and the carpenter. They are familiar with his rather modest origins, his low economic and social status, and they know for sure that he does not belong to the ruling political or religious elite. Challenged by this *im*modest man, speaking words of wisdom and performing deeds of power in their own synagogue, heart and center of their religious life, they react in a way that is natural and absolutely appropriate.

Twice they inquire after the source of this man's power and authority: "Where did this man get all this?" (vv. 54, 56), and in doing so, they ask the one critical and essential question that people always have asked when confronted with any kind of claim to power. The Nazarenes are right in not simply accepting Jesus' claim. Even in the presence of his powerful words and deeds, they are compelled to question the source of their former neighbor's authority.[1]

Pastoral Perspective

In a slightly sunnier take on Jesus' hometown than the take we find at the end of Matthew's thirteenth chapter, the nineteenth-century Presbyterian minister and hymnologist Louis FitzGerald Benson wrote: "O sing a song of Nazareth, of sunny days of joy, / O sing of fragrant flowers' breath, and of the sinless Boy; / For now the flowers of Nazareth in every heart may grow; / Now spreads the fame of his dear name on all the winds that blow."[1] If these four verses in Matthew's Gospel are to be believed, fragrant flowers do not describe the inhabitants of Nazareth in relation to Jesus, nor will Nazarenes be spreading the fame of his dear name on all the winds that blow. It seems that the "sinless Boy" has grown up to be a man who thinks a bit more highly of himself than he ought, according to those who remember him when. Why might they have thought this?

Was it because of what Jesus said that day in the synagogue? What we do not know in Matthew's account of Jesus' return to his hometown and to the synagogue where he grew up is the substance of what Jesus said. Perhaps he was interpreting the passage from Isaiah reported in Luke 4. Maybe he continued

---

1. Unintentionally reflecting "the purpose of Jesus' mission . . . to point to God, not to himself"; Stanley P. Saunders, *Preaching the Gospel of Matthew: Proclaiming God's Presence* (Louisville, KY: Westminster John Knox Press, 2010), 140.

1. *The Presbyterian Hymnal* (Louisville, KY: Westminster John Knox Press, 1990), #308.

Exegetical Perspective

The Merging of the Familiar with the Unfamiliar, the New with the Old. Context, text, and audience matter. Our story is immediately preceded by a trilogy of parables that utilize old and familiar images (hidden treasure, a pearl, and fishing) to develop a hermeneutic of the kingdom of heaven (13:47–53). In our text Jesus returns to his old neighborhood in Nazareth to teach with wise words accompanied by powerful deeds. Thus the familiar (Jesus) coalesces with the new (wise words and miracles) in an old context. In part one (v. 54a) Jesus returns to his hometown synagogue to teach. In part two, the hometown synagogue attendees are both astounded at and offended by Jesus' teaching (vv. 54b–57a). The final section (vv. 57b–58) records both Jesus' assessment of the people's response and the narrator's evaluative summary of Jesus' ministry in Nazareth, given the people's unbelief.

In the immediate context following our text (14:1–12), Herod Antipas is also disturbed. Herod's anxiety stems from the inexplicable miracles Jesus performed. Herod concludes that Jesus is performing miracles because he is the resurrected John the Baptist. Context and audience matter. Herod and the synagogue attendees at Nazareth attach different (in)significance to Jesus' miracles.

Homiletical Perspective

Unlike many Gospel passages, the social context of this story seems to transcend time and place. It could be any small town in today's United States, if not another part of the world. Close your eyes and you can hear the whispers in the hair salon, at the bridge table, and almost assuredly in the church parking lot:

> "Who does he think he is, coming back here all high and mighty!"
> "Was not his Daddy the town carpenter?"
> "Where did he get all this fancy learning, and where does he get off trying to tell us what's what in the world, as if he knows best!"

The aspirational young man returning home to a mixed reception is a common literary construct (think Thomas Wolfe's *You Can't Go Home Again*), one that preachers could exploit in bringing this story to life. On the surface, Jesus fits the mold. He grew up in the small village of Nazareth and left for reasons no one understood. While traveling, he gained a reputation for presumptuous teaching and debate; now he shows up surrounded by an entourage of followers and an avalanche of rumors. He starts teaching in the local synagogue and performs a few miracles, and not surprisingly his old neighbors

Theological Perspective

At the same time, they make a fundamental mistake by not truly allowing their valid and appropriate question to be just that: a sincere question. Their question instead appears to be a rhetorical device, a means to make a point, and one can almost hear the sneering and derisive tone in their asking about Jesus' parents and siblings. Of course, these questions about Jesus allow for only one answer. They are thinking, "We already know full well all we need to know about him, and it does not fit in the least with our expectations for a mighty prophet empowered by God. Where does he get all this from? Not from God; that much is sure."

They are not *testing* the spirits to see whether they are from God (1 John 4:1); they are not *asking*, "Are you the one who is to come, or are we to wait for another?" (Matt. 11:2). They have previously decided against Jesus. Consequently, their valid question turns into a mocking of this presumptuous neighbor, who dares to challenge and disturb their image and expectations of a God-sent prophet. By not staying inside the Nazarenes' predefined categories, Jesus is throwing them into a "theological crisis."[2] *That* is what makes him so annoying to the Nazarenes; that is his "offense." It is not his wisdom and powerful deeds that seem to scandalize them (v. 57, *eskandalizonto*), but Jesus' inherent claim—against all their expectations—to be a prophet from God.

If they want to keep their peace of mind, all they can do is to dismiss him completely—a reaction that Jesus seems to have expected. He responds in an almost sympathetic manner, quoting the proverbial saying about prophets without honor in their own country and house. As Matthew concludes the story, Jesus leaves his hometown without performing many deeds of power there—because of their *unbelief* (v. 58). With this last term, Matthew hands us the hermeneutical key to understanding and interpreting the whole episode from a theological perspective.

It is not the questioning that indicates unbelief in this text. Questioning, uncertainty, even doubting do not necessarily imply a lack of belief; quite the opposite. Such skepticism and searching may well contribute to our growth in faith, as, for example, the most recent confession of the Presbyterian Church in Canada, *Living Faith*, explains in section 6.2.2 on doubt: "Questioning may be a sign of growth. It may also be disobedience: we must be honest with ourselves. Since we are to love God with our minds, as well as our hearts, the working through of doubt

2. Thomas G. Long, *Matthew* (Louisville, KY: Westminster John Knox Press, 1997), 161.

Pastoral Perspective

to speak in parables, as he had spoken to the crowds beside the sea. However, Matthew's silence on the matter suggests that the issue for Matthew may not have been the content of Jesus' speech, even though the lesson astounded the congregation and caused them to acknowledge his wisdom. Rather, it seems that they were irritated because one of Mary and Joseph's many children had the audacity to speak of God and to act in God's name. They were offended that a person no better than they presumed to possess the authority to counter the usual word spoken and interpreted on the Sabbath by the regular teacher, the one who certainly knew his place. Part of the problem must have been the sort of familiarity that breeds contempt.

It also could be that they had come ready to be offended. Perhaps word had spread about Jesus' earlier encounter with his family. "Mr. Important" had been speaking to "the crowds" when word came to him that the woman who bore him and his younger male siblings were outside and needed to speak with him (12:46–50). Was this too much to ask? According to town gossip, he had denied any relationship to them, saying, "Who is my mother and who are my brothers?" Then he announced that his brothers were those who followed him (the adoring dozen) and his brother and sister and mother were those who did God's will (according to whom?). If that is how he treats his own flesh and blood, how dare he come home and expect a warm welcome, let alone an open-minded hearing! Another part of the problem is what might be called an "attitude" on the part of the congregation, given the single-minded obedience to God Jesus embodied and commanded.

However, the heart of the problem is not mentioned until the end. In the third place, unbelief characterized the congregation in Nazareth. Their unbelief was not a simple matter of failing to confess the faith with the right words or bear witness to the faith with righteous deeds. Given this unhappy encounter, the unbelief Matthew mentions at the end is the unbelief of people who reject revelation on behalf of religion. To paraphrase Karl Barth on this matter, on that day in Nazareth, revelation came to the gathered congregation in the person of Jesus. In his coming to them, God was telling them something utterly new, something that apart from Jesus they did not know and could not tell themselves or others.

On that day, as on most days in synagogues and sanctuaries, revelation was met with unbelief, even though these were religious people who had come to hear the Scriptures read and interpreted.

When Home Becomes a Place You Simply Return To (v. 54a). Jesus was born in a house (*oikia*) in Bethlehem (2:8–11), and he was raised in Nazareth of Galilee (2:22–23). After John the Baptist's arrest, Jesus left Nazareth and relocated to Capernaum (4:12–13). In our text, "hometown" refers to Nazareth. This is not the first time Jesus returned to his own city. In Nazareth, Jesus demonstrated his authority before the crowds (refuting the scribes) by forgiving the sins of and healing a paralytic man who was being transported by some people of faith (9:1–8). During that same visit to Nazareth, Jesus resurrected the synagogue leader's daughter (9:18–26//Mark 5:21–43). Here our text records the first time in the narrative that Jesus teaches in the synagogue at Nazareth. Matthew's Jesus is the paradigmatic teacher, who proclaims the good news in the synagogues of all the cities and villages around Galilee (4:23; 9:35). Jesus customarily participated in the synagogue gatherings, as did many Jews and God-fearers.

The Hometown Folk, a Tough and Sensitive Audience (vv. 54b–57a). A dissonance occurred between Jesus' wisdom and miracles and the people's familiarity with his family. The people try to understand Jesus' words and deeds in the context of his family. The father is mentioned first in terms of his occupation, but he is not named. Joseph is not mentioned beyond the birth narratives, where he is identified as Mary's husband and as a "just" man who did not abandon Mary when he discovered her pregnancy (1:16, 18, 19). Joseph's occupation as a carpenter provides a stark contrast with Jesus' miraculous deeds. Matthew's genealogy names only women who are considered exceptional, like Mary, Jesus' mother (see 1:5). Mary is significant, of course, as the virgin mother of Jesus. Jesus' sisters remain nameless. Their anonymity highlights the naming and quantifying of Jesus' four brothers. Of the four named brothers, Judas/Jude and James "the Just," who emerged as a leader at the Jerusalem council (see 27:56; Acts 1:13; 15:13; Jude 1), are mentioned outside of the Gospels.

Although Jesus regularly taught the good news of the kingdom in the synagogues, we do not know the specific content of his teaching here. We do know that previously Jesus had criticized some synagogue goers. While teaching on the mount, Jesus accused some synagogue attendees of being "hypocrites" (6:2, 5; cf. 6:7, 32). When commissioning the Twelve, Jesus warned them that the synagogues would be complicit in their persecution (10:16–17). Something

take offense. They greet him with mistrust, skepticism, and resentment.

If those neighbors had looked beneath the surface, however, they may have realized that in many important ways Jesus does not match the archetype. He departs from the familiar script of social or political ambition by refusing to follow the typical path of success and achievement. He eschews glory and honor; he does not mobilize military or secular power; he critiques the religious authorities instead of currying favor; he focuses not on self-promotion but on self-giving, sacrifice, and service.

An interesting interpretive possibility is that offense may have been taken, in part, because the neighbors *did* look beneath the surface. Perhaps they noted Jesus' departure from the script, a departure that served to deepen the offense. Standing before them is not simply a presumptuous prophet returning to his hometown; he is the Messiah, but—and this is critical—not at all the Messiah they expect. The Messiah was to be a great leader and king, a man surrounded by the military and political power needed to return the people of Israel to prominence among the nations. Jesus thoroughly betrays this expectation. He instead claims the mantle of the Suffering Servant, a far different model for messianic leadership.

The disconnect between the peoples' expectations and Jesus' unconventional manifestation as the Messiah is fruitful ground for the preacher to explore. Several modern classics of theology focus on this topic: *Practice in Christianity* by Søren Kierkegaard, *The Cost of Discipleship* by Dietrich Bonhoeffer, and *The Politics of Jesus* by John Howard Yoder. *Practice in Christianity* is essentially an extended meditation on the "offense" of a suffering Messiah. It is an image and an idea that upends our expectations, just as it did those of Jesus' hometown neighbors. With Christians of every era we face a moment of faithful decision in response: whether to welcome the presence of a savior whose life and purpose transcends our imaginations, or to take offense at a man who confounds our understanding.

Seeing Jesus as an unconventional, unexpected Messiah points to another possibility for sermon exploration: Where does Jesus, the Messiah, make his home? Whom does he call his friends and family? In Matthew 10:34–39 he tells his own disciples that they may need to leave family and friends behind for the sake of the gospel, and in Matthew 12:48–50 he calls anyone who does the will of God his brother and sister and mother. In that sense, this passage symbolizes the fact that Jesus' life and mission extend far beyond

Theological Perspective

is part of our growth in faith" (see http://presbyterian.ca/resources-od).

The unbelief referenced in Matthew prompts us instead to consider our own preferred presuppositions, categories, and images about God and Jesus. Are we so enamored by our constructions that we neglect to attend to their limitations and close ourselves to God's revelation? Do we place Jesus in our categories and expect him to stay put? In our varying interpretations, Jesus may be called the Pacifist, the Moral Teacher, the Feminist, Personal Savior, Liberator, Prophet, Judge, Brother, Friend, even Lord. However, all these interpretations risk becoming human-made idols if they are not continually and critically scrutinized with attention to their limitations as well as their strengths.

Such questioning demonstrates an openness that allows our understanding of Jesus Christ to be challenged and redefined by the witness of Scripture and the confessions of the church in past and present. It deepens our experience of Christ's presence when we remain open to the faith and life of our sisters and brothers, especially to those of us who live on the margins of the social, political, and religious contexts. As the Nazarenes knew, these were the margins where Jesus himself dwelt and where he is still active today.[3]

Like the Nazarenes, we too are not extraordinarily obstinate and malicious people, but we are held back by our own images of Jesus. We tend to shy away from the theological crisis that a real encounter with this man from Nazareth inevitably means for all believers. Instead, we defend our own notions of who we want, expect, and believe Jesus to be, over against all who disagree with us. There is no easy way out of this dilemma; there is only a helpful suggestion offered by Matthew's account of Jesus' rejection in his hometown. Before attempting to shape our understanding of Jesus, we need to keep asking, truly *asking*, as those who are truly and faithfully testing the spirits, while we open our minds and hearts to receive God's answer to our questions (who is Jesus Christ!).

MARGIT ERNST-HABIB

Pastoral Perspective

Nevertheless, they came with their own ideas of God and what God willed and would do. Jesus was not the revelation they had in mind. In a word,

> They did not believe. If they did, they would listen; but in religion, they talk. If they did, they would accept a gift; but in religion, they take something for themselves. If they did, they would let God Himself intercede for God; but in religion they venture to grasp at God. Because it is a grasping, religion is the contradiction of revelation, the concentrated expression of human unbelief.[2]

Earlier Jesus had described this very congregation to the disciples when they asked him why he spoke in parables: "seeing they do not perceive, and hearing they do not listen, nor do they understand" (13:13). Hearts grown dull, ears hard of hearing, eyes shut. Religion! Had they turned even slightly, he would have healed them. Instead, Jesus as much as wiped the dust off his feet in his own hometown.

The scene is familiar to both ministers and members of most congregations. If the minister's single-minded allegiance is to the Word written and spoken in the pulpit, signed and sealed at the font and Table; and if on the best of Sundays and by God's grace alone, the minister manages to say the Word that he or she has been set apart to say (a Word human beings could not know apart from Jesus Christ, could not say to themselves or to each other), then it likely will contradict the many other words by which both the minister and the congregation live. It will be a Word that is not the word people have in mind when they walk into the sanctuary and assume their usual place in the pew.

The temptation, of course, is to stick to religion, lest the congregation take offense and the conversation in coffee hour turn to who the minister thinks she is or on what authority he thinks he can say such disturbing things in God's name. Better to look on the sunny side of Nazareth—or learn how to speak in parables.

CYNTHIA A. JARVIS

3. Cf. Luis G. Pedraja, *Teología. An Introduction to Hispanic Theology* (Nashville: Abingdon, 2003), 162.

2. Karl Barth, *Church Dogmatics*, I/2, *The Doctrine of the Word of God* (Edinburgh: T. & T. Clark, 1956), 302–3.

Exegetical Perspective

Jesus said or did caused the synagogue attendees to be offended (*skandalizō*).

Rabbi and theologian Abraham J. Heschel once observed, "To be a prophet is both a distinction and an affliction."[1] People take offense, it seems, when new interpretations are introduced that challenge both traditional interpretations and the people's own self-understanding in light of those interpretations (cf. Luke 4:23–28). Jesus had anticipated some stumbling at his teaching and pronounced a blessing on those who would not find occasion to be offended (*skandalizō*) in him (11:6; cf. 18:6–9).

Every Prophet Dishonored in His Hometown (vv. 57b–58). Jesus in Matthew's Gospel understands his ministry within the context of the prophetic tradition. He is the prophet who is now being dishonored in Nazareth. Jesus came to fulfill the Torah and the Prophets (5:17). When Jesus enters Jerusalem, the crowds call Jesus a prophet "from Nazareth in Galilee" (21:11; cf. 21:26). King Herod and his disciples also view Jesus as a prophet (14:5; 16:14). Jesus himself quotes the prophet Isaiah: "Isaiah prophesied rightly about you when he said, 'This people honors me with their lips'" (15:7–9; cf. Luke 4:17–19). Jesus is dishonored like God's servants, including the prophets. Jesus resembles the servants in the Servant poems in Isaiah (42:1–4; 49:1–4; 50:4–11; 52:13–53:12), and he quotes from them. After Jesus healed Peter's mother-in-law, many brought to Jesus people who were demon possessed and sick to be healed. These exorcisms and healings were explained as a fulfillment of a line from one of Isaiah's Servant Songs: "He took our infirmities and bore our diseases" (8:17; Isa. 53:4). Although YHWH's Servant is "honored in the sight of" YHWH, he is despised and rejected by those to whom he is sent (Isa. 49:5c; cf. 52:14).

It is only in the prophet's hometown (*patria*) and home (*oikia*) that he is dishonored (*atimos*) (cf. John 4:44; Amos 7:10–17). This dishonoring is manifest in a lack of belief in the prophet's words, which limits the prophet's ability to perform many miracles for the people. Matthew ties a paucity of miracles done in Nazareth to the people's disbelief (*apistian*, v. 58; cf. Mark 6:6). If the narrator's final statement is any indication, the people may have refused to believe Jesus' teaching despite the accompanying miracles (*dynameis*). Previously Jesus declared that "wisdom is vindicated by her deeds" (11:19), except, it seems, in one's hometown.

MITZI J. SMITH

---

1. Abraham J. Heschel, *The Prophets* (New York: Harper Perennial Classics, 2001), 21.

Homiletical Perspective

the confines of geography, culture, and religious tradition. His home is no longer in the town where he grew up; his home is now among sinners and strangers, the poor and diseased, and anyone whose heart is open to God's healing grace and love. Needless to say, this has implications for the church. As followers of Jesus, where ought we to find our home (i.e., not in places of comfort and familiarity)?

Another interpretive approach to this passage becomes apparent when the preacher considers its location within Matthew's Gospel. The passage comes at the end of a string of parables highlighting the kingdom of heaven. The parables focus on the rare gift and treasure of such a kingdom and on its accessibility to those with eyes to see and ears to hear. The implication of this passage, then, is that the kingdom of heaven is coming, in and through Jesus himself. The priceless pearl, the treasure in the field, the net full of fish: these are imperfect analogies that point us toward the real and perfect gift, Jesus himself. He is the tangible symbol of God's generous grace, hidden in plain sight, and available and accessible to us all.

Indeed, Luke's version of this story, in the fourth chapter of that Gospel, is explicit on this point, and a preacher may wish to compare and contrast the two versions to draw out this idea. In Luke's telling, Jesus unrolls a scroll from Isaiah and declares good news for the poor, release for the captives, and recovery of sight to the blind. He proclaims the year of the Lord's favor, often interpreted as the jubilee year, and he concludes by saying that the Scripture has been fulfilled in their hearing. His words imply the inauguration of a new kingdom then and there through him. Luke's version is not only more explicit than Matthew's, but it also has political and economic overtones that cause the congregation to drive him out of town with the intention of killing him. This contrasting interpretation points to an ongoing and interesting debate about the nature of God's reign and its implications for earthly power and priorities.

JOHN D. ROHRS

Contributors

Charles L. Aaron, Pastor, Whaley United Methodist Church, Gainesville, Texas

David R. Adams, Retired Biblical Scholar, Episcopal Priest, Etna, New Hampshire

Mark S. Adams, Coordinator, Presbyterian Border Ministry, Frontera de Cristo, Douglass, Arizona

Carmelo E. Álvarez, Affiliate Professor of Church History and Theology, Christian Theological Seminary, Chicago, Illinois

Dale P. Andrews, Distinguished Professor of Homiletics, Social Justice and Practical Theology, Vanderbilt Divinity School, Nashville, Tennessee

Susan R. Andrews, General Presbyter, Hudson River Presbytery, Scarborough, New York

Maryetta M. Anschutz, Founding Head, The Episcopal School of Los Angeles, Los Angeles, California

Anne H. K. Apple, Interim Associate for Congregational Life, Idlewild Presbyterian Church, Memphis, Tennessee

John A. Azumah, Associate Professor of World Christianity and Islam, Columbia Theological Seminary, Decatur, Georgia

David L. Bartlett, Professor Emeritus of New Testament, Columbia Theological Seminary, Decatur, Georgia

Jonah Bartlett, Associate Pastor, Congregational Church of New Canaan, New Canaan, Connecticut

Timothy A. Beach-Verhey, Pastor, Faison Presbyterian Church, Faison, North Carolina

Nancy Elizabeth Bedford, Professor of Applied Theology, Garrett-Evangelical Theological Seminary, Evanston, Illinois

Shelley D. Best, President and CEO, The Conference of Churches, Hartford, Connecticut

Barbara Blaisdell, Interim Pastor, Tacoma First Christian Church, Tacoma, Washington

Dave Bland, Professor of Homiletics, Director of Doctor of Ministry Program, Harding School of Theology, Harding University, Memphis, Tennessee

Larry D. Bouchard, Professor of Religious Studies, University of Virginia, Charlottesville, Virginia

Matthew Myer Boulton, President and Professor of Theology, Christian Theological Seminary, Indianapolis, Indiana

Henry G. Brinton, Pastor, Fairfax Presbyterian Church, Fairfax, Virginia

Reginald Broadnax, Pastor, Trinity A.M.E. Zion Church, Woodruff, North Carolina

Gennifer Benjamin Brooks, Associate Professor of Homiletics, Garrett-Evangelical Theological Seminary, Evanston, Illinois

William F. Brosend II, Professor of Homiletics, Sewanee School of Theology, Sewanee, Tennessee

Wallace W. Bubar, Pastor, Overbrook Presbyterian Church, Philadelphia, Pennsylvania

Mark R. Burnham, Pastor, First Presbyterian Church Asheville, Asheville, North Carolina

Katherine M. Bush, Chaplain, St. Mary's Episcopal School, Memphis, Tennessee

Patricia J. Calahan, Pastor, Cornwall Presbyterian Church, Cornwall, New York

Cynthia M. Campbell, President Emerita, McCormick Theological Seminary, Chicago, Illinois

Timothy B. Cargal, Interim Associate for Preparation for Ministry/Exams, Office of the General Assembly, Presbyterian Church (U.S.A.), Louisville, Kentucky

William J. Carl III, President and Professor of Homiletics, Pittsburgh Theological Seminary, Pittsburgh, Pennsylvania

Warren Carter, Professor of New Testament, Brite Divinity School at Texas Christian University, Fort Worth, Texas

Cláudio Carvalhaes, Associate Professor of Worship and Liturgy, Lutheran Theological Seminary at Philadelphia, Philadelphia, Pennsylvania

Christine Chakoian, Pastor, First Presbyterian Church of Lake Forest, Lake Forest, Illinois

Gary W. Charles, Pastor, Central Presbyterian Church, Atlanta, Georgia

Diane G. Chen, Associate Professor of New Testament, Palmer Theological Seminary of Eastern University, King of Prussia, Pennsylvania

Jin Young Choi, Assistant Professor of New Testament and Christian Origins, Colgate Rochester Crozer Divinity School, Rochester, New York

Ashley Cook Cleere, Chaplain, Piedmont College, Demorest, Georgia

John W. Coakley, Professor of Church History, New Brunswick Seminary, New Brunswick, New Jersey

Ronald Cole–Turner, Professor of Theology and Ethics, Pittsburgh Theological Seminary, Pittsburgh, Pennsylvania

Adam J. Copeland, Faculty Director for Faith and Leadership, Department of Religion, Concordia College, Morehead, Minnesota

Stephanie Buckhanon Crowder, Adjunct Faculty, McCormick Theological Seminary, Chicago, Illinois

Lisa Wilson Davison, Professor of Hebrew Bible, Phillips Theological Seminary, Tulsa, Oklahoma

Marva J. Dawn, Teaching Fellow in Spiritual Theology, Regent College, and Preacher/Teacher, Christians Equipped for Ministry, Vancouver, Washington

Kathy L. Dawson, Associate Professor of Christian Education, Director of Master of Practical Theology program, Columbia Theological Seminary, Decatur, Georgia

Amos Jerman Disasa, Organizing Pastor, Downtown Church, Presbyterian Church (U.S.A.), Columbia, South Carolina

Lewis R. Donelson, Professor of New Testament Studies, Austin Theological Seminary, Austin, Texas

Mark Douglas, Professor of Christian Ethics, Columbia Theological Seminary, Decatur, Georgia

Pam Driesell, Pastor, Trinity Presbyterian Church, Atlanta, Georgia

Stacey Simpson Duke, Co-Pastor, First Baptist Church, Ann Arbor, Michigan

Steven P. Eason, Pastor, Myers Park Presbyterian Church, Charlotte, North Carolina

Adam E. Eckhart, Associate Pastor, First United Church of Christ (Congregational), Milford, Connecticut

Robert J. Elder, Interim Pastor, First Presbyterian Church, Vancouver, Washington

Margit Ernst-Habib, Theologian, Ubstadt-Weiher, Germany

James H. Evans, Professor of Systematic Theology, Colgate Rochester Crozer Divinity School, Rochester, New York

Wendy Farley, Professor of Theology and Ethics, Emory University Department of Religion, Atlanta, Georgia

Mary F. Foskett, Professor of Religion and Director of WFU Humanities Institute, Wake Forest University, Winston-Salem, North Carolina

Chris Glaser, Author and Speaker, Metropolitan Community Church, Atlanta, Georgia

Howard Gregory, Bishop of Jamaica and the Cayman Islands, Kingston, Jamaica, West Indies

Richard William Harbart, Pastor, Douglas Avenue Presbyterian Church, Des Moines, Iowa

Trace Haythorn, Executive Director, The Frazer Center, Decatur, Georgia

Christopher A. Henry, Pastor, Shallowford Presbyterian Church, Atlanta, Georgia

David Schnasa Jacobsen, Professor of the Practice of Homiletics, Director of the Homiletical Theology Project, Boston University School of Theology, Boston, Massachusetts

Cynthia A. Jarvis, Minister, The Presbyterian Church of Chestnut Hill, Philadelphia, Pennsylvania

E. Elizabeth Johnson, J. Davison Phillips Professor of New Testament, Columbia Theological Seminary, Decatur, Georgia

Stephen C. Johnson, Associate Professor of Ministry, Dean of the Honors College, Abilene Christian University, Abilene, Texas

Peter Rhea Jones, Professor of Preaching and New Testament, McAfee School of Theology, Atlanta, Georgia

Deborah J. Kapp, Associate Professor of Urban Ministry, McCormick Theological Seminary, Chicago, Illinois

Mark A. Lomax, Pastor, First African Presbyterian Church, Lithonia, Georgia

David Lower, Pastor, Winnetka Presbyterian Church, Winnetka, Illinois

Lois Malcolm, Associate Professor of Systematic Theology, Luther Seminary, St. Paul, Minnesota

Judith M. McDaniel, Professor of Homiletics Emerita, Virginia Theological Seminary, Alexandria, Virginia

Kathleen A. McManus, Associate Professor of Theology, University of Portland, Portland, Oregon

Erick R. Olsen, Pastor, Church of Christ Congregational (United Church of Christ), Norfolk, Virginia

Bonnie L. Pattison, Independent Calvin Scholar, Lombard, Illinois

Sandra Hack Polaski, Professor of New Testament, Union Presbyterian Seminary, Richmond, Virginia

John Proctor, Director of New Testament Studies, Westminster College, Cambridge, United Kingdom

Andrew Purves, Professor of Reformed Theology, Pittsburgh Theological Seminary, Pittsburgh, Pennsylvania

Mark Ramsey, Pastor, Grace Covenant Presbyterian Church, Asheville, North Carolina

Michelle Voss Roberts, Assistant Professor of Theology and Culture, Wake Forest University School of Divinity, Winston-Salem, North Carolina

John D. Rohrs, Rector, St. Andrews Episcopal Church, Norfolk, Virginia

Karen C. Sapio, Pastor, Claremont Presbyterian Church, Claremont, California

Stanley P. Saunders, Associate Professor of New Testament, Columbia Theological Seminary, Decatur, Georgia

Leah D. Schade, PhD Candidate in Homiletics, Lutheran Theological Seminary at Philadelphia, Philadelphia, Pennsylvania

Nancy Hastings Sehested, Co-Pastor, Circle of Mercy Church, Asheville, North Carolina

Donald Senior, President, Professor of New Testament Studies, Catholic Theological Union, Chicago, Illinois

Timothy R. Sensing, Professor of Ministry, Director of Academic Services, Abilene Christian University, Abilene, Texas

Melinda McGarrah Sharp, Assistant Professor of Pastoral Theology and Ethics, Phillips Theological Seminary, Tulsa, Oklahoma

Mitzi J. Smith, Associate Professor of New Testament and Early Christianity, Ashland Theological Seminary, Detroit, Michigan

Thomas R. Steagald, Pastor, Lafayette Street United Methodist Church, Shelby, North Carolina

Chandler Brown Stokes, Pastor, Westminster Presbyterian Church, Grand Rapids, Michigan

Laura C. Sweat, Assistant Professor of New Testament, Seattle Pacific University, Seattle, Washington

Haruko Nawata Ward, Associate Professor of Church History, Columbia Theological Seminary, Decatur, Georgia

Richard F. Ward, Professor of Homiletics and Worship, Phillips Theological Seminary, Tulsa, Oklahoma

Theodore J. Wardlaw, President, Austin Presbyterian Theological Seminary, Austin, Texas

Judith Hoch Wray, Scholar-at-Large, Indianapolis, Indiana

Seung Ai Yang, Associate Professor of New Testament, Chicago Theological Seminary, Chicago, Illinois

Brett Younger, Associate Professor of Preaching, McAfee School of Theology, Mercer University, Atlanta, Georgia

Author Index

Katherine M. Bush — Matthew 6:24–34 PP; 7:1–6 PP; 7:7–11 PP

Patricia J. Calahan — Matthew 3:7–12 PP; 3:13–17 PP; 4:1–11 PP

Cynthia M. Campbell — Matthew 9:18–26 EP; 9:27–34 EP; 9:35–10:4 EP

Timothy B. Cargal — Matthew 7:12 PP; 7:13–20 PP; 7:21–29 PP

William J. Carl III — Matthew 8:1–4 PP; 8:5–13 PP; 8:14–17 PP

Warren Carter — Matthew 7:12 EP; 7:13–20 EP; 7:21–29 EP

Cláudio Carvalhaes — Matthew 8:1–4 TP; 8:5–13 TP; 8:14–17 TP

Christine Chakoian — Matthew 4:23–25 HP; 5:1–12 HP; 5:13–16 HP

Gary W. Charles — Matthew 5:17–20 HP; 5:21–26 HPP; 5:27–32 HP; 10:5–15 EP; 10:16–23 EP; 10:24–33 EP

Diane G. Chen — Matthew 8:18–22 EP; 8:23–27 EP; 8:28–9:1 EP

Jin Young Choi — Matthew 4:23–25 EP; 5:1–12 EP; 5:13–16 EP

Ashley Cook Cleere — Matthew 8:18–22 PP; 8:28–9:1 PP

John W. Coakley — Matthew 8:18–22 TP; 8:23–27 TP; 8:28–9:1 TP

Ronald Cole-Turner — Matthew 12:9–14 TP; 12:15–21 TP; 12:22–32 TP

Adam J. Copeland — Matthew 12:9–14 PP; 12:15–21 PP; 12:22–32 PP

Stephanie Buckhanon Crowder — Matthew 4:12–17 EP; 4:18–22 EP

Lisa Wilson Davison — Matthew 5:17–20 EP; 5:21–26 EP; 5:27–32 EP

Marva J. Dawn — Matthew 9:2–8 PP; 9:9–13 PP; 9:14–17 PP

Kathy L. Dawson — Matthew 9:18–26 PP; 9:27–34 PP; 9:35–10:4 PP

Amos Jerman Disasa — Matthew 6:7–15 PP; 6:16–18 PP

Lewis R. Donelson — Matthew 10:34–39 EP; 10:40–11:1 EP; 11:2–19 EP

Mark Douglas — Matthew 10:5–15 TP; 10:16–23 TP; 10:24–33 TP

Pam Driesell — Matthew 10:34–39 PP; 10:40–11:1 PP

Stacey Simpson Duke — Matthew 12:33–37 PP; 12:38–42 PP; 12:43–45 PP

Steven P. Eason — Matthew 5:33–37 HP; 5:38–48 HP; 6:1–6 HP

Adam E. Eckhart — Matthew 13:18–23 PP; 13:24–30 PP; 13:31–32 PP

Robert J. Elder — Matthew 6:7–15 TP; 6:16–18 TP

Margit Ernst-Habib — Matthew 13:47–53 TP; 13:54–58 TP

James H. Evans — Matthew 13:18–23 TP; 13:24–30 TP; 13:31–32 TP

Wendy Farley — Matthew 13:33–35 TP; 13:36–43 TP; 13:44–46 TP

Mary F. Foskett — Matthew 11:20–24 EP; 11:25–30 EP; 12:1–8 EP

Chris Glaser — Matthew 10:5–15 PP; 10:16–23 PP; 10:24–33 PP

Chandler Brown Stokes	Matthew 2:13–15 HP; 2:16–23 HP; 3:1–6 HP	Theodore J. Wardlaw	Matthew 10:5–15 HP; 10:16–23 HP; 10:24–33 HP
Laura C. Sweat	Matthew 2:13–15 TP; 2:16–23 TP; 3:1–6 TP	Judith Hoch Wray	Matthew 8:1–4 EP; 8:5–13 EP; 8:14–17 EP
Haruko Nawata Ward	Matthew 12:33–37 TP; 12:38–42 TP; 12:43–45 TP	Seung Ai Yang	Matthew 3:7–12 EP; 3:13–17 EP; 4:1–11 EP
Richard F. Ward	Matthew 9:18–26 HP; 9:27–34 HP; 9:35–10:4 HP	Brett Younger	Matthew 4:12–17 HP; 4:18–22 HP